HUMAYMA EXCAVATION PROJECT, 2
NABATAEAN CAMPGROUND AND NECROPOLIS, BYZANTINE CHURCHES, AND EARLY ISLAMIC DOMESTIC STRUCTURES

AMERICAN SCHOOLS OF ORIENTAL RESEARCH
ARCHEOLOGICAL REPORTS

Kevin M. McGeough, Editor

Number 18

Humayma Excavation Project, 2
Nabataean Campground and Necropolis,
Byzantine Churches, and Early Islamic Domestic Structures

HUMAYMA EXCAVATION PROJECT, 2

NABATAEAN CAMPGROUND AND NECROPOLIS, BYZANTINE CHURCHES, AND EARLY ISLAMIC DOMESTIC STRUCTURES

By

JOHN PETER OLESON *and* ROBERT SCHICK

Including Contributions by

KHAIRIEH ʿAMR, KHALED AL-BASHAIREH, ERIK DE BRUIJN, DENNINE DUDLEY,

MICHAEL FINNEGAN, DAVID F. GRAF, NORMAN HERZ,

ELIZABETH HOLMQVIST-SAUKKONEN, JANET JONES, MAHMOUD Y. EL-NAJJAR (†),

MEGAN PERRY, JENNIFER RAMSAY, DAVID S. REESE, GREGORY D. ROWE,

LESLIE SHUMKA, MICHELLE SMITH, AND JOHN SOMOGYI-CSIZMAZIA

AMERICAN SCHOOLS OF ORIENTAL RESEARCH • BOSTON, MA

Humayma Excavation Project, 2

Nabataean Campground and Necropolis,
Byzantine Churches, and Early Islamic Domestic Structures

by

John Peter Oleson and Robert Schick

The American Schools of Oriental Research © 2013

ISBN 978-0-89757-037-4

Cataloging-in-Publication Data is available from the Library of Congress

— 2010040809

Printed in the United States of America on acid-free paper.

To the Memory of
Jerome and Ruth Oleson
and to
Edwin and Barbara Schick
with Love and Gratitude

Contents

List of Illustrations

In the years before 1998, J. P. Oleson took photographs alongside S. Coliton, B. Douglas, and C. Mundigler, often sharing the same equipment and film, so it has not been possible to attribute photographs to any particular individual. Photographs contributed by other individuals have been attributed. Unless otherwise indicated, drawings are by J. P. Oleson. Original object drawings were prepared by K 'Amr, A. Bidawy, P. Denholm, D. Emery, Y. Gerber, S. Hardin, C. Luna, M. Malkawi, J. Mason, L. Muh'dieh, C. Mundigler, L. Najjar, J.P. Oleson, M. Qudah, B. Seymour, Q. Tweissi, and R. Wazni. J. P. Oleson, C. Mundigler. R. Post, and M. Siklenka processed most of the object drawings, plans, and sections in Victoria for publication. The ceramic profiles are reproduced at 1:2 (50%), except for some large vessels reproduced at 1:3 or 1:4 (as indicated in the figure captions). For plates in which all the ceramic profiles come from the same locus, the locus designation is given only at the start of the caption list; for ceramic plates with mixed loci, the locus designation is given after each object number. For each ceramic profile, the most likely date based on the parallels cited is given at the end of that entry, in parentheses. An attempt has been made to reproduce the non-ceramic artefacts at the same scale on each particular page, as indicated by the scale ruler on that page.

List of Tables

Preface and Acknowledgements

This is the second volume of the final report on the Humayma Excavation Project. The first manifestation of this long-running project was the Humayma Hydraulic Survey, which started with a survey and probing of the regional water-supply system of ancient Hawara/Hauarra (modern Humayma), carried out under Oleson's direction in 1986, 1987, and 1989. The first volume — J. P. Oleson, *Humayma Excavation Project, 1: Resources, History, and the Water-Supply System*. Boston: American Schools of Oriental Research, 2010 (abbreviated in this volume as *HEP 1*) — is concerned for the most part with this early work, along with the history, topography, and resources of the site. In 1991, Oleson turned his attention to excavation of the settlement centre of Hawara, the original Nabataean name of the site, directing field seasons in 1991, 1992, 1993, 1995, 1996, 1998, 2000, 2002, 2004, and 2005. Co-Directors and Assistant Directors of the excavation project were Khairieh 'Amr (1991–1996), Robert Schick (1991–1998), Rebecca Foote (1994–2005), M. Barbara Reeves (2000–2005), Erik de Bruijn (2000–2005), and Andrew Sherwood (2002–2005), and all remain involved in the ongoing publication programme. Dr. Khairieh 'Amr also served as the Department of Antiquities Representative for the years in which she co-directed the excavation. Reeves (in the years 2008, 2010, 2012), Foote (in the years 2002, 2008), and Schick (in the year 2009) have also directed their own excavations at the site. Judy Logan of the Canadian Conservation Institute served as our conservator for every field and study season from 1993 to 2005. Susan Coliton was photographer in 1991, and Bronwyn Douglas made an attempt at it in 1992. Chris Mundigler was our very hard-working photographer, administrator, and draughtsman for the project from 1992–1996; he has continued to contribute essential drawings to the publications since then. Oleson took many photographs as well in the early years and served as photographer in the 1998–2005 seasons. This book has benefited from the efforts and the advice of all of these individuals.

I would also like to thank the many work-study students at the University of Victoria who helped me with the processing of data and images from the Humayma project nearly every year since 1991, in particular Ruben Post and Miranda Siklenka.

This volume for the most part reports on the results of excavation between 1991 and 1996 in the Nabataean necropolis and campground, and in the Byzantine churches, several of which were re-used as habitations during the Early Islamic period. There were some small-scale follow-up excavations in some of these areas in 1998 and 2009. The reports on our extensive excavations in the Roman Fort, Bath, and *Vicus* structures have been reserved for the third and fourth final report volumes. We had hoped to include in this volume D. Grubisha's report on the steatite vessels found at Humayma, but her schedule and available space in this volume did not allow it; this material will appear in volume three. The excavation of the Abbasid family manor house (F103) and the splendid finds from that structure will appear in a subsequent volume written by R. Foote. Numerous interim reports on all these seasons have appeared in print, along with preliminary analytical discussions (see the References entries for Oleson, Oleson et al., Foote, Reeves, and Schick).

Transliteration from Arabic to English is always difficult and at best an approximation, and the modern name of Humayma is no exception. During the 1970s and early 1980s, "al-Humayma" was the most widely accepted transliteration, and Graf, Eadie, and I accepted that version for our publications. In 1988, however, the Department of Antiquities published a General Index to *ADAJ* volumes 1–30 (1951–86), in which an "official" transliteration as "el-Humeima" appeared (p. 55), and I adopted this transliteration for my publications from 1989 through 2000. In 1997 the Royal Jordanian Geographic Centre once again adopted "al-Humayma" as the official transliteration, and I have returned to that spelling since. In the text, wherever possible, I use Hawara in discussions specific to the Nabataean settlement, Hauarra for discussions specific to the Roman period settlement, and Humayma for discussions specific to the early Islamic settlement, the modern period, or the archaeological site in general across time. It has not been possible to be completely consistent. I have not inserted diacritics in transliterated Arabic words, except in quotations from other works and in the titles of Arabic publications.

I have not abbreviated the names of ancient authors; the titles of the individual works have, however, been abbreviated according to the system used by the *Oxford Classical Dictionary*, 4th ed. (2012). According to this system, the titles of some single surviving works, such as Herodotus' *Histories* are not used, while others are cited, such as Vitruvius, *De arch.* None of this, of course, has much value as a logical system, but consistency can assist the reader, and the *Oxford Classical Dictionary*[3] is easily available for reference. Where no abbreviations are suggested in the *OCD*[3], abbreviations of the works of Greek authors have been taken from Liddell and Scott, *Greek–English Lexicon* (9th ed., rev. by H. Stuart Jones; suppl. by E. A. Barber. Oxford: Oxford University, 1968) and of Latin authors from the *Oxford Latin Dictionary* (P. G. W. Glare, ed. Oxford: Oxford University, 1982).

The fieldwork between 1986 and 2005 was funded mainly by the Social Sciences and Humanities Research Council of Canada (SSHRC), with supplementary funding provided by the Taggart Foundation, the Max van Berchem Foundation, the American Schools of Oriental Research, the American Center of Oriental Research, Dumbarton Oaks, the Department of Antiquities of Jordan, and the University of Victoria, and by the many self-supporting volunteers who participated in the excavation. I am very grateful for this generous support over so many years. Our fieldwork in Jordan was assisted in innumerable ways by the American Center of Oriental Research and its directors over that period and up to the present: David McCreery, Bert De Vries, Pierre Bikai, and Barbara Porter, along with Associate Director Christopher A. Tuttle. The support of the Department of Antiquities was also crucial, as was the kindness of its former Directors Adnan Hadidi, Ghazi Bisheh, Safwan et-Tell, and Fawwaz al-Khraysheh. Dr. Sawsan al-Fahkry, the Aqaba District Inspector for the Department of Antiquities, gave crucial assistance on many occasions. For all of the field seasons between 1991 and 2005, dormitory accommodations for the team were generously provided by the directors of the al-Mureighah Secondary School.

I am very grateful to everyone who has taken part in the project for sharing their energy and time, in particular to the participants in these field seasons.

1991: Field Supervisors were J. P. Oleson (Field B100), R. Schick (Field C101), and K. ʿAmr (Field F). Square supervisors were Susan Coliton, Erik de Bruijn, Dennine Dudley, Kelly Low, Carla Luna, Robert Moldenhauer, and Sabrina Rampersad. Martha Oleson assisted with excavation and processing finds for two weeks. Photographers were J. P. Oleson and Susan Coliton, and Brian Cannon and Peter Denholm served as architects.

1992: Field Supervisors were J. P. Oleson (Field B100), R. Schick (Field C101), and K. ʿAmr (Field F102). Square supervisors were Erik de Bruijn, Dennine Dudley, Rebecca Foote, John Somogyi-Cysizmazia, Judith Mitchell, Faida Abu-Ghazaleh, and Ruba Saleh al-Wazani. Student excavators were Darlene Emery, Leslie Shumka, John Howard, and Sarah Taylor. Martha, Olaf, and Patience Oleson assisted with excavation and processing finds for two weeks. Photographers were J. P. Oleson and Bronwyn Douglas; Stephen Copp served as the architect.

1993: Field Supervisors were J. P. Oleson (Field B100), R. Schick (Field C101), K. ʿAmr (Field F102), and R. Foote (F103). Square supervisors were E. de Bruijn, Cindy Davison, D. Dudley, Chris Nelson, and John Somogyi-Cysizmazia. Student excavators were Linda Clougherty, Iain Glover, Paul Shrimpton, and Rachel Wenstob. Photographers were J. P. Oleson and Chris Mundigler; S. Copp served as the architect. Judy Logan of the Canadian Conservation Institute was conservator.

1995: Field Supervisors were J. P. Oleson (Field E116), K. ʿAmr (Fields F102, E122), D. Dudley (Field E121), and R. Foote (Field F103). Square supervisors were Janet Boyer, E. de Bruijn, Fatma Ishak, Mark Lancaster, Bob Lane, Ken Lee, Edward Normington, Alexandra Retzleff, and Paul Shrimpton. Student excavators were James Cook, Francis

Dearman, Barbara Fisher, Vicky Karas, Joel Kinzie, M. Barbara Reeves, and Paul van Nieuwkuyk. Photographers were C. Mundigler and J. P. Oleson; Steve Nickerson served as the architect and systems analyst. J. Logan of the Canadian Conservation Institute was conservator. I. Glover and Naif Zeben Ahmad consolidated the architecture of the Bath Building (Field E077) and the Mosque in Field F103.

1996: Field Supervisors were J. P. Oleson (Field E116), K. 'Amr (Fields E122, E125), D. Dudley (Field C124), R. Foote (Field F103), and R. Schick (Field B126). Square supervisors were Janet Boyer, J. Cook, E. de Bruijn, D. Dudley, B. Fisher, Anne-Marie Forget, V. Karas, Ken Lee, Megan Perry, M. Barbara Reeves, and Paul van Nieuwkuyk. Student excavators were Aspen Price, Susan Reedy, Pauline Ripat, and Shelly Russell. Photographers were C. Mundigler and J. P. Oleson; Sean Fraser served as the architect. J. Logan of the Canadian Conservation Institute was conservator. Tawfiq Hunaity and Naif Zeben Ahmad consolidated the architecture of the Lower Church in Field C101 and the Mosque in Field F103.

2009: Director was Robert Schick. Square supervisors were Anja Heidenreich, Isabelle Rubin, Ilse Sturkenboom, and Steven Werlin.

Many scholars over the years have assisted our research concerning Humayma, most of all the collaborators named above. In the Preface to Volume 1, I named the individuals who assisted me with the research concerning the water-supply system of the settlement, and some of that advice obviously was of benefit for this volume as well. For this second volume, I owe a particular debt of gratitude to Erik de Bruijn, who has been a stalwart friend and indispensable colleague at every field season since 1987, and to Dennine Dudley, who served as an indispensable staff member from 1991 to 2000. I am also deeply grateful to M. Barbara Reeves, who started with the project as a student excavator in 1995, worked her way up to Co-Director of the project, and took on the burden of starting and directing a new excavation project at Humayma in 2008. This book is dedicated with love and gratitude to the parents of the two editors. Most of all, however, I am grateful to my wife Martha, who put up with many long periods of separation and their attendant hazards during my work at Humayma without losing faith in me.

In addition to the individuals mentioned above, many other scholars assisted our work at Humayma in its early years, and over the following years of study and excavation. We apologize if we have unwittingly omitted anyone from this list: Simon Barker, Leigh-Ann Bedall, Ueli Bellwald, Glen Bowersock, Christoph Eger, Tali Erickson-Gini, the late William L. Jobling, Martha S. Joukowsky, David L. Kennedy, the late Manfred Lindner, Burton MacDonald, Yiannis Meimaris, S. Thomas Parker, Yehuda Peleg, Dino Politis, the late Kenneth W. Russell, Jane Taylor, Mohammed Waheeb, Robert Weir, Robert Wenning, Donald S. Whitcomb, and Fawzi Zayadine. K. al-Bashaireh, who wrote Section 13.A.9, would like to thank Dr. David Dettman from the University of Arizona for the isotopic analysis, and Prof. Mahmoud Wardat for reading and editing the manuscript. Janet Jones, who wrote Chapter 14, would like to thank the generous efforts of several students at Bucknell University: Mallory Smith and Kris Baker, who organized and oversaw the creation of the plates; Marisa Ableson, Barry DeSain, Bonnie Wright, Rebecca Little, and Tracy Steneken, who helped with the processing of thousands of fragments; Phoebe Schweitzer, Ryan Crytzer, Keith DiMarco, Annelie Kahn, Mallory Smith, and Kris Baker drew hundreds of fragments and created most of the final drawings. Michael Finnegan, who wrote section 10.B on faunal remains would like to thank students who were of particular help in the reading of the bones: R. Lane, A. Campbell, D. Eckert, S. Meitl, C. VanSickle, and J. Bellew. Robert Lane also worked at Humayma during the summer excavation season in 1995 and Caroline VanSickle worked closely with me on the tables. The exercises were particular to those students who went on to graduate schools in various disciplines. Sara Stringfield, of the Department of Statistics, Kansas State University, was very helpful with canned statistical packages and setting up the original analysis.

Two anonymous readers provided very useful suggestions concerning the original manuscript, and the wonderful editor at ISD, Susanne Wilhelm, once again worked her magic. The publication subvention was provided by grant money from the Taggart Foundation, for which we are very grateful.

Addenda to Humayma Excavation Project, 1

The following book and articles are closely relevant to topics presented in Vol. 1, but were published or came to my attention too late to be taken account of in that volume: Ogden 1888, Bellwald 2008, Ohlig 2008, Erickson-Gini 2012, Nehmé 2012. In addition to Ogden, David Kennedy kindly pointed out three more references regarding early visitors to Humayma: Ridgaway 1876: 130, 134 (2 April 1874); E. L. Wilson 1885: 11 (ca. 25 March 1882), 1990: 69 (same account). Both Ridgaway and Wilson appear to have stopped only at Cistern no. 26 (*HEP 1*: 131–33), where Maughan's camels were watered in 1874, although Ridgaway also mentions the aqueduct and one of the off-take cisterns.

Abbreviations

AA	*Archäologischer Anzeiger*
AAE	*Arabian Archaeology and Epigraphy*
AASOR	*Annual of the American Schools of Oriental Research*
AB	Abbasid (mid-8th to early 10th century AD)
ABD	D. N. Freedman, ed., 1992. *Anchor Bible Dictionary.* 6 vols. New York: Doubleday.
ABSA	*Annual of the British School in Athens*
ADAJ	*Annual of the Department of Antiquities of Jordan*
AE	*L'Année épigraphique*
AJA	*American Journal of Archaeology*
ANRW	H. Temporini, W. Haase, eds., 1972–. *Aufstieg und Niedergang der römischen Welt.* Berlin: de Gruyter.
asl	above mean sea level
AY	Ayyubid (late 12th to late 13th century AD)
BA	*Biblical Archaeologist*
BASOR	*Bulletin of the American Schools of Oriental Research*
BEFAR	*Bulletin de l'École Française d'Athènes et de Rome*
BICS	*Bulletin of the Institute of Classical Studies, London*
BY	Byzantine (late 4th to mid-6th century AD)
cum	cubic metre
CAJ	*Cambridge Archaeological Journal*
CIS	*Corpus Inscriptionum Semiticarum* (1881–)
DOP	*Dumbarton Oaks Papers*
EANE	E. M. Meyers, ed., 1997. *Oxford Encyclopedia of Archaeology in the Near East.* 5 vols. Oxford: Oxford University.
EB	Early Byzantine (4th century AD)
EMC	*Echos du monde classique / Classical Views*
EN	Early Nabataean (1st century BC to early 1st century AD)
ER	Early Roman (late 1st century BC to late 1st century AD)
ETSA	Eastern Terra Sigillata A
EZ I	A. Bignasca et al., 1996. *Petra, ez Zantur I: Ergebnisse der Schweizerisch-Liechtensteinischen Ausgrabungen 1988–1992.* Mainz: Philipp von Zabern.
EZ II	S. Schmid, B. Kolb, 2000. *Petra, ez Zantur II: Ergebnisse der Schweizerisch-Liechtensteinischen Ausgrabungen.* Mainz: Philipp von Zabern.
EZ III	D. Keller, M. Grawehr, 2006. *Petra: ez Zantur III.* Mainz: Philipp von Zabern.
FA	Fatimid (mid-10th to mid-12th century AD)
FgrH	F. Jacoby, 1923–. *Fragmente der griechischen Historiker.* Leiden: Brill.
HD	Epigraphische Datenbank Heidelberg. Http://edh-www.adw.uni-heidelberg.de/home.
HEP 1	J. P. Oleson, 2010. *Humayma Excavation Project, 1: Resources, History, and the Water-Supply System.* Boston: American Schools of Oriental Research.

IEJ	*Israel Exploration Journal*
IGLS	M. Sartre et al., eds. 1929–. *Inscriptions greques et latines de la Syrie.* Paris: Geuthner.
JAS	*Journal of Archaeological Science*
JFA	*Journal of Field Archaeology*
JGS	*Journal of Glass Studies*
JNES	*Journal of Near Eastern Studies*
JRA	*Journal of Roman Archaeology*
JRS	*Journal of Roman Studies*
LA	*Liber Annuus*
LB	Late Byzantine (mid-6th to 7th century AD)
LN	Late Nabataean (late 2nd to 4th century AD)
LR	Late Roman (late 3rd to 4th century AD)
MA	Mamluk (late 13th to 15th century)
MB	Middle Byzantine (late 4th to mid-6th century AD)
MCM	manufactured construction material (i.e., plaster or mortar)
mcm	million cubic metres
mm	millimetre
MN	Middle Nabataean (mid-1st to mid-2nd century AD)
MPL	Maximum preserved length
MPW	Maximum preserved width
NEA	*Near Eastern Archaeology*
NEAEHL	E. Stern, A. Lewinson-Gilboa, J. Aviram, eds., 1993. *New Encyclopedia of Archaeological Excavations in the Holy Land.* 4 vols. New York: Simon & Schuster.
NFW	Nabataean fine ware
NISP	Number of identified (animal bone) specimens
NPFW	Nabataean painted fine ware
OT	Ottoman (16th to early 20th century AD)
PEF	*Palestine Exploration Fund*
PEQ	*Palestine Exploration Quarterly*
QDAP	*Quarterly of the Department of Antiquities in Palestine*
RBib	*Revue Biblique*
RCRFActa	*Res Cretariae Romanae Fautorum Acta*
RE	A. Pauly, G. Wissowa, W. Kroll, eds., 1893–1980. *Real-Encyclopädie der klassischen Altertumswissenschaft.* Munich: Druckenmüller.
RF	Roman foot, Roman feet, *pes monetalis;* equals 0.296 m.
RO	Roman (1st to 3rd century AD)
SHAJ	*Studies in the History and Archaeology of Jordan*
StDev	Standard Deviation
Th	Thick, thickness
UM	Umayyad (mid-7th to to mid-8th century AD)
UTM	Universal Transverse Mercator
ZDPV	*Zeitschrift des deutschen Palästina-Vereins*
ZPE	*Zeitschrift für Papyrologie und Epigraphik*

Chapter 1

Project Objectives and Excavation Areas, Field D120

by John P. Oleson and Robert Schick

1.A. OBJECTIVES OF THE HUMAYMA EXCAVATION PROJECT

In the course of initially mapping the site, the Director and the architects divided it up into six excavation fields for the purpose of administration and recording (see site plan, fig. 1.1). Field A incorporates all structures within a one kilometre radius of the base datum point in the settlement centre that are not part of some other excavation field, along with random surface finds. Field B incorporates the structures in the vicinity of Reservoirs nos. 67 and 68. Field C incorporates the field of ruins around the C101 Church and extending up the hill to the west. Field D incorporates the two areas of rubble north of Area B, and isolated structures in the vicinity. Field E incorporates the Roman Fort, Reservoir no. 63, the Bath, the Vicus, and the structures in their vicinity. Field F includes the Abbasid family Manor House and the structures to the south of it. Field Z, rarely used, has been reserved for surface finds or isolated structures that are found in the region of Humayma, but outside the radius of Field A.

Volume 1 of the Humayma Excavation Project report (*HEP 1*) concentrated on the topography, resources, and history of the site, and on the water-supply system that made the settlement of Hawara

possible, relying mainly on surveys and probes in 1986 and 1987, and excavation in 1989 and a few following seasons. The 1991 excavation areas were selected with the goal of obtaining a good sample of different types of structures, and of associated ceramics belonging to a wide chronological range (fig. 1.2). A prominent mound immediately to the north of Reservoir no. 68, in the very centre of the settlement (Field B), was selected as one excavation area, since a number of substantial wall stubs were visible on its surface, along with fragments of carefully worked Nabataean architectural mouldings. It was hoped that this area, registered as B100, might contain a major Nabataean public structure. Oleson directed excavation in this field with the assistance of de Bruijn and Dudley and has prepared the report. The second area, C101, consisted of the Lower Church, which had already been identified, since it had been partly cleared by the Department of Antiquities in 1962. Schick supervised the excavation of this field and prepared the report. The third field, F102, was selected because it seemed to be a well-preserved house associated with a circular cistern of Nabataean design. Some of the surface ceramics around the structure were Umayyad in character, suggesting that excavation might reveal a sequence of occupation across the whole period of Humayma's existence. In addition, it was thought

1

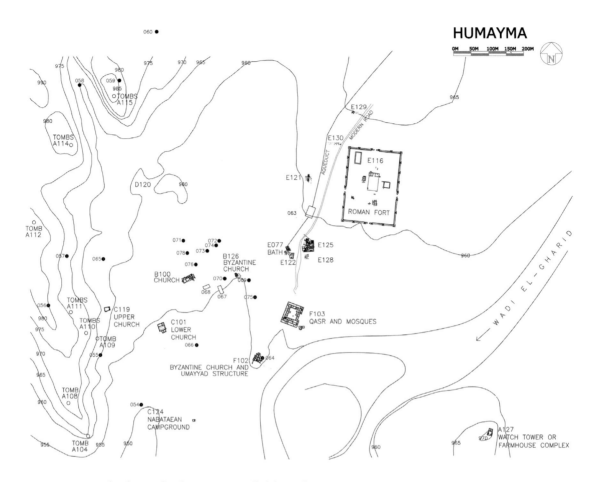

Fig. 1.1　*Topographical map of settlement centre. Filled dots indicate cisterns.*

that cultural material excavated near the edge of the settlement might show some interesting differences with that excavated in Field B, at the centre. 'Amr supervised the excavation of this field and wrote the preliminary reports on the basis of which J.P. Oleson prepared Chapter 5. The churches in Fields C119 and B126 were excavated in subsequent seasons by Schick as they came to the attention of the team, and they are included here because of their chronological relationship with the C101, B100, and F102 Churches. The Necropolis was surveyed and probed in 1992 and 1993 by J. Somogyi-Csizmazia to see how it related to the occupation history of the settlement centre.

During the last week of the 1993 season, Schick excavated two small probes in a large, multi-roomed structure at the northwest part of the site, given the identification number of D120 (on fig. 1.1, northwest of Cistern 071). In 1983 Eadie, without

any real justification, had identified the structure as an "Islamic Fort" (Eadie and Oleson 1986: 53). Schick's probes were designed to collect a sample of pottery that might provide evidence for dating the structure and to assess its potential as the target of further excavation (Schick in Oleson et al. 1995: 336–37). Although no overall plan of the structure was produced, the surface remains reveal a cluster of rooms grouped around two irregular courtyards; at least one of the rooms had a flat roof carried by a cross arch, and the interior wall surfaces were plastered white (figs. 1.3–4). The wall tumble suggests that the structure was a massive one, but there is no particular reason to identify it as a fort. There is also nothing specifically Islamic about the plan or building style, although elsewhere in the central part of the site structures visible on the surface have proven to be Early Islamic in date. Late Byzantine, Umayyad, and Abbasid sherds predominated in

FIG. 1.2   *Aerial view of settlement centre with indication of main excavation areas (Photo: W. Myers 21/07/1992, neg. H-1 no. 3).*

Fig. 1.3   *Area D120, Square 01.*

both probes. Because of the small scale of these probes, we have put this brief report into the introduction rather than include it as a separate chapter in the book.

The selection of these structures proved prescient, since they have produced data allowing reconstruction of the development and way of life of Hawara/Hauarra during the Nabataean, Byzantine, and Early Islamic periods. The excavation of the Roman Fort (E116), to be reported in *HEP 3*, filled in our knowledge of Roman and Early Byzantine Hauarra. The excavation of the Vicus structures (E125, E128), Late Roman Bath (E077), and Abbasid Family Manor House and Mosque, to be reported in HEP 4–5, have rounded out our knowledge of the rich and eventful history of the site. The structures presented in this volume are arranged in more or less chronological order: the Nabataean Campground in Chapter 3, the Necropolis in Chapter 4, the Nabataean through Early Islamic structures of F102 in Chapter 5, the Nabataean through Early Islamic structures of B100 in Chapter 6, the C101, C119, and B126 Byzantine

Churches in Chapters 7–9. Since the topic is relevant to the stratigraphic dating in the accounts of excavation, a discussion of the ceramic history of the site precedes them as Chapter 2. The ecofacts and artefacts are presented in Chapters 10–14.

Because of the volume of architectural and artefactual material produced by the excavations at Humayma, the major structures at the site have had to be divided among five volumes, as noted above. While this makes sense in terms of the types of structures and their chronology, it tends to obscure the overall development of the site, and the interrelationships among the structures. A discussion of the urban development of the site and its functioning is presented in *HEP 1* (pp. 21–62). Of the structures described in this volume, there must have been a great deal of interaction among the churches and the Early Islamic farm-houses, but we can only guess at its character. The data are not sufficient to interpret whether or not the five churches had specific or varying functions, but this seems likely in such a small community (see p. 553). The necropolis was undoubtedly a product

FIG. 1.4   *Area D120, Square 02.*

of the Nabataean inhabitants of Hawara, but the various tomb shafts were reused in the Byzantine and Early Islamic periods. Little is yet known about the houses of Nabataean Hawara and Byzantine Hauarra, and future excavation will have to fill in our knowledge of the urban framework of the site. Nevertheless, the structures and artefacts recorded here provide important information about the ways of life in an isolated desert settlement in the Nabataean, Byzantine, and Early Islamic periods.

Chapter 2

Ceramic Analysis

by John P. Oleson, Khairieh 'Amr, and Elisabeth Holmqvist-Saukkonen

2.A. SYSTEM OF RECORDING AND ANALYSIS

When 'Amr was asked to analyse the ceramics for the new Humayma Excavation project in 1991, relatively little was known about the ancient ceramic wares of Southern Jordan, particularly the coarse wares and kitchen wares. Excavation at Petra had produced some data (e.g. Hammond 1965; Johnson 1990; Parr 1970; Zeitler 1990), but with a focus on the fine wares of the Nabataean phases. Russell's work in this area (1990) was cut short by his premature death, although he had shared his results informally with many scholars, including 'Amr and Oleson. The ez-Zantur Project, which over several decades has produced spectacular documentation of ceramics and many other aspects of Nabataean and later cultures at Petra, only began in 1988 (Stucky 1990). 'Amr (1991) continued the excavation of kiln sites at Zurrabah, between Petra and Wadi Musa, begun in 1980. Villeneuve's excavation at Khirbet edh-Dharih was still in its early stages, but it provided some good parallels (Villeneuve 1990). Whitcomb's work at Aqaba naturally for the most part involved the Early Islamic period (Whitcomb 1987; 1988; 1989a–b), and Gichon (1974) reviewed some of the fine Byzantine wares in Southern Israel. Survey work in the region by Graf (1979) and Parker (1976; 1986; Parker et al. 1987) had produced some data, but in the absence of excavation the dating and attribution of wares remained tentative. The small excavation and survey by Eadie and Graf at Humayma in 1983 resulted in a brief report on the ceramics at the site (Eadie 1984: 220–24), but without any real documentation of the attributions.

The approach of the Humayma project from the start was a complete count of sherd numbers and weights from all excavation buckets, recorded by major ware categories, and a count of sherd numbers by individual wares. Since in 1991 'Amr was working for the most part in unknown territory, she set up a system for categorizing the various wares, both known and unknown, by means of the colours and surface treatment of the wares, under six major categories of Fine (F), Coarse (C), Kitchen (K), Storage (S), Handmade Wares (H), and Terracottas (T). The Fine Ware category included all fine and glazed wares and lamps. Coarse Wares included all vessels that were used for serving or temporary storage of food and drink, and Kitchen Wares all vessels that showed signs of being used for cooking or were known cook pot forms. Storage Wares included heavy vessels used for the storage or shipping of foodstuffs, while Handmade Wares included vessels not turned on the wheel, generally cups, bowls, and basins, along with *tabun* fragments. Many of these handmade vessels probably were produced locally, possibly by female specialists like those who produced handmade "Village Wares" up to the recent past in Jordan, or by itinerant potters. Johns (1998: 77–84) speculates on the social and economic reasons for the rise of handmade wares in the region. A few of the larger Storage Ware vessels were in fact partially hand-made, but by professionals, and with wheel-turned rims. Terracottas included hand-made and moulded figurines, along with bricks, roof tiles, flue pipes, and water pipes. Ultimately, the classification included 224 categories: Fine, 33; Glazed, 10; Lamps, 19; Coarse, 55; Kitchen, 20; Storage, 42; Handmade, 39; Terracottas, 6 (see Appendix 2.1). Oleson had suggested the main categories based on his previous archaeological excavation experience, which was in Italy, mainly at Cosa and Cetamura (Oleson and Oleson 1987: 243–44). Given this background, the distinction between Coarse and Kitchen Ware seemed logical. It turned out, however, that this categorization did not translate well to Southern Jordan, where many shapes were shared by vessels used for the presentation and serving or short term storage of food stuffs ("Coarse Ware") and by vessels used for cooking ("Kitchen Ware"). In hindsight, it would have been better to lump the two categories together as Coarse Ware or Utilitarian Ware.

Since new categories were created as new wares were identified, without prior knowledge of how important they might be, a significant number of categories included only a small number of examples. The full list of abbreviations, with the number of sherds noted for each category, is provided in Appendix 2.1. The abbreviations were intended to be descriptive, for easier recording, but length and formatting were constrained by the database system, rendering some abbreviations more opaque than others.

The goal of this categorization was the analysis of large amounts of ceramic material — particularly other than fine wares — that did not yet have ware names or chronological attributions, and to base this as much on fabric types from body sherds as on rim and base profiles. Many of the Fine Ware categories were directly associated with known ware types. The idea behind the system was to record the full spectrum of the ceramic varieties at the site, to determine which of them constituted distinct ware types, and to trace the evolution of the various wares through time. 'Amr set up an especially large number of categories for the Coarse, Kitchen, Storage, and Handmade Wares because she was trying to see in particular how much variation there was in these poorly known wares, and how the variations interrelated. The ware abbreviations were set up in a relational database run on a Macintosh computer by FoxBase©, which later was updated and made slightly more user-friendly in 1993 as FoxPro©. The input screens and relational processing program was written by John Howard in 1992 and 1993, and updated by Peter Cross in 2004. The program made it possible for 'Amr to compare the synchronic and diachronic relationships among selected wares.

Several problems, however, were involved with this approach. The greatest difficulty was the sheer amount of excavated pottery that had to be examined and sorted daily, a task 'Amr could not delegate because the classification system was intricate and subject to constant expansion or adjustment. In addition, there turned out to be very few chronologically distinct strata in the structures at Humayma, every stratum tending to contain residual ceramics from nearly every preceding period of occupation. Residual ceramic are an obvious and frequent issue in archaeological interpretation (e.g., Evans and Millett 1992; Van de Weghe et al. 2007), but the phenomenon is particularly intense at Humayma. Apparently, in antiquity, as today, potsherds littered the ground, where they were broken into fragments, moved around, and churned into the soil by the constant passage of sheep and goats. The sharp hooves of these animals eventually broke discarded vessels into sherds the size of which corresponds very closely to the fineness of the ware: the thinner the ware, the smaller the sherd, and the thicker, the larger. As a result, it was difficult to document the chronological evolution of the coarser wares simply by following their changes through a series of single period, closed deposits. For all these reasons, during the 1993, 1995, and 1996 excavation seasons, 'Amr applied her categorization only to the more archaeologically significant or interesting deposits, rather than to all the loci. During the analysis of the ceramic material presented in this volume, it has naturally been possible to make use as well of the numerous more recent publications of ceramics from the better stratified sites in Southern Jordan, particularly Aila, Petra, and Wadi Musa.

Finally, in 2000 Microsoft ceased to support FoxPro©, and the program (which was at best quite difficult to use) eventually could no longer function under the evolving Macintosh system files. After the 1996 season 'Amr had to move on to other responsibilities for the Department of Antiquities, and the work of ceramic analysis was undertaken by Yvonne Gerber, who has processed the material from the 1998 through 2005 seasons in a very different manner; her work will appear in the third and fourth volumes of the final report series. In 2005 the data, including all the ceramic abbreviations, were transferred to Excel© files. The relational analyses presented here are for the most part derived from laborious manipulation and comparison of the Excel© databases, but Oleson made use of heritage hardware and software to obtain some final results from the FoxPro© program in 2011–12.

2.B. WARE IDENTIFICATIONS AND RELATIONAL ANALYSES OF THE COARSE AND KITCHEN WARES

Despite all these difficulties, we have ware data for 93,081 sherds (out of 121,264 processed) over the first five excavation seasons, including all the structures presented in this volume: Fine Wares, 11,729 sherds; C Wares, 59,415 sherds; K Wares, 6,954 sherds; S Wares 10,799 sherds; H Wares, 1,693 sherds; T Wares, 2,491 sherds. The T Wares can be broken down as 219 brick fragments, 2,013 roof tile sherds, 116 flue tile sherds, 118 sherds of pipes, 22 fragments of handmade figurines, and 3 moulded figurines. A portion of these totals belongs to trenches at the Roman Fort (E116), Abbasid family Manor House (F103), and Roman *vicus* (E125), excavated on a small scale in 1995 and 1996, and to be reported on in the next volume of final reports. The total number of sherds recorded for the structures published in this volume is 50,975: B100, 12,067 (23.7% of the total for this group); C101, 21,247 (41.7%); F102, 15,022 (29.5%); C119, 226 (0.4%); C124, 2,366 (4.6%); Necropolis, 47 (0.1%). Although not comprehensive, this clearly is a very substantial data set. Since some of the categories set up by 'Amr in the end contained few, and occasionally no sherds, Appendix 2.2 presents a list of what she determined to be the most prevalent wares, with indications of chronology where known. Except for some of the widely-known fine wares, all categories for which fewer than 10 sherds were registered have been omitted from this appendix, or collapsed into a more comprehensive category. Because of the omissions, the sherd totals vary from those given above. Appendix 2.3 provides sherd counts for these prevalent wares for all the structures treated in this volume except the Necropolis, along with percentages of the collection for each structure for wares exhibiting 100 or more examples.

2.C. PRESENTATION OF CERAMIC CHRONOLOGIES FOR EXCAVATED LOCI

The classification system outlined above had some chronological value for the non-Fine Wares, and, with the assistance of known dates for various wares established by archaeological work elsewhere and comparison with datable non-ceramic finds from the same loci, 'Amr attributed dates to the ceramic material in the excavation buckets. A series of two-letter abbreviations was established for the main historical and cultural phases at the site, with approximate chronological boundaries. These abbreviations, supplemented by memo notes where appropriate, were entered on the ceramic bucket sheets during processing, and the data were entered into the FoxPro© database. Given the enormous amount and significant variety of the ceramic material excavated at the structures with which this volume is concerned, details and drawings of the individual sherds or vessels excavated can only be presented for selected loci of special importance, or for vessels of particular interest. Unfortunately, through recording errors, the ware descriptions and Munsell readings for about 18 percent of the illustrated vessels have been lost. For most of the text in this book, the ceramic evidence is cited only by the two-letter abbreviations noted in Table 2.1. Sometimes these abbreviations are cited directly in the narration of the excavation, sometimes in

Table 2.1 Chronological abbreviations used in the ceramic and non-ceramic databases.

ABBREVIATION		EXPANDED TERM	CHRONOLOGY
EN	=	Early Nabataean	1st century BC–early 1st AD
MN	=	Middle Nabataean	mid-1st–mid-2nd century AD
LN	=	Late Nabataean	late 2nd–4th century AD
ER	=	Early Roman	late 1st century BC–late 1st AD
RO	=	Roman	1st–3rd century AD
LR	=	Late Roman	late 3rd–4th century AD
EB	=	Early Byzantine	4th century AD
MB	=	Middle Byzantine	late 4th–mid-6th century AD
LB	=	Late Byzantine	mid-6th–7th century AD
UM	=	Umayyad	mid-7th–mid-8th century AD
AB	=	Abbasid	mid-8th–early 10th century AD
FA	=	Fatimid	mid-10th–mid-12th century AD
AY	=	Ayyubid	late 12th–late 13th century AD
MA	=	Mamluk	late 13th–15th century
OT	=	Ottoman	16th–early 20th century

parentheses along with the locus number or numbers involved in the narration. In order to save space and laborious periphrasis, we have avoided expanding the two-letter abbreviations. The effect can be a little brutal, but the presentation of our data is more efficient. These same abbreviations were used in the database entries for non-ceramic finds. Some of the chronological ranges we used for our ceramic analysis are slightly different from those traditionally used in the region (esp. LR, EB, MB, LB), but the ranges made sense to our team, are used consistently, and are set out in Table 2.1. Similar terms are used for the glass artefacts catalogued in Chapter 14, but some of the chronological ranges specified by Jones are slightly different from those used for the ceramics. Given the beginning of site occupation in the first century BC, it seemed unlikely that confusion would arise between the abbreviations EB, MB, and LB and the similar abbreviations for "Early, Middle, and Late Bronze Age" used at other sites in the Near East.

Since the labels have both cultural and chronological meaning, there is a certain amount of overlap, making the system less mechanical than it might at first appear. Early Nabataean, for example, overlaps chronologically with Early Roman, but a sherd of Nabataean painted fine ware Phase 2a would be attributed to the first category, a contemporary sherd of an imported Western Terra Sigillata vessel to the latter. A Phase 4 Nabataean painted fine ware bowl would be assigned to Late Nabataean, while a sherd of a contemporary Class 47 amphora would be labelled as Late Roman. The same approach was followed during the processing of non-ceramic artefacts, such as Nabataean as opposed to Roman coins, or Late Byzantine chancel screen fragments as opposed to contemporary Umayyad steatite vessels. The loci presented in the account of the excavation naturally have been assigned their chronological labels based on both the ceramic and non-ceramic artefacts contained in them. Because of the constant churning up of the strata, few loci later than the beginning of the Middle Nabataean period could be designated as closed, single period deposits and awarded a single chronological indicator.

The following section indicates the named wares that most commonly triggered the abbreviated chronological indicators they are associated with, along with a selection of the excavation reports that provided appropriate parallels for the unnamed Coarse, Kitchen, and Storage Wares encountered at Humayma. Perusal of this list makes it clear that the civilian inhabitants of ancient Humayma imported nearly all their ceramics from a fairly limited number of sites in Southern Jordan. The soldiers in the Roman Fort (Field E116) cast their net more widely, as the analysis of the ceramics found there — to be presented in the next final report volume — will show. Twelve seasons of excavation at Humayma have yielded no evidence for the local production of wheel-made wares; only the more humble handmade wares are likely to have been produced locally. This importation of ceramics is not surprising, given the absence in the immediate area of clay and robust fuel, the scarcity of water, and the relatively small population. Although the ceramic sample analyzed for this volume is vastly larger than that presented in *HEP* 1: 231–325, the short characterization of the regional connections of the corpus provided by Oleson in *HEP* 1: 327–28 for the most part holds good.

By far the largest portion of the ceramics at Humayma find their best parallels at Petra or at sites equally as dependent on Petra as was Humayma. These vessels were produced at Petra and exported to Humayma through at least the Late Byzantine period. The wares include painted and unpainted Nabataean fine ware, along with Nabataean storage jars, jars, cooking pots, bowls, juglets, and lamps, and a variety of Late Roman and Byzantine coarse wares and lamps. A smaller percentage of the corpus was imported from Aqaba, such as the so-called Aqaba Ware (Dolinka 2003), Mahesh Ware (Whitcomb 1989b), amphoras, and large jars. The Nabataean so-called Cream Ware (or Green Ware) was also imported, although the production site has not yet been identified. Other imports from farther afield include Parthian glazed ware, Eastern Terra Sigillata A (Southern Anatolia?) and B (Eastern Aegean or Western Asia Minor?) (Hayes 1985: 10, 49–50; Slane 1997: 272, 380), Roman factory lamps, and North African Red Slip. The array of non-local wares found at Aila (Parker 2002: 423–25; Dolinka 2003: 70–74) is in broad outlines similar to that found at Humayma, although more extensive in variety. Holmquist (oral communication 22 November 2008; pp. 16–23) has proven through laboratory analysis of ceramic fabrics that cooking pots were exported from Petra and Khirbet edh-Dharih to Aila, and that Aila (Aqaba ware) amphoras were exported to Petra, Khirbet edh-Dharih, and Elusa. Analysis of Aila amphoras found as far off as Yemen and Ethiopia has shown that they all originated in Aqaba (Parker 2009a: Tomber 2008: 70–71, 80–81).

Combined with the results at Humayma, these data testify to a lively regional trade in all types of ceramic vessels, but with Humayma always at the receiving end. Much of the trade in ceramics from Petra south and from Aila north would have passed through Humayma on the *Via Nova Traiana* and its predecessor. Nevertheless, the number of wares from outside the region is more restricted at Humayma than at the sea port of Aila, or the large commercial and population centre of Petra.

2.C.1. Selected Correlations between Chronological Designations and Ceramic Wares or Sites

It would not be feasible or even particularly useful to cite here all the publications that provide parallels to the Humayma ceramics. The point here is to provide a sense of the basis on which 'Amr assigned chronological indicators to the ceramic excavation buckets, along with an indication of the sites with which the Humayma ceramic corpus shows the most parallels.

Early Nabataean (EN)

Nearly all the Fine, Coarse, and Kitchen wares found at Humayma in this period were produced at Petra. They are thoroughly documented by Schmid and Brogli in *EZ* I, by Schmid in *EZ* II, and by Grawehr in *EZ* III; see also Alcock et al. 2010: 161–65. The Nabataean Painted Fine Ware (NPFW) of Phase 2b (30/20–21 BC) is fairly rare in the areas excavated up through 2005, but it is present. The absence of Phases 1 and 2a of this ware reinforces evidence suggesting that the founder of the town was Aretas IV rather than Aretas III (see *HEP* 1: 50–52). This was also the period when Aila was founded (Parker 2009b). The piriform unguentaria presented by Johnson (1990) are relatively common. The Coarse and Kitchen Wares of Petra described by Gerber (1994; 1997) find many parallels at Humayma in this phase (Gerber 2008a).

Middle Nabataean (MN)

The ground at Humayma is carpeted with Nabataean Fine Ware sherds, both painted and unpainted, belonging to this period, particularly Schmid Phases 3a, 3b, and 3c (Schmid in *EZ* I and *EZ* II; Bikai and Perry 2001). A small amount of Nabataean Sigillata appears as well: B100, 2 sherds; C101, 6; F102, 3; E116, 18; E125, 22. This is a different ware than that termed "Nabataean Sigillata" by Negev (1972; 1986: 26–35; cf. Gunneweg et al. 1983: 7, 14), involving the small-scale production of vessels with local Petra clay, but distinguished by the use of a heavier and thicker slip. 'Amr (oral communication, September 2011) believes that this ware may have been an experiment, soon abandoned. The Coarse and Kitchen Wares described by Gerber (1994; 1997; 2001c) and others (Bikai and Perry 2001) at Petra and at Khirbet edh-Dharih (Villeneuve 1990) find many parallels at Humayma in this phase (Gerber 2008b), along with the Cream Ware or Green Ware found throughout Southern Jordan ('Amr 1992; *EZ* I: 138-39; Negev 1986: 71–72). Some pipes from Wadi Musa are similar to contemporary pipes at Humayma ('Amr and al-Momani 2001: 271; cf. *HEP* 1: 331), and identical disk-like hypocaust support tiles and box flues (*tubuli*) are found at both sites (Petra: Kolb and Keller 2000: 361–63; S. Schmid, oral communication, December 2009; Humayma: *HEP* 1: 223–30; Oleson 1990). Square tiles have been found as well at both sites (Wadi Musa: 'Amr et al. 1997; Oleson 1990). M.B. Reeves and C. Harvey are preparing a study of all the ceramic building materials in the region.

Late Nabataean (LN)

Petra remains the main source of ceramics in this period as well, for both Fine Wares (Schmid in *EZ* I and *EZ* II; 'Amr 2004), and Coarse and Kitchen Wares (Gerber 1998; 2001a).

Early Roman (ER)

Only one sherd of Western Terra Sigillata was identified in the Humayma corpus presented here, in a mixed context in Room 03 outside the C101 Church. The general absence of ER material is not surprising, since Roman occupation of the site did not begin until after the conquest of 106.

Roman (RO)

The structures presented in this volume saw little Roman occupation. While a number of Roman wares are found in the Fort (E116) and *vicus* (E125), elsewhere on the site one indicator of this period are second-century sherds of Eastern Terra Sigillata (ETSA; *EZ* I: 133–36; Hayes 1985: 9–48), which in all cases survives as scraps mixed in with earlier and later wares. Four sherds of this ware appeared in B100, 33 in C101, 11 in F102. In C101 the sherds of this ware were found for the most part below the Church pavement, as part of an enormous dump of pottery and soil brought in from elsewhere on the site and used to level the area for construction. There is undoubtedly some overlap among the RO Coarse and Kitchen Wares at Humayma and the MN Coarse and Kitchen Wares described by Gerber (1994; 2001c) and others (Bikai and Perry 2001; Alcock et al. 2010: 161–65) at Petra and at Khirbet edh-Dharih (Villeneuve 1990). The bricks, roof tiles, flue tiles, and pipes are typically associated with RO, LR, and EB period structures at Humayma (*HEP* 1: 327–31, although one pipe found re-used in the Fort resembles the pipes of the first-century BC pipeline in the Petra Siq (*HEP* 1: 429, fig. 8.10; Bellwald 2008: 49–55; Bellwald and al-Huneidi 2003: 55–60).

Late Roman (LR)

The LR wares at ez-Zantur in Petra (Fellman Brogli in *EZ* 1: 219–82) provide some good parallels for Humayma. African Red Slip Ware (ARS; Hayes 1972; 1985), an indicator of trade with the Mediterranean, particularly from the mid-third century onward, is more evenly distributed around the site than the Roman ETSA, perhaps because the sample recovered so far is twice as big: B100, 18 sherds; C101, 46 sherds; F102, 23 sherds. It is not clear whether the import of ARS continued into EB and LB. There are also many good parallels between Petra and Humayma in the Coarse and Kitchen Wares (*EZ* I: 219–40; Gerber 2001a; 2008a–b). The bricks, roof tiles, flue tiles, and pipes are typically associated with RO, LR, and EB period structures (*HEP* 1: 223–30, Oleson 1990), but during this period there is much more evidence from the Roman

Fort. It is notable that the site apparently lacks significant quantities of the other imported fine wares attested elsewhere in the region. No sherds were identified as Egyptian Red Slip, only one sherd of Phocaean Red Slip has been found (in Field E077, the Roman-Byzantine Bath), and only a few sherds of Cypriote Red Slip were recognized (in E116, the Roman Fort). Egyptian Red Slip is common at Aila, and the other two wares are common even in inland Palestine. It is curious that these fine wares did not reach Humayma in significant quantities, even during the Byzantine period, when the inhabitants were importing substantial quantities of marble from the Mediterranean.

Early Byzantine (EB)

African Red Slip Ware (ARS) continues as an indicator of indirect trade with the Mediterranean. There continue to be good parallels between Petra and Humayma in the Coarse and Kitchen Wares (*EZ I*: 219–40; Gerber 2001a; 2008b). The bricks, roof tiles, flue tiles, and pipes are typically associated with RO, LR, and EB period structures, but at this period there is much more evidence from the Roman Fort.

Middle Byzantine (MB)

African Red Slip Ware (ARS) continues as an indicator of trade with the Mediterranean. The curious Deir 'Ain 'Abata salt-glazed ware (Freestone et al. 2001; Politis et al. 2012: 206–9), a grey cooking pot ware, appears in small amounts at Humayma. There continue to be many good parallels between Petra (Petra Church, ez-Zantur, Jabal Harûn, Zurrabah kiln) and Humayma in the Coarse and Kitchen Wares ('Amr and Momani 1999; Gerber 1998; 2001a; 2001b; 2008b).

Late Byzantine (LB)

The close parallels between Petra (Jabal Harûn) and Humayma in the Coarse and Kitchen Wares (Gerber 2000; 2001d; 2002; 2008a–b), and for a number of Coarse and Storage Ware types at Aqaba (Melkawi et al. 1994). A type of Fine Late Byzantine Ware is found in Southern Israel as well

as at Humayma (Gichon 1974; Waliszewski 2001: 97, 105, fig. 6.8). Magness (1993: 193–201) argues that this ware originated in southern Palestine, perhaps around Jerusalem, and was produced in various forms from the mid-fifth century into the tenth century.

Umayyad (UM)

There continue to be many good parallels between Petra (Jabal Harûn) and Humayma in the Coarse and Kitchen Wares (Gerber 2000; 2001d; 2002; 2008a–b). A type of Kitchen Brown Ware is frequent at Humayma in the LB to UM transition and continues on into the AB. Also frequent are large Storage vessels in a cream ware, often Aila amphorae ('Amr and Schick 2001; Whitcomb 2001) and large, partly handmade storage jars turned on a slow wheel, found at Aila, Petra, Khirbet edh-Dharih and elsewhere ('Amr and Schick 2001; Melkawi et al. 1994; Villeneuve 1990; Walmsley 2001a; Whitcomb 2001). Red-coloured wares with a fine calcite temper produced at al-Zurraba outside Petra represent a continuation of the Byzantine tradition ('Amr and al-Momani 2011: 206); these vessels were exported to Humayma as well. The many thick, handmade *tabun* fragments (smooth and burned on the interior, usually rough on the exterior, cream to reddish brown) begin to appear in this period and continue up to the present. *Tabun* ovens have been built and used throughout the Near East from the Bronze Age through the present. At Humayma, however, they appear in our excavation record only with the Umayyad period, since that is when the structures on which we have focussed attention begin to be abandoned and used for purposes not associated with worship or habitation.

Abbasid (AB)

More of the cream wares appear in this period at Humayma. In northern Jordan the painting on these wares is very indicative of UM or AB: red ware with white paint was typically UM (Smith et al. 1973: pls. 30–31, 45, Pella), but by the end of UM to early AB it became a cream ware with red painting (Najjar 1989). There is little of this painted ware at Humayma; just some surface sherds. A brown Kitchen Ware is typical of this period at Humayma, along with unglazed, cream Mahesh Ware (Whitcomb 1989b; 1990–91). There were 65 sherds of a cream, frit-body ware with blue glaze common in the Late Abbasid. This may be the ware formerly referred to as Raqqa ware, or a blue-green glazed storage jar from Southern Iraq (Whitcomb 1990–91: 53, fig. 8), the latter of which is tenth-century in date. A small number of typical moulded Abbasid lamps with tendril decoration (Gerber 2008b, Holmqvist 2011: figs. 5–6, Jabal Harûn; Hadad 1999, Bet Shean; Khalil and Kareem 2002: 140-43, Khirbat Yajuz) have appeared at Humayma. Some of the handmade wares may belong to this period, to judge from parallels at Gharandal (Walmsley and Grey 2001: 153–59). Because of their very nature, local handmade wares often show similarities in functional shapes, but they are unlikely to share in geographically widespread traditions of decoration. At Gharandal, coarse handmade wares, both painted and unpainted, seem to appear only after 850–900, alongside wheel-made wares (Walmsley and Grey 2001: 153–59, figs. 10–12). Some of the simple geometric patterns painted with brownish-red to pink matte paint bear a generic resemblance to those on the painted handmade pots at Humayma (see figs. 5.48, 49, 56, 59, 55; 6.10, 17, 28), but given their generic simplicity it is unnecessary to postulate a direct connection. There are many parallels in the enormous corpus of Early Islamic pottery at Hesban (Sauer and Herr 2012: 507–38). It is interesting that some sixth to seventh-century wheel-made bowls at Tel Jawa carry similar, carelessly painted motifs (Daviau 2010: 188, 195). The handles at Humayma vary from circumferential ridges, to ridges with projecting flat lug handles, to small pointed lugs.

Fatimid (FA)

The typical handmade cream wares with linear, geometric, or dotted red-brown painting are common in this period at Humayma and Aila (Johns 1998; al-Salameen et al. 2011: 239). Some of the vessels also show impressed dots, or incised lines, as at Aila (Whitcomb 1988: 214–15). There are parallels at Khirbat an-Nawafla ('Amr et al. 2000: fig.

18.1, 4) for the long lines and geometric patterns of impressed dots seen on some handmade wares at Humayma (e.g., fig. 5.48). This was a period of instability and decline at Aila (Whitcomb 1990–91: 56), and Humayma most likely was even worse off.

Ayyubid (AY), Mamluk (MA), Ottoman (OT)

It is difficult to distinguish among the wares of these periods other than by archaeological context, because the wares are so generic, and so few parallels in the south have been published (cf. Brown 1988: 236–41, Shobak; Sinibaldi 2009, Petra; Schmid 2010: 232–33, Petra; Whitcomb 1988: 211–18, Aila). The small vessels at Humayma, mainly cups and bowls in a brown fabric thick with chaff impressions, often show mottled colours ranging from orange/yellow to red to grey/black (cf. Milwright 2008: 146–54). Thirty-one examples had red paint on the surface, and many were decorated with punctuations or incised lines. A large deposit of this material from Umayyad to Ottoman levels in the Abbasid Manor House (F103) awaits publication. The complete absence of Ottoman ceramic tobacco pipes at Humayma may suggest that Ottoman occupation ended by the seventeenth century (Sinibaldi and Tuttle 2011: 448).

2.D. CHRONOLOGICAL STATISTICS FOR THE FIVE MAIN EXCAVATION AREAS

Table 2.2 shows the number of "bucket occurrences" by chronological period for the five excavation fields, in other words, the number of excavation buckets for each area that contained sherds from that particular period. Since nearly all the buckets contained sherds from more than one period, the total occurrences for period or field add up to 4,539, far more than the 1,422 buckets registered in those five excavation fields. MN, LN, and LB sherds logged 2,475 out of the 4,539 occurrences (54.5%), highlighting both the importance and persistence of the Nabataean occupation of the site, and the construction and heavy use of the churches in the Late Byzantine period. In Field C124, the LN and MN occurrences constituted 81% of the total, underlining the overwhelmingly Nabataean character of the occupation of the Campsite area. For the other

Table 2.2 The number of "bucket occurrences" by chronological period for the five excavation fields.

	MN	LN	ER	RO	LR	EB	MB	LB	UM	AB	FA	AY	MA	OT	No. of bucket occurrences	No. of buckets for field
B100	214	91	11	19	6	13	23	267	244	217	14	6	5	8	1,138	356
C101	360	224	52	37	22	11	70	358	246	113	1	0	0	1	1,495	463
F102	296	184	19	21	10	7	22	385	359	283	52	29	27	70	1,764	509
C119	11	8	2	0	1	0	0	14	14	7	0	0	0	0	57	29
C124	60	1	2	7	3	3	3	2	2	0	0	0	0	2	85	65
Total Occurrences	941	508	86	84	42	34	118	1026	865	620	67	35	32	81	4,539	1,422

Note that most buckets contained sherds from more than one period, so the totals for period or field add up to more than the 1,422 buckets registered.

four excavation fields, UM and AB sherds logged 1,483 out of the 4,539 occurrences (32.7%), while sherds of the periods FA to OT logged only 213 out of the 4,539 occurrences (4.7%) and 84 percent of those were found in Field F102. Clearly Fields B100, C101, and F102 were occupied during the Umayyad and Abbasid periods, and the architectural records of these areas reflect the fact. There is, however, much less ceramic evidence for the later periods. There were almost no post-Abbasid sherds in Field C101 (the Lower Church), and the sherds of that period recorded in Field B100 (Byzantine church and Early Islamic Farm House) constitute only 2.9% of the bucket occurrences in that field, indicating abandonment sometime in the ninth century. There was, however, some degree of continued occupation at the Early Islamic farm-house built into the Byzantine church in Field F102: 178 out of 1,764 bucket occurrences were attributed to the Fatimid through Ottoman periods, or 10.1%. The majority of these occur at either end of that long period. This later occupation may have been attracted to this part of the site by contemporary reoccupation of the Abbasid Manor House (F103; see pp. 93, 154–55).

2.E. OBSERVATIONS ON FREQUENCY PATTERNS OF SELECT WARES IN THE CERAMIC CORPUS

Appendix 2.3 provides data concerning the frequency of occurrence of various ceramic wares in

the structures published in this volume. Although the frequent appearance of earlier wares in later strata makes a nuanced discussion impossible, some deductions can be drawn from the data. Distribution patterns within the various structures will be discussed in the chapters concerning the structures themselves.

By far the most common fine wares in these structures were Nabataean painted and unpainted fine ware (11% of the corpus, 95.6% of the fine ware). The Nabataean campground (C124) has highest proportion of fine ware by far: 28%. This is not surprising, given the one-period, Nabataean character of that field, and the fact that the vast proportion of fine ware at the site is Nabataean. The C119 Church had the next highest proportion of fine ware (15%), which might seem surprising for a one-period, Byzantine church, but the sample is small. In addition, the proportion of kitchen wares naturally is very small, which skews the proportions of the other wares. Fine wares constituted 13.7% of the ceramics in the C101 Church, which might also seem high, but most of the fine ware, including both Nabataean wares and ETSA, was found in the fill below the pavements. This fill, brought in to level the building site, contained large amounts of ceramics from elsewhere on the site. The F102 Church and house site had the smallest proportion of fine ware (9.5%), and much of this came from Nabataean levels in Square 1, below and predating the Church. The sample of vitreous glazed wares was very small (n=25), and all of it came from F102, perhaps because of the longer Early Islamic occupation of that area. The sample of lamps (n=145) from the areas described in this volume is too small to allow much discussion, since the vast majority of lamps found at the site as a whole (n=841) are Nabataean and Roman lamps from the Roman Fort (E116, n=430) and the *vicus* (E125, n=196). The largest concentration in the areas presented here was 18 Umayyad lamps found in the later occupation strata of F102. Two Abbasid lamps were found in B100, and an interesting handmade Fatimid lamp in F102.

The coarse wares show fewer divergences in proportions, although overall this ware was less common in the C101 Church than elsewhere. The most common of these wares were coarse red ware with cream slip (c_rd_crs), coarse red ware (c_rd), coarse red ware with a grey black surface (c_rd_gbs), and ribbed coarse red ware with a grey black surface (c_rd_gbsr). C_rd constitutes nearly half of C124 sample, which suggests it might be early, while c_rd_gbs and c_rd_gbsr constitute a low percentage, which suggests they might be later wares. The high proportion of c_rd_gbsr in C119 supports the same chronology. Coarse red ware with a brown surface (c_rd_brs) is particularly concentrated in B100.

Areas B100, C101, and F102, where there was later domestic reoccupation, naturally show the highest proportion of kitchen wares. Most common is kitchen red ware with grey-black surface (k_rd_gbs), which is most common in B100, least common in the Byzantine church C119 and the Nabataean campground C124, then ribbed kitchen red ware with grey-black surface (k_rd_gbsr), which shows the same pattern. The next most common ware is ribbed kitchen red ware with brown surface (k_rd_brsr), which is prevalent in C101 and F102, rare in C119 and C124.

The highest proportion of storage wares appears in B100, reflecting the use of this structure as a farm-house, while it is lowest in the Nabataean campground (C124), possibly because of the transitory character of the occupation. The proportion is also high in the C119 church, but the sample size is low (n=34). The most common wares are ribbed red ware with cream surface (s_rd_crsr), which are a high proportion in C119 and B100, but nearly

absent from C124. The proportion of red ware with cream surface (s_rd_crs) is low in C119 and C124, and higher in F102. The proportion of red ware with grey-brown surface (s_rd_gbs) is higher in F102, low in C101, C119, and C124.

No handmade wares were found in C119 or C124, where there was no reoccupation in the Islamic period. The highest proportion was found in F102, where there was significant later occupation, probably up through the Ottoman period. The most common ware is red ware (h_rd), prevalent in C101, then F102. *Tabun* fragments (h_tab,) are most common in the later occupation phases of F102 and C101.

Bricks, tiles, pipes, and terracottas are a very small proportion of the ceramic sample (n=139, 0.3%), and nearly all of this material was found in B100 and F102. If the churches had gabled roofs with roof tiles, the tiles were salvaged prior to their destruction, since only 89 fragments were found; see the discussion on pp. 157–58. Only 33 brick fragments were recovered, probably from bricks salvaged from Roman or Early Byzantine period structures elsewhere in the site and carried in for reuse.

2.F. CHEMICAL CHARACTERISATION (ED-XRF) OF HUMAYMA COARSE WARE CERAMICS
(E. Holmqvist-Saukkonen)

At present, any indications of on-site ceramic manufacture, e.g., ceramic wasters or the like, are absent from Humayma. The relatively small-sized community may have had little demand for localized pottery manufacture, and fuel, water, and suitable clay resources were restricted in the vicinity of the site (*HEP* 1: 327). Therefore, it appears more likely that the coarse ware ceramic corpus found at the site comprises of imported vessels, presumably originating from a number of sources. Known ceramic workshops nearest to Humayma are located in Petra and Aqaba/Aila (Melkawi, 'Amr et al. 1994; 'Amr and al-Momani 1999; Whitcomb 2001). The proximity and economic relevance of Aila and Petra, and the transport links connecting the three sites — Humayma is located half-way down the main Aila–Petra route — make them very likely sources of ceramic supply to Humayma, although there may have been also other, currently unidentified ceramic workshops in the region. Ceramic transport from Aila has already been attested by macroscopically identified Aqaba amphorae found in Humayma ('Amr and Schick 2001). This links the site with the inland transportation network of the Aqaba containers, transported to al-Sadaqa, Petra, Khirbet edh-Dharih, Elusa and possibly further away ('Amr and al-Momani 2011: 313; Holmqvist 2010). The Aqaba amphorae were also transported by ship throughout the Red Sea Region (Tomber 2004: 398–400; Parker 2009a). In addition to the Aila links, typological comparanda for many ceramic forms recovered in Humayma can be found in Petra (see, e.g., Fellmann Brogli 1996; Gerber 2008b; Gerber and Holmqvist 2008), which may indicate a common source.

This report summarizes preliminary results of the energy dispersive x-ray fluorescence spectrometry (ED-XRF) of selected ceramic samples from Humayma (figs. 2.1–2), carried out in order to approach the question of provenance of coarse ware ceramics recovered at the site.[1] The analytical instrument employed was a Spectro XLab 2000 polarizing ED-XRF spectrometer, based at the Wolfson Archaeological Laboratory, Institute of Archaeology, University College London. The analytical specimens were prepared by following a scientific protocol (described in detail in Holmqvist 2010), in which a sample of ca. 8 grams was cut from the sherd, ground into a fine powder of which a subsample of ca. 4 grams was pressed into a pellet. All compositional values presented in this report are mean values of three XRF runs, with oxygen added by stoichiometry. The results are normalized to 100% by weight. Standards ECRM 776 1, NIST 76a, and SARM 69 were included in each analytical run to control the data precision and accuracy.

In addition to the chemical characterization, the sampled Humayma ceramics were integrated in a wider research project. This enabled comparative analysis with ceramic compositional data acquired from other sites, particularly Aqaba and Jabal Harûn in Petra (Holmqvist 2010), and examination of ceramic exchange between these locations. The sampled ceramics are domestic and utilitarian forms typical of the Byzantine and Islamic periods

in southern Transjordan, from the fourth to eleventh centuries AD. A detailed typo-chronological assessment of the sampled ceramics is beyond the scope of this report, and only a restricted number of regionally focused ceramic parallels will be given in the following catalogue. Similar forms and their geographical distribution are discussed in detail in Holmqvist 2010 and Holmqvist-Saukkonen (forthcoming). A more detailed typo-chronological discussion will be included in a forthcoming publication of the wider project.

The results of the first 20 Humayma samples (H1–20) analysed with ED-XRF are displayed in Table 2.3. As expected, the clearest compositional links can be found between the three amphora sherds recovered in Humayma (H14–16) and the Aqaba reference group composition (based on Holmqvist 2010, Table 1 showing mean values of selected reference group samples). The compositional patterns of H14–16 correlate with the local Aqaba fabric, characterized by high CaO, SrO, and BaO values, confirming their statuses as imports from Aqaba. The same source may also apply to samples H2 (comb decorated bowl/basin), H10–11 (comb decorated cream ware jars), H12–13 (containers, latter with comb decoration) and H17 (coarse ware bowl) that are compositionally relatively similar to the Aqaba fabric. This assignment should be treated as tentative and confirmed by microstructural analysis, at least in the case of H2 and H10 which present BaO concentrations uncharacteristically high for the Aqaba reference group (at ca. 810 and 990 ppm, respectively, compared to less than 500 ppm on average). In addition, H10 and also H17 display CaO values (ca. 22 wt %) above the reference group average (ca. 14 wt %), and the same applies to the K_2O value of H12 at 4.6 wt %. Scanning electron microscopy analysis (SEM-EDS) of Aqaba reference group samples showed quartz, plagioclase, K-feldspars, biotite and garnet group minerals embedded in a calcareous ceramic matrix (Holmqvist 2010), and related microstructure may later confirm the Aqaba source for H2, H10, H12 and H17. The elemental concentrations of these samples, however, may also be indicative of a Negev source (Holmqvist 2010: 201–2, 236).

The analysed open-form cooking pot (sample H1) is a compositional outlier in the Humayma

Table 2.3   ED-XRF compositional data. Reference groups based on Holmqvist 2010. Thirteen most significant elements only.

		Na₂O %	MgO %	Al₂O₃ %	SiO₂ %	K₂O %	CaO %	TiO₂ %	MnO %	Fe₂O₃ %	ZnO ppm	SrO ppm	ZrO₂ ppm	BaO ppm
HUMAYMA SAMPLES														
Cooking pot	H1	0.17	1.01	14.34	72.20	1.49	0.88	1.12	0.15	8.29	122	187	340	517
Basin/bowl	H2	0.92	1.50	14.39	59.79	2.08	14.61	0.64	0.11	5.26	97	682	205	813
Basin/bowl	H3	0.40	4.42	11.96	56.95	1.66	13.62	0.61	0.06	5.31	51	220	218	129
Jar	H4	0.45	1.55	17.38	65.69	2.31	5.19	0.79	0.04	6.10	112	312	277	510
Jar	H5	0.07	1.06	12.77	74.37	2.29	3.32	0.79	0.03	5.01	76	158	459	350
Jar	H6	0.20	1.51	13.86	64.40	1.91	11.52	0.64	0.05	5.46	77	344	204	348
Jar	H7	0.24	1.09	17.04	70.80	2.07	1.43	0.70	0.02	6.00	56	95	174	102
Jar	H8	0.28	4.61	13.52	59.23	1.78	13.16	0.69	0.13	6.15	57	368	244	199
Jar	H9	0.18	0.93	18.32	71.57	1.76	0.64	0.80	0.02	5.52	64	89	246	138
Jar	H10	0.49	2.10	14.88	51.78	2.51	21.67	0.61	0.09	5.27	97	724	182	991
Jar	H11	1.01	2.47	14.79	54.86	1.69	17.06	0.70	0.14	6.57	142	558	199	539
Jar	H12	1.97	2.42	12.81	58.38	4.13	13.07	0.62	0.10	5.07	105	516	274	677
Jar	H13	0.29	1.37	15.04	65.65	1.69	9.39	0.75	0.05	5.33	83	377	276	626
Amphora	H14	0.84	2.58	15.32	56.04	1.59	15.54	0.74	0.12	6.66	129	600	242	673
Amphora	H15	1.24	2.59	14.46	58.97	1.74	13.43	0.71	0.11	6.15	126	585	262	671
Amphora	H16	1.43	2.76	13.88	59.11	1.47	13.91	0.70	0.12	6.05	122	635	309	893
Bowl	H17	0.58	3.67	14.12	49.03	2.50	22.35	0.68	0.08	6.46	53	621	217	459
Brick	H18	0.35	3.10	13.05	61.51	1.89	13.51	0.67	0.07	5.45	55	291	254	179
Brick	H19	0.35	2.46	13.90	56.47	1.29	18.67	0.68	0.09	5.75	55	326	202	248
Lamp	H20	0.26	2.90	16.58	58.57	2.58	10.54	0.76	0.10	7.21	68	291	260	313
REFERENCE GROUPS														
Aqaba/Aila group	μ (n=9)	2.28	2.86	18.60	51.99	1.87	13.97	0.65	0.09	6.11	129	623	154	450
	σ	1.23	0.88	1.03	1.51	0.24	1.60	0.06	0.02	0.45	9	151	18	51
Negev cooking ware group	μ (n=4)	0.77	1.84	14.63	69.13	1.26	3.01	0.97	0.12	7.84	109	274	284	387
	σ	0.15	0.63	0.93	2.64	0.10	2.57	0.04	0.03	0.32	7	121	33	57
Petra (Jabal Harûn) group	μ (n=9)	0.53	2.75	21.12	60.88	2.14	3.94	0.81	0.05	7.04	73	181	249	142
	σ	0.21	0.51	1.13	1.33	0.19	1.65	0.04	0.01	0.32	11	64	18	18
Khirbet edh-Dharih group	μ (n=15)	0.51	3.78	18.04	55.95	2.89	9.85	0.73	0.07	7.26	84	411	178	200
	σ	0.22	1.61	2.94	3.65	0.53	3.09	0.09	0.02	0.51	18	142	57	104

data set. Its compositional pattern, representing a non-calcareous clay (CaO 0.9 wt %) with relatively high Fe_2O_3, ZrO_2 and BaO concentrations, is, however, notably similar to the Negev cooking ware reference group, formed by cooking pots recovered in Elusa and Abu Matar in Beer Sheva (Holmqvist 2010). The Humayma pot is also macroscopically and typologically similar to its Negev counterparts, further attesting to its Negev source. The presumably Negev-based workshop from which this pot may originate provided cooking wares for Elusa and Abu Matar in the late Byzantine period and possibly later (Holmqvist 2010). Its exact location remains unclear, but it is unlikely to have been the known Elusa workshop, which apparently concentrated on the manufacture of compositionally distinct jars (Holmqvist 2010; Goldfus and Fabian 2000; Fabian and Goren 2002; P. Fabian, personal communication). It is intriguing that a cooking pot apparently produced in the unknown Negev workshop reached Humayma, although it is perhaps not surprising, considering the inter-regional traffic and road network connecting southern Transjordan and the Negev. Although this pot alone does not allow for much socio-economic interpretation, future analysis may reveal more substantial inter-regional cooking ware exchange. It has already been shown (Holmqvist 2010) that cooking pots were imported from Petra to Aila, and the Petra origin pots form a significant percentage of the pottery assemblage recovered in Aila (S. T. Parker, personal communication), regardless of the fact that cooking wares were also locally manufactured in Aqaba. Ceramic transportation may be indicative of ceramic workshops specializing in the manufacture of certain forms, e.g., cooking utensils or transport containers — presumably dictated by the needs of the community in question and the nature of raw materials available — as is shown by the evidence from Aila, Petra, and Elusa (Holmqvist 2010). Domestic ware exchange has also been demonstrated in other regions (Adan-Bayewitz 1993).

Two of the analysed jars (H7 and H9) share some compositional similarity with the non-calcareous, low ZnO, SrO, and BaO Petra reference group (Table 2.3), although with some variation, and thus they may originate from the Petra region. The con-

centrations of the Petra and Khirbet edh-Dharih reference groups (the latter of calcareous nature) illustrate that separate workshops that operated in southern Jordan exploited chemically very similar ceramic recipes due to the geological homogeneity of the region, although they probably used different clay sources (Holmqvist 2010). Similarly, samples H18 and H20, for instance, appear, to a certain extent, compositionally related to the Khirbet edh-Dharih reference group ceramics, presumably manufactured in the relative vicinity of Khirbet edh-Dharih (no evidence of ceramic production was found at the site itself), although they probably represent another, fairly similar, ceramic recipe from southern Jordan. At this point, samples H3–5, H8, and H18–20 (representing a bowl/basin, three jars, bricks and a lamp fragment) cannot be associated with any of the reference groups presented here. Later analysis may help to conclude whether some of these samples represent variation among the products of a single workshop, or whether all of them originate from different manufacture. As these samples cannot be associated with the reference groups with any certainty, they may well be the products of pottery workshops located in the more immediate vicinity of Humayma.

2.F.1. Conclusions

To conclude, the results indicate that Aqaba was probably at least one of the main sources of ceramic import to Humayma. On the other hand, most of the ceramics shown here to be of Aqaba origin were containers, presumably transported as by-products of other goods. Further studies may reveal whether also other ceramic forms were transported from the port town. In addition, the heterogeneous data set indicates that there were also alternative sources of ceramic supply, probably located in the Negev, the Petra region and elsewhere in southern Jordan.

2.F.2. Descriptions and context information of ceramic samples selected for the ED-XRF analysis.

Ware colour descriptions are according to Munsell Soil Color Chart 2000 edition. Cf. figs. 2.1–2.

H1. Wheel-made open-form cooking pot, reddish-brown ware 5YR 4/4, context: bucket 1987.188, H87-68-P2, Loc. 02, 4C–5C; parallels: 'Amr and Schick 2001: 124, fig. 9:23–26; Melkawi, 'Amr et al. 1994: 456–58, fig. 9a–e; Magness 1993: 211–15; Waliszewski 2001: 104, fig. 5; Nikolsky and Figueras 2004: 197–98, figs. 45, 46: 1–6; suggested date 5C–8C/9C.

H2. Wheel-made bowl/basin, D ca. 0.20 m, combed wavy-lines on rim, light reddish brown ware 5YR 6/3; context: surface find, Humayma centre; parallels: Walmsley and Grey 2001: 154, fig. 9:1; Whitcomb 1989b: 279–80, figs. 2–3, Magness 1993: 206–9; suggested date 7–9C.

H3. Wheel-made bowl, D ca. 0.20 m, very pale brown ware 10YR 7/3; context: surface find, Humayma centre.

H4. Wheel-made jar with a short, straight neck and a grooved rim, rim D 0.09 m, light red ware 2.5YR 6/8; context: bucket 1987.159, H87-63-P12, Loc. 02; parallels: Fellmann Brogli 1996: 249, fig. 755, no. 28; suggested date: 4C.

H5. Wheel-made jar, mouth D 0.10 m; light red ware 2.5YR 6/6; context: surface find, Humayma centre; parallels: Fellmann Brogli 1996: 251, fig. 760, no. 33, suggested date: 4C–5C.

H6: Wheel-made jar, ribbed on the shoulder, reddish yellow ware 7.5YR 7/6; context: bucket 1987.099, H87-62-P6, loc. 4; parallels: Fellmann Brogli 1996: 252–53; figs. 761, 763 nos. 34, 36; suggested date: 4C–6C?

H7. Wheel-made jar with a thickened, folded rim, wide groove on rim, mouth D 0.12 m, light red ware 2.5YR 6/6; context: 1993.0264, C101.04.28; parallels: 'Amr and Schick 2001: 121, fig. 6:10–11; Kareem 1999: 196–97, fig. 7: 16–17; Pappalardo 2002: 427, fig. 30:7–8; suggested date 7C–8C.

H8. Wheel-made jar with a thickened, folded rim, mouth D ca. 0.10 m, light brownish grey ware 2.5YR 6/2; context: bucket 1987.183, H87-76-P5 Loc. 03; for parallels and suggested date, see H7 above.

H9. Handmade dolium, grey ware 7.5YR 5/1; context: bucket 1987.54, H87-54-P2 loc. 4.

H10. Wheel-made jar with combed wavy-line decoration, cream ware, pale yellow ware 8/4; context: surface find, Humayma centre; parallels: Whitcomb 1989b: 269; suggested date: mid-8C–11C.

H11. Wheel-made jar, combed lines and wavy-lines, cream ware, pale yellow ware 2.5YR 8/4; context: 1996.0107, F103.86.06; for parallels and suggested date see H10 above.

H12. Handmade dolium, engraved zigzag patterns on both surfaces, reddish brown ware 5YR 5/4; context: surface find, Humayma centre; parallels: Holmqvist 2010, no. A016.

H13. Wheel-made jar/jug, neck-to-shoulder vertical handle, rim/neck unpreserved, combed wavy-lines, light red ware 10R 6/6; context: bucket 1987.129, H87.63-P9 Loc. 1; suggested date: mid-8C–9C?

H14. Wheel-made amphora, grooved exterior; greenish, pale yellow ware 5Y 7/4; context: bucket 1987.62 H87-63-83 Loc. 03; parallels: Melkawi, 'Amr et al. 1994; Whitcomb 2001: 298; suggested date: 7C–mid-8C.

H15. Wheel-made Aqaba amphora, grooved exterior, greenish, pale yellow ware 5Y 7/4; context: bucket 1987.81, H87-62-P6 Loc 02; for parallels and suggested date, see H14 above.

H16. Wheel-made amphora, grooved exterior, greenish, pale yellow ware 5Y 7/4; context: bucket 1987.63, H87-63-P3 Loc. 04; for parallels and suggested date, see H14 above.

H17. Coarse, handmade bowl/cup; flat base, D ca. 0.12 m, coarse, reddish brown ware 2.5YR 5/4; context: 1992.0278, F103, surface find; parallels: Walmsley and Grey 2001: 153, 158, fig. 9:6–10; suggested date: mid-11C or later.

H18. Brick, coarse, light reddish brown ware 5YR 6/4; context: area of the Roman bath.

H19. Brick, coarse, light brown ware 7.5YR 6/4; context: area of the Roman bath.

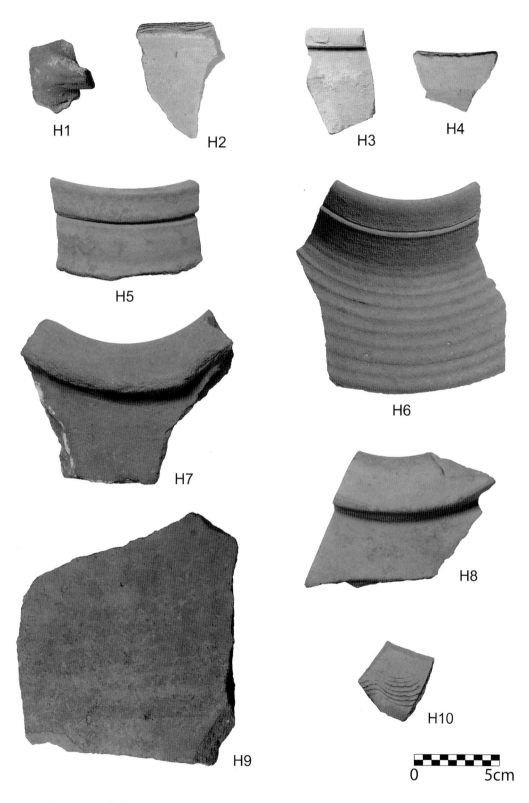

FIG. 2.1   *Ceramic samples from Humayma subjected to ED-XRF analysis, Samples H1 to H10.*

Fig. 2.2   *Ceramic samples from Humayma subjected to ED-XRF analysis, Samples H11 to H20.*

H20. Lamp fragment, ring-base, dot and circular motifs, fine, grey ware, 7.5YR 6/1; context: bucket 1987.176, H87-17-P5 surface find; parallels: Grawehr 2006: 342, No. 479; suggested date: late 4C–6C.

2.G. INTRODUCTION TO THE CERAMIC PLATES IN THE TEXT

In the captions to the ceramic plates, preference is given to citing parallels from Petra and surroundings, from Khirbet edh-Dharih, and from Aqaba. If close parallels are found at those sites, no attempt was made to cite parallels farther afield. If "cf." precedes citation of a parallel, the parallel is only approximate. The date in parentheses at the end of each entry is the date ascribed to that particular Humayma vessel. The ceramic profiles are reproduced at 1:2 (50%), except for some large vessels reproduced at 1:3 or 1:4 (as indicated in the figure captions).

NOTE

1   The sherds for the analysis were selected by Prof. John Oleson. Barbara Porter and Christopher A. Tuttle offered invaluable help during the process. The author would like to thank Prof. Jaakko Frösén, Dr. Zbigniew T. Fiema, Prof. S. Thomas Parker, Prof. Steven A. Rosen, Prof. Isaac Gilead, Dr. Haim Goldfus, Dr. Peter Fabian, Prof. Francois Villeneuve, and Prof. Zeidoun al-Muheisen for permission to study unpublished ceramics from their excavations. Full analytical results of ED-XRF and SEM-EDS study of Jabal Harûn, Aila, Beersheva Abu Matar, Elusa, and Khirbet edh-Dharih ceramics are presented in Holmqvist 2010. For excavation reports, see, e.g., Gilead, Rosen, and Fabian 1993; Goldfus and Fabian 2000; Villeneuve and al-Muheisen 2000; Parker 2003; Fiema and Frösén 2008. This study is part of the author's post-doctoral research project, funded by the Ella and Georg Ehrnrooth Foundation.

Appendix 2.1   Ceramic Database Categories

The three columns present the abbreviation used in the database, the number of sherds recorded in each for the 1991 through 1996 excavation seasons, and the expanded ware description. In addition to the excavation areas reported on in this volume, the database sums in this appendix and Appendix 2.2 also include sherds excavated in E116 (the Roman Fort) and E125 (the Vicus) during that period. The database contains information about 93,089 sherds, of which 50,928 (54.7%)were recovered from the excavation areas reported on in this volume. Appendix 2.3 reports on the main wares found in these particular excavation areas.

CERAMIC CATEGORY	ABBREVIATION	# OF SHERDS	EXPANDED DESCRIPTION
FINE WARES	f_np	2,352	fine-Nabataean painted
	f_np_c	1	fine-Nabataean painted-combed
	f_np_rd	8	fine-Nabataean painted-red paint
	f_nrd	7,871	fine-Nabataean red
	f_nrd_c	1	fine-Nabataean red-combed
	f_nrd_crs	137	fine-Nabataean red-cream surface
	f_nrd_gbs	64	fine-Nabataean red-grey/black surface
	f_nrd_rds	4	fine-Nabataean red-red surface
	f_nr	273	fine-Nabataean rouletted
	f_n_st	15	fine-Nabataean stamped
	f_ncr	14	fine-Nabataean-cream
	f_ngb	315	fine-Nabataean-grey/black
	f_lb_i	2	fine-late Byzantine-impressed
	f_lr	120	fine-late Roman (African Red Slip)
	f_lr_t	1	fine-late Roman-rouletted
	f_br	5	fine-brown ware
	f_br_crs	1	fine-brown ware-cream surface
	f_cr_rds	1	fine-cream ware-red surface
	f_gb_c	1	fine-grey/black ware-combed
	f_lb	32	fine-Late Byzantine
	f_rd_brs	2	fine-red ware-brown surface
	f_rd_c	1	fine-red ware-combed
	f_rd_crs	11	fine-red ware-cream surface
	f_rd_crsgbp	4	fine-red ware-cream surface-grey/black paint
	f_rd_i	2	fine-red ware-incised
	f_rd_rds	5	fine-red ware-red surface
	f_cs	7	Cypriot Sigillata
	f_etsa	103	Eastern Terra Sigillata A

Ceramic Category	Abbreviation	# of Sherds	Expanded Description
	f_etsb	1	Eastern Terra Sigillata B
	f_etsc	10	fine-Nabataean Sigillata
	f_wts	1	Western Terra Sigillata
	f_gb	11	fine-grey/black ware
	f_gb_gbs	14	fine-grey/black ware-grey/black surface
Vitreous Glazed Wares	g_cr_blg	33	glazed-cream ware-blue glaze
	g_cri_trg	1	glazed-cream ware incised-turquoise glaze
	g_crblgclg	8	glazed-cream ware-blue glaze-clear glaze
	g_crblgwtg	19	glazed-cream ware-blue glaze-white glaze
	g_cr_gbg	1	glazed-cream ware-grey/black glaze
	g_crgrgclg	1	glazed-cream ware-green glaze-clear glaze
	g_crgrgwtg	1	glazed-cream ware-green glaze-white glaze
	g_crtrgblg	4	glazed-cream ware-turquoise surface-grey/black glaze
	g_rdclggbp	2	glazed-red ware-clear glaze-grey/black paint
	g_rd_oyg	2	glazed-red ware-orange/yellow glaze
Lamps	l_abb_m	2	lamp-Abbasid moulded
	l_bc	30	lamp-Byzantine-cream surface
	l_br_m	1	lamp-brown ware-moulded
	l_cr	2	lamp-cream ware
	l_cr_gbs	2	lamp-cream ware-grey/black surface
	l_gb_gbsm	4	lamp-grey/black ware-grey/black surface-moulded
	l_gb_m	6	lamp-grey/black ware-moulded
	l_ib	26	lamp-Umayyad
	l_mb	1	lamp-Middle Byzantine
	l_lb_mrd	1	lamp-Late Byzantine-moulded-red ware
	l_nb	5	lamp-Nabataean
	l_n_ros	10	lamp-Nabataean-rosette
	l_ns	11	lamp-Nabataean-sunray
	l_rd_brsm	3	lamp-red ware-brown surface-moulded
	l_rd_crsm	33	lamp-red ware-cream surface-moulded
	l_rd_m	74	lamp-red ware-moulded
	l_rd_rdsm	40	lamp-Nabataean-red-slipped, moulded
	l_cr_m	3	lamp-cream ware-moulded
	l_rd_gbsm	13	lamp-red ware-grey/black surface-moulded

Ceramic Category	Abbreviation	# of Sherds	Expanded Description
Coarse wares	c_br	53	coarse-brown ware
	c_br_r	5	coarse-brown ware-ribbed
	c_br_rdpi	2	coarse-brown ware-red paint-incised
	c_cr	2,209	coarse-cream ware
	c_cr_c	188	coarse-cream ware-combed
	c_cr_gbs	10	coarse-cream ware-grey/black surface
	c_cr_i	11	coarse-cream ware-incised
	c_cr_r	519	coarse-cream ware-ribbed
	c_cr_rds	7	coarse-cream ware-red surface
	c_cr_t	4	coarse-cream ware-rouletted
	c_cr_u	1	coarse-cream ware-unslipped
	c_gb	1,458	coarse-grey/black ware
	c_gb_brsr	2	coarse-grey/black ware-brown surface-ribbed
	c_gb_c	8	coarse-grey/black ware-combed
	c_gb_crs	9	coarse-grey/black ware-cream surface
	c_gb_crsr	5	coarse-grey/black ware-cream surface-ribbed
	c_gb_gbsr	7	coarse-grey/black ware-grey/black surface-ribbed
	c_gb_gbs	142	coarse-grey/black ware-grey/black surface
	c_gb_gbsc	3	coarse-grey/black ware-grey/black surface-combed
	c_gb_r	407	coarse-grey/black ware-ribbed
	c_oy	4	coarse-orange/yellow ware
	c_rd	14,244	coarse-red ware
	c_rd_brs	83	coarse-red ware-brown surface
	c_rd_brsr	10	coarse-red ware-brown surface-ribbed
	c_rd_c	87	coarse-red ware-combed
	c_rd_crs	16,163	coarse-red ware-cream surface
	c_rd_crsc	377	coarse-red ware-cream surface-combed
	c_rd_crse	2	coarse-red ware-cream surface
	c_rdcrsgbp	159	coarse-red ware-cream surface-grey/black paint
	c_rd_crsi	99	coarse-red ware-cream surface-incised
	c_rd_crsu	10	coarse-red ware-cream surface-unslipped
	c_rdcrsrdp	16	coarse-red ware-cream surface-red paint
	c_rd_crsr	7,189	coarse-red ware-cream surface-ribbed
	c_rdcrsrc	10	coarse-red ware-cream surface-ribbed-combed
	c_rd_crsri	7	coarse-red ware-cream surface-ribbed-incised
	c_rd_gbp	109	coarse-red ware-grey/black paint
	c_rd_crst	1	coarse-red ware-cream surface-rouletted
	c_rd_gbs	9,821	coarse-red ware-grey/black surface

Ceramic Category	Abbreviation	# of Sherds	Expanded Description
	c_rd_gbsc	164	coarse-red ware-grey/black surface-combed
	c_rd_gbsci	2	coarse-red ware-grey/black surface-combed-incised
	c_rd_gbsi	59	coarse-red ware-grey/black surface-incised
	c_rd_rdsi	4	coarse-red ware-red surface-incised
	c_rd_gbsr	3,627	coarse-red ware-grey/black surface-ribbed
	c_rdgbswtp	3	coarse-red ware-grey/black surface-white paint
	c_rd_i	36	coarse-red ware-incised
	c_rd_u	6	coarse-red ware-unslipped
	c_rd_oys	3	coarse-red ware-orange/yellow surface
	c_rd_r	1,710	coarse-red ware-ribbed
	c_rd_rdp	6	coarse-red ware-red paint
	c_rd_rds	294	coarse-red ware-red surface
	c_rd_rdsc	6	coarse-red ware-red surface-combed
	c_rd_rdsr	36	coarse-red ware-red surface-ribbed
	c_rd_wtp	1	coarse-red ware-white paint
	c_rd_t	7	coarse-red ware-rouletted
	c_rd_oysr	1	coarse-red ware-orange/yellow surface
	c_oygbprdp	9	coarse-red ware-orange/yellow surface-grey/black paint-red paint
Kitchen (Cooking) Wares	k_br	47	kitchen-brown ware
	k_br_gbsr	1	kitchen-brown ware-grey/black surface-ribbed
	k_br_r	46	kitchen-brown ware-ribbed
	k_cr_r	6	kitchen-cream ware-ribbed
	k_gb	119	kitchen-grey/black ware
	k_gb_r	54	kitchen-grey/black ware-ribbed
	k_rd	415	kitchen-red ware
	k_rd_brs	163	kitchen-red ware-brown surface
	k_rd_brsr	579	kitchen-red ware-brown surface-ribbed
	k_rd_crs	1,194	kitchen-red ware-cream surface
	k_rd_crsc	5	kitchen-red ware-cream surface-combed
	k_rd_crsr	974	kitchen-red ware-cream surface-ribbed
	k_rd_crsri	21	kitchen-red ware-cream surface-ribbed-incised
	k_rd_gbs	1,608	kitchen-red ware-grey/black surface
	k_rd_gbsc	15	kitchen-red ware-grey/black surface-combed
	k_rd_gbsr	1,233	kitchen-red ware-grey/black surface-ribbed
	k_rd_i	2	kitchen-red ware-incised

Ceramic Category	Abbreviation	# of Sherds	Expanded Description
	k_rd_r	458	kitchen-red ware-ribbed
	k_rd_rds	7	kitchen-red ware-red surface
	k_rd_rdsr	7	kitchen-red ware-red surface-ribbed
Storage Wares	s_br_gbs	2	storage-brown ware-grey/black surface
	s_br_r	6	storage-brown ware-ribbed
	s_cr	289	storage-cream ware
	s_cr_c	11	storage-cream ware-combed
	s_cr_r	548	storage-cream ware-ribbed
	s_cr_rds	1	storage-cream ware-red surface
	s_cr_gbs	8	storage-cream ware-grey/black surface
	s_gb	15	storage-grey/black ware
	s_gb_gbs	7	storage-grey/black ware-grey/black surface
	s_gb_r	8	storage-grey/black ware-ribbed
	s_hcr	8	storage-handmade-cream ware
	s_hgb	10	storage-handmade-grey/black ware
	s_hgb_gbs	968	storage-handmade-grey/black ware-grey/black surface
	s_hgb_gbsc	9	storage-handmade-grey/black ware-grey/black surface-combed
	s_hrd	156	storage-handmade-red ware
	s_hrd_crs	363	storage-handmade-red ware-cream surface
	s_hrd_crsr	18	storage-handmade-red ware-cream surface-ribbed
	s_hrd_gbs	424	storage-handmade-red ware-grey/black surface
	s_hrd_gbsi	5	storage-handmade-red ware-grey/black surface-incised
	s_rd	487	storage-red ware
	s_rd_brs	2	storage-red ware-brown surface
	s_rd_c	8	storage-red ware-combed
	s_rd_crs	2,972	storage-red ware-cream surface
	s_rd_crsc	59	storage-red ware-cream surface-combed
	s_rd_crsi	38	storage-red ware-cream surface-incised
	s_rd_crsr	2,986	storage-red ware-cream surface-ribbed
	s_rd_crsrc	5	storage-red ware-cream surface-ribbed-combed
	s_rd_crsri	22	storage-red ware-cream surface-ribbed-incised
	s_rd_crsrdp	7	storage-red ware-cream surface-red paint

CERAMIC CATEGORY	ABBREVIATION	# OF SHERDS	EXPANDED DESCRIPTION
	s_hrd_gbst	3	storage-handmade-red ware-grey/black surface-rouletted
	s_rd_gbp	2	storage-red ware-grey/black paint
	s_rd_gbs	882	storage-red ware-grey/black surface
	s_rd_gbsc	9	storage-red ware-grey/black surface-combed
	s_rd_gbsr	123	storage-red ware-grey/black surface-ribbed
	s_rdgbsrc	2	storage-red ware-grey/black surface-ribbed-combed
	s_rd_i	3	storage-red ware-incised
	s_rd_r	317	storage-red ware-ribbed
	s_rd_rc	2	storage-red ware-ribbed-combed
	s_rd_rds	9	storage-red ware-red surface
	s_rd_rdsr	1	storage-red ware-red surface-ribbed
	s_gb_rc	0	storage-grey/black ware-ribbed-combed
	s_rd_oys	4	storage-red ware-orange/yellow surface
HANDMADE WARES	h_br	38	handmade-brown ware
	h_br_c	1	handmade-brown ware-combed
	h_br_ch	68	handmade-brown ware-chaff impressions
	h_br_ech	3	handmade-brown ware-chaff impressions
	h_br_gbs	3	handmade-brown ware-grey/black surface
	h_br_rdpch	2	handmade-brown ware-red paint-chaff impressions
	h_cr	15	handmade-cream ware
	h_cr_gbs	5	handmade-cream ware-grey/black surface
	h_cr_rds	1	handmade-cream ware-red surface
	h_rd_uch	5	handmade-red ware-thumb print-chaff impressions
	h_tab	549	handmade *tabun*
BRICKS, TILES, PIPES, TERRACOTTAS	t_br	219	brick
	t_ti	2,013	roof tile
	t_fl	116	flue pipe
	t_pi	118	pipe
	tc_h	22	handmade terracotta
	tc_m	3	mould-made terracotta

Appendix 2.2   List of Prevalent Ceramic Wares, with Indication of Chronology

In this list, the ceramic categories in Appendix 2.1 containing fewer than 10 sherds have been omitted or subsumed within more comprehensive, related categories, except for some cases of widely recognized fine wares, reducing the number of categories from 224 to 88. The three columns present the abbreviation used in the database, the number of sherds recorded in each expanded category for the 1991 through 1996 excavation seasons, the expanded ware description, and chronology (where known). In addition to the excavation areas reported on in this volume, the database sums in this appendix and Appendix 2.1 also include sherds excavated in E116 (the Roman Fort) and E125 (the *Vicus*) during that period. The database contains information about 93,089 sherds, of which 50,928 (54.7%)were recovered from the excavation areas reported on in this volume. Appendix 2.3 reports on the main wares found in these particular excavation areas.

Ceramic Category	Abbreviation	Total # of Sherds	Description/Chronology
Fine Wares	f_np	2,365	Nabataean painted (1C BC–3C AD).
	f_nrd	8,186	Nabataean red (1–2C)
	f_nrd_crs	137	Nabataean red-cream surface (1–2C)
	f_nrd_gbs	64	Nabataean red-grey/black surface (1–2C)
	f_nr	288	Nabataean rouletted (1–2C) (see Khairy 1982)
	f_ncr	14	Nabataean cream or green ware (1–mid-2C).
	f_lr	120	Late Roman (African Red Slip, 2–6C)
	f_lb	32	Late Byzantine (see Waleszewski 2001: 97, 105, fig. 6.8; Gichon 1974; 7–8C)
	f_cs	7	Cypriot Sigillata (ea. 1C BC–mid-2C AD)
	f_etsa	103	Eastern Terra Sigillata A (mid-2C BC–late 2C AD)
	f_etsb	1	Eastern Terra Sigillata B (late 1C BC–AD 150)
	f_etsc	10	Nabataean Sigillata (1C)
	f_wts	1	Western Terra Sigillata (1–2C).
Vitreous Glazed Wares	g_cr_blg	33	cream ware-blue glaze (Raqqa ware? Late Abbasid).
	g_crblgwtg	19	cream ware-blue glaze-white glaze
Lamps	l_abb_m	2	Abbasid moulded (8–9C)
	l_bc	35	Byzantine-cream ware (standard Byzantine lamp (5–6C)
	l_gb_gbsm	10	grey/black ware-grey/black surface-moulded
	l_ib	26	Islamic-B (Umayyad)
	l_lb_mrd	2	late Byzantine-moulded-red ware (7C)

Ceramic Category	Abbreviation	Total # of Sherds	Description/Chronology
	l_nb	26	Nabataean (1–2C).
	l_rd_crsm	33	red ware-cream surface-moulded (non-distinctive category, chronology unknown).
	l_rd_m	74	red ware-moulded
	l_rd_rdsm	40	red ware-red-slipped, moulded (Roman type discus lamps; 2–3C).
	l_cr_m	3	cream ware-moulded (Early Islamic, 7–8C).
	l_rd_gbsm	13	red ware-grey/black surface-moulded (Roman or Byzantine).
Coarse Wares	c_br	60	brown ware
	c_cr	2,220	cream ware
	c_cr_c	199	cream ware-combed
	c_cr_r	519	cream ware-ribbed
	c_gb	1,634	grey/black ware
	c_gb_r	407	grey/black ware-ribbed
	c_rd	14,262	red ware
	c_rd_brs	93	red ware-brown surface
	c_rd_c	87	red ware-combed
	c_rd_crs	16,163	red ware-cream surface
	c_rd_crsc	379	red ware-cream surface-combed
	c_rdcrsgbp	159	red ware-cream surface-grey/black paint
	c_rd_crsi	99	red ware-cream surface-incised
	c_rdcrsrdp	16	red ware-cream surface-red paint
	c_rd_crsr	7,189	red ware-cream surface-ribbed
	c_rdcrsrc	17	red ware-cream surface-ribbed-combed
	c_rd_gbp	109	red ware-grey/black paint
	c_rd_gbs	9,857	red ware-grey/black surface
	c_rd_gbsc	164	red ware-grey/black surface-combed
	c_rd_gbsi	61	red ware-grey/black surface-incised
	c_rd_gbsr	3,627	red ware-grey/black surface-ribbed
	c_rd_r	1,710	red ware-ribbed
	c_rd_rds	336	red ware-red surface (occasionally ribbed).
Kitchen Cooking Wares	k_br	94	brown ware (7–8C)
	k_gb	119	grey/black ware
	k_gb_r	54	grey/black ware-ribbed
	k_rd	415	red ware
	k_rd_brs	163	red ware-brown surface

Ceramic Category	Abbreviation	Total # of Sherds	Description/Chronology
	k_rd_brsr	579	red ware-brown surface-ribbed
	k_rd_crs	1,194	red ware-cream surface
	k_rd_crsr	1,000	red ware-cream surface-ribbed
	k_rd_gbs	1,608	red ware-grey/black surface
	k_rd_gbsc	15	red ware-grey/black surface-combed
	k_rd_gbsr	1,235	red ware-grey/black surface-ribbed
	k_rd_r	458	red ware-ribbed
	k_rd_rds	14	red ware-red surface
Storage Wares	s_cr	857	cream ware (usually Aila amphorae; mid-7c).
	s_gb	30	grey/black ware
	s_hcr	1,961	handmade-cream ware (large storage jars with fat rim, turned on slow wheel; 7c).
	s_rd	497	red ware
	s_rd_crs	2,972	red ware-cream surface
	s_rd_crsc	59	red ware-cream surface-combed
	s_rd_crsi	38	red ware-cream surface-incised
	s_rd_crsr	2,986	red ware-cream surface-ribbed
	s_rd_crsri	27	red ware-cream surface-ribbed-incised
	s_rd_gbs	882	red ware-grey/black surface
	s_rd_gbsc	14	red ware-grey/black surface-combed
	s_rd_gbsr	123	red ware-grey/black surface-ribbed
	s_rd_r	319	red ware-ribbed
	s_rd_rds	10	red ware-red surface
Handmade Wares	h_br	41	brown ware
	h_br_ch	443	brown ware-chaff impressions (mottled colours, from orange/yellow to red to grey/black; sometimes red paint; Ayyubid, Mamluk, Ottoman, late 12–early 20c).
	h_cr	21	cream ware
	h_gb	88	grey/black ware
	h_rd	550	red ware (cream to red to grey/black surface, frequently red paint, surface often combed, incised, or rouletted)
	h_tab	549	*tabun* fragments (very thick, smooth and burned on interior, usually rough on exterior, cream to reddish brown, Umayyad through Ottoman, 7–20c).

Ceramic Category	Abbreviation	Total # of Sherds	Description/Chronology
Bricks, Tiles, Pipes, Terracottas	t_br	219	brick (red-brown, often with cream or pink surface; 2–5C).
	t_ti	2,013	roof tile (red-brown, often with cream or pink surface; 2–5C).
	t_fl	116	flue pipe (light grey to pink ware, surface often soot stained; 2–4C).
	t_pi	118	pipe (cream to pink ware; Nabataean to Early Byzantine, 1–4C).
	tc_h	22	handmade terracotta
	tc_m	3	mould-made terracotta (1–2C).

Appendix 2.3   Occurrences of Prevalent Ceramic Wares by Area and Structure

This list is based on the same list of main categories as Appendix 2.2, but for reasons of space only the ware abbreviations are included, while the number of occurrences of wares in each category has been added. The totals given are for only the five excavation areas indicated and for prevalent wares and consequently are lower than those in Appendix 2.1 and 2.2. Percentages are provided for wares for which the count is 100 or more, or for which there are interesting anomalies. The percentages below the sample totals in the tables indicate the percentage of all the sherds found in that particular area.

Total of sherds examined		B100	C101	F102	C119	C124
	50,928	12,067	21,247	15,022	226	2,366
Percentage of overall total:		23.7%	41.7%	29.5%	0.4%	4.7%

Fine Wares	Total	B100	C101	F102	C119	C124
	6536 (12.8%)	1,503	2,906	1,429	34	664
	Percent of area:	12.5%	13.7%	9.5%	15.0%	28%
f_np	1,496	327	863	282	0	24
	2.9%	2.7%	4.1%	1.9%	–	1.0%
f_nrd	4,685	1,120	1,872	1,037	32	624
	9.2%	9.3%	8.8%	6.9%	14.2%	26.4%
f_nrd_crs	67	12	23	25	0	7
f_nrd_gbs	29	9	4	13	0	3
f_nr	90	10	55	22	2	1

FINE WARES	TOTAL	B100	C101	F102	C119	C124
f_ncr	11	1	10	0	0	0
f_lr	73	19	29	23	0	2
f_lb	21	1	14	6	0	0
f_cs	2	1	0	1	0	0
f_etsa	62	3	36	20	0	3

VITREOUS GLAZE	TOTAL	B100	C101	F102	C119	C124
	25 (0%)	–	–	25	–	–
Percent of area:		–	–	0.2%	–	–
g_cr_blg	15	0	0	15	0	0
g_crblgwtg	10	0	0	10	0	0

LAMPS	TOTAL	B100	C101	F102	C119	C124
	145 (0.3%)	31	21	36	2	2
Percent of area:		0.3%	0.1%	0.2%	0.9%	0.1%
l_abb_m	2	2	0	0	0	0
l_bc	7	6	0	0	0	1
l_gb_gbsm	4	2	2	0	0	0
l_ib	24	5	1	18	0	0
	0.05%	16.1%	4.8%	50%	–	–
l_lb_mrd	1	1	0	0	0	0
l_nb	0	0	0	0	0	0
l_rd_crsm	13	3	3	6	1	0
l_rd_m	26	9	10	6	0	1
l_rd_rdsm	13	3	3	6	1	0
l_cr_m	0	0	0	0	0	0
l_rd_gbsm	2	0	2	0	0	0

COARSE WARES	TOTAL	B100	C101	F102	C119	C124
	31,708 (62.3%)	7,233	12,906	9,857	146	1,566
Percent of area:		59.9%	56.9%	65.6%	64.6%	66.2%
c_br	26	8	15	3	0	0
c_cr	1,300	475	200	617	1	7
	2.6%	3.9%	0.9%	4.1%	0.4%	0.3%

Coarse Wares	Total	B100	C101	F102	C119	C124
c_cr_c	76	30	9	37	0	0
c_cr_r	293	132	82	74	3	2
	0.6%	1.1%	0.4%	0.5%	1.3%	0.1%
c_gb	1,191	280	587	289	2	33
	2.3%	2.3%	2.8%	1.9%	0.9%	1.4%
c_gb_r	251	64	120	63	2	2
	0.5%	0.5%	0.6%	0.4%	0.9%	0.1%
c_rd	7,741	1,267	3,079	2,304	33	1,058
	14.5%	10.5%	14.5%	15.3%	14.6%	44.7%
c_rd_brs	65	55	7	3	0	0
c_rd_c	35	7	11	17	0	0
c_rd_crs	8,342	1,766	3,505	2,866	40	165
	16.4%	14.6%	16.5%	19.1%	17.7%	7.0%
c_rd_crsc	168	46	45	76	1	0
	0.3%	0.4%	0.2%	0.5%	0.4%	–
c_rdcrsgbp	137	0	115	22	0	0
	0.3%	–	0.5%	0.1%	–	–
c_rd_crsi	44	12	26	6	0	0
c_rdcrsrdp	5	1	0	4	0	0
c_rd_crsr	3,719	985	1,584	1,057	10	83
	7.3%	8.2%	7.5%	7.0%	4.4%	3.5%
c_rd_gbp	44	1	31	12	0	0
c_rd_gbs	5,191	1,353	2,206	1,492	38	102
	10.2%	11.2%	10.4%	9.9%	16.8%	4.3%
c_rd_gbsc	81	14	33	28	0	6
c_rd_gbsi	12	6	4	2	0	0
c_rd_gbsr	3,627	455	878	601	14	40
	7.1%	3.8%	4.1%	4.0%	6.2%	1.7%
c_rd_r	816	195	297	255	2	67
	1.6%	1.6%	1.4%	1.7%	0.9%	2.8%
c_rd_rds	183	81	72	29	0	1
	0.4%	0.7%	0.3%	0.2%	–	–

Kitchen Wares	Total	B100	C101	F102	C119	C124
	3,904 (7.7%)	1,128	1,635	1,046	6	89
	Percent of area:	9.3%	7.7%	7.0%	2.7%	3.8%
k_br	60	6	40	14	0	0
k_gb	69	38	26	5	0	0
k_gb_r	43	24	11	8	0	0
k_rd	159	43	109	0	1	6
	0.3%	0.4%	0.5%	–	0.4%	0.3%
k_rd_brs	146	17	64	65	0	0
	0.3%	0.1%	0.3%	0.4%	–	–
k_rd_brsr	539	64	230	244	1	0
	1.1%	0.5%	1.1%	1.6%	0.4%	–
k_rd_crs	414	92	189	113	0	20
	0.8%	0.8%	0.9%	0.9%	–	0.8%
k_rd_crsr	277	71	111	67	1	27
	0.5%	0.6%	0.5%	0.4%	0.4%	1.1%
k_rd_gbs	1,116	422	396	272	2	24
	2.2%	3.5%	1.9%	1.8%	0.9%	1.0%
k_rd_gbsr	792	306	339	137	1	9
	1.6%	2.5%	1.6%	0.9%	0.4%	0.4%
k_rd_r	277	44	113	117	0	3
	0.5%	0.4%	0.5%	0.8%	–	0.1%
k_rd_rds	12	1	7	4	0	0

Storage Wares	Total	B100	C101	F102	C119	C124
	4,865 (9.6%)	1,484	1,758	1,557	34	32
	Percent of area:	12.3%	8.3%	10.4%	15.0%	1.4%
s_cr	189	104	11	74	0	0
	0.4%	0.9%	0.1%	0.5%	–	–
s_gb	18	0	15	3	0	0
s_rd	148	21	70	57	0	0
	0.3%	0.2%	0.3%	0.4%	–	–
s_rd_crs	1,452	324	568	539	4	17
	2.9%	2.7%	2.7%	3.6%	1.8%	0.7%
s_rd_crsc	48	14	14	20	0	0

STORAGE WARES	TOTAL	B100	C101	F102	C119	C124
s_rd_crsi	34	4	27	3	0	0
s_rd_crsr	2,193	838	842	480	28	5
	4.3%	6.9%	4.0%	3.2%	12.4%	0.2%
s_rd_crsri	13	2	9	2	0	0
s_rd_gbs	552	117	98	327	2	8
	1.1%	1.0%	0.5%	2.2%	0.9%	0.3%
s_rd_gbsr	43	11	15	17	0	0
s_rd_r	175	49	89	35	0	2
	0.3%	0.4%	0.4%	0.2%	–	0.1%

HANDMADE WARES	TOTAL	B100	C101	F102	C119	C124
	858 (1.7%)	143	361	354	0	0
	Percent of area:	1.2%	1.7%	2.4%	–	–
h_br	37	3	1	33	0	0
h_br_ch	21	2	0	19	0	0
h_cr	21	2	4	13	0	0
h_gb	81	20	18	43	0	0
h_rd	404	5	283	116	0	0
	0.8%	–	1.3%	0.8%	–	–
h_tab	296	111	55	130	0	0
	0.6%	0.9%	0.3%	0.9%	–	–

BRICKS, TILES, PIPES, TERRACOTTAS	TOTAL	B100	C101	F102	C119	C124
	139 (0.3%)	86	9	44	0	0
	Percent of area:	0.7%	–	0.3%	–	–
t_br	33	22	1	10	0	0
t_ti	89	55	5	29	0	0
t_fl	7	6	0	1	0	0
t_pi	1	1	0	0	0	0
tc_h	7	1	2	4	0	0
tc_m	2	1	1	0	0	0

Chapter 3

Field C124: Nabataean Campground

by John P. Oleson

3.A. LOCATION AND DESCRIPTION

Field C124 occupies part of a modern orchard and agricultural field located 225 m SSW of the Lower Church (C101), 380 m from Reservoir no. 67 at a bearing of 218 degrees. This field is on the southwest periphery of the settlement area of Hawara, at the lowest point on the site (figs. 1.1–2). Wall stubs and rubble, probably associated with Byzantine and Early Islamic structures, are visible on the surface just across the modern dirt road that skirts the northeast edge of the area. Occasional worked blocks and rubble appear in the modern ploughed field, but no coherent structural remains can be seen at present other than Cistern no. 54 and the wall in Squares 02 and 03 discussed below. The run-off from the large Pleistocene lakebed north of the settlement, which flowed through the ancient centre and filled the built reservoirs and round domestic cisterns, now splits on the south edge of the settlement into several channels that drain into the Wadi el-Gharid. In antiquity as today some of this water reached the C124 area, bringing with it the sandy loessal soil that characterizes the ploughed field.

A cylindrical cistern roofed with slabs carried on cross arches was constructed at the slightly higher, northwest edge of the modern field sometime in the first century AD (D 5.80–5.83 m; depth 6.25 m; cap. 166 cum; elev. of curb 951.98 m) (*HEP*

I: 199–202, 305–7). The intended run-off field was a bowl-shaped catchment to the west that still functions well today. Although Cistern no. 54 is identical in general design to the six other Nabataean cylindrical cisterns found in the settlement centre, it is unique in that it is an isolated structure; the others are all located in the courtyards of houses. As a result, Oleson (1988: 166–68; *HEP* 1: 199–201) speculated that this cistern was the only surviving example of a domestic cistern at Hawara constructed to serve a family or clan and not later on incorporated in a permanent house. The other cisterns in the group probably all started off as isolated structures serving owners accommodated at the site from time to time in tents, but they were ultimately surrounded by stone structures as the owners settled permanently.

During the 1980s, the Bedouin landowner made an attempt to establish a small grove of olive, plum, and almond trees along the southwest, lowest portion of the field, and he protected the area with a barbed wire fence. The rest of the field was lightly ploughed or harrowed most years of that decade and into the early 1990s, and planted with wheat (fig. 1.2). Sometime late in 1995 or early in 1996 much of the field was ploughed more deeply, churning up large quantities of Nabataean fine ware vessels, particularly in a portion of the field 20 m east of Cistern no. 54. The ceramics inspired the digging of a dozen robber pits, which in turn at-

FIG. 3.1   *View of C124, Square 01 to west (final).*

FIG. 3.2   *View of C124, Squares 02–03 to west (final).*

tracted our attention to the area. Given the unique architectural isolation of the cistern it was suspected that the ceramics might indicate the presence of an ancient campground. An excavation square (01) was laid out in the area where ceramics were appearing, and excavated during the 1996 season (fig. 3.1). Two more squares (02–03) were laid out and excavated in the same season 160 m east of the cistern, along a wall exposed by the ploughing at the northeast corner of the field (Oleson et al. 1999:

FIG. 3.3   *View of C124, Square 01 Locus 08.*

411–14) (fig. 3.2).[1] Either from a lack of interest, or because of insufficient run-off, the agricultural field was not seeded between 1998 and 2009, and the trees gradually died off. In May 2009 only a few of the trees had any green leaves. At some time in the first half of 2005, vandals intentionally scooped away most of occupation level around Square 01 with a front-end loader, exposing sterile soil.

It was not clear at the start what we might find in this area other than ceramics, but ancient and modern Bedouin campsites have some characteristic features. At a modern camp, rocks are cleared from tent site, leaving a border, and platforms of large flat stones are built for storing *laban* skins, or as sleeping areas. Arcs of stones outline hearths, and there are goat and chicken huts, and storage areas. Primary and secondary dumps are often present, but refuse location does not necessarily

indicate where activities took place (Simms 1988). Ancient camps in the Negev highlands were characterized by circles of stones for tents or other shelters, hearth circles, stone heaps, and scattered sherds (Haiman 1989). A first to third-century winter camp in the Negev had similar stone features, and a small collection of ceramics including cooking pots, jars, jugs, and lamps (Rosen 1993). Rosen comments that most sherds could be joined with nearby sherds, as in Field C124, indicating very little mixing of the material since deposition.

Because of the apparently special character of the habitation in Field C124, the sherd count and weight of the various classes of ceramic wares are generally provided in this chapter, alongside mention of chronology and specially distinctive ware names. Sherd count is given first, followed by total weight (e.g. "fine wares 304/867 g" indicates 304

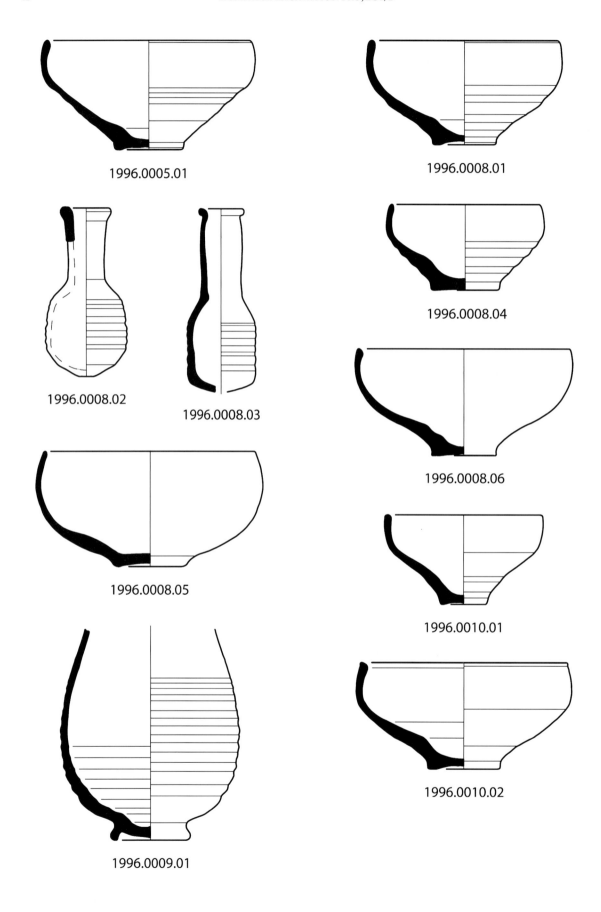

1996.0005.01

1996.0008.01

1996.0008.02

1996.0008.03

1996.0008.04

1996.0008.06

1996.0008.05

1996.0010.01

1996.0009.01

1996.0010.02

sherds weighing altogether 876 g). The chronological range based on pottery readings is given with the usual abbreviations.

3.B. EXCAVATION AND PHASING

3.B.1. *Square 01*

Square 01 (5 m × 5 m) was laid out 20 m east of Cistern 54, in an area of very fine, hard loessal soil only superficially affected by ploughing (surface elev. ca. 950.46 m). After collection of the surface ceramics (Locus 00; MN, MB, LB, UM), the fill that had been removed from a small modern robber pit (D 1.5 m) was excavated, exposing the undisturbed strata in the northern 2 m of the square. The surface sherds were predominantly fragments of first-century coarse ware bowls. Several metres south of the square a Byzantine *follis* was found on the surface, not far from a corroded, possibly Nabataean coin (p. 421, nos. 7–8). The spoil from the robber pit contained 620 small, weathered sherds, predominantly late first-century in date: fine wares 185/288 g; coarse wares 414/1476 g; cooking wares 14/92 g; storage wares 7/130 g. Of the fine ware, five sherds belonged to phase 3b NPFW bowls, and 175 to NFW vessels of the same period, predominantly bowls. Removal of a layer of light brown soil (Locus 02; Th 0.11 m) revealed a stratum of compact ashy soil across the entire square (northern half, Locus 03; southern, Locus 04). Locus 02 contained an array of MN ceramics similar to Locus 01, late first-century in date: fine wares 86/210 g; coarse red wares 211/1010 g; cooking wares 14/155 g; storage wares 5/145 g. Of the fine wares, 2 sherds belonged to phase 3b NPFW bowls, 84 to NFW vessels, mainly bowls,

A trench 2.0 m wide was laid out along the west side of the square, and the eastern half (Locus 03) was left undisturbed. Excavation of the slightly ashy, light brown soil in the trench (Loci 4 to 9) yielded a large amount of pottery (fig. 3.3; elev. ca. 950.23 m), predominantly small, first-century NFW bowls and NCRD bowls with string cut bases (figs. 3.4–6): fine wares 304/867 g; coarse wares 1668/10,820 g; cooking wares 31/549 g; storage wares 12/379 g. Only six sherds were identified as possibly dating to the EB, LB, or UM periods. Several of the bowls were intact, others were broken but complete; some of the bowls were found stacked one on top of another. A bronze coin of Rabbel II and Gamilat (101/2) was recovered from Locus 05 (p. 421, no. 5). There were occasional small fragments of glass throughout these loci. A possible installation was identified in association with these artefacts, a rough semi-circle (D 0.40 m × 0.14 m) of cobbles (Locus 12; top elev. 950.30 m) that rested on a layer of ashy, compact soil (Locus 13; elev. 950.19 m) (figs. 3.1, 3.6). Ceramics were found both inside and outside the feature.

Very little ceramic material was recovered from Locus 13, all of it late first-century Nabataean wares: fine wares 10/21 g; coarse wares 15/56 g. A Nabataean coin of Rabbel II and Hagru, dating to around AD 106 (p. 421, no. 6), was recovered at the bottom of this locus. Removal of Locus 13 exposed sandstone cobbles in a light brown soil (Locus 16), which was archaeologically sterile. Several large flat stones extending into the south baulk were investigated by means of a small extension of the square. The soil beneath them (Locus 17; Th 0.09 m, bottom elev. 950.03 m) contained a small amount of first-century Nabataean ceramics: fine wares 7/5 g; coarse wares 22/55 g; cooking wares 2/5 g; storage wares 1/5 g.

Examination of the sherds recovered from the surface in the eastern half of the square (above Locus 03) revealed a large number of ring-base

---

FIG. 3.4   *(Opposite page) Ceramic profiles from C124 Square 01, Locus 06. For the bowls with flat, generally string-cut bases, see 'Amr and al-Momani 1999: fig. 9.4–5, Wadi Musa kiln, late 1C to 150. These vessels should all date to the first or early second century. 1996.0005.01: C124.01.04, NFW bowl, ware 2.5YR 6/6. 1996.0008.01: C124.01.06, NFW bowl, ext. 2.5YR 6/5 with patches of 10YR 5/2, 10YR 6/4, int. 1.5YR 6/5. 1996.0008.02: C124.01.06, NFW unguentarium (Bikai and Perry 2001: fig. 9.12, Petra, 20–100). 1996.0008.03: C124.01.06, NFW unguentarium, 2.5YR 6/8 (EZ II: no. 317, 1C, Petra; Bikai and Perry 2001: fig. 9.11, Petra, 20–100) (1C). 1996.0008.04: C124.01.06, NFW bowl, ext. 2.5YR 6/5 with patches of 10YR 5/2, 10YR 6/4. 1996.0008.05: C124.01.06, NFW bowl, ware 2.5YR 6/5 with patches of 10YR 5/2. 1996.0008.06: C124.01.06, NFW bowl. 1996.0009.01: C124.01.06, jug (Bikai and Perry 2001: fig. 6.2, 20 BC to AD 80). 1996.0010.01: C124.01.06, NFW bowl, 2.5YR 6/8. 1996.0010.02: C124.01.06, NFW bowl, 2.5YR 6/8, core N5/0.*

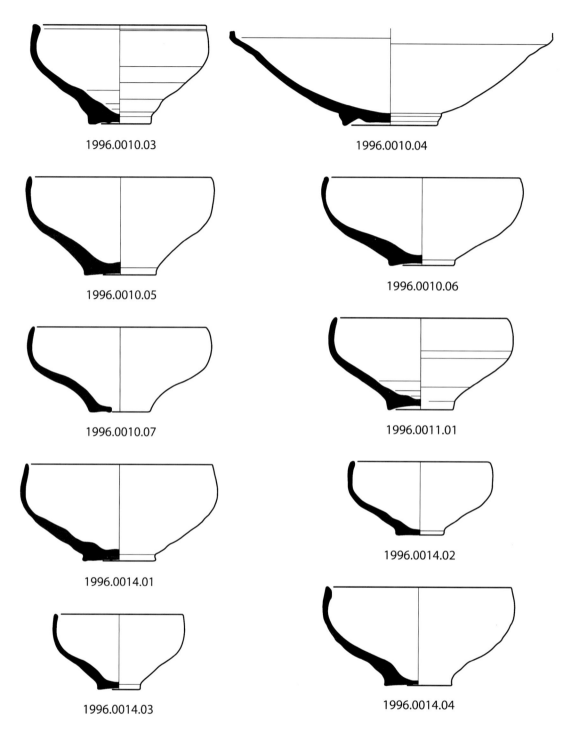

1996.0010.03

1996.0010.04

1996.0010.05

1996.0010.06

1996.0010.07

1996.0011.01

1996.0014.01

1996.0014.02

1996.0014.03

1996.0014.04

FIG. 3.5 *Ceramic profiles from C124 Square 01, Locus 08. For the bowls with flat, generally string-cut bases, see 'Amr and al-Momani 1999: fig. 9.4–5, Wadi Musa kiln, late 1C to 150. These bowls should all date to the first or early second century. 1996.0010.03: C124.01.08, NFW bowl, ware 2.5YR5/6 with patches of 2.5Y 6/3. 1996.0010.04: C124.01.08, NFW bowl. 1996.0010.05: C124.01.08, NFW bowl, ware 2.5YR 6/8; core N5/0. 1996.0010.06: C124.01.08, NFW bowl, ware 2.5YR 6/8. 1996.0010.07: C124.01.08, NFW bowl, surfaces 2.5 YR 6/5 with patches of 10YR 5/2 and 10YR 6/4, base 2.5YR 5/4. 1996.0011.01: C124.01.09, NFW bowl, 2.5YR 5/4 with patches of 2.5YR 4/2 and 2.5Y 7/4. 1996.0014.01: C124.01.08, NFW bowl. 1996.0014.02: C124.01.08, NFW bowl. 1996.0014.03: C124.01.08, NFW bowl. 1996.0014.04: C124.01.08, NFW bowl.*

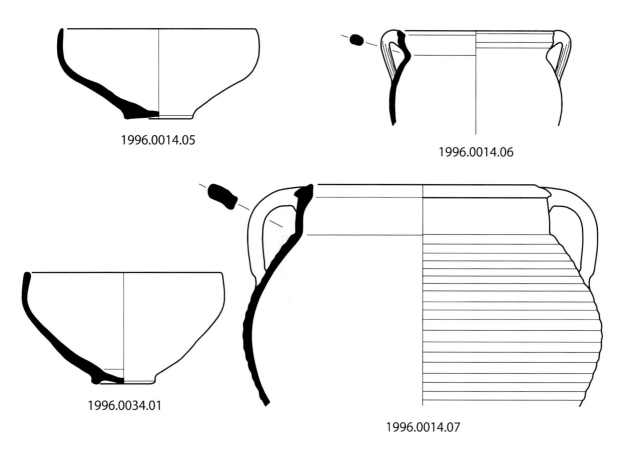

1996.0014.05

1996.0014.06

1996.0034.01

1996.0014.07

FIG. 3.6 *Ceramic profiles from C124 Square 01, Locus 08. 1996.0014.05: C124.01.08, NFW bowl (1C). 1996.0014.06: C124.01.08, NFW pot (cf. EZ II: fig. 272, Phase 3b; fig. 277, UK chronology) (1C). 1996.0014.07: C124.01.08, cook pot (Bikai and Perry 2001: fig. 9.13, 20–100, Petra; Gerber 2001: fig. 1.13, 2nd ½ 1–ea. 2C, Petra Church) (1–ea. 2C). 1996.0034.01: C124.01.06/08, NFW bowl, ware 2.5YR 6/6 with patches of 5YR 7/6, inner surface 2.5YR 6/6 (1C).*

vessels, and a higher proportion of fine ware than had been recovered in the western portion of the square: fine wares 70/204 g; coarse wares 4/42 g. The southern half of the remaining unexcavated portion of Square 01 was divided into two 1.5 × 2.5 m trenches: 01A and 01B, which were excavated in sequence to determine whether there was a shift in ceramic types over the square from west to east (fig. 3.7). There was some disturbance from robber pits. The concentration of ceramics in Loci 04–09 was found to continue into extension 01A Locus 03, but faded out short of extension 01B (fig. 3.8): fine wares 1058/6676 g; coarse wares 64/829 g; storage wares 2/190 g. The fine wares included eggshell ware bowls, sharp footed ring bases, NPFW bowls of Phase 3a, and roulette decorated bowls. The bottom half of a Nabataean rosette lamp was re-

covered, along with a coin possibly of Aretas IV (p. 421, no. 3). The large ceramic deposit in 01B (Loci 02–05) was not contiguous with those found in 01 or 01A, but it contains essentially the same blend of ceramic fabrics and types: fine wares 2,771/24,743 g; coarse wares 164/3,771 g; storage wares 2/630 g. The NPFW bowls belonged to both Phase 3a and 3b.

Analysis of Square 01

No architecture was found in this square, and only one possible feature. The artefacts date the strata to the second half of the first century and beginning of the second century. Given the small amount of ash that was present and the small number of bone fragments recovered (50 g), the deposits are unlikely to represent a garbage dump. Furthermore, the large number of intact and complete vessels, and the apparent stacked arrangement of some of the bowls indicate some other site-formation process. The absence of any obvious hearth and the very small relative proportion of cooking and storage vessels indicate that this is not a typical occupation deposit, but at the same time several of the soil loci have the appearance of packed earth floors (e.g., Locus 13). In addition, the high proportion of fine bowls and cups suggest activities involving frequent eating and drinking in a comfortable environment. Both of the complete NPFW and NFW bowls found in C124 cluster around a weight of 100 g. Although the equation is only approximate, the 30,122 g of fine ware sherds found in Square 01 consequently represent approximately 300 fine ware bowls. This is a significant but not unbelievable total, however the predominance of fine ware drinking vessels in the ceramic corpus requires explanation.

The absence of any architecture other than a cistern, the deposition of the undisturbed ceramics,

and the slight evidence for spatial sorting by chronology suggest that this portion of Field C124 was a Nabataean campground. It is likely that Square 01 has exposed a portion of campsite, possibly a location where a tent was erected repeatedly over a period of time, this portion of the area serving for entertainment or hospitality. The cooking ware, storage ware, and hearths would have been located in a different part of the hypothetical tent. Excavation of Nabataean period campsites in the Negev revealed the presence of stone circles, heaps of stones, occasional stone slabs, hearths, and scattered sherds that frequently joined nearby sherds (Haiman 1989: 187, 1995: 31; Rosen 1993; Finkelstein 1995: 23–30). These characteristics accord with what was found in Square 01, although the ceramics at the Negev sites were fewer in number and included a much higher proportion of coarse and cooking wares, and lamps. At Petra, the first phase of occupation at ez-Zantur involved tents rather than architecture, and the ceramics included many fine

FIG. 3.7   *View of C124, Square 01, Loci 12 and 17.*

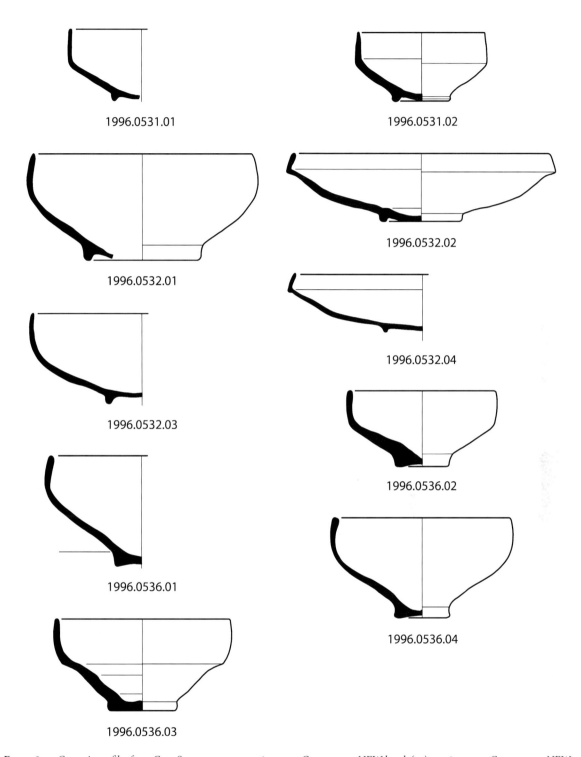

1996.0531.01

1996.0531.02

1996.0532.01

1996.0532.02

1996.0532.03

1996.0532.04

1996.0536.01

1996.0536.02

1996.0536.03

1996.0536.04

FIG. 3.8 *Ceramic profiles from C124 Squares 01A–B. 1996.0531.01: C124.01B.02, NFW bowl, (1C). 1996.0531.02: C124.01B.02, NFW bowl, (1C). 1996.0532.01: C124.01B.04, NFW bowl (EZ II: fig. 42, late 1C BC) (late 1C BC). 1996.0532.02: C124.01B.04, NFW bowl (EZ I: fig. 654, 20–100; Bikai and Perry 2001: fig. 9.2, AD 20–100) (1C). For the following bowls, with flat, generally string-cut bases, see 'Amr and al-Momani 1999: fig. 9.4–5, late 1C to 150; Wadi Musa kiln. 1996.0532.03: C124.01B.04, NFW bowl, (EZ II: fig. 42, late 1C BC) (late 1C BC). 1996.0532.04: C124.01B.04, NFW bowl, (1C). 1996.0536.01: C124.01A.06, NFW bowl, string cut base, ext. 2.5YR 6/6, int. and core 2.5YSR 6/6 (1 C). 1996.0536.02: C124.01A.06, NFW bowl, (1C). 1996.0536.03: C124.01A.06, NFW bowl, (1C). 1996.0536.04: C124.01A.06, NFW bowl, (1C).*

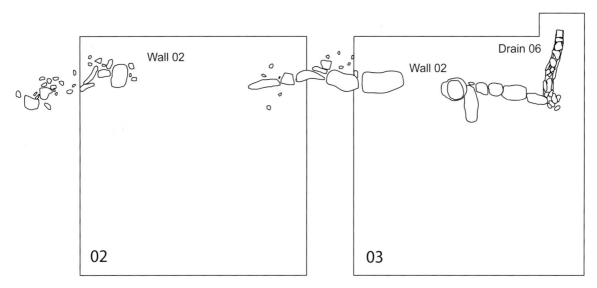

FIG. 3.9   *Plan of C124, Squares 02–03.*

ware vessels (*EZ* I: 14–17). A study of occupation patterns in modern Bedul Bedouin tents at Petra determined that the location of refuse does not necessarily correspond to the location of the activities that produced it (Simms 1988: 207; Cribb 1991: 84–112).

It is not surprising, given the flexible character of Nabataean urbanism, that tents should still be in use alongside well-constructed houses (Köhler-Rollefson 1987; Finkelstein 1995: 37–50; *EZ* 1: 14–17). It is possible that Cistern 54 was constructed to serve a family or related group of families who pitched their tents nearby when staying in town to harvest crops or to join in market activities. Unlike the other six cylindrical cisterns in the habitation centre, Cistern 54 never attracted the construction of a house. The economic or social structure of the proprietary family may have required a greater degree of nomadism than commitment to a house would have allowed. The location of the cistern on the periphery of the habitation centre may also have had something to do with this anomaly. Perhaps the cistern water was used mainly to water vegetable crops and fruit trees in the adjacent field; it would not have been practical to attempt to irrigate grain crops with cistern water. The hypothetical presence of a garden suggests other possible motives for location of the tent at this point: protection of the crops, and enjoyment of the greenery during occasions of hospitality. The nearly

complete absence of artefacts later than the early second century may have something to do with the disruption caused by the Roman occupation of Hawara, or it may simply reflect the relocation of the campsite to a slightly different spot.

3.B.2. *Squares 02 and 03*

Near the southeast corner of the modern field, just south of a modern wadi barrier and 140 m east of Square 01, two worked sandstone blocks were observed set into a 7.0 m long line of unshaped stones (Wall 02; top elev. 949.42 m; base elev. ca. 949.20 m) extending across the gentle slope for approximately 7 m at a bearing of 295 degrees. Since this was the only indication of architecture in the C124 area besides Cistern 54, two 5.0 × 5.0 m squares (02 and 03) were laid out to explore it (figs. 3.2, 3.9). Square 02 remained unexcavated, but the westernmost portions of the wall are visible on the surface there.

Removal of the light brown surface soil south of the wall (Loci 01, 03) yielded a significant amount of mixed ceramics dating from the first to third centuries (MN, ER, LR): fine wares 18/40 g, coarse wares 111/1138 g; storage wares 1/114; roof tiles 10/1188 g. A corroded bronze coin, possibly Nabataean, was also recovered (p. 421, no. 4). The ceramic material looks like scatter from houses to the north and east. Excavation of the more

Fig. 3.10 *Drain 06 in C124, Square 02.*

compact brown soil below the surface (Locus 04; elev. 949.20 m) revealed that the wall was only one course high. Locus 04 contained a great many cobbles, possibly fallen from a structure built on top of Wall 2. Excavation of the soil north of Wall 02 exposed 1.4 m of a drainage channel (Locus 06; interior H 0.20 m, W 0.17 m) sloping down from north to south and extending under the east end of the wall (fig. 3.10). The channel was carefully constructed: partly trimmed sandstone slabs (Th 0.10 m) set end to end formed the sides and cover, while the floor was paved with small, flat stones (elev. 949.24 m). Five of the northernmost cover slabs were found *in situ*. The channel was followed to the north until it disappeared beneath a modern earthen run-off barrier. A probe (Square 04) failed to locate any continuation of the drain north of the barrier, although several fragments of a handmade Ottoman bowl were recovered, and the blank for a stone bead (p. 507, no. 2).

The light brown soil below Wall 02 and adjacent to Drain 06 (Locus 08) was excavated to a depth of 0.11 m (elev. 949.11 m). A small amount of first-century pottery was recovered from the fill: fine wares 1/ 4 g; coarse wares 3/10 g; cooking wares 2/15 g. A probe next to and below a somewhat disjointed section of Wall 02 in the northwest corner of the square (Loci 10–14) recovered mainly first-century ceramics, along with a small amount as late as the third century: fine wares 10/23 g; coarse wares 56/257 g; cooking wares 11/75 g; storage wares 9/210 g. Sterile, silty soil (Locus 15) appeared at elev. 948.52 m. The sherds recovered from Square 03 resemble the random scatter of worn sherds on the edges of the habitation area, rather than specific occupation debris.

Drain 06 appears to have been constructed to assist in channelling water into the field. The most likely explanation of its function is that the topography of the field has changed little and that in antiquity there was a need for a wadi barrier in almost exactly the same location as exists today. The ancient barrier may have been washed or blown away (as has happened to some sections of the modern construction), leaving behind only the stone foundation and the drain. The barrier might have been intended to detain the water until it could flow into the field through drains such as the one recovered. This strategy of drained detention basins, which also was used at Petra to protect the Siq (Bellwald and Huneidi 2003; Bellwald 2008), would have protected the field from erosion and fostered more effective absorption of the run-off. A more monumental example, of the Umayyad period, can be seen at Wadi al-Qanatir (Genequand 2001: 650–51). The ceramics associated with the channel are predominantly first-century in date, but the structure could be later. The construction technique is simple, and it appears on a larger scale in the rebuilt intake for Reservoir no. 68 and in Drain no. 76, both probably Byzantine in date (*HEP* 1: 193–94, 220–22, 289–90, 321–22). In any case, the wall and drain have no apparent functional relationship with the campsite in Square 01, although they both may have been part of the same property.

3.C. CONCLUSIONS

The occupational remains in Field C124 Square 01 are very different from those in Squares 02–03. No architecture was found in Square 01, and the ceramics are overwhelmingly fine ware Nabataean drinking vessels. The ceramics and associated coins indicate occupation in the first century. One pos-

sible explanation for these occupation deposits is the erection of a large tent or group of tents belonging to inter-related families at this spot from time to time, adjacent to the Cistern no. 54. The occupants and their guests engaged in wine drinking, and were refreshed as well by the cistern water. The tent may have been pitched here because the occupants owned the cistern and adjacent field and did not have a house in the settlement centre. There may have been a garden in the field, watered from the cistern or from runoff channels similar to those found in Square 03. During growing season, the occupants of the tent could have busied themselves tending the garden, which in turn would in turn would have constituted a refreshing amenity for the wine drinking. Alternatively, the C124 area may have accommodated merchants and other travellers moving north and south along the King's Highway. The field is adjacent to the probably routed of the road, and close enough to the settlement centre to be convenient to any services or markets located there. In this case, water from the Cistern 54 may have been sold by the family that owned it.

The structural and occupational remains in Square 03 were very different, although possibly in their original stage contemporary with the tent site. The wall and drain were possibly intended to manage irrigation of the eastern portion of the field with run-off water. No standard occupation deposits were found in this area, and the ceramic material appears to be surface scatter that has worked its way down from the settlement to the north.

NOTE

1   Dennine Dudley supervised the excavation and was assisted by Anne-Marie Forget. This report is based on their excavation notes.

Chapter 4

Field A: The Necropolis

by John P. Oleson and John Somogyi–Csizmazia

4.A. LOCATION OF THE NECROPOLIS

Rock-cut tomb shafts dot the countryside around Humayma, although by far the greatest concentrations are found on the tops of the ridges immediately above the settlement centre, to the west and northwest (figs. 1.1, 4.31, 4.44). There are only two tomb façades that qualify as monumental, and one of these had only been partly blocked out on a smoothed sandstone face with preliminary excavation of a central door (A115.T1; fig. 4.41). The other façade, a smooth, undecorated square façade with central door at the south end of the same ridge, is clearly visible from the settlement centre (A114.T12–13; fig. 6.51, background to the left). Unfortunately, this complex was badly disturbed and re-cut some time in the recent past to serve for habitation or storage, so we could only record the two shaft graves visible among the debris. Otherwise, the tombs consist of shafts cut down into the Umm Ishrin sandstone, singly or in groups, for single or multiple burials or *loculi*. In her study of the necropoleis at Petra, Wadeson (2012: 101–3) refers to this type of grave as "pit grave," and reserves "shaft grave" for tombs in which a vertical shaft provides access to a rock-cut chamber with several "pit graves." The nineteenth-century visitors to the site do not comment on the presence of the tombs (*HEP* 1: 9–13), although Ogden (1888: 139) appears to describe the A114.T12–13 complex without identifying it as a tomb chamber.

After a good deal of squabbling and threats of returning, we managed to get off March 21, going via Wady el-Ithum. On the third day we passed the ruins of Humeimah. They cover a large area, and contain a number of cisterns and tanks for collecting rain water. The principal ruin now is a room, an almost perfect cube in shape, of about twenty feet each way. Just outside is a hole, the size of an ordinary bucket, cut or drilled in the rock, and in it a spring that always just fills it and never overflows or dries up. A little south of Humeimah we passed over one of the battle-fields of Ibrahim Pasha, where cannon-balls and iron bullets lay on the ground in great numbers.

Ogden is unique among the early visitors in completely ignoring the Roman fort. His mention of a battlefield of Ibrahim Pasha, however, appears to be unparalleled.

Musil (1926: 60) states that he spent "two hours" searching the hills west of the site but "did not see a single rock tomb." It seems unlikely that he missed all the shaft tombs, so he may have been looking for façade tombs and did not consider the others worthy of mention. It is not clear why he neglects to mention the A114.T12–13 façade; perhaps it had already been turned into a shelter and he assumed it had been created as such. Frank (1934: 237, pl. 37A) mentions both *Gräber* (shaft tombs) and

Felsgräber, by which he means façade tombs, since he illustrates Tomb A115.T1. *Felsgräber* probably corresponds to Musil's term "rock tomb." Alt (1936: 95) knew of the tombs, but he says he did not have time to visit them. Eadie and Graf carried out the first significant examination of the area in 1981 and 1983. Eadie (1984: 220) mentions a total of "forty-five shaft tombs" and speculates on the possibility that they originated in the Byzantine period.

A survey of the tombs on the ridges close to the settlement was conducted by J. Somogyi-Csizmazia in 1992 and 1993 under the direction of Oleson, with the goals of determining the chronology of original construction and of subsequent reuse, the development of tomb design, the location and organization of the necropoleis, and the average number of individuals within each shaft or tomb (Oleson et al. 1993: 486–87, 1995: 330). As expected, because of their highly visible location looters had plundered all the rock-cut tombs surveyed. The character of the information most likely lost through this plundering can be reconstructed from better preserved tombs at Petra, the Amman Airport Excavation, and Umm el-Jimal (Perry 2002b; Ibrahim and Gordon 1987; Brashler 1995; Cheyney et al. 2009): clothing, footwear, jewellery and other personal effects, ceramics, patterns of deposition of bodies, and repositioning of bones for subsequent interments. Furthermore, although the context is different, intact tombs of both Nabataean and Byzantine date were found cut into the soil in Fields B100, F102, and below the C101 Church. It is interesting that no evidence was found in the intact tombs at Humayma for multiple simultaneous or successive burials. In the course of the two seasons of survey and excavation 11 more or less distinct clusters of tombs and four solitary tombs were mapped, drawn, and catalogued; 94 individual burial locations in all. Unless otherwise indicated, the tomb plans and sections were prepared by Somogyi-Csizmazia, Copp, and Oleson. The tomb groups were given the field designations A105, A106, A107, A109, A111–A115, and A117–A118; the solitary tombs field designations A104, A108, A110, A119. The serial number 116 was allotted to the Roman Fort (E116) while the tomb survey was still in progress, interrupting the numerical sequence. Nine tombs were selected on the basis of their design or condition for excavation

or for the collection of any surface pottery within 1 m of the tomb shaft. A conservative estimate of the minimum total number of individuals buried in the tombs is 114. Although there were no sealed contexts, a significant ceramic sample was recovered, along with coins, and fragments of four inscribed headstones, one in Greek, and three in Nabataean script (see pp. 492–95). The only tomb we noted in the countryside farther afield from the centre was a beautifully built, vaulted Nabataean chamber tomb near the caravanserai on the *Via Nova Traiana,* 6.5 north of the settlement (*HEP* 1: 29, note 1), but this was outside our permit area.

4.B. TOMB TYPES, NECROPOLIS DESIGN, AND CHRONOLOGY

There are several different tomb designs. The most common is the single shaft with one or two compartments arranged in vertical sequence, cut down into the sandstone bedrock (e.g., figs. 4.22–23, 33, 36). The typical location was the top surface of one of the relatively flat outcroppings of red Umm Ishrin sandstone that form the ridges around the site. Several tombs are quite large and almost square in plan (e.g., A115.T2; fig. 4.43). The tomb groups were usually arranged in rows (e.g., A115.T1–T15; fig. 4.44), or in two instances radially around a square central court (A112.T3–T11; A117. T8–T17; fig. 4.29–30). A113 seems to follow the same arrangement, although the central court was encumbered by spoil. The regularity in the arrangement and execution of some of the tomb groups suggests some degree of contemporaneity. Most of the shafts (except those arranged around a central pit) are oriented approximately east–west, which is very common in the region from the Nabataean through the Early Islamic period (see pp. 91–92). There appears to have been only one chamber tomb (A114.T12–13), but another may have been begun and abandoned (A115.T1).

The tool marks in the side walls suggest that hammers and pointed chisels were used to finish the shafts (e.g., fig. 4.22), although simple heavy picks may have been used for the preliminary work (Bessac 2007: 40–42, figs. 20–22; Rababeh 2005: 59–65, 84–98). The upper portions of the shafts often have rounded corners (e.g., fig. 4.8, 4.13), as if a hafted tool was used for the first cutting. The lower portions of the shafts have square corners above the burial area, and typical Nabataean diagonal finishing executed with a chisel. Although the quality of the stone working varies from tomb to tomb, in general, the execution is crisp. The layout of adjacent shafts was usually measured and executed with care as well, resulting in a very regular appearance (fig. 4.8). The most prominent and larger capacity tombs, such as A104, show a much better quality of stone working than isolated tombs such as A107.

Some tomb shafts were designed for a single interment (or at least had cuttings for only a single, relatively shallow compartment), while others extended downwards to accommodate as many as five compartments in a vertical sequence (figs. 4.5–6). Each compartment was marked by either a pair of narrow, projecting, horizontal stone offsets on each side of the shaft to hold capstones, or by horizontal grooves into which the capstones were slipped. Some shafts show both types of support. Except for the last burial in each shaft, the slabs served both as capstones for the lower interment and flooring for the upper interment. No evidence survives concerning the possible use of apparently single *loculi* for multiple interments.

The capstones at the surface of the bedrock occasionally were set into an inset frame carved around the periphery of the shaft (figs. 4.13, 4.15). More often, there was an offset ca. 0.20–0.30 m below the surface, which, given the meagre clearance for a human corpse, was probably intended for slabs subsequently covered with a layer of earth (fig. 4.22). Small mounds of earth often surround the shaft of plundered tombs, even when the entire area around the tomb is bedrock (fig. 4.47). These deposits are probably the spoil from removal of the earth seal above the topmost level of cover slabs. It is possible that there was always a layer of earth above the topmost level of insets or offsets for cover slabs, designed to conceal the smell of decomposition and to protect the remains from scavengers. The fact that the shafts sometimes have square corners above the first offset, but rounded corners below shows a distinction between these two areas and tends to support this hypothesis. Nevertheless, in many cases the depth below ground level al-

lowed for this protective seal seems excessive (e.g., A114.T10, 0.80 m; fig. 4.38). We have accepted or rejected the possibility of a burial immediately below surface level depending on the design and dimensions of each shaft.

In most examples of multi-burial tombs, the tomb shaft contracted slightly in dimensions as it progressed below the surface, diminished by the cumulative dimensions of the offsets (e.g., A114.T9–T10; figs. 4.36). Occasionally, however, the offsets were undercut slightly, allowing nearly the same shaft width for each burial (e.g., A104.T1; fig. 4.5). Since shaft tombs for multiple burials could not be expanded downward once the first interment was in place, the decision on the final capacity of each tomb shaft must have been made at the time of initial construction. We have no idea how the desired capacity was calculated, although spousal pairs would be a likely priority. In any case, there is no guarantee that each shaft was filled to capacity during its period of use, or whether, if enough time had passed to allow previous interments to become completely skeletonised, they were occasionally filled beyond design capacity. There is no evidence in the intact graves found in F102, B100, and C101 for multiple burials in a single tomb. Very occasionally capping slabs that were found in position showed traces of hard, sandy white mortar that sealed the seams and held the slabs in place (fig. 4.46). Although we have no evidence for precise practices, it is logical that ground level cover slabs would be installed and sealed after each interment in a multi-level shaft, to prevent the living from falling into the shafts, and to keep vermin and rainwater out of them. All of these practices and characteristics are paralleled in the shaft tombs at Petra (Schmid et al. 2008; Wadeson 2011, 2012; Gorgerat and Wenning 2013).

The ceramics and coins found in association with the tombs date from the first century to the fifth or sixth century, with the bulk of the material dating to the first or second century, and only very occasional Umayyad material (cf. fig. 4.51). Although all the tombs had been badly disturbed, the impression is that the tombs were first excavated and used by the Nabataean inhabitants of Hawara, and that there may have been some reuse through the Late Byzantine period. The arrangement of *loculi* around a central court in groups A112. T3–T11, A117.T8–T17, and possibly in A113.T1–T5, is a design typical of first through fourth-century chamber tombs in this part of the Near East (e.g., Hegra, Nehmé 2006: 82, fig. 38; Petra, McKenzie 1990: pl. 124, 153, 161, 164; Jericho, Kenyon 1971: 29, fig. 17; Abila, Mare 1991: 215–19; Beit Zar'a, Khadija 1974: tomb 1; Tel Qedesh, Edelstein 2002; Silet edh-Dhahr, Sellers and Baramki 1953). We have not found any parallels for the unroofed examples seen at Hawara, and the poor quality of the bedrock at the site may have precluded construction of a shallow roofed chamber. Alternatively, the thin bedrock room may simply have collapsed and weathered away, leaving an open, debris filled pit. A first-century Nabataean chamber tomb with radial *loculi* was found at Sadaqa (Kurdi 1972). It is possible that at least some of the ceramics found around these tombs result from the smashing of vessels after a funerary banquet, a practice for which evidence was found at Mampsis (Negev 1971: 125–26).

4.C. CATALOGUE OF THE TOMBS

In accordance with the system worked out for designating the excavation fields around the large site of Humayma, the tombs are all in "Field A," the field designated for isolated structures or locations within 1000 m of the central datum point on Reservoir no. 67, but outside the central mounds of occupation debris. Each isolated tomb or group of tombs was assigned a structure number in this field (e.g., A104), and within groups of tombs, each tomb was also assigned a tomb number (e.g., A105.T2). In the catalogue, the dimensions of each tomb are given, along with the orientation, number of pairs of offsets, and the probable number of individuals interred. In the tomb descriptions, L indicates the length of the shaft or *loculus,* W indicates the width. The orientation of the grave is also given, the number of pairs of offsets to allow stacked interments, and the probable capacity. Unless otherwise specified, the design is that of a simple

FIG. 4.1   *Tomb A104.T1, view from northwest; knoll in left background carries A105.*

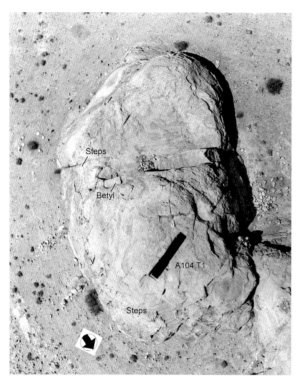

FIG. 4.2   *Tomb A104.T1, aerial view (W. Meyers, 21/07/1992, neg. H-5 no. 6).*

shaft tomb. All compass bearings refer to magnetic north; the magnetic deviation at Humayma in 1992 was approximately 3.5 degrees west of true north. Portable GPS systems were not available at the time the survey was carried out, so those coordinates are absent. Instead, the necropoleis are located by radial and distance from a nearby landmark or from the Humayma central datum point (the northeast corner of Reservoir no. 67). Several of the necropoleis unfortunately are just outside the site map, but they can be found by means of the polar coordinates given below. The main tomb groups are indicated on the overall site plan (fig. 1.1), so map references are not given in the catalogue.

4.C.1. A104.T1

On a low knoll at the south end of the ridge of Umm Ishrin sandstone west of the settlement centre (figs. 4.1–2).

T1.   L 4.0 m, W 0.61 m, depth 2.49–2.44 m; orientation 62 degrees. No. of offsets, 4; capacity, 8?

This tomb, the most capacious in the Hawara area, was cut into the top of a prominent, isolated knoll clearly visible to the southwest of the settlement centre. The side of the knoll facing away from the settlement has been in part quarried away (fig. 4.3), but above the quarry face a square betyl ("Dushara block") has been carved partly in relief and partly in the round (fig. 4.4). Virtually identical betyls in relief can be seen adjacent to tombs at Petra and Hegra (Brünnow and Domaszewski 1904–9: I, p. 321–23; Nehmé et al. 2006: 90, fig. 52). The tomb is reached by a curving, rock-cut staircase that starts from ground level at the north and ends at the eastern end of the tomb, ca. 4.0 m above (figs. 4.1–2). The tomb shaft was cut very carefully, with square corners all the way down. Four pairs of neat offsets (W ca. 0.05 m), the uppermost set below surface level, allow for four stacked compartments that decrease slightly in width with each successive downward stage (figs. 4.5–6). The bottom compartment (W 0.45 m) is 0.16 m narrower than the topmost. It is unlikely that a fifth burial compartment could have been provided at the top, because the bedrock slopes to the east, leaving that end of the long shaft open. The small amount of earth and a few broken roofing slabs inside the tomb were cleared in 1992, and the very small and worn potsherds on the bedrock surface around the opening were collected for dating. A bronze coin of Valentinian I or II, Valens, or Gratian was recovered from the surface spoil around the shaft, along with a glass and a quartz bead, and a cowrie shell perforated for suspension (pp. 421–25, no. 9; p. 507, nos. 3–4). The coin should date to a phase of re-use of the tomb in the Byzantine period. The only artefact found within the tomb was a small square clipping of bronze sheet. A few small fragments of human bone were recovered, including teeth and a portion of the cranial vault. The pottery shows a sequence from the late first century BC to the third century AD. The reason such a high population is reconstructed for this tomb is that the shaft is long enough to accommodate two individuals head to foot in each compartment.

As one of the two largest and visually most prominent tombs in the Hawara area (cf. A114. T12–13), T104 must have belonged to a particularly prominent family. It is not clear to what period

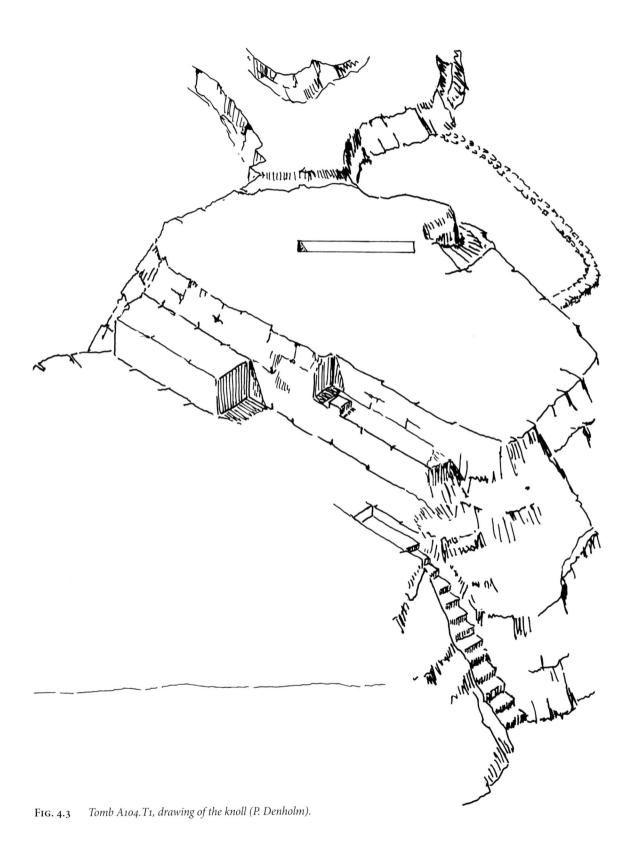

FIG. 4.3   *Tomb A104.T1, drawing of the knoll (P. Denholm).*

FIG. 4.6   *Tomb A104.T1, view of shaft.*

FIG. 4.4   *Tomb A104.T1 area, betyl on south slope.*

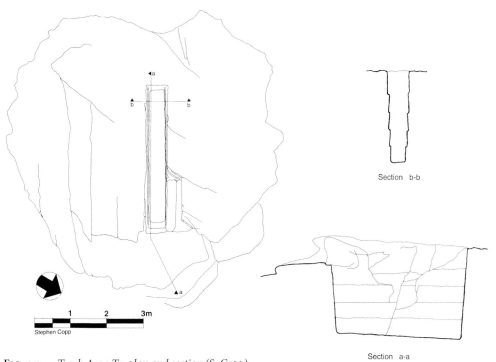

Section b-b

Section a-a

FIG. 4.5   *Tomb A104.T1, plan and section (S. Copp).*

belongs the curving wall foundation that marks off a semicircular space below the main stairs (figs. 4.1–3), but it is only one course high. It may have supported a mudbrick wall for a corral, built long after the tomb had been closed

4.C.2. A105.T1–T4

On top of a low ridge of Umm Ishrin sandstone, 150 m southeast of A104.

T1.   L 2.09 m, W 0.59 m, depth 1.21 m; orientation 63 degrees. No. of offsets, undetermined; capacity, probably ≥ 2. (fig. 4.7).

A single compartment shaft tomb in which the shaft has been expanded sideways from 0.20 m below the surface to provide a wider space. The interior could not be examined closely because it was filled with rubbish and several modern cover slabs were in place. Given the similarity in design and dimensions with A106.T3, however, it is likely that there were two shaft tombs within the chamber.

T2.   L 1.96 m, W 0.60–0.40 m, depth 1.52 m; orientation 65 degrees. No. of offsets, 2; capacity, 2.

T3.   L 2.00 m, W 0.54 m, depth 1.79 m; orientation 65 degrees. No. of offsets, 2; capacity, 2

T4.   L 1.84 m, W 0.56 m, depth 0.66–0.48 m; orientation 65 degrees. Unfinished.

A group of three tombs lined up next to each other 50 m south of T1 (fig. 4.8–9). T2 and T3 show an average quality of stone workmanship, while T4 had been finished only down to the first offset. The shafts, separated by sandstone partition walls (Th 0.19 m), have sharp corners above the first offsets, rounded corners below.

4.C.3. A106.T1–T3

On top of a low ridge of Umm Ishrin sandstone south of the settlement centre, 30 m southeast of A107 (figs. 4.10–11).

T1.   L 1.86–1.96 m, W 0.55 m, depth 0.62 m; orientation 152 degrees. No. of offsets, 1; capacity, 1.

T2.   L ca. 2.00 m, W ca. 0.55 m, depth undetermined; orientation 152 degrees. No. of offsets, undetermined; capacity, ≥ 1.

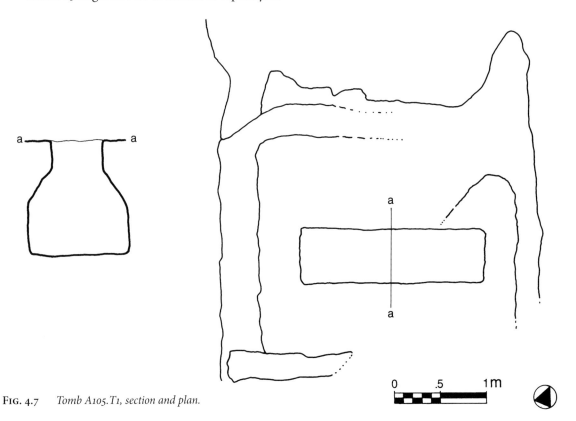

0   .5   1 m

FIG. 4.7   *Tomb A105.T1, section and plan.*

FIG. 4.8   *Tombs A105.T2–T4, view.*

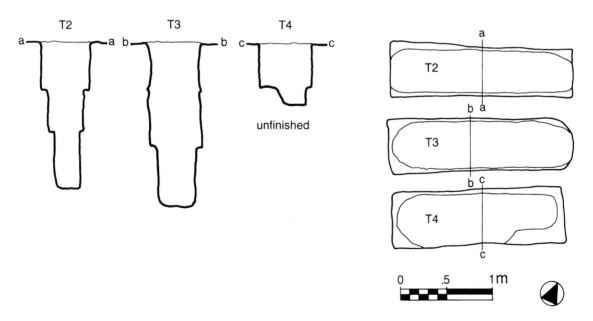

FIG. 4.9   *Tombs A105.T2–T4, section and plan.*

FIG. 4.10   *Tombs A106.T1–T3, view.*

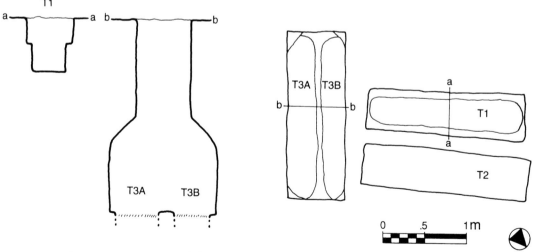

FIG. 4.11   *Tombs A106.T1–T3, section and plan.*

T3. L 1.96–1.99 m, W 0.71 m, depth 2.19 m; orientation 42 degrees. No. of offsets, 2; capacity, ≥ 2.

A group of 3 tombs. T1 is a standard single interment shaft tomb with rounded corners below the offset. T2 was filled with sand, making measurement of depth impossible. T3 consists of two shaft tombs in a chamber that begins as a shaft 0.71 m wide, then at 1.12 m below the surface expands to a chamber 1.32 m wide. Two narrow shafts (T3A and T3B) were cut in the floor of the chamber side by side, separated by a bedrock wall. Unfortunately, because this tomb was in use as a refuse pit, accurate measurements of the shafts could not be taken. This type of multiple loculus shaft tomb can be seen at Petra (Zayadine 1974: 140–41, 1C BC; 1979: 186, 1C AD; Wadeson 2012: 101–3). The juxtaposition of single shafts with a multiple burial shafts, however, is atypical at Humayma.

4.C.4. A107.T1–T2

On top of a low ridge of Umm Ishrin sandstone south of the settlement centre, 34 m south of A105 (figs. 4.12–14).

T1. L 2.09–1.98 m, W 0.55 m, depth 0.61 m; orientation 56 degrees. No. of offsets, 1; capacity, 1. (figs. 4.13–14).

T2. L 2.0 m, W ca. 0.60 m, depth undetermined; orientation 56 degrees. No. of offsets, undetermined. Capacity, ≥ 1.

T1 was excavated in order to sample the ceramics and determine the chronology. The narrow ends of the shaft are curved. Numerous badly decayed human bone fragments were found inside and on the surface around the shaft, and the presence of a human mandible at the western end of the grave might indicate where the head rested. The bones were those of an adult, but sex could not be determined (see p. 322). The pottery recovered was nearly all first to second century in date; the single UM/AB sherd is probably intrusive. One small spherical carnelian bead and a small seashell were found in the tomb.

A107.T1   A107.T2

FIG. 4.12 *Tombs A107.T1–T2, view.*

FIG. 4.13   *Tomb A107.T1, detail.*

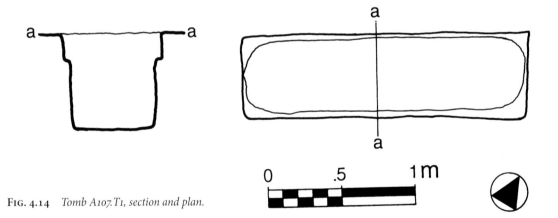

FIG. 4.14   *Tomb A107.T1, section and plan.*

4.C.5.A108.T1

On top of the ridge of Umm Ishrin sandstone west of the settlement centre, 100 m northwest of A104 (fig. 4.15–16).

T1. L 2.14–2.10 m, W 0.79–0.81 m, depth 2.22 m; orientation 43 degrees. No. of offsets, 2; capacity, 1?

The shaft was oriented across a fairly steep stone slope, and a shallow up-slope diversion channel protected it from runoff. The same arrangement can be seen on shaft tombs at Hegra (Nehmé et al. 2006: 86, fig. 45). The tomb was very carefully carved, and the shaft seems extraordinarily deep for a single burial. The upper offsets are 0.23 m below the surface, sufficient to allow an earth sealing above slabs, but the lower set is 1.45 m deep. The

Fig. 4.15   *Tomb A108.T1, view.*

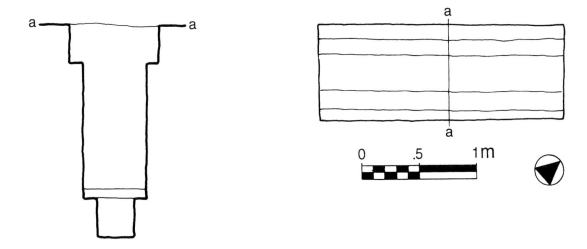

Fig. 4.16   *Tomb A108.T1, section and plan.*

1.22 m difference seems wasted space, unless the owner intended to add more offsets as they were needed but for some reason never did so. One capstone is still in place on the lower set of offsets, but the tomb was thoroughly looted. The small amount of surface pottery dates MN, LN, LB. No other artefacts were found. Several bone fragments of an adult were recovered, but the sex could not be determined.

4.C.6. A109.T1–T2

On the lower slope of the ridge of Umm Ishrin sandstone west of the settlement centre, 40 m NNW of Cistern 55 (fig. 4.17).

T1.　L 1.86 m, W 0.44–0.47 m, depth 0.58 m; orientation 63 degrees. No. of offsets, 1; capacity, 1

T2.　L 1.09–1.08 m, W 0.57 m, depth 0.34 m; orientation 50 degrees. No. of offsets, 1; capacity, 1

Since there are no offsets and the carving is careless, these tombs may be unfinished.

4.C.7. A110.T1

On the upper slope of a ridge of Umm Ishrin sandstone, 70 m NNW of Cistern 55 (figs. 4.18–19).

T1.　L 1.91 m, W 1.86 m, depth 0.64 m; orientation uncertain. No. of offsets uncertain; capacity, ≥ 1.

Erosion of the sandstone has blurred the outlines of this tomb, making measurement difficult, but it appears to be a roughly square shaft that may have given access to *loculi*. The design resembles a small,

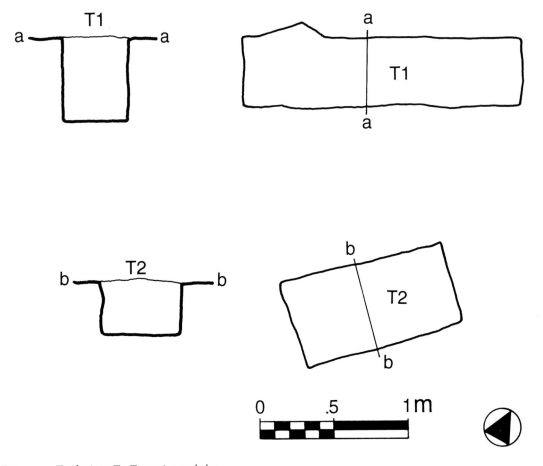

FIG. 4.17　*Tombs A109.T1–T2, section and plan.*

FIG. 4.18   *Tomb A110.T1, view.*

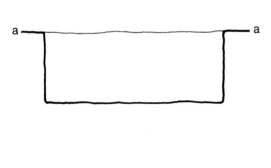

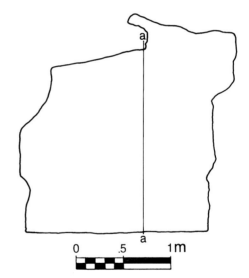

FIG. 4.19   *Tomb A110.T1, section and plan.*

unfinished cistern, but the location does not have a runoff field and is typical of a necropolis. The earth fill was not excavated, so the number of *loculi* — if any — is unknown, along with their orientation.

4.C.8. A111.T1–T5

On the upper slope of the ridge of Umm Ishrin sandstone west of the settlement centre, 150 m NNW of Cistern 55.

T1. L 1.94 m, W 0.49–0.43, depth uncertain; orientation 139 degrees. No. of offsets uncertain; capacity, ≥ 1 (figs. 4.20–21).

T2. L 2.23–2.43 m, W 2.85–2.90 m, depth 1.32–1.74 m; orientation uncertain. No. of offsets uncertain; capacity, ≥ 1 (figs. 4.20–21).

T3. L 1.89 m, W 0.49–0.54 m, depth 1.61 m; orientation 159 degrees. No. of offsets, 2; capacity, 1 (figs. 4.22–23).

FIG. 4.20   *Tombs A111.T1–T2, view.*

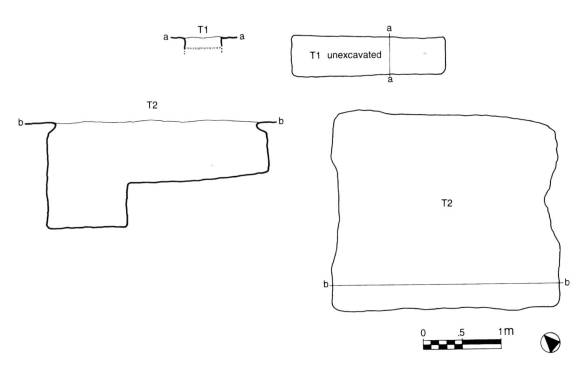

FIG. 4.21   *Tombs A111.T1–T2, section and plan.*

Fig. 4.22 *Tomb A111.T3, view.*

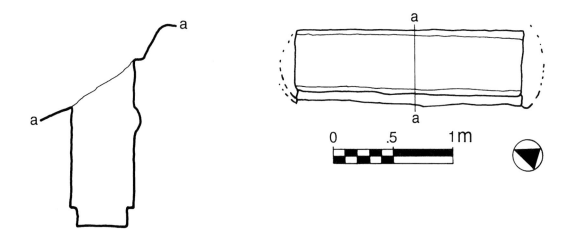

Fig. 4.23 *Tomb A111.T3, section and plan.*

FIG. 4.24   *Tomb A111.T4, view.*

T4. L 2.00 m, W 0.55–0.57 m, depth 1.40 m; orientation 146 degrees. No. of offsets, 0; capacity, ≥ 1 (figs. 4.24–25).

T5. L 1.98–1.95 m, W 0.49–0.52 m, depth 1.34 m; orientation 146 degrees. No of offsets, 2; capacity, 1 (fig. 4.25).

These tombs were built across a bedrock slope, possibly explaining their atypical orientation. Since T1 and T4 were filled with soil, the depths could not be measured. Half of T2 was filled with soil. It is not clear what design was intended for T2; what survives is a large square depression with a possible grave shaft cut along the west wall. In design and dimensions it resembles A110.T1. A groove has been carved at the uppermost portion of the shaft in T3 and T5, allowing capstones to be manoeuvred into place instead of resting on top of a stone lip. T4 and T5 were lined up end-to-end, 1.34 m apart. T3 was close by, but at a different orientation. The ceramics were mostly MN first to early second-century in date, but LB ceramics occurred as well.

T4 was selected for excavation because of its proximity to the rock-cut cistern and the Byzantine Upper church. The numerous cobbles and larger rocks that filled the shaft were cleared out. A deposit of modern goat bones was encountered at 1.31 m below the surface, and floor of the shaft at 1.40 m below datum, but no ancient artefacts were found.

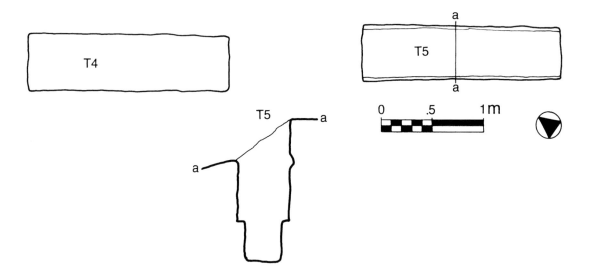

FIG. 4.25   *Tombs A111.T4–T5, plan and section.*

4.C.9. A112.T1–T11

On the upper slope of the ridge of Umm Ishrin sandstone west of the settlement centre, 135 m northwest of Cistern 57.

T1. L 1.96–1.95 m, W 0.63–0.61 m, depth 1.32 cm; orientation 105 degrees. No. of offsets, 1; capacity, 1 (figs. 4.26–27).

T2. L 3.79–3.78 m, W 0.76–0.73 m, depth 1.57 cm; orientation 189 degrees. No. of offsets, 2; capacity, 2 (fig. 4.28).

T3. L 2.00 m, W 0.53 m, depth uncertain; orientation 70 degrees. No offsets; capacity, ≥ 1 (fig. 4.29).

T4. L 2.15 m, W uncertain, depth uncertain; orientation 70 degrees. No offsets; capacity, ≥ 1 (fig. 4.29).

T5. L 2.00 m, W 0.52 m, depth uncertain; orientation 160 degrees. No offsets; capacity, ≥ 1 (fig. 4.29).

T6. L 2.00 m, W 0.52 m, depth uncertain; orientation 160 degrees. No offsets; capacity, ≥ 1 (fig. 4.29).

T7. L 2.12 m, W 0.54–0.61 m, depth uncertain; orientation 70 degrees. No offsets; capacity, ≥ 1 (fig. 4.29).

T8. L 1.88–2.25 m, W 0.32–0.38, depth uncertain; orientation 70 degrees. No offsets; capacity, ≥ 1 (fig. 4.29).

T9. L 2.00 m, W 0.74 m, depth uncertain; orientation 160 degrees. No offsets; capacity, ≥ 1 (fig. 4.29).

T10. L 1.96 m, W 0.55 m, depth uncertain; orientation 160 degrees. No offsets; capacity, ≥ 1 (fig. 4.29).

FIG. 4.26 *Tomb A112.T1, view.*

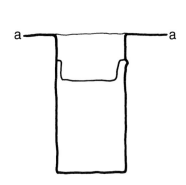

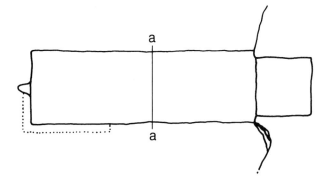

FIG. 4.27 *Tomb A112.T1, section and plan.*

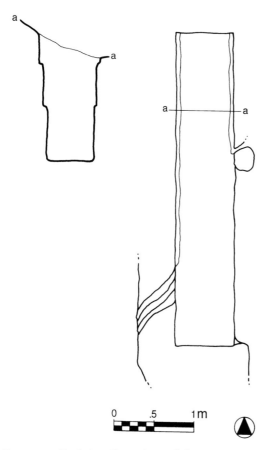

FIG. 4.28　*Tomb A112.T2, section and plan.*

T11. L 2.01 m, W 0.54 m, depth uncertain; orientation 160 degrees. No offsets; capacity, ≥ 1 (fig. 4.29).

T1–T2 were very carefully carved and may represent a pair. There appears to be a small drainage channel carved at the southern end of T2 and at the eastern end of T1. Another atypical feature at the eastern end of T1 is a shelf with an offset for a covering slab carved into the sandstone at a depth of 0.24 m, possibly for the display of offerings. No offsets were found in the interior of the tomb. Pit grave no. 2 in the Renaissance Tomb at Petra appears to have a similar offering shelf (Schmid et al. 2008: 141, fig. 15), and Tomb 779 (Wadeson 2011: 225).

　　T3–T11 form a distinct group of tombs, cut into the bedrock on four sides of a small court excavated into the stone: T3–T4 on the east, T5–T6 on the north, T7–T8 on the west, T9–T11 on the south. The whole complex has been very badly disturbed, and the tombs and court are partly filled with soil dumped by the looters, making measurement and analysis difficult. The surface pottery dated MN to LB. The *loculi* on each side were cut down side by side from the surface, separated by bedrock partition walls 0.19–0.34 m thick. The inner end of each

FIG. 4.29　*Tombs A112.T3–T11, view.*

loculus appears to have been open to the court, which would have required the use of covering slabs at that point, as well as along the upper surface. The complex appears to be an odd variation on the covered, rock-cut chamber tomb with *loculi* carved radially outward from the central chamber, a popular tomb design during the Roman and Byzantine period in Jordan (see above). The bedrock is not thick enough to allow reconstruction of a covered chamber whose bedrock roof has fallen in, and there is no sign of a dromos. A plan could not be prepared in 1993, and prior to re-survey in 2007 the area of A112 and A113 was incorporated into a closed military zone.

4.C.10. A113.T1–T5

On the upper slope of the ridge of Umm Ishrin sandstone west of the settlement centre, 100 m northwest of Cistern 57 (fig. 4.30).

T1. L 1.75–1.79 m, W 0.60 m, depth 1.37 m; orientation 90 degrees. No. of offsets, 3; capacity, 2.

T2. L 1.78–1.95 m, W 0.54–0.69 m, depth 1.11 m; orientation 0 degrees. No. of offsets, 1? capacity, 1?

T3. L 2.08–2.17 m, W 0.57–0.63 m, depth 1.48 m; orientation 0 degrees. No. of offsets, 3; capacity, 2.

T4. L 1.82–1.85 m, W 0.59 m, depth uncertain; orientation 0 degrees. No. of offsets uncertain; capacity, ≥ 1.

T5. L 1.90 m, W 0.57 m, depth uncertain; orientation 0 degrees. No. of offsets uncertain; capacity, ≥ 1.

The shafts seem to have been arranged radially around a central court, as were A112.T3–T11 and A117.T8–T17. The area has been heavily disturbed

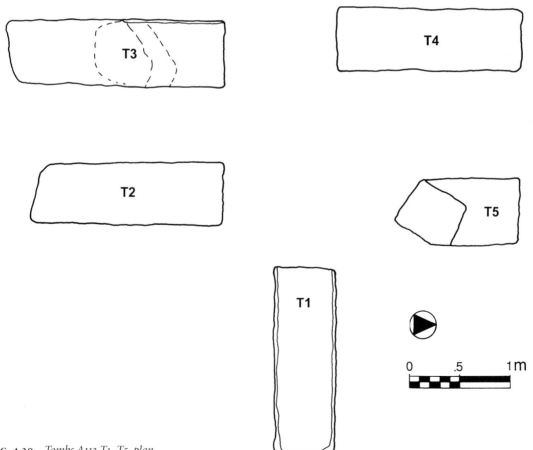

FIG. 4.30   *Tombs A113.T1–T5, plan.*

FIG. 4.31 *A114 Necropolis ridge, view from the north.*

by looters, making accurate assessment and measurement difficult. No surface pottery was observed, but a workman turned in five coins that he claimed to have found in the surface soil prior to our excavation. One of these was Nabataean, the others fourth-century in date (p. 425, nos. 10–14).

4.C.11. A114.T1–T13

On top of a prominent knoll of Umm Ishrin sandstone, 570 m northwest of Reservoir no. 67 (figs. 4.31–40).

T1.　L 0.65 m, W 0.38–0.48 m, depth 0.37 m; orientation 181 degrees. No. of offsets, 0; capacity, 0 (fig. 4.32).

T2.　L 2.21–2.23 m, W 0.92–1.02 m, depth 1.39 m; orientation 181 degrees. No. of offsets, 1; capacity, ≥2? (fig. 4.32).

T3.　L 1.97–2.07 m, W 0.49 m, depth 1.80 m; orientation 87 degrees. No. of offsets, 2; capacity, 1? (fig. 4.33).

T4.　L 1.79 m, W 0.46–0.51 m, depth 1.63 m; orientation 87 degrees. No. of offsets, 3; capacity, 2 (fig. 4.33).

T5.　L 1.86–1.89 m, W 0.45–0.47 m, depth 0.49 m; orientation 57 degrees. No. of offsets, uncertain; capacity, ≥ 1 (figs. 4.34–35).

T6.　L 1.78 m, W 0.48 m, depth 0.42 m; orientation 57 degrees. No. of offsets, uncertain; capacity, ≥ 1 (figs. 4.34–35).

T7.　L 1.80 m, W 0.45 m, depth 1.45 m; orientation 57 degrees. Number of offsets, 2; capacity, 1? (figs. 4.34–35).

T8.　L 1.79–1.82 m, W 0.45–0.47 m, depth 1.32 m; orientation 57 degrees. No. of offsets, 2; capacity, 1? (figs. 4.34–35).

T9.　L 1.93–1.96 m, W 0.51–0.53 m, depth 1.89 m; orientation 95 degrees. No. of offsets, 3; capacity, 3? (fig. 4.36).

T10.　L 1.96 m, W 0.41–0.47 m, depth 1.90 m; orientation 108 degrees. No. of offsets, 4; capacity, 3 (figs. 4.37–38).

T11.　L 2.06–2.10 m, W 0.46–0.52 m, depth unfinished; orientation 108 degrees. Number of offsets undetermined; capacity, ≥ 1 (figs. 4.37–38).

T12. L 1.89–1.92 m, W 0.42–0.46 m, depth uncertain; orientation 105 degrees. No. of offsets, uncertain; capacity, ≥ 1 (figs. 4.39–40).

T13. L 1.93 m, W 0.45 m, depth uncertain; orientation 105 degrees. No. of offsets uncertain; capacity, ≥ 1 (figs. 4.39–40).

T1–T2 are located on top of a sandstone bluff. T1 may be a short, unfinished shaft tomb, or it may have had some other function entirely. T2 is wide enough to have accommodated two individuals side by side. There is a small square depression (0.47 × 0.52 m) near the southeast corner of this shaft that was not registered as a tomb. T3–T4 were cut side by side, separated by a sandstone wall 0.22 m thick. Erosion has affected this wall and both shaft tombs. The four shaft tombs T5–T8 are situated side by side. T5 and T6 are filled with soil,

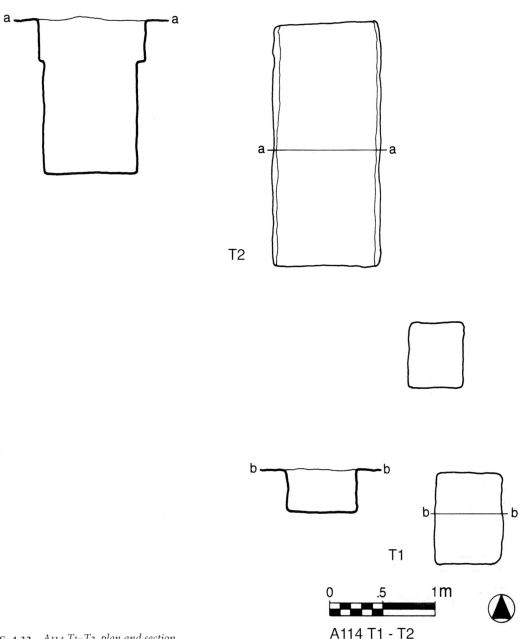

FIG. 4.32 *A114.T1–T2, plan and section.*

A114 T1 - T2

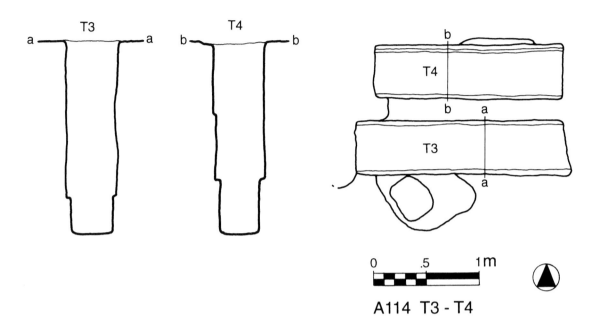

FIG. 4.33 *A114.T3–T4, section and plan.*

FIG. 4.34 *A114.T5–T8, view.*

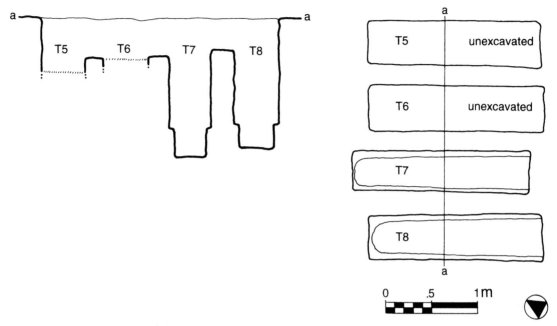

FIG. 4.35 *A114.T5–T8, section and plan.*

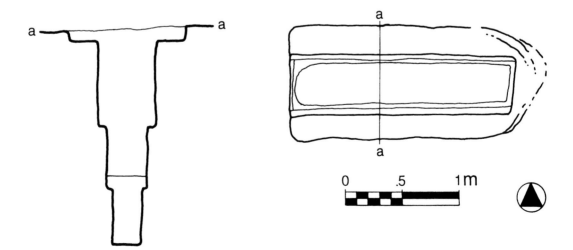

FIG. 4.36 *A114.T9, section and plan.*

Fig. 4.37 *A114.T10–T11, view.*

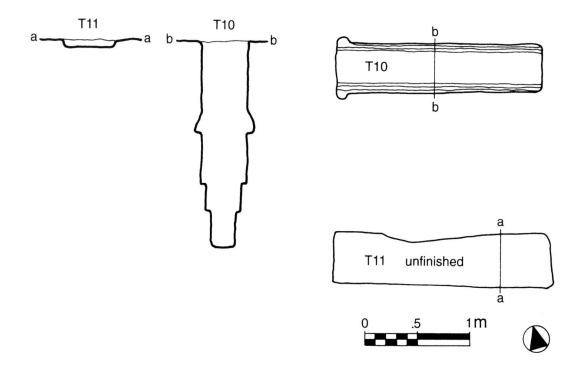

Fig. 4.38 *A114.T10–T11, section and plan.*

FIG. 4.39   *A114.T12–T13, view of chamber.*

possibly fill removed from T7 and T8 by looters. Erosion has badly worn the walls separating these tombs. A recess was carved around the top of T9 to allow the capstones to be placed flush with the surface, making it possible that three individuals were accommodated, rather than two. There may be a drain at the eastern end of the tomb. Grooves were carved into the sides of T10 to allow the uppermost capstones to be manoeuvred into place. There are two side niches at the western end of the tomb. The shaft for T11 had been cut only a few centimetres into the stone, providing an excellent example of the early stages in carving a shaft tomb. T3, T4, T7, T9, and T10 all have particularly deep shafts, but not always extra pairs of offsets. Due to the very exposed nature of this necropolis, on the narrow summit of a sandstone ridge, no identifiable sherds could be associated with the tombs.

The T12 and T13 *loculi* were originally located in a large chamber (W ca. 4 m, L ca. 5 m) carved in the side of a sandstone bluff, in the manner of the chamber tombs at Petra and Hegra, both those with façades and those without (Nehmé 2006: 80–84).

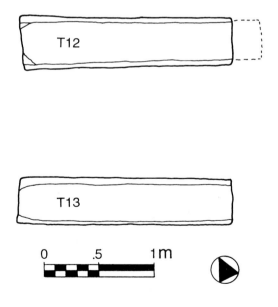

FIG. 4.40   *A114.T12–T13, plan.*

Unlike the larger façade tombs at Petra, however, there is no evidence at this tomb for associated triclinia, cisterns, or courtyards. Nevertheless, the unique character of this façade tomb at Hawara, and its prominent location dominating the site (e.g., fig. 6.51, background to the left), suggest that it was built for a particularly important family (cf. shaft tomb A104.T1). Unfortunately, the bedrock roof collapsed at some point, and the façade either fell or was removed when the chamber was turned into a storage space or house sometime in the past century. The present façade was constructed of reused blocks, and wooden beams supported a mud roof. The tomb *loculi* were filled with refuse and soil, so the depth could not be measured. They are located on either side of the chamber, and three more *loculi* may well occupy the space between them, and a second row of five the space to the rear, a type of arrangement seen at Petra in the Renaissance Tomb and other chamber tombs (Schmid et al. 2008: 137–40). This whole area is now encumbered with earth and rubble.

4.C.12. A115.T1–T17

On top of a prominent knoll of Umm Ishrin sandstone across a valley from A114, 600 m northwest of Reservoir no. 67 (figs. 4.41–46).

T1. L 0.98 m, W 0.88 cm; depth 1.60 m; orientation of entrance 260 degrees. Unfinished (figs. 4.41–42).

T2. L 1.96 m, W 1.25 m, depth 1.37 m; orientation uncertain. No. of offsets uncertain; capacity, ≥ 1 (fig. 4.43).

T3. L 1.77 m, W uncertain, depth uncertain; orientation 80 degrees. No. of offsets uncertain; capacity, ≥ 1 (fig. 4.44).

T4. L 190/187 m, W 42, depth uncertain; orientation 88 degrees. No. of offsets uncertain; capacity, ≥ 1

T5. Dimensions and capacity undetermined.

T6. L 1.82 m, W 0.59 m, depth 0.84 m; orientation 97 degrees. No. of offsets, 1; capacity, 1 (figs. 4.44–45).

FIG. 4.41 *A115.T1, view of façade.*

T7. L 1.80 m, W 0.52–0.56 m, depth 0.84 cm; orientation 97 degrees. Number of offsets, 1; capacity, 1 (figs. 4.44–45).

T8. L 1.94 m, W 0.57 m, depth 0.67 cm; orientation 97 degrees. No. of offsets, 1; capacity, 1 (figs. 4.44–45).

T9. L 1.84 m, W 0.55 m, depth 0.73 m; orientation 97 degrees. No. of offsets, 1; capacity, 1 (figs. 4.44–45).

T10. L 1.87 m, W 0.59 m, depth uncertain; orientation 97 degrees. No. of offsets, uncertain; capacity, ≥ 1 (figs. 4.44–45).

T11. L 1.79–1.82 m, W 0.53–0.60 m, depth uncertain; orientation 97 degrees. No. of offsets, uncertain; capacity, ≥ 1 (figs. 4.44–45).

T12. L 1.87 m, W 0.55 m, depth uncertain; orientation 97 degrees. No. of offsets uncertain; capacity, ≥ 1 (figs. 4.44–45).

T13. L 1.79–1.89 m, W 0.60 m, depth 0.86 m; orientation 97 degrees. No. of offsets, 1; capacity, ≥ 1 (figs. 4.45–46).

T14. L 1.79 m, W 0.58 m, depth uncertain; orientation 97 degrees. No. of offsets uncertain; capacity, ≥ 1 (figs. 4.44–45).

T15. L 1.70 m, W 0.58 m, depth uncertain; orientation 97 degrees. No. of offsets uncertain; capacity, ≥1 (figs. 4.44–45).

T16. L 1.81 m, W 0.45–0.47 m, depth 1.14 cm; orientation 47 degrees. No. of offsets, 1; capacity, 1.

T17. L 1.97–2.00 m, W 0.48 m, depth 1.82 m; orientation 95 degrees. No. of offsets, 2; capacity, 1.

T1 appears to be an unfinished chamber cut into the face of a sandstone cliff, like A114.T12–13, directly across the valley. Alternatively, it may be a large, unfinished niche for a betyl, such as that seen at the south end of the settlement by Structure no. 48 (*HEP* 1: 144–45, fig. 3.89). This side of the ridge has been regularized by quarrying, a situation that often attracted representations of betyls (e.g., A104), possibly carved by stonemasons in the course of their work. T2 is a large square shaft that may have had several offsets, but the rock face has been heavily eroded. There is a groove along the northern wall, but it is not clear whether it has been carved or is the result of erosion. T3 and T4 were located on

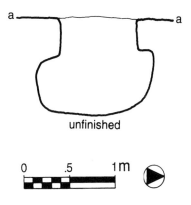

unfinished

0   .5   1 m

FIG. 4.42   *A115.T1, section.*

FIG. 4.43   *A115.T2, section and plan.*

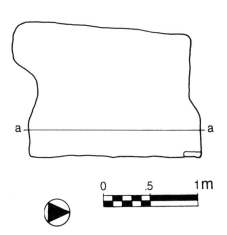

0   .5   1 m

FIG. 4.44　*A115.T6–T15, view to south.*

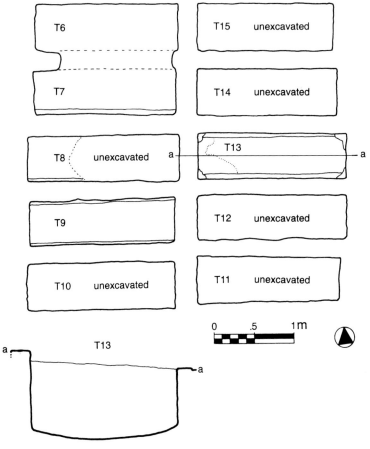

FIG. 4.45　*A115.T6–T15, plan and section.*

FIG. 4.46 *A115.T13, view.*

end, perhaps for offerings. The floor of the tomb was slightly concave. A 0.05 m offset was carved along the north and south walls at 0.56 m below the upper edge to support capstones. Some of the original light brown, sandy mortar packing that covered these slabs survived in each corner, 0.28 m above the offset (fig. 4.46). The shaft contained ceramic fragments dating MN, LN, LB, UM, AB, fragments of blue glass, and a few human and mammal bone fragments.

A block-built structure carefully constructed in an inset into the east side of the ridge just below the tombs may have had something to do with the necropolis, but it has been so badly damaged by looters that no clear plan could be made out.

T16 is an isolated tomb shaft 50 m east of the A115 necropolis.

T17 is the only tomb near Hawara that had been cut in the white Disi sandstone rather than the red Umm Ishrin sandstone typical of the slopes closer to the settlement centre. This tomb, with a particularly deep shaft above the first offset (1.39 m) possibly intended to provide room for further stacked burials, is located on a white sandstone outcropping 100 m north of the A115 necropolis. It should probably have been registered as a distinct burial area.

4.C.13. A117.T1–T17

Necropolis A117 is located at the top of a north/south ridge 250 m northwest of the A115 group (figs. 4.47–50).

T1. L 2.01–2.07 m, W 0.41–0.43 m, depth 1.33 m; orientation 91 degrees. No. of offsets, 1; capacity, 1 (figs. 4.47–48).

T2. L 2.03–2.09 m, W 0.54 m, depth unknown; orientation 91 degrees. No. of offsets unknown; capacity, ≥ 1 (figs. 4.47–48).

T3. L 2.01–2.03 m, W 0.51–0.55 m, depth 0.89 m; orientation 91 degrees. No. of offsets unknown; capacity, ≥ 1 (figs. 4.47–48).

T4. L 2.08 m, W 0.63–0.69 m, depth unknown; orientation 96 degrees. No. of offsets unknown; capacity, ≥ 1 (figs. 4.47–48).

top of the sandstone bluff, on the same orientation and 2.14 m apart. Unfortunately, the locals were using these tombs as storage bins covered with stone slabs, making some measurements impossible. T5 was almost completely covered with earth thrown up by the tomb robbers, making determination of its dimensions impossible. Farther along the ridge, T6–T15 appear to form a small necropolis, organized in two rows of five graves aligned in an east/west direction. Bedrock walls ca. 0.18 m thick separate the narrow ends of the shafts, bedrock walls ca. 0.15 m think separate them from side to side. The area has been heavily disturbed by looters, who have left most of the tombs are obstructed with heaps of soil. As a result, the depth could be determined only for T6–T8.

T13 was cleared out in a search for datable ceramics. The contents had already been disturbed. Because the shaft was cut into the sloping edge of the ridge, the ground level is 0.26 m higher at the east end of the shaft than at the west end. A 0.18 m inset was carved into the rock along the east

FIG. 4.47 *A117.T1–T6, view.*

T5. L 1.87–1.91 m, W 0.40–0.42 m, depth unknown; orientation 96 degrees. No. of offsets unknown; capacity, ≥ 1 (figs. 4.47–48).

T6. L 1.91 m, W 0.45 m, depth 0.63 m; orientation 96 degrees. No. of offsets unknown; capacity, ≥ 1 (figs. 4.47–48).

T7. L 1.97–2.02 m, W 0.57–0.60 m, depth 1.83 m; orientation 79 degrees. No. of offsets, 1; capacity, 1 (fig. 4.49).

T8. L 2.02 m, W 0.70–0.74 m, depth 1.49 m; orientation 180 degrees. No. of offsets, 1; capacity, 1 (fig. 4.50).

T9. L 2.02 m? W 0.47 m? depth unknown; orientation 180 degrees. No. of offsets unknown; capacity, ≥ 1.

T10. L 2.02 m? W 0.47 m, depth unknown; orientation 180 degrees. No. of offsets unknown; capacity, ≥ 1.

T11. L 2.04 m, W 0.46 m, depth unknown; orientation 91 degrees. No. of offsets unknown; capacity, ≥ 1.

T12. L 2.04 m? W 0.64 m, depth unknown; orientation 91 degrees. No. of offsets unknown; capacity, ≥ 1.

T13. L 2.02 m? W 0.52 m, depth unknown; orientation 180 degrees. No. of offsets unknown; capacity, ≥ 1.

T14. L 2.02 m? W 0.47 m? depth unknown; orientation 180 degrees. No. of offsets unknown; capacity, ≥ 1.

T15. L 2.02 m? W 0.47 m? depth unknown; orientation 180 degrees. No. of offsets unknown; capacity, ≥ 1.

T16. L 2.04 m? W 0.46 m? depth unknown; orientation 91 degrees. No. of offsets unknown; capacity, ≥ 1.

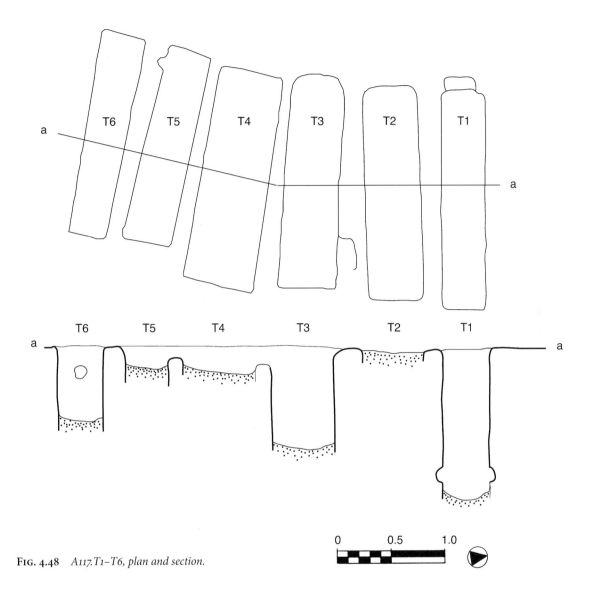

FIG. 4.48 *A117.T1–T6, plan and section.*

T17. L 2.04 m, W 0.46 m, depth unknown; orientation 91 degrees. No. of offsets unknown; capacity, ≥ 1.

There are two sets of tombs at this area. There is one small necropolis in which six shaft tombs were oriented side by side (T1–T6), and a seventh (T7) set slightly apart at the south end. A parallel arrangement can be found at A114.T5–T8 and A115. There is a second cluster of tombs, or necropolis nearby, with ten *loculi* (A117.T8–T17) branching outward from a small central courtyard: T8–T10 on the north, T11–T12 on the east, T13–T15 on the south, and T16–T17 on the west. Parallels for this arrangement can be seen at A112 and A113

(figs. 4.29–30). Several sandstone blocks carefully finished with Nabataean type stone dressing were found near the T8–T17 group, probably used to supplement the bedrock, or to monumentalize the façades.

There was a large quantity of small, weathered fragments of pottery on the surface around the two groups of tombs, collected as three separate loci. Locus 00A was confined to a 2.0 m radius around T1–T7; Locus 00B comprised the area between 2 m and 4 m from the tombs. A roughly 2 m radius around the second necropolis (T8–T17) was given designation Locus 00C. Locus 00A yielded only MN and LN fine wares, suggesting the original chronology of the shaft tombs (fig. 4.51). Locus

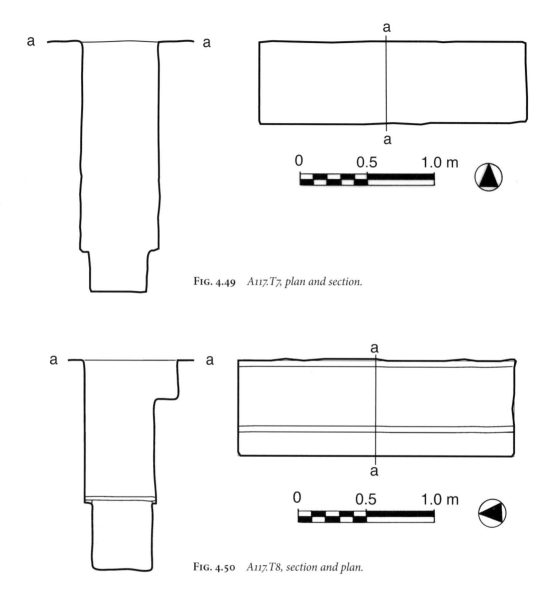

FIG. 4.49   *A117.T7, plan and section.*

FIG. 4.50   *A117.T8, section and plan.*

OOB yielded MN and MB ceramics; the collection was predominantly second-century in date, with some fourth to fifth-century wares. The second-century to fifth-century date fits the typology of the courtyard and *loculus* tomb arrangement well.

Two tombs from A117 were selected for excavation. T8 was chosen because of the presence of human bones on the surface around the tomb as well as within the tomb. The tomb had been looted, but several MN potsherds were recovered, smeared with the mortar used to seal the capstones. There was a ledge near the surface to support an upper set of capstones, although it seems very wide for this purpose. There is a second set of ledges at 1.01

m depth below the surface, on which a second set of capstones was placed (fig. 4.50). Capstones were still in situ mortared into place at the southern end of the tomb. Several human bones were recovered, including left half of a mandible.

The second tomb to be excavated was A117.T7. This tomb appeared to have been already looted in the past, so a probe was dug at the western end of the loculus to determine depth and other features. The ledge for the capstones was found at 1.51 m below the surface, with capstones still *in situ* at the eastern end of the tomb. Remains of mortar could be seen holding the capstone in place, as well as along the ledge. At the bottom of the tomb, there

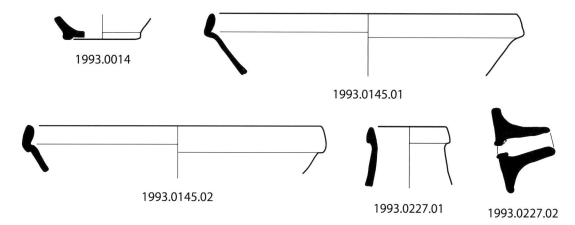

FIG. 4.51   *Ceramic profiles from tomb group A117. 1993.0014: A117.00, NFW small vessel base (cf. Bikai and Perry 2001: fig. 8.9, 20–100) (1C). 1993.0145.01: A117.00, NFW bowl, ware 2.5YR 6/8 (EZ I: fig. 652–53, 50 BC–AD 20; Bikai and Perry 2001: fig. 9.1, 20–100) (ea. 1C). 1993.0145.02: A117.00, NFW bowl, ware 2.5YR 6/6, rim 2.5YR 6/2, core N5/0 (cf. 1993.0015.01) (mid-1C). 1993.0227.01: A117.T7.01, small jar, probably NFW (ES IIL fig. 284, 50 BC–AD 106). 1993.0227.02: A117.T7.01, nipple spout from jug. Although these spouts are used into the LB and Early Islamic period (Jerash: Uscatescu 2001: fig. 8.3, 9.3, 6C; Pella: Smith and Day 1989: pl. 54.8, 700–725) in the context of the necropolis an early ware is more likely (cf. 'Amr 1992: fig. 3.160, 1–ea. 2C; Aqaba: Dolinka 2003: 129, no. 22, mid-1C; Parker 1987: fig. 91.15, 1C) (1C).*

was a layer of dark soil containing fragments of wood, possibly the remains of a coffin. Fragments of four inscribed headstones were found in the tomb fill (pp. 492–95, nos. 1–4). One fragment preserved two Greek letters forming part of a funerary formula or a name; the other three carried names in Nabataean script. The inscriptions cannot be positively attributed to this particular tomb since the context was badly disturbed. The pottery found within the tomb and the associated fill was MN, placing the tomb in the late first or early second century. Freestanding, inscribed tombstones are rare in the Nabataean cultural area (Schmid et al. 2008: 139).

4.C.14. A118.T1–T11

The A118 necropolis is located on a small knoll of Umm Ishrin sandstone 350 m north of necropolis A115 (figs. 4.52–59).

T1.   L 1.97 m, W 0.46–0.49 m, depth 1.79 m; orientation 80 degrees. No. of offsets, 1; capacity, 1 (fig. 4.52).

T2.   L 1.94–1.97 m, W. 0.48–0.50 m, depth 1.48 m; orientation 80 degrees. No. of offsets, 1; capacity, 1 (fig. 4.52).

T3.   L 1.88 m, W 0.46–0.48 m, depth 1.30 m; orientation 80 degrees. No. of offsets, 1; capacity, 1 (fig. 4.52).

T4.   L 1.96–2.00 m, W 0.49 m, depth 1.57 m; orientation 80 degrees. No. of offsets, 1; capacity, 1 (figs. 4.53–54).

T5.   L 2.00 m, W 0.52 m, depth 1.96 m; orientation 80 degrees. No. of offsets, 1; capacity, 1 (figs. 4.53–54).

T6.   L 2.03 m, W 0.51–0.56 m, depth 1.97 m; orientation 90 degrees. No. of offsets, 1; capacity, 1 (fig. 4.55).

T7.   L 1.79–1.90 m, W 0.41–0.45 m, depth 0.69 m; orientation 80 degrees. No. of offsets unknown; capacity, ≥ 1 (fig. 4.56).

T8.   L 1.80–1.83 m, W 0.47 m, depth 1.48 m; orientation 80 degrees. No. of offsets, 1; capacity, 1 (fig. 4.56).

T9.   L 1.96–1.99 m, W 0.44–0.49 m, depth 1.68 m; orientation 58 degrees. No. of offsets, 1; capacity, 1 (figs. 4.57–58).

T10. L 1.96 m, W 0.49 m, depth 1.75 m; orientation 58 degrees. No. of offsets, 1; capacity, 1 (figs. 4.57–58).

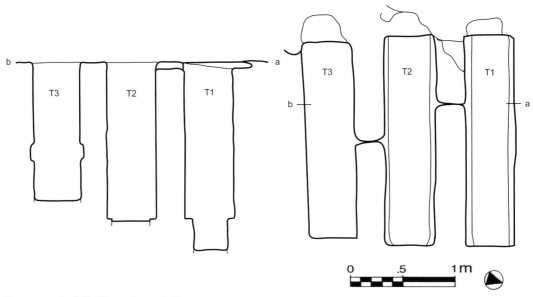

Fig. 4.52   *A118.T1–T3, section and plan.*

Fig. 4.53   *A118.T4–T5, view.*

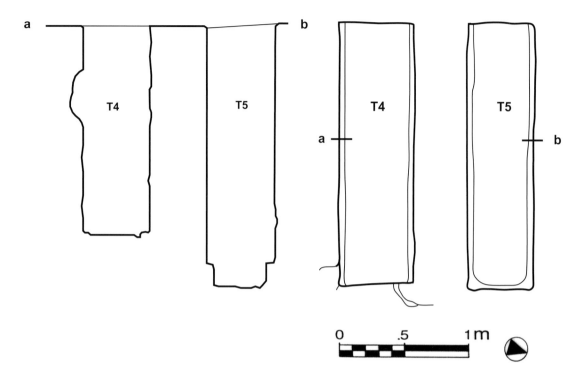

FIG. 4.54   *A118.T4–T5, section and plan.*

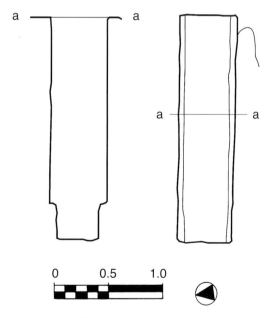

FIG. 4.55   *A118.T6, section and plan.*

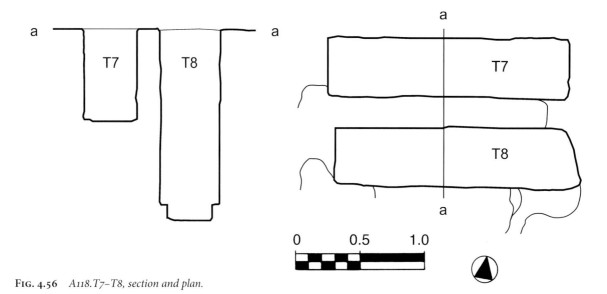

FIG. 4.56   *A118.T7–T8, section and plan.*

FIG. 4.57   *A118.T9–T10, view.*

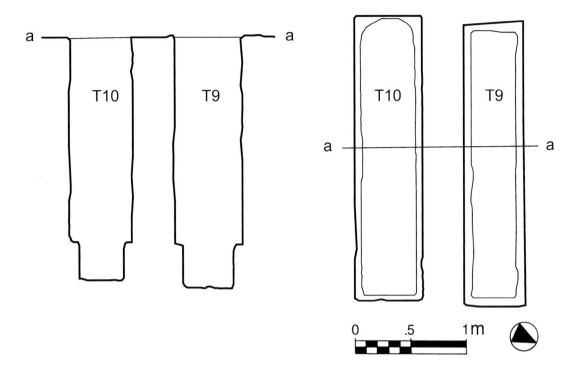

FIG. 4.58 *A118.T9–T10, section and plan.*

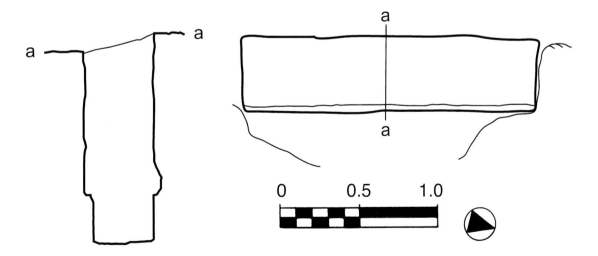

FIG. 4.59 *A118.T11, section and plan.*

FIG. 4.60   *A119.T1, view.*

T11. L 1.84–1.88 m, W 0.43–0.46 m, depth 1.77
      m; orientation 143 degrees. No. of offsets, 1;
      capacity, 1 (fig. 4.59).

The tombs are standard single person shaft tombs,
spread out along the ridge, all oriented more or
less east/west except for T11, which is oriented to
the southeast. The small number of potsherds recovered from the surface around the tombs dated
MN, LN, and MB, late first to early third century,
with a few fourth to fifth-century wares.

    T4 was chosen for excavation on the basis of its
apparently less disturbed condition; several cover
slabs were still in position, although they may not
belong to the original interment. Since the slabs are
held in place with mud packing rather than lime
mortar, they may have been put in place in the
early modern period, when the tomb shafts were
reused for storage for tools or grain. A probe was
placed at the eastern end of the tomb to see if any
artefacts could be found, as well as to clarify the
tomb design. The probe in T4 produced several

possibly human bone fragments, as well as a few
very non-diagnostic potsherds possibly dating to
the third century. Several cover slabs still in place
on T10 may be ancient, since there are traces of
mortar around the bottom edges.

4.C.15. A119.T1

A solitary tomb cut into an outcropping of Disi
sandstone 50 m northeast of A118 (fig. 4.60).

T1. L 1.71–1.81 m, W 0.42–0.50 m, depth 0.42 m;
     orientation 92 degrees. No. of offsets, 1; capac-
     ity, 1.

The surface pottery dated MN and LN, from the
second and third century AD. The tomb itself is
of poor workmanship and is not very deep when
compared to the others, plus it is slowly eroding
away from wind erosion. No other notable features
were found.

4.D. CONCLUSIONS

The tomb survey recorded 11 groups of tombs and
four isolated tombs along the ridges of Umm Ishrin
sandstone just west of the settlement centre. While
there are undoubtedly other rock-cut tombs in
the vicinity of Humayma, none were noted during searches several hundred meters west of those
that have been recorded here, or in the white Disi
sandstone hills to the east of the settlement. Clearly
it was felt important that the burial places be near
the settlement and be visible from it. Five of the
necropoleis contained 10 or more separate tombs.
The total number of separate shafts of *loculi* was 94,
with a potential population of at least 100 individuals. The most capacious tomb was A104.T1, with an
estimated capacity of 8 burials. There were 15 shaft
tombs with more than one pair of offsets (anywhere
from 2 pairs to 4 pairs): 2 pairs, A105.T2, A105.T3,
A106.T3, A108.T1, A111.T3, A111.T5, A114.T3, A114.
T7, A114.T8, A115.T17; 3 pairs, A112.T2, A113.T1,
A113.T3, A114.T4, A114.T9; 4 pairs, A104.T1, A114.
T10. A114 has the highest proportion of stacked
burial positions, perhaps indicating significant
family size or social coherence among the individuals buried there. There were two sunken courts
surrounded by single person *loculi* open above and

at their inner end (A112.T3–T11, A117.T8–T17); A113. T1–T5 may be another example of this type. Only two shafts were left unfinished: A105.T4, A115.T1. There is evidence that tombs were often reused in Nabataean, Roman, and Byzantine Jordan and the Negev (e.g., Cheyney et al. 2009: 329; Perry 2002b; Schmid et al. 2008; cf. Nagar and Sonntag 2008), but even so, 94 burial positions clearly could not have accommodated even a small portion of the cumulative population of Nabataean, Roman, and Byzantine Hawara/Hauarra, even with multiple burials in each position. Most of the dead must have been buried in cist tombs cut into the soil in and around the settlement centre, such as those found in B100, C101, and F102. It is likely that there was a separate military cemetery for the soldiers of the Roman Fort. One possible location for the military burial ground is a gently sloping field 740 m west of the Roman Fort, below the ridge on which the A115 necropolis was located (Oleson et al. 2008: 333–34). There has been some clandestine digging in this area, and several tomb markers inscribed with crosses or inscriptions have turned up (fig. 4.61; Oleson et al. 2003: 54–55). In addition, potsherds in the area frequently are found to have been exposed to very hot fires that left them melted,

possibly during the cremation ceremony typical of Roman military burials (cf. Negev 1971).

In the necropoleis with more than one tomb, there was a clear tendency for most or all of the shafts to have the same orientation, for example, A105, A114, or A115. The tombs organized around a central court naturally radiated outward in all four directions. The shaft tombs show a tendency to be oriented east–west, most likely considered as facing east, since in all three tombs excavated beneath B100 and F102 the bodies were laid out on their backs with the head at the west end. The 76 shaft tombs for which the orientation could be determined fall into three clusters: 42 (55.3%) ranged from 79 to 108 degrees, 17 (22.4%) ranged from 40 to 70 degrees, and 17 (22.4%) ranged from 139 to 189 degrees. Little evidence for the orientation of burials at Petra has been published, but an adult female skeleton buried in the mid-first century in a stacked shaft tomb in the chamber of a tomb in the Wadi Mataha is reported to have been on her back, head to the south, face turned to the east (D. Johnson, in Keller et al. 2012: 734). The 50 shaft tombs ("pit graves") around the Aslah Triclinium Complex, however, seem to be placed only in reference to the immediate topography (Gorgerat and

FIG. 4.61 *Christian grave marker from necropolis below A115.*

Wenning 2013: 224, fig. 2). All the skeletons in the burials at Wadi Faynan were found on their backs, with their skulls at the west end of the cist (Findlater et al. 1998: 72). The same is true for the intact tombs found at Khirbet edh-Dharih (Lenoble et al. 2001: 110–11, 132–43, 146), for the second to third-century tombs at the Amman airport (Ibrahim and Gordon 1987), and for Byzantine Christian burials at many sites in the Negev (Nagar and Sonntag 2008: 88). In his discussion of the shaft tombs at Hegra, Tholbecq (2006) does not provide statistics concerning their orientation. He does, however, state that the ordinary shaft tombs did not follow any preferred orientation, but corresponded to the topography (Nehmé et al. 2006: 88). Nevertheless, one site map of the Jabal al-Khraymat necropolis (Nehmé et al. 2006: 77, fig. 32) shows a large number of shaft tombs, all apparently oriented between east and southeast. In the courtyard tombs one might expect all the burials to be oriented with the head toward the central court for ease of insertion, but no evidence survives. Schmid (Schmid et al. 2008: 144) does not find any obvious prevalent orientation. At Hawara, as at Petra and the rest of the Nabataean cultural region, free-standing inscribed tombstones are rare (Schmid et al. 2008: 139, 143).

We can only speculate as to the reasons for the absence at Hawara of the elaborate Nabataean façade tombs seen at Petra and Hegra. One chamber tomb was recorded at Hawara (A114.T12–T13), but any elaborate façade — if there was one — has been lost. The location, however, gave little scope for elaborate architectural designs. Geology was not the reason for the absence of such façades, since the simple tombs of Hawara were carved in the same stratum of Umm Ishrin sandstone utilized for the magnificent tombs at Petra. The reasons for the differences in practice were probably social and economic; the noble and the rich were less likely to live and die in the small settlement of Hawara, than at Petra. Furthermore, time and tradition may have conferred on the Petra necropoleis a greater degree of sacredness than could be mustered for Hawara. There are, however, hundreds of parallels at Petra for the single and multiple shaft tombs seen at Hawara, both out in the open and inside the chambers behind the elaborate façades (Musil 1907–8: vol. 2, p. 50–52, "Senkgräber;" Horsfield

and Horsfield 1938: 94, pl. 48, 52; Hammond 1973: 76–77, "shaft and ledge types;" Lindner et al. 1984: fig. 2, pl. 21.1; Sinibaldi 2009: 458, fig. 17; Wadeson 2012: 101–3, "more than 800…pit graves;" Gorgerat and Wenning 2013: 223–24). Two undisturbed first-century shaft tombs with multiple burials excavated at Petra in 2011 show many of the features less well-preserved at Humayma (Keller at al. 2012: 734, 738–39): rubble and earth fill above carefully fit roofing slabs, plaster sealing around the stones, wooden coffins, and ceramic and metal grave goods. Some of the clusters of tombs elsewhere at Petra are arranged in neat rows like those in fields A115 and A117 at Hawara, others clearly have been laid out to fit the topography. Although the necropoleis at Hegra are less well-known, Tholbecq has so far counted nearly 500 shaft tombs (Nehmé et al. 2006: 84–87). The great majority of these shafts are quite shallow, less than 0.30 m deep, and apparently not organized side by side in groups. Tholbecq suggests that to accommodate the corpses, the shallow depressions were supplemented by dry stone or mudbrick walls around the periphery carrying cover slabs, all now lost or scattered. This was possibly the arrangement for the tombs in F102. There was also a less numerous class of deeper shaft tombs, with a single pair of offsets in the shaft for slabs, allowing either single or double burials. These deeper shafts often occupied "positions privilégiées, au sommet de massifs rocheux" (Nehmé et al. 2006: 87), and they were often organized in pairs.

Although different in character, the monumental, early second-century Tomb C1 at Khirbet edh-Dharih provides some parallels for multiple, stacked burials and celestial orientation. The structure, which was built of blocks rather than rock-cut, contained six shafts, each with five pairs of offsets, for a potential total capacity of 30 burials (Delhopital et al. 2009; Lenoble et al. 2001: 100–104). The structure was oriented to 116 degrees.

The burial practices at Hawara clearly correspond well with those at ancient Petra, slightly less closely with those at Hegra, but all three sites testify to a well-established tradition of Nabataean burial practices. It would be useful to have more extensive statistics on the celestial orientation of the shaft tombs at Petra and Hegra, to determine whether this aspect, too, is shared.

Chapter 5

Field F102: Nabataean Cistern, Byzantine Church, and Early Islamic House

by Khairieh 'Amr and John P. Oleson

5.A. LOCATION, DESCRIPTION, AND PHASING

Extensive excavation was carried out from 1991 to 1995 in an area designated as Field F102, a large domestic structure and associated cistern at the southeast edge of the settlement (figs. 1.1–1.2; Oleson et al. 1993: 476–84; 1995: 337–43). The excavation was directed by K. 'Amr. The cistern (Survey no. 64; *HEP* 1: 207–9) lies 150 m southeast of central Reservoir no. 67. The building itself was one of approximately 15 structures, clearly visible in aerial photographs and on the ground, stretched out along a triangular plot of ground between the Wadi Qalkha on the southeast, the outflow channel of the through-settlement drainage on the northwest, and the open ground south of Reservoir no. 67 (fig. 1.2). The Abbasid Family Manor House (F103) is set slightly apart from this group of structures, but it is only 40 m northeast of the nearest one. The buildings all appear to have been constructed of heavy blocks of Umm Ishrin sandstone mixed with various types of rubble. The six largest structures, all rectangular or square in plan, with numerous rooms and usually a courtyard, were built along a low rise just above a gully that feeds run-off to the Wadi Qalkha. Presumably this higher ground provided more protection against occasional flooding

during run-off events. The neighbouring structures to the west were smaller and more scattered.

Structure F102, the southernmost of the six large structures, was selected for excavation because of the apparently good preservation of its walls and clarity of its plan, and the presence of a Nabataean type cylindrical cistern as part of the complex (fig. 5.1). It seemed possible that excavation might reveal a sequence of Nabataean, Byzantine, and Early Islamic structures that made use of the cistern water. Potsherds on the surface between F102 and F103 showed a significant proportion of Umayyad, Abbasid, and Mamluk wares. Since nothing was known in 1991 about the arrangement of the settlement or the chronology and purpose of the Abbasid Manor House, it also seemed wise to balance excavation at B100 in the centre of Humayma with excavation near the periphery of the site.

At the commencement of excavation, the F102 structure appeared to consist of a single complex approximately 27 m square, with a more or less rectilinear plan oriented approximately 20 degrees east of north. Excavation over the first three seasons, however, revealed a structure the scale and complexity of which was puzzling, and whose identification as a domestic structure was complicated by the presence of several Byzantine cist graves seem-

FIG. 5.1   *Aerial view of F102, with indication of room designations (W. Meyers, 21 July 1992, neg. H-3 no. 8).*

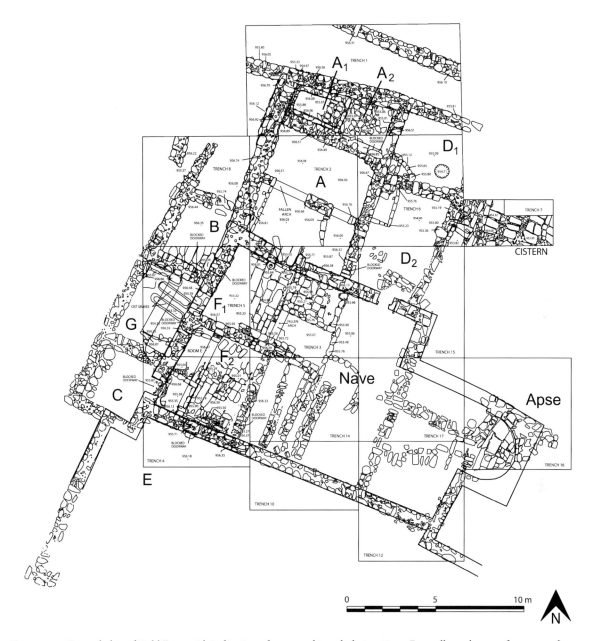

FIG. 5.2 *General plan of Field F102, with indication of room and trench designations. For wall numbers see figs. 5.15 and 5.40.*

ingly inside the east wall (figs. 5.68–72). Excavation in 1991 focussed on Trenches 01, 03, and 04, the north and south boundaries of the structure and its core. Trench 01 revealed only layers of fill and dump in an empty passageway between the north wall of F102 and the south wall of the structure immediately to the north. Excavation in Trenches 03 and 04, however, immediately revealed a complicated sequence of both well-built and poorly built

walls on or associated with a slab pavement, obviously the result of several phases of construction. In 1992 excavation continued in Trench 01, which continued to yield significant quantities of ceramics and occupation rubbish, and in several trenches adjacent to those finished in 1991: Trenches 02, 05, and 06. A deep sounding in Trench 05 revealed the surprising presence of three graves. An energetic campaign in 1993 resulted in the clearing of

Trenches 07, 08, 09, 10, and 12, and the completion to sterile soil of a probe in Trench 01, but many aspects of the structure remained puzzling. Finally, in 1995, excavation in the southeast portion of F102 (Trenches 13–17) uncovered an apse and revealed that the core of the structure was a Byzantine church with associated rooms to the north and west, rebuilt for habitation in the Umayyad, Fatimid and Ottoman periods (fig. 5.3). Once this key identification had been made, the chronology and phasing of the complex became clearer. As the primary aim of the 1995 season's work was architectural definition, only the tops of walls identified in that season were cleared in Trenches 14, 15 and 17, and floor levels were reached only inside the Apse in Trench 16. The phasing of most of the uncovered walls, however, can be deduced from their relationships with the walls uncovered in other trenches. In the published preliminary reports by 'Amr the phasing was numbered sequentially from the latest to the earliest, but here it has been reversed, to give a clearer view of the succession of structural changes across time. To allow comparison with the published field reports, however, the 'Amr numbering is repeated here in parentheses.

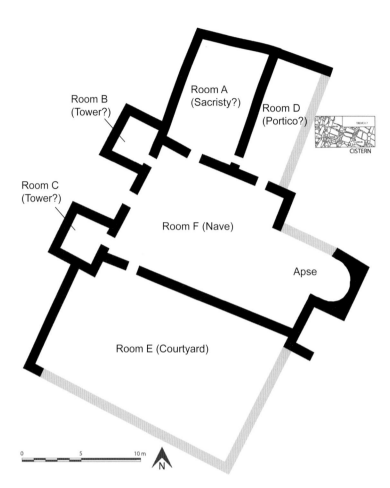

FIG. 5.3   *Wall lines of F102 Byzantine Church Complex; shaded lines are unsure or restored.*

Phase I: Construction of Cistern no. 64 (Late 1st C BC or early 1st C AD) ('Amr Phases VII/VIII).

Phase II: Burials (2nd–5th C) ('Amr Phases VII–VIII).

Phase III: Church Complex (mid-6th or early 7th to mid-8th C) ('Amr Phase V).

Phase IV: Abbasid period house (mid-8th to 9th C) ('Amr Phase IV) built into Nave, Apse, and Room A.

Phase V: Further subdivision of the Nave and Room A for housing (9th C) ('Amr Phase III).

Phase VI: Renovation of some housing areas, then abandonment (10th C to 12th C) ('Amr Phase II).

Phase VII: Squatter occupation (13th to ea. 20th C?) ('Amr Phase I).

FIG. 5.4   *View of Trench 01 to west.*

5.B. DESCRIPTION OF THE EXCAVATION

5.B.1. *Arrangement of the Trenches*

The squares in F102 (termed "trenches" by 'Amr) were opened and numbered as the excavation progressed, so the sequence of square numbers does not follow the logic of the structures involved. As various rooms were identified in the course of excavation, most of them overlapping several trenches, they were given letter designations. These designations, as reported in the field notes and preliminary published reports, have been changed slightly here to follow a more logical pattern across the structure. Only the northern half of Trench 01 was excavated once it had become clear that the area north of Wall 01.05 was a passageway or open space between the main F102 structure and the structure to the north. The nave and apse of the Phase III Church Complex are designated as "Nave" and "Apse," while the original peripheral rooms and those created by later partition walls follow

the sequence of letter designations. The cistern, partly exposed in Trench 07, is designated as the "Cistern." Most of the trenches measured 6 × 6 m, in order to allow for 1.0 m wide baulks between excavated areas 5.0 m on a side. Trenches 01 and 09 were laid out as 6 × 12 m and 4.5 × 12 m in order to fit better the associated structural remains. For the same reason Trenches 10, 14, and 17 were made somewhat smaller than the standard dimensions. Surface clearing was carried out in Trench 11 at the northeast corner of the structure, in order to trace the south wall of the structure north of the F102 complex. No excavation was carried out in Trench 13, laid out 1.0 m west of Trench 09, or along the south wall of the courtyard south of the Church.

Description of the excavation follows approximately the chronology of exposure of the various rooms but is organized according to the units of the ancient structure, which sometimes were defined over several seasons. Trench 01 is also described first because it contains the longest sequence of strata in the field, several of which provide dates for

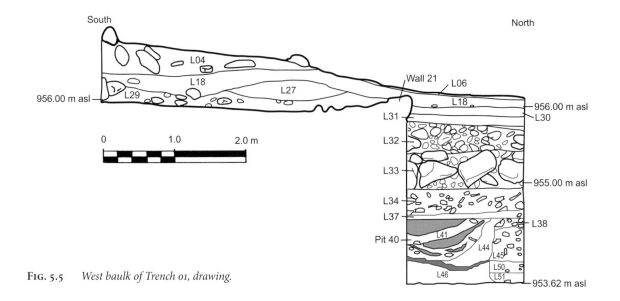

FIG. 5.5   *West baulk of Trench 01, drawing.*

the Church structure. Excavation of Trench 05 and the Tombs in it is described last, both because it is outside the Church proper and because of its complex relationship with the structure. Although most of the Church complex is oriented approximately 20 degrees east of north, for ease of description the walls, rooms, and features are described as if they were oriented due north.

5.B.2. Trench 01

Clearing of the topsoil across Trench 01 exposed several poorly defined layers of sandy, brown to red loess (Loci 04, 06) containing many tumbled blocks and rubble, a small amount of ash, bone, and glass fragments, and scattered sherds dating MN, LN, LB, UM, and possibly FA. Removal of this fill exposed the walls forming Room A and A1, and it was decided to clear part of the open area north of Walls 05, 13, and 21 (which formed the north edge of the complex) to determine the date and relationship of the walls and to expose any paving or features in the passage between F102 and the structure to the north (fig 5.8). In this area the upper layer of tumbled blocks lay on a more compacted stratum of blocks and rubble in a brown soil (Locus 16), mixed with sand and ash, along with fragments of glass, wall plaster, and bone, and a small amount of LB and UM ceramics (figs. 5.4–7). This stratum, most likely tumble from Walls 05 and 13, rested on

a substantial (Th 0.10–0.30 m) layer of light ashy soil (Locus 18) containing scraps of iron and glass, fragments of mortar, basalt and limestone quern fragments, and steatite cooking vessels, along with bones and egg shells (p. 504, nos. 2–5). Apparently a dump of occupation refuse, the locus contained sherds dating to nearly every period of occupation at the site: MN, LN, LB, UM, AB, FA, AY, and OT. This locus was cleared for the entire length of Trench 01, exposing a layer of light brown sand (Locus 30) that occupied the entire space between the two structures and sloped gently east toward the wadi tributary. Since it contained very little cultural material, other than a sandstone quern fragment (p. 505, no. 6), this may be a windblown deposit laid down during the Phase VI abandonment period. The passageway between the two buildings tapers from approximately 3.0 m at its northwest end to approximately 2.0 m at the southeast end, above the cistern. This interval is wide enough to accommodate humans and donkeys or camels carrying panniers (fig. 5.8).

The character of the structure immediately to the north of the F102 complex remains undetermined, but it most resembles a habitation (figs. 1.2, 5.1, 5.8). The carefully constructed south wall (Wall 01.11; Th ca. 0.70 m) was traced for a total length of 15 m. At ca. 8.5 m east of the east end of Trench 01 there is a 90-degree bend to the north, at which point the wall disappears beneath fill.

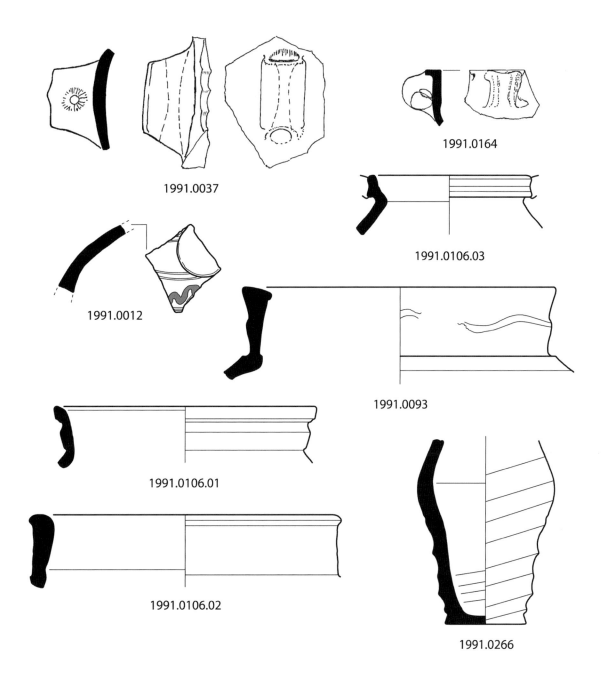

1991.0037

1991.0164

1991.0012

1991.0106.03

1991.0093

1991.0106.01

1991.0106.02

1991.0266

FIG. 5.6 *Ceramic Profiles from F102 Trench 01, Loci 01–26. 1991.0037: F102.01.06, jug handle with vertical perforation. 1991.0164: F102.01.18, saucepan (Wadi Musa kiln, 'Amr and Momani 1999: fig. 9.11, 2C?) (1–2C). 1991.0012: F102.01.01, body sherd decorated with red-brown paint. 1991.0106.03: F102.01.12, jar, grey core and surface. 1991.0093: F102.01.12, jar (cf. Petra, EZ I: fig. 753, last quarter 4–ea. 5C) (late 4–ea. 5C). 1991.0106.01: F102.01.12, jar, 7.5YR 8/4, slip grey. 1991.0106.02: F102.01.12, jar, ware 2.5YR 4/6, slip 2.5YR 5/2. 1991.0266: F102.01.23, jar, core and surface 5YR 7/6, traces of white slip (cf. Whitcomb 1988: fig. 6.m, Fatimid) (mid-10–mid-12C).*

Given the length of Trench 01, it was decided to probe deeply only a 3.0 m section at the west end, which might provide information about the sequence and chronology of Walls 02, 05, and 13 (fig. 5.10). The upper layers of fill (top elev. 956.00 m) consisted of a thin layer of light brown sandy soil (Locus 30, Th 0.13 m) over a layer of yellow sand with lenses of decayed red-brown mudbrick (Locus 31, Th 0.10–0.17 m). Locus 31, associated with the use of Wall 13, contained ceramics dating to MN, LN, LB, UM, and AB (fig. 5.9). This occupation layer rested on a layer of levelling fill (Locus 32, Th ±0.40 m), over what appears to be a stratum of earthquake collapse (Locus 33, Th ±0.50 m), mainly tumbled blocks. Locus 32 consisted of loose brown sand containing many cobbles, sherds of MN, LB, UM, and AB wares, and scraps of iron and glass, steatite

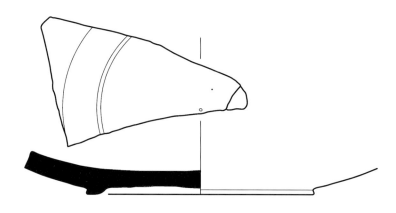

1991.0285

FIG. 5.7   *Ceramic Profile from F102 Trench 01, Locus 26. 1991: 0285: F102.01.26, fineware plate with dull red gloss surface, possibly Eastern Sigillata B (Hayes 1985: pl. IV.14, ETSA Form 30, 10–50; pl. XIII.19, ESB Form 55, 70–150) (1–2C).*

cooking vessels, marble chancel screen fragments (pp. 479–80), wall plaster, and bone. Locus 33 consisted of reddish sandy soil with a great many sandstone blocks, large pieces of rubble, cobbles, fragments of wall plaster, pockets of ash, and a small amount of the rubbish seen in Locus 32. The range of ceramics was the same as well, although

FIG. 5.8   *View of passage between F102 and structure to north (Trench 01, locus 30 surface), from the east.*

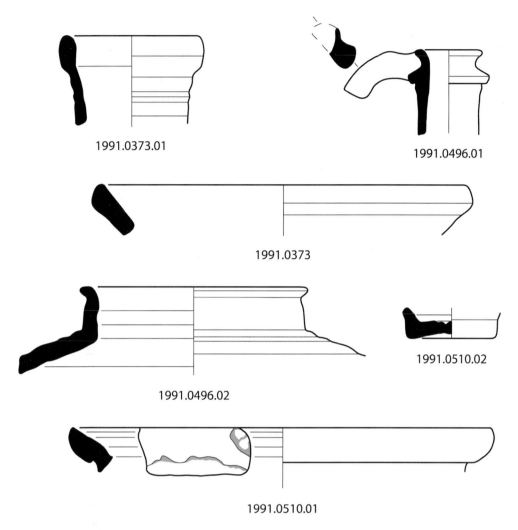

1991.0373.01

1991.0496.01

1991.0373

1991.0496.02

1991.0510.02

1991.0510.01

FIG. 5.9   *Ceramic Profiles from F102 Trench 01, Loci 31–34. 1991.0373: F102.01.31, jug or bottle, ware 2.5Y 8/4. 1991.0496.01: F102.01.33, jug, ware 5YR 6/8, slip 10YR 8/4. 1991.0373.02: F102.01.31, heavy bowl, 2.5YR 6/8. 1991.0496.02: F102.01.33, jug, ware 5YR 6/8, slip 10YR 8/4 (Petra, Gerber 1994: fig. 15.O, 2nd half 1C BC) (late 1C BC). 1991.0510.02: F102.01.34, jug base, core and surface 10YR 8/4, ext. slip 2.5Y 8/2. 1991.0510.01: F102.01.34, bowl, core and surface 10R 6/8, polychrome paint on interior (MB?).*

the AB sherds were doubtful. This debris rested on a stratum of compacted brown soil with a high clay content (Locus 34, Th 0.11–0.16 m, elev. 954.90 m), containing a few cobbles, fragments of wall plaster, and ceramics dating MN, LN, MB, LB, UM, and AB (fig. 5.9).

The foundation trench for Walls 02 and 05 (Locus 35, bottom elev. 954.67 m), which bond and form the northwest corner of the Phase III Church complex, was cut into Locus 34 (fig. 5.5). The fill in the trench (Locus 36), a loose, reddish sandy soil, contained only a few small body sherds,

MN and LB in date. The Locus 34 layer should be the occupation level associated with the planning, construction, and early use of the Church. If the debris in Locus 33 was produced by the earthquake of AD 749 (Russell 1985: 47–49 dates it to 748; Fiema and Frösén 2008: 148, n. 191), then the original construction of Structure F102 must pre-date AD 749. Unfortunately, the date of construction remains imprecise. Some time in the sixth century is likely, since that was the most active period of church building in the region, but it may have been as late as the early seventh century (Michel 2011: 236).

FIG. 5.10   *Trench 01, Northwest corner of Church complex.*

At this point, excavation of Trench 01 had determined the sequence of walls outside the northwest corner of Room A, and hinted at the sequence of building phases. The northwest face of Wall 02 (Wall 02.1) is a late addition built against the original face of Wall 02 and its north end rests on top of Wall 21. Wall 21, which is only one course high, in turn abuts the original (Phase III) northwest face of Wall 02 (fig 5.10). Pottery found in the stratum of ash and decayed mudbrick that extends under Wall 02.1 (Locus 29) dates as late as the Fatimid period (MN, LB, UM, AB, FA), but other loci associated with this phase (Phase VII) produced Ottoman handmade "village ware" pottery. Ottoman ceramics and other artefacts were found under the top levels in all excavated trenches, along with high concentrations of stone rubble, most probably due to an earthquake. Two scrappy walls also most likely of the Ottoman period project from the northwest corner of Room B, at the north end of Trench 08. Surface cleaning produced

a steatite cooking pot, and a handmade bowl with exterior punctate decoration.

Excavation continued in the Trench 01 probe in order to shed light on the earlier phases of use of Area F102. Removal of Locus 34 exposed a thin layer of light brown sand (Locus 37, Th 0.03–0.12 m) lacking construction debris such as cobbles or wall plaster, and containing only a few fragments of glass and bone, along with a few MN, MB, and LB (?) sherds (fig 5.6). This deposit, perhaps representing a period of abandonment, capped an irregular stratum of compact brown, sandy soil (Locus 38, elev. 954.54 m) containing lenses of ash (Locus 39) and decayed mudbrick, along with a scattering of ceramics dating MN, LN, MB, and LB (fig. 5.11), and a faience bead. A possible pit (Locus 40) contained deposits (Loci 44, 45, 50, 51) of compact brown, sandy soil with decayed mudbrick and ceramics dating up to the fourth century (MN, RO, LR, and MB) (fig. 5.12). A mudbrick feature separated this deposit from a deposit of

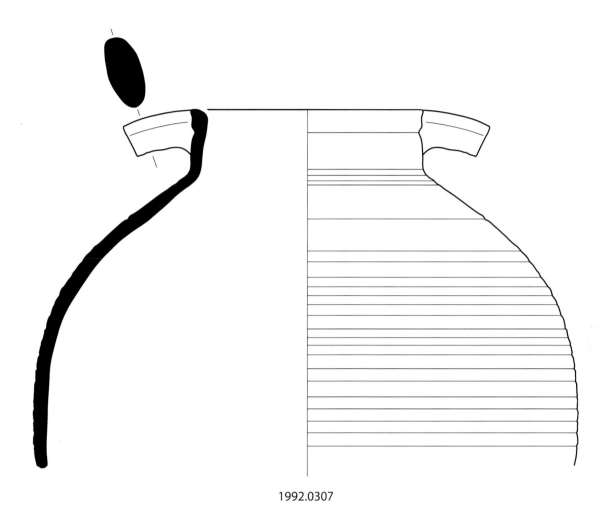

1992.0307

FIG. 5.11   *Ceramic Profile from F102 Trench 01, Loci 38–39. 1992.0307: jar, outer core 2.5YR 6/6, outer surface 10YR 4/1, with traces of 10YR 8/1 slip (cf. EZ I: fig. 765, last quarter 4–ea. 5C) (last quarter 4–ea. 5C).*

ashy red-brown soil (Locus 41) containing MN, RO, and EB ceramics (figs. 5.13–14), and a fragment of mother of pearl inlay. A lens of ashy soil (Locus 49) extending across much of the probe, beneath the mudbrick feature, contained only MN ceramics of the first to early second century. Between this deposit and the undisturbed sandy red soil typical of the pre-occupation level at Humayma (Locus 54; elev. 953.62) there were lenses of a hard, red, sandy, decayed mudbrick (Loci 52 and 53) that contained small fragments of first and early second-century Nabataean ceramics, and a small bronze coin that remained illegible after cleaning.

The first to early second century occupation deposits at the bottom of the probe correspond with the Phase I construction and use of the cistern in Trench 07. It is possible that the decayed mudbrick and the mudbrick feature associated with these deposits testify to Phase I structures, but proof will only come from further excavation beneath the Church complex.

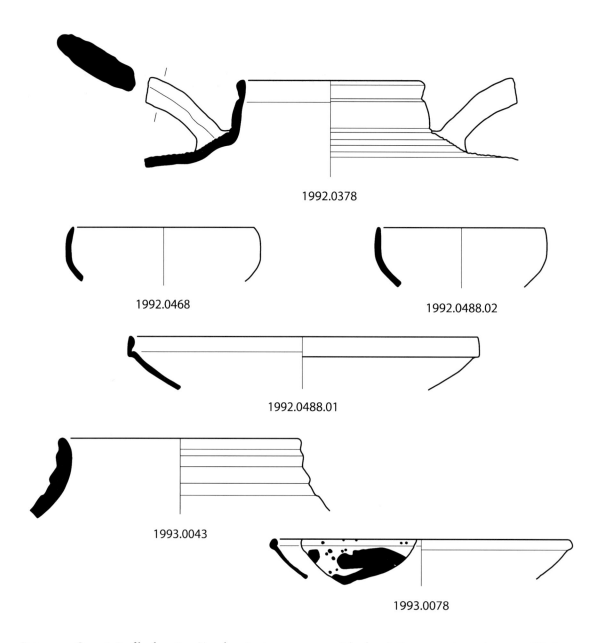

1992.0378

1992.0468

1992.0488.02

1992.0488.01

1993.0043

1993.0078

FIG. 5.12 *Ceramic Profiles from F102 Trench 01, Loci 44–49. 1992.0378 (scale 1:3): F102.01.44, storage jar, core 10YR 7/3, ware 5YR 6/6, ext slip 10YR 8/3 (Petra, Gerber 1997: fig. 6, 2nd half 1C; Wadi Musa, 'Amr and Momami 1999: fig. 12.25, 2C?) (1C). 1992.0468: F102.01.49, NFW bowl, ware 5YR 6/8, slip 2.5YR 7/6 (Petra, EZ II: fig. 42, late 1C BC?) (late 1C BC). 1992.0488.01: F102.01.44, NFW bowl, 10YR 6/4 (Petra, EZ II: fig. 51, 20–100) (1C). 1992.0488.02: F102.01.44, NFW bowl, ware 7.5YR 5/6, surface 7.5YR 6/4 (see 0488.01). 1993.0043: F102.01.46, storage jar, inner core 2.5YR 7/2, outer core 2.5YR 5/8, slip 10YR 7/2 (Petra, Alcock et al. 2010: fig. 11.12, Late Roman; Aila, Dolinka 2003: 128, nos. 20–21, 1–ea. 2C) (2–3C). 1993.0078: F102.01.46, NPFW bowl, ware and int. 10R 5/8, ext. 10R 6/6, int. paint 10R 4/3 (Petra, EZ II: fig. 94, Phase , 2–3C) (2–3C).*

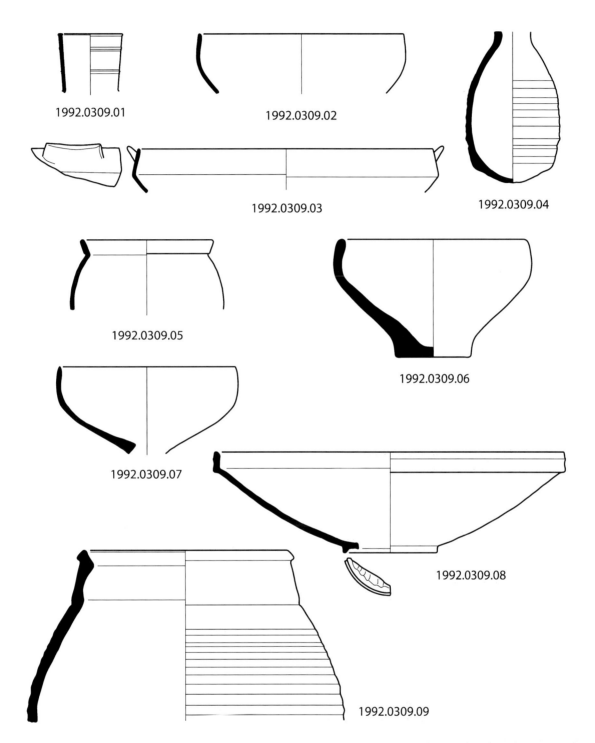

1992.0309.01

1992.0309.02

1992.0309.03

1992.0309.04

1992.0309.05

1992.0309.06

1992.0309.07

1992.0309.08

1992.0309.09

FIG. 5.13 *Ceramic Profiles from F102 Trench 01, Locus 41. 1992.0309.01: NFW bottle 2.5YR 6/8, slip 2.5YR 7/8 (Petra, cf. EZ II: fig. 339, late 1–ea. 2C)(late 1–ea. 2C). 1992.0309.02: NFW bowl, ware 2.5YR 6/8, slip 2.5YR 7/8 (Petra, EZ II: fig. 59, late 1–2C) (late 1–2C). 1992.0309.03: NFW bowl with horizontal lug handle, burned, ware 2.5YR 6/8, slip 2.5YR 7/8. 1992.0309.04: NFW unguentarium, ware 2.5YR 6/8, ext slip 2.5YR 7/4 (Bikai and Perry 2001: fig. 9.12, 20–100) (1C). 1992.0309.05: NFW honey pot, ware 2.5YR 6/8, slip 2.5YR 7/8 (Petra, EZ II: fig. 250–51, 3rd quarter 1C) (late 1C). 1992.0309.06: NFW bowl with string cut knob base, ware 7.5YR 7/4, slip 7.5YR 7/3 (cf. figs. 3.4–5) (1C). 1992.0309.07: NFW bowl, grey core, surface 2.5YR 7/8 (cg. fig 3.5) (1C). 1992.0309.08: NFW bowl (Petra, EZ II: fig. 52, late 1C; Bikai and Perry 2001: fig. 9.5, 20–100) (1C). 1992.0309.09: cook pot, ware 5YR 6/8, off-white slip (Petra, Bikai and Perry 2001: fig. 9.14, 20–100) (1C).*

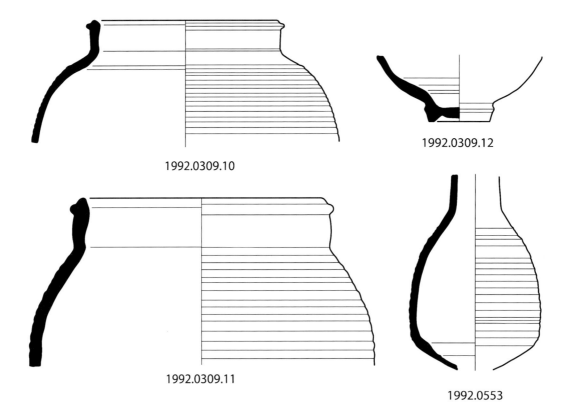

1992.0309.10

1992.0309.12

1992.0309.11

1992.0553

FIG. 5.14 *Ceramic Profiles from F102 Trench 01, Locus 41. 1992.0309.10: cook pot, ware 2.5YR 6/6, ext slip 7.5YR 6/4 (Petra, EZ I: fig. 730, last quarter 4–ea. 5C; Gerber 2001: fig. 3F, 4C) (4C). 1992.0309.11: cook pot, ware 2.5YR 6/8, slip 2.5YR 7/6 (Petra, EZ I: fig. 731, last quarter 4–ea. 5C) (1C). 1992.0309.12: jug, ware 2.5YR 6/8, ext slip 2.5YR 5/4 (1C). 1992.0553: NFW unguentarium, ware 2.5YR, ext slip 7.5YR 8/3 (Petra, Bikai and Perry 2001: fig. 9.12, 20–100) (1C).*

5.B.3. Nabataean Cistern (Trench 07)

Although the original context is now lost, the cistern, the earliest structure in the F102 complex, was built in a cylindrical hole dug into the sterile, red sandy soil at the southeast edge of the habitation area (see the full report in *HEP* 1: 207–9). The structure is very similar in design to the six other built, circular cisterns that served families living at Hawara, but it has by far the smallest capacity (43 m³ as opposed to the average of 130 m³). Like Cistern no. 54 in Field C124 (*HEP* 1: 199–202), it is located some distance from the settlement centre. This cistern probably was filled by diverting water from a major, south-flowing wadi tributary 20 m east of the intake channel. The immediate area has been badly disturbed in the modern period, and the fill over the cistern has been carried away, leaving a depression roughly 18 m long (east–west) and 7 m wide (north–south), exposing the roofing

slabs (figs. 5.1, 5.15–16, 5.19). As a result, the original configuration of the area is unclear. A set of steps, however, appears to have connected the cistern with a slightly higher courtyard (Room D) opening off the east side of the adjacent Church Complex. In recent times (although not since 1983) water was brought to the cistern by an earth trench dug from the wadi to the edge of the settling tank (L 2.08 m; W 1.84 m; depth 0.98 m; cap. 3.8 m³). The original intake, however, was a block-built channel (W 0.32 m; H 0.26 m) at the northwest corner of the tank. The settling tank was roofed with stone slabs carried on a single transverse arch (W 0.50 m) that still survives in place. The interior was waterproofed with a very thick (Th 0.13–0.22 m), very hard, pale brown plaster heavily tempered with poorly sorted, rounded sand and pebbles. A block-built channel (W 0.41 m; H 0.27 m) roofed with slabs leads from the top of the south end of the west wall of the settling tank 1.20 m west into

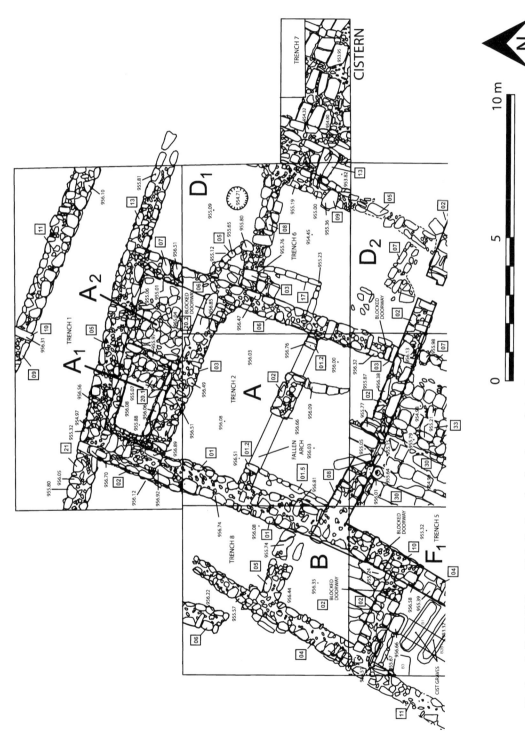

FIG. 5.15   *Northern half of Field F102, with indication of wall and room designations.*

the main cylindrical tank (D ca. 3.8 m; depth >4.50 m, >3.80 m below overflow; cap. >43 m³).

The cistern roof, built of sandstone slabs carried by three (?) transverse arches, survives intact, except for the removal of a portion of one slab near the east edge to open a new draw hole. The upper surface (elev. 954.26 m; fig. 5.16) is 1.0 m to 0.80 m below the level of the paving in the later Church Complex. The original draw hole consisted of a circular opening (D 0.34 m) cut through a sandstone roofing slab (Th 0.40 m); there is a slight inset around the mouth in which a lid could sit. The circular cistern wall was constructed of blocks and waterproofed with a sandy white plaster containing numerous pebbles. Two marl conduit blocks laid edge to edge to form a sort of pipe (opening W 0.12 m; H 0.28 m) have been built into the cistern wall close to the modern draw hole to serve as an overflow pipe (*HEP* 1: fig. 4.34); the floor of the channel is 0.70 m below the slab roof, 3.80 m above the present floor level. A sounding on the exterior (H89-64-P01) revealed that this conduit emptied into a larger drain built of stone slabs (W 0.21 m; H 0.30 m) that survives for a length of 0.80 m. Excavation of the upper layers of rubble and soil fill outside the cistern wall in 1993 yielded a rich

FIG. 5.16 *Trench 07, Nabataean Cistern, view of cistern roof, view to east.*

1993.0377

FIG. 5.17 *Ceramic Profile from F102 Trench 07, Cistern. 1993.0377: F102.07.12, cook pot rim and base, base burnt, ware and int. 10R 5/7, ext. 10R 4.5/6 to 10R 4.5/4 (cf. 1992.0558.11, below, fig. 5.37; Humayma, Gerber 2008a: fig. 23.26, 2–3C (2–3C).*

FIG. 5.18
(Opposite page) Ceramic Profiles from F102 Trench 07, Cistern. 1993.0253: F102.07.10, cream ware pilgrim flask, burned, int. core 2.5Y 3/2, ext. core 2.5Y 6/3 (Khirbet edh-Dharih, Villeneuve 2011: 318 fig. 2, mid-7C; cf. 1992.0511.02, below Fig. 7.70; Aqaba kilns, Melkawi et al. 1994: fig. 10.j, mid- to late 7C) (mid- to late 7C). 1993.0414.02: F102.07.15, NFW bowl with burnished surface, ware 10R 6/8, surfaces 10R 6/4 (EZ I: fig. 642, phase unknown) (ea. 2C). 1993.0252: F102.07.10, cook pot, ware 10R 5/7, ext. slip 2.5YR 4/2 (Petra, EZ I, p. 243 fig. 731, last quarter 4C–ea. 5C) (ea. 5C). 1993.0413: F102.07.14, jar, ware 2.5YR 6/8, ext. slipped grey, smoke blackened. 1993.0414.01: F102.07.15, cook pot, ware 10R 6/6, ext. slip 2.5YR 5/2 (Humayma, Gerber 2008a: fig. 22.5, lt. 1–1st half 2C) (ea. 2C).

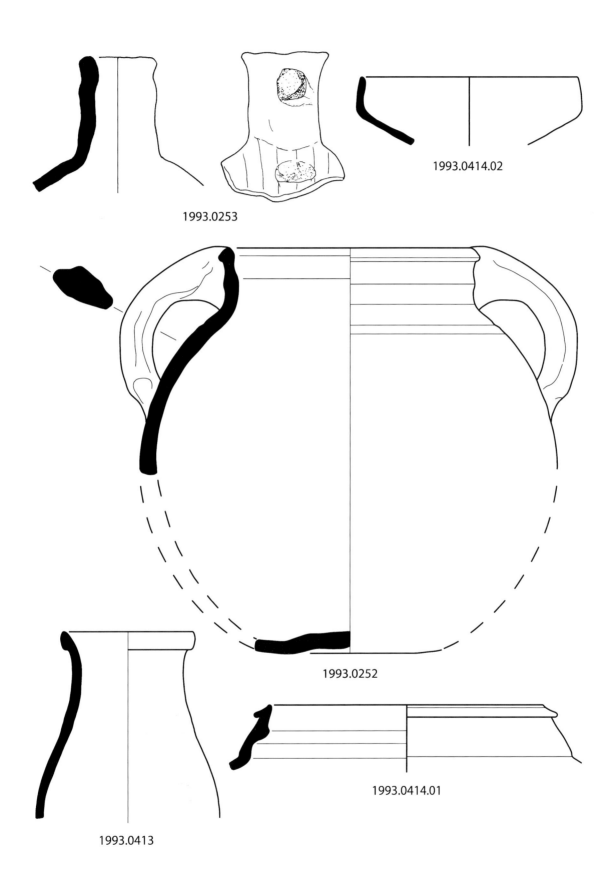

1993.0253

1993.0414.02

1993.0252

1993.0413

1993.0414.01

FIG. 5.19   *Trench 07, Nabataean Cistern, view of cistern, curb, and steps, view from the east.*

selection of MN, RO, MB and UM ceramics (fig. 5.17–18). The lowest occupation level, above what seems to be sterile soil (Locus 06), yielded only MN and RO ceramics (see *HEP* 1: 305–7).

5.B.4. Room A (Trenches 01, 02, 03, 06, 08)

Clearing of the surface rubble and topsoil across Trenches 01 and 02 (elev. 956.50–956.90 m) exposed the tops of walls forming a large room, portions of which extended into Trenches 03, 06, and 08. Descriptions of the excavation will treat the feature, termed Room A, as a unit. As a result of the overlap across trenches, some walls are designated here by two numbers (e.g., Wall 06/07), and some loci with both trench number and locus number (e.g., Locus 01.08). The walls, constructed of sandstone blocks and rubble, bond at all corners except the southeast, which is occupied by a door (fig. 5.2, 5.15). There was also a door in the middle of the south wall. The north wall (Wall 05) could

be traced east of its join with the east wall (Wall 06/07), down the slope toward the cistern. Room A is a trapezium in shape: north wall inside L 5.08 m, south wall (Wall 02/08) L 5.79 m, east wall L 7.65 m, west wall (Wall 01/02) L 8.55 m. The walls vary in thickness from 0.80 m to 0.95 m and after excavation were found to be preserved to heights between 1.0 m and 1.5 m. Traces of a sandy white plaster adhered to the interior surfaces at several points, particularly where protected by later partition and spur walls. Excavation to the foundation of the north wall in Trench 01 revealed that this room was constructed as part of the Phase III Church Complex. A worn, incomplete sandstone block (L 0.56 m, H 0.18 m, W 0.18 m; fig. 5.20) was found in the surface rubble above Trench 03. A neat Latin cross (H 0.15 m, W 0.10 m) was carved deeply into one face, oriented across the short axis and presumably at the centre of the block, which would put the original length at 0.62 m. The block seems too short to have served as a door lintel in the Church, so it

FIG. 5.20   *Lintel block with cross, found in the rubble above Room A.*

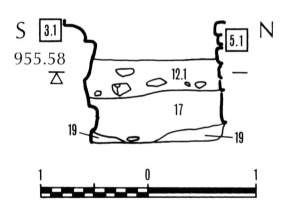

FIG. 5.21   *Room A1 (Trench 01), west baulk.*

may have served as a window lintel. This is the only artefact bearing a cross to be found in the Church.

The upper layer of fill within Room A, below the surface rubble (Locus 00), consisted of a light brown, very sandy soil mixed with rubble and cobbles (Loci 01.08, 02.04, 02.05, 06.07; fig. 5.22). The mixed and worn potsherds dated MN, LN, LB, UM, AB, MA, OT, and possibly FA. A marble chancel screen fragment was recovered, along with a limestone quern (p. 505, no. 7; p. 480). Removal of this stratum exposed Wall 03 (Th ca. 0.80 m), a cross wall with door at the east end that partitioned off a trapezoidal area at the north end of Room A (L 5.08 m, W 2.21–2.42 m). Excavation within this area (see below) identified an interior partition wall (Wall 15), and the two subdivisions were named Room A1 (on the west) and A2 (on the east; fig. 5.2, 5.15). In Room A proper, removal of that stratum to an elevation of 956.03 m also exposed two arch imposts built up against the inside faces of the east and west wall, 3.40 m north of the south wall. Their position aligns with a sturdy central pier (Wall 02, L 3.08 m, Th 0.70 m) built of blocks and rubble. The imposts were built up against the Phase III plaster of their respective walls and presumably carried arches that sprang from the central pier as well. In a still later phase, a rough stone wall marked off a bin between the west impost and the south wall of the room, a poorly preserved spur wall was built from the south

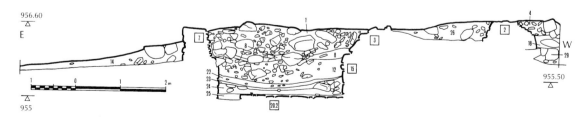

FIG. 5.22   *Room A2 (Trench 01), south baulk.*

FIG. 5.23   *Room A1 (Trench 01), earth floor (Locus 19) above stone paving (Locus 20).*

face of the central arch pier, and the doors leading to Room A2 and exiting the southeast corner of Room A were blocked up.

As a result of time constraints, approximately a metre of fill (top elev. 956.03 m) was left in the central portion of Room A, and only the door in the south wall and the interior of Room A1 and A2 were taken down to the floor. Clearing of the south door opening revealed a fallen lintel block (L 1.40 m) resting on a packed earth floor (Locus 03.02.3, Th. 0.06 m) containing a few MN, LB, and UM ceramics. This floor had been laid directly on a pavement composed of large, roughly rectangular sandstone slabs (elev. 955.05 m). In the southeast corner, removal of a stratum of firm, dark brown soil with cobbles (Loci 09–10) to a level of 956.87 m exposed the infill of the door in that corner. The ceramics dated LN, LB, UM, and AB.

Cleaning of the walls around Room A1 revealed that the partition wall on the east (Wall 15,

Th 0.20–0.24 m) bonded with similar thin walls built up against the outer walls of the Phase III structure on the north (Wall 05) and west (Wall 02), and against the Phase IV partition wall on the south (Wall 03) (fig. 5.24). Excavation within Room A1 removed a layer of yellow brown soil with a significant component of clay (Loci 12 and 12.1), containing scattered blocks and cobbles, fragments of steatite cooking vessels, and ceramics dating MN, LN, LB, UM, and AB (fig. 5.21). A thick layer of silty, yellow brown soil (Locus 17, Th 0.23–0.30 m) below was deposited by wind during a period of abandonment. The few sherds were MN, LN, LB, UM, and possibly AB in date. This stratum lay on a packed brown earth floor (Locus 19) containing LN, LB, AB and possibly UM ceramics, and fragments of steatite cooking vessels (fig. 5.23). The earth floor lay directly on the Phase III slab floor identified at the south end of Room A (Locus 20.2, elev. here 955.07 m). The same sequence of strata was found

FIG. 5.24   *Room A1–A2 (Trench 01), view to west.*

in Room A2, with particularly clear layering in the wind and water-deposited strata (Loci 22, 23, 24), and ceramics of the same chronological spread. The mud floor (Locus 25) contained MN, LB, and UM ceramics and lay directly on the slab pavement. This locus also yielded a decorated bronze handle for an incense burner with many regional parallels in the mid-eighth to ninth century (pp. 429–32, no. 1).

Room A was built sometime in the mid-sixth or early seventh century as part of the Phase III Church Complex. A door in the south wall opened into the Nave, and a door in the southeast corner opened into Room D, a walled courtyard or room on the east. The room was paved with the same neat sandstone slabs found in the rest of the complex, and the walls were covered with a sandy white plaster. There is no indication of how this room originally was roofed. In Phase IV, of the mid-eighth century, a partition wall built part way across the north end of the room isolated a small room accessed through a door at the east

end of the partition. Arch imposts and a central pier were built at this time in the south half of the room to carry arches supporting a flat roof, and the stone paving was covered with a beaten earth floor. Later on, either during Phase IV or as part of the Phase V renovation, Room A1 was defined by a partition wall and lining walls, perhaps to serve as a bin, and a second bin was built between the west arch impost and the southwest corner of the larger room. During Phase VI (tenth century?) the door in the southeast corner of the room was blocked up, along with the door providing access to Room A2.

5.B.5. *Room B (Trenches 05, 08)*

Only the southeast corner of this room (at the north edge of Trench 05) was excavated to the Phase III pavement, while the rest of the room (Trench 08) was cleared only of surface debris to reveal the walls (figs. 5.1–2, 5.15, 5.25). The room is roughly square: the east and west walls approximately L 2.57 m, the north and south walls approximately L 2.28 m; they bond at the corners. The north wall is offset slightly north of the north wall of the Nave. Like the walls in the rest of the Phase III structure, they are constructed of an untidy mix of blocks, rocks, and cobbles, approximately 0.76 m thick. Excavation of the surface rubble (Locus 00, upper elev. 956.77 m) and cleaning of the walls revealed a walled up door in the east wall (Wall 10), just north of the southeast corner. There may have been another walled up door in the south wall (Wall 02). The surface rubble contained potsherds dating MN, LN, LB, and OT. Beneath the surface, the same loose yellow brown soil with blocks, large rocks, and cobbles formed a thick deposit (Locus 14, Th 0.65) containing fragments of bones, glass, wall plaster, and potsherds dating MN, RO, MB, LB, and UM. A slightly more compact layer of light brown to reddish sandy soil (Locus 24, Th 0.41) containing bones, ash, and potsherds dating MN, LB, UM, and AB lay on a compact brown clay floor (Locus 31). The clay floor, seen also in Room A, contained many fragments of glass, bones, wall plaster, and ceramics dating MN, LB, UM, and AB. Removal of the packed floor revealed the same sandstone slab pavement (Locus 20, elev. 955.24; fig. 5.26) found in Room A.

FIG. 5.25   *Room B and Trench 08, view from northwest.*

FIG. 5.26   *Room B (Trench 05), paving in southeast corner (Locus 20).*

5.B.6. Room C (Trenches 04, 09)

This room is balanced symmetrically with Room B, on the opposite side of the Nave (figs. 5.2–3, 5.40). The visible wall configuration makes Room C slightly larger than Room B and the form less regular: north wall L 2.66 m, west wall L 2.76 m, S wall L 2.76 m, E wall L 2.95 m. The walls are 0.70–0.80 m thick. Like the north wall of Room B, the south wall is set slightly outside the line of the adjacent wall of the Nave. A door near the north end of the east wall, blocked up at a later phase, allowed entrance from the Nave. Other than the door opening, the only excavation in this room involved exposing the top of the walls to allow drawing of the plan. Some illicit digging subsequent to the 1993 excavation season exposed a stretch of the typical Church paving along the inside face of the west wall of the room.

Rooms B and C are part of the Phase III Church, placed symmetrically outside the northwest and southwest corners of the Nave. A single door in the east wall provided access to each room.

The projecting structures, possibly a pair of towers, framed a wider door in the centre of the west wall of the Church, the main entrance to the Nave (fig. 5.3). All these doors were blocked up in later phases of occupation. The absence of any traces of paving in so-called Room G, framed by Rooms B and C, indicates that this space was not part of the interior of the Phase III Church (see pp. 145–53). Churches with symmetrical towers framing the façade were not uncommon in Byzantine Syria (Beyer 1925: 152–53), and this feature is seen at Umm Qeis/Gadara (al-Daire 2001: 177–79). Twin façade towers appear to be represented on a church illustrated on the mosaics found in a Byzantine church at Zay, near Salt (Piccirillo 1993a: fig. 677).

5.B.7. Room D (Trenches 01, 06, 15)

In addition to Rooms A, B, and C, Room D and Courtyard E were part of the original Church complex, but peripheral to the Nave. Room D at the northeast corner of the complex has been assigned to the Phase III Church Complex because

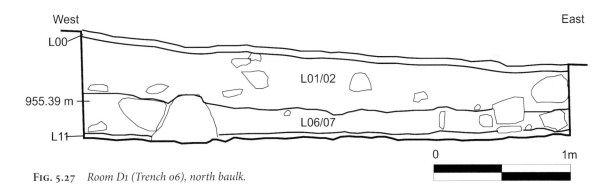

FIG. 5.27 *Room D1 (Trench 06), north baulk.*

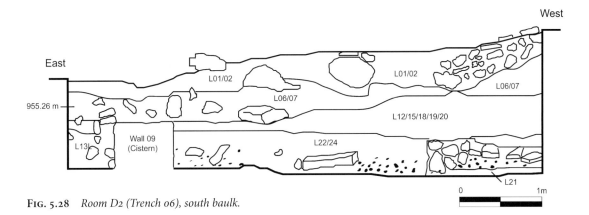

FIG. 5.28 *Room D2 (Trench 06), south baulk.*

FIG. 5.29   *Room D2 (Trench 06), southwest corner, with walled up Door 03.*

it is defined on at least the north, west, and south by Phase III walls (fig. 5.2–3, 5.15). Although the northeast corner of the room was not excavated, it is likely that the north framing wall (Wall 01.13) terminated on line with the end of the south wall, at the northeast corner of the Nave. This arrangement would have produced a regular rectangular space ca. 8.65 m long and ca. 4.85 m wide. The paving seen elsewhere inside the roofed areas of the Church was not found in Room D, despite excavation to levels well below that at which the pavement was typically found. As a result, this area may originally have been an unroofed or lightly roofed courtyard open on its east side towards the Nabataean cistern and adjacent wadi. A door at the southwest corner of the space provided access from Room A, and a door in the centre of the south wall provided access from the Nave. There are traces of stone steps outside the east wall (Wall 09), ca. 0.50 m below the level of the probable earth floor that may have provided access to the cistern. If Room D was in fact originally open-sided and unpaved,

the space may have served for the storage of agricultural implements and the temporary confinement of animals. The proximity of the cistern fits a functional interpretation, as does the atypically large number of spherical pounding stones found on the Phase IV floor. In the later phases of use, walls were added to provide habitation areas.

Removal of the surface stratum of sandy yellow-brown soil (Locus 00 and 01; Th 0.30 m) across the whole trench yielded sherds dating from nearly every period of occupation at Humayma other than EB and MB: MN, LN, LB, UM, AB, MA, OT, and possibly AY and FA. Another metre of loose, sandy red brown soil containing a great deal of rubble lay beneath (Locus 06.06, 15.04; figs. 5.27–28), with fragments of steatite cooking vessels and potsherds dating to MN, LB, UM, AB, and OT. Removal of these strata exposed a wall crossing the room from east to west (Wall 08; Th ca. 0.67 m), roughly constructed of reused stones and blocks (fig. 5.15). This wall abuts Wall 06 on the west and Wall 09 on the east. Wall 09 (Th 0.50–0.67 m),

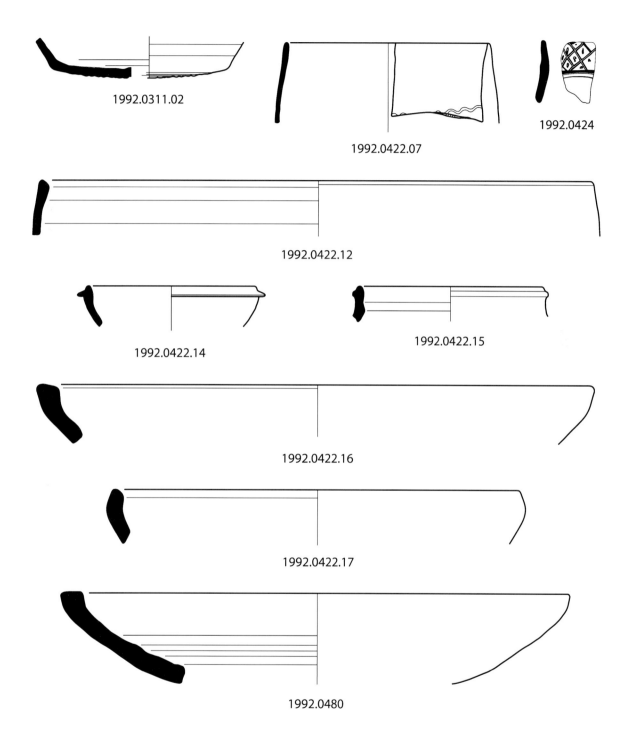

1992.0311.02

1992.0422.07

1992.0424

1992.0422.12

1992.0422.14

1992.0422.15

1992.0422.16

1992.0422.17

1992.0480

FIG. 5.30   *Ceramic Profiles from F102 Room D, Loci 06–16. 1992.0311.02: F102.06.06, casserole base, ware 2.5YR 5/6, ext. burned (UM?). 1992.0422.07: F102.06.12, core black, surface 10R 6/8, slip 5YR 7/6 (LB–UM). 1992.0424: F102.06.16, jug body sherd, white painted filled lozenge motif on ext., black core, ware 2.5YR 6/8, Egyptian import? 1992.0422.12: F102.06.12, bowl, core 7.5YR 8/4, slip 10YR 8/2. 1992.0422.14: F102.06.12, bowl with flanged rim, ware 10R 6/6. 1992.0422.15: F102.06.12, cook pot, core grey, ware 7.5YR 6/6, surface black, burned (Petra, Gerber 2001: fig. 3.F, 4C; Gerber 2008b: fig. 3.40, 2nd half 4–5C) (4–5C). 1992.0422.16: F102.06.12, bowl, core and surface 10R 7/6, slip 5YR 8/4. 1992.0422.17: F102.06.12, bowl, core and surface 10R 6/8, slight traces of whitish slip. 1992.0480: F102.06.12, heavy bowl, ware 10YR 8/6, int. slip 5YR 7/6, ext. slip 10YR 8/3.*

FIG. 5.31   *Room D1 (Trench 06), tabun (Locus 14).*

equally poorly constructed, closed off the east side of the room south of Wall 08, termed Room D2, its south end abutting the north wall of the Nave. Both these walls should belong to Phase IV and were intended to enclose and subdivide Room D for habitation. Wall 09 appears to continue past the junction with Wall 08, to close off the east side of Room D1, but it was not excavated at that point. If Wall 09 extended as far as Wall 13 on the north, there must have been a door in the east wall to provide access to Room D1. The Phase III door in the north wall of the Nave provided access to Room D2, while the Phase III door in the south-west corner of the room was blocked up (fig. 5.29). In Trench 15, the southern end of Room D2, there was an area of ashy soil and stones below the fallen blocks, which contained plaster, fragments of glass and iron, and ceramics dating RO, LB, UM, AB, and OT (fig. 5.30). Excavation of this layer exposed a roughly built wall or platform (Wall 15.07, L 1.80 m, W 0.25 m) slightly off-axis with the nearby walls. Since the feature would have impeded access to the

door at the south end of the room, which is only 0.67 m away, it may belong to the Ottoman phase of reoccupation. Excavation in Trench 15 was limited to defining wall tops, so the precise character of Wall 15.07 is unclear. The concentration of Ottoman ceramics in the southern part of Room D2 suggests that the late squatters occupied areas defined by the more substantial walls of the Nave.

Removal of a stratum of sandy, reddish brown fill north of Wall 08 (Locus 07, Th 0.25 m) exposed a packed mud floor (Locus 11, Th 0.05 m; elev. 955.13 m). Locus 07 contained household debris and potsherds dating MN, LB, UM, and AB. A circular *tabun* pit (Locus 14, D 0.26 m; fig. 5.31) that had been dug into the southeast quadrant of Room D1 contained brown, ashy soil (Locus 16) with fragments of bone, glass, and potsherds dating MN, LN, LB, UM, and AB. Excavation of the various levels of fill inside Room D2 also exposed a rough wall of small stones (Locus 05; L 1.30 m, H ca. 0.53 m, Th ca. 0.20 m) that closed off the southwest corner of the room to form a bin. The Locus 11 mud floor,

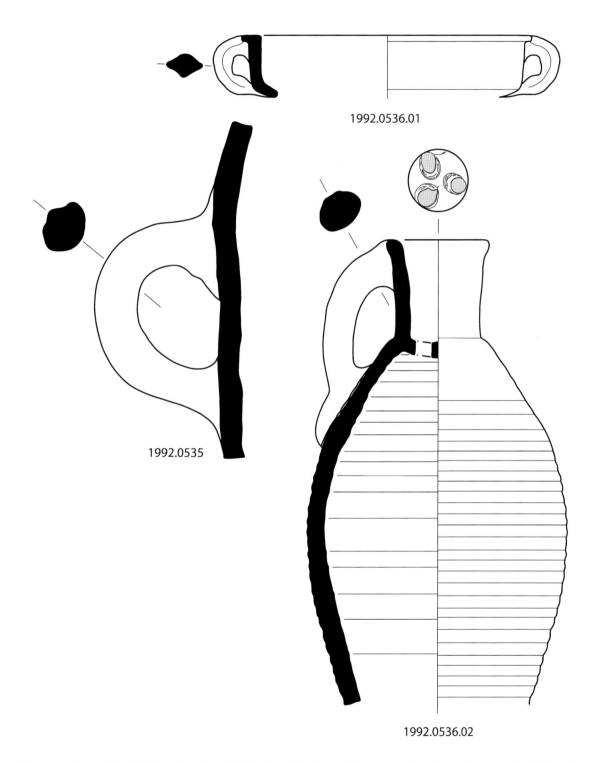

1992.0536.01

1992.0535

1992.0536.02

FIG. 5.32 *Ceramic Profiles from F102 Room D (Trench 06), Loci 20 and 22. 1992.0536.01: F102.06.22, casserole with handles, core and surface 10R 6/6, slip 5YR 6/2 (Humayma, HEP 1: 284, fig. 87.141.8–9; Humayma, Gerber 2008a: fig. 22.12, 2nd half 1–1st half 2C; Petra, Gerber 1994: fig. 161, lt. 1–ea. 2C; Wadi Musa kiln, 'Amr and Momani 1999: fig. 9.11, 2C?) (lt. 1–ea. 2C). 1992.0536.02: F102.06.22, strainer jug with circular rim, ware 5YR 5/8, ext. slip 10YR 8/2, mica present (Parker 1987: fig. 118.210, 502–551; Aqaba kiln, Melkawi et al. 1994: fig. 10.C, 7C; Whitcomb 2001: fig. 2.c, lt. 7–mid-8C) (mid-8C). 1992.0535: F102.06.20, storage jar handle, core 2.5YR 6/4, slip 10YR 7/2 (LB–UM).*

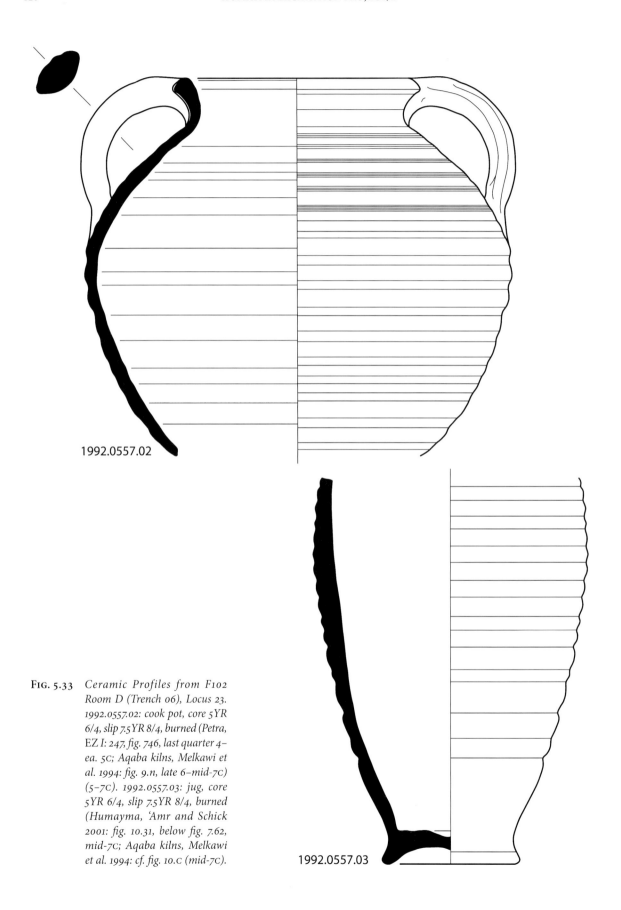

1992.0557.02

1992.0557.03

Fig. 5.33 *Ceramic Profiles from F102 Room D (Trench 06), Locus 23. 1992.0557.02: cook pot, core 5YR 6/4, slip 7.5YR 8/4, burned (Petra, EZ I: 247, fig. 746, last quarter 4– ea. 5C; Aqaba kilns, Melkawi et al. 1994: fig. 9.n, late 6–mid-7C) (5–7C). 1992.0557.03: jug, core 5YR 6/4, slip 7.5YR 8/4, burned (Humayma, 'Amr and Schick 2001: fig. 10.31, below fig. 7.62, mid-7C; Aqaba kilns, Melkawi et al. 1994: cf. fig. 10.C (mid-7C).*

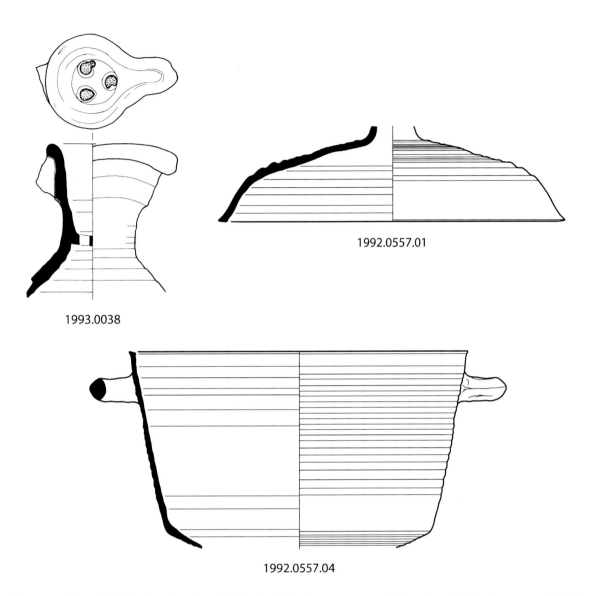

1992.0557.01

1993.0038

1992.0557.04

Fig. 5.34 *Ceramic Profiles from F102 Room D (Trench 06), Loci 23–24A. 1993.0038: F102.06.24A, strainer jug, ware 2.5YR 5/6, ext. slip 10YR 8/1.5 (Aqaba kilns, Melkawi et al. 1994: fig. 10.c, mid to late-7C; Humayma, 'Amr and Schick 2001: fig. 10.30, mid-7C; Jabal Harûn, Gerber 2008b: fig. 5.113, 6–mid-7C) (mid-7 C). 1992.0557.01: F102.06.23, casserole lid, core 2.5YR 5/6, slip 2.5YR 4/4 (Aqaba kiln, Melkawi et al. 1994: fig. 9.a, mid-6-7C). 1992.0557.04 (scale 1:3): F102.06.23, casserole with horizontal handles, core and surface 10R 5/6. ext. blackened (Aqaba kiln, Melkawi et al. 1994: fig. 9.b–d, mid-6-7C; Khirbet edh-Dharih, Waliszewski 2001: fig. 5.9, 6–7C; Jabal Harûn, Gerber 2008: fig. 5.118, late 4-7C) (6–7C).*

which contained fragments of steatite cooking pots, glass, and bone ran up against the base of the wall of the bin. The bin contained a hard packed light grey soil with fragments of glass and sherds dating MN, LB, UM, and AB.

In Room D2, removal of a layer of rubble and loose ashy soil (Locus 10) exposed a compacted layer of grey, ashy soil (Locus 12; fig. 5.28). These

strata contained MN, LB, UM, and AB potsherds, along with fragments of glass and bone (fig. 5.30). Locus 12 enveloped a rectangular bin (Locus 17, L 2.40 m, W 1.0 m) neatly built of reused blocks and slabs in the northwest corner of the room. The technique resembles that of the rectangular Bin 15 in Room A. The soil inside was not excavated. Locus 12 rested on a beaten, grey-brown mud floor

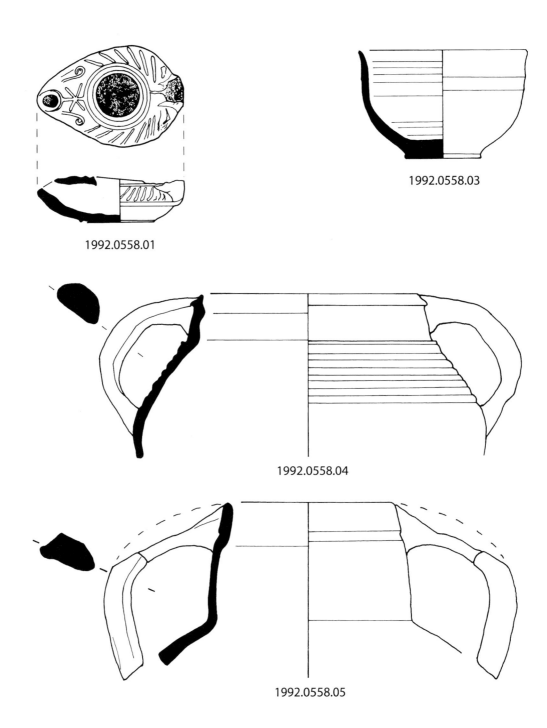

1992.0558.01

1992.0558.03

1992.0558.04

1992.0558.05

FIG. 5.35 *Ceramic Profiles from F102 Room D (Trench 06), Locus 24. 1992.0558.01: lamp, outer surface brown-grey, partially burned (Pella, Da Costa 2001: fig. 3.4, 5C; cf. EZ III: fig. 506–7, 510, 521, last ¼ 4–ea. 5C) (late 4–ea. 5C). 1992.0558.03: cup. 1992.0558.04: cook pot, 2.5YR 5/8, slip 5YR 6/2 (Humayma, Gerber 2008a: 339, fig. 22.8, lt. 1–1st ½ 2C; Wadi Musa, ʿAmr et al. 1998: fig. 4.12, 1–2C; Petra, Bikai and Perry 2001: fig. 9.13, 20–100) (1C). 1992.0558.05: slot-rim jug, rim 5YR 4/1 core and surface (Petra, EZ I: fig. 761, 300–363) (4C).*

(Locus 15, Th 0.07 m, elev. 955.05 m) that contained fragments of a steatite cooking vessel, glass, bone, and potsherds dating MN, LN, RO, LB, UM, and AB. The coincidence of level and ceramic chronology suggests that this floor is contemporary with the Locus 11 floor in Room D1. These mud floors, found throughout the F102 structure, belong to Phase IV, as do the bins along the walls. The mud floor covered three layers of what appears to be household rubbish mixed with slightly ashy, pebbly brown soil (Loci 18, 19, 20, total Th 0.18 m). The

rubbish included two iron buckles, numerous corroded fragments of iron fittings and spikes, glass, bone, ash, mortar, four flint pounding stones (pp. 509–11), and numerous small sherds of MN, LN, LB, UM, and AB wares. The soil below (elev. 954.87 m) is more sandy and has a reddish brown tinge (Loci 22, 23, Th 0.20 m) but contains a similar array of rubbish, with the addition of several fragments of a marble slab. The ceramic fragments are larger and include cook pots and several large, handmade storage ware vessels (figs. 5.32–34).

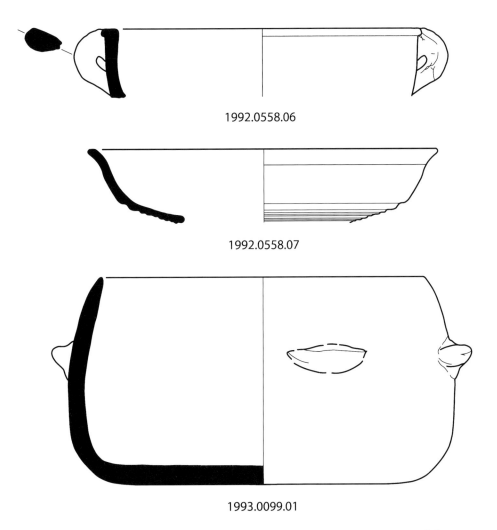

1992.0558.06

1992.0558.07

1993.0099.01

FIG. 5.36 *Ceramic Profiles from F102 Room D (Trench 06), Loci 24–26. 1992.0558.06: F102.06.24, ledge rim casserole with ear handles, 5YR 6/8, slip 5YR 7/2 (Humayma, HEP 1: 284, fig. 87.141.8–9; Humayma, Gerber 2008a: fig. 22.12, 2nd half 1– first half 2C; Petra. Gerber 1994: fig. 161, lt. 1–ea. 2C) (lt. 1–ea. 2C). 1992.0558.07: F102.06.24, ETSA (?) bowl (cf. Hayes 1985: pl. VIII.2, ETSA, 2C?) (2C?). 1993.0099.01: F102.06.26, handmade bowl with lug handles, core N4/0, ext. and int. mottled 2.5YR 6/6 to 5YR 7/4, many chaff impressions (Aqaba, Whitcomb 1988: fig. 5.h, Fatimid; Karak, Milwright 2008: 146–54) (late 19th–early 20th C).*

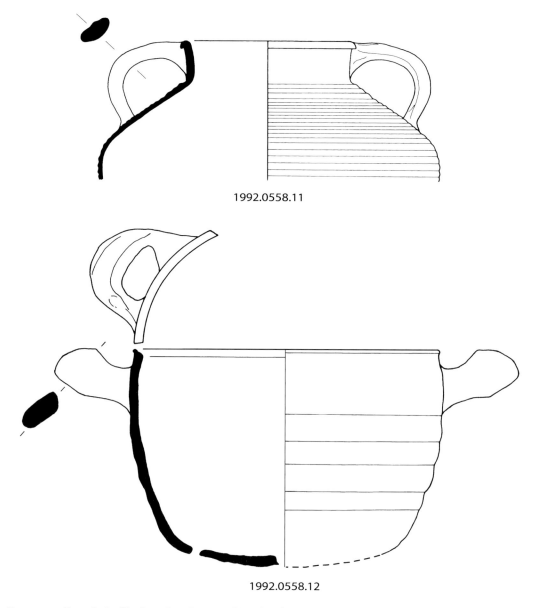

1992.0558.11

1992.0558.12

FIG. 5.37   *Ceramic Profiles from F102 Room D (Trench 06), Locus 24. 1992.0558.11: jar, core and surface 5YR 4/1 (cf. 1993.0377, above fig. 5.17; Humayma, Gerber 2008a: fig. 23.26, 2–3C) (2–3C). 1992.0558.12: casserole with horizontal handles, inner core 2.5YR 6/8, outer core 7.5YR 6/3 (Petra, EZ I: fig. 772, 775, lt. 4–ea. 5C; Waliszewski 2001: fig. 5.4, 6–7C) (6–7C).*

The lowest level excavated in Room D2 was Locus 24/26 (Th 0.12 m, bottom elev. 954.45 m), a deposit of brown, ashy soil containing a high proportion of rubbish: many fragments of iron, bronze, and glass artefacts, two ivory beads, perforated stone loom weights (?), pounding stones, bones, seashells, and potsherds dating MN, LN, ER, RO, LB, and UM, including a LB oil lamp and handmade bowl (figs. 5.34–39; pp. 509–11).

The glass included an alembic, which seems out of place in a farm-house (p. 543, no. 38). Several sherds recovered from Locus 23 join with sherds from Locus 24/26. Locus 24/26 abuts Walls 08, 09, and 17. It appears as if at some point in the Abbasid period household trash that had accumulated in Room D2, or was carried to Room D2 from elsewhere in the F102 structure, was levelled out and covered with Floor 15.

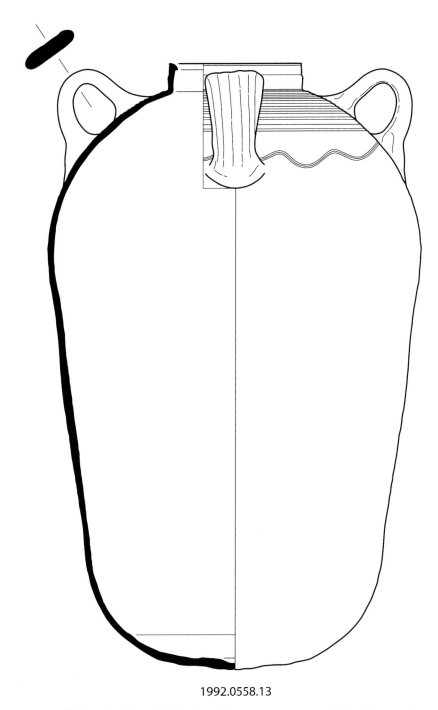

1992.0558.13

FIG. 5.38   *Ceramic Profile from F102 Room D (Trench 06), Locus 24. 1992.0558.13 (scale 1:4): storage jar, ware 2.5YR 5.5/8, ext.
mottled slip 10YR 7.5/4 to 5YR 6/6 (mid-7C) (cf. 1992.0133.04 below, fig. 7.64, mid-7C) (7C).*

Just east of Wall 09, excavation of loose yellow
brown soil with rubble (Locus 13) exposed four
stone steps constructed out of stone slabs, descending north and east toward the west edge of the
cistern (fig. 5.19). The ceramics in the fill above the
steps dated MN, LN, RO, LB, UM, and AB. Unless
the steps were constructed by the Ottoman period
squatters, they should date to Phase III, since the
wall blocks access to them from inside Room D.

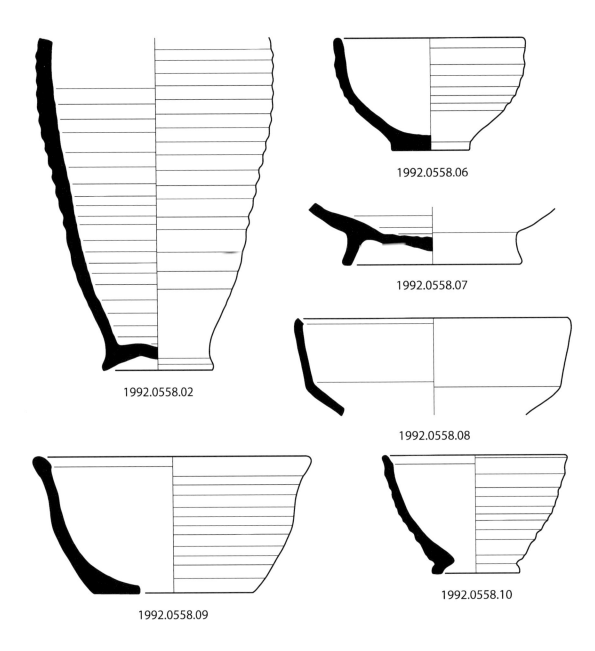

1992.0558.06

1992.0558.07

1992.0558.02

1992.0558.08

1992.0558.09

1992.0558.10

FIG. 5.39   *Ceramic Profiles from F102 Room D (Trench 06), Loci 24/26. 1992.0558.02: F102.06.24, jug or jar, interior core 5YR 6/8, exterior core 7.5YR 6/6, slip 2.5YR 6/6 (Humayma, 'Amr and Schick 2001: fig. 10.31, below fig. 7.64, mid-7C; Aqaba kilns, Melkawi et al. 1994: cf. fig. 10.C) (mid-7C). 1992.0558.06: F102.06.24, ledge rim casserole with ear handles, 5YR 6/8, slip 5YR 7/2 (Humayma, HEP 1: 284, fig. 87.141.8–9; Humayma, Gerber 2008a: fig. 22.12, 2nd half 1–1st half 2C; Petra. Gerber 1994: fig. 161, lt. 1–ea. 2C) (lt. 1–ea. 2C). 1992.0558.07: F102.06.24, ETSA (?) bowl (cf. Hayes 1985: pl. VIII.2, ETSA, 2C?) (2C?). 1992.0558.08: F102.06.24, casserole, core and surface 2.5YR 5/6, ext. slip 10R 5/4 (Petra, cf. EZ I: fig. 774, lt. 4–ea. 5C) (lt. 4–ea. 5C?). 1992.0558.09: F102.06.24, bowl, 5YR 6/8, slip 7.5YR 7/4. 1992.0558.10: F102.06.24, cup with ridged exterior surface, core and surface 2.5YR 6/8 (Petra, EZ I: fig. 784, lt. 4–ea. 5C) (lt. 4–ea. 5C?).*

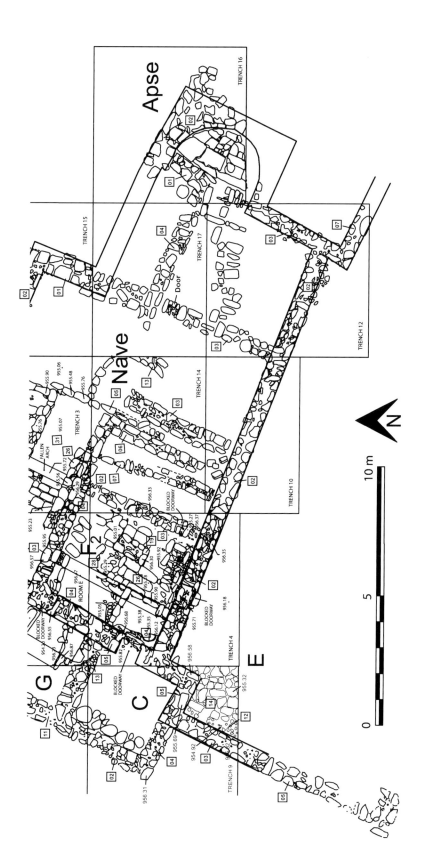

Fɪɢ. 5.40 *Southern half of Field F102, with indication of wall and room designations.*

FIG. 5.41   *Courtyard E, view of pavement and bench.*

5.B.8. *Courtyard E (Trenches 04, 09)*

Little is known for certain about the configuration of the Church Complex south of the Nave. There is only one doorway in the south wall of the Nave, located 2.15 m east of the west wall, as opposed to two in the north wall (figs. 5.3, 5.40). Furthermore, this door is narrower than the corresponding door in the north wall that led to Room A, significantly off axis with that doorway, and less well-defined. Since the door is centred on the Phase IV Room F2, it may have been inserted into the Nave wall at that time. Whatever the chronology of the door, it provided access to an area south of the Church at least part of which was paved with the same sort of sandstone slabs seen in the other roofed portions of the Church, and at more or less the same level (elev. 955.32 m). The only excavation in this area took place in the southeast corner of Trench 09, where the paving was exposed (fig. 5.41). This pavement abutted both the south face of the south wall of Room C (Wall 04/05) and a long, well-built wall (Wall 03, L >6.6 m, Th 0.70 m, MPH 1.60 m)

that in 1993 could be traced for 6.6 m south of Wall 04/05. There was no opportunity to follow it further at that time. Wall 03 abuts Wall 04/05, but the stratigraphy (see below) indicates that it belongs with the Phase III Church Complex. By 2010, erosion of the surface soil had exposed the top surface of the rest of this wall, and two others enclosing a large court attached to the south wall of the Nave (figs. 5.3, 5.42). At a point 9.3 m south of the Nave, Wall 03 makes a 90 degrees turn to the east, continues for 20 m and turns to the north, more or less on line with Wall 12.03, the east wall of the Nave. The join, however, was not exposed. It seems likely that Room E was open courtyard (ca. 9.3 m × 20 m), paved at least in the area near the single entrance door. These dimensions are nearly identical to those of the Nave, suggesting coordination between the two, and probably the same construction phase.

Clearing of the rubble collapse across the southeast corner of Trench 09 exposed the walls mentioned above, yielding a quern fragment, fragments of glass and steatite cooking vessels, and

FIG. 5.42 *View of Courtyard area; black lines indicate the course of the walls, which were in part faintly exposed by surface cleaning.*

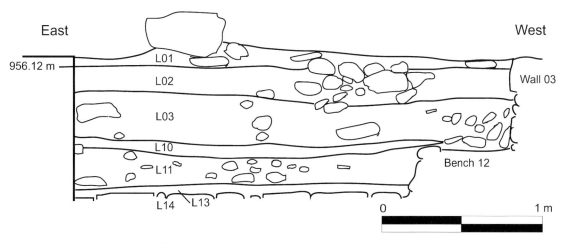

FIG. 5.43 *Courtyard E, south baulk of probe.*

ceramics dating MN, LN, LB, UM, AB, FA, and OT. Excavation of several layers of loose brown ashy soil (Loci 8, 9, 10; Th 0.50 m; fig. 5.43) exposed a compacted layer of sandy soil with ash (Locus 11; Th 0.08 m) containing animal bone, sea shell, glass fragments, and a small stone basin (see p. 511, no. 31). The associated ceramics dated MN, LN, LB, UM, AB, and possibly FA. Apparently a dump, this stratum rested on loose, wind-deposited sand (Loci 13, 16; Th 0.10 m) that

FIG. 5.44 *Room F1, excavated area, looking north.*

5.B.9. Nave and Apse (Trenches 03, 04, 05, 10, 12, 14, 15, 16, 17)

The discovery of the curved inside wall of the Apse of the Phase III Church in 1995 provided the key to an understanding of the main structural phase of Area F102, which in turn clarified the organization of the later phases of occupation. The Nave (internal dimensions ca. 19.3 m east–west × 9.4 m north–south) spread across portions of nine excavation trenches, not all of which were excavated to pavement level, and it was subdivided by walls representing several later phases of occupation (figs. 5.1–3, 5.40). As a result, the narration of the excavation will follow the structures, beginning with the Apse and Nave, rather than the progress of exposure. The sequence of occupation and deposition from pavement to the modern surface was most clear in Trenches 03, 04, and 16 (the Apse), so those areas are described first.

Trench 03 (Room F1)

Removal of the surface rubble and associated light brown loessal soil (Locus 01; top elev. 956.40 m) revealed the top of Wall 02, which was the north wall of the Nave, Wall 04, a Phase IV partition wall parallel to Wall 02, and Wall 07, another Phase IV partition wall extending south from Wall 02. Excavation in Trench 05 in 1992 revealed the west wall of the Nave (Wall 05.10) and the continuation of Wall 04 (as Wall 05.03). On the west, this substantial and relatively well-built wall (Th 0.70 m) terminated against the rubble infill of the central Church door. The space enclosed by these walls, occupying approximately the northwest quarter of the Nave was called Room F1 (ca. 3.8 m × 6.27 m) (figs. 5.44–46). The original door leading from the Nave to Room B may have remained open during Phase IV. The ceramic material in Locus 01 dated MN, LN, LB, UM, and AB. Further cleaning revealed the Phase III door (W 1.19 m) connecting the Nave with Room A. Below Locus 01, an irregular stratum of light, reddish brown soil with

had accumulated on a flagstone pavement during the Phase VI abandonment. The pavement (Locus 14; elev. 955.32 m) abutted a low bench (Locus 12; L 2.40 × W 0.55 × H 0.28–0.32 m) built of blocks against the east face of Wall 11. A pit (Locus 15; D 0.50 m, depth 0.30 m) had been dug through the pavement at the north end of the bench (fig. 5.41). Removal of a portion of the pavement revealed a layer of compact brown soil (Locus 17; Th 0.35 m) containing a small amount of MN and LB pottery, abutting Wall 11. An indistinct layer of sandy soil and cobbles below it (Locus 18; Th 0.10 m; elev. 954.83 m) also abutted Wall 03, and contained only six LB sherds. Given the small amount of cultural material and the absence of Early Islamic ceramics, Loci 17 and 18 may represent fill brought in to level the area south of the Church for installation of the pavement.

FIG. 5.45   *Room F1, excavated area, looking east.*

FIG. 5.46   *Room F1, excavated area, view of west baulk.*

significant amounts of rubble (excavated as Loci 05, 06, 08, 09, 10, and 32; top elev. ca. 956.33–955.99 m) covered most of the trench (figs. 5.46–47). This was a very mixed deposit, including potsherds dating LN, LB, UM, AB, MA, OT, and possibly AY and FA, a marble chancel screen fragment, and household rubbish such as bones, sea shells, ostrich egg shells, scraps of iron tools, a bronze spike, steatite cooking vessels, pounding or rubbing stones, and small fragments of glass vessels (pp. 433, no. 5, 435, no. 13), all

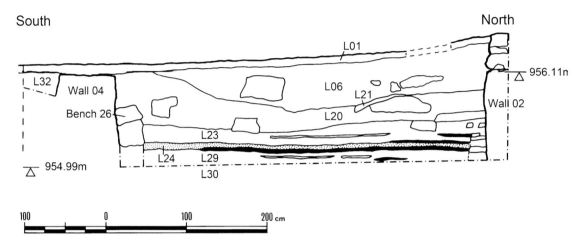

FIG. 5.47   *Room F1, excavated area, drawing of west baulk.*

in very poor condition (figs. 5.48–49). A single iron forging bloom was found (p. 437, no. 19, fig. 12.13.19), very similar to those found in association with a forge in the Roman Fort (E116, Area H; Oleson et al. 1999: 419–20). Since significant forging would have generated large amounts of ash and more than a single bloom, this artefact may simply have been carried here from the Fort long after if had formed. Ostrich egg shells were often associated with the *polykandela* in Byzantine churches (see p. 295).

The stratum below (Loci 12, 13, 20, 21; Th 0.10 m; top elev. 955.84 m) consisted of firmly packed light brown soil containing household rubbish similar to that of the loci above, but with a smaller component of rubble. The numerous potsherds dated to more or less the same chronological range: MN, LN, LB, UM, AB, FA, MA, AY, and OT. Given the presence of Ottoman ceramics, it is likely that this stratum represents the Phase VII occupation level of the squatters from that period, and that the rubble above was deposited as earthquake debris.

Removal of the Ottoman occupation level revealed the thin, poorly built walls (Walls 17, 19, 33) of a bin or similar feature (L 2.55 m × W 2.15 m; fig. 5.50) occupying the northeast corner of Room F1. Wall 07 mentioned above forms the east wall of the bin. The outside walls of the bin bond with each other, but only abut the south face of the Nave wall. The voussoirs of a fallen arch occupied the passage (W 1.55 m) between the southwest corner of the bin and the south wall of the room. It is likely that this arch spanned the entire width

of the room, supporting the roof beams, and that the stones from the northern half of the arch had been salvaged. Excavation of the strata associated with the walls of the bin revealed that, like the bin in Room A, it had been built on the neat stone slabs forming the Church pavement (Loci 30, 33, elev. 954.99 m). Excavation also revealed the presence of a low bench built up against the central portion of the south wall (Locus 26; H 0.56 m, W 0.48 m, L 3.04 m; elev. 955.56 m).

The uppermost layer of soil within the bin (Locus 14) appeared to be a continuation of the packed earth floor of the Ottoman period, but it contained only earlier ceramics: MN, LB, UM, AB, and possibly FA. Below this layer, a packed surface of brown soil with clay (Locus 16; Th 0.14 m; fig. 5.50) extended across the entire bin, containing scraps of glass and bone, and ceramics dating MN, LN, MB, LB, UM, AB. Removal of this stratum exposed a layer of loose, light brown soil and rubbish: bones, plaster, fragments of tiles and steatite cooking vessels, fragments of glass, and potsherds dating LB, MN, UM, and AB. One LB potsherd had a *graffito* on the exterior surface (p. 443, no. 2, fig. 12.18.2). Since this locus was laid directly on the Church paving (Locus 33; elev. 955.07), it seems likely that soon after the bin was constructed the level of the floor inside was raised by means of this mixed fill, and the packed earth floor typical of the Phase IV reoccupation of the Church was laid on top of it. Elsewhere in Room F1, the Phase IV earth floor was laid directly on the Phase III paving.

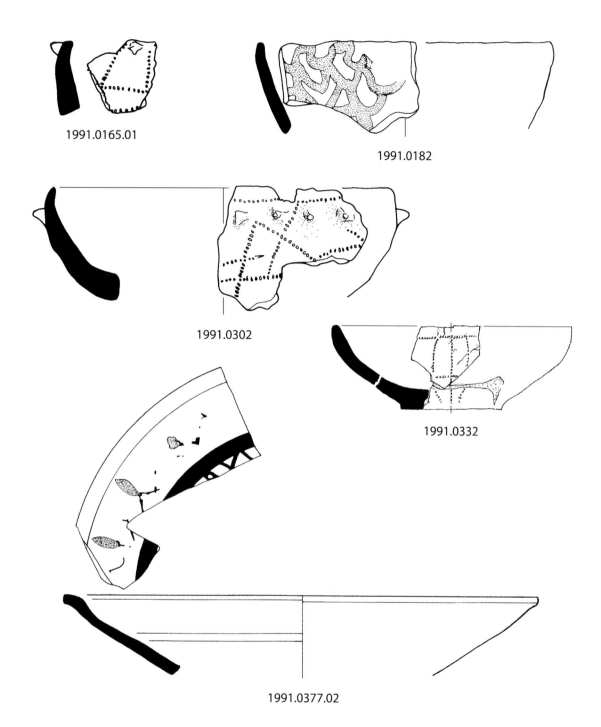

1991.0165.01

1991.0182

1991.0302

1991.0332

1991.0377.02

FIG. 5.48 *Ceramic Profiles from F102 Room F1 (Trench 03), Loci 04–24. There are a few parallels for the painted decoration on 1991.0182 (8C to Ottoman), but few good parallels for the geometric patterns of impressed dots; see the discussion pp. 13–14. 1991.0165.01: F102.03.05, handmade bowl with exterior punctate decoration, stub handle, outer core 10R 6/6, surface 10YR 6/2 (Late Islamic). 1991.0182: F102.03.13, handmade bowl with interior painted decoration, core 10YR 7/2, ext 10YR 6/6, paint 10R 6/8 (Late Islamic). 1991.0302: F102.03.20, handmade bowl with external punctate decoration and nipples, core 10R 5/6, 10YR 7/2 slip (Wadi Nawafla, 'Amr 2000: fig. 18.4) (Fatimid? Late Islamic?). 1991.0332: F102.03.04, handmade bowl with exterior punctate decoration, core 10YR 7/4, surface 7.5YR 7/6 (Fatimid? Late Islamic?). 1991.0377.02: F102.03.24, bowl with faint traces of polychrome paint on interior, core and surface 10R 6/8 (Ayyubid? Egyptian import?).*

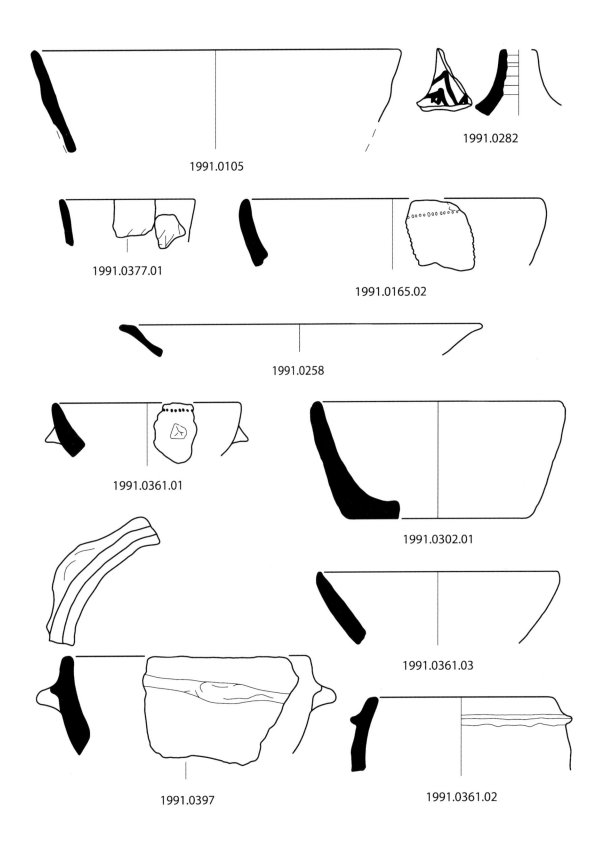

1991.0105

1991.0282

1991.0377.01

1991.0165.02

1991.0258

1991.0361.01

1991.0302.01

1991.0361.03

1991.0397

1991.0361.02

FIG. 5.50   *Room F1, Bin, with Locus 16, Phase IV surface.*

South and west of the bin, the upper strata of firm, light brown soil (Loci 22, 23, 28) consisted of another mixed deposit of habitation debris: bones, ostrich egg shell fragments, sea shell jewellery, fragments of corroded iron, steatite cooking vessels, grinding stones, small fragments of glass, and ceramics dating MN, LN, RO, LB, UM, AB, FA, and possibly AY and MA. A firmer layer of soil beneath (Locus 24; elev. 955.28 m; figs. 5.48–49), containing

the same sort of debris, as well as a fragment of iron knife blade (p. 435, no. 15), a fragment of a bronze pin (p. 435, no. 11), and a coin of the House of Constantine (p. 425, no. 18) that lay on the Phase IV earth floor (Locus 29). The floor deposit contained bones, scraps of iron, copper alloy, and glass, fragments of steatite vessels, and ceramics dating MN, LN, LB, UM, and AB. A sandstone column drum recut as a mortar was found at the west side of the

FIG. 5.49   *(Opposite page) Ceramic Profiles from F102 Room F1 (Trench 03), Loci 05–24. Parallels for the handmade wares are only approximate, and they run from the eighth century through the Ottoman period; see the discussion p. 14. 1991.0105: F102.03.05, handmade bowl, core grey, ware 2.5YR 7/8, off white slip. Late Islamic. 1991.0282: F102.03.20, neck fragment of small jug (?) with painted exterior, core 7.5YR 7/6, ext slip 10YR 8/2, dark paint ext 10YR 6/4 (cf. Gharandal, Walmsley and Grey 2001: fig. 10.7; Fatimid?) (mid-10–mid-12C). 1991.0377.01: F102.03.24, jug rim with fine incised lines on exterior, ware 2.5Y 8/2 (Ayyubid?). 1991.0165.02: F102.03.05, handmade bowl with punctate decoration on exterior, core black, outer core 10R 6/6, slip 7.5YR 7/2 (Late Islamic). 1991.0258: F102.03.20, wheel-made bowl. 1991.0361.01: F102.03.24, handmade bowl with punctate decoration on ext., sharp lug handles, core 10YR 7/3, ext 10YR 6/3 (Wadi Nawafla, 'Amr 2000: fig. 18.4, Fatimid) (Fatimid). 1991.0302.01: F102.03.20, handmade bowl, core black, surface 2.5YR 6/6, variable slip (Late Islamic). 1991.0361.03: F102.03.24, handmade bowl, core 7.5YR 7/6, surfaces 7.5YR 8/4 (Late Islamic). 1991.0397: F102.03.22, handmade bowl with external ridge below rim, core black, surface 2.5YR 6/6 (Late Islamic). 1991.0361.02: F102.03.24, handmade bowl with external ridge below rim, core black, surface 5YR 7/6–7.5YR 8/4) (Late Islamic).*

FIG. 5.51   *Room F1, Ottoman tabuns and in-filled door to Room B.*

FIG. 5.52   *Room F2 looking east after surface clearing and definition of walls.*

door in the north wall, resting on the clay floor (D
0.45 m, MPH 0.44 m; pounding cup D 0.20, depth
0.21) (fig. 5.44). There is a square peg hole (0.05 ×
0.05 × 0.05 m) in the lower surface for centering the
drum. Column drums of the same diameter were
found reused in the last phase of the Roman Fort,
probably salvaged from the peristyle courts in the
Principia and *Praetorium* (Oleson et al. 2008: 321).
This drum may have been brought from the Fort.

Clear evidence of the Ottoman period of occupation was found in the western half of Room F1,
excavated as part of Trench 05 in 1992. Immediately
below the surface soil, a layer of loose sand soil
and rubble (Locus 05) contained scraps of bones,
glass, and potsherds dating MN, LN, LB, UM, AB,
MA, and OT. The deposit may have been produced
either by gradual decay or by earthquake damage.
Removal of this stratum revealed a layer of ashy
soil (Locus 18) associated with two *tabuns,* one
in the northwest corner of the room (Locus 16; D
0.05 m), the other in the southwest corner (Locus
19; D 0.60 m) (fig. 5.51). Locus 18 contained fragments of glass, bones, and seashells, and ceramics
dating MN, LN, LB, UM, AB, and OT. The *tabuns*
were roughly circular, constructed of mud that had
fired to a dark red-brown, nearly brick-like texture.
The fill inside *Tabun* 19 consisted of fine ash with
ceramics dating UM, AB, and possibly LB. A large
ash lens between the two *tabuns* (Locus 23; elev.
955.47), which should represent the occupation
level associated with it, produced the same type of
rubbish, along with a fragment of marble chancel
screen and potsherds dating MN, LN, RO, LB, UM,
AB, AY, MA, and OT. Since the compacted layer
of grey-brown soil below the *tabuns* (Locus 30;
elev. 955.42) did not produce any artefacts, it may
represent clean fill brought in to level the floor for
the Phase VII squatters. Nevertheless, the Ottoman
floor level here is ca. 0.35 m lower than that in the
eastern half of the room. Excavation stopped at
this level, above the Church pavement.

Although the upper levels of stratigraphy are
not well-defined, the overall sequence of occupation in Room F1 is clear enough. After abandonment of the Phase III Church in the mid-eighth
century, partition walls were built in the Nave to
facilitate habitation, and an earth-clay floor was
laid or gradually developed on the paving slabs of

the original floor. At some point early on in this
phase a bench was built along the central part of
the south wall of the room, along with a large bin
in the northeast corner. It is not clear whether
there was a door in the east wall, or instead the
space between the bin and south wall was left open.
After abandonment in the ninth century, the room
gradually filled with rubble and earth. No architectural features can be assigned to Phases V to VII,
but ceramic remains and the two *tabuns* testify
to occupation by squatters. The packed surfaces
forming Loci 03.20, 03.22, and 05.30 may represent
the floors of the Phase VII Ottoman occupation.

Trench 04 (Room F2)

Removal of the light brown surface soil and rubble
across the trench (Loci 00, 01; elev. ca. 956.80 m)
exposed the southwest corner of the Church and
the Phase IV north–south partition wall built between the south wall of the Church (Wall 04.02)
and the south wall of Room F1 (Wall 04.03; Th
0.57 m) (figs. 5.52–54). The rubble contained rough
limestone querns, and a fragment of a well-cut
Nabataean pilaster base or moulding of Ma'an
limestone (pp. 506, nos. 10–11, 498, no. 6). The
roughly square space exposed was termed Room
F2 (ca. 3.71 m east–west × 4.37 m north–south).
The northern portion of Room F2 extends into
Trench 05 and the northeast corner into Trench
14. The west wall of the Nave (Wall 05.10/04.05)
forms the west wall of both Room F1 and Room
F2. The door leading from Room F2 into Room C
was blocked up at some point during the Phase IV
occupation when a bin was built in front of it (fig.
5.54). The door in the middle of the south wall of
Room F2, possibly an original Phase III door allowing direct access from the Nave to the courtyard
or space along the south side of the Church, was
also blocked up at some point. Yet another blocked
up door was identified close to the centre of Wall
04.03/14.02, and either of the two doors could have
provided entry into Room F2 during Phase IV. As
in Room A, several impost piers for arches crossing
the room from north to south were built up against
the Phase III wall plaster. One pair projected from
the north and south walls of the room ca. 1.0 m
from the west wall, and traces of two others can

FIG. 5.53 *Room F2 looking east, with central pier (Locus 19), partition Wall 03, and door to southern courtyard.*

FIG. 5.54 *Room F2, southwest corner, looking west across bins and door to Room C.*

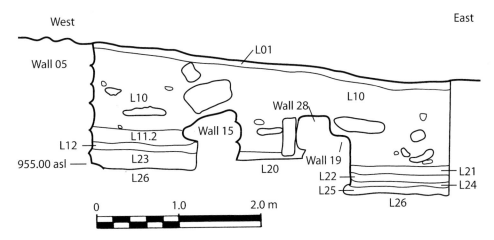

FIG. 5.55 *North baulk of Room F2.*

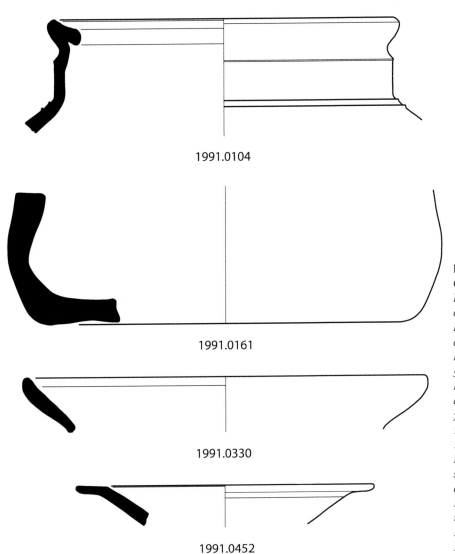

FIG. 5.56
Ceramic profiles from F102 Room F2 (Trench 04) Loci 07–27. 1991.0104: F102.04.07, jar with rim overhanging interior (cf. EZ I: figs. 752, 754, late 4–ea. 5C) (ca. 400). 1991.0161: F102.04.09, handmade bowl, core black, surface mottled 7.5YR 7/6 (Whitcomb 1988: fig. 5, Fatimid) (mid-10–mid-12C). 1991.0330: F102.04.10, bowl, core and surface 10R 6/6, traces of white slip. 1991.0452: F102.04.27, bowl with ledge rim, surface slipped red (cf. Hayes 1985 : 42, pl. VIII.9, ETSA, late 2C) (2C?).

FIG. 5.57   *Room F2, interior of bin in southwest corner, with mud floor (north to the left).*

be seen projecting from the south wall at 1.0 m intervals, continuing into Trenches 10 and 14. Since Wall 04.03 was built up against the easternmost of these piers, that wall was probably not part of the original Phase IV arrangement. As a result, it is likely that Room F2 originally extended as far east as Wall 14.06, which bonds with the south wall of Room F1 at a right angle, on line with the east end of that room. The sequence of occupation in Room F2 corresponds well with that in Room F1.

The bulk of the fill within the room consisted of a firm, light brown soil with a small amount of tumbled rubble (Locus 10; fig. 5.55), and a great deal of mixed occupational debris: fragments of bone, egg shell, bronze clippings, corroded iron fragments, fragments of steatite cooking pots, and a thin-walled, lathe-turned alabaster vessel (fig. 5.56; p. 511, no. 27). Close to the south wall the fill contained many fragments of the Phase III white wall plaster. The numerous potsherds date MN,

LN, LB, UM, AB, MA, and possibly FA, AY, and OT. An Ottoman period iron scissors (pp. 435, no. 16) was found wedged among rubble blocks well down in the north baulk, indicating at least some disturbance of this stratum during Phase VII.

Removal of this stratum revealed thin partition walls built of re-used blocks: Wall 15 (Th 0.20 m) ran north–south 1.25 m east of the west wall of the room; Wall 14 (Th 0.23 m) ran east–west, 1.80 north of the south wall of the room, marking off a roughly square subdivision of the larger bin (figs. 5.53–54). Excavation of Locus 10 also revealed the remains of a pier or stand (Locus 19; 1.86 m × 0.70 m, H 0.83 m; elev. 956.30 m) just east of the centre of the room. The south face of this feature is aligned with Wall 14. Another partition wall (Locus 17), poorly preserved, may have linked the pier and Wall 15. All of these Phase IV structures were built on the same compacted mud floor (Loci 12, 21) typical of Phase IV elsewhere in the Church Complex. In

Room F2, however, the floor was laid over layers of ash (Loci 22, 23, 24, 25; a destruction layer?) rather than directly on the Phase III Church pavement.

Within the bin, removal of Locus 10 exposed a stratum of loose, brown sand with lenses of clay (Locus 11; top elev. 955.45 m, Th 0.18 m), probably deposited by wind during the period of abandonment after the Phase IV occupation, since the ceramics were dated as LB, UM, and AB. A steatite cooking pot lid and faience bead were recovered in this fill (p. 511, no. 32). This deposit rested in turn on the compact mud floor (Locus 12; elev. 955.29 m, Th 0.07 m) that ran under the bin walls and up against the doorsill of the entry to Room C (fig. 5.57). The floor contained fragments of white wall plaster and potsherds dating LB and UM. At some point, possibly prior to the construction of the bin, but after blocking of the door to Room C, a fire pit (Locus 13; D 0.30 m, depth 0.05 m) was dug into the floor in the southwest corner of Room F2 and lined with mudbrick (fig. 5.57). A deposit of loose brown soil under the door sill but above the Church paving contained well-preserved ceramics dating MN, RO, and possibly UM, along with a steatite cooking vessel.

The mud floor had been laid over the stratum of loose, dark ash and soil (Locus 23; elev. 955.22, Th 0.07 m) mentioned above, containing LB and UM ceramics, and small fragments of bone, wall plaster, and glass. This deposit, possibly associated with the destruction of the Church, lay directly on the Church pavement (Locus 26; elev. 955.01 m). The same sequence was found elsewhere in the room. The mud floor (Locus 21; elev. 955.30 m, Th 0.09 m) outside the bin contained more cultural material: MN, LN, LB, UM, and AB potsherds, fragments of corroded iron and bronze, glass, steatite cooking vessels, and bone. This deposit rested on lenses of light grey and dark grey ash (Loci 22, 24) containing fragments of wall plaster and potsherds dating MN, LN, LB, UM, AB, and a lens of light yellow-brown sand (Locus 25) containing fragments of wall plaster, bone, glass, a thin-walled alabaster vessel, and potsherds dating MN LB, UM, and AB. Outside the bin, the Church paving (Locus 26; fig. 5.54) lay at an elevation of 955.05 m, nearly the same as that seen elsewhere in the Church Complex.

Eastern Portion of Nave (Trenches 10, 12, 14, 15, 17)

Surface clearing was carried out across the southeast portion of the F102 complex in 1993 (Trenches 10, 12) and 1995 (Trenches 14, 15, 16, 17) in an attempt to determine the extent of the structure and identify its character (figs. 5.40, 5.58, 5.61). Once the Apse had been identified and excavated in Trench 16, excavation in the rest of the area was restricted simply to defining the outlines of the Church. Other than the Apse, the walls in this area were heavily disturbed by apparent earthquake damage and subsequent stone robbing. The potsherds in the surface deposits removed included MN wares, and wares dating to every period from LB to OT (fig. 5.59). These deposits also included the same sort of occupation rubbish found in the rest of the complex: fragments of bones, ash, many fragments of glass, fragments of steatite cooking vessels, a marble chancel screen fragment, and, particularly along the south wall of the Church, large quantities of white wall plaster. Very few fragments of metal were recovered. There were numerous ash deposits in the topsoil, probably the result of occupation in the Ottoman and modern periods.

The precise line of the northern side of the Nave remains somewhat problematic, as Wall 15.02 bonds with the north–south Wall 15.01 at a right angle, thus making the northern wall of the Church approximately 4.5 m shorter than the southern wall (figs. 5.2–3). Close inspection of Wall 15.01 showed it to have a south "face" 3.4 m south of its outer corner with Wall 15.02, in alignment with the northern end of Apse wall 16.02, which is of the same width (0.90 m). Beyond this point to the south (where it becomes Wall 17.03) the construction is of inferior quality, probably the result of rebuilding. The obvious reconstruction is an east–west wall directly joining the Apse with Wall 15.01, making for an asymmetrical plan. It is worth noting that the Apse wall is the highest preserved wall in F102 while the area to the north of it is badly eroded, sloping steeply towards the cistern, the presence of which may have fostered the inset in the plan of the Nave. There was unfortunately not time to verify this detail with excavation.

In Trenches 10 and 12, the south wall of the Church was only poorly preserved. It had been re-

FIG. 5.58 *Nave, Phase IV partition walls, looking east.*

duced to a heap of rubble on the surface, but to the south, several portions of the wall that had escaped stone robbing could be seen lying horizontally in the fill as they had fallen (cf. fig. 5.42 on the right). At the southeast corner of the Church, the east wall continues 0.88 m south of its junction with the south wall, then turns to the east. There may have been a tower at this corner of the Church, as well as at the northwest and southwest corners, but there was not time to excavate the area.

Clearing in Trench 14 revealed a perplexing series of poorly preserved north–south walls (fig. 5.58). As noted above, Wall 06 was found to bond at a right angle with the partition wall between

Room F1 and Room F2 (Wall 05.03/03.04/14.08). There is room for a door at the south end of the wall, which most likely was the original east wall of the Phase IV Room F2. Since three arch imposts at approximately 1.0 m intervals were found along the south wall of this room in Trench 04, Wall 14.07, approximately 1.0 m east of the last of these imposts, may represent the remains of a fallen arch. The arch just to the west of it (Wall 04.03/14.02) was filled in with a wall at some point in Phase IV, and provided with a door in its centre that opened inward to the west. It is not clear what function was served by the scrappy remains of three walls at the east end of Trench 14 (Walls 03, 13, 16).

FIG. 5.59 *(Opposite page) Ceramic Profiles from F102 Trenches 08, 09, 14–16, eastern portion of Nave. 1993.0178: F102.08.01, handmade bowl with punctate decoration, numerous chaff impressions, ware 5YR 6/4, core 5YR 5/1, ext. 2.5YR 6/6 to 2.5YR 5/2, int. 2.5YR 5/3 (Aila, Whitcomb 1988: 214–15; Karak, Milwright 2008: 146–54) (late 19–early 20C). 1995.0085: F102.15.03, handmade bowl with traces of pink paint on ext. and int. (Fatimid?). 1995.0073: F102.14.01, handmade bowl with punctate decoration on ext., core 10YR 7/4, surface 7.5YR 7/6 (Fatimid?). 1995.0053.01: F102.15.03, handmade lamp, core 10 YR 4/1, outer surface mottled 10YR 6/3, 7.5YR 7/4, 10 YR 4/1, inner surface 10YR 4/1 ('Amr et al. 2000: 247, fig. 18.4–5, Fatimid) (Fatimid). 1995.0227.01: F102.16.18, small jar with pointed base, ware 5YR 4/4, slip 5YR 7/6 with patches of 2.5YR 7/6, painting on rim 10R 5/8 (Egyptian, ca. 700–750). 1993.0297: F102.09.11, bowl, core 5YR 5/8, slip 7.5YR 7/4, white grits and mica.*

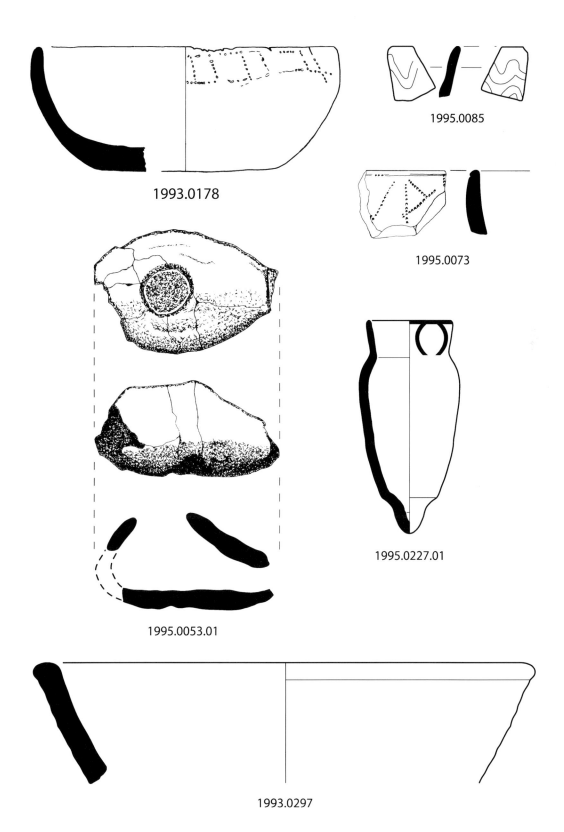

1995.0085

1993.0178

1995.0073

1995.0227.01

1995.0053.01

1993.0297

FIG. 5.60 *Apse wall and paving, with Phase IV partition wall 16.01A on left.*

Excavation in Trench 15 was focussed mainly on definition of the south end of Room D2. Nevertheless, surface clearing within the northeast corner of the Nave identified the Phase III door connecting the Nave with the Room D area, and documented the northeast corner of the Church. The topsoil within this portion of the Nave (Locus 03) yielded ash and bone fragments, fragments of glass, part of a painted ostrich eggshell, and potsherds dating MN, LR, LB, UM, AB, and OT. A complete handmade Late Ottoman lamp (fig. 5.59) was recovered, along with a fragment of a marble chancel screen (p. 480). Ostrich egg shells were often associated with the *polykandela* in Byzantine churches (see p. 295).

Finally, clearing of topsoil and a large amount of surface rubble in Trench 17 revealed two poorly preserved partition walls (Walls 17.04 and 12.03) that possibly formed a square room (3.61 m × 4.28 m) built into the southeast corner of the Nave. There was a walled up door at the northwest corner of the room in Wall 03, and a bin (Locus 05; 0.90

m × 1.08 m) built of reused blocks in its northeast corner. The cultural material included animal bones, ostrich egg fragments, fragments of glass, the runner stone for a quern (D 0.37 m), and a fragment of a marble chancel screen (pp. 480, 506, no. 15). Potsherds in the fill dated MN, LB, UM, AB, AY, and OT.

Apse (Trench 16)

Clearing of the surface soil and rubble across Trench 16 exposed the thick wall forming the Apse, which had a diameter of approximately 3.09 m, precisely 10 Byzantine feet (see pp. 155–57; figs. 5.40, 5.60). The side walls of the Apse continue approximately 0.80 m beyond the diameter of the curve, giving the Apse a U-shape (inside W 3.09 m, L 3.89 m). Although the larger stones along the upper portion of the outer face of the Apse structure had been robbed out, spilling the rubble core, it appears that the Apse was accommodated within a square block of masonry projecting approximately 2.30 m east from the back wall of the Church. The inner face of the Apse wall is constructed almost entirely of limestone ashlars with a few marl blocks. All of the stones had been cut specifically for this location, since each was cut to fit the curve of the Apse. They were laid in alternating thick and thin courses. During Phase IV, a partition wall (Wall 16.01A = Wall 12.03) was constructed across the front of the Apse, leaving an opening ca. 0.80 m wide to provide access (fig. 5.61). The fill between this wall and the inside face of the Apse was excavated.

The top 0.85 m of fill within the Apse consisted of dusty brown to light red soil (Loci 00, 03, 04, 05; fig. 5.62) containing much rubble, some fragments of greyish white plaster, and potsherds dating MN, LN, LB, UM, AB, and OT. Removal of this material exposed a layer of ash (Locus 09) possibly produced by a *tabun*, and the first of several layers of yellow-brown packed earth with clay (Locus 10; Th 0.08 m). These layers resemble floors but may be simply the product of eroding mudbricks from the upper levels of the structure; they alternate with softer, striated layers of silty soil that appear to have been laid by wind and water during the Phase VI period of abandonment. Locus 10 contained bone

FIG. 5.61   *Apse, Phase IV partition wall 16.01A and Nave area, looking west.*

fragments, one stone mosaic tessera, and potsherds dating MN, LN, possibly RO and LB, and UM and AB. The layers of loose red soil and silt below Locus 10 (Loci 11, 15) contained fragments of glass, bone, greyish-white plaster, and potsherds dating MN, ER, LB, UM, and possibly AY and OT. Another packed earth surface, with some gravel content (Locus 16; Th 0.10 m), appeared at 955.80 m. It contained the usual fragments of bone, glass, and plaster, along with two chancel screen fragments of blue-grey marble (p. 480), and potsherds dating MN, LB, UM, and possibly AB. Below, a layer of yellowish red sand and gravel (Locus 17), containing fragments of bone, glass, and iron, and ceramics dating MN, UM, and AB, was associated with the foundation of Wall 02. Another packed surface of yellow soil and clay (Locus 18; Th 0.04 m) was revealed at 955.60 m, in this case probably representing the Phase IV mud floor seen elsewhere in the Church Complex, since it rests directly on a layer of greyish-white plaster (Locus 19), that originally covered the flagstone pavement of the Apse (Locus 20; elev. 955.55) and continued up the

wall. The mud floor contained many fragments of ash and bone, along with a large portion of a mid-eighth century cup with knob base (fig. 5.59), possibly imported from Egypt. The pavement in the Apse is 0.40 to 0.50 m higher than that in the aisles, suggesting there was a raised chancel area, as in the other churches at Humayma.

The plaster on the Apse paving seems to belong to the Phase III Church, since it extends up on to the interior wall of the Apse. At least two marl blocks appear were installed at the western edge of the Apse, perhaps as a base for an altar table or chancel screen. The top and western face of this feature was concealed beneath Wall 16.01B, but parallels from the churches in B100 and C101 suggest that these were reused aqueduct conduit blocks oriented so that the upright chancel screen slabs could be fit into their central troughs. Numerous fragments of marble chancel screen and/or altar table were recovered from various parts of the F102 Church Complex. The greyish-white floor plaster from the pavement slopes up on to the face of at least one of the marl blocks.

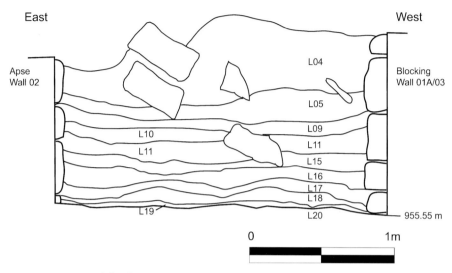

East

West

Apse
Wall 02

L04

Blocking
Wall 01A/03

L05

L10

L09

L11

L11

L15

L16

L17

L18

L19

L20

955.55 m

0   1m

FIG. 5.62   *Apse, South baulk.*

Wall 03

Wall 04

Wall 19

Arch impost

Phase III door

Phase IV
door

Arch impost

FIG. 5.63   *F102 Church entrance passage (Room G, Trench 05) and in-filled central door to Nave. Bin and possible fire pit in southeast corner.*

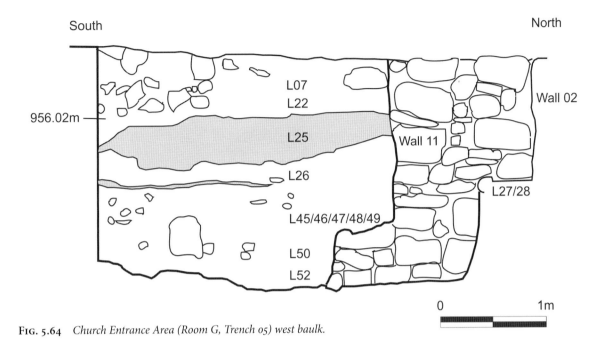

FIG. 5.64 *Church Entrance Area (Room G, Trench 05) west baulk.*

Further evidence for the mid-seventh century date for construction of the Phase III Church Complex came from a small sounding under the Apse pavement. The removal of two paving slabs exposed a hard, red sandy soil (Locus 21), similar to that found at the bottom of Trench 01 and associated with the burials below Room G. During the removal of 0.10 m of this fill, numerous small fragments of bones and glass were recovered, along with numerous small potsherds dating MN, LN, LB, and UM. The latest datable potsherd was the body sherd of an Aila amphora, dating to the mid-seventh century. A rim fragment of a large marble platter or altar table was also recovered (p. 480). In contrast to the well-built Apse wall above the pavement, the foundations below are composed of smaller blocks of various stones, some of which have Nabataean dressing; none are curved in the manner of the upper Apse ashlars.

5.B.10. Entrance Area and Cemetery (Room G, Trenches 05, 09)

The west wall of Room G (Wall 11) unfortunately was not well-defined during the excavation. The top of the wall was cleared in Trench 09, but only a small portion of the northern end of the wall was excavated. The junction with Wall 02, the north wall

of the room, was excavated only to the level of the Ottoman rebuild (Loci 27/28 bin, elev. 955.67 m). Given the presence of the central Church door in the middle of the east wall of the room, however, it is clear that Room G is a creation of the Phase IV or Phase VII reoccupation activity, and that the space was originally a recessed approach to the Church flanked by two towers (figs. 5.2–3, 5.40, 5.63). The central door was walled up during Phase IV to accommodate the new partition wall between Rooms F1 and F2. Probably at the same time, the west wall of Room G was inserted between the two towers, and a new door was opened in the west wall of Room F1 (Wall 04/10) close to its north end, to provide access to the new space. If Room G had already existed, it seems more logical that the partition wall would have been built farther to the north or south to preserve access to the room. The resulting space (2.70 m × 3.70 m) had a roof carried by an arch that sprang from imposts built up against the centre of the north and south walls of the room. The fact that the Phase III white wall plaster found behind the Phase IV arch imposts in Rooms A and F is absent in Room G also suggests that this space was not part of the Church interior, as does the absence here of the slab paving found elsewhere inside the structure.

The upper 0.65 m of fill within Room G (Loci 00, 07, 08, 12; fig. 5.64) consisted of a large amount

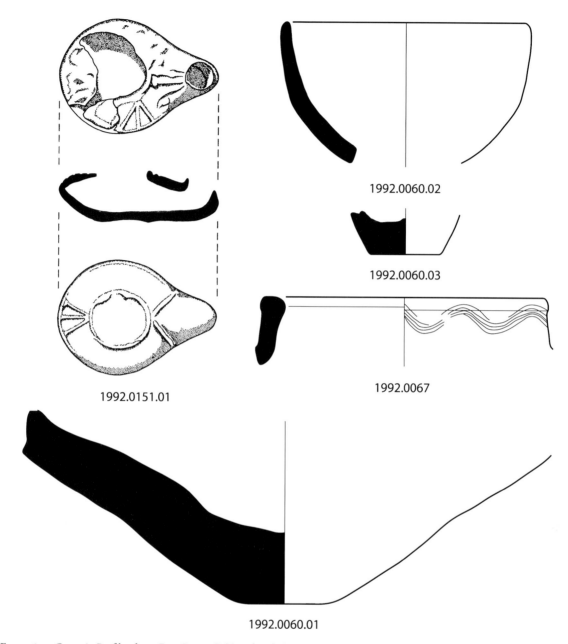

1992.0060.02

1992.0060.03

1992.0151.01

1992.0067

1992.0060.01

FIG. 5.65 *Ceramic Profiles from F102 Room G (Trench 05), Loci 05, 14. 1992.0151.01: F102.05.14, lamp (Petra, EZ I: fig. 914; Khairy 2001: fig. 368, no. 10, 6C) (6C). 1992.0060.02: F102.05.14, bowl. 1992.0060.03: F102.05.14, jar (Early Islamic?). 1992.0060.01 (scale 1:3): F102.05.14, storage jar base (cf. 1993.0266.02, fig. 7.53, mid-7C) (mid-7C). 1992.0067: F102.05.05, jar with wavy combing on exterior of rim and neck, core 5YR 6/8, surface 5YR 7/6 (Early Islamic?).*

FIG. 5.66 *(Opposite page) Ceramic Profiles from F102 Room G (Trench 05), Loci 18–29, 48. 1992.0153: F102.05.18, small two-handled jar, core and surface 5Y 7/3 (cf. 1992.0133.02 below, fig. 7.64, mid-7C) (mid-7C?). 1992.0161: F102.05.23, handmade bowl, core and surface 7.5YR 7/4 (Late Islamic). 1992.0169.03: F102.05.27, jug base, core and surface 10R 6/6, slip 5YR 7/3. 1992.0169.02: F102.05.27, fragment of knob-topped handle and cup (?) rim, traces of fine impressed rosette or leaf motifs on exterior, ware 2.5Y 8/4 (Qal'at Sem'an, Orssaud 2001: fig. 1.3–7, fig. 2.17–19, 20, 8–9C; Hira, Rousset 2001, late 8–9C) (8–9C). 1992.0295: F102.05.25, knob-topped handle with fragment of cup (?) rim, core 10YR 8/3, surface 2.5Y 8/3 (see previous) (8–9C). 1992.0272: F102.05.24, jar, ware 10YR 8/4, surface 2.5Y 8/2. 1992.0356: F102.05.29, handmade, disk-shaped jar lid, inner core 10YR 7.6, outer core and surface 5Y 8/2 (Early Islamic). 1992.0169.01: F102.05.27, cup with handle, exterior decorated with fine impressed rosette or leaf motifs, core 10YR 8/3 core, slip 10YR 8/2 (Qal'at Sem'an,*

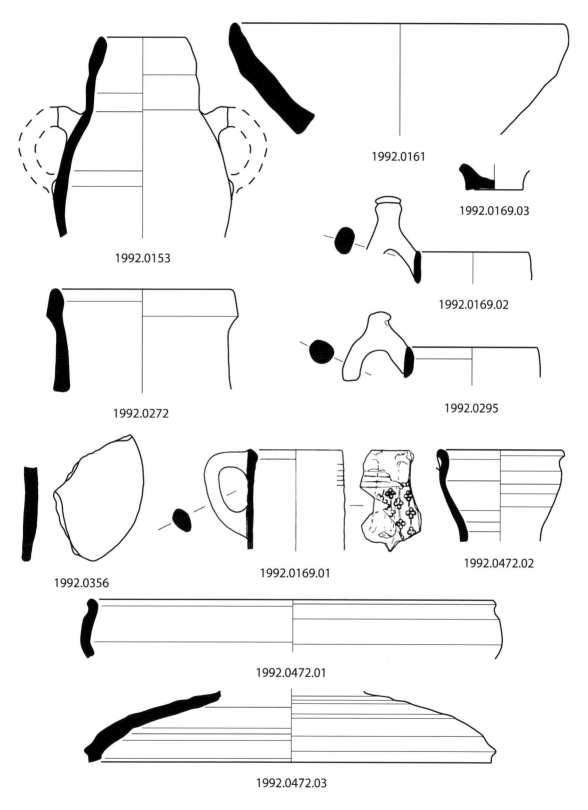

1992.0161

1992.0169.03

1992.0153

1992.0169.02

1992.0272

1992.0295

1992.0356

1992.0169.01

1992.0472.02

1992.0472.01

1992.0472.03

Orssaud 2001: fig. 1.3–7, 8–9C; Hira, Rousset 2001, late 8–9C; Oboda, cf. Negev. 1986: 62–66, no. 503, "Nabataean stamped ware," 1–2C) (7–8C). 1992.0472.02: F102.05.48, jug, ware 10YR 7/6, slip 5YR 6/1 Gerber 2008: 293 no. 51, 7–mid-8C) (7–mid-8C). 1992.0472.01: F102.05.48, bowl, ware 2.5YR 6/8. 1992.0472.03: F102.05.48, bowl or lid, ware 2.5YR 6/6, burning at rim.

FIG. 5.67   *Layer of Plaster (Locus 36) extending beneath foundations of Walls 02 and 04.*

of fallen rubble mixed with light, windblown soil and cobbles and miscellaneous household debris: a basalt quern, fragments of steatite cooking vessels, marble slabs, and a *follis* of Anastasius I (491–518) (p. 425, no. 21). The ceramics dated MN, LN, LB, UM, AB, and OT (figs. 5.65–66). The arch that had supported the room (Locus 09, W 0.55) was found fallen neatly between the two imposts, on a thick layer of ash and soil (Loci 22, 25; Th 0.40 m, top elev. 956.15 m). This stratum, apparently a destruction level, contained animal bones, pounding stones, a stone spindle whorl, a fragment of marble chancel screen, fragments of glass, and potsherds dating to virtually every period of occupation in this area: MN, LB, UM, AB, FA, MA, and OT (p. 480). Along the west wall, this stratum overlay a layer of loose, light brown soil (Locus 26) containing a similar range of material (MN, LN, RO, LB, UM, AB, FA, OT). Phase VII occupation debris was associated as well with two bins defined by light stone walls running between the arch imposts and the north-west (Locus 28, L 1.20 m, W 0.27 m) and southeast corners (Locus 12, L 1.20 m, W 0.52 m; fig. 5.63) of the room. The loose, ashy soil inside the bin in the northwest corner of the room (Locus 27) contained

numerous animal bones, glass fragments, and ceramics dating LN, LB, AB, and FA. Outside the bins, the room was filled with mixed soil and ash (Locus 26) containing a flint hammer stone and ceramics dating MN, LB, UM, AB, FA, MA, and OT (p. 509, no. 15). There was a deposit of rubble in the southeast corner of the room (Locus 22).

This layer of Phase VII debris, presumably produced by a destructive fire, rested on a very compact layer of soil and clay (Locus 29; elev. 955.37 m) that may have been laid down to serve as the Phase VII floor. It contained numerous animal bone fragments, sea shells, fragments of glass, a hooked bronze rod possibly from a *polykandelon* (p. 435, no. 9), a coin of the House of Constantine (p. 425, no. 23), and ceramics dating MN, LN, LB, UM, and AB (fig. 5.66). At this same elevation, there is an offset in Wall 04, the west wall of the Church, which may represent the top of the foundation level. The latest cultural material below this level is Late Byzantine in date.

A stratum of loose yellow-brown soil with cobbles (Loci 34, 49, 50, 52) occupied most of the room. It contained a coin of Anastasius I (dating post 512), and ceramics dating MN, LN, EB, LB,

FIG. 5.68 *Trench 05; exposed cover slabs of Burial 1, with indication of Burials 2 and 3. Note plaster layer in northeast corner of room.*

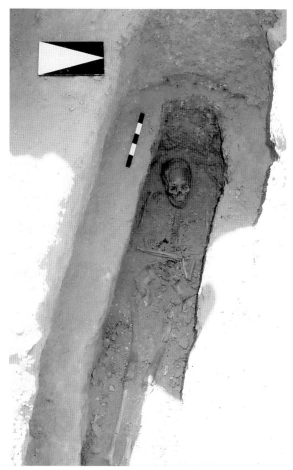

FIG. 5.69 *Trench 05; skeleton of Burial 1.*

UM, AB) (p. 425, no. 25). This debris lay on a thin layer of plaster (Locus 36; Th ca. 0.01 m, elev. 954.67 m) that extended beneath the foundations of Walls 02 and 04, the north and east walls of the room (figs. 5.67–68). Although badly weathered, the plaster is too thin and unsupported to represent a floor level; it may be debris from the plastering of the Phase III Church, or the remains of the plastering of some other structure in the vicinity prior to the construction of the Church. In any case, the plaster clearly sets the Phase III Church apart from the Phase II graves found beneath it.

Remains of three burials were found: one adult female (Locus 43; Burial 1) toward the north side of Room G, and an adult male (Locus 56, Burial 2) toward the south side (figs. 5.68–72). The tip of a third burial projected from the west baulk in Trench 05, but it was not excavated (fig. 5.68). The upper portion of each burial shaft was cut through or marked off by a material similar to mudbrick

(Th ca. 0.46 m; top elevation at Burial 1, 954.23 m), above an offset composed of the same hard, sandy red soil seen below the foundations of the F102 complex in Trench 01, and at close to the same level. A striking example of what an entire necropolis using such marking walls might look like can be seen at Roman Scupi in Macedonia (Brunwasser 2012: 24–25). The compartments for the bodies were cut into this same soil: Burial 1, Locus 40; L 1.93 m, W 0.62 m, H 0.42 m; Burial 2, Locus 56; L 1.67 m, W 0.50, H 0.36 m. Five roughly rectangular sandstone cover slabs were laid across the offsets above each cist, but the cuttings were not lined with vertical slabs (figs. 5.69, 5.71). The cover slabs of Burial 1 were at an elevation of 953.77 m; those covering Burial 2 were at 953.60 m. All three graves were oriented approximately east-southeast (110/290 degrees), close to the orientation of the

FIG. 5.70   *Trench 05; upper portion of skeleton of Burial 1.*

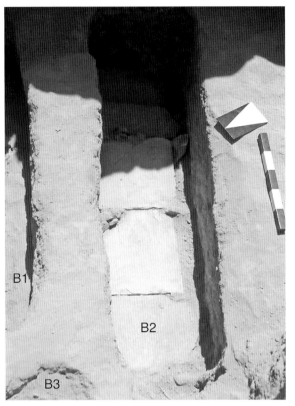

FIG. 5.71   *Trench 05; exposed cover slabs of Burial 2.*

Church Complex, the same orientation typical of other graves at Humayma (see pp. 91–92, 175–76). The two excavated skeletons lay on their backs, with the heads at the west end of their respective cists. Some LN and LB potsherds were found with Burial 1, probably introduced from surrounding soil during the excavation. There were no ceramics in Burial 2. The artefacts from these two burials are described on pp. 381–84; the skeletal material is described on pp. 322–23.

The corpse in Burial 1 had been wrapped or dressed in coarse, dark brown woollen cloth, of which a few scraps survived (fig. 11.1.11), and possibly placed in a wooden coffin, of which there were also small traces (figs. 5.69–70). Two thin, simple silver rings and one iron ring were found on her right hand, four similar silver rings, one copper alloy ring, and one iron ring were found on her left hand (fig. 11.1.1a, 1b, 4, 5). A seashell ornament was found near the skull, possibly an ear or hair decoration, along with seventeen stone, amber, and glass beads (fig. 11.1.8). The arms were

crossed at the time of burial. The male in Burial 2 had also been wrapped or dressed in dark brown woollen cloth, of which a few scraps survived. Scraps of a leather sandal survived by the feet (fig. 11.1.1c). His hands were at his side, but his legs appear to have been crossed at the ankle. No burial offerings survived.

There is no reason to identify these burials as Christian in character, and they appear to date significantly earlier than the Church complex. As with the B100 Church, however, it is possible that the juxtaposition of church structure and probably pagan burials was not coincidental. Both these churches may have been constructed on their particular locations in order to commandeer places previously used for pagan burials or religious rites, as at the B100, and the church at Jabal Harûn (Fiema 2012). The type of burial, in a long trench covered with stone slabs but without any upright slabs lining the cist, is paralleled at Humayma only in C101 Burial 4, possibly suggesting a chronology earlier than the sixth century date of the

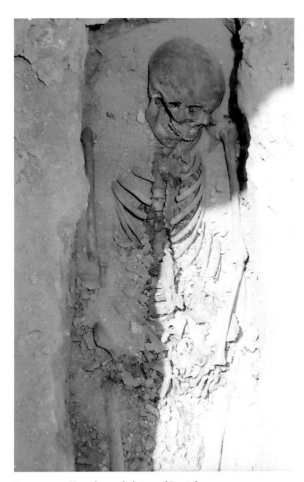

FIG. 5.72   *Trench 05; skeleton of Burial 2.*

C101 burials. Although the absence of side slabs may only reflect economic contingences or haste, the practice is seen at many Late Roman or Early Byzantine sites in the region, for example Umm al-Jimal (Cheyney et al. 2009), Mampsis (Negev 1971), and other sites in the Negev (Nagar and Sonntag 2008). See the discussion of burial procedures pp. 241–52, 400–401. Fragments of copper alloy rings, a woollen shroud, leather sandals, and a wooden coffin were found at Umm al-Jimal in Tomb AA.23 associated with RO, LR, EB, and MB potsherds. Since the F102 burials themselves provide no artefactual evidence for dating, other than priority to the Church, Phase II might theoretically date anywhere between the first and the sixth century. The absence of the MN ceramics so numerous in Nabataean contexts, however, suggests a date after the first century. Of the 509 excavation buckets recorded for Field F102, 385 (75.6%) contained LB

ceramics, as might be expected given the presence of the Church. The basic ceramic evidence for the second through fifth century, in contrast, is exiguous: RO, 21 out of 509 buckets (4.1%), LR 10 out of 509 (2.0%), EB, 7 out of 509 (1.4%), MB 22/509 (4.3%). The absence of ceramics may indicate a low level of activity in the immediate area over this period of time, and that very absence of domestic or other occupation might well have made this peripheral portion of the site suitable for a necropolis. It seems best to date these tombs, and thus Phase II, to the broad range of second to fifth century.

5.C. ANALYSIS OF STRUCTURAL HISTORY AND FUNCTIONS

5.C.1. *Phasing, Reconstruction, and Function*

Based on the excavations described above, seven phases of occupation and development can be documented for the site. Some, naturally, are better documented than others. The 'Amr phasing numbers are given here in parentheses in order to allow comparison with her published preliminary reports on the site (Oleson et al. 1994: 476–84; 1995: 337–43).

PHASE I: Construction of Cistern no. 64 (Late 1st C BC or early 1st C AD) ('Amr Phase VII/VIII). Probes executed in 1989 revealed that Cistern no. 64 was constructed on an unoccupied site, probably in the late first century BC or the beginning of the first century AD. The cistern, by far the smallest of seven cylindrical, block-built cisterns built by Nabataean families around the central Hawara occupation area (*HEP* 1: 377–79), nevertheless held 43.0 cubic metres of water. This handy source of water serviced nearby tents or a habitation structure that generated extensive dumps of first to second-century ceramics. Since F102, like C124, involves a cistern on the periphery of the habitation centre, the clan that owned this cistern may also have been content to live in tents. In any case, the cistern remained in use through at least the ninth century, and was reopened once more sometime in the early or mid-twentieth century. The presence of this water source, along with the Phase II cemetery, may have influenced the choice of this site for the Phase III Church Complex.

PHASE II: Burials (between 2nd and 5th c) ('Amr Phase VII–VIII). At some point during this phase, for which there is little ceramic evidence around Field F102, at least three cist graves were dug into a hard red-brown sandy clay ("bricky material," Locus 40/58) in front of the point later occupied by the central Church door. The same deep layer of undisturbed soil was noted in Trench 01. It is likely that more graves exist west of the Church façade and possibly beneath the Nave. No structural remains were associated with the burials other than possibly low mudbrick peripheral walls, and it may be that the cemetery was located here because the location was peripheral to central Hauarra, and largely unoccupied.

PHASE III: Church Complex (early 7th to mid-8th c) ('Amr Phase V) (fig. 5.3). During this phase a single-apse church with three aisles and a flagstone pavement, along with several ancillary rooms and courtyards, occupied nearly the entire F102 area. The construction date is not entirely clear and may be slightly earlier, but given the absence of evidence for the construction of completely new churches in this region after 636 (Gatier 2011:27; Michel 2011: 235–41), the first quarter of the seventh century is the latest likely period. The selection of this location for the Church Complex may have been influenced as much by the presence here of a pre-existing pagan or Christian graveyard, as by the convenience of the Phase I cistern. The Church may have been intended to subsume the previous pagan religious importance of the site, or to reinforce any importance to local Christians. The same factors may have influenced location of the B100 Church, although that location was very central and probably busy. A single apse church was built inside the Nabataean temple at Khirbet edh-Dharih in the sixth century, and a Christian tomb was installed in the crypt, disarming the pagan history (Schick 1995a: 372; Villeneuve and al-Muheisen 2000: 1558–60; Kennedy and Bewley 2004: 129; Villeneuve 2011: 319–23). Although the evidence is not entirely clear, it seems most likely that the F102 Nave was not symmetrical, the north wall making a jog to accommodate the pre-existing cistern. There were three symmetrical doorways in the west wall, the north and south doors leading to small square rooms (B and C), possibly support-

ing towers. The central entrance door was set back between the towers. There was a raised chancel in front of the Apse, with a marble chancel screen. The paving in the Apse reveals no evidence for installation of a *synthronon*, but the support for an altar may survive at the front of the Apse.

A door in the west end of the north wall led to Room A, a long room that may have served any number of purposes, including sacristy, meeting room, or rectory. A door toward the east end of the north wall of the Nave lead to a small, probably unpaved courtyard (Courtyard D) framed by a wall to the north. Steps led down from here to the Phase I Cistern. This space, possibly partially roofed with a light portico, may have been used for the storage of equipment or the accommodation of animals. Rooms A and D were connected by a door at the south end of the wall separating them. A door at the west end of the south wall of the Nave led to a large, partially paved courtyard (Courtyard E) close to the dimensions of the Nave itself. Courtyards are commonly associated with Byzantine church complexes in this region (see below).

Because of renovations in the later phases, it is not clear how the Nave and Rooms A, B, and C were roofed. The arch imposts found in Room A and F2 were built up against the Phase III wall plaster during Phase IV. Room A (W 5.79 m) might possibly have been roofed with wooden trusses supporting a gabled roof, but the Nave seems too wide (W 9.4 m) for a gabled roof without intermediate supports. No Phase III support piers were identified in the Nave, but that is not surprising given the extensive remodelling of the space in later phases, and the incomplete excavation. It is likely that there were two rows of three piers down the Nave, as in the B100 and C101 Churches, forming two side aisles and supporting east–west arcades on which cross beams or trusses rested.

PHASE IV: Abbasid period house (mid-8th to 9th c) ('Amr Phase IV) (fig. 5.2). The Church may have been destroyed in the earthquake of 749 (see above p. 101), possibly reflected in the tumbled blocks and debris in Locus 01.33 and the neatly fallen blocks of the south wall of the Nave. The growing islamization of the region, along with an economic decline after the departure of the

Abbasid family for Iraq, would have made rebuilding difficult. This was the period in which the abandonment of churches accelerated significantly (Michel 2011: 250). In any case, after the Church ceased to be used for religious purposes, the Nave, Apse, and Room A were broken up by partition walls. A cross wall near the north end of Room A formed the long, narrow Room A1, accessed through a door at the east end of the partition. Either in Phase IV or Phase V a second partition wall set off the west half of Room A1, possibly as a large bin or storage area; the eastern end, Room A1, remained accessible through the original door. Two imposts toward the southern end of Room A supported a cross arch that helped hold up roof beams or roof slabs. Another bin was built in the southwest corner of Room A, and some kind of support pier in the centre of the room between the two imposts.

Beaten earth floors covering the Phase III flagstone pavements are typical of this phase throughout the complex, either laid down to smooth the floors, or resulting from the gradual accumulation of soil from outside. The cistern remained accessible.

Walls built across Courtyard D and along its east side formed two rooms: Room D1 on the north, possibly open on the east to the Cistern, and Room D2 on the south, enclosed by the new partitions. There was a *tabun* in the southeast corner of Room D1. A rough bin was built into the northwest corner of Room D2, which remained accessible to Room A through a door in its southwest corner.

The western half of the Nave was divided into two more or less equal spaces by an east–west wall, forming Rooms F1 and F2, and blocking the in-filled central entrance door to the Nave. A large bin occupied the northeast corner of Room F1, the roof of which was supported by at least one north–south arch. A bench was built along the central part of the south wall of this room during this phase. It is not clear whether the east end of Room F1 was closed with a wall. Room B remained in use, accessible from Room F1 through the original door in the west wall of the Nave.

Room F2 occupied the space south of the dividing wall, roofed by two north–south arches set on imposts built against the Phase III wall plaster.

At some point during this phase the door leading into Room C was walled up, a fire-pit was built in front of it, and ultimately a bin as well. The east end of the room appears to have been closed off by a wall with a door at its south end. A door in the south wall providing access to Courtyard E may belong either to this phase, or to Phase III. A wall built across the face of the Apse to create another room may belong to this phase.

PHASE V: House (9th c) ('Amr Phase III). This phase is poorly understood, but it seems that further subdivision of the Nave and Room A took place, either to house more persons or families or to accommodate more functions. The Apse was completely closed off with a wall during this period. The cistern remained accessible.

PHASE VI: Renovation and abandonment (10th c to 12th c) ('Amr Phase II). Several walls in the Nave seem to have been renovated, the Apse was closed off completely, and soon afterward the site was abandoned for approximately 300 years. During the abandonment period, thick layers of silt and sand accumulated in the Apse and several other rooms within the Church complex, and rubble piled up on the cistern roof.

PHASE VII: Squatters (13th to ea. 20th c?) ('Amr Phase I). Several partition walls were built in the ruins of the earlier structure, particularly at the northwest corner of the complex. At some point tumbled rubble was cleared off the cistern, and the roof was sealed with a layer of soil with clay. *Tabuns* were set up here and there around the complex, probably in the shelter of surviving wall stubs. An iron scissors and a handmade Ottoman lamp suggest occupation by squatters in the early 20th c in several rooms that still had some standing walls. The earthquake of 1927 may have driven out these squatters. Oleson observed a Bedouin man drawing water from the cistern in 1983, but it has been dry and abandoned since then.

5.C.2. *Planning and Modules*

It is clear that the Church was laid out according to carefully determined modules (fig. 5.73). Measuring from centreline to centreline, the north wall of Room A (east end), the north wall of the Nave, the south wall of the Nave, and the south wall of

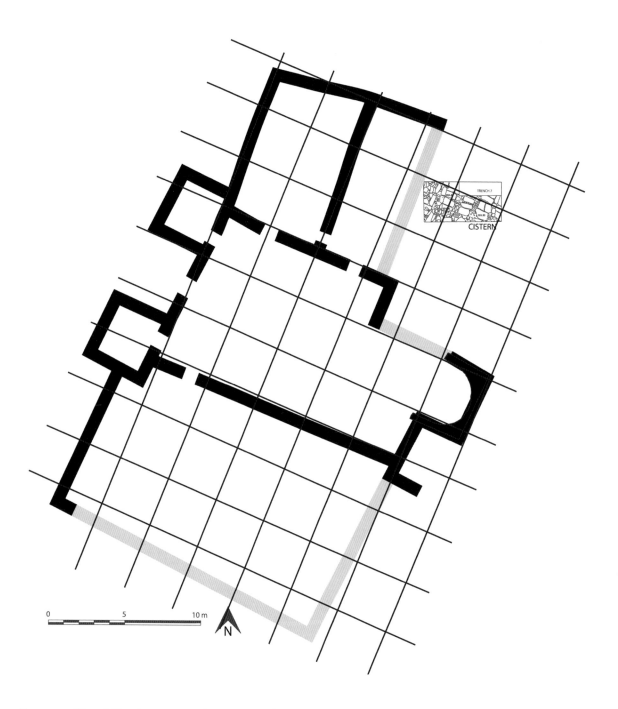

Fig. 5.73 *Plan of Church structure with superimposed grid of squares 10 Byzantine feet on a side. The slight deviations from the grid planning may be due to careless surveying, or to drift of the wall lines during the period of reuse and the subsequent period of abandonment.*

Courtyard E are all 9.5 m apart. This dimension equals 30.75 Byzantine feet of 0.3089 m (with an error of 2.5%), the same unit of measurement used in the C101 and B100 Churches, along with the Church of the Blessed Virgin at Petra (Oleson 2010: 399–401; Fiema et al. 2001: 163–64). Butler (1929: 182–83) flirts with the idea that a similar "Greek foot of 308 mm" was used in some Syrian churches, along with a cubit of 555 mm. Measuring from the midpoint of the west wall of the Nave to the midpoint of the back wall of the Apse, the length of the Church is 18.53 m, or precisely 60 Byzantine feet. The width of the apse is 3.09 m, precisely 10 Byzantine feet. The courtyard, although the same width as the Nave, is slightly longer, about 20 m, or 64.7 Byzantine feet. It is not clear why the west wall of Room A is slightly shorter than the east wall, but the width of the room from wall centre to wall centre is 6.08 m, or 19.68 Byzantine feet. Clearly the plan of the complex was laid out in multiples of 10 Byzantine feet. Rooms B and C do not provide convincing multiples of this dimension, but these two features (tower bases?) and the space between them allowing access to the central Church door each occupies close to one third of the total width of the façade.

5.C.3. *Local and Regional Parallels for the Church*

Of the five known Hauarra churches, the general configuration of the F102 Church is closest to that of the B100 Church, although the F102 Church is smaller: F102, 30 × 60 Byzantine feet, B100 40 × 70 (?) Byzantine feet. What sets the F102 Church apart, however, is its orientation east-southeast (110 degrees), rather than east-northeast (62–72 degrees) like the other four Hauarra churches (fig. 15.1). There is no obvious topographical reason for this anomaly, and in the absence of any evidence for a pre-existing structure beneath the Church that influenced the builders, we can only guess at the reasons. The most likely cause was the location of the large adjacent building on the north, combined with the slope leading to the small wadi on the east, but the deviation 20 degrees south of east may have no more significance than the deviation of the other churches 18 to 28 degrees to the north.

There is apparently no extensive published discussion of the degree of adherence to an eastward orientation among Byzantine churches in the east (Schick, oral communication 2012). Butler (1929: 182) notes "wide variation" among the churches in Syria, and up to 12 degrees deviation south of east. Curiously, he found only one example that deviated north of east. He notes the possibility that builders used the point of sunrise at the time they laid out the plan on site, which would vary by time of year, but cites the lack of data to prove this hypothesis.

The Church was built late in the major period of Byzantine church construction in Jordan, which took place during the sixth and early seventh century (Michel 2011: 236). Although the eastern half of both the F102 and B100 Churches have suffered badly from later occupation, both had a rectilinear block projecting from the east wall to contain the apse and a raised chancel in front of the apse. The surviving floor and wall plaster in the F102 Apse show no trace of a *synthronon* bench, suggesting that this common feature was absent (Michel 2001: 57–58). *Pastophoria* may have framed the apse of the B100 Church, and there is room for the same features in the F102 Church, although the surviving remains are not clear. Like the B100 Church, the F102 Church probably had a series of freestanding piers carrying two arcades that supported the roof structure and formed three naves. Around 80 percent of the Byzantine churches in Jordan had three naves (Michel 2001: 24). It is possible that the roof was gabled (Michel 2001: 38), although only 29 roof tile fragments were recorded during the excavation. The intact tiles may have been salvaged for reuse elsewhere, but the number of fragments still seems small in comparison with the several thousand tiles that would have required careful removal. The same problem of a paucity of roof tiles occurs at the B100 Church, where only 55 tile fragments were found, and the C101 Church, which yielded only five fragments. It seems unlikely that so many tiles could have been reused on some other structures at Humayma at this late period without having left significant surface traces, so export of the material to Aila or Petra must be considered. The alternative to gabled roofs with tiles is the flat, plastered clay roof laid on a framework of beams, cross-beams, and rushes or canes. Traces of the clay foundation packing of such roofs were found in the barracks and *Principia* of the Roman Fort, where there are also problems with the relatively small number of surviving roof tiles (see *HEP* 1: 328–29). Although Barker (oral communication January 2013) is not aware of any published archaeological examples of roof tiles reused as roof tiles, he cites a late republican *graffito* at Pompeii that appears to offer salvaged roof tiles for sale (Barker 2010: 132 n. 46; Frank 1938; *Inscriptiones Latinae Liberae Rei Publicae* no. 1121). He notes that the practice is also documented in late fifth-century BC Eleusis: cf. *IG* XI.314.113–20, XII.313.103–110.

Like the C101 Church, the F102 Church was built as part of a complex including rooms on the north flank and a large courtyard on the south flank. There appear to have been rooms adjoining the C119 Church as well. There is no evidence for rooms flanking the B100 Church, and the topography to the north and proximity of the Reservoir no. 68 on the south preclude any major annexes. The large Entrance Hall (Room 4) and Sacristy (Room 2) of the C101 Church may have served some of the same functions as Room A in the F102 Church, but the absence of a major exterior entrance to Room A, and its connection by means of a small door with a small courtyard (Room D) and the Cistern suggest a more diverse set of activities.

The Church fits into Category AI of Qaqish's typology (2007: 304–5). Among the 160 Byzantine churches in Jordan, there is only one close parallel for the plan we reconstruct for the F102 and B100 churches (a single apse inscribed in a block projecting beyond the east wall of a church; Michel 2001: 13), the sixth-century Church 29 at Khirbat as-Samra, northeast of Zarqa. This church has an irregular square plan, slightly wider than long (13.5 m × 12.6 m) (Humbert and Desreumaux 1998: 52–53; Desreumaux and Humbert 2003: 29–30). Piers separate the wide nave from the side aisles. There was a raised chancel with chancel screen in front of the single apse, which is set into a block that projects from the east wall of the church. There is a central door in the west wall, a door in the north aisle (which is shorter than the south aisle), and two doors in the south wall, one of which led to a small room (sacristy?). Church 79 at the same site has a similar plan (Humbert and

Desreumaux 1998: 54; Desreumaux and Humbert 2003: 31), but there is a *pastophorion* to the right of the apse and the north side of the projecting apse block meets the northeast corner of the church at an angle. Another good parallel for the plan of the F102 Church is the basilica at Sussita-Hippos in Galilee, where the apse is inscribed in a block projecting from the east wall (Epstein and Tzaferis 1991). There was a projecting chancel in front of the apse, protected by a screen. The apse contained a *synthronon,* and there were no *pastophoria.* A three-apse baptistery was built against the north wall of the church in the late sixth century, accessed through a door in the north wall. The Church of Photios at Huarte near Apamaea in Syria, dated by a mosaic to 483–485, also has a projecting apse block (Canivet 2003: 189–94; Canivet and Canivet 1987: 189–206; Donceel-Voûte 1988: 19–102). There are three doors in the west wall, three in the north (one leading to a sacristy), and two in the south wall. A courtyard, baptistery, and slightly smaller church with interior apse adjoin the Church of Photios on the north. A church built over the Temple of Echmoun at Sidon has an apse block that projects beyond the east wall of the church on the north side but is encompassed within it on the south (Duval 2003: 103 fig. 41.c).

The areas outside the Apses of both the F102 and B100 Churches were disturbed and in part destroyed during later phases of occupation, but the balance of the archaeological evidence supports the somewhat atypical configuration of their apses proposed here, and there are good parallels elsewhere in the Near East for the design. This plan cannot be connected with any regional school of design alternatives, or with any particular ecclesiastical function; it probably simply represents one of several straightforward approaches to the layout of a modest, single apse church.

There are numerous examples throughout the region of churches with rooms or courtyards on the north or south flanks of a church structure, accessed through doors in the side walls of the nave or aisles, e.g., the St. George complex at Khirbat al-Mukhayyat, Church of Julianos at Umm al-Jimal, and the West Church at Bakirha. In Syria the courtyards usually run the whole length of the church, as with the F102 Church, and are found on the south side, perhaps to catch the sun, with two doors into the church (Butler 1929: 207).

5.C.4. Local and Regional Parallels for the Early Islamic House

While the F102 Church can be expected to reflect the plans of contemporary churches built elsewhere in the region, the Early Islamic house or houses may well look very different than contemporary houses because it had to adapt its plan to a pre-existing structure. Churches could be turned into mosques, as for example the churches of St. Sergius and Bacchus at Umm al-Surab and of St. George at Sama in either the eighth or the twelfth to fifteenth centuries, and in some cases this conversion involved closing off the apse with a wall (King 1983), as happened to both the F102 and B100 Churches. In addition, a *mihrab* apparently was not necessary at first, or at least could not be identified in the two churches at Umm al-Surab and Sama, and a bell tower could be transformed into a minaret with little obvious modification. Nevertheless, It is assumed here that the Early Islamic structures of F102 were houses, because of the frequent bins and *tabuns* found in them, and the domestic character of the occupation debris. Furthermore, given the mixed pastoral and agricultural economy of Hauarra/Humayma (*HEP* 1: 49–50, 401–10), the term "farm-house" is probably appropriate.

Given the wholesale adaptation of the F102 Church Complex as a residence, it is not surprising that it does not reflect closely the plans of contemporary "farm-houses" built on open sites. The Early Islamic rural houses identified in the West Negev Highlands Survey do not follow a uniform plan, but three or more rooms are involved, access to the interior is usually through the largest room, which might also be a courtyard (Haiman 1995: 35–37), with small square rooms opening on to it on one or two sides. This plan can be seen at Hauarra/Humayma in the Early Islamic phases of the E122 and A127 Houses (Oleson et al. 1999: 426–30). The roots of this rural house plan may well lie in the Byzantine period (Helms 1990: 126–27). A version of this basic plan can be seen in the Early Islamic house at Jawa (Daviau 2010: 26–27), and a larger, less coherent version of this plan can be seen in the

Umayyad house at Jerash (Galikowski 1992). The F102 House is much more compact, linking Rooms A, B, and C with subdivided spaces in the Nave. The eastern portion of the Nave may have been an open court in Phase IV, along with Room D, but the plan nevertheless cannot be said to resemble the basic Early Islamic house design noted above.

Although the plan of the F102 Farm-house does not find obvious parallels elsewhere, the interior details find parallels in rural houses in the region from the Early Islamic period up to the recent past. The arch-supported roof, of course, goes back to at least the first century BC in this region (*HEP* 1: 482–87). The packed dirt floors over pre-Islamic stone pavements were found in the Islamic structures in the sanctuary at Khirbet edh-Dharih, along with mangers (Villeneuve and al-Muheisen 2000: 1561). At Khirbat al-Nawafla near Wadi Musa ('Amr and Momani 2011: 368) and Khirbet Faris on the Kerak plateau, Early Islamic through recent farm-houses show many features similar to those of the F102 House: walls of dry stone masonry with some traces of mud mortar, impost walls built against inside walls to support transverse arches carrying light roofing materials, bins built between or beside the impost walls, stone platforms and benches. Houses 1 and 2 were particularly good examples (McQuitty and Falkner 1993: 41, 52–53). The arches and bins were characteristic enough to give rise to the term "arch and grain-bin type", in which bins set up in the space between the arch imposts. This practical arrangement has continued in use in the region through the early twentieth century, for example at al-Smakieh (McQuitty and Falkner 1993: 52–53) and 'Aima (Biewers 1992, 1993), and these details can be seen as well in the early twentieth-century Bedouin houses built into the ruins at Humayma. The debris found in the bins and occupation levels at Khirbet Faris sound very similar to that from F102: collapsed building materials, ash, dumped debris including mixed sherds from the Iron Age through Umayyad periods. At Faris, as in F102, collapse of the roofing arches was followed by the introduction of *tabun* ovens and handmade pottery, then covered by more rubble and wind-blown silt (McQuitty and Falkner 1993: 41–43).

Chapter 6

Field B100: Byzantine Church
and Early Islamic House

by John P. Oleson

6.A. LOCATION, DESCRIPTION, AND PHASING

Before excavation, B100 appeared as a prominent mound ca. 2 m in height in the very centre of the ancient settlement area (Field B), 25 m north of Reservoir no. 68 (figs. 1.1–2, 6.1–2). Stubs of a number of substantial walls were visible on its surface, along with fragments of carefully worked architectural mouldings (e.g., p. 498, no. 9). Since the mound itself was well-defined and centrally located, it seemed possible that it concealed substantial remains of a major public structure or structures originating in the Nabataean phase and reused or rebuilt during one or more of the later cultural phases. Three seasons of excavation in 1991, 1992, and 1993 revealed a Byzantine Church, of which only the Apse was partly visible in 1991.[1] A sounding was carried out in 1995 to define the west wall of this structure. The Church had been built above a Nabataean necropolis, possibly associated with a Nabataean temple that remains to be found. This Church was cleared out in the Umayyad period and subdivided into a large structure with a south-facing courtyard. Most likely at some later date, the Umayyad complex was extended 10 m to the west, and two more rooms were added along the north wall. Later still, another room was added outside the west wall. The final complex was 41 m long from east to west, and 15 m wide (fig. 6.3).

All the construction subsequent to the Byzantine period seems to belong to the Early Islamic period, although there is some ceramic evidence that parts of the complex were occupied as late as the Ottoman period.

At the start of the 1991 excavation, 5 × 5 m squares separated by 1 m baulks were laid out over the highest part of the B100 complex in the hope that this area would provide the most information about its nature, function and chronology. In order to reveal the overall plan of the latest stage of the complex, the surface soil was cleared from most of the mound during this 1991 season, while several deep probes were excavated in an attempt to define the character of two particularly interesting features and the chronology of structural development in the area. Between 1991 and 1993 deep excavation was carried out in Square 02 (Room E, the Apse) and Square 03 (Room B), along with superficial clearing and shallow excavation in the other 14 squares. This activity revealed the presence of a ramshackle structure consisting of 11 or 12 rooms following more or less the same approximately east–west orientation, and sharing many party walls and doors (fig. 6.4). The ceramic finds indicated a date in the Umayyad or Abbasid periods for this structure, which probably was domestic in character. At the core of the mound, however, a large, well-built, west-facing Apse (Room E) was exposed, the foundation deposits

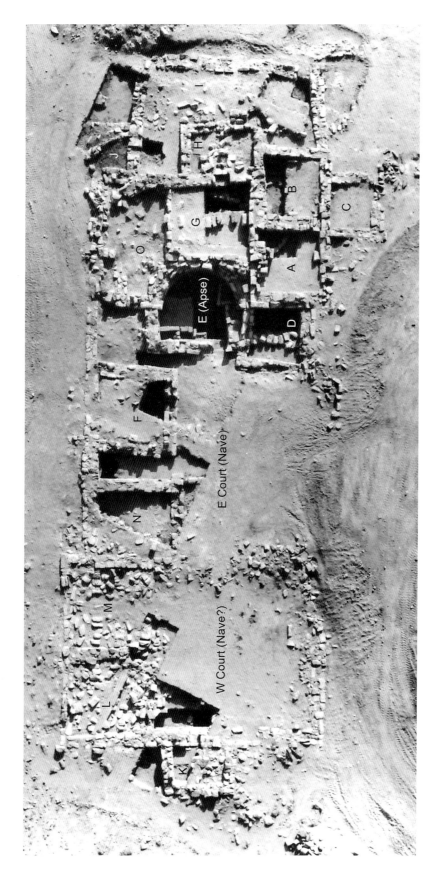

FIG. 6.1   *Aerial view of Field B100, with indication of room designations (W. Meyers, 21/07/1992, neg. H-3, no. 5).*

Fig. 6.2   *General view of Field B100, from northwest.*

of which dated to the Byzantine period (fig. 6.5). This Apse was associated with a solid wall forming the north sides of Rooms A and B, and the west wall of Room A. In addition, the deep probe in Room B revealed the presence of a substantial wall of Byzantine date, the foundations of which had been excavated into Nabataean strata. At the end of the 1991 season, it was noted that the B100 complex continued to the west for another 20 m, forming a large rectangle.

Excavation in 1992 focused on defining the chronology of the Apse and its relation to the rectangular feature apparently framing Rooms A and B, determining the character of the early structures below the centre of the B100 mound, and exposing the western portion of the complex. The accessible portions of Room E were excavated down to sterile soil, a deep probe was also sunk down to sterile strata in Room G, and the layout of the western portion of the complex, which extends 28 m west of the Apse, was defined and probed. By the end of the season, we had revealed a multi-roomed early Islamic habitation complex 41 m long from east to west, and 15 m wide, built in two main phases around a Byzantine Church that backed up against some outbuildings.

At the beginning of the 1993 season, three weeks were spent resolving some remaining questions. The sandstone feature below Room E had been disturbed by clandestine diggers over the winter and was shown to have covered a neatly built Nabataean cist tomb, probably part of a necropolis excavated into hard, silty sterile soil before the area had been extensively built upon (figs. 6.14–16). Furthermore, probes revealed the north and south walls and pavement of the Church, a corner of the chancel, and four piers that had supported the roof. Although the west wall was not identified, it was clear that the remains were those of a single-apse Byzantine Church 12.75 m wide and somewhere between 19 m and 26.5 m long from the back of the Apse to the front wall (fig. 6.4). In 1995 a long trench and several probes were excavated in an unsuccessful attempt to document the west wall and entrance to the Church.

The surface clearing yielded pottery that dated mainly to the late Byzantine, Umayyad, and Abbasid periods. The presence of a few Mamluk sherds and *tabuns* testify to light activity in the B100 area in later periods, after the Early Islamic structures had been abandoned and fallen (see Table 2.2). A small room was built at the west end of the complex in the Ottoman period.

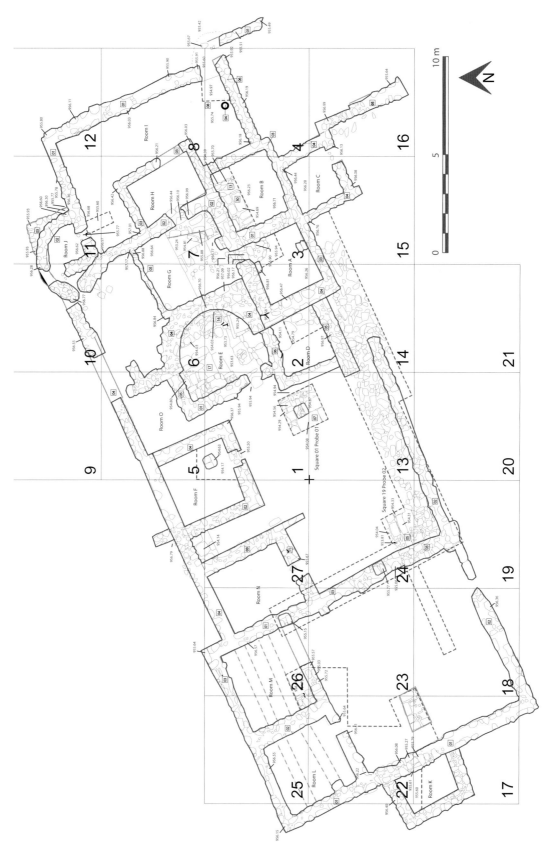

FIG. 6.3   *Stone by stone plan of Field B100, with square numbers.*

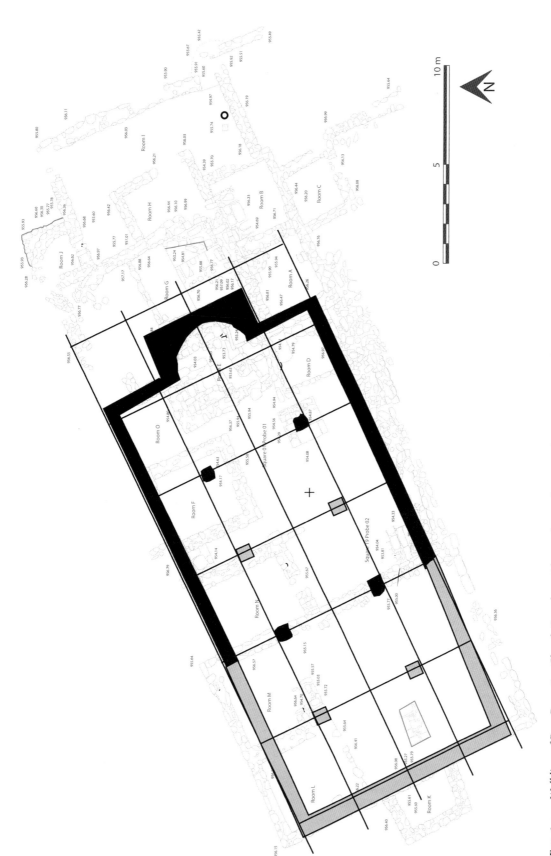

FIG. 6.4   *Wall lines of B100 Byzantine Church Complex, with superimposed squares of 10 × 15 Byzantine feet. Shaded walls and piers are uncertain or restored.*

FIG. 6.5 *View of Apse from southwest.*

The phasing of the complex can be outlined as follows:

Phase I: Nabataean necropolis and possible sanctuary (1st–3rd C).

Phase II: Byzantine Church (5th–6th C).

Phase IIIA: Re-use of the Church as a habitation (7th C).

Phase IIIB: Expansion of the Phase IIIA structure west and east of the Church (7th–8th C).

Phase IV: Abandonment and collapse, possibly with some squatter occupation (8th–15th C).

Phase V: Construction of Room K, and squatter occupation (probably Ottoman, 16th–early 20th C).

6.B. DESCRIPTION OF THE EXCAVATION

The initial grid of 16 5 × 5 m squares laid out over the B100 mound had to be expanded to the east and west in the course of excavation to cover portions of the structure previously undetected, ultimately reaching a total of 27 squares in three discontinuous series (fig. 6.3). Once the surface fill had been removed, however, and the rooms making up the structure were identified one by one, the room designations superseded the square coordinates, and the configuration of the architecture determined the logic of the excavation within it. In consequence, the initial excavation squares are seldom referred to in this description of the excavation. The rooms and walls were assigned identification letters and numbers as they were exposed, so these reflect the sequence of identification rather than the logic of the structure. The sequence of room designations seen on the plan (fig. 6.3, Rooms A to O) consequently reflects the progress of the excavation, running for the most part from south to north along the east end of the complex, then from west to east along its north wall. In order to follow the logic of the structure, the excavation of its core — the Church and its re-occupation — is presented first (Rooms D, E, F, N, O, and Probes 1 and 2), then the later west (Rooms K, L, M) and east extensions (Rooms A, B, C, G, H, I, J).

6.B.1. Room E: The Apse (Squares 01, 02, 05, 06)

Description begins with Room E, since it constituted the largest single unit of the structure to be excavated and is critical to an understanding of Phases I–IV.

Removal of surface soil and loose stones immediately revealed the existence of a semi-circular feature constructed of blocks of white sandstone. This Apse, as it was later identified, was backed on the east by a retaining wall and packing (Wall 04; figs. 6.3–5). It was flanked on the south by an ashlar wall 0.86 m thick, constructed in part of finely dressed blocks with drafted edges, and with a bearing of 60/240 degrees. This last wall (surviving top level at 956.81 m) subsequently proved to be a later construction, the north wall (01) of Room A. The upper courses of white sandstone blocks (at 956.70 m) forming the Apse were badly eroded, but the lower courses revealed by excavation were well-preserved, with a marked curve on their interior surfaces. In all, seven courses were preserved, the bottom of the lowest course at 954.60 m, on a foundation extending down to 954.20 m. The upper levels of fill in the Apse (fig. 6.6; Locus 00, 03, 06) consisted for the most part of tumbled blocks— including many facing blocks from the Apse wall and rubble packing from behind it—indicating that the original structure was considerably higher. The blocks of the Apse wall are not always tightly laid,

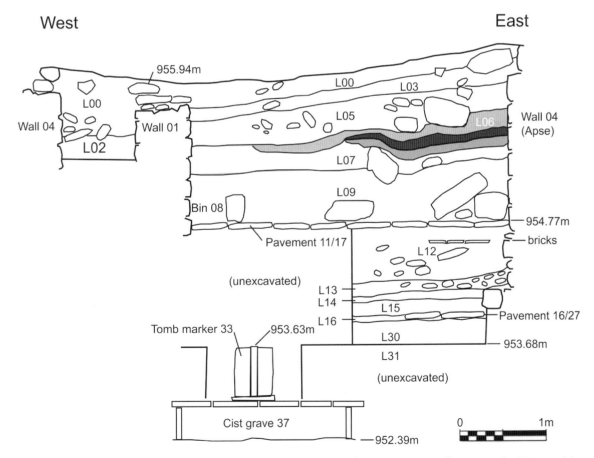

FIG. 6.6 *North baulk of Room F and Apse (Squares 02 and 01; Room E). The cist grave is actually 1.4 m south of the rest of the section line plane.*

FIG. 6.7   *Tabun in Room E.*

and the resulting gaps were chinked with small stones. Some traces of crumbly white mortar and hard, white wall plaster were found between and on the lower courses. The diameter of the Apse was 4.18 m; the longitudinal orientation of the Church was 62/242 degrees. The long-term defining influence of the Church structure is indicated by the approximate adherence of virtually all the later walls to the same orientation or its perpendicular. The presence in the upper layers of fill of Nabataean limestone moulding fragments (figs. 13.15.7–19, 13.16.9, 13, 17), Umayyad steatite cooking vessels, and an Abbasid lamp (fig. 6.10) is testimony to the mixing that has gone on.

The surface (Locus 00) and subsurface (Locus 03) strata consisted of a dusty, light brown soil surrounding tumbled blocks and rubble down to 956.29 m, at which point the tumble continues, but the soil gradually becomes dark with ash and charcoal bits (Locus 06). All these layers slope gently down to the west. A substantial lens of ash was encountered within Locus 06 in the northern part

of the Apse interior at 955.60 m. The ash had been produced by two clay-lined *tabun* ovens (Locus 02 at 955.52 m and Locus 03 at 955.48 m), neatly built and carefully floored with heat-retaining flint cobbles. One of the ovens was of typical beehive shape, framed in rubble, and mud-plastered on its interior. The other had lost its upper structure (fig. 6.7). Such ovens are common at the site, and in this case indicate post-destruction cooking activities by squatters in the windbreak provided by the Apse, possibly individuals associated with the Phase V occupation of Room K. The *tabuns* in C101 and F102 also were placed in abandoned areas, usually after the roof had collapsed, The same behaviour by recent squatters can be seen at Khirbat Faris (McQuitty and Falkner 1993: 43).

The ceramics in all of these upper strata — as in virtually all Phase III and IV strata — included MN, LB, UM, and AB wares, a few small clippings of bronze, very small and badly degraded fragments of glass vessels, and animal bones. A fragment of a quern may have had some association with the squatters who used the *tabuns,* but it is a fairly common artefact at Humayma (p. 506, no. 19). A small altar was found at 955.63 m at the intersection of the Apse wall and the north baulk, reused as construction material for Phase IIIA (p. 501, no. 1). A second and larger altar of white sandstone was found in the upper course of the Apse retaining Wall 04 where it intersects Wall 02 (p. 501, no. 2). The discovery of two altars within the apsidal feature, along with numerous fragments of carefully cut stone blocks and mouldings, suggests the existence of a Nabataean religious structure in this area.

Just below the ash, a row of six fallen sandstone voussoir blocks was exposed at the top of a lighter coloured, more sandy fill containing MN, LN, LB, UM, and AB ceramics (fig. 6.8; Locus 07), their lower surfaces at a level of 955.41 m. The blocks are aligned with the centre of the Apse (on a bearing 236 degrees) and a block-built impost pier (upper surface at 955.38 m) projecting from the centre of the west wall of Room E (01). No corresponding impost was found on the east. The Apse of the nearby Byzantine Church B126 was adapted to habitation in the 1950s by the construction of an arch in just the same orientation (fig. 9.4). Loci 07 and 09, which rest on a flagstone pavement (Locus 11/17; fig. 6.9) at 954.77 m, are composed of a sandy, pebbly, yellow-brown earth containing only a few blocks and a small number of sherds (MN, LN, LB, UM, AB). This material probably derived from the gradual decay of portions of the mudbrick or mud-plastered walls and roof, culminating in the collapse of the arch. Iron nails were recovered, and fragments of marble chancel screens (p. 475). There are patches of a possible packed earth floor directly above the paving stones, containing MN, LB, UM, and late AB or early FA ceramics (fig. 6.10), fragments of glass, corroded iron nails, bronze clippings, fragments of marble, Ma'an limestone, and alabaster revetment slabs, and numerous animal bone fragments. A similar deposit was found above the church paving in F102.

A flagstone floor, constructed with a wide variety of reused blocks, including some marble

FIG. 6.8   *Fallen arch and south bin from Early Islamic reoccupation of Room E.*

chancel screen fragments and a Nabataean cornice (p. 500, no. 13) is preserved across the north and east portions of the room (fig. 6.9); the portion of the floor near the back of the Apse was slightly elevated at a neat north–south edge, perhaps as a sleeping platform. There are similar floors at the same level as Floor 11/17 in Room D to the south (Locus 10, 954.79 m) and Room B to the east (Locus 30, elev. 954.89 m). The well-preserved floor in Room D shows that the gaps in the paving were carefully filled with clay. The proximity of the door may have allowed weathering to destroy such paving in Room E. This floor belongs to Phase IIIB and represents the last use of Room E, in the Early Abbasid period.

There were traces of a possible earlier floor partly paved with bricks below Floor 11/17 at a level of 954.54 to 954.58 m (Locus 12). Five bricks were

FIG. 6.9   *Early Islamic west blocking Wall 01, Bin 08, and paving in Room E.*

found, four of them laid adjacent to the interior of the Apse wall. They have mortar adhesions indicating that they were salvaged from somewhere else, probably the Fort (E116) or the Late Roman Bath (E077). Most have an X-mark on at least one side, made by a pair of fingers pushing the unfired clay into the mould, and intended to increase the bite of the mortar. The bricks were not associated with any identifiable surface in the room but were laid at the bottom level of the last ashlar course of the Apse wall. Brick 1992.0236.01: 0.215 × 0.215 × 4 m; hard sandy clay, 5YR 7/6 with off-white surface;

both surfaces smooth, with traces of grey mortar. Brick 1992.0236.02: 0.215 × 0.21 × 0.03 m; hard sandy fabric (5YR 7/6), surface 2.5Y 8/2.

During Phase III, the room was defined on the north and south by Walls 05 and 06 (L 0.75 m) built against the west face of the Apse structure, just outside the corners, and on the west by Wall 01. There was a door (W 0.75 m) toward the south end of the crosswall. The doorsill was damaged, but it seems to have been set at approximately elevation 954.90 m, with a higher outer threshold at 955.11 m (figs. 6.9, 6.11). There was a second, blocked

FIG. 6.10   *(Opposite page) Ceramic Profiles from Room E (the Apse). 1991.0070: B100.E.03, Abbasid lamp, ware 2.5YR 6/8, core 10YR 7/5, outer surface 10YR 7/5 (cf. fig. 6.31, 1992.0502.01; Jabal Harûn, Gerber 2008b: fig. 2.b, 3.a, 65, 116, 162–63, 8c; Hadad 1999; Khalil and Kareem 2002: 140–43) (late 8–9c). 1991.0193: B100.E.09, "Boot shaped lamp," ware 2.5YR 6/8, core 10YR 7/5, outer surface 10YR 7/5 (Petra church, Khairy 2001: 369 no. 16, 5–6c; Petra, EZ III: 349–51, 5–7c) (5–7c). 1992.0187.01: B100.E.12, small handmade cup, core pink, outer and inner surfaces red, thin white slip on upper body, exterior and interior of rim; traces of burning on lower body and broken part of rim (burning after breakage) (10–11 C?). 1992.0197.01: B100.E.17, bowl rim, core and surface 10R 6/8. 1992.0197.02: B100.E.17, bowl with incisions on exterior, core and surface black. 1992.0197.04: handmade bowl, serrations along rim, core and surface 10YR 8/3. 1992.0238: B100.E.23, juglet base, core black, surface 10R6/6. 1992.0238.20 (scale 1:4): B100.E.23, basin rim (UM–AB).*

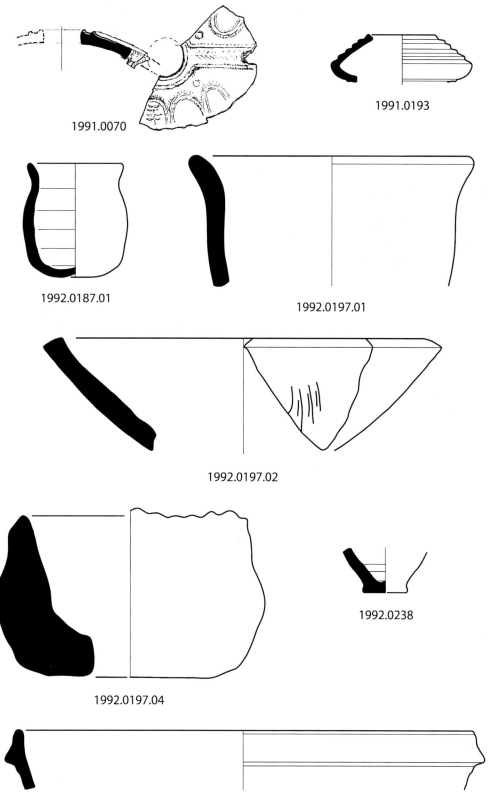

1991.0070

1991.0193

1992.0187.01

1992.0197.01

1992.0197.02

1992.0197.04

1992.0238

1992.0238.20

FIG. 6.11   *South door and step down into Room E.*

door in the northern half of this wall, behind the Locus 08 bin, perhaps closed up when the bin was constructed (fig. 6.9). There may be another closed door in wall 06, just west of its intersection with the Apse and behind Bin 15. The doorjambs are not clear, but there appears to be a door sill at 954.36 m. This door, too, may have been walled up when the adjacent bin was constructed. All of these walls, fairly well-built of a wide variety of re-used blocks and rubble set in mud, were constructed in Phase IIIA. They define a room 4.7 m wide from north to south, and 3.9 m deep. The room was fitted out with three storage bins or earth-filled platforms constructed of large, upright blocks and slabs, two (Loci 15 and 16; upper edges at 954.41 and 955.24) along the south wall, and one (Locus 08, upper edge at 955.16–955.45) at the north end of the west wall (fig. 6.9). Similar features can be seen in the reoccupation phase of F102, and in Rooms 03 and 05 adjacent to the C101 Church. The southern half of Bin 08 was filled with ash and appears to have

been used as a hearth area. Below the ash layer, the bin was lined with small, thin stone slabs and fragments of square bricks similar to the complete examples found next to the Apse wall. All three rest on Floor 11/17 or the corresponding earth floor. A cupboard (W 0.30 m, H 0.36 m, depth undetermined, floor elev. 955.79 m) was built into the north wall just east of the northwest corner of the room (fig. 6.9). Two shallow fire-pits (Loci 19, 20, D approx. 0.50 m) occupied the centre of the room; they contained MN, LB, UM, and AB ceramics.

Pit 19 had been re-laid with clay over an earlier installation (Locus 21), a roughly square marl block (L 0.32 m, W 0.32 m, H 0.14 m) framed by cobbles and fragments of marble and carrying a shallow central depression lined with plaster (L 0.215 m, W 0.215 m, elev. 954.76 m). The installation was not used as a hearth but may have supported a large jar or a post; its function remains enigmatic, in part because it belongs to Phase IIIA and its original context was lost in the Phase IIIB renovation.

FIG. 6.12 *Foundation of Apse, detail.*

The basin block in turn rested on a cornice block of Ma'an limestone (p. 500, no. 15, fig. 13.15). This feature is embedded in Loci 22 and 23, composed of a very compact red-brown soil containing much sand and pebbles (954.46 m). These loci form a single deposit, the division between them being arbitrary, and extend down to 954.13 m. Although no distinct levels were visible in this stratum, it appears to consist of the gradual accumulation of household occupation debris: small fragments of bones, sea shells, egg shells, carbon bits, fragments of plaster, clippings of copper and iron, small fragments of glass and steatite vessels, several corroded bronze coins — including one of Aretas IV of 4–3 BC, a stone bead (p. 513, no. 39; p. 527, no. 58), and numerous small potsherds (EN, MN, LN, MB, LB, UM, AB) of every type of ware from fine to storage (fig. 6.10). This elevation is almost precisely the same as the base of Wall 01, the pier for supporting the roof arch, and the base of the foundation packing for the Apse. The pavement extends beneath

Wall 05 to the north, beneath the Locus 08 bin and wall described above, and beneath the north half of Wall 01 to the west. The pavers extending under Wall 05 are smoothly dressed slabs of Ma'an shelly limestone rather than the typical sandstone. Clearly, at the beginning of Phase IIIA, the early Islamic re-occupiers of the Church cleared out the original pavement in the Apse—possibly to provide more headroom below the top level of a partly destroyed Apse wall—and walled the Apse off to form a separate space. The Church pavement survives to the west of this room. The Apse in the F102 Church was also walled off during a later occupation phase, although the pavement was left in place.

The foundation courses of the Apse wall consist of unworked blocks, rubble, and re-used worked stone blocks. Substantial stone packing (Loci 13–15, 25, Th 0.14 m) sloped down from the Apse wall for 1.0 m into the interior of the Apse (fig. 6.12). At first this appeared to be foundation packing for the Byzantine Church, but the ceramics

Fig. 6.13 *Foundation of Apse, and tomb shafts in Locus 30.*

ment or foundation (Locus 16/27) belonging to Phase II (fig. 6.13). It seems likely that this sloping layer of rubble and blocks set in a hard mud was intended to reinforce the footings of the Apse, either immediately after removal of the Byzantine floor and foundation deposit in Phase IIIA, or after a short interval once signs of stress appeared in the wall.

The layer of clay (Locus 16) above the Phase II pavement contained the usual variety of ceramics (MN, LN, LB, UM, AB). The feature itself (elev. 953.67 m) was constructed of substantial, reused blocks and slabs, some more than 0.18 m thick, including a re-used Nabataean pilaster base or capital. Although only a restricted portion of the Apse could be cleared to this level, the edge of the feature was found, just inside the baulk line, 1.02 m out from the central point of the Apse wall. The regular edge has a bearing of 160/340 degrees, nearly 90 degrees to the longitudinal axis of the Church. Only sterile, hard yellow silt was found in a probe beneath it to 953.39 m.

Removal of the accessible portions of the compacted earth surface (Locus 26) west of this feature exposed a very hard, level surface of yellow-brown, sterile, water-deposited silt (Locus 31, 953.68 m; fig. 6.13). Although only a restricted area of this surface could be exposed, two rectangular cuttings into it were visible, extending into the north and south edges of the probe. The north cutting (W >0.48 m, L >1.25 m) was filled with a loose red-brown sand (Locus 35) containing a small number of MN and LN sherds. There were some broken sandstone slabs in the upper level. Although no distinction in the fill could be made, the locus was changed (Locus 36) at 952.69 m and excavation continued to 952.11 m without recovering any further cultural

found in it — in addition to the usual Middle and Late Nabataean and Late Byzantine — included Umayyad, and possibly Abbasid wares. In addition, there was a selection of habitation debris very similar to what was found in Loci 22 and 23. Inside this fill and placed against the footing blocks directly below the Apse wall were two large blocks of a hard sandstone carefully cut to a curve (top elev. 954.01 m; figs. 6.5. 6.13). The curve, however, had a significantly smaller radius than the curve of the Apse, indicating that the blocks were reused from elsewhere. These blocks and the rubble packing rest on a thin layer of hard, water-deposited clay (Locus 16; elev. 953.71 m) covering a flagstone pave-

material. At this point the space became too restricted to allow further excavation.

Excavation of the similar reddish sandy fill on the south side of the clay feature (Locus 32) exposed a curious cross-shaped construction (Locus 33, top elev. 953.63 m) (figs. 6.13–14). It was built of two white sandstone blocks with Nabataean dressing on their upper surfaces, upended to frame and support two thinner slabs held between them at right angles. The blocks rested on large, thick stone slabs and blocks, and what looked like a slab pavement (elev. 952.81 m). The lower slabs penetrated into the south baulk. A significant number of animal bones were found in the fill around the feature (Loci 31, 32, 34), and the ceramic finds ranged from EN to LN. Two sherds were dated to the late first century BC, and the latest material was dated to the late fourth century AD. A coin of Aretas IV dating 39–40 was also recovered (p. 427, no. 60). There was much more ceramic and non-ceramic material on the south side of the clay feature than on the north.

Because of time constraints, the great difficulty involved in

FIG. 6.14   *Tomb marker below Apse.*

working in the restricted space around Feature 33, and the consequent need to totally destroy the feature in order to excavate deeper, it was covered with backfill at the end of the 1992 season. During the following winter, clandestine diggers from the locality ripped out the cross-shaped construction and exposed a neat row of white sandstone slabs (elev. 952.79 m) forming the roof of a cist grave (Locus 37, L 1.96 m, W 0.46 m, H 0.40 m) (fig. 6.15). Several of these slabs were then smashed to give access to an extended inhumation burial within, the feet oriented to the east. The broken slabs were thrown on top of the backfill, and most

of the contents of the grave dumped on top of it. The fill and cist tomb were examined and excavated in 1993, although the contexts had already been removed or disturbed.

The grave was constructed of neatly cut slabs of white sandstone lining the sides of a trench cut into the very hard silt of Locus 31. The floor was earth. Further slabs were laid across the cist to cover it, and the cross-shaped feature was apparently built above as a marker — although one below the level of the original backfill. The covering slabs were 0.90 m below the original ground level. The pit to the north may have been excavated for another burial,

Fig. 6.15 *Tomb cist below marker in Apse.*

but apparently it was not used. Both pits had the same orientation (60/240 degrees). The burials below the F102 Church were also located close to each other (pp. 150–52).

The heap of robber spoil immediately to the north of the burial was assumed to have originated within the cist, and it was excavated down to the level of the smashed sandstone cover slabs as Locus 38. This soil contained many fragments of human bone, some still embedded in a very hard matrix of concreted sand. The eastern 0.80 m of the fill within the grave (Locus 39) was undisturbed and still contained the lower legs and feet of the individual interred there (fig. 6.16). Examination of the skeletal remains revealed that the individual was a mature male (see pp. 326–27). The soil within the cist consisted of coarse reddish sand alternating with lenses of fine silt, all concreted to a very hard consistency. The bones were removed in a matrix of sand, which was then cleaned off at the laboratory. Unfortunately, no potsherds were directly associated with the bones. A probe 0.10 m into the floor

of the cist revealed only sterile sand. The only grave goods recovered were a polished bone ornament, a few small fragments of bronze beads, and a few small and worn sherds of MN coarse ware that may in fact have washed into the grave. The ceramics in the fill immediately above the grave, excavated in 1992, were MN and LN in date. Together with the sherds collected from the grave itself, the ceramics suggest that the tomb was closed early in the Late Nabataean period, several centuries before the Byzantine Church was built above it. The Church has the same orientation as the tomb cist.

6.B.2. Room D

The removal of a small amount of surface soil and rubble (Locus 00; fig. 6.3) exposed Room D, immediately to the south of Room E and sharing a party wall (Wall 08). The ground slopes off to the west at this point, from the high, strong west wall (04) of Room A towards the disturbed tumble of the south wall (02) of the B100 complex. As a result, the upper portions of the west (09) and south (05) walls of Room D were in poor condition, and surface clearing could not verify the existence of a door in those walls. Walls 04 and 05 were built on top of the east and south walls of the Church, and walls 08 and 09 do not bond with them, being partition walls of Phase IIIA designed to isolate a room at this point. The resulting space was an irregular square approximately 2.60 m (N–S) by 2.75 m (E–W). Removal of the upper layer of light, wind-blown sand and rock tumble within the room (Locus 01) revealed the presence of a collapsed arch (Locus 07, L 2.60 m, W 0.65 m, Th 0.70 m) that spanned the centre of the room from north to south. Locus 01 contained an enormous variety of ceramics (MN, LB, UM, AB, FA?, MA, OT), along with miscellaneous glass, metal, stone, bone, and shell rubbish.

This fill overlay a layer of light ash with a few small stones (Locus 02; top elev. 955.64 m) that had been generated by a *tabun* (Locus 03, D 0.45 m) built of mudbrick in the northwest corner of the room. The fire-hardened oven was floored with 45 fist-sized flint cobbles intended as a heat sink. The spreading ash layer surrounding the oven contained numerous carbonized beads of goat dung, presumably remains of the usual fuel. This oven,

FIG. 6.16   *Lower portion of the skeleton in situ at east end of tomb cist.*

FIG. 6.17   *Handmade clay bowl on pavement in Room D.*

Fig. 6.18 *Probe in Room D, with Church paving and edge of chancel step.*

like the identical examples in Room E, belongs to Phase IV, after the structure had been abandoned and fallen into ruin, or the limited re-occupation in Phase V. Their elevations and relation to the layers of collapse are the same.

The eastern half of the room, between Wall 04 and the arch tumble, was excavated to clarify the architecture of Walls 04 and 08. The *tabun* had been built on a layer of sandy soil containing numerous chunks of mudbrick debris and tumble (Locus 06), the results of the gradual decay of the structure of the room and its roof in Phase IV. Locus 06 contained a few small fragments of glass, copper, iron, and bone, along with a variety of ceramics (MN, MB, LB, UM, AB, FA). The decayed mudbrick came to predominate just above a carefully laid floor (Locus 10, elev. 954.79 m) consisting of irregular large slabs chinked with smaller stones and covered with mud plaster. At several points there was only mud paving. Two bricks were set into the floor against the south wall, and an unfired, handmade clay bowl was set into the floor just in front of them (Locus 11; fig. 6.17; rim D 0.165 m; base D 0.11 m; H 0.10 m; high base and simple rim, thick walls;

coarse, very pale brown, 10YR 7/3, ware with large chaff impressions, exterior wet smoothed; there was a deposit of clay inside the bowl).

This paving is at the same level as the Locus 17 pavement in Room E (elev. 954.80 m) and resembles it closely in design, suggesting that they belong to the same construction period, in Phase IIIB. There is a slight offset in Wall 04 at this level (elev. 954.75 m), possibly indicating the level from which the fallen Church walls were rebuilt in Phase IIIA or B. This level also corresponds with two horizontal blocks that may be threshold blocks, built into what may have been a door in the north wall (Wall 08), leading into Room E. There is a vertical line of blocks in this north wall, 0.50 m out from the east wall of the room, but the opening could not be cleared because the whole wall was very unstable. This door may have been walled up for some reason at the time of abandonment.

The northernmost paving slab in floor 10, a very large, thick slab of red sandstone adjacent to this possible door, was removed, revealing a compact stratum (Loci 12–13) of sand mixed with pebbles and cobbles. The fill contained a few fragments of metal, glass, plaster, and bones, and MN, LB, UM, and AB ceramics, predominantly large fragments of Islamic storage vessels. A greenish plaster with a smooth surface and fine, hard texture survived in patches at the corner formed by Walls 08 and 04.

Beneath was another floor (Locus 14; elev. 954.35 m), built of rough stones set in mud and containing LB, UM, and AB sherds. Small fragments of metal, stone and shell artefacts were associated with this floor. The wall plaster continued past this level, and removal of the floor revealed that it had been built directly on top of a step (Locus 15, elev. 954.31 m) associated with another floor (Locus 15, elev. 954.11 m). The visible part of Floor 15 consists of large rectangular blocks of yellow sandstone (fig. 6.18). The wall plaster terminated just below its upper surface. Probe 01 later revealed that this step is the south edge of the chancel of the Byzantine Church, and that the paving belongs to the southern side aisle. The design, materials, alignment, and elevation of the features in Room D correspond precisely to those of the southwest corner of the chancel

platform revealed more extensively in Probe 01. The plaster that survives over the joint in the northwest corner of the room just below Floor 10 indicates that the lower portion of Wall 04 and of the easternmost end of Wall 08 belong to the Phase II Church. In fact, the lower portion of Wall 08 is most likely a pier, similar to those identified elsewhere in the structure. The upper edge of the plaster terminates at the same level (elev. 954.79 m) as the tops of the piers in Room F and Probe 01. Furthermore, the interval between this pier and that in Probe 01 (3.70 m) is approximately correct for the reconstructed intervals between those in Probes 01 and 02 (fig. 6.4).

The fill beneath the step (Locus 16) was probed, revealing a firm, brown sand with some pebbles and cobbles, containing a few small fragments of ceramic that could be either LB or UM. At an elevation of 953.39 m the probe had to be abandoned due to the constraints of space. Wall 04 seems to continue downward, but the foundation levels of Wall 08 appear to lie just below Floor 15. Unfortunately, it was not possible to reach any remains of the Phase I level at this point.

FIG. 6.19 *View of Rooms D, E, O, F, N, M, L, and K, from the east; cf. figs. 6.1, 6.3.*

6.B.3. *Room O*

Room O was explored only through limited surface clearing to expose the tops of the walls (figs. 6.3, 6.19). Nevertheless, its general outlines are clear, and the more thorough examination of Rooms D and E allow some deductions to be made. The entrance to Room O in Phase III was through a narrow passage (L 1.75 m, W 0.80–0.70 m) formed by Wall 01 of Room E and Wall 04 of Room F. No doorjamb blocks appear in the portions of the walls exposed, suggesting that the space to which the passage leads (N–S 2.83 m, E–W 3.05 m) was in fact a casual by-product of the construction of Rooms E and F, and possibly unroofed. The narrow corridor between Rooms F and N is a possible parallel. The north and east walls of the room most likely were built up on top of the walls forming the northeast corner of the Church, similar to the arrangement in Room D.

6.B.4. *Room F*

Removal of a surface layer (Locus 00) consisting of a loose, dusty soil containing a large quantity of fallen rubble and blocks, exposed a large square room (3.70 m N–S, 3.40 m E–W) built against the north wall of the B100 complex (figs. 6.3, 6.20). The surviving wall tops slope downward towards the interior of the complex, from elevation 956.79 m to 956.37 m. The walls (Locus 04, Th 0.70–0.74 m), roughly constructed with a variety of re-used blocks and rubble, bond with the north wall of the complex (Locus 04); the upper portion of this wall belongs to Phase IIIA or B, constructed on top of the north wall of the Phase II Church. Nevertheless, the walls follow the orientation of the Church very closely. There is a doorway (Locus 07, 0.71 m wide) in the south side of the room, set slightly to the east of the centre line. Portions of the east and west jambs are still in place, built of L-shaped blocks

Fig. 6.20 *Interior of Room F, with Phase II Church pier and paving, and Phase III doorway. The south and west edges of the top of the pier have been highlighted to bring out the contrast.*

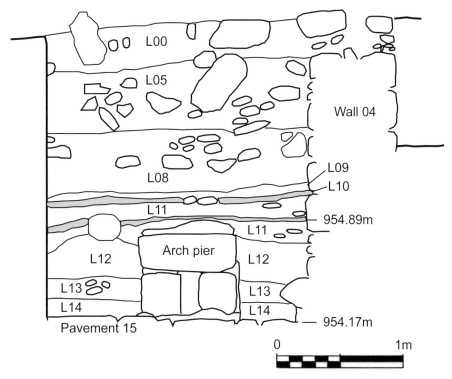

FIG. 6.21 *North baulk of Room F.*

oriented so that the door would swing inward, the same arrangement seen in many other rooms in Phase IIIA–B of this complex. A small hole was cut through the flange on one block of the west jamb, most likely to serve as a door latch, indicating that the door was swung inward to the right.

The fill in the southeast quadrant of the room was excavated (fig. 6.21). The upper half of the room was filled with enormous quantities of large stone blocks and rubble (Loci 05, 08) down to 955.42 m, where there was an irregular surface of mud or clay (Locus 09), possibly a floor. Loci 05 and 08 contained large quantities of potsherds (MN, MB, LB, UM, AB) and many small fragments of glass, plaster, and bone (fig. 6.22). The elevation of the possible Floor 09 corresponds approximately with the upper, outside threshold in the door (Locus 07, elev. 955.50 m). This was not the original floor in the room, however, for there is a lower threshold at 955.30 m.

Below this surface was a thick ash layer (Locus 10, Th 0.24 m; elev. 955.36 m), resting on a surface of burnt red sandy soil. A small amount of pottery (MN, LN, LB) was recovered from the ash

layer, which may have been produced by a hearth inside the room. There was a clear layer of habitation debris below (Locus 11, elev. 955.12 m), 0.23 m thick, consisting of compact light brown soil containing fragments of iron, glass, stone, many bones, and small potsherds (MN, LN, LB, UM, AB). This stratum, which extends down to 954.89 m, must be the original Phase IIIA floor, because it rests on a stratum of destruction or reconstruction debris (Locus 12) surrounding the top of one of the piers of the Church. The presence of this pier just inside the doorway would have made it very difficult to enter or use the room, indicating that it was largely covered with rubble before the room was built. The walls of the room bottom out at an elevation of 954.77 m, close to the level of the top of the pier (fig. 6.20).

The pier (0.65 × 0.65 m) survives to an elevation of 954.79 m, its upper surface covered with a 0.013 m thick layer of mortar containing pebbles and cobbles. Locus 12 was composed of an ashy soil containing large quantities of mortar and plaster fragments, carbon bits, pebbles, blocks, and fragments of marble revetment or chancel screen,

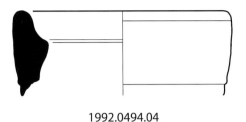

1992.0494.04

FIG. 6.22 *Ceramic profile from Room F. 1992.0494.04:
B100.F.13, Aila amphora rim, ware 7.5YR 8/4,
surfaces 2.5Y 8/2 (Aqaba kilns, Melkawi et al. 1994:
fig 10.e, mid to late 7C; Humayma, 'Amr and Schick
2001: fig. 3.1, mid-7C; Red Sea region, Tomber 2004:
398–400, mid-7C) (mid-7C).*

along with numerous bones. The ceramics (MN,
LB, UM, AB) included a considerable number of
fragments of large Abbasid storage vessels used as
packing for the wall foundation. This debris, and
that of Loci 13 (elev. 954.58 m) and 14 (elev. 954.33
m) below it, probably derives from the destruction
of the Church, its use as a dump during a period
of abandonment, and the shifting and levelling of
walls, piers, and rubbish to allow re-occupation in
Phase IIIA. Loci 13 and 14 contained more or less
the same sort of material as Locus 12, but a higher
proportion of ash and rubble, and larger amounts
of ceramic material (MN, LB, UM, AB) (fig. 6.22).
The carefully laid sandstone paving of the Church
(Locus 15; elev. 954.17 m) was revealed at a slightly
higher elevation than elsewhere in B100, but it was
constructed in the same manner and with the same
materials. The pier, surviving only two courses
high, was built of pairs of large sandstone blocks
(for the most part reused) alternately coursed N–S
and E–W to bond and framing smaller blocks or
rubble. Traces of a hard, sandy, off-white plaster
adhered to the pier near its base.

6.B.5. Room N (Squares 26, 27)

Continued clearing of the extensive surface rubble
and light loessal soil sloping southward from the
north wall (Wall 04) of the B100 complex west of
Room F quickly revealed a second room built up
against the north wall (figs. 6.3, 6.19). Room N (3.28
m × 4.0 m) is slightly larger than Room F, but was
constructed in the same careless fashion with re-

used blocks and rubble. A narrow, dead-end corridor (L 4.75, W 0.80–0.69) separates the two rooms.
Room N is framed by Wall 04 on the north, Wall 03
on the east, Wall 11 on the south, and the west wall
(01) of the Phase IIIA complex on the west. There
is a door with L-shaped doorjamb blocks in Wall
11, slightly to the left of the centreline of the room.
Only the top 0.75 m of surface rubble (Locus 05)
was removed in this area, so no further information about the fill or furnishings is available. The
light. loessal soil contained the usual rubbish along
with a few potsherds (LN, LB, UM, AB). Cleaning
of Wall 01, however, revealed the presence of one
of the Church piers built into its fabric during the
Phase IIIA re-occupation, precisely on line with
the pier in Room F and the north face of the Apse.
Probe 02 revealed a corresponding pier on the
south (figs. 6.3–4).

The corridor separating Rooms F and N
seemed less encumbered with fallen blocks than
the interior of either room, so it was probed to
verify the presence of the north Church wall below Wall 04. The thin layer of surface soil (Locus
00, elev. 956.60 m) concealed tumbled blocks
and rubble, surrounded by a light tan loessal soil
containing a few sherds (LN, LB, UM, AB). Most
of the rubble fall ceased at a compact layer of ash
(Locus 06, elev. 955.65 m), probably produced by
a nearby *tabun*. Clearing of Locus 06 revealed that
the top three courses of Walls 02, 03 and 04 were
much more poorly constructed than the courses
below, which probably belonged to Phase II. Below
this point (elev. 955.61 m) only the northernmost
metre of fill in the corridor was excavated (fig. 6.23).

Locus 06 rested on a thick layer of decayed
mudbrick and plaster (Locus 09, elev. 955.61 m)
with a few large pieces of rubble, probably representing the gradual decay of the structure prior to
the collapse of the walls. Locus 09 bottomed on a
lighter soil (Locus 12, top elev. 955.11 m) containing numerous lenses of ash, sand, and a great deal
of rubble or brick. Below, two thin layers of ash
(Loci 13, 14) covered a thin layer of light brown
sand (Locus 15) that extended down to the church
pavement, at approximately 954.14 m. Wall 02 on
the east bottoms out at 954.70 m (cf. the elevation
of 954.77 m in the southwest corner of Room F),
and Wall 03 at 954.96 m. There does, however,

seem to be a particularly thick concentration of rubble and cobbles below each, which may represent intentional foundation packing. The ceramics in Loci 06, 09, and 12 date to LN, LB, UM, AB. Beneath were found two further thin (Th 0.10) layers of ash and plaster bits (Loci 13, 14), above a thin layer of sandy silt (Locus 15; Th 0.03 m) deposited directly on the flagstone pavement of the Church (Locus 16; elev. 954.14 m). Locus 15 was probably deposited by wind and water during a period of abandonment, Loci 13–14 by a destructive fire that followed. Debris from the destruction of the Church fell on top, then rubbish was deposited, and subsequently the site was prepared for the Phase IIIA construction. Loci 12–14 in Room F show the same sequence. The floor was made up of sandstone slabs of various sizes; one in the centre of the probe was 0.76 m square. A ragged patch of firm white wall plaster survives along the lower edge of the north wall, behind Loci 13–15, and is smoothed over the joint with the floor. No artefacts were found at this level, but the rubble foundation footings of Walls 02 and 03 rest on the pavement.

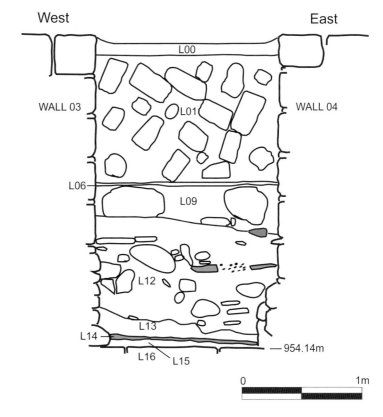

FIG. 6.23 *Corridor between Rooms F and N (Square 27), E–W baulk.*

6.B.6. Square 01, Probe 01

In 1993, an attempt was made to find another support pier belonging to the Church by excavating a 2.0 by 2.0 m probe laid out over a point in the south aisle corresponding to the location of the pier in Room F (figs. 6.3–4). The level of the light, loessal soil at this point was fairly low (elev. 955.60 m) suggesting that the pier might be just below the surface. The upper strata (Loci 00, 02, 04, elev. 955.60–954.86 m) in the probe consisted of fine wind and water deposited soil, free of ash and carbon bits, containing a few fragments of glass and bone and quantities of pottery (MN, LB, UM, AB, FA?), for the most part rubbish that washed into this low-lying courtyard during Phase IV (figs. 6.24–25). No evidence was found for later structures in the vicinity of this probe, and it seems likely that they were only built against the north wall of B100, and that the area of the probe lay within a courtyard. Two possible floors, one of beaten earth/mud (Locus 04, elev. 955.01 m), the other of beaten earth and cobbles (Locus 03, elev. 955.04 m) could be associated with such a courtyard, as they lie not far above the remaining courses of the pier.

The top of the pier (Locus 08, 0.66 × 0.64 m, elev. 954.87 m) appeared in Locus 05 (elev. 954.86 m), which, like the loci surrounding the pier in Room F and above the pavement in the corridor, contained significant quantities of ash, charcoal, plaster, mortar, glass and bone. The ceramics were the same as those in the upper strata. Beneath it was a deposit of light brown soil (Locus 06, elev. 954.56 m) containing less ash, but more plaster and

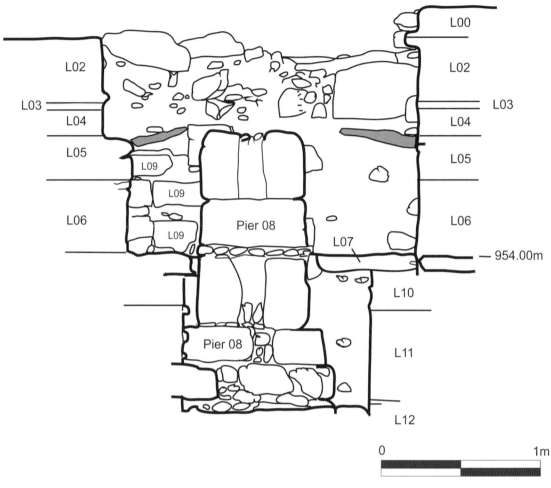

FIG. 6.24 *Square 01, Probe 01, section with pier.*

construction debris, and numerous potsherds (MN, LN, ER, LB, UM, AB) (fig. 6.26). The sandstone pavement of the Church (Locus 07, elev. 954.08 m) lay beneath (fig. 6.25). Ceramic material in the loci above the pavement range from Middle Nabataean to Abbasid. Locus 06 contained many large fragments of restorable amphorae. Similar large sherds were found in the locus immediately above the Church pavement exposed in Room F; this deposit appears to constitute intentional fill, as no associated living surface was found. An ash layer encountered in Locus 05 at an elevation of 954.86 m resembles those found in Rooms E and F.

The pier (Locus 08) was constructed of courses of sandstone blocks and rubble arranged in pairs and held together with a hard white mortar. Many of the blocks had been reused and showed

Nabataean dressing. The pier lined up precisely with the piers in Room F and Probe 02, and with the south termination of the Apse, and its sides have the same orientation. The elevation of the pavement is very close to that of the traces exposed elsewhere in B100. The large, rectangular paving slabs (e.g., L 1.10 m, W 0.66 m, Th 0.075 m) are laid parallel to the axis of the structure. Small patches of a smooth, cream-coloured plaster remain in place on the bottom course of the pier and extend onto the flagstone pavement.

On its north and east sides, the pier is bonded to a set of two steps that represent the southwest corner of the raised chancel platform (Locus 09; the lower at elev. 954.29 m, the upper at elev. 954.56 m) (fig. 6.25). The lower chancel step on the south is aligned with similar mortared blocks exposed at the north side of Room D, forming the south edge of the chancel area. The juxtaposition of piers and chancel steps can also be seen in the C101 Church. The steps to the north of the pier are constructed of re-used cornice blocks cut from Ma'an limestone; those to the east are built of sandstone blocks. Plaster extends from the pier onto the chancel steps. A marl conduit block northeast of the pier and bonded to the top north chancel step is reused as the base for a chancel screen (top elev. 954.65 m). The conduit channel has been partially filled with white mortar into which the lower edge of a marble screen was set; removal of the screen had left a narrow channel W 0.025 m.

Removal of one of the Locus 07 pavers west of the pier revealed that the pier continued for one more course (H 0.44) below the floor; the west face is partially covered with mortar and plaster (fig. 6.24). The footing (top elev. 953.69 m) beneath this course was roughly constructed of irregular blocks and mortared rubble; its orientation is 00/180 de-grees, 30 degrees west of the orientation of the pier itself. The top of the footing extends out 0.17 to 0.23 m from the west face of the pier and 0.09 m from its south face and rests on a pavement (Locus 12, elev. 953.12–953.18 m). The fill around the footing (Loci 10, 11) contained fragments of glass, marble, metal, mortar, a bone pin (p. 444, no. 5), bones, and charcoal, along with numerous ceramics (EN, MN, LN, LB, UM). The lower pavement consists of roughly fitted large and small sandstone and limestone slabs laid in a hard-packed silt. This floor resembles the slab floor (Locus 27, elev. 954.09 m) associated with the foundation of the Apse in Room E, and below which only sterile silt was found, but it was not possible to lift the slab at this position. It is possible that this feature belongs to some undefined Phase I structure.

The architectural elements exposed by this probe prove that the apsidal structure within the B100 complex was a basilica Church consisting of a nave, two side aisles, and a raised chancel. The

FIG. 6.25 *View of Square 01, Probe 01, pier, chancel steps, and church paving.*

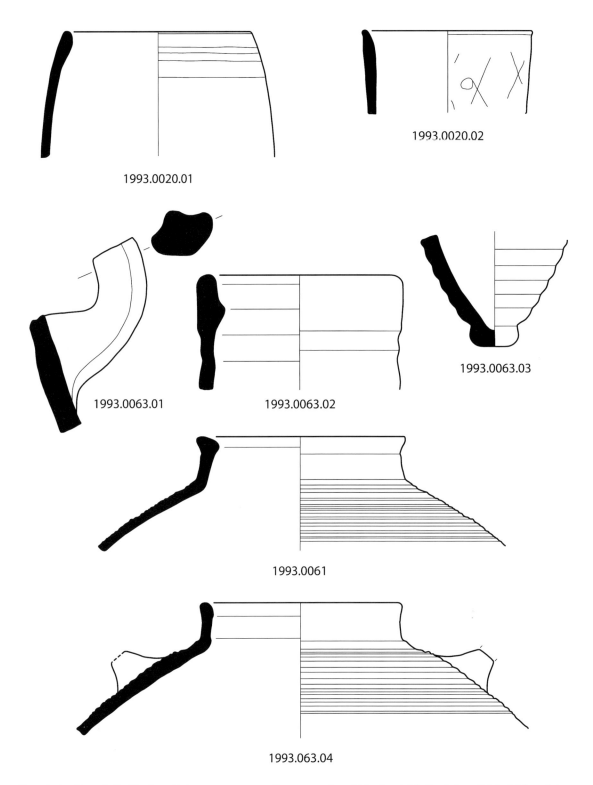

1993.0020.01

1993.0020.02

1993.0063.01   1993.0063.02   1993.0063.03

1993.0061

1993.063.04

FIG. 6.26 *Ceramic Profiles from Probe 01. 1993.0020.01: P01.02, cup rim with horizontal fluting below slightly thickened rim, core 2.5YR 6/6, exterior slip 5YR 5/6. 1993.0020.02: P01.02, cup rim with exterior cross-hatching, core 5YR 7/8, slip 7.5YR 7/4. 1993.0063.01: P01.06, storage jar handle. 1993.0063.02: P01.06, Aila amphora rim, ware 5YR 7/5, ext. 7.5YR 7/4, int. 10YR 8/3, mica flecks (Aqaba kilns, Melkawi et al. 1994: fig. 10.e, mid to late 7C; Humayma, ʿAmr and Schick 2001: fig. 3.1, mid-7C) (mid-7C). 1993.0063.03: P01.06, Aila amphora base, ware 7.5YR 8/4, surfaces 2.5Y 8/2 (Aqaba kilns,*

FIG. 6.27   *Square 19, Probe 02, Walls 03 and 05, from the east.*

Locus 07 flagstone pavement appears to belong to a later phase in the structure's existence. Ceramic materials found in Loci 10 and 11 below this upper floor range from Early Nabataean to Umayyad/Abbasid, suggesting a rebuilding or renovation of the pavement in the early Islamic period, possibly to shore up the foundations of the pier. These loci also contained much non-ceramic evidence of human occupation, and probably represent fill brought in to support the upper flagstone pavement floor (Locus 07). This fill also contained fragments of marble and shelly limestone, as well as fragments of mouldings. Since such mouldings were also used in the chancel steps, these spolia may be the remains of an earlier phase of the Church or of a Nabataean structure associated with the lowest slab pavement (Locus 12).

The upper courses of this pier, like those of the pier in Room F were lost through collapse or

removal of the blocks. The fact that the upper remaining sandstone courses are weathered indicates that the destruction of the Church associated with the Locus 07 pavement was substantial and left the interior unroofed, and that the remains were exposed to the elements for some time before later occupation.

6.B.7. Square 19, Probe 02

A 2.0 by 2.0 m probe was excavated at the conjectured junction of the west (Wall 03) and south (Wall 02) walls of the B100 complex, in an attempt to find the west and south walls of the B100 Church (fig. 6.3). A substantial wall was exposed (Wall 03) running 160–340 degrees across the B100 complex to its north perimeter wall (fig. 6.27). Top elevation is 955.69 m within the probe area. The upper three courses were crudely laid without mortar. The

Melkawi et al. 1994: fig. 10.m, mid to late 7C; Humayma, 'Amr and Schick 2001: fig. 3.1) (mid-7C). 1993.0061 (scale 1:3): P01.06, jar, ware 2.5R 6/8, ext white/grey slip (Petra, cf. EZ I: fig. 765, lt. 4–ea. 5C) (lt. 4–ea. 5C?). 1993.0063.04 (scale 1:3): P01.06, storage jar, core 5YR 6/6, exterior slip 10YR 8/3, (Petra, EZ I: fig. 742, last quarter 4–ea. 5C) (last quarter 4–ea. 5C).

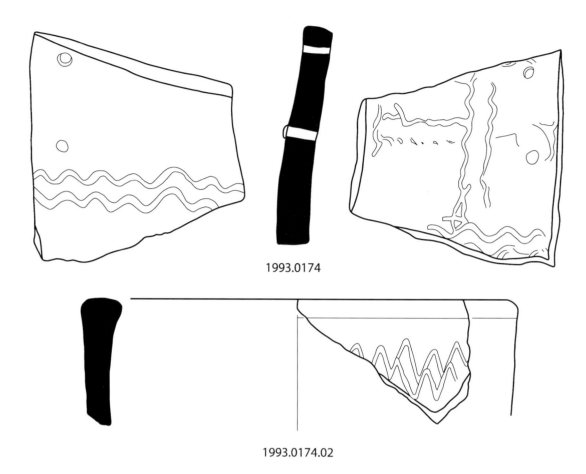

1993.0174

1993.0174.02

FIG. 6.28 *Ceramic profiles from Square 19, Probe 02, Locus 04. 1993.0174.01: handmade basin body sherd, ware, 2.5YR 7/6, incised pairs of wavy line decoration on interior and exterior, mending holes, one with lead plug (Aila, Whitcomb 1988: fig. 5.g, h, j, Fatimid; Hesban, Sauer and Herr 2012: fig. 4.8.15, Umayyad; Khirbat Yajuz, Khalil and Kareem 2002: fig. 11.11, Abbasid) (UM–AB). 1993.0174.02 (scale 1:3): handmade basin, ware 7.5YR 7/4, surface 2.5Y 8/3, incised wavy line decoration on exterior (Aila, Whitcomb 1988: fig. 5.h, j, Fatimid; Hesban, Sauer and Herr 2012: fig. 4.8.15, Umayyad) (UM–AB).*

fourth course below (top elev. 955.00 m), however, and the courses below it lie slightly to the east of the upper courses. These lower courses are built of carefully cut and well-laid, mortared ashlar blocks, resembling the lower courses of the north wall exposed in previous seasons.

The upper strata of fill against this wall (Locus 00, elev. 955.58 m; Locus 01, elev. 955.37 m; Locus 02, 954.94) consisted of rubble mixed with loose loessal soil, scraps of metal, and a variety of coarse ware and storage ware ceramics (LN, UM, AB). Below, also extending throughout the probe, was a stratum of packed earth and rubble (Locus 04, elev. 954.64 m) sloping from south to north, towards the centre of the square. There was a significant

amount of occupation debris — fragments of iron, bronze, glass, bones, shells, and ceramics (MN, LN, LB, UM, AB) — in the fill, but no identifiable floors (fig. 6.28; 1993.0174). The deposit most likely represents a dump from Phase IIIA or B. Removal of this deposit exposed an irregular wall built of large stone slabs (Wall 05, elev. 954.31 m), abutting wall 03, and disappearing into the east baulk (fig. 6.27). The orientation of this feature (70/250 degrees) does not match that of the rest of the B100 complex. The fill to the south of Wall 05 (Locus 06, elev. 954.17 m) consisted of a compact, sandy reddish soil containing pebbles and cobbles, numerous animal bones, a fragment of marble moulding, and a wide variety of ceramics (EN, MN, LN, LB, UM, AB) (fig.

6.28). This deposit rested directly on a pavement (Locus 10, elev. 953.81 m) constructed of roughly fitted slabs and rubble. This pavement may not be related to the similar, lower slab pavement (Locus 12) uncovered in Probe 01, which lies at a considerably lower elevation (953.12–953.18 m). North of wall 05, removal of a further small deposit of soil and rubble (Locus 07, elev. 954.18 m) exposed the flagstone pavement of the Church (Locus 08, elev. 954.10 m). At this point, however, the pavement has been badly disturbed, the slabs tipped and some stacked on one another. The paver at the NW corner of the probe was not in place, and the compact sandy soil beneath it (Locus 09, elev. 953.96 m) was excavated, exposing the Locus 10 pavement (elev. 953.81 m). This fill contained fragments of bronze, bone, shell, and ceramics (MN, LN, LB, UM, AB).

While the lower courses of Wall 03 at first seemed a likely candidate for the original west wall of the Church, surface cleaning north of the probe exposed two piers built into this wall and not bonded to it (fig. 6.3). The piers are identical in dimensions to the piers exposed in Room F Square 01, and Probe 01 and are aligned with them. The location of these piers makes it likely that at least one more bay existed between the piers in Wall 03 and the front wall of the Church 3.25 m to the west. Probes in 2005 between Wall 03 and the west wall of the B100 complex failed to locate the front wall of the Church, so determination of the length of the structure must await further excavation. Crosswall 03 may be part of a rebuilding of the structure after partial destruction, truncating its length but preserving the east half. Alternatively, it may be part of the Phase III renovation. Only one possible doorway was identified in Wall 03, situated 0.14 m north of the north baulk of the probe; it was blocked up. The width of the doorway is 1.03 m, and the elevation of the sill is 954.41 m. The south side of the southern imbedded pier forms the north edge of the doorway. This door appears to be related to the floor that belongs to the bottom edge of the wall plaster on Walls 03 and 11. Surface cleaning north along the east face of Wall 03 did not reveal any other doors.

On the south side of the probe, an untidy ashlar wall (Locus 11; top elev. 954.63 m) was exposed. This wall has been considerably disturbed either through collapse or stone robbing, and only a short

section was visible within the area of the probe. In terms of placement, it is a likely candidate for the Church's south wall, but further excavation would be required to make a definite identification. The lower courses of Wall 03 abut this wall, while its upper courses abut Wall 03. It is probable that Wall 11 predates Wall 03, and that the upper courses of both walls are later additions.

Patches of a hard, off-white wall plaster remained in place on Walls 03 and 11, including the corner intersection of the two walls. The bottom edge of the plaster (elev. 954.26 m) curves inward from the walls unto the Locus 10 floor. Since the plaster also spreads onto the west block of Wall 05, which extends across the probe (top elevation 954.31 m), the latter is most likely part of a disturbed flagstone floor associated with the Locus 08 pavement.

Ceramics recovered from Loci 06 and 09 above the Locus 10 floor range from Early Nabataean to Abbasid, indicating that this floor may date to the Abbasid period, and that the Locus 08 flagstone pavement, like the flagstone pavement in Square 01, Probe 01 was installed at some later time during the Abbasid period, probably when the Church was renovated or rebuilt for habitation. It should be noted that ostrich egg fragments and fragments of thin glass, possibly from lamps, were found above this floor, and that these are often associated with the *polykandela* in Byzantine churches (see p. 295).

This flagstone pavement appears to have been disturbed at some later time when the floor associated with the wall plaster on Walls 03 and 11, and of which Wall 05 may have been part, was installed. A noticeable difference between this probe and Square 01, Probe 01 and Room F was that the locus above the flagstone floor did not include the large number of amphora sherds found in the other areas above the related flagstone pavement.

While Wall 11 is a likely candidate for the south wall of the Church, the long heap of tumbled blocks visible at present makes the issue difficult to resolve (fig. 6.1–2, 6.19). There are traces of a substantial wall south of the line of Wall 11, extending east from Wall 03, but it is difficult to trace its track in the tumble. This feature may also be part of other structures lying outside but contiguous to the Church. The whole area was badly disturbed when Reservoir no. 68

just to the south was partly cleared out by the local Bedouin in the 1960s. If the possible walled-up door in Wall 03 is rejected as the main Church entrance, the only other possible location for an entrance to the Church and/or the later B100 Complex is at some point along this south wall. This would be a logical location, since it would have provided easy access to the centre rather than the periphery of the complex, and convenient access from inside to the adjacent reservoir.

6.B.8. West End of Complex: Rooms K (Square 22), L (Square 25), M (Square 26)

Clearing of surface rubble and soil west of Room N and Probe 02 revealed that the structure continued for a further 12.5 m to the west, forming a large, N–S rectangle more or less on the axis of the Apse in Room E, 14.75 m wide from north to south — approximately 2 m wider than the Phase IIIA complex and the Church (figs. 6.1–3, 6.19). Two rooms were built up against the north wall (later identified as Rooms L and M), and there was also a feature projecting from the outside of the west wall of the structure (later identified as Room K). The extra width gives this feature the appearance of a later Annex to the Church, although the west wall of the Church has to lie farther west than the Crosswall 05, beneath either the wall separating Rooms L and M or the west wall of the complex. Removal of a dump of soil excavated by the Bedouin from Reservoir no. 68 that extended over the southern portion of the complex revealed the presence of Wall 02 closing the south side. Excavation was undertaken in 1992 to clarify the plan of this Annex, and its relationship to the central portion of B100. Although the relationship could not be documented conclusively, aspects of the construction technique, plan, and floor levels suggest that the Annex is a Phase IIIB addition to the core of the B100 complex, overlying the western portion of the Phase II Church. Room K was probably a still later addition, in Phase V. It was not possible to locate conclusively the west wall of the church.

The north wall of the Annex, Wall 03 (L 10.40, W 0.70), was constructed of a mixture of re-used blocks and rubble, tied together with long slabs and blocks of hard, red sandstone. This construction technique is somewhat heavier and more careful than that of the visible sections of the north wall of the rest of the complex to the east (Wall 04), with more frequent use of the Umm Ishrin sandstone. Furthermore, Wall 03 is set 1.30 m to the north of Wall 04. Unfortunately, the join between the offset wall (Wall 01) and Wall 04 was badly disturbed, making it impossible to determine the sequence of construction. The same problem occurs along the south wall of the two complexes, since here the walls are even more disturbed. The surface of this whole area slopes down gradually from the north wall (elev. 955.64–956.15 m) to the south wall (elev. 955.36 m), with a marked depression indicating the central courtyard.

Room M

Clearing of surface rubble south of Wall 03 revealed a north–south wall (Wall 02, L 4.38, Th 0.70) built in the same manner as Wall 03 and seeming to bond with it. This wall marked off two rooms occupying the whole northern side of the Annex: Room L on the west and Room M on the east. The dimensions of Room M were 4.07–4.40 m east–west, 4.20–4.65 m north–south. The remains of two fallen transverse arches that bridged the room in an east–west direction could be seen in the surface fill (elev. 956.29–956.14 m). A probe in the doorway revealed that the arches sprang from impost piers built out 0.045 m from the walls. There was a door (Locus 07, W 0.65) 0.75 m east of Wall 02, framed by L-shaped doorjamb blocks identical to those of Rooms F and N (fig. 6.29).

The loose soil and tumble inside the door opening was excavated, along with a 1.5 m square inside the room, in an attempt to find doorsills and pavement. The room was filled nearly to the surviving wall tops with a large amount of fallen rubble and blocks in a matrix of soft, brown, slightly sandy soil (Locus 06, top elev. 955.85 m; fig. 6.30). Even though the area of the probe was small, it is remarkable that no ceramic material was recovered during removal of this thick layer of collapse. The absence may indicate both that the collapse was sudden, and that it came after abandonment of the site, when inhabitants were no longer shifting rubbish around the area. Although the soil remained

FIG. 6.29   *Room M, door and paving; fallen roofing arch in background.*

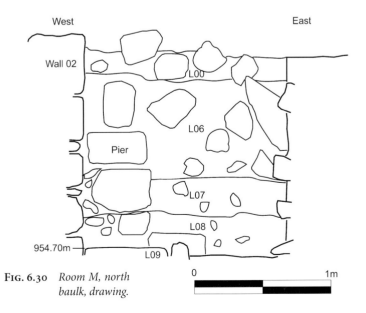

FIG. 6.30   *Room M, north baulk, drawing.*

the same, there was markedly less rubble in the level of fill below (Locus 07, elev. 955.30 m), and a small amount of ceramic material was recovered (MN, LB, UM, AB), along with an illegible bronze coin (p. 427, no. 67). Below Locus 07, the fill was a soft, light brown loess with a few cobbles (Locus 08, elev. 954.97 m). An Umayyad lamp was found in this fill (fig. 6.31). A high outer doorsill was found (elev. 955.03 m), stepping down to a lower threshold (elev. 954.70 m). One of the piers for the arches that crossed the room to support the roof was visible in the baulk. Although it is difficult to be certain without further excavation, it is possible that this pier rested on top of Locus 08. No obvious floor level, however, was found.

Locus 08 rested on a neatly laid pavement of sandstone slabs (Locus 09, elev. 954.70–954.64 m; fig. 6.29), covered in part with packed clay. Although only a small area of the pavement could be cleared, a portion of the floor west of the doorjamb is elevated 0.06 above the rest of the floor and separated from it by a curb. It is significant that this pavement is approximately 0.50 m above the level of the similar pavements in the central portion of the B100 complex (Rooms E, F, and D) but corresponds exactly with the level of a hard packed clay floor at the base of Wall 01, in front of the door to Room K. The discrepancy in floor levels reinforces interpretation of the Annex as a later addition to the western portion of the Church.

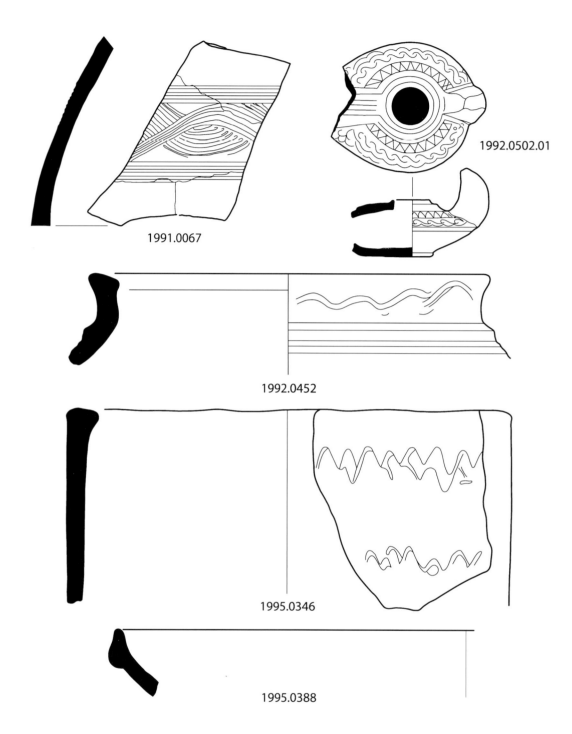

FIG. 6.31 *Ceramic profiles from Squares 04, 11, 21, 26, and 27. 1991.0067: B100.04.00, combed body sherd (Aqaba, cf. Whitcomb 1988: fig. 4.g, Fatimid; Pella, Smith and Day 1989: pl. 50.24, 6–ea. 7C; el-Muwaqqar, Najjar 1989: fig. 5.11, Abbasid) (8–9C). 1992.0502.01: B100.26.08, Abbasid lamp, ware 2.5YR 6/8, core 10YR 7/5, outer surface 10YR 7/5 (cf. fig. 6.10, 1991.0070; Jabal Harûn, Gerber 2008b: fig. 162–63, fig. 2.b, 3.a, 11.c, 162–63, 8C; Wadi Nawafla, 'Amr 2000: fig. 15.2; Bet Shean, Hadad 1999: figs. 6–7; Khirbat Yajuz, Khalil and Kareem 2002: 140–43) (late 8–9C). 1992.0452: B100.27.12, jar rim, ware 2.5YR 6/8, slip 10YR 8/6 (LB–UM?). 1995.0346 (scale 1:4): B100.21.02, basin rim with wavy lines painted on exterior (Tel Jawa, for the motif cf. Daviau 2010: fig. 8.12.5–6, 6–7C) (UM–AB). 1995.0388: B100.21.02, basin with hammerhead rim (UM–AB).*

Room L

Clearing of surface rubble and soil in the northwest corner of the Annex revealed an enormous heap of red and white sandstone blocks and rubble, extending 6.5 m south of the corner and sloping gradually down and in toward the courtyard (elev. 956.15–955.62 m). Ultimately, through careful removal of the blocks, a spur wall (Wall 09, L 2.50, Th 0.63, top elev. 955.94 m) was found that bonded into Wall 01 and extended to the east at a right angle. One metre east of the intersection, the wall blocks tumbled to the south in a great heap. Clearing of the surface tumble and loose soil revealed the continuation of Wall 09 to the east and a door (Locus 05, W 0.52) 2.5 m east of Wall 01, 1.18 m west of the east wall of the room. This wall is on line with the south wall of Room M (Wall 05). Like most of the Phase III doors, this one was framed by L-shaped doorjamb blocks. Walls 01, 03, 02, and 09 thus framed a room (Room L) 3.94 m square on the interior. Because of the enormous mass of rubble, the surface fill was cleared in the door opening only to a level of 956.31 m. Removal of some surface rubble within the room revealed the blocks of two fallen, east–west arches (W 0.50 m), directly on line with those in Room M: 0.93 m and 2.25 m south of their north walls. The few sherds recovered during the clearing were LB, UM, and AB.

A number of factors indicate that Rooms L and M and the courtyard in front of them were part of a single construction period, and that this was subsequent to the Phase IIIA construction in the core of the complex. Although Room M is slightly wider than Room L, they are roughly the same length, their interior arches line up with each other, their doors are placed close to each other, and all the walls forming them bond, with the exception of the east end of Wall 05, the south wall of Room M. This wall abuts a pier of the Phase II Church, built into the N–S Wall 01 that marks off the Annex from the rest of the complex. Furthermore, there are no obvious doors in Wall 01/03 allowing communication between the two parts of the complex. The only place for an entrance to the Annex is in its south wall (Wall 02), which cannot be traced with confidence along its central section. Furthermore, this wall faces the adjacent reservoir, probably a frequent destination for humans and their animals. The Annex was probably made wider north to south than the eastern courtyard of B100 simply to provide more enclosed space.

Room K

Deep excavation in the Annex was undertaken only in and around the central portion of the west wall (Wall 01), where a feature projected westward from the wall. Clearing of the surface rubble revealed a small, slightly irregular room (Room K) with the interior dimensions 1.92/2.04 m (south and north walls) by 3.02/2.79 m (east and west walls) (figs. 6.1, 6.3, 6.33). The walls (Th 0.59 m) are built of large, roughly trimmed sandstone blocks facing a core of cobbles and earth. The present upper surface of the north wall is at 955.99 m, the base of the finished

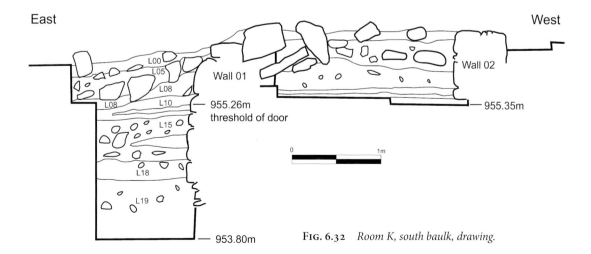

East   West

Wall 01   Wall 02

L00
L05
L08
L10   — 955.26m
L15   threshold of door   — 955.35m
L18
L19

0   1m

— 953.80m   **FIG. 6.32** *Room K, south baulk, drawing.*

Fig. 6.33   *Room K, view from east.*

surface at 954.65 m, and the base of the cobble foundation at 954.16 m. A large amount of wall rubble
occupied the surface level (Locus 00), containing a
few LB, UM and AB potsherds (fig. 6.32). Beneath
the level of the wall tops more large rubble was
found in a matrix of light brown loess and reddish
brown sand (Locus 06, elev. 955.90 m) devoid of
ceramics, like the rubble layer (Locus 06) within
Room M. Beneath the rubble there was an irregular
layer of reddish-brown, clay-like soil with a few
cobbles and an occasional piece of larger rubble
(Locus 13, elev. 955.74 m), probably representing
decayed mudbrick and mud plaster fallen from the
walls. This locus yielded fragments of glass vessels,
bone, seashells, and some MN, LN, LB ceramics,
including 1 OT sherd. A beaten clay floor (Locus 14)
was encountered at 955.60 m; it contained MN, LB,
UM, and AB ceramics (fig. 6.34). The floor, in turn,
lay on a layer of a very soft, light cream-coloured
loess (Locus 16, elev. 955.44 m) containing a large
amount of ash and numbers of fish, fowl, and mammal bones, along with LN, UM, and AB pottery.

This layer ran under the cobble packing forming
the foundation of the north and west walls of the
room, providing a *terminus post quem.*

Essentially the same sequence and approximately same levels were found outside the north
wall of the room (fig. 6.35). In this case, however,
the rubble spill (Locus 04, elev. 955.90 m) contained an abundance of potsherds (MN, LB?, UM,
AB) and fragments of steatite cooking vessels. The
rubble lay on a stratum of decayed mudbrick and
plaster (Locus 07, elev. 955.55 m), which in turn covered a lens of soft, ashy loess (Locus 11, elev. 955.50
m) containing numerous bones and MN, LN, and
LB ceramics. This layer of rubbish extended under
the north wall of Room K, and approximately 1.5
m out to the north. Below it, a stratum of a very
sandy, dark-reddish soil (Locus 12, elev. 955.47 m)
was probed and yielded some UM, AB, and possibly LB ceramics.

Wall 01 (L 14.70, Th 0.64–0.73, bearing 160/340
degrees, north elev. 956.15 m, south elev. 955.55 m),
forming the east wall of Room K and the west wall

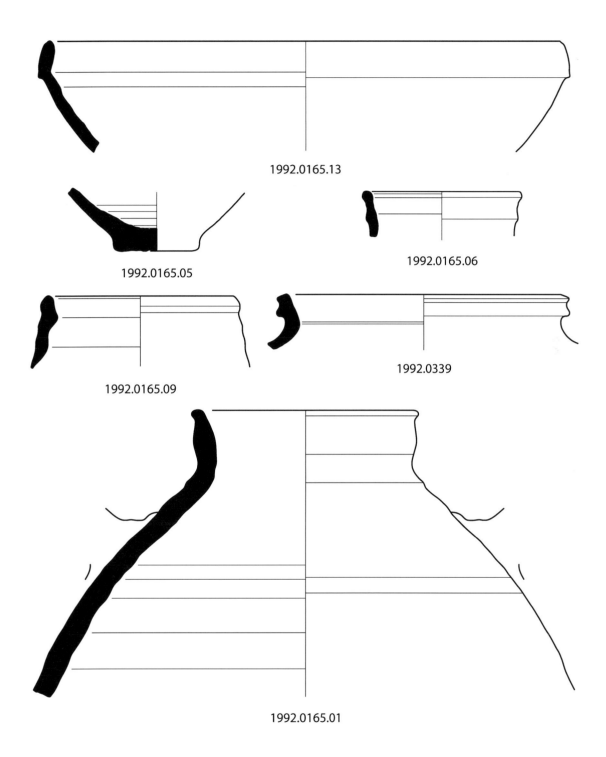

1992.0165.13

1992.0165.05

1992.0165.06

1992.0165.09

1992.0339

1992.0165.01

FIG. 6.34 *Ceramic profiles from Room K (Square 22), Loci 15, 18. 1992.0165.13 (scale 1:3): B100.22.15, basin, inner core 2.5Y 7/6, outer core 2.5Y 7/3, mica visible (UM–AB). 1992.0165.05: B100.22.15, jug base, core 2.5YR 6/6, slip 2.5YR 5/2. 1992.0165.06: B100.22.15, jar, black core, black surface, no slip. 1992.0165.09: B100.22.15, jar, core and surface 2.5YR 6/8, no slip. 1992.0339: B100.22.18, cook pot, core 10R 6/6 core, slip 7.5YR 8/2 (Humayma, Gerber 2008a: fig. 23.25; Petra, Gerber 2001: 11, fig. 2.C–D, 2–3C; Gerber 2005: 731, fig. 1.2 2–3C (2–3C). 1992.0165.01: B100.22.15, bag amphora, 2.5YR 6/8 (cf. 1992.0133.03 below fig. 7.37; Tel al-Fara, Tubb 1986: fig. 4.1, 2, 6–7C; Caesarea, Adam Bayewitz 1986: fig. 1.5, 1.7, 630–660 (6–7C).*

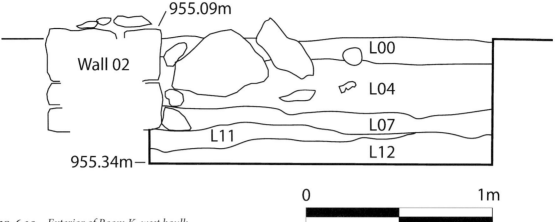

FIG. 6.35   *Exterior of Room K, west baulk.*

of the complex, was founded at a much lower level than the walls of Room K (base of foundation elev. 954.16 m) and does not bond with them. Entry into Room K was provided by a door (Locus 17, W ca. 0.50–0.63 m) approximately in the centre of its east wall (fig. 6.33). Although this feature is weathered and disturbed, the rough finish and absence of L-shaped doorjamb blocks suggests that the door was knocked through Wall 01 at a time subsequent to the original construction period. The irregular outline of the room suggests the same. Nevertheless, the door is only ca. 0.20 m north of the central point of Wall 01, possibly indicating some interest in symmetry with the pre-existing structure. It had a high interior sill (W 0.63 m, elev. 955.65 m) and lower exterior sill (W 0.05 m, elev. 955.27 m).

A trench 1.25 m wide was excavated to the east of Wall 01, to determine the relationship of the door and the wall to any possible courtyard pavement. At its very north end this trench exposed Wall 09, the south wall of Room L, which bonded with Wall 01 and extended east from it (fig. 6.33). The fill east of Wall 01 consisted of a layer of tumbled blocks and cobbles (Locus 05, west elev. 955.59 m) sloping down to the east from the wall, set in a compacted loess and sand, above an eastward tapering layer of fine, loose, light-brown sandy soil with a few blocks and cobbles (Locus 08, west elev. 955.34 m) (fig. 6.32). The rubble of Locus 05 contained MN, LB, UM, and AB ceramics. Locus 08, which has the appearance of a windblown deposit that built up around gradually accumulating tumble, contained a rich variety of ceramics, dating MN, AB, MA,

and 2 possible OT sherds, and a quern fragment (p. 506). Locus 08 overlay a dense layer of crumbly, decayed mudbrick, or possibly a packed clay paving (Locus 10, west elev. 955.30 m). Within it, at 955.25 m, there is a slightly harder, eastward-sloping layer of clay. The correspondence of level between this layer and the outside sill of Door 17 suggests that it is either an intentional paving or was produced by traffic through the door. It contained fragments of glass vessels, bone, and MN, LB, UM, and possibly AB ceramics.

This possible paving overlay a thick (Th 0.40 m) deposit of sandy loess (Locus 15, west elev. 955.18 m), containing numerous loosely-seated cobbles and lenses of decayed mudbrick and ash, along with a few tumbled blocks, along with an abundance of ceramic material from nearly every period represented at the site: EN, MN, LN, LR, LB, UM, AB, and possibly MA, along with a single OT sherd (fig. 6.34). There were also many bird, mammal and fish bones, and clippings of bronze. The loose fill beneath Locus 15 (Locus 18, elev. 954.72 m), probed along the south 2.5 m of the trench, consisted of an ashy soil with many cobbles, much ash, and numerous bones and potsherds. The ceramics follow a wide range: MN, LN, LB, UM, AB, and possibly MA. One Ottoman sherd found in the bucket from this locus during processing is probably intrusive (see below), as may be the Ottoman sherd in Locus 15. The lower surface of this stratum, at 954.52 m, is just above the lowest course of the east face of Wall 01 (lower edge at 954.45 m) and should represent the earliest period of use of the Annex. The foundation trench for the wall, consisting of sandstone cobbles set in a very hard, red-brown clay, was cut into a harder, crumbly, light brown to red layer of sandy soil (Locus 19, elev. 954.45 m) containing numerous white sandstone cobbles. The packing of sandstone cobbles extended down to 954.16 m, but the Locus 19 fill was probed down to 953.80 m without any change being noted. The ceramics in this fill include EN, MN, LN, LR, MB, LB, and possibly UM wares.

The character and chronology of Room K remain enigmatic. The room probably was added to the Annex after the original Phase IIIB construction, but it is not possible to say exactly when. The single sherd of Ottoman handmade pottery in Locus 18 might be taken to indicate that Wall 01 — and by implication the whole Annex — belongs to that period, but if that were the case, there would surely be much more evidence for Ottoman occupation, such as large quantities of this ceramic, and scraps of early modern metal artefacts. As it is, only 14 sherds of Ottoman handmade wares were found in the B100 complex (Table 2.2); all of them — except the sherd mentioned, one sherd just above in Locus 15, and four in Locus 13 — were found in ones or twos in surface loci (eight B100 buckets in total). In excavations over the entire site (with the exception of F103) between 1991 and 2005, Ottoman sherds or other artefacts have been found in only 51 loci: 36 at F102, 8 at B100, 2 at C124, 2 at E125, 2 at E122, and 1 at E116. At F103, which had an extensive Ottoman phase, 187 buckets out of 985 excavated between 1992 and 2002 produced Ottoman sherds or other artefacts (19%; Table 15.1). For the entire site, the ratio was 274 buckets out of 5,929 (4.6%); for the entire site apart from F103, the ratio was 87 buckets out of 4,944 (1.8%). If a structure as large as the Annex had been built entirely in the Ottoman period, clearly there would be more ceramic evidence for this chronology.

The Ottoman sherd found in Locus 15, just below the Locus 10 surface connected with the door is more easily explained away, since it could have been trodden into the layer below or carried there down a rodent or snake hole. A more likely explanation, however, is that both of these sherds actually derive from Locus 08, the loose locus filled with rubbish just in front of the door, in which two further Ottoman sherds were found, and

that they fell from the baulk into the lower levels during excavation. This would allow the Annex an Early Islamic date. The four Ottoman sherds found inside Room K, in Locus 13, however, are more convincing. Combined with the four sherds restored to Locus 08, they represent over half the Ottoman material from B100, and the only reliable non-surface context. As a result, it seems likely that there was some sort of Ottoman occupation in Room K, which can be termed Phase V. Since the room is an addition to the Annex, its walls and door less carefully laid out, and its foundations more shallow, it is quite possible that Room K is an Ottoman structure. It seems too small to have served for habitation, but it may have been intended to provide shelter for a guard over the adjacent cisterns, or storage for water-dipping equipment. It is at least possible that the *tabuns* in Room E and D date to this period, but for the present they are attributed to Phase IV.

During the winter of 1994, weathering caused the collapse of the east baulk across from the door to Room K, exposing the edge of a large pier or platform (fig. 6.36). The feature was carefully built of large blocks facing a fill of cobbles and soil (elevation of northwest corner 954.91 m); the west face was only 1.0 m east of the east wall of Room K. Extension of the square exposed the northeast corner, revealing that the north edge of the structure was 1.90 m long, oriented 66/246 degrees, almost perpendicular to the west wall of the complex. The stratigraphy was the same as that in front of Room K. There was no time to completely excavate this structure, which may belong to either the Church or the Phase IIIB complex.

6.B.9. East End of Complex: Rooms A, B, C, G, H, I, J (Squares 3–4, 6–8. 10–12, 15–16)

For the most part, the architecture of the east end of the B100 complex was poorly built and is poorly preserved, particularly along the north and east slope of the mound, where it was exposed from time to time to run-off water from the north (figs. 6.1–6.3, 6.37). The crown of the mound, especially over Rooms G and H, was covered with a layer of tumbled sandstone blocks and rubble over a metre thick, most likely collapse from the Church

FIG. 6.36   *Feature east of Room K.*

FIG. 6.37   *East end of the B100 Complex, from the south.*

FIG. 6.38   *Room G from the north.*

Apse and Phase III structures. Nevertheless, careful removal of the blocks and the matted layer of surface soil exposed the walls of a series of interrelated rooms. All the walls were built of dry-stone masonry, including re-used blocks with careful trimming of typical Nabataean character, rubble, soil, and unworked boulders. As is typical of the entire B100 complex in Phases I–V, only the two outer faces of the walls were built of large blocks laid with a modicum of care, while the interiors were filled with rubble and soil.

Room G

The area later defined as Room G was of particular interest because of its location at the crest of the mound and in proximity to the Apse. Removal of the surface rubble (highest elev. ca. 957.65 m), most of which seems to have fallen from Wall 02 on the east and Wall 02/09 on the south, exposed a roughly rectangular room: 3.95–4.10 m east–west, 4.30–4.50 m north–south (fig. 6.38). The walls defining the room were a great mix of styles, dimensions, and orientations. Wall 04 on the west (L 4.30 m) was

well-built with reused, but for the most part square, blocks, and oriented at 145/335 degrees, 5 degrees east of the orientation of the Church proper. Wall 02/09 and a stub of Wall 01 framing a door on the south (L 4.10) were less well-built, composed of a great mixture of blocks, rubble, and cobbles of a wide variety of dimensions and materials, oriented to approximately 61/241 degrees. Wall 01, west of the door, was 0.84 m thick; Wall 04 does not bond with it. Wall 02/09 east of the door varied in thickness from 0.55 to 0.83 m. The east end of this wall bonds with Wall 02, the east wall of the room, which was very poorly built of re-used blocks of white sandstone. This wall, which extends north of Room G, has an approximate bearing of 150/330 degrees but has shifted at its north end. The total length of this wall was about 7.0 m and its width 0.68 m; the first 4.5 m form the east wall of Room G. The north side of the room is formed by Wall 05 (L 3.95, Th 0.45), which seems more like a narrow, lightly built partition wall than a structural support. It has a bearing of 59/239 degrees.

The fallen rubble of Locus 00 ended quite abruptly on a surface of water-deposited silt (Locus

West   East

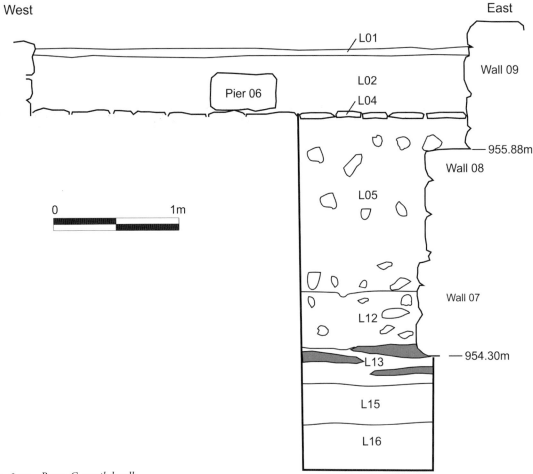

FIG. 6.39 *Room G, north baulk.*

01, elev. 956.75 m), probably from the Phase IV abandonment, which contained a few AB sherds and the fragment of a quern (p. 506, no. 17). Below was a fill consisting of a fine, light brown soil (Locus 02, elev. 956.62 m; fig. 6.39) containing chunks and lenses of decayed mudbrick, some lenses of ash and a large amount of fine, coarse, cooking, and storage ware pottery (MN, LB, UM, AB), clippings of metal, fragments of glass vessels, bones, and egg shells. Locus 02 rested on a pavement (Locus 04, elev. 956.23 m) carefully constructed of large, irregular slabs of sandstone set in a mud/clay mortar. The east and south walls and the arch impost retained some of their original plaster surface. At the bases of each wall the plaster filled the joint to make a smooth join with the floor plaster. The voussoirs of the arch that spanned the room from south to north lay on this floor in a line, north of the project-

ing, block-built pier that had supported one end of the arch (fig. 6.38). The voussoirs still preserved significant traces of the mortar in which they had been set. Although Locus 02 was not excavated in the north half of the room, approximately 0.50 m of the north wall (05) projects above it but without any traces of an impost pier corresponding to the one on the south. This absence, combined with the very weak construction of Wall 05, suggest that it may be a partition wall associated with a re-occupation of the room after the fall of the roof. In this case, Locus 02 may be a habitation deposit.

Pavement 04 was associated with doors in the east and south walls; both had been intentionally walled up with roughly laid blocks chinked with cobbles at the time the building was abandoned (fig. 6.38, 6.40–41). The layers of fill below the blocking included sand and some small rubble

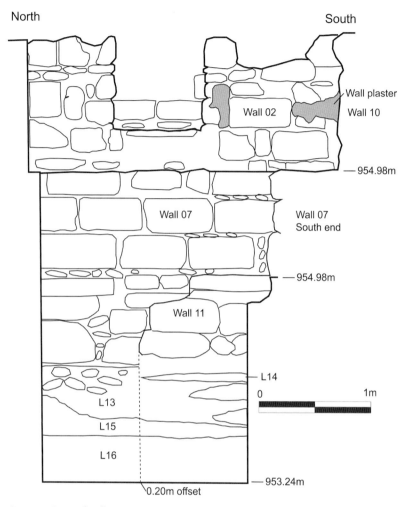

FIG. 6.40 *Room G, Room G, east baulk.*

on top of decayed mudbrick, indicating that the structure had begun to decay before the doorway was blocked. The fill in the east door contained, among other mixed cultural material, one of the few EN coins found at the site so far, a bronze coin of either Aretas II or III (pp. 427, no. 64), a residual survival into this late context. The pattern of fill in the south doorway (Locus 10.1) was the same. The east door contained a large sill block (elev. 956.26 m) set 0.03 m above the level of the floor, and between the doorjambs there was an outer threshold (H 0.25 m) stepping up into Room H (fig. 6.41). One L-shaped doorjamb block survived on the south, oriented so the door opened inward towards Room G. Given the pattern in the other rooms of the complex, this orientation suggests that the east door is the original outside entrance

to Room G and the two rooms connected with it (Rooms A and B). This conclusion is reinforced by the absence of a high threshold in the south doorway; Pavement 04 continues right into the door opening, and both the north (elev. 956.18 m) and south (elev. 956.17 m) sills have the same elevation. An intact Byzantine lamp was recovered from the sand fill just under the blocking in the east doorway (fig. 6.42.1), but it predates the deposition of the fill, since Locus 02 contains material up to the Abbasid period.

The east portion of Pavement 04 (W ca. 1.5 m) between the fallen arch and Wall 09 was removed to allow a deep probe beneath it (figs. 6.39–40, 6.43). The floor was laid on a very thick layer (Locus 05, elev. 956.11 m to 954.78 m) of loose, reddish-brown sand with cobbles and a few pieces of stone

Fig. 6.41   *Room G, east door, and Wall 07.*

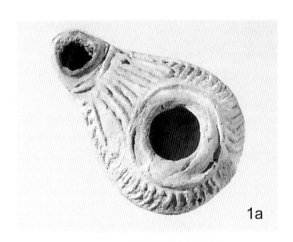

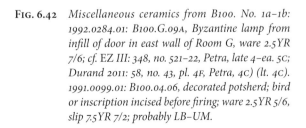

Fig. 6.42   *Miscellaneous ceramics from B100. No. 1a–1b:*
1992.0284.01: B100.G.09A, Byzantine lamp from
infill of door in east wall of Room G, ware 2.5YR
7/6; cf. EZ III: 348, no. 521–22, Petra, late 4–ea. 5C;
Durand 2011: 58, no. 43, pl. 4F, Petra, 4C) (lt. 4C).
1991.0099.01: B100.04.06, decorated potsherd; bird
or inscription incised before firing; ware 2.5YR 5/6,
slip 7.5YR 7/2; probably LB–UM.

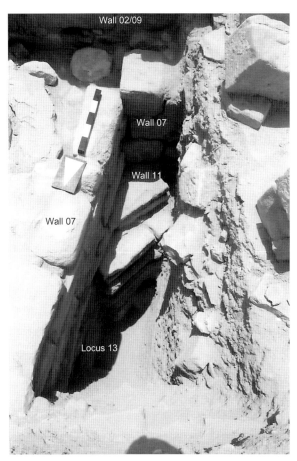

FIG. 6.43 *Room G probe, with Walls 07 and 11.*

The top 0.20 m of this fill was removed, yielding fragments of glass, bone, copper, and marble, an illegible bronze coin (p. 427, no. 65), and a few MN and possibly LN sherds. Below the south wall of Room G, Wall 07 makes a 103-degree turn to the west, 2.12 m south of its appearance in the north baulk. Both the east and south walls of Room G rest directly on Wall 07 or its packing, the change in orientation and in building styles making the transition obvious.

A stepped foundation (Locus 11) was built across this corner, bonding with both segments; the top step was one course high (elev. 954.81–954.98 m), the lower step two courses high (elev. 954.30–945.81 m) (fig. 6.43). This stepped feature rested on the same cobble foundation as the rest of the wall (elev. 954.30 m). At a level even with the top surface of the bottom step, the consistency of the surrounding fill of reddish-brown sand (Locus 12, elev. 954.78 m) became firmer, with fewer stones. Although there was no apparent difference in the sand itself, the upper levels of Locus 12 contained only LB ceramics, the lower levels strictly MN and LN ceramics, along with a few scraps of copper alloy, a fragment of a Ma'an limestone architectural moulding, and fragments of bones and seashells. The loci below (Loci 13, 15, 16) contained only EN, MN, LN, and ER ceramics and should belong to Phase I of the B100 complex.

The fill around and below the foundations (Locus 13, elev. 954.30–953.96 m) consisted of a very loose, red-brown sand containing lenses of pebbles, firm sand, and silt, apparently water-deposited. This deposit rested on a slightly firmer layer (Locus 15, elev. 953.96–953.66 m) of the same material. The pebble layers in both loci contained large quantities of fragmentary ceramics (EN, MN, LN) dating from the first to third and possibly fourth centuries, indicating that this is a Phase I deposit, probably wash from occupation areas farther up the hill. Locus 15 lay on a deposit of very fine, hard silt containing a small number of MN sherds (Locus 16, elev. 953.66 m). Excavation ceased at 953.24 m. This layer of water-deposited silt corresponds to Locus 29 (elev. 953.63 m) in Room E, into which the Phase I tombs were cut. The identification of the Phase II structure revealed in this probe is discussed below.

tumble. This fill contained a very uniform mix of rubbish: iron nails, copper clippings, fragments of glass vessels, a few corroded coins (illegible after cleaning), two fragments of architectural mouldings (pp. 500–501, no. 18), and a few bones. The ceramics dated EN, MN, LN, ER, LB, UM, AB. The lack of any visible layering suggests that this fill was brought in intentionally to level the site.

This fill lay above and around another wall (Wall 07, W >1.0 m, elev. 955.88 m, bearing 346 degrees), carefully built of large sandstone blocks chinked with cobbles down to the foundation courses (top elev. 954.98 m), which were built of less regular blocks and rubble (fig. 6.40). The foundation rested on a packing of cobbles in clay (elev. 954.30–954.05 m). Behind this facing, the wall was filled (or topped) with cobble-sized stones and compacted sand (Locus 08, elev. 955.88 m).

Room A

Room A (2.90 m N–S by 3.31 m E–W) lies south of the structure of the Apse and the western half of Room G; its location and orientation clearly were determined by the Phase II wall at the head of the south aisle of the Church and the outside face of the south wall framing the Apse. The north and west walls were visible before excavation began, and removal of the tumbled blocks and rubble above and inside the room (Loci 00, 02) revealed all four generally well-preserved walls (fig. 6.37). There was a small amount of sherd material in these loci (MN, LN, ER?, MB, LB, UM, AB). The northern wall (Wall 02, L 3.55 m, Th 0.86 m, bearing 70/250) was carefully built of large, reused Nabataean blocks. It bonds with the west wall (Wall 04, L 4.40 m, Th 0.87 m, bearing 150/330 degrees), which resembles it in materials and design. Although the south wall (Wall 03, L 8.60 m, Th 0.48–0.57 m, bearing approximately 60/240) bonds with the west wall, it is thinner and more poorly built, using smaller, less regular blocks of sandstone and marl with less interior packing. The east wall is formed by the party wall shared with Room B (Wall 01, L 4.05 m, Th ca. 0.70–0.81 m, bearing 173/343 degrees), which is approximately 0.70–0.82 m thick and abuts the south wall of Room G. A doorway (W 0.60 m, elev. 956.17 m) in the northeast corner of the room provided access to Room G; it was blocked up with a rubble wall at the end of Phase IIIB, leaving a recess 0.39 m deep. There is an arch impost (W 0.55 m, top elev. 955.83 m) roughly built of sandstone blocks, 0.45 m west of the door. A corresponding impost was found on the south (W 0.53 m).

Clearing of Locus 02 exposed a stratum (Locus 03, elev. 956.22 m) of very fine and soft, light brown loessal soil, containing a few small pieces of rubble and a modest amount of ceramic material (MN?, LN, LB, UM). Excavation of this stratum to 955.94 m exposed a bin (Locus 04, 1.30 × 0.90 m) in the northeast corner, below the door, built of small pieces of rubble arranged in a curve from the arch impost pier to the east wall (fig. 6.37). The soil in Locus 03 appears to have been deposited by wind and water during a period of abandonment. The elevation of the upper edge of the bin is essentially the same as the threshold to the door and the floor

in Room G, suggesting some sort of levelling for the later stage of use. A small amount of ceramic material was recovered (MN?, LN, LB, UM). The fill inside the bin (Locus 05) was identical to the soil of Locus 03, except slightly looser. Its removal to 955.52 m revealed that the wall of the bin was only two courses high (H 0.34) its base (elev. 955.86 m) at the same elevation as the base of the arch pier. It contained several stone blocks, one of which may have served as an earlier step (elev. 956.02 m) to the door, and MN, LN, LB, UM, AB ceramics. A second door (W 0.65, elev. 955.95 m) at the southeast corner of the room provided access to Room B, until it too was walled up.

Room B

The north (Wall 02) and west (Wall 01) walls of Room B were visible before excavation in this area began, and removal of the surface rubble (Locus 00) quickly revealed the presence of the south (Wall 03) and east (Wall 04, L 4.25 m, W 0.56 m) walls, which defined a slightly irregular square room, (3.10–3.17 m N–S, 3.30–3.33 m E–W) (figs. 6.3, 6.37). Walls 01 and 02 do not bond at the northwest corner of the room, but walls 02, 04, and 03 do bond at the northeast and southeast corners. All four walls are constructed in the same general manner, the inside and outside faces built of reused blocks and partly trimmed boulders, the interior filled with cobbles and earth. Walls 03 and 04 are 0.57 m thick, while Wall 01 is 0.81 m thick.

As is typical of B100, the surface Locus (Locus 00, elev. 956.80 m) was composed mostly of fallen blocks and rubble, surrounded by a small amount of loose, ashy soil, and numerous potsherds (MN, RO, LB, UM, AB) (figs. 6.44–45). Below was a layer of tumbled blocks set in a reddish sandy soil (Locus 03, elev. 956.69 m) containing LB, UM, and AB ceramics. Only a few blocks were found in the stratum below (Locus 05, elev. 956.44–956.31 m), composed for the most part of a reddish-brown sandy soil containing small fragments of glass vessels, steatite cooking pots, an occasional iron nail, and MN, LB, and AB ceramics. The entire room was cleared to the level of the top of Locus 06 (elev. ca. 956.28 m), and the remaining loci were excavated only in a 1.5 m wide sounding along the north wall.

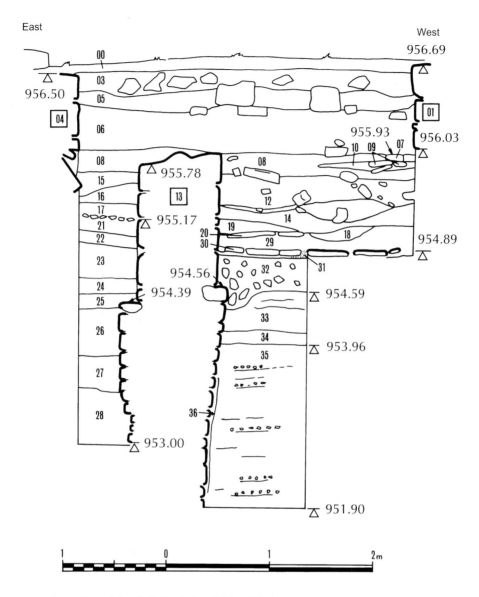

Fig. 6.44 *Room B, south baulk (P. Denholm, C. Mundigler).*

Locus 06 consisted of a hard mix of crumbled clay lumps with straw temper, lime and carbon bits, and reddish-brown sand, lying on a spotty clay floor level with a plastered stone and brick step (Locus 07, elev. 955.93 m). Although there were no obvious floor levels within Locus 06, it contained a wide assortment of refuse, including numerous fragments of animal bones, glass vessels, iron, steatite cooking pots, and carbonized twigs, along with MN, LN, RO, LB, UM, AB, possibly FA ceramics. The clay may be the result of the decay of mudbrick, or clay roofing or wall plaster. A couple of low, plastered steps project from the south baulk 0.30 m into the room. The surface of hard, white plaster is smoothed on to the east face of wall 01 and conceals the hard red tiles and sandstone slabs out of which the steps were built. Wall 01 on the west survives to more or less the same level (elev. descending from 956.49 m at the northwest corner of the room to.955.80 m at the south face of the sounding, 1.0 m farther south), and Wall 04 on the east tops out approximately 0.50 m lower (elev. ca. 955.97 m).

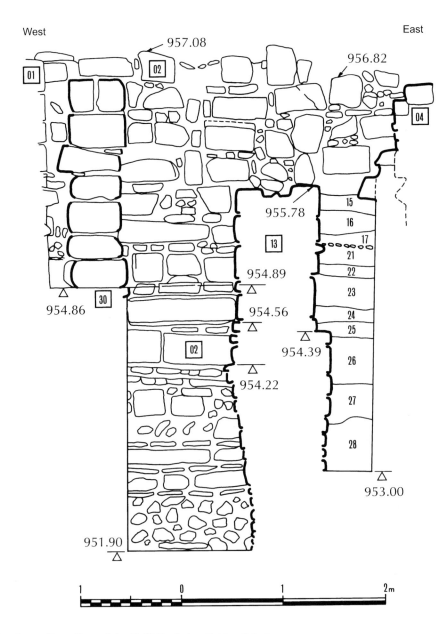

FIG. 6.45   *Room B, north baulk (P. Denholm, C. Mundigler).*

Floor 07 lay on a layer of fine, moderately loose, sandy loess, containing many specks of carbon and a few small stones, along with fragments of glass, iron, and bone and MN, ER?, LB, UM, and AB ceramics (Locus 08, elev. 955.93 m). Excavation of this locus exposed the ragged top of Wall 13 (elev. 955.78 m, Th 0.82 m, bearing 155/335 degrees), solidly built of large blocks of sandstone with mortared seams and a mortared rubble core. This wall, the foundation of which lies below 953.00

m, belongs to Phase II. Locus 08 also contained a lens of ash (Locus 10, elev. 955.90 m) extending out 0.15 m from the Locus 06 steps.

Above this point, Wall 02, forming the north side of the trench, was poorly built out of reused sandstone and limestone blocks and rubble with a rubble core. Below an elevation of approximately 955.50 m, however, the structure is solid, built of large, well-cut sandstone blocks set in mortar, with occasional levelling courses of thin slabs (figs. 6.45,

FIG. 6.46 *Northwest corner of Room B.*

6.46). Wall 13 bonds with this lower portion of Wall 02 at an approximate 90-degree angle, and both walls share the same foundation offset and packing. This lower portion of Wall 02 does not extend beyond Wall 13 on the east.

Below the top of Wall 13, the strata east and west of the wall were given separate locus numbers, although for the most part they seem to be the same deposit. West of the wall, sandy, very fine light brown loess containing a few cobbles and blocks and bits of charcoal, extends from just below the top of the wall to a pavement (Locus 20, elev. 955.18 m; fig. 6.44, 6.47). Two loci were distinguished for purposes of excavation, but they seem to belong to the same deposit: Locus 12 (elev. 955.73–955.51 m) and Locus 14 (elev. 955.51–955.26 m). They contained fragments of copper, steatite vessels, lead, glass, bones, plaster, and MN, LB, UM, and AB ceramics, along with a complete Late Byzantine lamp (figs. 6.48–49).

Locus 20 was an uneven, poorly laid pavement (elev. 955.18 m) built with a few large, approximately rectangular sandstone pavers chinked with a few smaller flat stones set in clay, that extended 1.5 m west of the wall. A lens of decayed mudbrick on the floor adjacent to the wall (Locus 19) contained only LB pottery. The west end of the floor had been pulled up and left in a pile along the edge of a pit (Locus 18, L 0.43, W 0.32, elev. 955.26–955.10 m) filled with soft, ashy loess, along with bones and sherds of LB and possibly UM cooking wares. Pavement 20 sealed off a stratum of very loose, sandy loess (Locus 29, elev. 954.98–954.86 m) mixed with ash, cobbles, occasional lenses of clay and plaster, and a great deal of rubbish: numerous potsherds (MN, LN, MB, LB, and possibly UM), scraps of glass, iron, bronze, and lead, a bronze statuette base (p. 439, no. 23), bronze buckle, some small lumps of sulphur (D 5–15 mm), bones, and ash. Unfortunately, only one of the 16 coins was legible after cleaning (p. 426, no. 37, Constantius II), but their general dimensions suggest an EB date. This deposit has the appearance of an intentional dump, probably thrown in during a period

FIG. 6.47   *Room B, soundings on either side of Wall 13.*

of neglect rather than as fill brought in to raise the floor. The pavement below it (Locus 30, elev. 954.86–954.80 m) is of much better quality, and not much lower in elevation.

Pavement 30 was carefully levelled and well-built with sandstone slabs, re-used sandstone blocks, and a piece of alabaster revetment, extending out from Wall 13 into the baulk. The base of the north pier for the N–S arch spanning the room rested on this pavement, which was the lowest preserved pavement in the room (figs. 6.45–47). Below it was a thin deposit of yellow brown loess (Locus 31, elev. 954.85 m) containing a few fragments of glass, an unreadable bronze coin, and some LB ceramics. The ashlar blocks facing the west side of Wall 13 and south side of Wall 02 terminate above a foundation offset (W ca. 0.10 m) at 954.56 m, in association with a loose fill composed for the most part of cobbles with some yellow-brown loessal soil (Locus 32, elev. 954.75–954.59 m) (fig. 6.44). This deposit clearly was intended to serve as levelling for Pavement 30. Locus 32 contained fragments of glass,

bone, an unreadable coin, and MN, LN, RO, and LB ceramics. Below the offset, the foundation of the wall consisted of unshaped sandstone and limestone rubble and cobbles laid in a very hard red-brown clay that puddled on the exterior (Locus 36). This packing, containing LN, LB, and MB ceramics, had been set in a foundation trench 1.0 m wide and more than 2.66 m deep. At the level of the east and west foundation offsets on Wall 13, the wall is 1.04 m wide; following the profile of the trench, the packing gradually tapers to 0.70 m across. Excavation had to be abandoned at a level of 951.90 m without reaching the bottom of this very deep foundation, because of the lack of working space.

The strata into which the foundation had been cut (Locus 33, elev. 954.59 m; Locus 34, 954.22 m; and Locus 35, 953.82 m) extend directly up to the face of the foundation. Locus 33 and 34 consisted of dark red-brown sand with a significant component of clay and probably represent a single deposit. Locus 33 contained a few small fragments of MN, LN, MB, and possibly LB ceramics, along with a small amount of bone and mortar. Locus 34 contained some of the earliest ceramics so far identified at Humayma, Early Nabataean cup fragments of the first century BC, but in combination with MN, LN, and MB wares. Locus 35, extending from 953.96 m to the bottom of the trench at 951.90 m, was sterile. It consisted of a series of very hard, water-deposited layers of clay, sand, and pebbles, into which the foundation trench for the wall had been dug. This same stratum was identified in Room G (Locus 16, elev. 953.66 m), and Room E (Locus 29, elev. 953.63 m).

The sequence of strata on the east side of Wall 13, outside the room framed by it and Wall 02, was

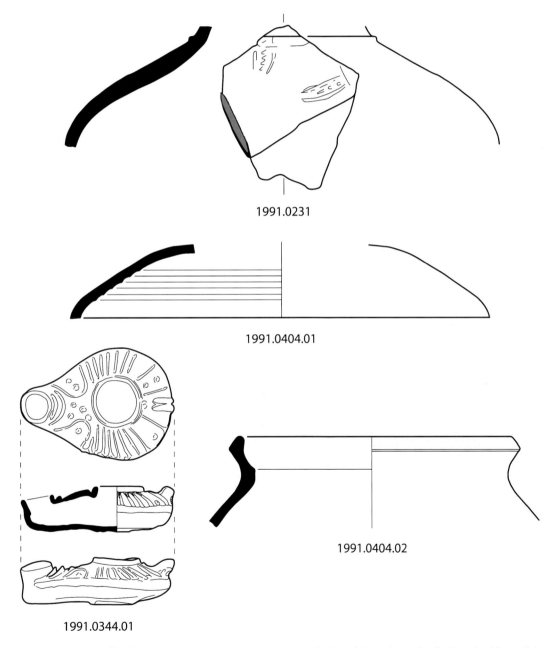

1991.0231

1991.0404.01

1991.0344.01

1991.0404.02

FIG. 6.48 *Ceramic Profiles from Room B, Loci 00, 14, 29. 1991.0231 (scale 1:3): B100.B.00, sherd of jar shoulder with incised decoration (UM–AB?). 1991.0404.01: B100.B.29, casserole lid (MB). 1991.0344.01: B100.B.14, moulded lamp, 2.5YR 7/6 (Petra, EZ III: no. 508, 4–6C) (4–6C). 1991.0404.02: B100.B.29, jar rim.*

essentially the same (figs. 6.44–47). Loci 15, 16, 17, 21, and 22 consisted of poorly distinguished layers of light brown loess, red sand, and lenses of clay, pebbles, and cobbles, containing a few potsherds (MN, LN, ER, LR?, EB, LB, UM, AB) and small scraps of copper, iron, glass, and bone. Locus 23 (elev. 954.93 m) was a thick layer of clay, mud plaster, and decayed mudbrick, possibly the result of the decay of the structure. It contained a small amount of MN and possibly MB ceramics. The

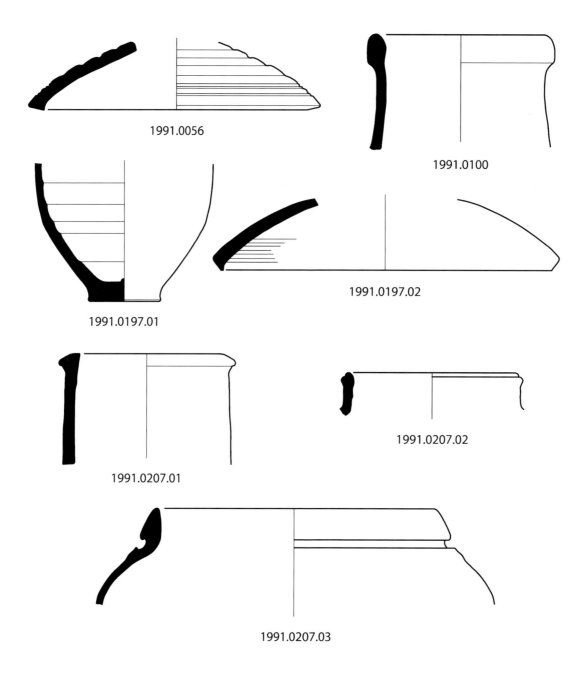

FIG. 6.49   *Ceramic Profiles from Room B, Loci 03, 06, 14, 15. 1991.0056 (scale 1:3): B100.B.03, casserole pot lid (LB–UM). 1991.0100: B100.B.06, jar rim. 1991.0197.01: B100.B.14, NFW string-cut juglet base (1–2C). 1991.0197.02: B100.B.14, casserole lid (MB–LB). 1991.0207.01: B100.B.15, jar rim (MB?). 1991.0207.02: cook pot rim (Petra, EZ I: fig. 731, last quarter 4–ea. 5C). 1991.0207.03: jar rim (Petra, EZ I: fig. 760, no. 33, 300–363) (4C).*

FIG. 6.50 *Room B, foundation offset on east side of Wall 13 (top of Locus 26). North is to the left.*

foundation offset on the east was slightly lower than on the west, at 954.39 m (fig. 6.50), and was surrounded by red-brown sand (Locus 24, elev. 954.61 m; Locus 25, elev. 954.46 m) containing flecks of carbon, scraps of glass and bone, and MN, LN, RO, UM, and AB ceramics. Below the offset, to the top of sterile soil at 953.74 m, the foundation had been dug into a stratum of loose red-brown sand containing scraps of glass and bone, and numerous potsherds (MN, LN, ER, RO?, LB). The original ground level at this point was 0.22 m lower than on the west side of the wall.

Room C

Several ramshackle walls were visible on the surface south of Rooms A and B, but only Room C could be defined, and only the lowest courses of its walls survived (fig. 6.51). It is bounded on the north by the south wall of Room B (Wall 03), and on the east and west by spur walls (W 0.66 to 0.72 m, elev. 956.76–956.08 m) that abut the south face

of this wall just to the west of its intersection with Walls 01 and 04 of Room B: west wall L 3.11 m, W 0.50 m, bearing 150/330 degrees; east wall L 3.10 m, W 0.66 m, bearing 160/340 degrees. Only the very bottom courses of the south wall (L 2.48 m, W 0.73 m, bearing 60/240 degrees) survive, but a single doorjamb block at the east end of the wall shows that there was a door (W ca. 0.70 m, sill elev. 956.13 m) in the southeast corner of the room. All these walls were very poorly built of reused blocks, unshaped boulders, and cobbles, set in mud. Removal of 0.20–0.30 m of loose surface fill (Locus 00) to a level of 956.05 m did not reveal any paving or packed earth floor.

To the southeast of Room C there are badly damaged traces of a wall (05, L 5.40 m, W ca. 0.80–0.87 m, bearing ca. 160/340 degrees, elev. 956.43 m). The top of the wall is at 956.43 m, and its width varies from 0.80 to 0.87 m. It was constructed of boulders and un-mortared, mixed sandstone and marl rubble, but was too disturbed to justify excavation.

FIG. 6.51　*Room C, from the south.*

FIG. 6.52　*East end of B100 Complex, from the north. Reservoir 67 is in the background.*

Rooms H and I

The structures on the east slope of the B100 mound were poorly preserved, in part because of their poor construction, but also because of exposure to run-off water from the north that from time to time follows a natural hollow along the east side of the mound (figs. 6.1–3, 6.52). In addition, this slope is adjacent to the path herds of goats and sheep often follow on their way to Reservoir 67, cleared out for re-use in the 1960s. Clearing of the very dusty surface soil across the east slope revealed a possible courtyard (Room I, L 9.50, W 6.0) formed by Spur Wall 06 (L 5.0, W 0.70, bearing 63/243 degrees) extending east from the east wall of Room B and the L-shaped Wall 01 (L 9.50 m, W ca. 0.90 m, bearing ca. 120/300 degrees; return, L 7.0 m, W 0.53–0.68 m, bearing ca. 80/260 degrees) that joined the east wall of Room G on the north. The walls are irregular in plan and direction, constructed of reused blocks and rubble set in dirt.

A door or gate (W 0.70 m) is formed by the south end of Wall 01 and east end of Wall 06. There are traces of another, possibly later wall just outside the gate. Removal of the surface soil (Locus 00) in a probe laid out over the opening revealed a compact surface of soil packed with pebbles (Locus 08, elev. 955.74–955.60 m) on which Walls 06 and 01 were built. There was a shallow circular depression (Locus 09, D 0.45 m, depth 0.06, elev. 955.74 m) 2.4 m inside the gate, filled with yellowish clay that retained impressions of plant materials. The upper surface of this material was concave, as if it was intended to support and brace a heavy object, perhaps a stone mortar like that found in Field F102 (fig. 5.44). Excavation of a portion of Locus 08 yielded many LN, MN, LB, UM, AB sherds (including one blue-green glazed late AB sherd), fragments of steatite cooking vessels and a moulding (p. 501, no. 19), and fragments of bone. Below was a stratum of loose, grey-brown sand (Locus 13, elev. 955.64 m) containing many pebbles and small stones, scraps of iron, copper, glass, and bone, numerous potsherds (MN, RO, LB, UM, AB?), and a small stone betyl or chess piece (pp. 503–4, no. 3). This stratum overlay a layer of coarse sand (Locus 14, elev. 955.09 m) with lenses and thin layers of gravel, probably water-deposited,

and containing MN, LB, and possibly UM ceramics. A very hard, apparently sterile sand and gravel layer (Locus 15) was reached at 955.05 m, possibly the pre-disturbance ground level, although only 0.12 m could be excavated. This same sequence was found on the south side of Wall 06.

The clearing of a large heap of tumbled sandstone blocks east of Room G revealed the badly damaged walls of a small room (Room H, N–S 3.50–3.69 m, E–W 2.16–2.23 m) built on to the east wall of Room G (figs. 6.1–3, 6.52). The side walls of Room H (W 0.50–0.53 m) abut the east wall of Room G. All the walls were badly built of re-used blocks and rubble set in dirt. Traces of a threshold block (elev. 956.21 m) and a northern doorjamb block were found in the centre of the east wall, approximately on line with the door in the east wall of Room G (elev. 956.44 m). The interior of this room was not excavated.

Room J

The situation at the northeast corner of the B100 complex is very confused, because the walls were poorly built and have been badly disturbed. Nevertheless, there seems to have been a small room (Room J, ca. 2.0 m N–S, 1.75 m E–W) at the north edge of the structure, entered by a narrow door (W 0.53 m) through the north wall of Room I, near its west end (figs. 6.3, 6.52). The doorway was well-delineated by large, carefully cut stones that bonded with both faces of the wall. The interior of the doorway had been blocked with courses of small stones, above a stone doorsill (elev. 955.77 m) and corresponding, compacted earth floor. The north wall (Wall 02, elev. 956.28 m) of Room J has a distinct curve, but its course and termination have been disturbed. At least in part it is founded on what appears to be a projecting square platform (Locus 03, elev. 955.93 m) of cobbles faced by larger and more carefully squared rubble and blocks, founded on an indistinct surface (Locus 05, elev. 955.45 m) of sand and rubble. In fact, this poorly made and collapsing curved wall may be a windbreak or other unrelated addition constructed in Phase V, and Feature 03 may have been the north and east wall of Room J. This interpretation is better in tune with the rectilinear design of the rest of the complex.

The deposits around all these walls were soft, ashy, and filled with roots and animal burrows. Most of the ceramics found in the fill around these walls were MN, LB, UM, and AB coarse ware vessels, and there was also an interesting concentration of fragments of decorated steatite cooking vessels of the Abbasid period displaying burn marks on the exterior. Several pieces of marble chancel screen were recovered, and a carved bone toothpick or pin (p. 445, no. 8). A fragment of marl water conduit had been reused as the pivot block for a door.

6.C. ANALYSIS OF STRUCTURAL HISTORY AND FUNCTION

6.C.1. *Phasing, Reconstruction, and Function*

*Phase I. Nabataean to Roman,
        first to third centuries*

Only a very small area of the Phase I development of the B100 site was exposed, and the excavation raised more questions than it answered. One or possibly two Nabataean cist graves were found, their cover slabs 1.35 m below the top of the pavement inside the later Byzantine Church. Neither grave could be completely exposed, but the Locus 37 cist (interior dimensions L 2.50 m, W 0.47 m, H 0.40 m) was constructed of neatly cut slabs of white sandstone lining the sides of a trench cut into the hard soil. The tomb was aligned at more or less the same orientation as the later Church (60/240 degrees), but this is not surprising given the tendency to orient both Nabataean tombs and Byzantine churches to the east. The floor of the cist was earth. Further slabs were laid across the cist to cover it, and a cross-shaped feature was built above, perhaps to serve as a marker, although it may have been concealed below the level of the original backfill. This backfill contained Middle and Late Nabataean ceramics and a first-century Nabataean coin, probably of Aretas IV. A second excavation for a cist could be seen in the baulk to the north, but it appeared to be empty.

The burial found in Square 01 presents some interesting problems. It is probably Late Nabataean in date, rather than Late Byzantine, so it cannot be associated with the Church. Burials do occur in habitation areas at Petra (e.g., at the North Ridge area), but segregation seems the normal practice. It is also possible that a Nabataean temple or sanctuary were located at B100, close to the reservoirs on which the settlement depended, and that these structures attracted burials. The numerous fragments of Nabataean architectural elements, a betyl, and an altar block found reused in the later B100 structures might have originated in a Nabataean temple at this location. The pier of the Byzantine Church located in Square 01 Probe 01 rested on a pavement of neat stone slabs that may belong to a Phase I structure. This paving was laid on sterile silt at an elevation of 953.18 m, close to the elevation of the slabs above the cist grave (952.81 m). Elsewhere in B100, the hard layer of red sand, clay and pebbles below the Apse, into which the cist graves had been cut (Locus 29, elev. 953.63 m), was observed in the probes below Room G (Locus 18, elev. 953.66 m) and Room B (Locus 36, elev. 953.96 m).

Tombs have been found in the vicinity of the Nabataean temples at Khirbet edh-Dharih (Lenoble et al. 2001) and Wadi Ramm (Perry and Jones 2008). Middle Nabataean cist tombs of the type found below the Apse in B100 have been found at Mampsis (Negev 1971), Khirbet edh-Dharih (Lenoble et al. 2001; Delhopital et al. 2009), but as far as I am aware, the distinctive grave marker does not have parallels elsewhere. Khirbet edh-Dharih provides an example of the construction of a church with apse inside a Nabataean temple (Villeneuve 2011: 323–25), although much of the temple structure survived there, whereas it has disappeared or not yet been traced at Humayma. The transition from Nabataean sanctuary to Christian church and monastery, designed to subvert the pagan worship, has been well-documented at Jabal Harûn near Petra (Fiema 2012).

Phase II. Byzantine, fifth to sixth centuries

The major structural event in B100 was the building of a large Church in the fifth or sixth century. The Church, oriented approximately ENE (60/240 degrees) had a central nave and two side aisles separated by block-built piers, and a single Apse (D 4.20 m) set into a block of masonry projecting

1.9 m from the east wall of the Church (fig. 6.4). Clearing of the Apse and its flooring in Phase III removed any evidence there might have been for a *synthronon*. The floor was paved with neat slabs of sandstone, and a large chancel was raised up on two steps. A marble chancel screen was mounted in the gutter groove of Nabataean marl conduit blocks set back on the top step. These features are all found in the F102 Church as well. Traces of hard white plaster remained on some of the surviving wall surfaces. No signs of *pastophoria* survived, but it is possible that such features may lie hidden beneath Room D and Room O. The structure of the Church was 12.75 m wide (outside dimensions) and at least 19 m long. Four piers that supported the clerestory and roof were identified, the easternmost pair 4.43 m west of the wall framing the Apse, forming a central aisle that was 4.86 m wide. The second pair of piers was found built into Wall 03, which appears to close off the west end of the Church but in fact is later. There should be a third, intermediate pair of piers beneath the east wall of Room N and south of it in the Phase IIIA eastern courtyard (see p. 218). The piers in Wall 03 do not bond with the wall structure, and the paving of the aisles continues under it, so the original west wall of the Church must lie farther west. In addition, there is no trace of any central entrance door through Wall 03 into the Church. Unfortunately, several probes west of Wall 03 failed to discover any convincing original west wall. It remains possible that the west wall of the Church lies beneath the west wall of the over all B100 complex, and that the entrance to the Church was in the south wall of the nave.

It is tempting to suggest that the later walls of the west extension of the B100 complex were built on top of the walls of an atrium in front of the Church, explaining the greater width from north to south. Atria are seen, for example, in front of Church of the Blessed Virgin (Fiema et al. 2001: 42, fig. 50) and the Ridge Church at Petra (Bikai 1996), and in the later phases of the Jabal Harûn Church (Fiema and Frösén 2008: 424, fig. 1). Michel (2001: 17–20) provides a complete list and discussion of church atria in Jordan. For reasons discussed above, however, the east wall of this courtyard cannot have formed the west wall of the Nave. If the west

wall of the Church lies beneath the west wall or somewhere within the west extension, however, the question arises of why the extension is wider than the eastern half of the Nave. This problem can only be resolved by further excavation.

Questions still remain as well concerning the character of the structures that formed the core of the mound at the east end of the B100 complex. Probes in Room B in 1991 and in Room G in 1992 revealed the presence of very substantial walls deep below the surface, possibly Byzantine in date, but with foundations extending deep into Nabataean levels. The function of the structures to which these walls belonged is still to be determined, but they may have belonged to ancillary buildings such as those found attached to the C101 and F102 Churches, and to many of the other Byzantine church complexes in the region (Michel 2001: 49–50).

Any evidence for the abandonment or destruction of the Church at some point in the seventh century has been compromised by its re-use in the Umayyad period, but some conjectures are possible. The floor was re-laid sometime at the beginning of the Islamic period, and the Church remained in use for an unknown period of time until its abandonment, possibly associated with destruction by fire. The earthen floor in Room N rested on two thin layers of ash and plaster fragments (Loci 13, 14) and a fine, tan sand (Locus 15) that covered the flagstone pavement of the Church (Locus 16). The sand may have been deposited by the wind during a period of abandonment, Loci 13–14 by a destructive fire that followed, probably some time in the seventh century. The abandonment of churches became more common in this region only after 700, so if the B100 church was already out of use in the seventh century, it is outside the norm (Michel 2011: 244–45).

Phase IIIA. Umayyad, seventh century

Rubbish was dumped or accumulated in the ruins of the Church during the Umayyad period, but at some point in the later seventh or early eighth century this fill was levelled off, partition walls built, and a few stretches of paving installed to allow domestic occupation of the structure. Wall

03 probably was constructed at this time, closing off the west end of a courtyard but allowing entry through a door at its south end. Room N and Room F, approximately the same dimensions, were built up against the north wall of the Church, or against an upward extension built on the original Church wall. No evidence was recovered for rooms along the south wall of the courtyard (fig. 6.3).

Spur walls built up against the outside face of the Apse defined Room E within the Apse, along with spaces to the north and south that we have termed Rooms O and D. The roof over the Apse was carried on an arch that sprang from a plinth at the centre of the back wall of the Apse and the centre of the wall closing it off. The roughly square Rooms F and N were roofed with transverse arches. Room O may have been open to the sky, perhaps as a small animal pen. Room D has the appearance of a ramshackle addition, perhaps during Phase IIIB. The doors to Rooms E, F, and N opened inward, and led to steps that descended to beaten earth floors well below the level of the high doorsill.

Although the B100 Phase IIIA complex is larger than any of the early modern structures at the site, with the exception of the enigmatic structure with standing walls just north of the modern schoolhouse, it probably served the same purposes. The small rooms probably served as habitations for one or more related nuclear families, and for storage of agricultural products, foodstuffs, and other property. The courtyard and other nooks would have been suitable shelters for poultry and some of the flocks, and for the storage of tents and farming equipment. Given the proximity of Reservoirs nos. 67 and 68, there was an assured supply of water. Cisterns nos. 70 and 76 were also close by, and one of them may have belonged to the family inhabiting B100. Given the relative comfort of the structure, the adjacent water supply, and the energizing presence of the Abbasid family as owners of the site by the last quarter of the seventh century, the structure may have been inhabited year-round. Like the early modern Bedouin, the proprietors could have sustained themselves with a mix of local and regional pastoralism, local agriculture, the exploitation of travellers, small-scale craft production, and hunting.

Phase IIIB. Early Islamic,
seventh to eighth centuries

The core of the Phase IIIA complex forms a neat, self-contained unit built within the nave and aisles of the Phase II Church. Since the structure west of this core is wider than the Phase IIIA structure and the walls do not bond with it, Rooms L and M and the courtyard they face (14.75 m N–S, 12.5 m E–W) are attributed to a slightly later phase, Phase IIIB. The adjacent Room K belongs to Phase IV. Unfortunately, it is not clear from the archaeological evidence whether the walls and rooms east of the Apse belong to Phase IIIA or IIIB. In consequence, both the west and the east extensions to what we define as the Phase IIIA structure have been assigned to Phase IIIB. The western unit is quite uniform in design and construction and may belong to a single construction period, while the eastern extension has the appearance of a longer period of agglomeration.

At the west end of the complex, Rooms L and M, like Rooms F and N, faced south on to an approximately square courtyard (8.65 m E–W, 9.19 m N–S). They were roofed with transverse arches that probably carried wooden beams, reeds, and a packed mud surface. As in the central courtyard, there is no evidence for rooms along the south wall, a position in which they would have faced the prevailing NW winds and lacked exposure to the winter sun. A door toward the south end of the east wall allowed passage into the eastern court (within the former Nave), and there may have been a wide door with heavy sill blocks at the east end of the south wall of the court. There is no evidence to propose a different function for the west extension of the post-Byzantine B100 complex than that hypothesized for the core of the complex: permanent or semi-permanent habitation combined with pastoral and agricultural activities. The stimulus for the extension may have been expansion in the number of human and/or animal occupants of the complex.

The east end of the complex is more difficult to unravel, but Rooms A, B, and G are defined by substantial, well-constructed walls, and the other rooms seem to have been added on later. Room G (3.95/4.10 m × 4.30/4.50 m) was built up against the outside wall of the Apse, on top of a substantial Phase II wall. A door in the east wall provided entrance from the outside, while a door in the south wall provided stepped access down into Room A/B (L 7.43 m; W 2.9–3.1 m). The position of the impost piers for the transverse arches that supported the roof, the position of the door, and the construction of the wall that separates them reveal that Rooms A and B were originally one long room. The only entrance was through Room G. At some point this space was divided by a partition wall with a door at its south end. Room C was built up against the south wall of Room B at some later stage, and Room H was built up against the east wall of Room G. It seems unnecessary to consider these additions a distinct phase, since they make the most sense as agglomerations on a still active residential complex. Access to Rooms G, A, and B was now provided through Room H. Although the walls were very poorly preserved, and bereft of intact cultural deposits, so-called Room I (ca. 4.5m × 10 m) has the appearance of another courtyard, only slightly smaller than the Phase IIIB courtyard at the west end of the complex. It is likely that the courtyard was constructed prior to the construction of Room H, which may have been built to store agricultural equipment or produce or to isolate Room G from agricultural and pastoral activities in the courtyard. Room J is too badly preserved to allow determination of its purpose, but a doorway in the south wall connected it with the courtyard. The size and location would be appropriate to a storage area, poultry coop, or latrine.

The western Phase IIIB addition resembles the Phase IIIA core structure in its neat rectilinear design and the provision of several rooms along the north wall facing south on to a courtyard. The eastern addition to the complex is organized differently, but it provides the same types of space. It is possible that three related families occupied the three units, and that the growth of the structure reflects the expansion by marriage and birth of a family occupying what must have been a prime location in the Umayyad or Abbasid settlement of Humayma. Our excavation recorded the gradual decay and abandonment of this complex, reflected in the accumulation of blown soil, the walling-up of doors, and the collapse of roofing arches and walls.

The bin that obstructs the blocked door into Room A presumably belongs to this period, along with the adjacent *tabun*. The *tabuns* in Room E should also belong to a period of neglect and abandonment, which presumably began with the departure of the Abbasid family in the mid-eighth century. The blocking of doors and presence of *tabuns* in derelict buildings is paralleled in modern Humayma.

Phase IV. Ottoman, 16th to early 20th centuries

The only structural addition to the B100 complex that can be attributed to a phase later than IIIB is Room K, on the centre line of the complex at its west end. A door was knocked through the centre of the west wall of the west extension to provide access to a small room constructed outside the wall. The walls were carefully built of large blocks facing a core of mud and rubble, but the plan was a trapezoid, forming a room with interior dimensions 1.92/2.04 m E–W and 2.79/3.02 m N–S. The walls were built on top of a rubbish heap of the Early Islamic period, including a large amount of faunal material and fish bones, but a scattering of Ottoman ceramics suggests occupation and most likely construction within that period. The rest of the B100 complex seems to have been in ruins at this time. Room K is too small for intensive occupation, but it may have served a custodian keeping watch over the adjacent reservoirs. Alternatively, a Bedouin family may have constructed it for the storage of property during periods of pastoral activity outside the Humayma area or for the storage of water-lifting equipment.

6.C.2. Planning and Modules

Since the western and eastern pairs of piers in the Nave of the Church are 9.15 m apart (centre to centre), there was most likely another pair of piers midway between them, as noted above. This arrangement would give a centre to centre pier spacing of 4.58 m. The centre to centre spacing across the nave is 5.72 m. Since the easternmost pair of piers, which touch the northwest and southwest corners of the chancel steps, are 4.58 m west of the east wall of the Church (face to face), 4.58 m seems to be a modular dimension. It equals 14.83

Byzantine feet of 30.89 cm, so the module was very likely 15 such feet (fig. 6.4). The Byzantine foot of 0.3089 m has been documented in use at a number of churches in Syria (Milson 2003), and it was used with margins of error well under one percent in the Church of the Blessed Virgin at Petra (Fiema et al. 2001: 163–64). The same foot was used to plan the C101 Church at Hauarra (ca. 60 × 40 feet), and the F102 Church (nave ca. 60 × 30 feet). There are further parallels among these three churches in dimensions and design (see pp. 155–57, 551–53; fig. 15.1).

It is probably not coincidental that the interval to the east wall of Room N also follows the module of 15 feet; the northern member of the missing pair of piers may have been built into it. It is striking that the wall separating Rooms L and M and Wall 01 forming the west end of the complex are also spaced at approximately the same intervals west of the piers in Wall 03. Extension of the Church to the westernmost wall (Wall 01) would result in a structure 24.6 m long (26.5 m including the Apse block) and 12.60 m wide, with four pairs of piers. The dimensions 24.6 × 12.60 m correspond very closely with 80 × 40 Byzantine feet, a very long, narrow plan, but not unprecedented. The F102 Church was also laid out with the length of the nave twice that of the width (30 × 60 ft.). If, however, the west wall of the B100 Church was located approximately below the wall separating Rooms L and M, the length would be around 19.3 m or 60 feet long (actually 62.5 feet). These dimensions of 40 × 60 ft. correspond with those of the nave of the C101 Church, although the latter is a three-apse basilica.

6.C.3. Local and Regional Parallels for the Church

The configuration of the B100 Church, with a single Apse probably projecting beyond the east wall of the Church within a square masonry block, most resembles that of the F102 Church. Although the dimensions of the B100 Church are greater, both these churches have a nave twice as long as it is wide. Regional parallels for the plan are discussed on pp. 157–58. The Church fits into category AI of Qaqish (2007: 192, no. 116, 304). A raised, projecting chancel with a pier at each front corner, and

a marble chancel screen held by upturned marl conduit blocks are details seen in both the B100 and the C101 Churches. It is possible that the roof was gabled (Michel 2001: 38), although only 55 roof tile fragments were found during the excavation. The intact tiles may have been salvaged for reuse elsewhere, but the number of fragments still seems small. The same problem of a paucity of roof tiles occurs at the F102 and C101 Churches, where only 29 and 5 tile fragments were found, respectively (see p. 157).

6.C.4. Local and Regional Parallels for the Early Islamic House

No evidence was recovered for rooms along the south wall of either the eastern or western courtyards, perhaps because this orientation would have exposed the doors to the prevailing northwest wind and would have kept the winter sun from entering the doorways. The traditional, nineteenth-century houses at al-Qasr on the Kerak plateau were also oriented away from the prevailing winter wind (Kana'an and McQuitty 1994: 131). The B100 plan in Phase III resembles that of the "combined cell blocks and courtyards" Helms identifies in several Early Islamic houses at ar-Risha: Structures F, G, and R (1990: 102–7, 123). Haiman (1995: 36, fig. 7) identifies several Early Islamic period farm-houses in the western Negev highlands with a similar plan. The Phase III rooms at the eastern end of the site resemble the Early Islamic settlement built into the sanctuary at Khirbet edh-Dharih (Villeneuve 2011). The rooms at both sites are simple square or rectangular, single story spaces with flat roofs held up by transverse arches that spring from piers built against the side walls. The rooms are linked in compact clusters that developed over a period of time. There are frequent manger bins and platforms. The artefacts were simple, rural in character, and for the most part local; some of the ceramics were imported from Petra and Aila, and the steatite cooking vessels were imported as well, from farther afield. Few coins were found from this period (7–8c) at Humayma or Khirbet edh-Dharih.

It is interesting that sometime after Alt's visit to Humayma in 1935, the Bedouin roofed the Apse of the Byzantine Church B126 in just the same manner as the Umayyad inhabitants roofed the Apse of the B101 Church, with an east–west arch springing from an impost built against its back wall. There are, in fact, numerous parallels of design and materials between the renovations of the Early Islamic period at Humayma and those carried out by the Bedouin during the twentieth century: the re-erection of transverse arches to carry roof rafters; the construction or re-use of doorjambs oriented so the doors open inward, often to steps leading down to a slightly subterranean floor; the construction of recesses in the walls to serve as cupboards; the assembly of upright slabs of stone next to the walls to serve as bins or earth-filled platforms; the walling up of doors to allow rooms to be filled with rubbish or to keep livestock out; and the installation of *tabuns* within rooms, either before or after abandonment. There are many parallels for these details in the early modern houses at Khirbat al-Nawafla ('Amr and Momani 2011: 368), 'Aima (Biewers 1992, 1993) and Khirbat Faris (McQuitty and Falkner 1993).

NOTE

1 Oleson directed excavation in this field with the assistance of E. de Bruijn and D. Dudley in 1991–93, of R. Foote and J. Somogyi in 1992–93, and of James Cook in 1995. Portions of this chapter are based on field reports submitted by de Bruijn, Dudley, and Cook.

Chapter 7

Field C101: Byzantine Church ("Lower Church")

by Robert Schick

7.A. LOCATION AND EXCAVATION HISTORY

The Church in Field C101, located toward the western edge of the ancient occupation centre, was designated the "Lower Church" in 1991 to distinguish it from the C119 "Upper Church" on the slope above, prior to the discovery of the other three churches at the site (fig. 1.1). The Church is a typical three-apse basilica, the interior divided into a wide central nave and narrower north and south aisles by two east–west rows of arches (figs. 7.1–2, 7.4). At the east end of the nave there is a raised chancel and an apse, and the two side aisles also terminate in semicircular apses on their east ends. Doors in the north aisle connect with a Sacristy (Room 2) and large Entrance Hall (Room 4), while several small rooms are built up against the outside of the south wall (fig. 7.3). The Church is the best preserved of the churches at Humayma and was a major focus of excavations in the 1991, 1992 and 1993 seasons, with limited further work being carried out in 1998 and 2009 (Oleson et al. 1993, 1995; *HEP* 1: 59–60; Schick 1995a: 311–13, 1995b: 324–35, 2001).

There had been previous excavation at the C101 Church. In 1962 the Department of Antiquities

under the direction of Muhammad al-Maghribi cleared much of the Church interior, but nothing was ever published about the work, and there is nothing on file at the Department of Antiquities Registration Centre. The work in the 1991 season revealed that the Department of Antiquities personnel in that year had cleared the apse, chancel area, and the north and south aisles down to the flagstone pavement found everywhere in the Church, but had cleared only part of the nave. They had left undisturbed an L-shaped deposit of soil in the east end of the nave and removed tumbled rubble in the rest of the nave, but left the lower deposits in place. They did not work in the rooms adjoining the Church to the north or south, nor did they trace the exterior faces of the walls. In 1983 a small team directed by John Eadie carried out some cleaning in the Church, but he postponed excavation for a future season that never took place (Eadie 1984: 219–20; Eadie and Oleson 1986: 52–53). Eadie's architect produced careful drawings of the structure, but once Oleson took over the permit for the site in 1986, Eadie reported those drawings as lost, along with the negatives of the photographs Oleson had taken in 1983.

After the 1962 clearance that had exposed the flagstone pavements in the north and south aisles

FIG. 7.1   *Aerial view of Field C101, with indication of room designations (W. Meyers, 21 July 1992, neg H-3 no. 3).*

and the chancel area, locals searching for treasure lifted a number of pavers out of position from the east central portion of the south aisle and the east portion of the north aisle, digging out some of the soil below the pavers. This intervention need not have been limited to a single episode. The stones had been lifted prior to 1983, although at least one additional paver with a cross carved on it (over Burial 6) was lifted after 1983.

The 1991 season thus began essentially with an undocumented church structure, with the objectives of quickly cleaning up the interior to enable the documentation of the architectural features, and of excavating a probe below the pavement to produce evidence for the date of construction. Recognition of the importance of the intact deposits in the Nave, however, soon justified a much greater investment of effort into the excavation of the Church than originally intended.

The Nave was excavated as Room 1 during the 1991, 1992, and part of the 1993 seasons. The Sacristy was partially excavated in 1991 and 1992 as Room 2, while a portion of the large north Entrance Hall was excavated in 1992 and 1993 as Room 4. To the south, the southeast room was partially excavated in 1991 and 1992 as Room 3, while the southwest room was completely excavated in 1992 as Room 5. Further rooms to the south were excavated briefly as Square 6 and Rooms 7 and 8 during the 1993 season. While work in the rooms south and east of the Church, as well as in the incompletely excavated Rooms 2, 3 and 4, would certainly have provided additional information about the Church complex, other areas at Humayma had a higher claim to attention in later seasons.

In the 1998 season a few days were spent investigating an illicitly dug burial below the pavement of the north aisle, and in 2009 a few days were spent

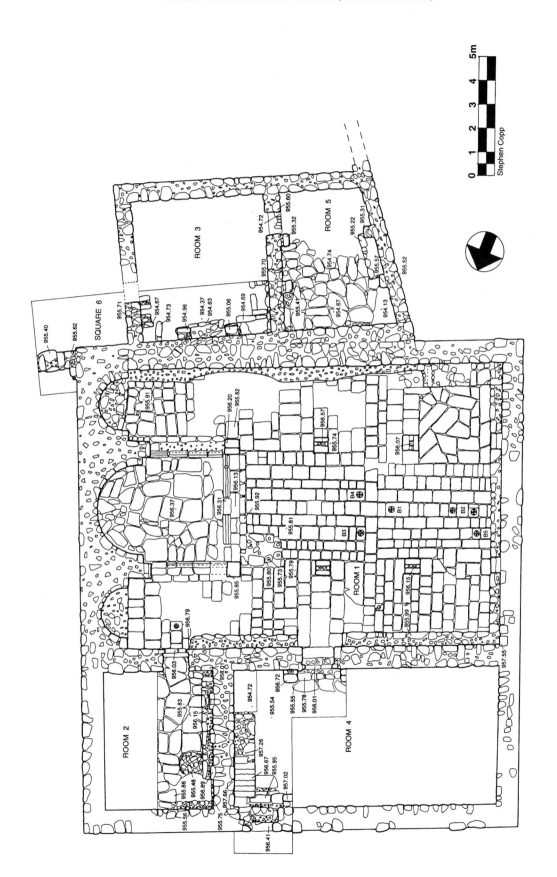

ROOM 3

ROOM 5

SQUARE 6

ROOM 1

ROOM 2

ROOM 4

5m

Stephen Copp

FIG. 7.2   *Stone by stone plan of C101 Church (S. Copp).*

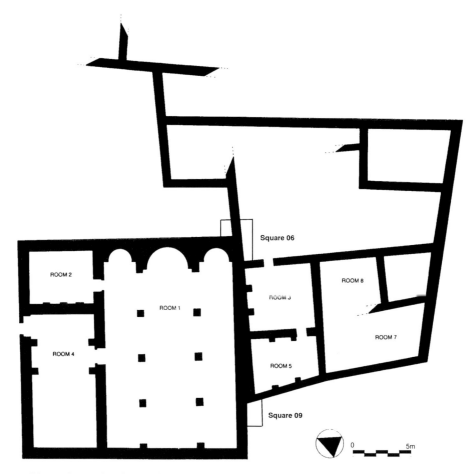

FIG. 7.3   *Wall lines of C101 Church Complex (S. Copp).*

FIG. 7.4   *General view of C101 Church nave in 2009, from southwest.*

FIG. 7.5   *Nave of C101 Church from the East, before consolidation.*

digging three small probes in the north side apse, in Square 06 outside the southeast corner of the Church, and in Square 09 outside the southwest corner of the Church, to resolve some specific stratigraphic questions.

Most of the excavation dumps from the 1962 season and the three 1990s seasons were removed by front-end loader and truck at the end of the 1993 season, although some dump from the 1990s still remains to the southwest of the Church, along with some 1962 dump around Rooms 7 and 8.

Oleson's excavation team carried out consolidation of the walls of the Church in 1996 and 1998, mainly re-pointing the walls and plaster. Sometime around 2005, Department of Antiquities personnel executed further wall consolidation, in the course of which they subtly altered some features of the Church. Specifically, they placed a course of capping stones at the top of the mudbrick benches along the Church walls, they placed flagstones in the side apses, and they replaced many of the stones in the steps up to the chancel on all three sides and in the steps in the southwest corner of the Church (compare figs. 7.4 and 7.7).

7.B. THE CHURCH NAVE AND AISLES (ROOM 1)

7.B.1. Architectural Features

The Church is oriented 20 degrees north of east, with interior dimensions of ca. 17.80 m long east to west and 11.80 m wide north–south. The two rows of east–west arches dividing the side aisles (W 3.20 m) from the Nave (W 5.40 m) were supported by engaged piers against the west and east walls and three pairs of free-standing arch piers (fig. 7.4). Benches made of blocks with rubble fill and capped with mudbricks were built up along the south, west, and north walls. A stairway in the southwest corner of the building led up to a gallery over the south aisle (fig. 7.6). Beneath the stairway is a cupboard. The pavement of the Church (elev. ca. 955.80 m) consists of large flagstones of bluish flaky slate and harder white sandstone, some approximately rectangular, others irregular in shape. At the east end of the nave, the chancel is raised up two steps from the nave and fronts a large semicircular apse, while the two side aisles end in semicircular apses.

FIG. 7.6   *West end of C101 Church from the north, before consolidation.*

FIG. 7.7   *Nave and Chancel of C101 Church from northwest, before consolidation.*

FIG. 7.8   *Chancel and north wall of C101 Church from south, before consolidation.*

There is no clear evidence for more than one building phase anywhere in the Church.

Exterior Walls

The walls of the Church are 1.0 m thick and are preserved to a height of generally under two metres, higher along the north wall than elsewhere. The highest elevation along the north wall near its east end is 957.97 m, while the top elevation in the northwest corner is 957.55 m. The walls are of uniform construction, composed of header and stretcher courses of dressed hard limestone and sandstone blocks facing a core of rubble and soil. The courses are more or less horizontal, although of somewhat variable height, with chinking stones in between. The interior faces of the walls were originally finished with plaster, traces of which survive along the north wall, on the arch piers, and on the apses (fig. 7.8). Traces of colour were observed on some plaster along the north wall

newly exposed during the cleaning in 1983 (Oleson, oral communication).

The exterior wall lines of the Church building were delineated by shallow excavation in the course of the 1991 season, except along the south wall, much of which has always stood clear of the surrounding debris and soil. Excavation along the exterior wall faces exposed no more than approximately a single wall course, except in Squares 6 and 9 at the southeast and southwest corners, respectively. Along the south side of the Church, the north walls of Rooms 3 and 5 run at a slightly different angle from the south wall of the Church. Although of similar construction, it appears that the north walls of the pre-existing Rooms 3 and 5 were sliced through for the construction of the south wall of the Church, without leaving a clear south face for the south wall of the Church, or a clear north face for the north wall of Rooms 3 and 5 (see below pp. 273–77). No traces of windows survive in any of the walls.

Arch Support Piers

Two rows of three freestanding piers between the side aisles and the nave, and corresponding engaged piers against the west and east walls supported two east–west rows of arches (fig. 7.3). The eastern arch pier (Locus 01.15) in the south row abuts the southwest corner of the chancel area. Three courses of dressed marl blocks in header and stretcher construction measuring 0.65 × 0.65 m survive, along with two original layers of plaster, a coarse inner backing layer and a finer outer layer with a smooth surface. A similar but less well-preserved eastern arch pier in the north row (Locus 01.16) abuts the northwest corner of the chancel area (fig. 7.8). Traces of two layers of plaster could be seen on its west face. The four other arch piers in the north and south rows are constructed in a similar fashion. They are preserved to varying heights; the lowest is the west pier of the south row, with an upper elevation of 956.07 m, while the highest is the east pier of the south row, at 956.57 m.

The two arch support piers flanking the central apse are 0.60 m wide and project 0.35 m from the end of the apse curve, with which they bonded. Seven courses of the northeast arch support pier are preserved (H 1.85 m); the bottom course extends below the apse pavement. The southeast pier survives to a height of five courses (H 1.60 m). The two piers abutting the west wall are 0.65 m wide and projected 0.55 m from the wall. They are abutted by the benches along the west wall. Six courses of the northwest pier survive (H 1.25 m from the pavement), five courses of the southwest pier (H 1.35 m).

Roof

The removal of all the tumbled stone deposits from the Church interior in 1962, except for the 6.00 m by 0.50 m deposit in the nave, eliminated the bulk of the evidence for the nature of the Church roof. The ash layers, chunks of charcoal and iron nails found in the undisturbed deposits in the nave, however, are most easily explained as remains of the wooden beams used to construct the roof (see p. 239). No stone slabs were recovered that are long enough to have served as an alternative to wood beams, and the distances to be spanned are in any case too long to have allowed this method with the stone available around Humayma. Most churches had roofs of a standard gabled form with a clerestory, but it has not been possible to determine the specific details of the design in this structure. Only five roof tile fragments were found in the Church. Their absence points to a flat roof, with larger wood beams spanning the east–west arches, along with thatch between the larger wood beams, all covered with compressed soil. Such a roof could be the source of the thin layer of clayey silt found directly in contact with the church pavement (Locus 01.19). No stone roller for compressing the roof was found, however, as in the Petra Church (Fiema et al. 2001: 156, 184–85). Reconstruction of the roof design for this Church, along with those of the B100 and F102 Churches, remains a difficult issue, since ancient representations of churches, for the most part on mosaics, always show them with gabled roofs (Duval 2003b) (see p. 157).

In some other buildings at Hauarra roof tiles appear to have been removed for reuse elsewhere when the structures were abandoned. The administrative structures in the Roman Fort (E116) provide a particularly good example (*HEP* 1: 328–29). But if this were the case for the C101 Church, one wonders how it could happen that the roof tiles could be all removed while leaving behind only five fragments to be recovered during the excavation. It would also be odd that the far more valuable wooden roof beams were not removed as well.

Apses

The three semicircular apses do not project beyond the east wall of the Church. The upper preserved courses of the three apses are built of yellow marl blocks (fig. 7.4), while the lower courses, like all the other building stones in the Church, consist of the local, brown to purple Umm 'Ishrin sandstone (*HEP* 1: 23–25). The two side apses belong to the initial construction period of the Church. The two side apses are too small to have accommodated the type of table that was installed at these positions in the Petra Church (Fiema et al. 2001: 54–55, 194–96).

The central apse is semicircular, about 3.75 m wide (W 4.50 m from pier to pier) and 2.10 m deep.

The yellow marl blocks formed the fourth and five courses up from the pavement. There is no trace of a *synthronon*. The flagstone pavement of the apse is the same as the pavement in the chancel area (elev. 956.37 m); nothing in the pavement marks the transition from the chancel into the area of the apse. A probe was dug below the pavement to clarify the chronology and sequence of construction (see below, pp. 230–31).

The north apse is also semicircular, about 2.10 m wide and 1.10 m deep. It is preserved to a height of seven courses; the fifth and sixth courses up consist of yellow marl blocks. A line of mudbrick (Locus 01.30; L 2.14 m, W 0.16 m, MPH 0.15 m) covered with white plaster delineated the open west end. As in the rest of the Church, the fine, smoothed outer layer of plaster is laid on a coarse bedding layer with many pebble inclusions. The appearance of plaster, and the similarity of the plastering technique with that elsewhere in the Church, indicate that this feature belongs to the period when the Church was in use. A

FIG. 7.9   *Probe in North Apse, view.*

small probe dug in the southeast edge of the apse revealed some disturbed cobbles set in silt (Locus 01.31), possibly the bedding for a stone pavement that may have extended below the blocks of the apse. Unfortunately, the area is disturbed, with only some tumbled blocks and cobbles remaining at the level where the pavement would once have been. The pavement visible now was laid during the recent consolidation work of the Department of Antiquities and does not necessarily reflect what was there originally.

In 2009 a trench was excavated in the southwest corner of the north apse below the pavement level in order to confirm whether the walls of the north side apse and the central apse bonded or abutted, i.e. whether they were constructed

simultaneously or the north side apse is a later addition. The question is significant because of the argument some scholars have made that early Christian church architecture underwent a development from churches with a single apse and two side rooms to churches with three apses (Negev 1989; Margalit 1989; Michel 2001: 30–33, Fiema et al. 2001: 53, 120–21). The north and south side apses appeared to bond with the central apse above the floor level, but it was necessary to determine whether the foundations bonded as well.

This trench (1.00 m north–south × 2.00 m east–west) was laid out against the interior face of the north side apse, the northeast arch pier, and the lowest step up to the chancel area (fig. 7.9). At this point the pavers that the Department of

Antiquities had recently laid as part of their work to consolidate the Church walls had already been disturbed, indicating that further illicit digging had taken place. The soil in the probe trench (Loci 1.81, 82, 83, and 91) consisted of disturbed silty soil with occasional blocks and cobbles, as well as some pieces of plastic and cigarettes, clearly the back-fill from the illicit digging. Excavation continued all the way down to the sterile orange sand at the level of the bottom of the foundation courses of the north apse wall and the northeast pier (elev. 953.85 m), 1.95 m below the level of the pavement (fig. 7.10). The sterile orange sand is substantially lower at this point than in the nearby Grave 6 probe; the reason for that anomaly was not determined. At a middle depth (within Locus 01.83) were found several disturbed blocks and capstones, along with a handful of human bones, probably part of the Burial no. 6, located immediately to the north of the probe trench. Numerous Byzantine-period sherds were found in the disturbed soil of the trench, along with Nabataean sherds, but no pottery datable to the early Islamic period was found.

The excavation of this trench revealed that the upper three foundation courses of sandstone blocks of the north apse bond with the northeast pier below the pavement, indicating their simultaneous construction (figs. 7.9–11). The lower three courses of the foundation, built of less regular, large blocks with courses of cobbles in between, rest on the subsoil at the same level, again pointing to their simultaneous construction.

The south apse is also semicircular, ca. 2.16 m wide and 1.13 m deep. Its six preserved wall courses are less regular than those in the north apse, but as in the north apse the yellow marl blocks appear in the fifth and sixth courses. The west end of this apse, however, is delineated in a different manner than the north apse: a line of mudbricks (Locus 01.32) extended across the opening, backed up by a row of cobbles (Locus 01.33) to its east. A small probe in the apse uncovered only disturbed cobbles and tumbled blocks at the level where a pavement would once have been. Nothing survived to indicate the nature of the original pavement and so no attempt was made to excavate any deeper here. The pavement there now was laid during the consolidation work of the Department of Antiquities and does not necessarily reflect what was there originally.

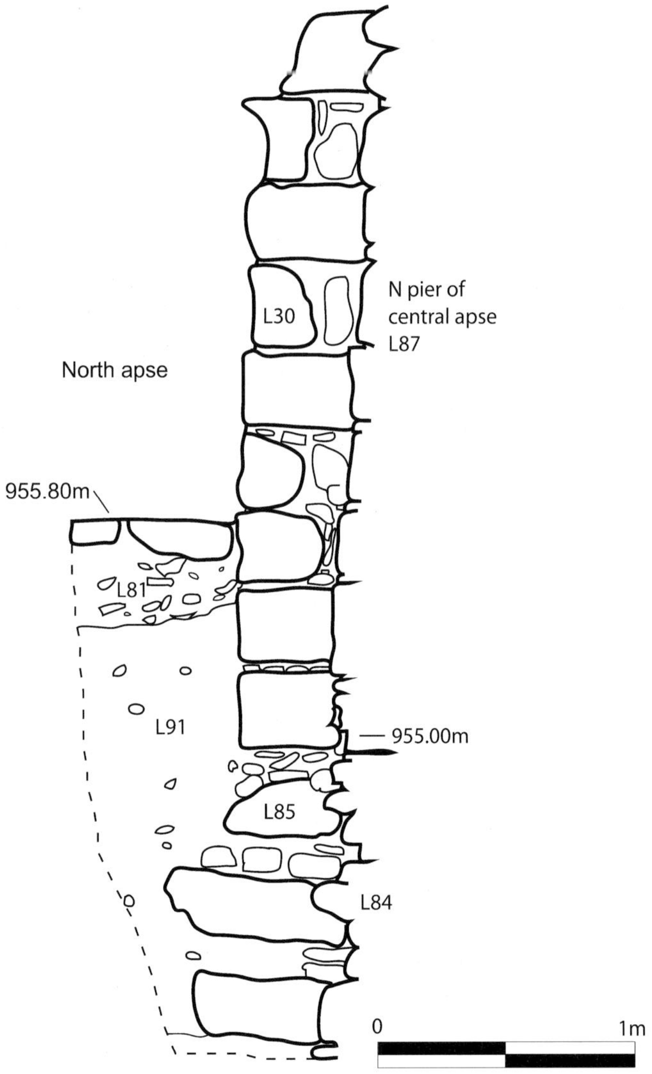

Chancel

The rectangular chancel area in front of the central apse is raised three steps above the level of the nave and side aisles and projects into the nave as far

FIG. 7.10 *Probe in North Apse, section and elevation looking east (A. Heidenreich, I. Sturkenboom, M. Siklenka).*

as the first arch piers (figs. 7.7–8, 7.12). The chancel and apse pavement (Locus 01.10; elev. 956.37 m) is composed of large, rather irregular flagstone pavers. No evidence for an altar remains. The steps up from the nave and side aisles are built for the most part of reused conduit blocks of yellow marl placed with the conduit channel face down. The most spectacular use of these typically Nabataean conduit blocks is in the core of the aqueduct system serving Hawara (*HEP* 1: 75–115), but they were also applied to local, small-scale water transport in the town. In consequence, the appearance of such blocks reused in the Church does not necessarily mean that the main aqueduct system had fallen out of use by the time the Church was constructed. Since the blocks fracture easily when exposed to the weather, the north and south steps exposed in the 1962 clearance are in poor condition, while the blocks are better preserved along the west side, where the soil covering them was not removed until 1991.

Along the west side of the chancel, the first step up from the nave pavement (Locus 01.14; H 0.10 m, W 0.25 m; elev. 955.91 m) consists of ordinary stone blocks; the second step consists of reused yellow marl conduit blocks placed upside down (Locus 01.13; H 0.22 m; W 0.40 m; elev. 956.13). The third step up (Locus 01.11), just 0.05 m below the level of the chancel pavement (Locus 01.10), is composed of blocks that served as the base for the marble chancel screen panels, along with a single threshold block at the entrance, in the centre of the west side (Locus 01.12; H 0.18; W 0.25 m; elev. 956.31 m). There is a gap in the west steps for 0.65 m south of the freestanding pier at its northwest corner, to allow room for installation of the ambo.

A row of reused yellow marl conduit blocks with their conduit channels placed face-up served as the base for the marble chancel screen panels along the front of the chancel. The marble panels

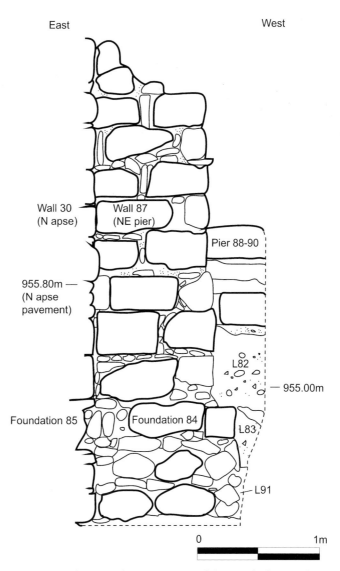

FIG. 7.11 *Probe in North Apse, section and elevation looking south (A. Heidenreich, I. Sturkenboom, M. Siklenka).*

were set into the grooves (W 0.12 m; deep 0.06 m) and held in place with mortar containing small sandstone cobbles. There is one long conduit block to the north of the entrance step to the chancel, extending 1.20 m to the location of the ambo, and one long and one short conduit block south of the entrance to the chancel, extending 1.80 m to the south arch pier. Along the less well-preserved north and south sides of the chancel, both 3.20 m long, four conduit blocks are installed to hold the panels of the screen, and no gaps can be seen for any entrances up from the north or south aisles.

FIG. 7.12   *View of Chancel and Apses from west.*

The surviving fragments of the marble chancel screens are discussed below (pp. 449–85).

Curiously, there is no trace along the line of the grooved conduit blocks for the rectangular holes where upright, vertically grooved posts were typically inserted to help support the chancel screen panels, as for example at the Petra Church (Fiema et al. 2001: 196–204). No obvious fragments of any chancel screen posts were found in the C101 Church, and the arrangement for supporting the chancel screen panels remains unclear. Chancel screen posts were found in the B100 Church and in F103 (possibly from the F102 Church).

The recent consolidation work of the Department of Antiquities along the steps entailed the replacement of some of the stones, so the current appearance of the steps and row of blocks for the chancel screen panels is different from what was originally there.

Ambo

Clear evidence was found for the presence of an ambo at the northwest corner of the chancel, abutting the south side of the east arch pier of the north row (Locus 01.16) as well as the north side of the west row of chancel screen blocks. A few rectangular blocks (Locus 01.20; L ca. 0.72 m; W 0.53 m;

elev. 956.38 m), similar to the blocks of the chancel steps, form the remnants of a step or two up into the raised ambo platform. Just west of the chancel, there is an area of irregularly set cobbles (Locus 01.21; elev. 955.81 m); four blocks set into this surface contain holes (D 0.14–0.17 m; 0.06 m deep) lined with mortar, and there are two similar holes on the east dug into the dirt fill (figs. 7.2, 7.8). These six holes served as the base for the colonnettes that supported the base of the hexagonal ambo. The presence of the blocks and the six postholes is sufficient to establish that the ambo was similar to those found in the Petra Church (Fiema et al. 2001: 204–8) and the Church of the Lions at Umm al-Rasas (Piccirillo 1992: 208–11), and elsewhere (Michel 2001: 81–87). Several scattered pieces of the hexagonal marble ambo base and the side panels were recovered (pp. 468–70). Such ambos seem to be a liturgical feature introduced around the beginning of the seventh century (Michel 2001: xiii, 87).

Doorways

There is only one entrance into the Church, located in the middle of the north wall, described as part of Room 4. A second doorway in the east end of the north wall leads into the Sacristy (Room 2) (figs. 7.3, 7.8). A cross is cut into one of the flagstone pavers in front of the door into Room 2. There are no doorways in the west wall, the usual location for entrance doors into churches, nor are there any doors in the south wall to connect with the rooms to the south. It is not clear why the only entrance to the Church in on the north, since there are no obvious buildings or other topographical obstacles on the west, but the location of the settlement centre to the north may have been a factor.

Staircase

In the southwest corner of the Church are the remains of a staircase with six preserved steps made up of irregular courses of dressed sandstone blocks, mounting from east to west and reaching at present 1.30 m above the Church pavement (figs. 7.6, 7.15); there is a second staircase in Room 4 (fig. 7.43). Whether the stairs led up to a gallery above the south aisle or simply provided access to the (flat?) roof cannot be determined. The steps are around 0.20 m to 0.22 m high, and the treads vary from 0.20 m to 0.30 m; the exposed top step is 1.17 m deep and so provides space to mount a few more step blocks. The bottom course of the staircase abuts the bench along the west wall; above the bottom course a space is left between the staircase and the west bench, creating a cupboard 0.90 m wide and 0.95 m deep; the bottom shelf of the cupboard is 0.40 m above the Church pavement. The recent consolidation work by the Department of Antiquities altered the appearance of the staircase. Another church with a similar arrangement of two staircases is the Church of the Lions at Umm al-Rasas (Piccirillo 1992: fig. 2 and plan I). One of the staircases at this church is in the southwest corner and the other along the middle of the exterior north face of the north wall, within a northern side room.

Benches

Benches (H 0.30–0.35 m; W 0.50 m) built of cobbles with rubble fill extend along the south, west and north walls of the Church (figs. 7.5–7). A capping of one course of mudbricks was partially preserved. The north bench extends from the west wall eastward as far as the door into the northeast room, with an interruption at the entrance door

into the Church from the Entrance Hall; the south bench continues all the way to the opening of the south apse. The benches along the west wall abut both western arch piers. The south bench is less well preserved than the others. The consolidation work by the Department of Antiquities here replaced the mudbrick with a course of stones.

Pavement

The pavement of the Church (Locus 01.09) consists of irregularly shaped flagstones of flaky bluish slate and harder white sandstone (fig. 7.2). While the distinction is not absolute, the sandstone pavers tend to be concentrated in the nave, while the side aisles and chancel area are paved mostly with slate. The reason for this distinction is not apparent. The elongated pavers in the nave are arranged in an east–west orientation in fairly orderly rows, while the more nearly square pavers in the side aisles are oriented in north–south rows. A number of irregularly shaped pavers oriented randomly appear at the west end of the south aisle. The elevations of the pavers are a few centimetres higher in the east than west, ranging from around 955.85 m elevation in the east to around 955.69 m in the west. In the nave, six of the pavers are marked with crosses, which indicate the location of graves below the pavement (figs. 7.2, 7.19–20). Illicit digging disturbed portions of the pavement in the north and south aisles after they were exposed in 1962.

7.B.2. Stratigraphy

The side aisles, apses, and chancel were cleared down to the pavement level in 1962, but enough of the accumulated tumble layers remained undisturbed in the nave, especially in a high L-shaped deposit west of the chancel, to provide a clear picture of the post-occupation deposits and the sequence of events that they represent.

Cleanup and Clearance

General clean-up of the Church interior and removal of soil and debris from collapse of the Church walls that had accumulated since both the 1962 clearance and 1983 work was conducted

FIG. 7.13   *North–South baulk in Nave, view from east (for a colour photograph see Schick 1995a: pl. 26).*

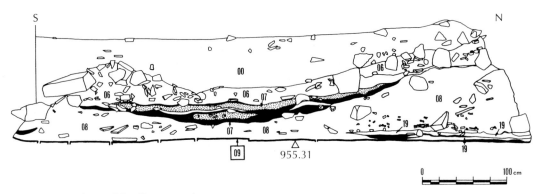

FIG. 7.14   *North–South baulk in Nave, drawing.*

throughout the 1991 season. Most of these deposits of silt and generally ash-free soil removed throughout the Church (Locus 01.00) were post-1962 deposits deriving from recent general deterioration of the Church walls, wind-blown soil and soil from the illicit digging below the disturbed pavers, and — in the east — from the disintegration of the chancel steps. This deposit was cleared from the east and centre of the south aisle, where the flagstone pavers had been lifted out of position (Locus 01.02), in the east end of the south aisle and the south apse (Locus 01.03), and in the east end of the north aisle and the north apse (Locus 01.04).

Stratigraphy of Excavated Areas

The area that had not been cleared in 1962 was irregular in shape. Undisturbed deposits below tumble that had been removed in 1962 covered about a quarter of the surface area of the church, extending from the west end of the chancel ca. 6 m north–south by 3.5 m east–west, as far as the east face of a high deposit of soil in the centre of the nave that included both undisturbed tumble and the soil deposits below. This relatively deep, undisturbed deposit extended ca. 6 m north–south and 0.50 m east–west (fig. 7.13). To its west were

FIG. 7.15   *East–West baulk in Nave, view from north (scale is on Locus 28).*

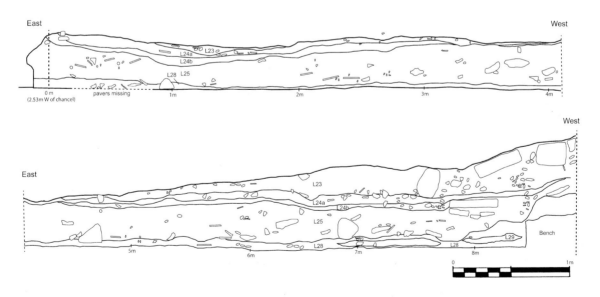

FIG. 7.16   *East–West baulk in Nave, drawing. Locus 23: sterile silt. Locus 24a: light coloured ash. Locus 24b: Dark coloured ash.*
Locus 25: soil and stones below the ash layers. Locus 28: compacted soil. (L. Shumka, J.P. Oleson).

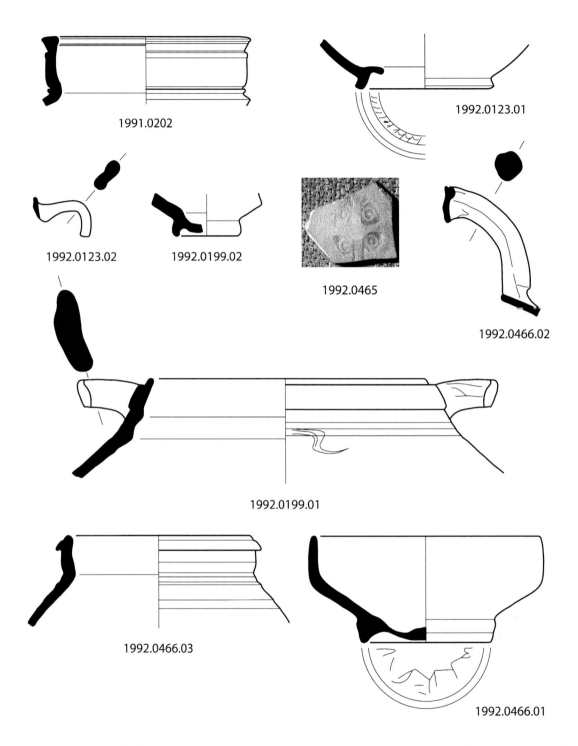

FIG. 7.17 *Ceramic Profiles from the Nave (Room 01), Loci 03, 25, 36, 37. 1991.0202: C101.01.03, jar (Petra, EZ I: fig. 753, last quarter 4–ea. 5C) (last quarter 4–ea. 5C). 1992.0123.01: C101.01.25, NFW bowl base with fingernail finish (Petra, cf. EZ I: fig. 659, 20–100) (1C). 1992.0123.02: C101.01.25, NFW double handle (1C). 1992.0199.02: C101.01.25, jar or jug base (Petra, cf. Bikai and Perry 2001: fig. 8.10, 20–100) (1C). 1992.0465: C101.01.36, Late Roman C bowl base with stamped cross, ware 5YR 6/6, slip 2.5YR 6/4 (Hayes 1972: 366, fig. 79 no. 79.p, q, r, s, late 5–mid-6C) (late 5–mid-6C). 1992.0466.02: C101.01.37, handle and rim of split rim jar, ware 7.5YR 6/4, ext 7.5YR 5/1 (Hesban, Sauer and Herr 2012: 240, fig. 3.17.6, 10, 37 BC–AD 73; Parker et al. 1987: fig. 102.101, AD 284–363) (4C). 1992.0199.01: C101.01.25, pot, zigzag incision on exterior, core 2.5 YR 6/8, slip 7.5YR 8/4 (Humayma, HEP 1: 237, Gerber 2008a: fig. 22.5, 2nd half 1–1st half*

further undisturbed low deposits below tumble that had been removed in 1962, extending all the way to the west wall, allowing isolation of baulks that provided continuous stratigraphy from ca. 3 m west of the chancel to the west wall (figs. 7.15–16). In the 1991 season the area between the chancel and the high deposit was excavated and the east face of the high deposit was trimmed and drawn as an especially informative north–south baulk section (fig. 7.14). In the 1992 season the high deposit west of that north–south baulk and the lower soil farther west in the nave were excavated (fig. 7.16). Almost all of the soil was sifted for artefacts.

Three major layers could be distinguished in the deposit west of the chancel and in the north–south baulk (fig. 7.14). These layers presumably once extended over the rest of the Church, but had been removed elsewhere in 1962. On top was a layer of firm, totally sterile silt and soil (in the deposit east of the baulk mostly removed as Locus 01.00, but excavated in part as Locus 01.17, and in the baulk deposit excavated as Locus 01.22). Below it was a layer of hard-packed, almost totally sterile soil with numerous large tumbled blocks and cobbles from the arches and walls (Loci 01.06 and 01.18 east of the baulk deposit and Locus 01.22 in the baulk deposit). These two layers represent the partial collapse of the building after it had been abandoned, followed by accumulations of wind-blown silt and sand. This sequence can be seen in most of the excavated structures at Humayma.

Below the compacted tumble was an ash deposit (Locus 01.07 east of the baulk and Locus 01.24 in the baulk). The ash varied in width and thickness across the area. It was thickest (around 0.40 m) in the centre of the nave at the north–south baulk, and it thinned out as it sloped up towards the north and south aisles and towards the chancel. There were a number of layers and lenses that split and merge, with non-ashy soil in between, but there appeared to be only one basic deposit of ash. The ash varied from black to light bluish grey, and the non-ashy soil associated with the ash was normally discoloured by heat, indicating that the ash was deposited hot. There was only a little charcoal, and no seeds were detectable on a macroscopic level. A modest amount of animal bone was found in the ash, along with numerous fragments of ostrich shell. Pottery was relatively scarce but contained the usual mix of Nabataean through Early Islamic sherds (MN, LN, LB, UM AB; cf. fig. 7.17). Some of the sherds were burnt. There were also numerous corroded iron nails and lumps of iron corrosion, a few glass fragments, and fragments of a marble chancel screen.

Below the ash was a layer of compacted silty soil (Loci 01.05 and 01.08 east of the baulk and Locus 01.25 in the baulk), with comparatively few cobbles or pebbles, up to 0.80 m thick (fig. 7.14). This layer was much richer in organic materials and pottery than the ash above. Small pieces of charcoal were found throughout the layer, particularly in the northwest, but no large pieces, nor any ash. This locus also produced many animal bones, and a large number of ostrich egg shell fragments, but no seeds were noticed on a macroscopic level. Many glass fragments were also found, some clearly from liturgical lamps, along with several dozen iron nails. Several hundred marble fragments from various panels belonging to the chancel screens and ambo were found, with particularly high concentrations very close to the pavement and near the chancel and ambo (pp. 453–60). The large quantities of pottery included Nabataean through Early Islamic types, and notably a substantial number of hand-made storage jars. In the north portion of the area just above the pavement was another thin layer of clayey silt with ash (Locus 01.19).

The extensive undisturbed deposits below the tumbled rubble that had been removed in 1962 continued to the west of the north–south baulk (Locus 01.23, 24, 25; fig. 7.16), above a few centimetres of compacted silt without ash, and a thin layer of yellow soil rich in clay directly on the pavement (Locus 01.28). The deposits were excavated in such a way that a temporary east–west baulk was left all the way to the west Church wall. In one area to the northwest of the north–south baulk there was

2C; Petra, Gerber 1994: fig. 16A, late 1–2C) (1–ea. 2C). 1992.0466.03: C101.01.37, cook pot, core 5YR 6/2, ware 2.5YR 5/6, slip 7.5YR 6/1 (Petra, Gerber 2001: fig. 2.F, 4C; EZ I: fig. 738, 300–363) (4C). 1992.0466.01: C101.01.37, NFW cup with fingernail finish, ware 5YR 6/4, surface 7.5YR 6/6, base slipped 7.5YR 6/4 (Petra, EZ I: fig. 661, 20–100; Bikai and Perry 2001: fig. 8.6, 20–100 (1C).

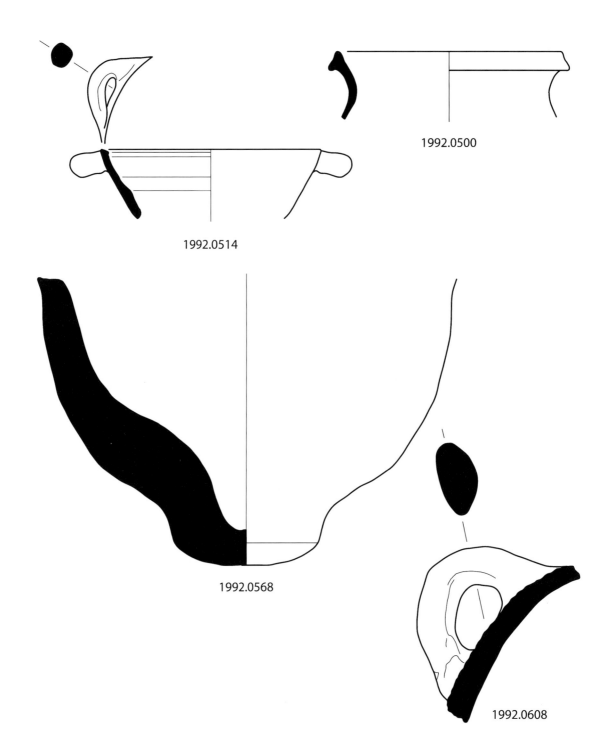

1992.0500

1992.0514

1992.0568

1992.0608

Fig. 7.18 *Ceramic Profiles from the Nave (Room 01), Loci 37, 39, 45, 52, 60. 1992.0500: C101.01.39, jar (cf. 1991.0133.02, below fig. 7.41; 1992.0377.01, below fig. 7.68; Humayma, ʿAmr and Schick 2001: fig. 9.20, mid-7C). 1992.0514: C101.01.45, casserole (4–5C). 1992.0568: C101.01.52, large pot, inner core 7.5YR 8/6, outer core and surface 5Y 8/3 (Humayma, ʿAmr and Schick 2001: fig. 9.21, mid-7C) (mid-7C). 1992.0608: C101.01.60, storage jar handle, 2.5YR 5/6, slip 2.5Y 8/3, (LB–UM).*

a distinct deposit of compacted soil (Locus 01.27), and in the far west there was a thicker pocket of ash (Locus 01.29 above Locus 01.28). Numerous iron nails and marble chancel screen fragments were found in these loci, mostly in Locus 01.25. A fair amount of animal bones was found, but little glass. All of these deposits were sifted.

The careful analysis of these intact layers in the nave revealed the sequence of events during the abandonment of the Church. The thin layer of yellowish clay directly above the pavement in some parts of the nave may represent soil introduced during the initial disintegration of the roof. The limited deposit of ash directly above the pavement around the northern portion of the north–south baulk section may represent the activities of squatters or individuals salvaging Church furnishings while the building was still intact. These squatters may also have been responsible for the *tabun* in Room 2. The compacted silty soil with small pieces of charcoal, seemingly from the roof, found directly above the thin clay and ash in other areas of the Church reflects a phase of abandonment of the church when the liturgical furnishings were removed while the building remained physically intact, along with an initial destruction of the roof. The Nabataean through Early Islamic pottery in this layer included numerous sherds of large handmade storage jars. The layer also produced many animal bones, hundreds of fragments of ostrich egg shell and glass, metal objects and many marble fragments, especially in the bottom few centimetres.

While many marble fragments were recovered, it is clear that the bulk of the marble had been removed from the Church. Only a few of the several hundred marble fragments join. Only about half of the most complete panel could be pieced together, and its fragments were found scattered throughout the area between the chancel, the north–south baulk, and Room 4 (see pp. 451–53). One of these fragments (Locus 01.19; p. 451; fig. 13.1) was blackened from fire although it joined with other unblackened fragments, suggesting destruction of the screen and dispersal of the pieces prior to the loss of the roof. Although the 1962 clearance operation presumably found additional marble pieces that have now been lost, the case for intentional salvaging of the marble is clear. Only a couple of pieces may have come from

the altar or colonnettes. Almost all of the marble fragments were found scattered and face up, which would not be the case had they been left as they had fallen randomly due to natural destruction such as an earthquake or accidental fire and collapse of the roof. Thus, the chancel screen and pulpit panels seem to have been deliberately broken up and most of the pieces removed in antiquity, leaving a few pieces scattered about. The same process occurred at the other churches around the site, and isolated fragments of chancel screen have turned up on the surface and in excavated strata throughout the habitation area. Presumably the salvaged marble was burned to lime for use in plastering or agriculture, although no trace of a lime kiln was found in any of the excavated areas (see p. 450).

Above the deposit of silty soil with charcoal and all the marble fragments was the main layer of thick ash, which was thickest in the centre of the nave and thinned out and disappeared as it sloped up towards the north and south aisles. The ash clearly derived from the burning of the large wooden beams that supported the roof. A C_{14} date for some charcoal from the layer (TO 3731) provided a date of 1510 ± 50 BP, or AD 580 (AD 540–620 at 68.3 confidence interval). In 2011, the Cologne Radiocarbon Calibration Package provided an adjusted date of 1420 ± 65 BP, or 530 ± 65 AD (465–595). These results provide an approximate date for the felling of the wood used in the construction of the roof. Pottery was scarce and consisted of the usual mix of Nabataean through Early Islamic types typical of the site as a whole. The hard-packed soil with large tumbled blocks and cobbles but very few artefacts above the ash derives from the collapse of the walls of the building after it had been abandoned. The deposit of sterile soil on top is wind-blown silt and sand that accumulated over the centuries.

It is thus clear that when the Church went out of use the building remained structurally intact. First, the marble chancel screen panels were broken up and mostly removed, along with the other liturgical furnishings. The ambo and altar were dismantled completely. These activities left a deposit of debris within a few centimetres of the pavement. At some point squatters, possibly resident in the Nave or the Entrance Hall, installed a *tabun* in the Sacristy. Later on, a fire burned down

FIG. 7.19   *Crosses above the burials in the Nave: 1, Burial 1;*
2–3, Burial 2; 4, Burial 3.

the roof, the walls collapsed, and the building then remained abandoned over the following centuries.

Sub-Pavement Probe in the Apse

In order to acquire evidence for the construction date of the Church, some pavers along the northeast edge of the central apse were lifted, and the uniform sandy fill below was excavated down to a depth of about 1 m in a sequence of more or less arbitrary loci (Loci 01.35, 37, 39, 45; MN, LN, RO, LR, LB; fig. 7.18), and then for another 0.30 m down to elevation 954.94 m (Locus 01.41, Locus

01.43; MN, LN, RO, LR, EB, MB, LB). Each of these layers contained small quantities of cobbles and pebbles, but no larger blocks. The upper loci contained large amounts of pottery and bones, but almost no other artefacts, although the quantity of pottery and bones low down (in Locus 01.41 and Locus 01.43) is less than in the upper layers. An Early Byzantine bronze coin was found in Locus 01.37 (p. 427, no. 69).

Removal of the silt (Locus 01.43) revealed a layer of irregularly shaped cobbles placed roughly horizontally in slightly compacted silty soil that was left unexcavated (Locus 01.47). The probe

FIG. 7.20   *Crosses above the burials in the Nave: 1, Burial 4; 2, Burial 5; 3, Burial 6; 4, Slab with cross from south aisle.*

excavated in the north apse in 2009 showed that this level is still about a metre above the bottom of the apse foundation courses and sterile soil (figs. 7.10–11). The cobbles lined the inside of the apse wall but did not extend for more than about 0.50 m inward towards the centre of the apse, where silty, sandy soil is free of cobbles. The cobbles represent a foundation course for the apse wall, and the layers of soil above represent layers of fill dumped on the inside of the foundation courses up to the pavement level. The pottery in the fill layers seems not to include any types datable to the Islamic periods, indicating a construction date

of the Church in the Byzantine period, most likely in the early sixth century.

7.B.3. Burial Probes in the Nave

At least eight crosses are carved into the pavers in the nave and north aisle, including six in the nave area covered by the soil deposits left undisturbed in 1962 (figs. 7.2, 7.19–20). The crosses are all similar in design and execution: a circle was inscribed on the stone slab, then segments of four circles of the same radius were inscribed across the circle from centres outside, outlining the four spreading, concave sided arms of the cross. The outer end of each arm could follow the circumference of the framing circle, could be flat, or could be concave. The spaces between and just outside the arms were then lowered by pecking the stone surface. There is no symmetry or apparent order to the distribution of the crosses, although most are located in the western half of the nave. In an attempt to understand the reason for their presence, one marked slab was lifted toward the end of the 1992 season, the fill below excavated, and Burial 1 was discovered. It then became an urgent priority to excavate beneath the other crosses before illegal digging disturbed the burials. The locals, in fact, spoke of additional burials below the north and south aisles, which they had found during illicit digging below the pavements after they were first exposed in 1962. One of these (Burial 6) was marked by the cross in a paver in front of the door into the Sacristy (Room 2). One cross was observed on the displaced paving slabs in the middle of the south aisle, but because of the disturbed nature of the deposits in the south aisle around the many missing pavers, no attempt was made to excavate there to confirm the presence of another burial.

The paving stones marked with crosses are close to but not always directly over the graves, with the greatest displacement at Burial 4. There are two crosses, close together but on separate paving stones, over Burial 2. In all but Burial 4, the grave cists are constructed in a similar manner: a rectangular pit was dug, rows of dressed blocks were set upright to form the sides, and flat sandstone slabs with irregular outlines were laid on top, approximately a metre below the pavement (figs. 7.22–23). In the case of Burial 4, the capstones were simply laid on the margins of an unlined trench cut in the soil (fig. 7.33). The latter method was used for the burials in F102 as well (figs. 5.69–72). The skeletons were oriented roughly east–west, on their backs with the head at the west end, and the hands crossed over the lower abdomen. All the skeletons were fully extended and articulated. Two of the bodies were placed in wooden coffins, but the other three were not; there was no apparent reason for that distinction. All these methods of burial were common in Jordan during the periods represented at Humayma, for both Christians and non-Christians (see the

FIG. 7.21 *View of Burials 1–5 after excavation.*

discussion on pp. 400–401). The fill layers in the five burial probes contained a great amount of pottery and animal bones, but almost no other artefacts. All the artefacts predate the Umayyad period.

These intramural burials, unique so far as we can tell among the churches at Humayma, can be classified as "privileged burials," in which individuals of high social or ecclesiastical status, or donors to the construction of a church, were granted the right to interment within the sacred structure (Sodini 1986; Goldfus 1997). There was ecclesiastical opposition to the burial of lay people within churches, especially those within city limits, so at least the children in Burials 1 and 2 and the female in Burial 4 must have come from prominent families, while the male burials may have been those of ecclesiastics. The rich burial goods associated with the girl in Burial 2 reinforce this interpretation (see the discussion pp. 385–98). These privileged burials were relatively common in the churches in the Negev, particularly after 630, but rare elsewhere. An

Fig. 7.22   *Burial 1, view of shaft and cover slabs.*

infant burial was documented in a church at Beʿer Sheva (Sodini 1986: 237). Fifth to sixth-century cist burials were found below the pavement in the church at Udhruh, but al-Salameen (2011: 239) seems to feel that some of them post-date the abandonment of the church. The appearance of this practice at Humayma is another indication of the geographical and cultural links between Humayma and the Petra hinterland (*HEP* 1: 460–78). The presence of a few burials within the Church raises the question of the location of the other Christian burials. Some Christians may have been buried adjacent to the possible military cemetery 740 m west of the fort (see p. 91), while others may have been interred in new or reused graves in the Nabataean necropolis.

Most of the excavation of Burials 1–5 was carried out at the end of the 1992 season, with some follow-up work in the 1993 season. The graves were backfilled and the pavers replaced at the end of the 1993 season (fig. 7.21).

A clear difference in the compaction of the fill below the pavement marked the edge of the soil dug out for each burial, demonstrating that the fill below the pavement was deposited when the Church was constructed and the pavement laid above. Only at a later date were the pavers lifted in selected locations, the fill below dug out, and the graves constructed. Looser fill was then deposited above the grave capstones and the paving stones replaced. The pottery in the old fill and the looser fill appears to be homogeneous, so the loose fill most naturally was simply a redeposit of the soil that had been dug out to install the graves. For a technical report on the human skeletons and identification of the wood species used for the surviving coffins, see pp. 384–400.

Burial Probe 1

The first burial probe excavated was marked by a large paver incised with a cross, on the centre line of the nave, slightly more than halfway between the chancel steps and the west wall (figs. 7.19.1, 7.21). The soil below the pavement was excavated in arbitrary loci (Loci 01.34, 36, 38, 40, 42), since it all consisted of a uniform fill of silt with some cobbles down to the top of the capstones of the grave cist (Locus 01.44; elev. ca. 954.66) just over 1.00 m below the level of the pavement. The six irregularly shaped sandstone capping blocks were oriented north–south, with some small chinking

FIG. 7.23   *Burial 1, view of grave cist after removal of cover slabs.*

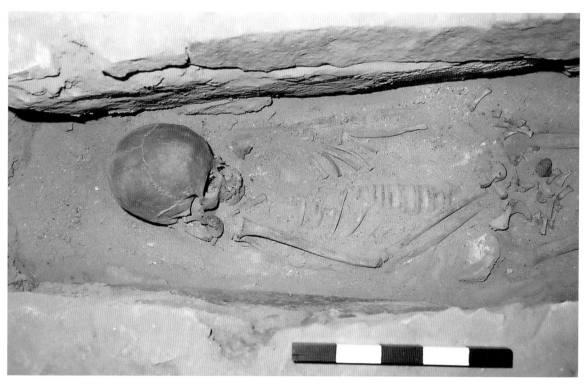

FIG. 7.24   *Burial 1, view of upper portion of skeleton.*

FIG. 7.25   *Burial 1, view of feet and remains of sandals.*

stones filling the gaps between them (fig. 7.22). The ceramics in the fill included MN, LN, ER, RO, LR, MB, and LB wares.

The internal east–west length of the cist is 1.70 m; it is 0.26 m wide at the west end, 0.30 m wide in the centre, and 0.25 m wide at the east end. The skeleton and surrounding soil (Locus 01.46) rested on a layer of orange-red sand (elev. 954.19 m), part of the extensive deposit of sand that predates the construction of the Church (figs. 7.23–24). It contained MN, LR, and MB sherds.

The bones belonged to fully articulated skeleton of a five-year old laid out on his back with the head on the west end. The right arm crossed over the pelvis and the right hand rested near the left hand along the left side of the body. A small bronze cross found on the chest (fig. 11.1.1d) probably had been worn on a necklace of leather or string. Remnants of leather sandals were found on the feet (fig. 7.25). The body had not been placed in a coffin.

Burial Probe 2

A second burial probe was excavated below two pavers with incised crosses close to one another near the west end of the nave, on line with Burial 1 (figs. 7.19.2–3, 7.21). The largely undifferentiated fill below the pavement (Loci 01.48, 50, 52, 57) contained exceptionally large amounts of pottery and animal bones. The ceramics in the fill included MN, LN, ER, RO, LR, MB, and LB wares, possibly into the seventh century. The capstones of the second cist grave appeared at a depth of around 1.20 m below the top of the pavement (elev. 954.48 m; fig. 7.26). Gaps left by the irregular covering slabs were sealed with smaller stones, mud, and plaster, The grave cist (Locus 01.61) has an internal east–west length of 1.56 m; the internal width is 0.31 m at the west end and 0.24 m at the east end.

The burial (Locus 01.62) contained the skeleton of a young girl laid on her back with her head at the west end (figs. 7.27–28). Remains of long black

FIG. 7.26 *Burial 2, view of shaft and cover slabs.*

FIG. 7.27 *Burial 2, view of grave cist after removal of cover slabs.*

FIG. 7.28   *Burial 2, upper portion of skeleton, with grave goods.*

hair lay by the left side of the skull. The right arm was draped across the lower torso with the hand resting above the pelvic area; the left arm lay at the side of the body. She was buried with jewellery and other objects (pp. 385–96, figs. 11.2–4), some of them possibly contained in a palm fibre basket on her stomach. The basket structure had almost entirely disintegrated, but the pattern of splayed, spiky fibres suggested a basket constructed with coils of palm fibres (fig. 7.29), as in some examples at Masada (Bernick 1994: 292–93, ill. 4) and Nahal ʿOmer (Baginsky and Shamir 1995: 31–33). A gold frontlet rested on the forehead, one gilded earring was located immediately below the left ear, another was recovered during flotation, and dozens of assorted stone, glass and amber beads were found at the base of the skull in a compact lump. A bronze cross pendant rested on the sternum. Vestiges of a small ivory doll or figurine were found at the outside of the left elbow along with textile fragments. A ring encircled the second finger of the left hand. Below the right forearm, which was partially covered by a large textile fragment, a figured wooden plaque rested face down. An ivory container lay just below the right side of the greater

FIG. 7.29   *Burial 2, remains of palm fibre (?) basket and spindle whorls.*

pelvic area, while above this, in the vicinity of the sacrum, a small mirror lay face up. Situated above and to the right of the container were three spindle whorls. Numerous small leather scraps were found among the foot bones, indicating the presence of footwear. After removal of the human remains and grave offerings, an agate pendant was found loose in the soil. Sifting brought additional items to light: fragments of two small bone crosses, a small misshapen item of gilded copper, and a jug-shaped bead. Traces of an unidentified textile were found

FIG. 7.30   *Burial 3, remains of coffin below cover slabs.*

FIG. 7.31   *Burial 3, view of grave cist after removal of cover slabs and coffin lid.*

FIG. 7.32 *Burial 3, desiccated remains of brain from inside skull.*

together with the skeletal remains in the cranial, abdominal, and pelvic regions. Whether these belong to clothing, a winding sheet, or both could not be ascertained.

The burial and surrounding soil (Locus 01.62) rested on the same compact orange sand layer (Locus 01.64) found below Burial 1. Excavation of the top few centimetres of this layer down to a level 1.74 m below the top of the pavement (elev. 954.01 m) yielded a few sherds datable to the first to third centuries (MN, LN, RO, LR).

Burial Probe 3

A third burial probe was excavated at the north edge of the nave, northeast of Burial 1. The cross is carved on a paver located over the west end of the grave (figs. 7.19.4, 7.21). Below the pavement were layers of silty fill with comparatively little pottery (Loci 01.49, 51, 59; MN, LN, ER, RO, MB, LB, UM) down to the top of the capstones (Locus 01.54), at elev. 954.79 m, ca. 1.00 m below the pavement, and the stone sides of the grave (Locus 01.55). The internal east–west length of the cist is 2.26 m; it is 0.49 m wide at the west end, 0.40 m wide at the east

end (figs. 7.30–31). Two of the capstones had broken and allowed soil to seep in on top of the burial. The removal of the broken capstones revealed the presence of a largely intact wooden coffin made of long planks (Locus 01.56). Some fragments of rope were found on top of the coffin, seemingly used to lower it into the grave. The bottom of the coffin had an elevation of 954.17 m.

Inside the coffin was the well-preserved skeleton of an adult male (fig. 7.31). Of particular interest was the unusual discovery of the desiccated, but intact brain still inside the skull (fig. 7.32). There were no associated artefacts. The presence of seventh-century ceramics in the fill above the burial indicates that the interment was made quite late in the history of the Church.

Burial Probe 4

The fourth burial probe was excavated below a cross in the nave, southeast of Burial 1 (figs. 7.20.1, 7.21). The fill above the burial consisted of layers of silt (Loci 01.53, 01.60; MN, LN, LR, MB, LB). A fragment of a marble paving slab (p. 473, no. 1) was found in a lens of ash there, along with part of sandstone pilaster base (p. 498, no. 3), and a fragment of a large vessel of polished, striped alabaster (p. 508, no. 6). Excavation at the end of the 1992 season proceeded to a depth of around 1.10 m without revealing any capstones, so in the 1993 season the area of excavation was extended beneath the row of paving slabs north of the row with the cross. Capstones for the grave cist were reached at elev. 954.43 m, some 1.25 m below the pavement, deeper than the other graves found at the Church.

In this probe the distinction between the more compacted original fill and the looser fill above the capstones of the grave was especially noticeable (fig. 7.33). The soil matrix that made up the looser fill (Loci 01.68, 69) was mixed with ash at the upper level and mottled throughout, with different colours of soil and including a significant number of MN, LN, MB, LB potsherds, and animal bones.

The interior of the grave was filled with soil (Locus 01.73; LN, RO), due to the collapse of the eastern capstones. An atypical feature of this grave was the absence of the side slabs associated with the other cist graves (fig. 7.33). Here the grave had

FIG. 7.33　*Burial 4, view of grave cist after removal of cover slabs.*

been dug into compact soil and simply roofed with capstones laid on the margins of the trench. The desire to provide a cist without the expense or trouble of providing stone slabs for the walls may explain the unique depth of the burial. It is possible that this was the first burial in the church, dug with a different construction technique than for the other, later ones, and that the position of the cross one row to the south of the actual burial indicates that the exact position of the burial had been forgotten by the time the locals decided to mark the burials with crosses.

The skeleton, that of an adult female, was moist and extremely fragile. Bone material began to crumble immediately. The body had been wrapped in a cloth shroud, which survived only as a dark discoloration on parts of the skeleton, especially the skull. The left arm was draped across the belly, while the right arm was draped across the pelvic region. The close proximity of the leg bones to each other suggests that the legs had been bound before burial.

A small bone pin with lathe-turned head (p. 392, fig. 11.4.1) was found among the left hand bones; it may have been a hairpin, or used to close up the burial shroud. A small bronze clasp or pendant (fig. 11.4.2b) was found underneath the vertebrae. Small, deteriorated fragments of a pair of leather sandals were found by the feet (fig. 11.4.3).

After removal of the burial (bottom elev. 953.99 m), excavation continued in the soil below, which contained only MN ceramics of the first to early second century (Loci 01.74, 01.76), to the level of the sterile, orange-red sandy soil (Locus 01.77; elev. 953.58 m), which was excavated for another 0.10 m.

Burial Probe 5

A fifth burial probe was excavated in the extreme west end of the nave, to the north of Burial Probe 2, separated from it by one row of paving slabs (figs. 7.21, 7.34). The paver marked with a cross was located above the west end of the burial (fig. 7.20.2). The soil

FIG. 7.34   *Burial 5, view of grave cist with skeleton.*

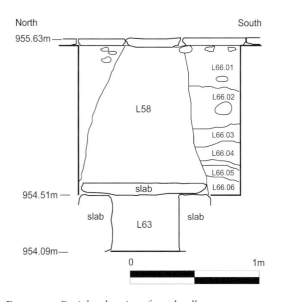

FIG. 7.35   *Burial 5, drawing of east baulk.*

below the pavement (Locus 01.58), which contained MN, LN, ER, RO, LR, and MB ceramics, was excavated down to the top of the capstones (Locus 01.65), at elev. 954.62, 1.00 m below the level of the pavement (fig. 7.35). The maximum interior east–west length of the cist is 2.07 m, the width is 0.51 m at its

west end, centre and east end. The remnant of soil (Locus 01.66; MN, LN, RO) between Burial Probes 2 and 5 was later excavated, as it began to collapse.

The grave contained a wooden coffin (Locus 01.63) in poor condition. Inside was the skeleton of an adult male. A single iron nail was the only artefact, other than very slight traces of sandals near the feet. The bottom of the coffin was 1.53 m below the surface of the pavement (elev. 954.09 m).

Burial Probe 6

Sometime after the 1996 season, illicit digging was carried out in the northeast area of the C101 Church, revealing a sixth grave below the Church pavement. The location of this grave had been marked by a paving stone with a faint cross, near the doorway into the northeast Room 2. This marker and the surrounding pavers had been lifted after the clearance of the north aisle by the Department of Antiquities in 1962, and prior to the 1991 season. Since it seemed likely that the grave had already been disturbed, it did not seem worth the effort to expose the grave again during the 1991–1993 seasons.

FIG. 7.36 *Burial 6, view of cist after clearing of looter's spoil.*

In the course of further illegal disturbance of the burial after the 1996 season, the fill above the grave and the soil within the grave were removed and heaped up nearby, making it easy to document the grave cist and recover any remaining bones or artefacts during the 1998 season. The remaining disturbed soil (Locus 01.78) in the grave was removed, exposing a typical burial cist constructed of one course of thin, upright stone slabs (H 0.40 m; Locus 01.79) (fig. 7.36) Only one of the cover slabs was still in place (top elev. 954.72 m), 1.08 m below the top of the pavement. There was no trace of a coffin, but a small amount of animal and human bone and a bone spindle or hairpin were found in the disturbed dirt (p. 445, no. 15). The bottom of the cist is at elev. 954.32 m, above the orange-red sandy layer (Locus 01.80) found everywhere under the Church foundations, but here remarkably high.

After the grave was documented, the disturbed soil originating from above and within the burial was placed back in the grave as backfill. A few fragments of human bone along with numerous animal bones were recovered during the process, but they were not kept.

7.C. THE NORTHEAST ROOM, SACRISTY (ROOM 2)

Excavation of the northeast room (Room 2), assumed to be a sacristy, had the objective of determining its function and documenting its occupational history (figs. 7.2–3). A door toward the east end of the north aisle provides access to the room (L ca. 6.0 m; W 4.5 m) (fig. 7.8), which originally was spanned by three east–west roofing arches springing from projecting piers in the east and west walls. The floor is paved with large, irregular slabs of sandstone, and a low bench ran along the west and south walls (fig. 7.37). Excavation was carried out in the 1991 and 1992 seasons in the western 2.75 m of the room, leaving a baulk section ca. 2.00 m deep across the full north–south length of the room.

FIG. 7.37   *Room 2, view from north.*

7.C.1. Architectural Features

The threshold (Locus 02.29) of the south door into the Church consists of a single yellow marl block (L 1.07 m; W 0.17 m), which bonds with the south wall. Its upper surface (956.03 m) is 0.22 m above the level of the pavement in the Church and 0.20 m above the pavement in the room. The south face is covered by plaster. A drain runs east–west just to the north of the threshold.

The walls of the room were constructed at the same time as the Church. The south wall of the room (Loci 02.06, 07; MPH 2.18 m) is simply a continuation of the north wall of the Nave, constructed of eight regular courses of blocks chinked

with smaller stones, with the highest preserved point at the southwest corner of the room at 958.01 m elev., ca. 2.18 m above the level of the pavement in the room. The west wall of the room (Locus 02.08; MPH 2.17 m), serving as well as the east wall of the northwest room (Room 4), is constructed in the same manner as the south wall, preserved for seven courses above the benches. The wall rests on several foundation courses of blocks below the pavement (Locus 02.34) extending down ca. 2.0 metres below the pavement (elev. 953.80 m), matching the depth of the wall of the north apse. The north wall of the room (Locus 02.09) is built of slightly smaller blocks in slightly less regular courses. This wall rests on a deep foundation packing of cobbles set in mud (Locus 02.35), exposed for 0.80 m below the pavement (elev. 955.03 m), without bottoming out. Irregular sandstone slabs, laid without apparent order, form the pavement of the room (Locus 02.28; elev. ca. 955.83 m).

A bench built of blocks facing rubble fill runs along the south wall west of the door (Locus 02.26; H 0.30 m; W 0.30 m; top elev. 956.15 m), turns the corner and continues along the west wall as far as the north arch support pier (Locus 02.27; H 0.32–0.37 m; W 0.35 m). The west bench is built in front of the two other piers, unlike the bench along the west wall of Room 1. The three piers along the west wall (Loci 02.10–12; W 0.55 m, projecting 0.10 m; MPH ca. 0.70 m) are built of careful header and stretcher courses of dressed blocks, extending for three courses above the height of the bench.

The room is one storey high. The amount of tumbled blocks found in the excavation is enough for a few more wall courses, but not for a second storey as well. Room I and the other northeast rooms in the Petra Church (Fiema et al. 2001: 153–58), by contrast, had a second storey. The absence of any roof tiles indicates that the roof was flat with wood beams spanning the arches, covered

FIG. 7.38   *Room 2, view of east baulk.*

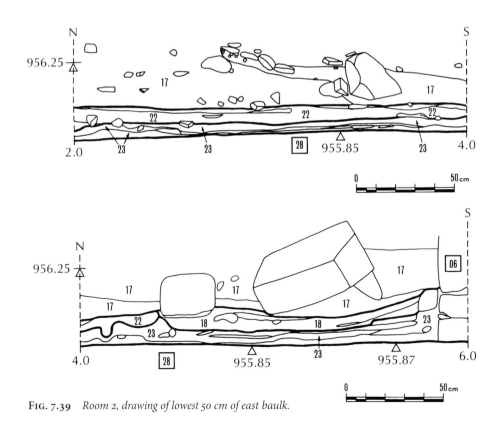

FIG. 7.39   *Room 2, drawing of lowest 50 cm of east baulk.*

by thatch and compressed soil. No trace survives of any windows in the walls of the rooms.

7.C.2. Stratigraphy

The upper layers of fill in Room 2 (Locus 02.01, 02, 03, and 04, all largely arbitrary) consisted of layers of rock tumble with many random boulders, cobbles and pebbles in loose sand and silty soil (figs. 7.38–39). No alignment of the tumble was observed. Below these loci, a layer of soil (Locus 02.05) contained a number of voussoirs from the three arches that had spanned the room. These layers were about 0.90 m thick.

The layers below Locus 02.05, ca. 0.50 m thick, contained less tumble (fig. 7.39). Ashy, sandy soil (Locus 02.13) occupied the north end of the room, perhaps representing the remains of transient cooking fires after the collapse of the Church complex, along with a nearly complete chronological sample of Humayma ceramics (MN, LN, ER, RO, MB, LB, UM, and possibly AB) and fragments of

glass and bone. A well-preserved Byzantine bronze lamp was found here (p. 441, no. 34, fig. 12.15.34), possibly a rare surviving example of the original furnishings of the Church, aside from the chancel screens. A silty soil without ash (Locus 02.14) occupied the rest of the room. Below these two deposits throughout the entire room were further layers of mixed loose silty soil with some ashy pockets and a few voussoirs in their original alignment (Loci 02.15, 16, 17), approximately at a level even with the top of the benches along the south and west walls. The substantial amounts of pottery in these layers were very mixed, Nabataean through Early Islamic in date; animal bones and glass were also present (fig. 7.41).

At approximately the level of the top of the door threshold in the south wall (elev. 956.03 m), the soil layers above the flagstone pavement (Th ca. 0.20 m), almost all of which was sifted, contained much ash (Locus 02.29), concentrated at the south end of the room. There, the deposit below the silty soil of Locus 02.17 was mostly ashy soil ranging from dark black

Fig. 7.40 *Room 2, northwest corner with recessed oven.*

ash to light bluish grey with lenses of non-ash mixed in (Locus 02.18). A thin layer of almost totally sterile silt (Locus 02.19) lay between the ash and the pavement in some parts of the south area. In the west central part of the room, there was generally sandier, non-ashy soil (Locus 02.20) above the pavers, while a higher proportion of ashy soil (Locus 02.22) was found above the pavers around the eastern central area. In the doorway itself was a deposit of generally silty soil without ash (Locus 02.21). The collection of ceramic fragments was again nearly comprehensive, indicating the open nature of the deposits: MN, LN, ER, RO, EB, MB, LB, UM, AB.

Within the non-ashy soil of Locus 02.20 there is an extensive hard clay surface (Locus 02.23, MN, LN, LB, UM, AB), which surrounded two paving stones that had been removed from their original position slightly to the north (in front of the north arch support pier) and shifted above the adjacent pavers. Dark ash containing many large storage jar fragments was found in the clay below the shifted pavers and also covered the space from which the pavers had been taken.

The ashy deposits were not present in the northwest area of the room. Several paving slabs were missing along the north part of the west wall,

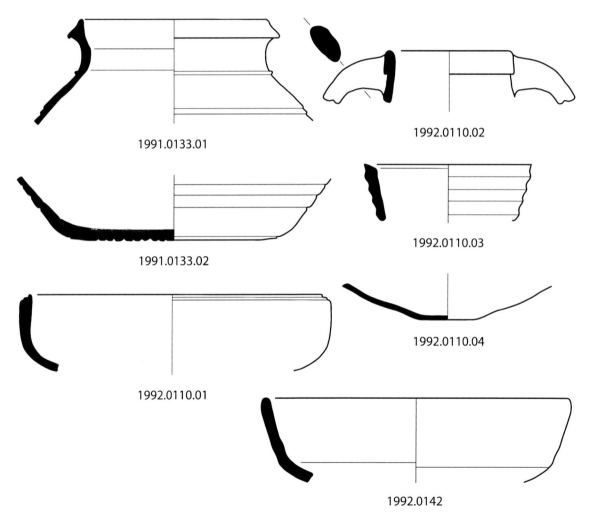

Fig. 7.41 *Ceramic Profiles from Room 2 (Sacristy), Loci 14, 42, 49. 1991.0133.01: C101.02.14, jar. 1991.0133.02: C101.02.14, jar (cf. 1992.0500, above fig. 7.18; 1992.0377.01, below fig. 7.69; Humayma, ʿAmr and Schick 2001: fig. 9.20, mid-7c; cf. Sauer and Herr 2012: 254, fig. 3.22.9–23, 73–135) (mid-7c). 1992.0110.01: C101.02.42, NFW bowl (Petra, EZ I: fig. 61, AD 20–1st quarter 2c) (1c). 1992.0110.02: C101.02.42, jar. 1992.0110.03: C101.02.42, bowl. 1992.0110.04: C101.02.42, NFW bowl (1c). 1992.0142: C101.02.49, bowl.*

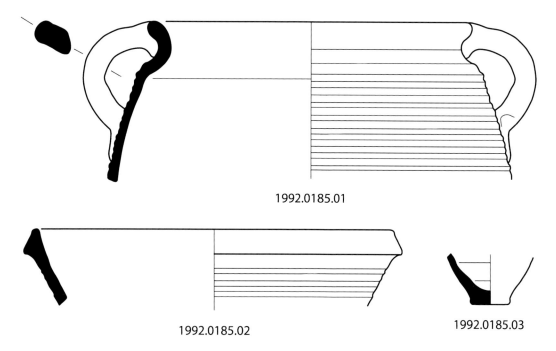

1992.0185.01

1992.0185.02

1992.0185.03

FIG. 7.42 *Ceramic Profiles from Room 2 (Sacristy), Locus 48. 1992.0185.01: cook pot (cf. Jabal Harûn, Gerber 2008b: 317, fig. 4.86, no good parallels) (6C). 1992.0185.02: bowl (6C). 1992.0185.03: juglet base.*

where the west bench did not reach, and along the north wall, where there also was no evidence for a bench (fig. 7.40). In place of the bench there was sandy, pebbly soil containing much ceramic material and bone, but very little glass (Locus 02.24, 30, 31, 32, and 33). The pottery from these loci was completely Byzantine with no Islamic period sherds.

Below the ashy deposit (Locus 02.23), the hole where the two pavers had been removed was filled with clumped, sandy soil (Locus 02.25) containing MN, LN, LB ceramics and many fragments of iron nails and liturgical glass lamps. Below this layer were the remnants of an oven lined with fired brick (Locus 02.36). It seems that the two paving stones were intentionally removed in order to install the oven below floor level. The oven is larger and better constructed than the *tabuns* in the other excavation areas. Removal of the ash deposit (Locus 02.37) directly above the oven and of a small quantity of non-ashy soil immediately outside it (Locus 02.38) revealed the oven floor, formed of roughly flat cobbles (elev. 955.46 m). Only a small portion of the fired brick sides of the oven survived.

The presence of the oven in the room helps to account for the large number of storage jars, some

burnt, the large amounts of animal bones, and the concentrated ash deposits in various parts of the room. It is likely the room was put to use for domestic occupation after the building had gone out of use as a church. Many fragments of glass liturgical lamps were also found mixed in the bottom ash layers, pointing to the original function of the room in its church phase as a sacristy storage room for the liturgical vessels.

After exposure of the oven, two paving stones were removed in the northwest corner of the room to enlarge for further excavation the narrow space along the north and west walls where the pavement is absent. A sequence of layers (Locus 02.39 to Locus 02.50) was then excavated until the bases of the north and west walls of the room were exposed at a depth of ca. 2.0 m below the pavement (elev. ca. 953.80 m), matching the depth of the wall of the north apse (elev. 953.85 m). Directly below the removed pavers was a thin layer of silt (Locus 02.39), and below that a more substantial layer of silt (Locus 02.40), above a layer of ashy silt (Locus 02.41) that extended to the level of the oven floor (elev. 955.46 m). Below this were variable layers of slightly ashy sandy silt and silt (Loci 02.42 to

02.49). The lowest stratum was the layer of sterile orange sand (Locus 02.50) found at the bottom of the other probes in the Church.

Those layers (Locus 02.42 to Locus 02.49) all appear to be intentionally deposited fill. None of them can easily be seen as a beaten earth floor or other occupational surface. All of the layers contained substantial quantities of potsherds (MN, LN, ER, MB, LB; fig. 7.41), a high proportion of them fourth to fifth-century in date, and none of them clearly Islamic. There were also scraps of iron and bronze, and animal bones, but — in contrast to the strata above the pavement — little or no glass. The only registered finds in this fill were an elongated, leaf-shaped bronze spoon from a cosmetic instrument and a crescent-shaped bronze sheet, both found in Locus 02.42. The character of this assemblage is consistent with carefully picked-over domestic rubbish collected from dumps elsewhere and brought in as fill.

7.C.3. Conclusions

Given its location off the east end of the north aisle, with no access from outside the Church, its size, and the presence of the bronze lamp and many fragments of liturgical glass lamps in the layers immediately above the pavement, the room can be identified as a sacristy. Similar rooms built to the north of three-apse basilicas can be seen in Room I at the Petra Church, where the papyrus scrolls were found (Fiema et al. 2001: 18–23, 138–50), as well as the Cathedral at Umm al-Jimal (Michel 2001: 173–74) and the Church of the Lions at Umm al-Rasas (Piccirillo 1992). In those last two cases, however, no finds from the rooms indicate their function.

After the building went out of use as a church, within the Umayyad period, occupants lifted a couple of the paving slabs and installed an oven. Given relatively close confines and the presence of substantial deposits of ash around the installation, the individuals using the oven may have lived elsewhere in the Church, or in a nearby structure. The roofing arches, possibly still carrying the roof, were still in place while the oven was in use. The layer of soil and rubbish above the ash deposits indicates that the room was abandoned for some time before the roofing arches fell.

The ashy deposits in the bottom few centimetres directly above the pavement of the room, however, appear to have been deposits of cooking ash from the oven, rather than remnants of burned wood from the roof. Unlike the roof over the nave of the Church, the roof over Room 2 did not burn down.

7.D. THE NORTHWEST ROOM, ENTRANCE HALL (ROOM 4)

Excavation of the eastern portion of Room 4, to the north of the church west of Room 2, involved a considerable effort during the 1992 and 1993 seasons. The wall lines were not visible on the surface before work began, but they were fully delineated during the 1992 season, revealing the room's interior dimensions to be ca. 12 m east–west by 6 m north–south. Clearing also revealed the sole entrance into the Church from the outside in the northeast corner of the room. The fill within the room was ca. 2.0 m deep, consisting of heavy, tumbled blocks and rubble in a hard soil matrix. Given the time constraints, excavation was focused on the eastern end of the room in an L-shaped trench that exposed both the north entrance door and the door into the north aisle of the Church, the centre line of which was 2.0 m west of the centre line of the north entrance door.

7.D.1. Architectural Features

Although only about a quarter of the room was cleared, some significant architectural features were revealed, in addition to the two doors.

Walls

The north wall and west wall of the room are in line with and bond with the north wall of the Sacristy and the west wall of the Church (figs. 7.2–3). The east wall (Locus 04.50) and the south wall (Locus 04.51) are shared with the Sacristy and the north aisle of the Church, respectively. The widths and methods of construction are also identical, indicating that all these walls belong to a single construction phase. The east and south walls were highest at the southeast corner (elev. 957.99 m) and dropped

Fig. 7.43 *North door to Church, and staircase in Room 4, view from N.*

down to the west and north (elev. 957.34 m). The north and west walls are preserved mostly at a uniform wall course around elev. 957.09 m, ca. 1.55 m above the level of the beaten earth floor in the room. There is no surviving trace of any windows or cupboards in the walls.

Arch Piers

A support pier for a north–south arch (Locus 04.65; top elev. 957.02 m) was uncovered along the interior face of the north wall just west of the north door. It extends into the west baulk and consists of five irregular courses of dressed sandstone blocks, 0.48 m north–south and 1.30 m high, placed in two rows with chinking stones. It is in line with a pier (Locus 04.53; top elev. 756.72 m), 0.50 m north–south and 0.60 m east–west just east of the south door. There is another arch pier (Locus 04.54; top elev. 956.70 m), immediately west of the

south door. This west pier, extending into the west baulk, is 0.50 m north–south and consists of three courses of marl and sandstone blocks in two rows with mud packing and chink stones. If intervals of ca. 2.0 m between the piers, and widths of ca. 0.60 m for the piers themselves continued along the rest of the room, there would have been four evenly spaced north–south arches to support the roof. The interval between the westernmost arch and the west wall of the room may have been slightly less than that between the easternmost arch and the east wall. The larger interval on the east is necessary to accommodate both the entrance door and the stairs. The presence of the south door also requires a 2.0 m interval.

Staircase

Immediately inside the north door are remains of a staircase (Locus 04.52; top elev. 957.46 m, 0.20 m lower than the immediately adjacent east wall) ascending southward (fig. 7.43), similar to the staircase in the southwest corner of the Church. The steps in this case, however, are made of re-used marl aqueduct blocks placed upside down on a support wall of blocks and rubble fill. Seven remain in position; they vary in height from 0.17 to 0.22 m, are 0.90 m wide, and extend for 3.55 m north–south. The steps provided access either to the roof over Room 4 or to a clerestory along the north side of the nave.

North Door and Pavement

The north door extends for 1.20 m east–west, starting 0.80 m west of the east wall of the room (fig. 7.44). The threshold of the door in the north wall consists of large flat-lying stones at two different levels. At the north end of the doorway is a large dressed sandstone threshold block (Locus 04.59, top elev. 956.41; L 1.20 m long east–west, W 0.35 m, Th 0.17 m). To the south is a step down ca. 0.21 m to the central part of the doorway to a layer of cobbles (Locus 04.60; elev. 956.16 m) with mud packing, covered with a layer of plaster (L 0.90 m east–west, W up to 0.35 m, Th 0.10 m). In the south part of the doorway, 0.10 m lower down, are three large flat sandstone blocks aligned north–south, with slight mud-packing (Locus 04.61; elev. 956.06 m), 0.90 m long east–west, up to 0.38 wide and 0.08 m thick; they were covered by the Locus 04.60 layer, which would have extended through the entire southern part of the doorway.

Immediately south of the doorway there is a step down to two large dressed sandstone blocks with mud packing (Locus 04.62; elev. 955.95 m; L 1.65 m east–west, 0.55 m north–south, Th 0.15 m). They are placed in part on top of two marl blocks (Locus 04.63; elev. 955.81; L 1.00 m east–west, 0.25 m north–south, Th 0.19 m), placed horizontally.

Farther south an additional large, sandstone block (Locus 04.64; elev. 955.71 m), seemingly an out-of-place paver, was uncovered during the excavation of the Locus 4.09 deposit. Its original position is not apparent; it is too large to be the missing landing for the staircase. There were no further pavers to the south, only a beaten earth floor (Locus 04.13 = 04.44; elev. around 955.60 m), until two pavers just inside the south door of the room at elev. 955.55 m.

South Door and Pavement

The door in the south wall leading into the north aisle of the Church is 1.40 m wide (fig. 7.45). The doorjambs on the east (Locus 04.55; top elev. 956.73 m) and on the west (Locus 04.56; top elev. 956.57 m) consist of two large, carefully dressed blocks. In the doorway on the south side is a single large paver at the same level as the pavement in the north aisle, then some cobbles, and then on the north side two narrower sandstone blocks (Locus 04.57; elev. 956.01 m). That threshold is ca. 0.22 m above the level of the pavement in the north aisle of the Church to the south, and 0.25 m above a row of five blocks to the north at elev. 955.76 m that extends for 2.00 m east–west between the two arch support piers that flank the door. To their north is a second step down to two large flat sandstone pavers at elev. 955.55 m.

Roof

No roof tiles were found anywhere in Room 4, indicating that the roof most likely was flat, with wood beams spanning the arches and covered with

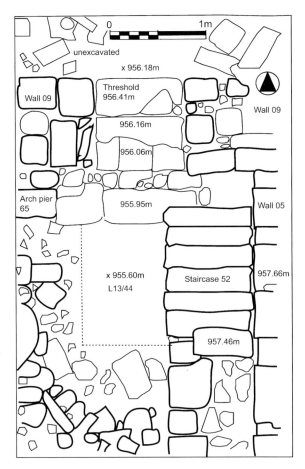

FIG. 7.44 *Northeast corner of Room 4, plan.*

thatch and compressed soil. The staircase most likely would have led to the roof rather than to a second storey, for which there is no evidence. The amount of tumbled blocks found in Room 4 are not sufficient to allow reconstruction of a second storey or a gallery above the north aisle.

7.D.2. Stratigraphy

In 1992, the surface of the room was cleaned up, and the interior face of the east wall and the exterior face of the north wall were clarified (Locus 04.00), revealing the location of the doorway in the north wall. Excavation then began with removal of topsoil (Locus 04.01) to just below the preserved wall tops, particularly in the eastern portion of the room where the soil was slightly higher than elsewhere. The top of the staircase was exposed during removal of topsoil in this area. The exterior

Fig. 7.45   *South door of Room 4, entrance to north aisle.*

face of the north wall is less well preserved than its interior face, which survives to a level one wall course higher over most of its extent.

As excavation proceeded, a trench 5 m north–south by 3 m east–west was laid out, extending from 2 m north of the inside face of the north door to 3 m to the south of the door, in order to sample both the interior and exterior of the room. Three superimposed layers of tumbled blocks and soil (Loci 04.02, 03 and 04) were revealed (fig. 7.46–47). At their bottom level, 1.30 m below the top of the east wall, the north wall and doorway of the room were fully delineated, so for further excavation different loci were assigned for the soil north and south of the doorway. Excavation continued to encounter tumbled blocks and soil both inside the room (Locus 04.05, 07) and outside (Locus 04.06, 08). Very few ceramics were encountered (MN, LN, MB, LB, UM, AB), but there was a modest amount of white wall plaster. At a point ca. 1.80 m below the top of the east wall, the rock tumble terminates

on a horizontal stratum of soil in both the interior and exterior of the room, leaving the threshold of the north door exposed (elev. 956.41 m) (fig. 7.45).

Outside the room, the rock tumble lay on a slightly compacted layer of silty, sandy soil (Locus 04.14), with a few cobbles and pebbles, but only a small amount of pottery (LB, UM, AB). Removal of this layer exposed a more compacted layer (elev. 956.18 m), left unexcavated, which probably represents the original ground level when the Church was in use, 0.23 m below the north threshold.

Beneath the rock tumble of Locus 04.07, around the same level as the first paver inside the room (Locus 04.62; elev. 955.95 m), further excavation exposed layers of silty, sandy soil with some ash down to the beaten earth floor of the room (Locus 04.13; elev. 955.60 m) (figs. 7.46–47). Excavation proceeded first with a 1.0 by 1.0 metre probe south of the doorway. This probe revealed two layers of silty, sandy soil with few if any cobbles or pebbles, separated by a layer of black powdery ash with

FIG. 7.46   *Southwest baulk in Room 4, view from east.*

some grey and white ash mixed in. Very little pottery was found in these three layers (Locus 04.09; MN, LN, LB, UM, AB), excavated to a depth of some 0.20 m. Excavation farther south in the room separated these three layers into the upper layer of loose silty, sandy soil with very few cobbles or pebbles and only a slight amount of pottery (Locus 04.10; MN, LB, UM; top elev. ca. 955.83 m), the ash below (Locus 04.11; MN, LB) and the compacted silt below the ash (Locus 04.12; MN, LB, UM; fig. 7.48), which contained virtually no pebbles, cobbles, or pottery.

The removal of Locus 04.12 revealed a beaten earth floor (Locus 04.13) composed of very compacted silt with embedded cobbles and pebbles. Its elevation of 955.60 m is some 0.20 m lower than the pavement in the Nave and in Room 2. Oddly, the flagstone pavement seen in the Sacristy, Church, and Room 5 is absent in the excavated areas of Room 4, aside from a few slabs in front of the north and south doors. Excavation of the beaten earth floor for a few

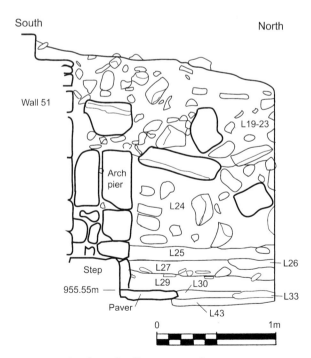

FIG. 7.47   *Southwest baulk in Room 4, drawing.*

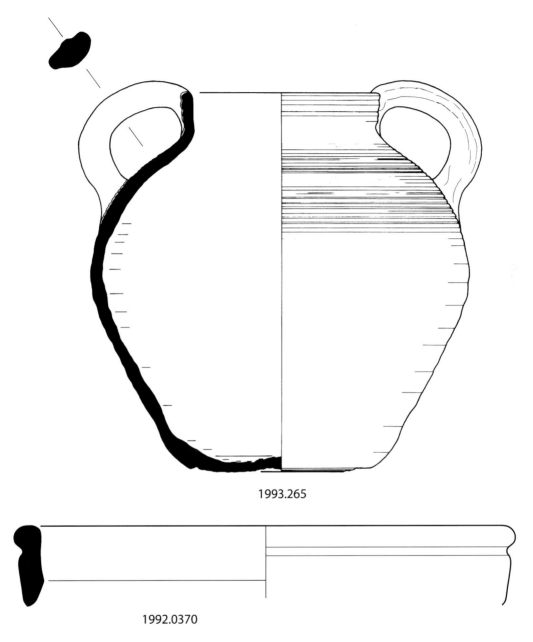

1993.265

1992.0370

FIG. 7.48 *Ceramic Profiles from Room 04 (Entrance Hall), Loci 12, 28. 1993.0265: C101.04.28, cook pot, ware and int. 5YR 6.5/5, ext. 5YR 6/4 to 5YR 5/6 (Humayma, 'Amr and Schick 2001: fig. 8.17; mid-7C) (mid-7C). 1992.0370 (scale 1:3): C101.04.12, large bowl, (Humayma, 'Amr and Schick 2001: fig. 12.37, mid-7C) (mid-7C).*

centimetres down to elev. 955.52 m produced a moderate quantity of pottery, the highest concentration being third-century to late fourth- or early fifth-century (MN, LN, LB), and animal bones.

Removal of the beaten earth floor revealed a cobble wall (Locus 04.18; top elev. 955.52 m), adjacent to the west side of the staircase, probably serving as its foundation. Only the initial few

centimetres of slightly compacted silty, sandy soil with some cobbles, pebbles, and ash to the west of the cobble wall was excavated, so the depth of this low wall remains undetermined. This deposit resembles the fill layers below the pavement in the adjacent Room 2.

In the northeast corner of the room interior, during the removal of tumble (Locus 04.07) a

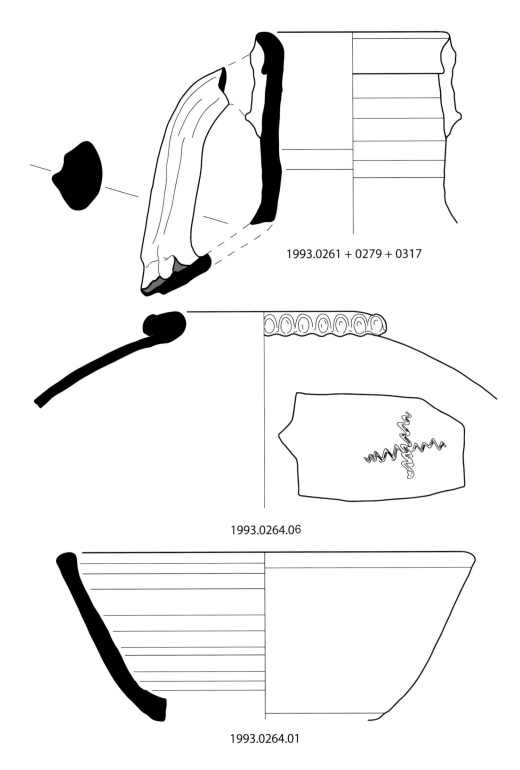

1993.0261 + 0279 + 0317

1993.0264.06

1993.0264.01

FIG. 7.49 *Ceramic Profiles from Room 04 (Entrance Hall), Loci 26, 28, 29. 1993.0261, 0279, 0317: C101.04.28, 26, 29, storage jar, core 5YR 4/2, ware 10R 5/8, rim ext. 2.5YR 6/7, ext. slip 5YR 5.5/2 to 5YR 6.5/3, int. 5YR 6.5/3 (Humayma, 'Amr and Schick 2001: fig. 3.4, mid-7c; Mt. Nebo, Bagatti 1985: fig. 16.7, 531–ea. 7c) (mid-7c). 1993.0264.06 (scale 1:4): C101.04.28, storage jar, ware 2.5YR 5.5/7, core 10YR 5.5/6 (Humayma, 'Amr and Schick 2001: fig. 6.10, mid-7c) (mid-7c). 1993.0264.01: C101.04.28, bowl, ware 5YR 6/4, surfaces 10YR 7.5/2 (Humayma, 'Amr and Schick 2001: fig. 11.36, mid-7c; Aqaba, Melkawi et al. 1994: fig. 8.n, mid- to late 7c) (mid-7c).*

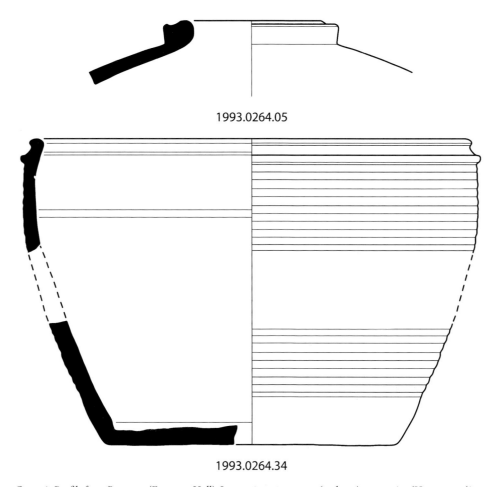

1993.0264.05

1993.0264.34

Fɪɢ. 7.50   *Ceramic Profile from Room 04 (Entrance Hall), Locus 28. 1993.0264.07 (scale 1:4): storage jar (Humayma, ʿAmr and Schick 2001: fig. 6.11, mid-7C). 1993.0264.34 (scale 1:4): basin (Humayma, ʿAmr and Schick 2001: fig. 11.34, mid-7C) (mid-7C).*

deposit of ashy soil about 0.70 × 0.70 m was encountered that covered the lowest step of the staircase, so this portion of the room was excavated separately from Loci 04.09 and 04.10–12. At the top (elev. 956.12), at a depth of 1.54 m from the top of the east wall and about the level of the plastered cobbles in the south part of the door (Locus 04.60), was some silty soil (Locus 04.15). Below it were layers of grey, white and black powdery ash with no pottery, and then an underlying layer of silty, sandy soil with a slight amount of pottery (Locus 04.16; LB, UM, AB) extending down to the level of the bottom of the lowest step of the staircase. Below, there is silty, sandy soil (Locus 04.17) with a moderate amount of pottery (MN, LN, LB). No further step or landing was found despite further probing down to elev. 955.85, 0.10 m below the top of the immediately adjacent northernmost pavers

(Locus 04.62). It is difficult to imagine that the staircase was built originally without a substantial landing at this point, but there is also no sign that a landing paver was removed.

In 1993, an area about 5.0 m east–west × 3.4 m north–south was excavated in the southeast area of Room 4 adjoining the 1992 trench in order to uncover fully the southern extent of the staircase, and to expose the doorway in the middle of the south wall that led to the north aisle of the Church. The same deposit of tumbled blocks and soil that had been found in 1992 was excavated in the room down to the southern continuation of the beaten earth floor, and then a probe was dug below the floor level along the east wall. The layers of tumble in silty, sandy soil (Loci 04.20, 21, 22, 23, 24) contained little pottery (MN, LN, RO, LR, MB, LB, UM, AB). Among the tumble were several reused marl

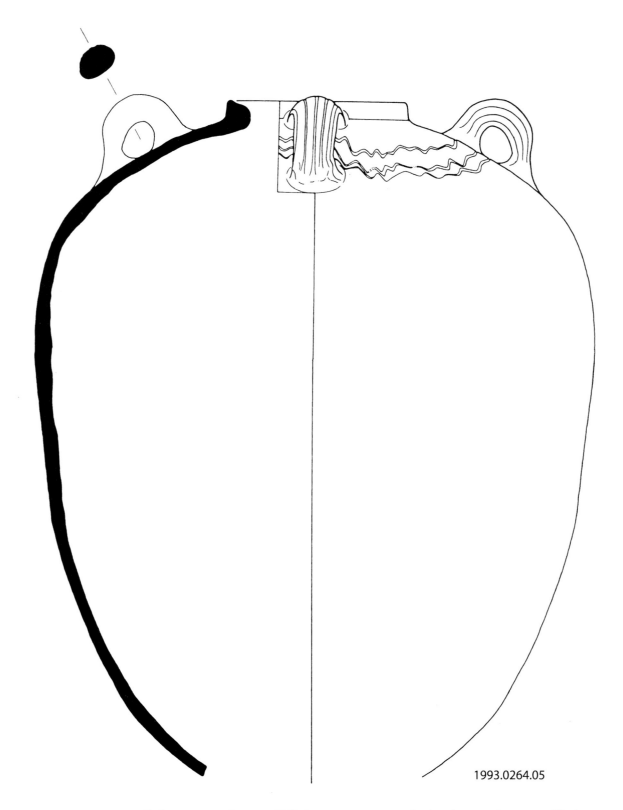

1993.0264.05

FIG. 7.51 *Ceramic Profile from Room 04 (Entrance Hall), Locus 28. 1993.0264.05 (scale 1:4): storage jar, ware 2.5YR 5/6, ext 7.5YR 8/3 to 2.5YR 6/6, int. 2.5YR 6/6 (Humayma, 'Amr and Schick 2001: fig. 7.13, mid-7C; Mt. Nebo, Bagatti 1985: fig. 16.7, 531–ea. 7C; Waiszewski 2001: fig. 2.2, 6–7C) (mid-7C).*

aqueduct blocks that had fallen off the staircase. No clear alignment of the tumble was observed, except in the west baulk, where several arch blocks from the easternmost north–south arch in the room remained in close juxtaposition.

At the bottom of these layers of tumble layers (elev. ca. 956.16–955.98 m) was a transition layer of tumble and sub-tumble (Locus 04.25) above a sub-tumble deposit of silt (Locus 04.26 = Locus 4.10 from 1992) that contained substantial quantities of pottery (MN, LN, ER, LB, UM), along with fragments of glass lamps and their suspension chains, scraps of iron, fragments of marble chancel screen, including one with a portion of an inscription (p. 460), and numerous animal bones. Below the silt in the north part of the trench there was a layer of alternating grey and black ash (Locus 04.27 = Locus 04.11 from 1992; MN LB, UM), ca. 0.17 m thick (variable bottom elev. ca. 955.80–955.69 m). This ash layer did not extend into the southeast corner of the room or near the door in the south wall. The nature of this ash layer is less clear than the ash in the Church from the roof burning down or the deposit of ash in Room 2 from the oven. Here the ash did not form a continuous layer across all of the excavated area. It was deposited after the artefact-rich layers, described below, and so does not seem to be an occupational deposit itself. Its origin in the burning of the roof seems the most likely explanation.

Below the Locus 04.27 ash was a layer of loose to compacted silt (Locus 4.28 = Locus 04.12 from 1992; top elev. ca. 955.80 m; Th 0.20 m) around the level of the row of blocks between the arch support piers flanking the south door. It contained approximately 30 kg of ceramic fragments, some of which were partly restorable with fragments from Loci 4.27 and 4.30, along with scraps of bronze, lead, and iron, fragments of glass, a decorated bone object (p. 447, no. 17, fig. 12.18.17), numerous animal bones, and several sea shells (figs. 7.48–54). There were also numerous marble chancel screen fragments, including several with fragments of inscriptions (p. 460, nos.1–8, figs. 13.4.3–4). This locus contained exceptionally large numbers of storage jar sherds that joined, from at least six vessels, a funnel, basin, large bowl, four cooking pots, and a North African Red Slip plate. The storage jar sherds were concentrated

immediately north of the arch pier (Locus 04.53) on the east side of the door in the south wall, but this is unlikely to have been the original location of the jars. Their placement so close to the door would have made access into the Church awkward. The rest of the deposit looks like a dump of occupation debris mixed with destroyed Church furnishings.

Below this Locus 04.28 layer of dump, in front of the door in the south wall, there was a lower layer of compacted sandy, silty soil with a lens of ash (Locus 04.29; bottom elev. 955.71 m) above a layer of compacted silty soil (Locus 04.30; bottom elev. 955.55 m). Both these loci, 0.27 m thick, contained sherds that joined with vessels in Locus 04.28. As one might expect in a dump, there was a great mix of ceramics from EN to RO, LB, and UM. Locus 04.30 lay above a few stone pavers (elev. 955.55 m) in front of the doors.

In the southeast corner of the room, below the ash layers, there were lower layers of silt associated with three circular stone installations (fig. 7.55). Here, below the sub-ash layer of silt (Locus 04.28) was a layer of compact silty soil (Locus 04.31; MN, LB; top elev. 955.61 m). A small portion of this layer in the south central area was excavated separately (Locus 04.38; MN, LB, UM). Immediately to the south of the staircase, below the silt of locus 04.28, in place of the Locus 04.31 layer, there was an installation (Locus 04.34), consisting of a layer of flat cobbles (top elev. 955.76 m) packed around a thin, circular sandstone slab (D ca. 0.45 m), resting on loose to slightly compacted silty, clayey soil. The feature had no clear function, although it could have served as a stand for some vessel or other object. Below it (Locus 04.35; LB; top elev. 955.71 m) was a further deposit of slightly compacted silty, clayey soil above some greenish ashy soil (Locus 04.36; LB; top elev. 955.68 m), ca. 0.05–0.10 m thick. At a level around the bottom of Locus 04.36 (elev. 955.63 m), to the southwest of the Locus 04.34–36 installation, and below the Locus 04.31 silt, a second installation was encountered, a roughly circular deposit (D ca. 1.20 m) of greenish ashy soil, some 0.05 m thick, with some deliberately placed cobbles in the centre (Locus 04.37; MN, ER, LB, UM; fig. 7.55). Its function is not clear.

The southeast edge of the greenish ash (Locus 04.37) was bounded by another installation in

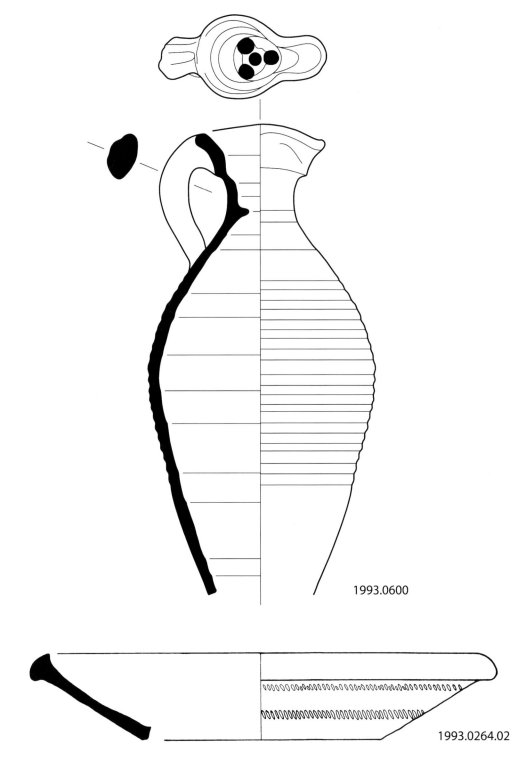

1993.0600

1993.0264.02

FIG. 7.52 *Ceramic Profiles from Room 04 (Entrance Hall), Loci 28, 28A. 1993.0600: C101.04.28A, strainer neck jug, ware and int. 2.5YR 6/7, ext. 2.5Y 8/2 with patches of 5YR 7/6, mica flakes (Humayma, 'Amr and Schick 2001: fig. 10.30, mid-7C; Aqaba kilns, Melkawi et al. 1994: fig. 8.n, mid- to late 7C) (mid-7C). 1993.0264.02 (scale 1:4): C101.04.28, "Aqaba basin," ware 2.5YR 5/8, ext. and int. 10YR 8/3, mica flakes (Humayma, 'Amr and Schick 2001: fig. 12.39, mid-7C; Aqaba kilns, Melkawi et al. 1994: fig. 8.j, mid- to late 7C) (mid-7C).*

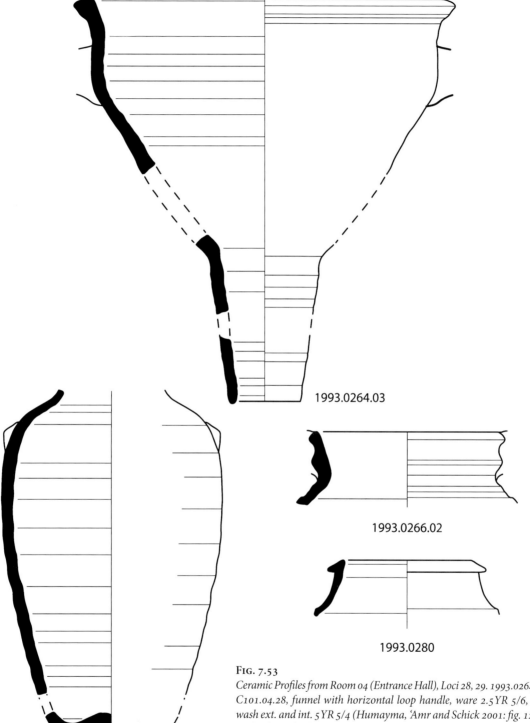

1993.0264.03

1993.0266.02

1993.0280

1993.0264.04

Fig. 7.53

Ceramic Profiles from Room 04 (Entrance Hall), Loci 28, 29. 1993.0264.03: C101.04.28, funnel with horizontal loop handle, ware 2.5 YR 5/6, thin wash ext. and int. 5 YR 5/4 (Humayma, 'Amr and Schick 2001: fig. 12.40, mid-7c) (mid-7c). 1993.0264.04: C101.04.28, jug, ware and int. 3.2 YR 6/8, patchy ext. slip 5 YR 5/3 to 5 YR 5/6 (Humayma, 'Amr and Schick 2001: fig, 9.28, mid-7c) (mid-7c). 1993.0266.02: C101.04.28, cooking pot, ware and int. 2.5 YR 5.5/8, thin ext. wash 5 YR 4/1 (Humayma, 'Amr and Schick 2001: fig. 8.16, mid-7c) (mid-7c). 1993.0280: C101.04.29, cook pot, ware and surfaces 2.5 YR 4.5/4 (Humayma, 'Amr and Schick 2001: fig. 9.22, mid-7c; Lejjun, Parker et al. 1987: 183, fig. 113, LB I–II) (mid-7c).

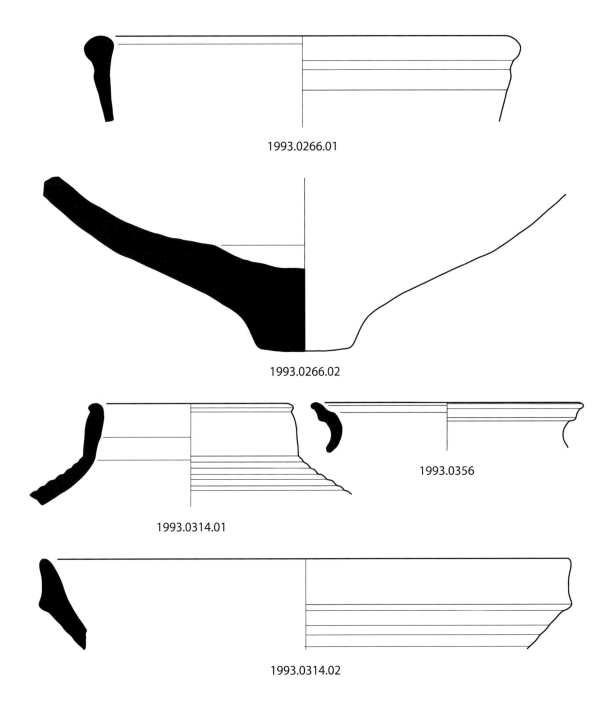

1993.0266.01

1993.0266.02

1993.0314.01

1993.0356

1993.0314.02

FIG. 7.54 *Ceramic Profiles from Room 04 (Entrance Hall), Loci 28, 29, 31. 1993.0266.01 (scale 1:3): C101.04.28, "Aqaba basin," ware 2.5YR 5/8, ext. and int. 10YR 8/3 (Humayma, 'Amr and Schick 2001: fig. 12.38; Aqaba kilns, Melkawi et al. 1994: fig. 8.j, mid- to late 7C) (mid-7C). 1993.0266.02: C101.04.28, storage jar base, ware 2.5YR 5/8, ext. slip mottled 10YR 7/3 to 2.5YR 6/6 (Humayma, 'Amr and Schick 2001: fig. 6.12; Khirbet edh-Dharih, Waliszewski 2001: fig. 2.8, 6–7C) (mid-7C). 1993.0314.01: C101.04.29, bag amphora, ware 2.5YR 5/8, ext. slip 10YR 7/3 to 5YR 6.5/4, int. 2.5YR 6/4 (parallels, 'Amr and Schick 2001: fig. 4.7, mid-7C) (mid-7C). 1993.0314.02: C101.04.29, "Aqaba bowl," ware 7.5YR 7/6, ext. and int. 2.5Y 8/2 (Humayma, 'Amr and Schick 2001: fig. 11.35; Aqaba kilns, Melkawi et al. 1994: fig. 8.n, mid- to late 7C) (mid-7C). 1993.0356: C101.04.31, jar, ware and int. 2.5YR 6/8, ext. slip 7.5YR 7/2 (Humayma, 'Amr and Schick 2001: fig. 8.15, mid-7C) (mid-7C).*

the extreme southeast corner of the room, which consisted of two phases. On top, below the Locus 04.28 silt, were three large dressed blocks placed in a quarter circle (Locus 04.39; top elev. 955.82–.72 m), framing a thin layer of ashy soil (Locus 04.32; top elev. 955.73), above a solid layer of flat cobbles and boulders with compacted silt around them (Locus 04.40; top elev. 955.64 m). One block within Locus 04.40 (top elev. 955.61 m) had the arm of a cross cut into it near its base; it clearly was a reused block, broken before it was placed here. Below the three blocks was the earlier phase of the installation, four blocks placed in a quarter circle (Locus 04.42; top elev. 955.65 m).

Throughout much of the southeast part of Room 4 below the layer of silt (Locus 04.31) and the two installations (Loci 04.34–36 south of the staircase and Locus 04.37) there was a deposit of hard compacted clay (Locus 04.44 = 04:13; top elev. ca. 955.61 m), representing the beaten earth floor of the room. However, below the third installation in the southeast corner (Loci 04.32, 39, 40) at this level was a layer of slightly compacted ashy soil (Locus 04.41; MN, LN, ER, MB, LB; top elev. 955.53 m; Th 0.18).

At least the first two installations in the southeast area of the room, and possibly the third, lay above the beaten earth floor. If the beaten earth floor is the primary floor of the room, then the installations could belong to the primary phase of the Church. But if the beaten earth floor is a secondary floor replacing the robbed out original flagstone paving, then the installations would belong to the first reoccupation of the building after it fell out of use as a church.

In the area near the south door, below the Loci 04.28–.30 dump deposit, at the level of the Locus 04.44 beaten earth floor, there is a deposit of ashy,

FIG. 7.55   *Southeast corner of Room 4.*

silty soil (Locus 04.33; top elev. 955.54 m), with many small MN and LB sherds, bronze clippings and a bronze perfume dipper (pp. 442–43, no. 40, fig. 12.17), fragments of glass, a few animal bone fragments, and a sea shell. This seems to represent the top of the fill deposited at the time of construction. Below it was a lower deposit of more ashy soil (Locus 04.43; top elev. 955.41 m) with small MN and LB sherds and animal bones, and occasional lenses of sandy, silty soil that resembled the sub-pavement fill layers of Room 2 (Locus 02.42 to Locus 02.49).

At the level of the beaten earth floor (Locus 04.44 = 04.13), projecting south some 0.20 m along

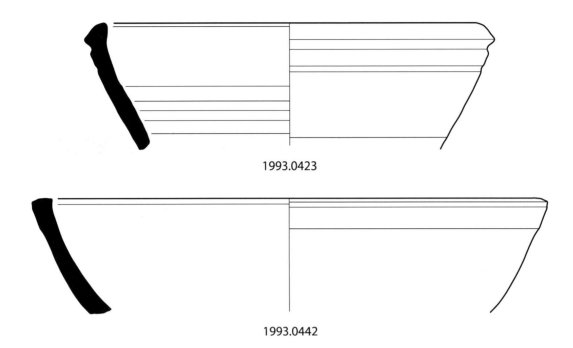

1993.0423

1993.0442

FIG. 7.56　*Ceramic Profiles from Room 04 (Entrance Hall), Loci 46, 49. 1993.0423: C101.04.46, bowl, inner surface 10R 6/6, exterior slip 5YR 7/2. 1993.0442: C101.04.49, bowl.*

the south edge of the staircase (Locus 04.52) to the east wall of the room (Locus 04.50) was a deep deposit of irregularly laid cobbles (Locus 04.45; top elev. 955.55 m) representing the sub-floor foundation for the staircase, found also to the west of the staircase in 1992 as Locus 04.18. A 1.0 m wide probe along the east wall below the beaten earth floor (Locus 04.44; bottom elev. 955.48 m) and the third installation in the southeast corner (Locus 04.42; bottom elev. 955.35 m) exposed a clumpy silt fill (Locus 04.46) with much MN, ER, LB pottery, fragments of glass, animal bones, and ash (fig. 7.56). Below was a lower layer of pebbly compact silt with pockets of ash (Locus 04.47; top elev. 955.30 m), and a still lower layer of ashy soil (Locus 04.48; top elev. ca. 955.10 m) with MN, LN, ER, and LB pottery, fragments of glass, and animal bone. Below this lower silt (Locus 04.48), a portion of another layer of silty soil (Locus 04.49; top elev. 954.91 m; MN, LB) was excavated further until work stopped at an arbitrary depth (elev. 954.72 m), not quite a metre below the level of the beaten earth floor and seemingly about 0.90 above the bottom of the east wall, as revealed in Room 2. The layers of fill resembled those excavated in 1992 below

the pavement in Room 2, and in the probe in the central apse of the Church.

7.D.3. Conclusions

It is odd that this room had only a beaten earth floor, rather than the flagstone pavements in all the other rooms, given the amount of traffic that the room saw. Everyone using the Church had to pass through it. It is conceivable that the few flagstones by the north door and the nearby stairs up to the roof as well as by the south door into the Church were part of a more extensive pavement that was later removed. But the intact floor of packed soil and clay in the room seems to be the primary church-phase floor.

Only the eastern quarter of Room 4 was excavated, which leaves the full use of the room undetermined. But given the exceptional plan of the church, with no doors in the west leading to a narthex or atrium there, Room 4 would have had to function as the narthex. The stone features in the southeast corner of the room are above the packed soil floor, leaving it ambiguous whether they date to the church or initial post-Church use of the building. The artefact-rich deposit inside the south door seem to belong to the post-Church phase of occupation, given the present of broken pieces of the marble chancel screens in it. The presence of storage jars there, with a parallel in the Petra Church (Fiema et al 2001: 80–81), could point to a post-Church use. It could be that the people who installed the oven in the Sacristy lived here after the church went out of use.

7.E. THE SOUTHEAST ROOM (ROOM 3)

The Southeast Room, along the eastern half of the south wall of the Church, is roughly square, with interior dimensions of about 6 × 6 m (figs. 7.2–3). An initial 2.0 by 2.0 m square was excavated in the northwest corner in 1991, and a second 3 × 2 m square in the northeast corner was excavated in 1992, clearing the northern third of the room to floor level. The objectives were to determine its function and clarify whether this room was part

of the original Church construction, since the west wall of the room did not bond with the south wall of the Church, and there was no door allowing direct access from the Church.

7.E.1. Architectural Features

The south wall of the Church was found to cut through the original north wall of the room, indicating that the room pre-dated the construction of the Church. The room was roofed by two north–south arches. Along the north wall, the west arch support pier (Locus 03.10; top elev. 955.06 m) measures 0.50 m E/W and 0.40 m N/S and consists of three dressed blocks, the space between the pier and the north wall chinked with small stones (figs. 7.57–58). The east pier along the north wall is similar, but less well preserved; some of the tumbled arch blocks were found still aligned with it to the south. The west pier is 1.50–2.00 m east of the west wall, with a space of 1.50 m between it and the east

FIG. 7.57 *Room 3, northwest corner.*

FIG. 7.58 *Room 3, northeast corner.*

pier, which is 1.50–2.00 m west of the east wall. The piers along the south wall were not exposed. The room is paved in the same manner as the Church interior, with irregular sandstone flagstones (Loci 03.15, 16; elev. 954.27 m). This pavement is ca. 1.50 m lower than that inside the Church and ca. 0.47–.43 m lower than the pavement in Room 5 to the west. Excavation did not proceed below the pavement.

A door into the room from Square 6 to the east is partially exposed in the north central portion of the east wall. A second doorway in the middle of the west wall, leading into Room 5, is exposed as part of the excavation of Room 5.

Two cupboards had been built into the north wall, between the west and east arch support piers (W 0.40 m, 0.50 m deep, H unknown) and between the east pier and the east wall (W 0.35 m, H 0.35 m, 0.45 m). The bottom of the cupboards, ca. 1.30 m above the level of the pavement, consists of thin stone slabs, while the sides are formed by stone blocks placed upright.

Excavation uncovered four other installations in the room, bins built of stone slabs set directly on the flagstone pavement. The first is located in the northwest corner between the west wall and the western pier (ext. L 1.50 m, W 0.80 m, 0.22 m deep; int. L 1.20 m, W 0.60 m) (fig. 7.57). An east–west row of three large blocks (Locus 03.06; top elev. 954.76 m), with a lower course of blocks below, forms its south edge, while a single block (Locus 03.13; top elev. 954.68 m) along the west wall forms the west edge. The north wall and the western pier form the north and east edges. The base consists of a solid layer of cobbles packed in soil (Locus 03.14; elev. 954.54 m), ca. 0.25 m above the level of the pavement elsewhere in the room; the cobbles were not removed. The silty soil inside the installation (Locus 03.05) contained a few MN, ER, LB, UM, AB ceramics and fragments of bone and sea shell, but did not differ much from the soil elsewhere in the room.

The second bin was built along the west wall, immediately south of the first; it extends into the south baulk, so it was not fully exposed (L 1.20 m, W 0.80 m, 0.48 m deep; int. L ca. 0.70 m, W 0.40 m). A single large block (top elev. 954.77 m) forms

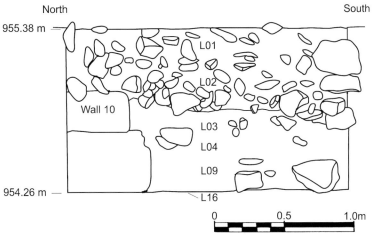

FIG. 7.59 *Room 3, drawing of east baulk.*

the north edge; three blocks (Locus 03.08; top elev. 954.60 m) form the east edge; a row of stones along the south baulk (Locus 03.11; top elev. 954.54 m) seems to form the south edge; two large blocks (Locus 03.12; top elev. 954.62 m) along the west wall form the west edge. The flagstone pavers (Locus 03.15; elev. 954.29 m), as elsewhere in the room, form the bottom, rather than the layer of cobbles as in the first installation. The silty soil (Locus 03.07) contained a few MN, LN, RO, LB, UM, and possibly AB ceramics, a fragment of rolled bronze sheet and bone fragments, but it was essentially the same as the soil elsewhere in the room.

The third bin (Locus 03.22) was built along the north wall between the two arch support piers (L 1.30 m, W 0.60 m, 0.32 m deep; int. L 1.20 m, W 0.40 m; fig. 7.58). An east–west row of three stones (top elev. 954.69 m) forms the south edge, while one block (top elev. 954.64 m) just east of the western pier forms the west edge. The north wall forms the north edge, while the eastern pier forms the east edge. The shallow interior is floored with cobbles and two larger blocks (elev. 954.58), as in the first installation, well above the pavement elsewhere in the room.

The fourth bin (Locus 03.23) is in the northeast corner of the room (L 1.30 m, W 0.80 m, 0.43 m deep; int. L 0.60 m, W 0.35 m) (fig. 7.58). A north–south row of two stones in two courses (top elev. 954.73 m) forms the west edge. The north and east walls form the north and east edges, while two courses of a single block form the south edge (top elev. 954.67 m), with two additional rows of blocks

(top elev. 954.54 m) immediately to the south. This fourth bin differs from the others in the absence of a stone floor. Rather it was filled with loose sandy, silty soil down to below the level of the pavement elsewhere in the room. No pottery or other artefacts were found within this installation. Three further blocks (top elev. 954.65) visible in the south balk to the south of the fourth installation may belong to a fifth installation.

The four installations were built after construction of the room, although it cannot be determined whether they were added immediately as a single construction phase, or singly over a period time as needed or as the function of the room changed. This type of bin built of stones against the wall of a room, making opportunistic use of corners and arch support piers to supplement and reinforce the added blocks, is common in domestic structures at Hauarra, e.g. in B100, F102, and F103. Exactly the same installations can be seen in the Bedouin houses built on ancient foundations around Humayma in the twentieth century (see pp. 313–14). Interpretation of the installations as either storage bins or feeding troughs for animals seems reasonable for both the ancient and the modern examples.

7.E.2. Stratigraphy

Excavation from the surface in 1991 exposed layers of tumbled blocks and stones (Locus 03.01, 02), devoid of artefacts, above compacted silty soil (Locus 03.03) (fig. 7.59). The first installation along the north wall of the room (Locus 03.06) appeared as this locus was removed. The silty soil (Locus 03.04, 09) surrounded the south side of the bin and occupied the rest of the room down to the pavement; it contained a modest amount of MN, LN, RO, LB, UM, and AB ceramics, animal bone fragments, and a small amount of ferrous slag.

Excavation in the northeast corner of the room in 1992 proceeded through the same sequence of layers, with topsoil (Locus 03.17 = Locus 03.01) above tumbled blocks and rubble (Locus 03.18 = Locus 03.02). This infill of rubble and soil rested on a fairly level deposit of silty soil that filled the rest of the room (Locus 03.19 = Locus 03.03 and 03.04 in the north centre; Locus 03.20 = 03.03 above and Locus 03.21 = Locus 03.4 below elsewhere). Within the silty fill (Locus 03.20, 21) were some large, carefully dressed blocks that clearly had fallen from the two arches that spanned the room. The fill contained MN, LN, LB, UM, and AB ceramics (fig. 7.60), a decorated sandstone loom weight (p.

508, no. 9, fig. 13.20.9), fragments of glass including window pane, several fragments of steatite cooking vessels with mending holes, and small amounts of animal bone and sea shell. There was no trace of ash or carbonized wood on the branches found in Room 5.

In addition to the excavation of the northern third of the room down to the flagstone pavement, the top layer of topsoil (Locus 03.17) was removed from the south two-thirds of the room, and the south wall and southern portions of the east and

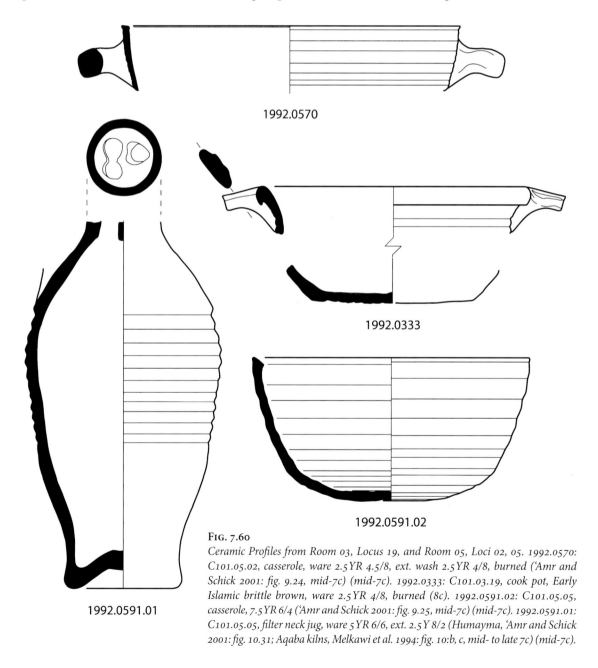

1992.0570

1992.0333

1992.0591.02

1992.0591.01

Fig. 7.60

Ceramic Profiles from Room 03, Locus 19, and Room 05, Loci 02, 05. 1992.0570: C101.05.02, casserole, ware 2.5YR 4.5/8, ext. wash 2.5YR 4/8, burned ('Amr and Schick 2001: fig. 9.24, mid-7c) (mid-7c). 1992.0333: C101.03.19, cook pot, Early Islamic brittle brown, ware 2.5YR 4/8, burned (8c). 1992.0591.02: C101.05.05, casserole, 7.5YR 6/4 ('Amr and Schick 2001: fig. 9.25, mid-7c) (mid-7c). 1992.0591.01: C101.05.05, filter neck jug, ware 5YR 6/6, ext. 2.5Y 8/2 (Humayma, 'Amr and Schick 2001: fig. 10.31; Aqaba kilns, Melkawi et al. 1994: fig. 10:b, c, mid- to late 7c) (mid-7c).

west walls of the room were fully cleaned off and delineated. No further walls were observed extending from the room on either the east or south sides.

7.F. THE SOUTHWEST ROOM (ROOM 5)

Room 5, to the west of Room 3 along the middle portion of the south wall of the church, was completely excavated in 1992, with the goals of determining its function and its relationship to the Church and to Room 3. The west wall of the room does not run parallel to the east wall, but forms a trapezoidal space ca. 6 m north–south and 4.5. m to 3.5 m east–west (figs. 7.2–3).

7.F.1. Architectural Features

As with Room 3, the south wall of the Church cut through the pre-existing north wall of Room 5 (Locus 05.13; Th 0.70 m), preserved to a height of six courses of dressed blocks and chink stones

above the pavement of the room. The west wall of the room (Locus 05.14) is preserved to a height of five irregular courses above the pavement in the south and seven courses above the pavement in the north (fig. 7.61). Two additional courses were exposed below the pavement in a probe in the northwest corner of the room. The west wall abuts the north wall and bonds with the south wall of the room (Locus 05.15; Th 0.70 m), which is preserved to only three courses. North of the door, the east wall of the room (Locus 05.16) is preserved to eight smaller, irregular courses (top elev. 955.70 m). South of the door (Locus 05.17) there are five preserved courses of variably sized, roughly dressed blocks with chinking stones (top elev. 955.60 m). The east wall abuts the north and south walls. In all these walls, the larger blocks face a rubble core.

Two piers on the inner face of the both the east wall (Loci 05.20, 21, top elev. 955.41 m, 955.32 m) and west wall (Loci 05.18, 19, top elev. 955.57 m, 955.31 m) originally carried two east–west arches

FIG. 7.61 *Room 5, view from south.*

FIG. 7.62 *Room 5, view of south baulk.*

that supported the roof (fig. 7.61). These piers are built in the same manner as those in Room 3, consisting of three carefully dressed blocks chinked with smaller stones where they abut the adjoining wall; the north pier on the west (locus 05.18) and the south and north piers on the east (loci 05.19 and 05.20) were 0.50 m wide and project 0.30 m; the south pier on the west wall (locus 05.19) is 0.45 m wide and project 0.25 m. A probe in the northwest corner of the room exposed a foundation of cobbles and small stones below the adjacent pier.

The north half of the room is paved with large, irregularly shaped flagstones (Locus 05.04) without any obvious orientation, at an elevation around 954.67 m, about 1.0 m lower than the pavement inside the Church and 0.40 m higher than the pavement in Room 3 to the east. Flagstones are absent in the south half of the room.

A bench or storage installation (Locus 05.22; H 0.48 m; top elev. 955.22 m) like those in Room 3 is built along the west wall between the two arch support piers (fig. 7.61). It consists of two courses of dressed blocks chinked with smaller stones; there may be a third course of blocks below the pavement level. A layer of cobbles forms the bottom, well above the level of the pavement of the room,

as with the first and third installations in Room 3.

A door in the east wall (W 0.90 m) connects Room 5 with Room 3. The threshold (Locus 05.23; elev. 954.72 m) consists of several large, aligned cobbles, which dropped down a step or two to the level of the pavement of Room 3 (elev. 954.27 m), although this southern area of Room 3 was not excavated. A concentration of corroded nails found nearby probably served as part of the door construction. There is no door connecting Room 5 with the Church, or with Room 7 to the south.

7.F.2. Stratigraphy

Excavation in the northwest corner of the room revealed the same sequence of strata seen in Room 3: topsoil (Locus 5.01), tumbled blocks and rubble (Locus 05.02), and undifferentiated silty soil with a few cobbles (Locus 05.03) above a flagstone pavement (Locus 05.04) (fig. 7.62). The topsoil (Locus 05.01) and tumble (Locus 05.02) contained only small amounts of pottery, but the chronological range is wide (MN, LN, ER, MB, LB, UM, AB), along with a coin of Elagabalus struck in Petra in 221/222 (p. 427, no. 75, fig. 12.8.75). The tumble bottomed out at a fairly uniform level and below

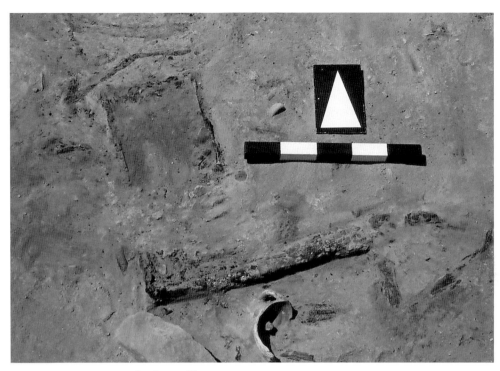

FIG. 7.63　*Room 5, view of carbonized box.*

is silty fill with ash at the top throughout the room (Locus 05.03), as well as *in situ* carbonized wood and smashed vessels. A Byzantine copper *follis* was found in Locus 05.03 (p. 427, no. 77; ruler uncertain). The carbonized wood represents branches forming part of a roof made of thatch and compressed soil. A C_{14} sample (TO-3732) of this charred wood provided a date of 1540 ± 50 BP, or 545 AD (AD 440–600 at 68.3 confidence interval). In 2011 the Cologne Radiocarbon Calibration Package provided an adjusted date of 1443 ± 60 BP, or 507 ± 60 AD (447–567). The carbonized wood lay directly on three or four broken vessels still *in situ* where they had fallen, either directly on the pavement or within a few centimetres of it. These dates agree well enough with those of the Byzantine bronze *follis* mentioned above, but the date of the ceramics (see below) is somewhat later, the mid-seventh century. The C_{14} dates, of course, indicate the date the wood was cut, which may well have taken place a century earlier than the fire that destroyed the roof of Room 5. Locus 05.03 also yielded a small, rectangular cosmetic pallet or revetment slab of black, grey, and red marble, possibly Africano marble from Teos in Western Turkey (p. 508, no. 8,

fig. 13.20.8). This artefact, which should date to the second or third century, may have been reused in the Church and subsequently salvaged from there.

The appearance of this intact, closed deposit of pottery, a rare phenomenon at Humayma, made it imperative to excavate the rest of the room. The ceramics in this deposit were published by 'Amr and Schick (2001), but because that publication is not easily found, and for the sake of completeness in this report, the information and drawings are repeated here. Excavation of the northeast quarter exposed the same sequence of topsoil (Locus 05.01) and tumble (Locus 05.02). The silty soil below the tumble (Locus 05.03) was excavated down to the level of the carbonized wood and smashed vessels (Locus 05.05) lying on the flagstone pavement (figs. 7.63–71). Several more *in situ* smashed vessels were found very close to or directly on the pavement. The powdery, burnt remains of a rectangular wooden box also appeared in Locus 05.05 (L 0.14 m, W 0.12 m) (fig. 7.63). The side and bottom panels of the box were ca. 6 mm thick, but it was not possible to determine the original height. Near the box lay a larger and thicker fragment of wood of uncertain function. A single small iron nail was

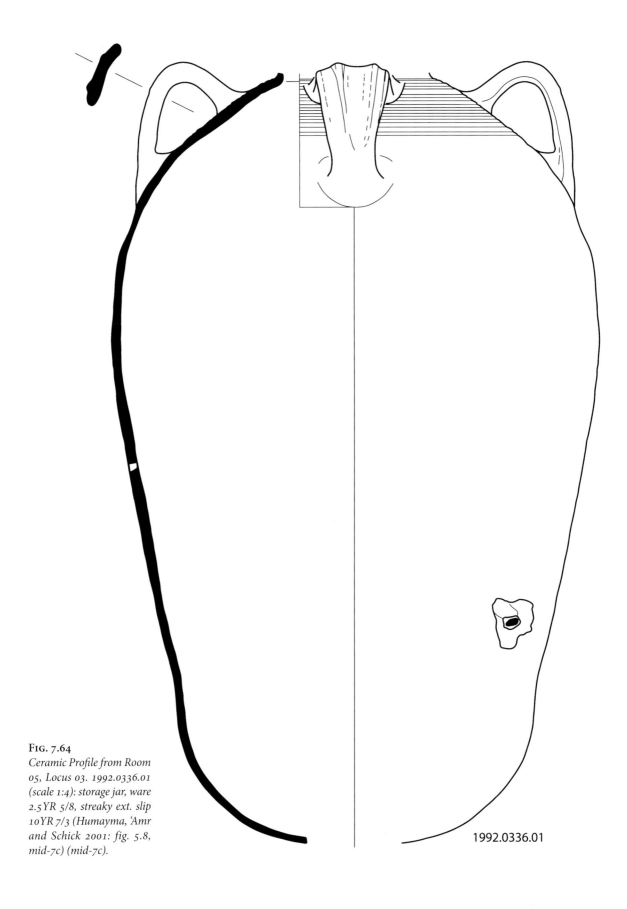

Fig. 7.64
Ceramic Profile from Room
05, Locus 03. 1992.0336.01
(scale 1:4): storage jar, ware
2.5YR 5/8, streaky ext. slip
10YR 7/3 (Humayma, 'Amr
and Schick 2001: fig. 5.8,
mid-7c) (mid-7c).

1992.0336.01

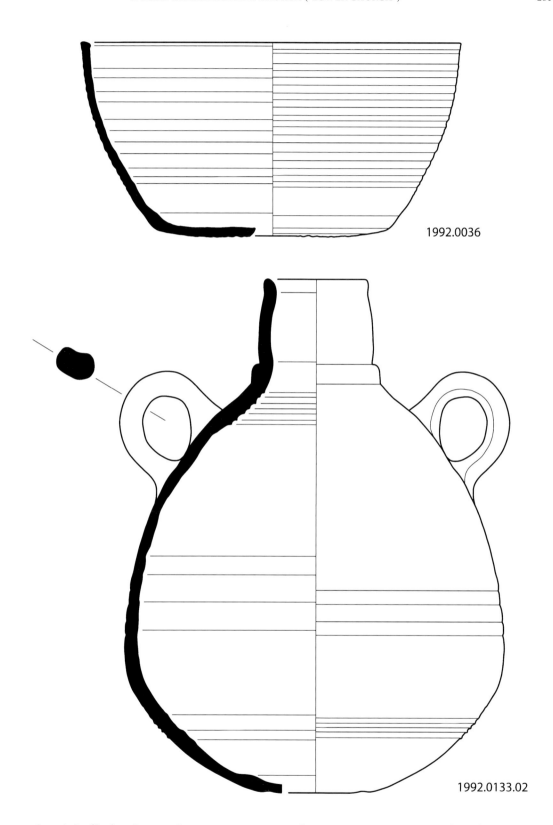

1992.0036

1992.0133.02

Fig. 7.65 *Ceramic Profiles from Room 05, Locus 03. 1992.0036: casserole, ware 2.5YR 5/8, ext. 2.5YR 4/6, burned (parallels, 'Amr and Schick 2001: 112, fig. 9.23; mid-7c) (mid-7c). 1992.0133.02: jar, 10YR 5/1 (Humayma, 'Amr and Schick 2001: 111, fig. 8.14, mid-7c) (mid-7c).*

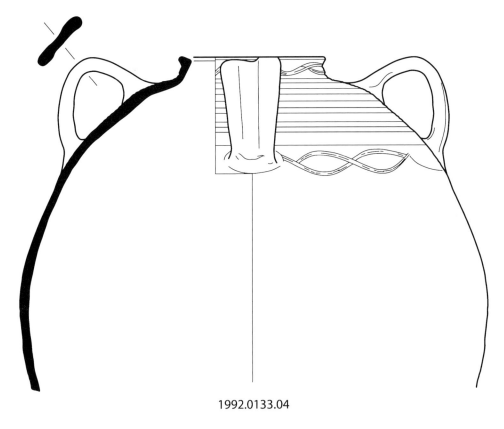

1992.0133.04

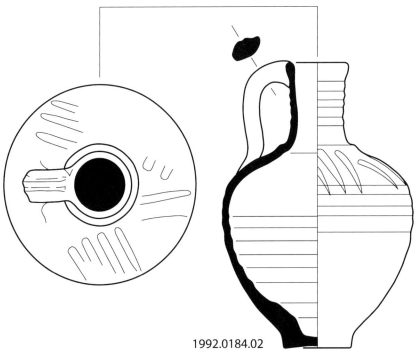

1992.0184.02

FIG. 7.66 *Ceramic Profiles from Room 05, Locus 03. 1992.0133.04 (scale 1:4): storage jar, ware 2.5YR 5.5/8, ext. mottled slip 10YR 7.5/4 to 5YR 6/6 (Humayma, 'Amr and Schick 2001: fig. 6.9, mid-7C) (mid-7C). 1992.0184.02: juglet, ware 2.5YR 6/8, slip 5YR 6/6 (Humayma, 'Amr and Schick 2001: fig. 9.29, mid-7C) (mid-7C).*

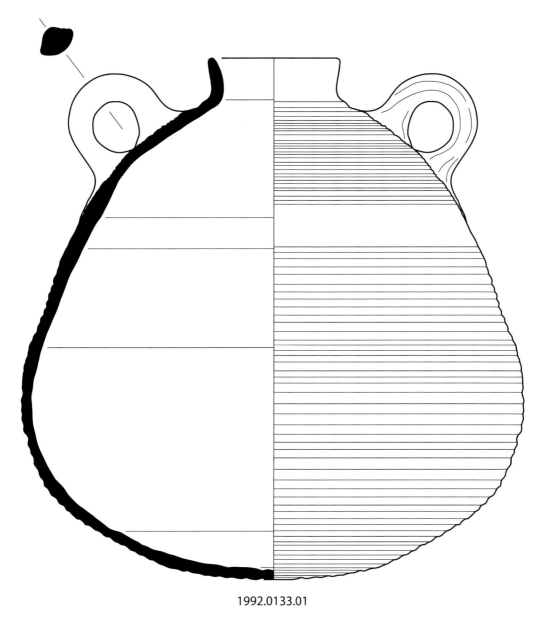

1992.0133.01

Fig. 7.67 *Ceramic Profile from Room 05, Locus 03. 1992.0133.01 (scale 1:3): bag amphora, ware 2.5YR 6/6, ext. 2.5Y 8/2 to 1.2Y 7/6 (Humayma, 'Amr and Schick 2001: fig. 4.6, mid-7c; Nessana, Baly 1962: pl. LV: 130.2, MB) (mid-7c).*

found in the vicinity of the box, presumably used to fasten the boards. The box contained only the silty soil of Locus 05.05.

Excavation of the southern half of the room exposed the same sequence of topsoil (Locus 05.01), tumble (Locus 05.02), and silt (Locus 05.09 = 05.03). An intact amphora was found in Locus 05.09, as well as several other vessels (figs. 7.72–73). Removal of Locus 05.09 exposed a thin but exten-

sive layer of ash and charcoal from the burned roof (Locus 05.10). It also contained two complete iron nails with bent tips (p. 443, no. 46). The silt below it (Locus 05.11) contained many additional smashed vessels. There was no sign that the southern half of the room had been paved, and instead, at the same level as the pavement in the north there was a lower layer of compacted silt (Locus 05.12, bottom elev. ca. 954.69 m) that contained a small

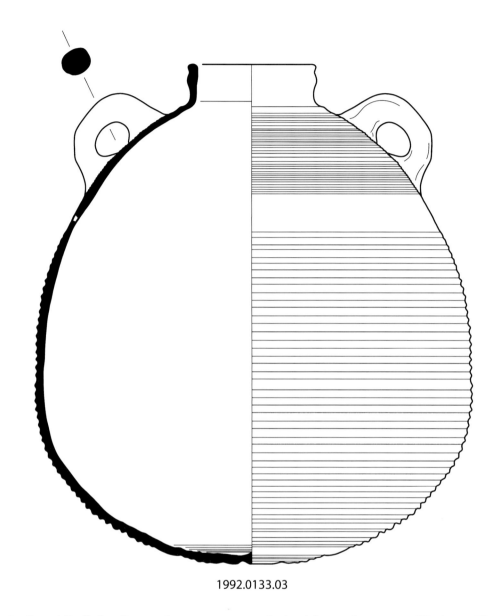

1992.0133.03

FIG. 7.68   *Ceramic Profile from Room 05, Locus 03. 1992.0133.03 (scale 1:3): bag amphora, ware 3.2YR 6/8, ext 5YR 6/6 to 10YR 7/4 (parallels, 'Amr and Schick 2001: fig. 4.5, mid-7c) (mid-7c).*

amount of pottery (MN, LN, RO, LB, UM). The south edge of the pavement formed a fairly straight east–west line about halfway across the room. A few irregularly placed cobbles near the west end, within which there was a small deposit of ash, may be the remnants of a hearth.

Several paving stones were lifted in the northwest corner of the room, allowing a probe below the pavement (1.5 m north–south × 1.0 m east–west). The probe was excavated to a depth of about

0.50 m, exposing the base of the north and west walls of the room. The stratum of silty soil (Locus 05.06) directly below the pavement contained a large quantity of first and second-century ceramics, along with a few of the third century (EN, MN, LN, ER), a few fragments of class, some lumps of corroded iron, some animal bones, and a few sea shells. The layer of ashy soil (Locus 05.07) below contained a great deal of first to second-century Nabataean fine ware, along with some MB and LB

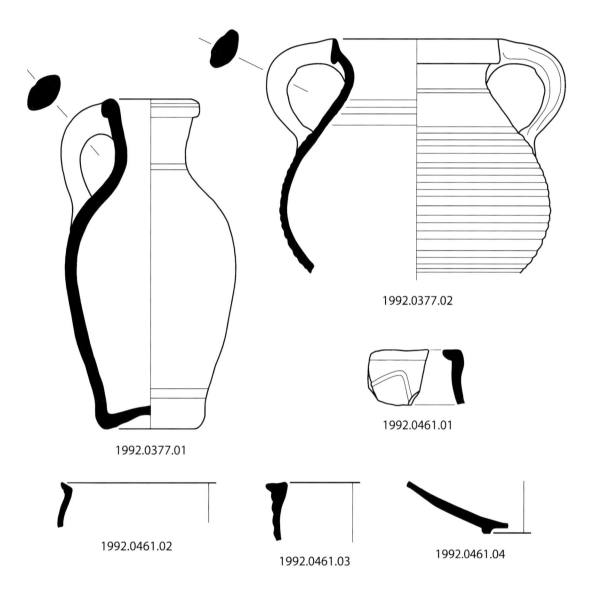

1992.0377.02

1992.0461.01

1992.0377.01

1992.0461.02

1992.0461.03

1992.0461.04

FIG. 7.69 *Ceramic Profiles from Room 05, Loci 05, 06. 1992.0377.01: C101.05.05, jug, ware 10YR 7/4, ext. and int. 5Y 8/2 (cf. 1992.0500, above fig. 7.18; 1991.0133.02, above fig. 7.41; Humayma, 'Amr and Schick 2001: fig. 9.27, mid-7C) (mid-7C). 1992.0377.02: cook pot, ware 3.2YR 4.5/6, core 5YR 3/1, ext. wash 3.2YR 4/4 (parallels, 'Amr and Schick 2001: fig. 9.20, mid-7C) (mid-7C). 1992.0461.01: C101.05.06, ledge rim casserole, incised wavy line below rim on ext., ware 2.5YR 5/8, slip 10YR 8/2 (2C). 1992.0461.02: C101.05.06, pot, 5YR 5/8, ext slip 2.5Y 8/3 (Petra, Gerber 1994: fig. 16.I, ea. 2C) (ea. 2C). 1992.0461.03: C101.05.06, bowl with horizontal fluting below rim, ware 2.5YR 6/8, surface slipped grey 2.5YR 8/1 (2C). 1992.0461.04: C101.05.06, NFW bowl base, ware 5YR 5/8, possible surface slip 5YR 6/6.*

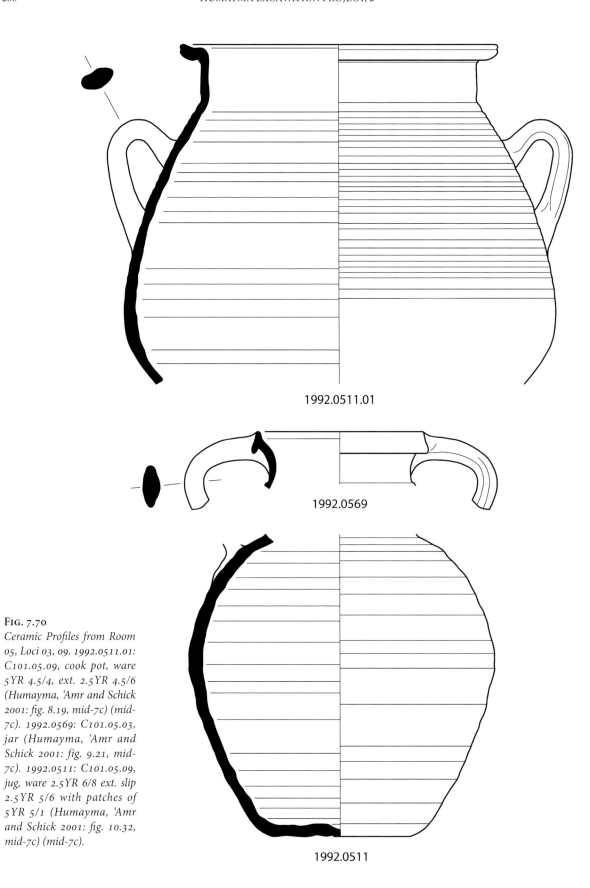

1992.0511.01

1992.0569

FIG. 7.70
Ceramic Profiles from Room 05, Loci 03, 09. 1992.0511.01: C101.05.09, cook pot, ware 5YR 4.5/4, ext. 2.5YR 4.5/6 (Humayma, ʿAmr and Schick 2001: fig. 8.19, mid-7c) (mid-7c). 1992.0569: C101.05.03, jar (Humayma, ʿAmr and Schick 2001: fig. 9.21, mid-7c). 1992.0511: C101.05.09, jug, ware 2.5YR 6/8 ext. slip 2.5YR 5/6 with patches of 5YR 5/1 (Humayma, ʿAmr and Schick 2001: fig. 10.32, mid-7c) (mid-7c).

1992.0511

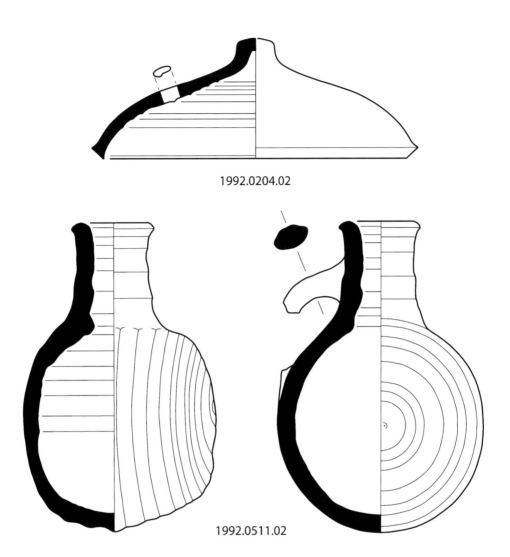

1992.0204.02

1992.0511.02

FIG. 7.71 *Ceramic Profiles from Room 05, Loci 03, 09. 1992.0204.02: C101.05.03, casserole lid, ware, 2.5YR 5/8, ext. 10YR 5/1 (Humayma, 'Amr and Schick 2001: fig. 9.26, mid-7C; Lejjun, Parker et al. 1987: 189, fig. 114, LB) (mid-7C). 1992.0511.02: C101.05.09, pilgrim flask, ware 2.5YR 6/8, ext. 10YR 8/2 (Humayma, 'Amr and Schick 2001: fig. 10.33, mid-7C; Khirbet edh-Dharih, Villeneuve 2011: 318 fig. 2, mid-7C; cf. 1992.0511.02; Aqaba kilns, Melkawi et al. 1994: fig. 10.j, mid- to late 7C) (mid-7C).*

cooking ware, glass fragments, and animal bones. At the bottom of the probe was a layer of orange sand and cobbles (Locus 05.08; elev. 954.13 m); the upper portion contained a modest amount of pottery of the first to early third century (MN, LN) and a few animal bones. The north and south walls of the room rested on this layer.

7.F.3. Conclusions

The excavation showed that Room 3 and Room 5, formed part of a single complex, probably intended for habitation, but possibly used to shelter animals as well. The structure was built before the Church, but the main occupation phase corresponds with

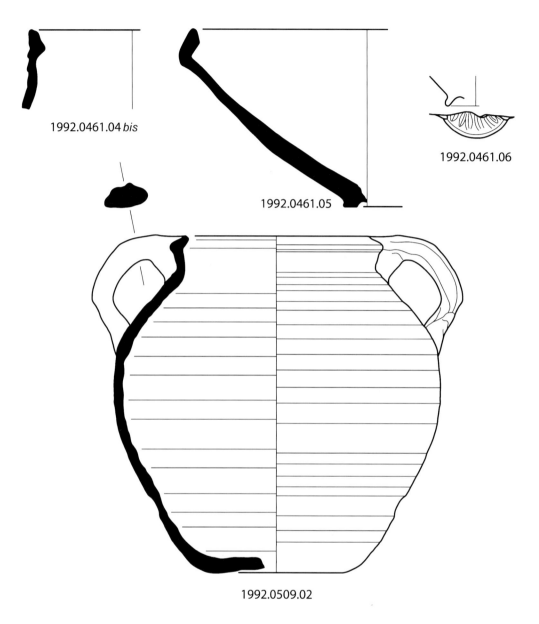

1992.0461.04 *bis*

1992.0461.06

1992.0461.05

1992.0509.02

FIG. 7.72 *Ceramic Profiles from Room 05, Loci 06, 09. 1992.0461.04bis: C101.05.06, bowl with horizontal fluting below rim, ware 5YR 5/8, ext slip 2.5Y 8/3 (2C). 1992.0461.05: C101.05.06, NFW bowl, 5YR 5/8, rim 10YR 8/2 (2C). 1992.0461.06: C101.05.06, NFW jug or jar base with fingernail finish (1C). 1992.0509.02: C101.05.09, cook pot, 2.5YR 5/8, core and ext. N 4/0, int. int. 10YR 5/2, (Humayma, ʿAmr and Schick 2001: fig. 8.18, mid-7C) (mid-7C).*

that of the Church, ca. 500–650 AD. Although adjacent to the Church complex, this structure was not necessarily functionally related to it. The mixture of cooking, serving, and storage vessels found smashed on the floor of Room 5 suggest that in its last phase of use, at least, the structure served as the habitation of a relatively well-off household.

The ceramics also indicate that the structure was destroyed unexpectedly by fire, and abandoned permanently, in the mid-seventh century. This event may have been contemporaneous with the fire that destroyed the roof of the Church complex, although the Church had been cleared of most of its furnishings before the roof burned. Without

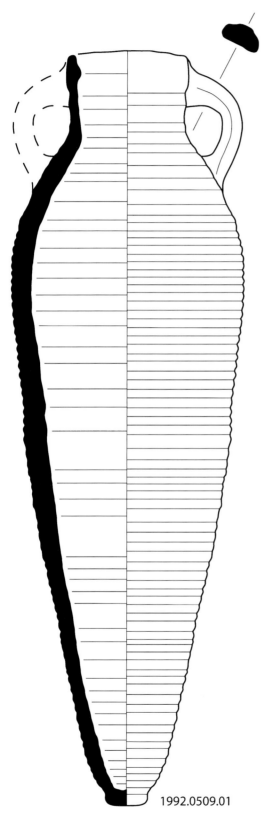

1992.0509.01

their roof, the two rooms gradually filled with wind and water-born silt, the roofing arches fell or were salvaged, and the upper portions of the walls fell in.

7.G. THE FAR SOUTHWEST SQUARE (SQUARE 9)

In 2009 a probe trench was dug outside the southwest corner of the Church in order to clarify the architectural phasing of the south wall of the Church and the north wall of Rooms 3 and 5. At ground level there is no clear south face of the south wall of the Church or clear north face of the north wall of Rooms 3 and 5. In order to determine the relationship of the two walls, a 1.5 × 1.5 m square was dug down to sterile soil in the exterior corner formed by the west wall of Room 5 (Locus 05.14) and the south wall of the Church (figs. 7.74–75). This square was on the opposite side of the west wall of Room 5 from the sub-pavement probe of loci 05:06–08.

Removal of the surface soil (Locus 09.01) exposed a thick layer of ashy soil (Loci 09.02, 04. 05; top elev. ca. 955.48 m), resting on a mortared surface (Locus 09.07; Th 0.05 m; top elev. 954.55 m) and its thin bedding layer (Locus 9.08), consisting of pieces of mortar and soil mixed with small stones, just below the level of the pavement in Room 5 (elev. 954.67 m). The next stratum consisted of soft, brown sandy silt (Locus 09.09, top elev. 954.40 m) above a layer of orange sandy silt (Locus 09.10), both containing many sherds of Nabataean fine ware. Sterile orange, sandy soil (Locus 09.11; elev. 954.14 m) was encountered at the same level as in the probe east of the wall in Room 5 (Locus 05.08), and roughly at the level of the sterile sand below the burials in the Church, but higher than the sterile soil in Square 6 to the east.

The probe revealed the foundation trench for the west wall of Room 5 (Locus 05.14). It contained ashy sandy silt (Locus 05.06) and was cut from the top of the ashy soil layer (Locus 09.02) down into the middle of the silty layer (Locus 09.09) or

FIG. 7.73 *Ceramic Profile from Room 05, Locus 09. 1992.0509.01 (scale 1:5): Aila amphora, ware 2.5YR 6/8, ext. 10YR 8/4, int. 2.5YR 6/6 (Humayma, ʿAmr and Schick 2001: fig. 3.1, mid-7C; Aqaba kilns, Melkawi et al., 1994: fig. 10.e, mid- to late 7C) (mid-7C).*

the top of the mortar surface (Locus 09.07). The foundation trench for the south wall of the Church was also revealed. It contained slightly orange silt with sand and clay (Locus 09.03), and, like the foundation trench for the west wall, was cut from the top of the ashy layer (Locus 09.02) all the way down to sterile soil (Locus 09.11). The bottom of the foundation trench was packed tightly with boulders and stones. The foundation trench for the south wall of the Church was cut after the construction of the west wall of Room 5, since the line of the foundation trench for the Church wall curves northwards as it reaches the west face of the foundation courses of that wall. It seems that the ground surface in the Byzantine period was not very different from that of today, since the first row of carefully dressed ashlars for the wall face are more or less at modern ground level.

The results of this probe produced evidence for Nabataean period use of the area as an ash and garbage dump, if nothing more. Room 5 was constructed later, given that the foundation trench for its west wall cut through the Nabataean ash layers. It is apparent that the north wall of Rooms 3 and 5 and the west wall of Room 5 were built before the south wall of the Church, which sliced through the north wall of Rooms 3 and 5 at a slightly different orientation.

7.H. THE FAR SOUTHEAST SQUARE (SQUARE 6)

Square 6 was excavated in 1992 and 1993 to investigate an east–west wall (Locus 06.05; Th 1.0 m) whose remains could be seen on the surface extending east from the southeast corner of the Church to meet further wall lines of additional rooms that were not investigated further. Square 6 was laid out

FIG. 7.74   *Square 09, view of square to the east.*

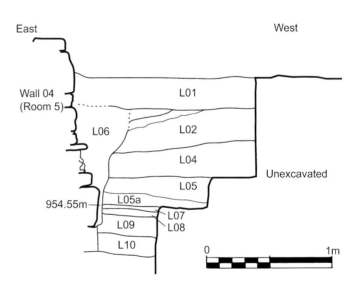

FIG. 7.75   *Square 09, drawing of south baulk (I. Ruben, J.P. Oleson).*

FIG. 7.76 *Square 06, view to north (1993).*

along the south wall of the Church for 4.0 m east of the east wall of Room 3 and straddling Wall 05 for a total of 4.0 m N/S (fig. 7.76). The objective was determination of the nature of the east–west Wall 05, its relation to the east and south walls of the church and to the east wall of Room 3, along with the nature of the occupation in the area. Substantial amounts of topsoil and surface rubble (Locus 06.01, 02) were removed from above and to the north of Wall 05 (down to elev. 955.50 m) to delineate it clearly, after which excavation proceeded south of Wall 05 in an L-shaped trench 1.0 m wide and 4.0 m long E/W along the south face of Wall 05 and the south wall of the Church (Locus 06.06) and 2.00 m N/S along the east face of the east wall of Room 3 (Locus 06.08) down to the foundations of the walls.

7.H.1. Architectural Features

The excavation exposed the south faces of the east–west Wall (Locus 06.05), the east wall of the Church (Locus 06.07), the south wall of the Church (Locus 06.06) and the east face of the east

wall of Room 3 (Locus 06.08) (fig. 7.76). The east–west Wall 05 abutted the east wall of the Church (Locus 06.07) and had two components. The upper portion consisted of five uneven courses of pairs of blocks in a header and stretcher arrangement (Th ca. 0.80 m) about 1.0 m high (top elev. 955.64 m, bottom elev. 954.60 m). This bottom level is coincident with the top of a layer of silt (Locus 06.04), which was an occupational deposit contemporary with the wall. The bottom portion of a cupboard (elev. 955.40 m; interior 0.67 × 0.60 m) is preserved in the topmost course of Wall 05. The lower portion of Wall 05 (H 0.90 m), from the top of the Locus 06.04 silt, as the below ground foundation courses (assigned Locus 06.14) is composed of ill-defined courses of roughly dressed rocks and cobbles with mud packing and chinking stones. The eastern portion projects ca. 0.20 m south of the upper wall courses of Wall 05. The lower foundation courses (Loc. 06.14; bottom elev. ca. 953.80–953.69 m) bottom out on a low silty layer (Locus 06.12), about 0.40 m lower than the east and south walls of the church (Loci 6.07 and 06; bottom elev. 954.10 m) and the east wall of Room 3 (Locus 6.08; bottom elev. 954.08 m).

The southeast corner of the Church drops down sharply in preserved height from the south apse to the southeast corner. The east wall of the Church (Locus 06.07), abutted by Wall 05, continues all the way to the southeast corner, where four courses are preserved above the Locus 06.04 silt layer. The east wall continues down to the same level as the south wall of the church and the east wall of Room 3.

It is difficult to interpret the constructional history of the south wall of the Church (Locus 06.06). The south face is built of less regular wall courses than the east wall, which it seems to abut (fig. 7.76). That detail seems to make the south face of the south wall an eastern continuation of the north wall of Rooms 3 and 5, and so predating the construction of the south wall of the church that sliced through it. In any event the south face of the south wall bottoms out on a layer of silt (Locus 06.10; elev. 954.10 m) that contained a large amount of MN, LN, ER, MB, and LB ceramics. This elevation corresponds to that of the bottom of the east wall of Room 3 (Locus 06.08; bottom elev. 954.08 m), but is higher than the lowest Locus 6.14 wall courses.

The east wall of Room 3 (Locus 06.08) is similar to the south face of the south wall of the Church (Locus 6.06), which it abuts, consisting of eight irregular courses preserved to a height of up to 2.00 m but dropping sharply down to the south. It bottoms out on a silt layer (Locus 06.10; elev. 954.08 m), at the same height as the bottom of the south wall of the Church, but higher than the bottom of Wall 05 (Locus 06.14). Wall 08 (Th 0.70 m) was constructed of roughly dressed stones chinked with smaller stones in mud packing. At the south edge of the excavated trench were traces of a door in the wall, perhaps blocked, leading into Room 3, but this door was not fully clarified during the excavation.

7.H.2. Stratigraphy

In the L-shaped trench described above, removal of the thick surface level of topsoil and tumble (Locus 06.01, 02, 03) exposed a layer of silty soil (Locus 06.04; Th ca. 0.20 m; upper elev. ca. 954.56 m) containing some lenses of ash and substantial

FIG. 7.77   *Square 06, east baulk south of Wall 05.*

numbers of MN, LN, EB, MB LB, UM sherds (fig. 7.77). This layer, ca. 0.85 m below the cupboard in the south face of Wall 05 (elev. 955.41 m), represents an occupational deposit from the time when the Church was in use.

Below the Locus 06.04 ashy, silty soil was a layer of silty, sandy soil (Locus 06.09; top elev. 954.40 m) with MN, LN, ER, LB and possible UM pottery, followed by another layer of silty, sandy soil (Locus 06.10; top elev. 954.27 m) with MN, LN, ER, MB, LB and UM sherds, down to the bottom of the south wall of the Church (Locus 06.06; bottom elev. 954.10 m) and the east face of the east wall of Room 3 (Locus 06.08; bottom elev. 954.08 m), but not yet the bottom of the east–west Wall 05 (Locus 06.14). Below the Locus 06.10 layer was a third layer of silty, sandy soil (Locus 06.11; top elev. 954.05 m), with MN, LN and LB sherds, near the bottom level of which Wall 05 (Locus 06.14) bottomed out at elevation of ca. 953.80–953.63 m.

Below the Locus 06.11 layer and the level of Wall 05 (Locus 06.14) was a fourth layer of silty,

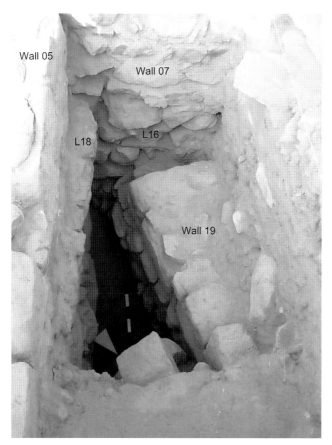

Wall 05

Wall 07

L18   L16

Wall 19

FIG. 7.78   *Square 06, view of Wall 06.19. Traces of the original plaster floor were found where the scale and arrow are located.*

sandy soil (Locus 06.12; top elevation 953.80–.63 m), with MN and LB sherds. The Locus 06.12 ashy silt layer lay above the sterile layer of orange sand (Locus 06.13; top elev. 953.52 m) found everywhere beneath the church, but here it is substantially lower than elsewhere.

These Loci 06.09–06.12 layers contained fragments of glass, bronze clippings, iron nails and lumps of corrosion, three small lumps of iron slag, substantial quantities of animal bone, and a few sea shells. The layers seem to be construction fill deposited at the time that the walls were built. A temporal distinction for the date of construction of the various walls could not be identified on the basis of the pottery, although based on stratigraphy, Wall 05 (Locus 06.14) was built first.

Only in the northwest corner of the trench formed by the south wall of the Church and east wall of Room 3, but at a depth below all the walls, is there a possible occupational deposit consisting

of a concentration of ashy soil at the bottom of Locus 06.11 and the top of Locus 06.12 that contained an especially large number of sherds of MN and LB date along with two stone beads (p. 509, nos. 10–11, fig. 13.20).

7.H.3. The 2009 Probe in Square 6

During the 2009 season further excavation was carried out in Square 6 to clarify the architectural phasing of the Church walls and the Locus 06.05 and 06.14 east–west wall that extended east from the southeast corner of the Church. Exposure of the south face of the east–west Wall 05 and the south face of the south wall of the Church (Locus 06.07) in Square 6 during the 1992–1993 seasons had not provided conclusive information about the phasing of the walls.

To generate more data, a 2.0 × 2.0 m square was laid out against the east wall of the Church (Locus 06.07) straddling Wall 05. The above-ground courses of the east wall of the Church are supported by a foundation of five alternating courses of large and medium-sized boulders and cobbles, all very roughly hewn, with a very coarse mud-mortar (Locus 06.16) projecting ca. 0.20 m to the east beyond the upper courses. There are three courses of cobbles below, resting on sterile soil (elev. 953.77 m).

Wall 05 rests on a foundation (Locus 06.18 = 06.14; upper elev. 955.00 m) consisting of four courses of large boulders and cobbles, resting on sterile soil at an elevation of 953.60 m (fig. 7.77). The foundation courses (Loci 06.16 = 6.18) of Wall 05 and of the east wall of the Church (Locus 06.07) bond.

Another wall (Locus 06.19) oriented NE–SW and so not aligned with the other walls, was uncovered at a lower level (variable upper elev. 955.23 m to 954.95 m) (fig. 7.78). It consists of one or two upper courses of roughly hewn blocks (bottom elev. 954.45 m), over four probable foundation courses of cobbles and small, unshaped boulders. The bottom foundation course rests on sterile soil (elev. 953.62 m) at roughly same level as the Locus 06.18 foundation courses of Wall 05 and the Locus 06.16 foundation courses of the east wall of the Church.

This NE–SW wall (Locus 06.19) belongs to a pre-Church wall that originally continued farther to the west beneath the walls of the Church.

The exposure of these wall courses entailed the removal of various soil layers to the north of Wall 05. On top was wind-blown soil (Loci 06.15). Below was a very coarse plaster floor (Locus 06.17; elev. 954.81 m), the best candidate for the ground level at the time the Church was constructed. Below the floor were layers of cobble and boulder fill (Loci 06.20, 21, 22), deposited to raise the ground level after the Church foundations had been built. At the bottom of the upper fill layer (Locus 06.20, elev. 954.25 m), just below the level of the finer-hewn upper courses of the pre-Church NE–SW wall (Locus 06.19, elev. 954.45 m), there was a plaster floor that seemed to be the floor associated with the pre-Church wall. This plaster floor was cut by the foundations (Loci 06.16 and 18) for the later Walls 05 and 07.

7.H.4. Conclusions

This area south of the southeast corner of the Church seems to have been an open courtyard rather than another room, with the bottom of Locus 6.04 the best candidate for ground level at the time the Church was in use. The presence of the cupboard in the south face of Wall 05 points to use of the courtyard, but the small area of the courtyard that was excavated did not add further information about any specific use to which it was put.

Pre-Church occupation in the area is shown by the wall predating the Church (Locus 06.19). A portion of that wall must have been dismantled when the east–west wall (Locus 06.05) was built, breaking any stratigraphic connection between it and the north wall of Rooms 3 and 5 to the west.

7.I. ROOM 7

A large room (9.50 m N–S × 4.5 m E–W) south of Room 5 was designated as Room 7 in 1993 (fig. 7.3). Numerous MN, LN, LB, and possibly UM sherds, including a sizable number of storage jar sherds, were collected during the removal of limited amounts of topsoil and surface rubble (Locus 07.01) to expose the wall lines. The wall lines of the

room were fully exposed everywhere except along the northern part of the east wall (shared with Room 8), where substantial excavation, including removal of 1962 excavation dump, would have been necessary to establish the presence of a door. There is no door in the north wall that would have provided access to Room 5.

7.J. ROOM 8

A room south of Room 3 was designated as Room 8 in 1993 (fig. 7.3). Its wall lines were traced by removal of surface soil and rubble, except along the north part of the west wall shared with Room 7. In order to trace the course of the east wall and expose any existing door, a north–south trench (5 × 1 m) was excavated to a depth of over 1.0 m through silty soil with tumble (Locus 08.01, 02), exposing the east wall. There is, however, no clear evidence for a door, leaving the question of access to Rooms 7 and 8 unresolved.

Further wall lines are clearly visible to the south and east of the Church, indicating the presence of additional rooms. There is no surface evidence, however, for any rooms adjoining the Church on the north and west sides. Further rooms and buildings are present in the area of the Church, but it is questionable whether any of them have any connection with the Church.

7.K. ANALYSIS OF STRUCTURAL HISTORY AND FUNCTION

7.K.1. Reconstruction, Phasing, and Parallels for the Design of the Church

The excavation of the C101 Church revealed a standard, rather large, triple-apse basilica (see Michel 2001: 141–43, figs. 87–89), built at some point in the fifth or sixth century, and probably abandoned at some point in the seventh century. The Church was built at the location of a pre-existing building from the Late Nabataean/Roman period, as shown by the pre-Church wall in Square 6, the north wall of Rooms 3 and 5, and the pre-Church dump deposit in Square 9. It is curious that the north wall of Room 3 and 5, which runs east–west at a slightly different angle than the Church, was sliced through when it was incorporated into the south wall of the Church, rather than being dismantled and rebuilt.

The excavations revealed that the core of the Church complex — the Church, the Sacristy, and Entrance Hall — were the result of a single construction phase, and that there were no later structural additions. No dedicatory inscription was found that could provide a precise date of construction, nor do any coins help narrow the date beyond what can determined from the generic Byzantine pottery in the various sub-pavement excavation probes An approximate construction date would be the first half of the sixth century, which was a very active period for church building in the region (Michel 2011: 235–37). The Church appears to have continued in use into the seventh century, as suggested by the presence of an ambo, a late development in churches (Michel 2001: xiii, 87). The tight pottery corpus from Room 5 is particularly valuable evidence for dating the last phase of use to around 650.

Enough fragments of glass lamps, ostrich egg shells and other small finds came to light during the excavation to show that the Church had the normal inventory of liturgical furnishings. The Church also had a full complement of panels made of imported marble for the chancel and ambo; no trace of the altar survived. The C101 Church, like the other churches at Humayma, lacked any floor or wall mosaics.

Ostrich eggs were a common feature of Byzantine period churches (Galvaris 1978), as well as mosques (Flood 2001: 42, n. 142), but their fragments, often very numerous, are rarely published in church excavation reports. Three such examples are the large number of ostrich egg shell fragments found at Sobata (Shivta) in the Negev (Baly 1935: 180) and those found at the church at Lejjun (Schick 1987: 367) and at Deir 'Ain 'Abata (Lot's Cave) (Sidell 2012). Only one small rounded ostrich egg shell fragment was found in the Petra Church (Bikai 2001: 411, 422, no. 104).

Ostrich egg shells were placed on the chains from which oil lamps are suspended. Baly (1935: 180) suggested that a practical purpose of having smooth eggs placed on the chains above the lamps was to prevent rats from getting at the edible olive oil in the lamps. The use of ostrich egg shells, or

ceramic, glass or metal equivalents, continues in Eastern Churches, such as the notable example of the Church of the Holy Sepulchre in Jerusalem (for photographs see Krüger 2000; Ghushah 2010).

A number of church-related burials were placed below the floor of the nave and side aisles. Such burials in churches are occasionally found at other sites, notably in the Negev (Nagar and Sonntag 2008). The closest parallels are the cist graves with covering slabs that were placed below the north and south aisles and central nave of the North Church at Rehovot (Tsafrir et al. 1988: 36–38, 193–209). But such burials within churches are less common elsewhere in Jordan (Michel 2001: 9; for the area of Mount Nebo see Sanmori 1998). The church burials in the Negev typically were accompanied with Greek funerary inscriptions (Negev 1981), which is not the case here.

The building seems to have been peacefully abandoned around the middle of the seventh century while still structurally intact, rather than abandoned after destruction. This is a fairly early date for abandonment, since around 660 between 82 and 96 percent of the dateable churches in the region of modern Jordan still continued in use (Michel 2011: 241–43). Later on, the marble and other liturgical furnishings were largely robbed out. Subsequently, at least part of the building was used for domestic occupation within the Umayyad period, as shown by the oven in Room 2, before the roof and walls of the Church were destroyed in a fire.

The structure stands out as the only verified three-apse church at Humayma, given the ambiguity of the plan of the B126 Church. The central apse does not project beyond the straight east wall of the building. The plan of the church corresponds to Type A.I.d of Qaqish (2007: 190 no. 30, 224–25), represented by 22 other examples in Jordan, including the Petra Church and Blue Chapel (Bikai 2002). The type is also common in the Negev, as in the North Church at Rehovot (Tsafrir et al. 1988), the South Church at Nessana (Colt 1962: 43–454), the churches at Shivta (Rosenthal-Heginbottom 1982), and the Cathedral at Elusa (Negev 1989).

The two side apses take the place of the *pastophoria* that appear in the C119 and B126 churches, but the side apses were part of the original con-

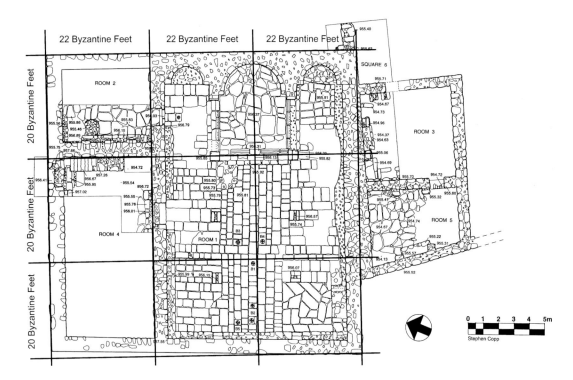

FIG. 7.79 *Stone by stone plan of C101 Church, with planning layout (S. Copp, J.P. Oleson).*

struction, rather than being converted from two side rooms, an architectural development that has been noted for some churches in the Negev (Negev 1989; Margalit 1989; Michel 2001: 30–33, Fiema et al. 2001: 53, 120–21).

One unusual feature of the church architecture is the lack of an entrance in the west side, resulting in the sole entrance being placed in the north wall. A handful of other churches in Jordan do not have an entrance in the west (Michel 2001: 22), but those churches are smaller and have multiple entrances on other sides; the Church of Wa'il at Umm al-Rasas, for example, has two entrances on the south and one on the east (Piccirillo 1993b).

7.K.2. Planning and Modules

Given the excellent preservation of the Church phase of the C101 complex in comparison with the other churches at the site, which were all reused for housing, it is important analyze the layout and planning procedures. It is clear that the planners laid out a nearly square outline (20.0 m north–

south, 18.3 m east–west), oriented at approximately 70 degrees magnetic, and a wall (Th ca. 1.0 m) was built on this plan with large limestone blocks and boulders, chinked with smaller stones, facing a rubble and mud core (fig. 7.79). It is not clear why the complex was not laid out as a proper square, but topography or the pre-existing structures at the southeast corner may have slightly truncated the east–west distance, or the desire to build on top of the pre-existing structures in Squares 03, 05, and 06 may have stretched the north–south measurement. In fact, since 18.3 m equals 59.3 Byzantine feet of 0.3089 m (henceforth simply "feet" or "ft."), while 20.0 m equals 65 such feet, the subsequent division of the block into thirds probably indicates that the more convenient 60 feet was the result intended. The same foot was very likely used to plan the B100 and F102 churches at Hauarra (see pp. 155–57, 217–18), along with the Petra Church (*HEP* 1: 399–401; Fiema et al. 2001: 163–64).

The east/west planning lines (22 Byzantine feet apart) correspond with the north edge of the north wall of the complex, the north edge of the north Nave wall, the centre line of the Nave, and the south edge of the south wall of the complex (fig. 7.79). The north/south planning lines (20 Byzantine feet apart) correspond with the outer face of the east wall of the complex, the west face of the wall separating Room 2 from Room 4, along with the centre point of the piers in front of the Chancel, the exterior face of the west wall of the complex, and a line equidistant between these last two. There is no obvious metrical pattern to the location of the three doors in the complex, although the door providing access to the Church proper is approximately halfway down the north aisle, and it lines up with the adjacent arch support piers. The door through the exterior wall into the Entrance Hall is out of alignment with the door into the Church, possibly to ensure privacy or to minimize distractions to the congregation during worship.

As a result of the nearly square shape of the Church Complex, and the restriction of the Church proper to the southern two-thirds of the block, the interior of the Church has the proportions of ap-proximately 2:3, width to length, but inside dimensions of only 11.8 × 17.8 m (38.2 × 57.6 ft.). The inside width of the Church may have been divided into 12 units of theoretically 3 feet (in fact, 3.18 Byzantine feet, or 0.98 m): 3 such units defined the distance from the north and south walls of the aisles to the outside faces of the arch support piers, leaving 6 units, minus the widths of the piers, for the width of the nave. These proportions also affected the widths of the apses, although they were also diminished in width by offsets from the measured lines. The length of the Church was divided up into 16 of the same units, measuring from the offsets on either side of the north and south apses to the inside of the west wall (15.74 m, 51 ft.). Measuring from this point, the east faces of the six freestanding arch support piers are very close to 4, 6, and 8 units distant from the offsets. Since the piers are each ca. 2 feet square, and the attached piers project 1 foot, the distance between the east and west piers and the free-standing piers along the length of the nave is slightly over 10 feet.

Chapter 8

Field C119: Byzantine Church ("Upper Church")

by Robert Schick

8.A. LOCATION AND EXCAVATION HISTORY

The small Church in Field C119, located midway up the hill on the far western edge of the site (figs. 1.1, 8.1), was designated the "Upper Church" in 1991 to distinguish it from the C101 "Lower Church" on the plain below, prior to the discovery of the other three churches at the site. There is a steep drop-off of ca. 8 m immediately east of the building down to the elevation of the C101 lower church, so the structure would have been prominently visible from the east at a significant distance. Schick carried out excavations in the church during the last two weeks of the 1993 season and again during a short season in 2009. Prior to the 1993 season, some limited illicit digging had been done around the area of the apse, but otherwise the church was undisturbed. During the 1993 season an overall plan of the building was produced, while the disturbed area around the apse was cleaned up and labelled as Room 01, and the southeast room flanking the apse, a *pastophorion,* was excavated as Room 02 (see Schick 1995b: 335–37).

Sometime in the first years of the twenty-first century extensive illicit digging took place in the interior and the northeast room of the church, the northern *pastophorion,* leaving heaps of churned soil and exposing some of the architectural fea-

tures. When Schick visited the church in 2008, he realized that additional information about the design and plan could now be generated with a minimum of effort, by cleaning up the disturbed soil in the church interior. For a few days during 2009, his team removed the churned-up deposits of soil in the north aisle and the north part of the chancel area (labelled as Square 04) to document the architectural features of the church. They also excavated a trench along the middle of the west wall of the church as Square 03 to sample the deposits in what appeared to be an undisturbed area, and to determine whether or not a door is present there. Square 04 was back-filled at the end of the 2009 season.

8.B. ARCHITECTURAL FEATURES AND PHASING

With the possible exception of the chancel steps, all of the architectural features appear to belong to a single phase, dating generally to the Late Byzantine period, i.e., sixth or beginning of the seventh century. The building is a basilica with a single apse flanked by two small *pastophoria* (figs. 8.2–3). The building is oriented north of east (long axis at about 72/252 degrees), and it is wider at its west end (9.5 m) than its east end (8.25 m); the outside length from east to west is about 14.5 m.

Fig. 8.1   *View of C119 at end of 2009 excavation, looking east, with the C101 and F102 Church complexes in the distance (Photo: R. Schick).*

The Church is only slightly larger than Michel's definition of a chapel (2001: 17; 5–8 × 12 m). There is one door in the middle of the north wall, another door in the middle of the west wall, and a third door near the south end of the west wall. There clearly are additional rooms to the south and west of the church, but their wall lines remain only partially traceable, and there has so far been no time to document them.

8.B.1. Walls

The walls of the structure are 1.00 m thick, consisting of two facing courses of dressed hard limestone and sandstone blocks, and a rubble core. The interior walls of the northeast and southeast rooms are 0.60 m thick. The walls are preserved to a significant height above the pavement (elev. ca. 963.66 m), those on the east had a top elevation of ca. 964.70 m, while the west wall is preserved to about 1.5 m higher, up to 966.23 m. The east wall

of the church is poorly preserved. Its exterior face had fallen away and tumbled down the sharp drop off to the east; it is preserved three courses lower than on its interior face. The northeast corner is also poorly preserved, and the northeast room is less well-preserved than the southeast room (Room 2). The recent illicit digging in the northeast and southeast rooms had churned up the soil inside the rooms and had caused the walls to collapse further.

The north wall of the church (Locus 04.02) is preserved up to four or five wall courses above the pavement, up to around 965.03 m (fig. 8.5), while the west wall of the northeast room and its doorway is preserved four courses above the pavement, up to 965.00 m on the south and up to 964.70 m on the north. A niche (W 0.26 m; 0.20 m deep) is built into the east wall immediately north of the northeast attached pier (1.05 m above the level of the pavement and 0.50 m above the top row of the chancel). The sides and bottom of the niche are plastered. Plain white plaster covered extensive

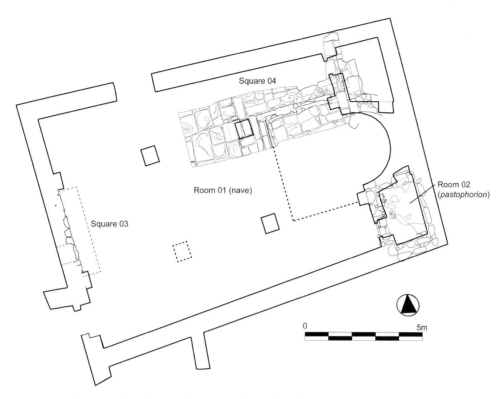

FIG. 8.2   *Stone by stone plan of excavated portions of C119 Church (A. Heidenreich, I. Sturkenboom, M. Siklenka).*

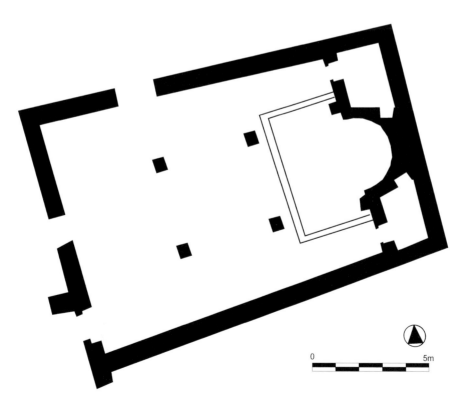

FIG. 8.3   *Reconstructed plan of C119 Church (S. Copp, J.P. Oleson).*

portions of the interior face of the north wall (Locus 04.02), the west wall of the adjacent northeast room (Locus 04.03), and the west wall of the church (Locus 03.02) A few fragments of red and green painted plaster were found in the area of the apse in 1993. No excavation was carried out below the floor level, so the characteristics of the wall foundations are unknown.

8.B.2. Doors

The three doors into the church are badly preserved. There is a door (width at door jambs 1.00 m) in the west wall ca. 0.50 to 2.00 m north of the interior southwest corner of the building but it was not exposed or clearly defined. In 1993 a door was noticed toward the centre of the west wall, ca. 4.00 to 5.20 m north of the interior southwest corner of the building. In 2009 the doorjambs were covered by the recently churned-up soil. Square 04 was excavated to clarify the existence of that door (fig. 8.4). Excavation revealed apparent doorjamb blocks at this point, approximately 1.75 m above the paving (elev. 965.55 m at the north; 965.31 m at the south), framing a door about 0.86 m wide. There

FIG. 8.4   *West door and bedrock step, looking south (Photo: R. Schick).*

is a level area with broken pieces of stone (Locus 03.06) at the point where a threshold should have been located. To the east is a single stone forming a doorstop ca. 0.20 m high and 0.20 m wide. Such a doorstop would have required a high step of 0.36 m down to the top bedrock step inside the church, but the arrangement is paralleled by the two doorways in the C101 Lower Church (pp. 259–60).

Possible traces of a door in the west portion of the north wall were noted in 1993, 3.30–4.80 m east of the interior northwest corner of the church, but this feature could not be identified in 2009.

8.B.3. Arch Piers

Two rows of three arches oriented east–west divided the two side aisles from the nave; they were supported by piers engaged to the east and west

walls and by two freestanding arch piers (fig. 8.3, 8.6). The two freestanding piers measured 0.55 × 0.55 m and are set 3.40 m apart. Two courses of the northeast engaged pier (Locus 04.04; 0.50 m north–south × 0.35 m east–west) are preserved (top elev. 964.76 m). There is a circular hole of undetermined function in the west face of its uppermost course. The southwest engaged pier at the south edge of Square 03 is composed of three preserved courses above bedrock, up to 965.43 m.

The northeast freestanding pier (Locus 04.10), fully exposed within square 04, consists of three preserved courses above the pavement. The southeast freestanding pier was exposed in the centre of a modern robber pit that was left unexcavated to the south of square 04. A small amount of excavation just to the west of Square 04 exposed the top of the northwest freestanding pier (Locus 04.16).

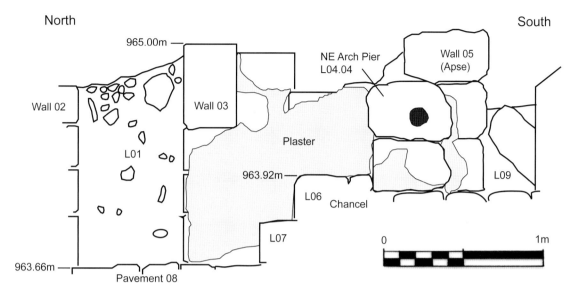

FIG. 8.5   *C116, elevation drawing of door into north* pastophorion, *wall plaster, and chancel steps (A. Heidenreich, I. Sturkenboom, M. Siklenka).*

8.B.4. Roof

Other than the piers, no evidence survived to provide specific details of the roof design. No roof tiles or nails were found. The nearly complete absence of remains of roof tiles from all the excavated churches at Humayma suggests that the roofs were flat and built out of wood beams covered by crossbeams, a thatch of rushes or sticks, and a plastered clay surface. Only 55 roof tile fragments were found at B100, 5 at C101, 29 at F102, and none at all at C119 and B126. An alternative idea that these roofing elements were thoroughly and carefully salvaged after the churches went out of use seems less likely (see p. 157).

8.B.5. Pavement, Apse, and Chancel Area

The portions of the north aisle and the central nave that were exposed were paved with flagstones (Locus 04.08; elev. 963.66 m; fig. 8.2, 8.6). There are some intact traces of floor plaster in the east, indicating that the pavers originally had been covered by plaster. There are no traces of any benches along the interior faces of the church walls. At the west end of the church, a flattened bedrock surface serves as the floor.

The interior of the small apse measures 3.00 m wide and 1.55 m deep. The east end of the apse is aligned with the east wall of the northeast and southeast rooms. The curved apse wall (Locus 04.05) is preserved above the pavement level in the chancel area for two to three courses, up to 965.06 m at the northwest corner. There was not sufficient time in the 2009 season to remove the disturbed soil and tumble throughout the apse.

The chancel is raised above the level of the north aisle and central nave and approached by two steps (figs. 8.5, 8.6–7). The lower step on the north side of the chancel (Locus 04.07) is 3.50 m long east–west, while the lower step on the west side of the chancel (Locus 04.15) was exposed for 1.00 m north–south. They both rise up 0.26 m from the pavement (to elev. 963.92 m). The upper step of the north edge of the raised chancel (Locus 04.11) consists of a course of eight blocks 2.68 m long and covered with plaster up 0.30 m from the lower step (at 964.10 m), while two blocks were exposed of the west edge (Locus 04.12). The north and west edges meet at a right angle, leaving a space of 0.30 m between the corner and the northeast free-standing pier, just enough for a person to squeeze past.

The lower north step (Locus 04.07) is not exactly parallel to the upper step (Locus 04.11); it is

FIG. 8.6   *North aisle and Chancel, looking east (Photo: R. Schick).*

0.34 m wide at the west and ca. 0.50 m wide at the east. At the east there are two additional blocks (Locus 04.06) between the lower and upper steps (0.76 m east–west, 0.30 m north–south; top elev. 964.20 m), a few centimetres below the level of the upper step. It seems that the lower step and these two blocks represent a first phase of the chancel, which was then redesigned in a second phase, at which point the upper row of blocks replaced the western continuation of the two blocks.

The groove in which the marble chancel screen panels were placed is well-preserved in the upper step along the west edge, but less clearly preserved in the upper step along the north edge. At the east end of the north step a layer of small stones is set into mortar.

Within the chancel there is a flagstone pavement (Locus 04.14; elev. 964.10 m), ca. 0.10 m lower than the top of the upper chancel steps (Loci 04.11, 04.12). The pavement extended below the top chancel steps, demonstrating that the construction of the pavement belongs to a phase prior to installation of the upper chancel steps. There is no trace of any plaster on the flagstones, as seen in the north aisle.

FIG. 8.7   *Northeast corner of Chancel, detail (Photo: R. Schick).*

FIG. 8.8   *Cupboard in north* pastophorion *(Photo: R. Schick).*

There is no trace of an altar or pulpit in the portion of the chancel area that was exposed within Square 04. One of the flagstones is missing and another one had clearly been lifted and replaced recently. During the short 2009 season, time ran out before any of the paving stones in the chancel or aisles could be lifted and the soil below dug down to bedrock. Thus there are no sub-floor finds here that could provide evidence for the date of the construction of the church.

8.B.6. Pastophoria

The southeast *pastophorion* room (Room 02) is roughly rectangular. The curving apse wall gives it variable dimensions of about 2.20–2.50 m north–south, 1.25–1.50 m east–west. The room is entered from the south aisle through a doorway (W 0.56 m) with jambs and a threshold (fig. 8.9). A cupboard with two shelves is built into the north wall (W ca. 0.70 m, ca. 0.40 m deep; bottom elev. 964.23 m).

The northeast *pastophorion* room is closely similar to the southeast room. It is roughly rect-

angular, 2.25–2.50 m north–south, ca. 1.25 m east–west. The room is entered from the north aisle through a doorway 0.64 m wide the jambs and a threshold (elev. 963.76 m) of which survive. A cupboard with two shelves in the south wall is 0.70 m wide (east–west) and 0.40 m deep (north–south); bottom elev. 964.10 m (fig. 8.8). The area around the cupboard was cleaned up for photographs, but otherwise the extensively churned-up soil and tumble in the room were not excavated.

8.C. STRATIGRAPHIC DEPOSITS

8.C.1. Square 04

In 1993, surface rocks and some small amounts of topsoil were removed from the general area of the C119 structure (Locus 01.01), including the churned-up soil around the apse, and extending about a metre into the chancel. Further cleaning in the church interior in 2009 showed that the soil layers throughout most of the interior had been churned up all the way down to the pavement in the north aisle, the nave, and the chancel area. The recent date of this disturbance was demonstrated by the presence of a few pieces of modern garbage directly on top of the chancel pavement. At least one paver in the chancel had been lifted and then replaced. Modern pits elsewhere within the walls indicated that most of the interior in the rest of the church had also been dug through recently.

The disturbed soil in the eastern part of the north aisle and the raised chancel area was excavated as Square 04 (figs. 8.6–7). The square was L-shaped, based on the area where the illicit digging had left large pits, measuring 3.50 m north–south by 6.50 m east–west, leaving a 1.0 m wide unexcavated strip along the north wall. Most of the soil that was excavated was clearly disturbed soil, with cobbles and blocks from the recent illicit digging; Locus 04.01 on top, and Locus 04.09 below down to the level of the raised chancel. Below the top level of the raised chancel, the soil in the north aisle and nave contained few to no cobbles (Locus 04.13). It was clear that the soil had been disturbed in most of the area, except possibly along the extreme west edge of Square 04, west of the churned-up pit around the eastern free-standing arch pier, In this area a layer of silty soil without any large blocks (Locus 04.13) above the pavement may have been undisturbed, as indicated by a small lens of ash directly above the pavement. The west baulk section, however, does not clearly reveal at this point a transition between the intact and disturbed deposits.

Finds from Square 04

Two pieces of marble were collected during the general clean up in 1993: a fragment of the edge of a panel or table, and a fragment of a panel (p. 478). Substantial numbers of amphora and storage jar sherds appeared in the disturbed soil. In 2009, two additional small fragments from chancel screen panels were found in the soil churned up by the illicit digging (p. 478). A few small pieces of glass, ostrich egg shells, and animal bones were also found in the soil directly above the chancel pavement (Locus 04.09), and above the aisle and nave pavement (Locus 04.13). Glass lamps and ostrich egg shells were often associated with the *polykan-*

dela in Byzantine churches (p. 295). A corroded iron nail was also found in the soil above the nave pavement. The pottery sherds found were mostly LB and UM, and included a few fragments of an Aqaba amphora of Umayyad date. A few glass oil lamp fragments were also found.

8.C.2. *Square 03*

Square 03 was excavated along the central portion of the east face of the west wall of the church (Locus 03.02), in order to delineate clearly the door into an adjoining room on the west, as well as reach the pavement of the church in a seemingly undisturbed area. This square was laid out for 5.00 m north–south from the north face of the southwest attached pier to the north wall of the church and 1.00 m east–west from the east face of the west wall. The top layer (Locus 03.01) consisted of soil with tumbled blocks that had fallen from the west wall of the church. Below the initial layer of tumble, the excavation area was reduced to the southern half of the square, revealing further layers of soil with tumbled blocks and rubble (Locus 03.03, 03.04, 03.05), ultimately resting on bedrock (fig. 8.4).

The west wall of the church is founded on bedrock, and the plaster covering the lowest course of the wall extends over the seam between the lowest block and the bedrock. The bedrock is highest beneath the west wall, two steps up from the level of flattened bedrock that here forms the floor of the church in place of pavers (fig. 8.4). Adjacent to the east face of the west wall, the bedrock has been levelled at an elevation of 964.95 m. This bedrock surface had a widely variable east–west dimension of some 0.10 m to 0.45 m before stepping down 0.10 m to a lower step (W 0.15–0.20 m). To the east the bedrock surface drops down as much as 0.39 m. That lowest level (elev. 964.46 m) was some 0.70 m above the level of the pavement farther to the east in the north and central aisle (elev. ca. 963.76 m). Two further bedrock steps in the 2 m of unexcavated soil between squares 03 and 04 presumably spanned this difference in height.

There is a gap in the west wall (Locus 03.02), around 3 m to 4 m south of the northwest inside corner of the church, indicating the location of a doorway (figs. 8.2, 8.4). No doorjambs are in place,

FIG. 8.9   *South* pastophorion *with earth floor and cupboard (Photo: J.P. Oleson, 1993).*

so the exact width of the door cannot be determined. A threshold and door stop, however, are present. About 0.80 m south of the door opening can be seen the southwest engaged pier, terminating the south row of east–west arches, preserved for three courses above bedrock.

Finds from Square 03

One stray piece of marble was found in low tumble (Locus 03.05; 2009.0042.01, p. 478), along with a few pieces of glass. The pottery found dated generally to the Byzantine period.

8.C.3. *The Southeast Room*
(Room 2, **Pastophorion***)*

Most of the southeast *pastophorion* room (Room 02; fig. 8.9) was excavated in 1993 in order to define

the stratigraphy and provide some evidence for dating the building. Excavation proceeded through topsoil (Locus 02.01) and tumble (Loci 02–04). Pottery was predominantly LB and UM. A bronze pin was found in Locus 02.03, and a bronze hook in Locus 02.04. Below the layers of tumble, ca. 1.5 m below the surviving tops of the walls, a layer of silt with Late Byzantine and Umayyad pottery (Locus 02.05) extended across the room. Associated with the lowest tumbled blocks and cobbles were two large fragments of a marble chancel screen panel with a cross, a large fragment of a marble colonnette shaft, and an additional small fragment of a marble panel (fig. 8.10; pp. 478–79).

A second layer of silt with no pottery (Locus 02.06) below Locus 02.05 contained several thousand fragments of glass from liturgical tumbler lamps and stemmed oil lamps, tightly packed in a layer a few centimetres thick (see pp. 529–32). There was no evidence indicating how the glass lamps had been stored in the room. When intact, they could not all have fit in the cupboard. Below the glass fragments there was yet another layer of silt (Locus 02.07) a few centimetres thick that seems to represent the occupational layer of the room, resting on a beaten earth floor. Across the north half of the room, excavation proceeded below the beaten earth floor, exposing a further layer of silt (Locus 02.08) associated with the top foundation courses for the room walls. Pottery from the bottom layers (Loci 02.07 and 02.08) were predominantly LB and UM. A bronze coin (Locus 02.08) was unreadable. The excavation did not reach sterile soil.

8.D. CONCLUSIONS

The C119 Upper Church is a small, three-aisled basilica with a standard plan involving an apse flanked by two side rooms (cf. Michel 2001: 145, fig. 91). This plan corresponds to Type A.I.f of Qaqish (2007: 191 no. 76, 269), represented by 50 other examples in Jordan, including the Ridge Church at Petra (Bikai 2002) and the Jabal Harûn Church (Fiema and Frösén 2008). It was the single most common plan for a church among Qaqish's 24 sub-types (2007). The construction date of the church, based on the pottery from the low layers of Room 2, cannot be narrowly defined within the Late Byzan-

FIG. 8.10   *South* pastophorion, *with deposit of salvaged marble furnishings (Photo: J.P. Oleson).*

tine period. Since there is little evidence elsewhere in Jordan for the construction of new churches after 636 (Schick 1995a: 119–23; Gatier 2011: 27; Michel 2011: 235–37), it is unlikely that this church could date post-636. The architecture of the church points to a single building phase. The only indication of a second phase in the church is the apparent re-working of the north step up to the chancel area. No clear indication was found for the placement of the altar and pulpit. Storage cupboards in the *pastophoria* flanking the apse are a typical feature (Butler 1929: 218), as in the Church of St. George at Khirbat al-Mukhayyat (Michel 2001: 343, fig. 322) and the Church of Wa'il at Umm al-Rasas (Michel 2001: 410, fig. 397), among other examples.

The excavation of the southeast room revealed that it had only a beaten earth floor, and that the room had been used for the storage of glass lamps. After the abandonment of the church and the breakage of the glass vessels stored in the southeast room, enough time passed for wind-blown silt to accumulate before the marble furnishings of the church were robbed out, and a few pieces dumped in the southeast room. The furnishings of the church were almost completely removed, and the major structural collapse of the building occurred afterwards.

Chapter 9

Field B126: Byzantine Church

by Robert Schick

9.A. LOCATION AND EXCAVATION HISTORY

The B126 church was built in the centre of the habitation area, east of the B100 excavation area and northeast of the large Reservoir no. 68. Albrecht Alt noticed the structure during his brief visit to Humayma in 1935 (1936: 94–95, plate 3B) (figs. 1.1, 9.1). He mentions recent digging by the Bedouin inhabitants at the three apses of a Byzantine church near the southeast edge of the ruin field, and he publishes a photograph facing northeast that shows the east end of the church, with seven courses of the central apse above the pavement level and seven courses of the north portion of a south apse curve and a doorway into a southeast room. That the building in the photograph is indeed the B126 building can be seen by a careful examination of the north portion of the apse curve, where the seven courses visible in the photograph remain in place today. The church building was incorporated into a modern barn built in the 1960s (fig. 9.2). No church features are visible from outside the 1960s structure. The Humayma staff had ignored the building, which had always been kept locked, until the 1996 season, when the owner had ceased to use it and left the door open. Once the apse had been recognized, Schick investigated the site for three days immediately after its rediscovery and then again for a few days in a short season in 2009.

According to one of the workmen, whose grandfather had used the building as a barn, the locals brought in an architect named ʿAli al-Hijazi in the 1960s to construct the various one-room buildings scattered around the site, including the B126 structure. His construction of this building incorporating the eastern portions of the church is commemorated by an Arabic inscription on the lintel of the south door that reads: "There is no god but God and Muhammad is the Messenger of God" (above), and "ʿAli al-Hijazi made this" (below). The locals preferred this reading to the alternative rendering "work of ʿAli al-Hijazi" (fig. 9.3). Such private building inscriptions with pious phrases have become common in Jordan in recent decades, although the fact that our building is a barn, rather than a house, and that the person named is the builder/architect, rather than the owner, is noteworthy.

Published parallels to our inscription prior to the late twentieth century are few, but there are two examples from the village of ʿAima in southern Jordan (Biewers 1997: 69, figs. 2.28 and 2.31). Her figure 2.28 shows the inscription "There is no god but God. Muhammad is the Messenger of God" crudely incised into a lintel. Her figure 2.31 shows a professionally-cut inscription on a specially prepared block recording "In the name of God the Merciful, the Compassionate" on line one and "Possession belongs to God" on line 2, followed by

words that are difficult to read in the photograph, and the date, which seems to be 1372/1952–1953. Additional examples from the mid-20th century are known in Palestine (Riwaq 2006, volume 2).

It is not clear why a circular central section of the slab was pecked away. The slab is very likely a re-used ancient block, so perhaps there was a cross or other inappropriate motif on it that had to be effaced, or maybe the date was for some reason removed. A similar case in an Ottoman house in Tayba in Palestine looks more like natural erosion (Petersen 2001: 297, pl. 335). There is an open hand (for good luck) on the right side of the pecked area, and a motif of unknown meaning on the left, consisting of an upright line joining a triangle above with a semicircle below. The latter may possibly be a *wasm* (camel brand), although it does not appear among the *wusum* commonly used by the Huweitat (K. ʿAmr, personal communication, Dec. 2012). After reconstruction the B126 building was used for storage of grain and then as a stable for sheep and goats.

After the discovery that the 1960s building incorporated the remains of a church, Schick spent

three days in 1996 removing some of the deposits in the church interior (Room 1) to clarify some of the original church features, and excavating a probe in the southeast room (Room 2). After a partial collapse of the flat wood and mud roof around 2005, the locals removed the remaining wooden roof beams in the winter of 2008–2009 for use elsewhere, making it easier to excavate and take photographs in the interior. In consequence, part of the two-week season in 2009 was spent excavating the interior to clarify the architectural features and determine what belonged to the original church and what belonged to the modern 1960s building.

9.B. Architectural Features and Phasing of the 1960s Building

The 1960s building incorporates the eastern portion of the church. It reuses the wall of the apse curve, but the other walls of the building all appear to be modern or completely rebuilt (figs. 9.4–6). The north and west walls are clearly modern, since their bottom courses rest directly on the original church pavement. The construction of the 1960s building

FIG. 9.2   *View of house built over B126 Church, from the south (Photo: R. Schick).*

FIG. 9.3   *Builder's inscription on ancient block (Photo: J.P. Oleson).*

FIG. 9.4   *View of apse from above, after robber activity (Photo: R. Schick).*

entailed the removal of the south apse curve shown in the 1935 photograph and the rebuilding of the south face of the apse curve as a straight wall (Locus 01.02) and the upper courses of the east wall (Locus 01.07), thus altering the east wall as shown in the 1935 photograph.

The 1960s building has two rooms with exterior dimensions of ca. 10 m north–south and ca. 7.5 m east–west. The walls are ca. 0.75 m thick, except for the irregular east wall, which is thicker (fig. 9.5).

Room 1 measures 8.50 m north–south and 4.70 m east–west. It incorporates seven courses of the original church apse (Locus 01.02), on which the roof was placed, and uses newly-built north (Locus 01.06), east (Locus 01.07), west (Locus 01.03) and south walls. The roof was supported by an east–west arch (Locus 01.04) spanning the 3.0 m distance from an arch support pier in the centre of the apse curve and a second arch support pier 0.50 m wide along the west wall (fig. 9.7). This arch was 2.20 m from the north wall. A second arch (Locus 08) spanned the 2.50 m east–west distance from the

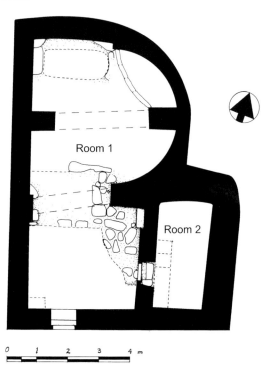

FIG. 9.5   *Plan of modern B126 structure incorporating ancient apse (S. Fraser).*

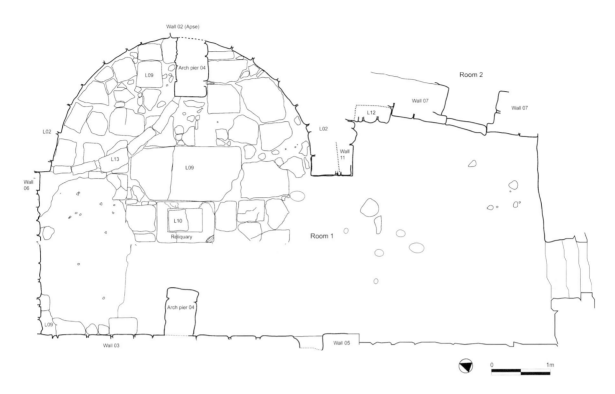

FIG. 9.6 *Stone by stone plan of interior of B126 structure (A. Heidenreich, I. Sturkenboom, M. Siklenka).*

southwest end of the apse curve to a support pier (Locus 01.05) 0.80 m wide along the west wall, slightly off-set by 0.30 m to the south; it was 2.20 m south of the first arch. The space between the south arch and the south wall of the building was 3.00 to 3.10 m north–south and 3.40 m east–west. A door in the south wall provided entrance into the building; a door in the east wall (Locus 01.07) led into the southeast room (Room 2) (fig. 9.8). The church paving stones were not present in this south area, which was left unexcavated.

The modern walls contained a number of cupboards. There were three cupboards in the north wall (Locus 01.06) west of the apse and six cupboards in the west wall (Locus 01.03); two of them re-use large, finely-dressed blocks of Ma'an shelly limestone as the side panels (figs. 9.7, 9.9). Those four blocks could originally have been steps up to the chancel area. They are similar to step blocks found in the B100 church, as well as in the Petra church (Kanellopoulos and Schick 2001: 193–94).

The post-1960s barn deposits of variegated dung and straw (Locus 01.01) were up to 0.30 m

thick above a layer of modern cement a couple of centimetres thick, laid directly on the original church pavement (Locus 01.09) and serving as the barn floor. The juxtaposition demonstrates that the modern occupants completely cleared out the collapse debris of the church down to the original pavement. A row of stones (Locus 01.13) one-course high in a curve along the west part of the apse, directly above the apse church pavement, delineated an area of grain storage (fig. 9.7).

The southeast room (Room 2) measures 3.20 m north–south and 1.80 m east–west. Its walls are modern. There is one cupboard in the east wall. The doorway into the room appears to be a rebuild of the doorway in the 1935 photograph.

9.C. ARCHITECTURAL FEATURES OF THE CHURCH

The 1960s building was constructed over only the eastern portion of the original church. The western and northern extents of the church are no longer detectable on the surface, and it would take the

FIG. 9.7 *Interior of B126 structure from doorway. The reliquary cover is visible in the middle distance (Photo: R. Schick).*

no trace of any pulpit or a chancel elevated above the side aisles and nave. The width of the apse is one of the few original features of the church structure that can be tested for use of the Byzantine foot of 0.3089 m. The resulting figure, just under 14 Byzantine feet, unfortunately does not confirm whether or not the foot was used.

In 1935, Alt identified the church as having had three apses. No trace is visible of any northern apse, which might still be buried in the high mound of rubble beyond the north wall of the 1960s building. No trace survives of the south curved wall clearly shown in the 1935 photograph; it has apparently been completely dismantled (figs. 9.1, 9.8). The south curved wall, now known only from Alt's photograph, is puzzling. At first glance one might think of it as the wall of a south apse, but it is difficult to understand how it could have functioned as such, given the apparent arch support pier (Locus 01.12) and the southeast room (Room 2) behind it. But if the curved wall was not part of a south apse, no obvious alternative function for the wall presents itself.

removal of substantial quantities of rubble and soil to determine the overall plan.

9.C.1. Apses

The apse has a north–south width of 4.30 m and an east–west depth of 2.40 m, wider and deeper than the central apse in the C101 Church (3.75 × 2.1 m) (figs. 9.4–6). The pavers (Locus 01.09; elev. 955.62 m) in the apse are mostly intact below the post-1960s barn deposits and consist of thin purple sandstone slabs, like the pavers in the C101 church (fig. 9.6). Along the centre of the west end of the apse there is one exceptionally large paver (1.85 × 0.90 m). None of the pavers show any markings indicating the location of the altar. There is also

9.C.2. Arches and Pavement

The south arch support pier in the west wall (Locus 01.05) is an original feature of the church. Several blocks continuing below the pavement level seem to be foundation courses, although that area was not excavated. The arch pier is set off 0.30 m to the south of the southwest end of the apse curve, from which the 1960s arch springs. The original church arch seemingly spanned the space between the west support pier (Locus 01.05) and a support pier in the east wall (Locus 01.12), consisting of two well-dressed ashlar blocks. That arrangement, however, would have worked only if the south curved wall in the 1935 photograph was not in fact a south apse.

FIG. 9.8   *Room 01 with door to Room 02 (Photo: R. Schick).*

An L-shaped trench 2.40 m north–south by 1.80 m east–west was excavated south of the apse curve (Locus 01.02) and west of the east wall (Locus 01.07), below the modern barn deposits, to clarify the phasing of the various architectural features. Excavation soon hit a solid layer (Locus 01.14; Th 0.50 m) of large, irregularly laid cobbles in sandy silt at a top elevation of ca. 955.50–955.35 m; bottom elevation ca. 954.95 m. The large cobbles were not removed, and excavation here did not proceed further; the top of the sterile orange sand layer probably lies ca. 0.70 m lower down. The excavation revealed that the two lower ashlar blocks of the presumed arch pier (Locus 01.12) and the lowest three courses of the west face of the east wall (Locus 01.07) are original church-phase features, but that the upper courses of the arch pier (Locus 01.12), the west face of the east wall (Locus 01.07) and the south face of the apse wall (Locus 01.02) belong to the 1960s building.

9.C.3. *Reliquary*

Although the original flagstone pavers had been lifted or removed in much of the interior of the 1960s building, one large, thick paver flush with the floor, located in the centre of the church immediately west of the exceptionally large paver in the apse, had been left undisturbed (Locus 01.10; 0.94 m N–S; 0.63 m E–W; Th 0.21 m; figs. 9.6, 9.10). A large rectangular recess had been cut in the centre of the block (0.52 × 0.38 × 0.03 m Th), leaving margins 0.13 to 0.20 cm wide. At the time of discovery, only the north half of the opening was filled by a stone slab, while the south half was filled with soil. When the recess was cleared out, the paver was found to cover an intact stone reliquary (figs. 9.11–13). There was a rectangular opening (0.22 × 0.35 m) cut through the paver toward the north end, and in the centre there was a circular hole (D 0.05 m).

FIG. 9.9   *West interior wall of B126 structure (Photo: R. Schick).*

The paver covered a block of sandstone (Locus 01.17; 0.65 × 0.34 m; Th ca. 0.34 m) forming the body of the reliquary. A rectangular receptacle (0.15 × 0.16 m; 0.10 m deep) occupies the north end, directly beneath the rectangular hole of the covering paver. The receptacle in the block and the hole in the covering paver are both lined by a layer of plaster that had to have been applied after the paver was in place (fig. 9.13). A circular receptacle (D 0.18 m; 0.12 m deep) is cut into the south end of the block; the circular hole in the covering paver is positioned just inside its north edge. There is no connection between the rectangular and circular receptacles. At the time of discovery, the circular receptacle was nearly filled with ordinary gritty sandy and silty soil, along with some stone chips and pebbles, and a very few small pieces of carbonized material (not remains of cremated bones), but no bones or any other artefacts of any kind. Regrettably, the soil was misplaced before flota-

tion could be carried out. The contents seem to be original, rather than soil that filtered in through the small hole after the abandonment of the church, in which case the soil would not have been lying flat but would have been higher below the hole, resting at a natural angle of slope; certainly some of the stone chips and pebbles are too large to have fit through the hole. The rectangular receptacle had only a little soil inside it.

The sandstone block was clearly a reliquary, and it was undisturbed, so it is puzzling that it did not contain any relics. The plaster lining that covered both the rectangular hole and rectangular receptacle was intact, which argues against the covering paver having been lifted at some later point to remove the relics. The reliquary and covering paver were deposited in the Humayma Visitors Centre.

The sandstone reliquary block had been installed in silty, sandy soil fill (Locus 01.16) with some cobbles, among which was a small fragment

FIG. 9.10 *Reliquary with covering slab in place (Photo: R. Schick).*

FIG. 9.11 *Reliquary with lid in place (Photo: R. Schick).*

FIG. 9.12 *Reliquary after removal of lid (Photo: R. Schick).*

of a Nabataean pilaster base (p. 498, no. 4). One
paver immediately to the north of the reliquary
was also removed and the similar soil under it
excavated (Locus 01.15,). Within a few days after
the 2009 season, some illicit diggers dug a deep
pit around the area where the reliquary had been,
through about a metre of the same soil, revealing
that there was no earlier phase below the church
pavement (fig. 9.4).

Some 44 reliquaries have been found in Jordan
(Michel 2001: 72–81; Duval 2003a: 79–82, 90–92);
a reliquary from Jabal Harûn (Fiema and Comte
2008) can now be added to Michel's list (see also
Israeli and Mevorah 2000: 76–77; Fulcherio 2007).
The Hauarra reliquary is of the box with lid type,
rather than the sarcophagus type, but is rather
larger than the other examples. The location of the
reliquary suggests that the altar was located there
as well, although no trace of it survives.

9.C.4. Southeast Room (Room 2)

In 1996, two days were spent digging a probe in
the southeast room (Room 2) along the west wall
(Locus 2.04 = Locus 01.07) and the doorway. The
trench ran the entire 3.50 m north–south length
of the room and was 0.50 m wide east–west. First,
the thin modern goat dung and straw layer was
cleaned off to reveal a horizontal layer (Th 0.30
m) of uniform sterile silt with very few cobbles or
pebbles (Locus 01). This silt layer was contiguous
with the threshold (Locus 2.03) in the west door
and overlay a deposit of two to three irregular layers of cobbles and pebbles in a matrix of sterile silt
(Locus 02; Th 0.30 m), matching the cobble layer to
the west (Locus 01.14). There was no trace in Room
2 of any pavers, as in the church. It may be that the
cobbles were the bedding for a now missing church
pavement, and that the top layer of silt (Locus 2.01)

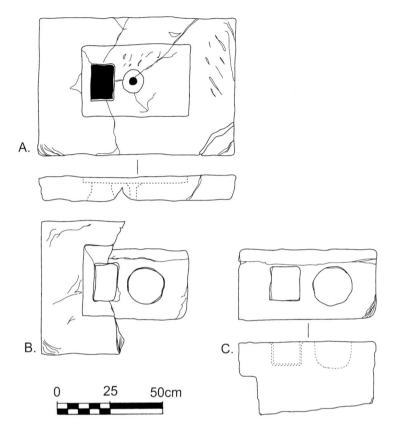

A.

B.

C.

0   25   50cm

contained large quantities of pottery in variegated layers of silt, sand, and ashy silt.

The excavation of these soil layers clarified some of the architectural features of the room. The doorway in the west wall (Locus 2.03) had thresholds of two phases. On the west was a single block placed sideways spanning the entire width between the door jambs (0.70 m north–south; elev. 955.80 m). That west block is a feature of the 1960s building. To the east are two flat, roughly-dressed blocks 0.23 m lower than the top of the west block, with small cobbles in between (elev. 955.57 m). They appear to have been the Byzantine phase threshold. The doorjambs consist of four courses of blocks.

The east face of the west wall of the room (Locus 2.04 = Locus 01.07), extends for 10 slightly irregular courses above the threshold and for three courses more below the threshold. The courses above the threshold utilize mud-packing and chink stones in between the variably sized, roughly-dressed blocks. Below the threshold, the upper two wall courses consist of dressed blocks with chink stones and so are the best constructed courses of the wall. The base is an irregular foundation course of cobbles.

The south wall (Locus 2.05) has nine courses above the level of the threshold that were a bit more irregular than in the west wall, using mud-packing, chink stones, and variably sized blocks. Below the level of the threshold are four courses, each smaller in size than the three courses in the west wall, again with the bottom course consisting of a foundation of cobbles. The south and west walls bond. The courses above the threshold level are 1960s construction, while the better-built foundation courses seem to be Byzantine features. The north and east walls were not exposed below ground level,

was fill placed during the 1960s construction of the room to produce a level floor surface, but the total absence of artefacts in those layers makes it impossible to date the deposits.

The cobble layer (Locus 2.02) was left unexcavated in the north part of the trench, which thus was reduced to only 2.20 m long north–south for the lower layers. Below is a thick layer of uniform, mostly sterile silt with occasional random cobbles and pebbles (Locus 2.06; Th ca. 0.90 m), extending all the way down to the bottom of the west and south walls (elev. 954.27 m), on top of the sterile orange sand layer (Locus 2.07) that underlies all the structures at Humayma. The fill (Locus 2.06) appears to be uniform, with no clear internal differentiation of content, although it does become sandier towards the bottom. Only 14 sherds of general LB and UM date were found. The nature of the fill here is radically different from the fill beneath the pavement of the C101 church, which

so whether the above-ground modern 1960s walls lie above Byzantine period walls remains unknown.

9.D. CONCLUSIONS

The church appears in general to be humbler than any of the other churches at Humayma, although it is difficult to judge its character without knowing the main dimensions and number of apses. Qaqish assigned the church to her Type A.I.d (2007: 190, no. 31, 225–26). No evidence was found that could serve to date the construction, use, or abandonment of the church beyond the generic designation that it must belong to the Late Byzantine period. The handful of undiagnostic sherds recovered from below the pavers (Loci 01.15, 01.16) and in Room 2 (Locus 02.06) do not help much in narrowing down the date of construction. The church would repay further, lengthier investigation to determine its overall dimensions and clarify whether it was indeed a triple-apse church.

The 1935 photograph showing the south apse reveals that the southeast Room 2 with its doorway lies immediately behind this feature. While there are some examples of an especially large room to the side of a single apse, e.g., the church at el-Lejjun (Schick 1987), the presence of a room as large as Room 2 behind a side apse is anomalous (see in general Michel 2001; Qaqish 2007).

Chapter 10

Human, Animal, and Plant Remains

by Megan Perry, Mahmoud Y. el-Najjar (†), Michael Finnegan,
David S. Reese, and Jennifer Ramsay

10.A. HUMAN REMAINS FROM B100, C101, F102, F125, AND THE NABATAEAN NECROPOLIS

(M.A. Perry and M.Y. el-Najjar)

In the course of the Humayma excavation project, human burials have been recovered from a number of contexts. Burials contemporary with Nabataean occupation at the site (first to second century AD) were found interred in shaft tombs cut into the bedrock to the west of the occupation area. Two of these shaft tombs (A107 and A108), each containing a single burial, were excavated in 1992 (see pp. 61–64). An additional first-century AD cist tomb (B100) was identified underneath the apse of the B100 Church (see pp. 175–76). In addition, individuals residing in Byzantine period Hauarra were buried in association with the ecclesiastical structures at the site. In 1992, two cist tombs dating to the fourth century AD were excavated in front of the east façade of the F102 Church (see pp. 150–53), although they probably predate its construction. In 1992 and 1993, five burials dating to the sixth century AD were recovered from below the floor of the C101 church (see pp. 241–52). This small sample of individuals who lived in ancient Hauarra can help to illuminate the quality of life of the city's residents compared to other contemporary populations in the region (Table 10.1). Furthermore, in 2004 an early

modern intrusive burial was excavated in the area of the E125 domestic complex. The bones from this burial are reported here for the sake of completeness.

Cleaning and initial examination of the skeletal material was carried out by J. Somogyi-Cyzismazia in the course of the excavation. Preliminary study of the burials excavated in 1992 and 1993 was completed by Mahmoud el-Najjar in 1993. In 1998, Megan Perry studied the adult burials from this sample that were held at ACOR and Yarmouk University, focusing on recording age, sex, and skeletal genetic traits. At that time, two adult burials could not be located, Burial 11 from underneath the B100 church, and Burial 8 from the C101 church. In 2004, an additional burial was recovered from within the E125 domestic complex (Burial 12) and was studied by Perry in 2006. Dr. Najjar's untimely death in January 2009 meant that he could not see this project to completion. Thus, this final report draws upon Najjar's preliminary report and subsequent analyses conducted by Perry.

10.A.1. Description of the Skeletal Remains

Study of the remains was conducted primarily by Mahmoud Najjar (MN). Additional information on preservation, age and sex estimation, taphonomy, and pathology for some of the burials was added by Megan Perry (MP), who collected these

Table 10.1   Burials excavated at Humayma in 1992, 1993, 2004.

BURIAL No.	BUCKET No.	LOCUS	CONTEXT	DATE	AGE	SEX
1	1992.0396	A107.T1.01	Nabataean necropolis	Late 1–early 2C?	older adult	indeterminate
2	1992.0397	A108.T1.00	Nabataean necropolis	2C?	adult	indeterminate
3	1992.0482	F102.05.43	F102 church no. 1	4C?	30–34 years	female
4	1992.0530	F102.05.56	F102 church no. 2	4C?	35–39 years	probable male
5	1992.0516a	C101.01.46	C101 church no. 1	6C	3–5 years	indeterminate
6	1992.0604	C101.01.62	C101 church no. 2	6C	8–11 years	indeterminate
7	1992.0606	C101.01.56	C101 church no. 3	6C	adult	male
8	1993.0063	C101.01.73	C101 church no. 4	6C	35–45 years	probable female
9	1992.0615	C101.01.63	C101 church no. 5	6C	25–34 years	male
10	1993.0019, 1993.0021	B100.E.37	Cist tomb beneath B100 church	1C	35–45 years	male
11	2004.0091	E125.19.26	Mound in ruin field	Early modern	adult	female

observations according to the *Standards for Data Collection from Human Skeletal Remains* (Buikstra and Ubelaker 1994). Complete skeletal inventories are not published here, as Perry only inventoried two of the burials during her analysis, and Najjar did not attempt complete inventories of the remains he studied.

Burial 1: Nabataean necropolis, Locus A107.T1.01 (observed by MN)

Description of the remains: Only a fraction of the skeleton was recovered from the tomb, and many of the bones were in a fragmented state due to robbing that had occurred in the rock-cut shaft tomb.
Age and sex: This individual was determined to be an adult individual, perhaps an older adult, based on the dental wear and completed union of epiphyses. The remains were not complete enough for sex estimation
Pathologies: None.

Burial 2: Nabataean necropolis, Locus A108.T1.00 (observed by MN)

Description of the remains: The second tomb in the Nabataean-period necropolis also had been plundered, which destroyed most of the human skeleton. The only remnants of this burial include very small bone fragments of the post-cranial human bones that were gathered from the surface around the shaft tomb opening.
Age and sex: Based on fusion of the epiphyses, the human bones are those of an adult individual. However, the fragmentary nature and small number of the bones available for examination precluded any estimation of sex.
Pathologies: None.

Burial 3: F102 Burial 1, Locus F102.05.43 (observed by MN and MP)

Description of the remains: The remains were found in an undisturbed cist grave below the entrance to the later F102 Church (see pp. 151–53; figs. 5.68–72). Faunal remains also were recovered from the fill within the tomb. The skeletal remains were in extremely good condition with a large proportion of the bones recovered.
Age and sex: Age estimation was accomplished via morphological assessment of the left and right pubic bones, which both point to this individual being a female. Age estimation relied on pelvic degeneration. The right pubic symphysis was scored as a 6 (30–35 years) according to Todd's standards (Todd 1921), and the left and right auricular surfaces were

FIG. 10.1 *Burial 4 (F102 Burial 2), vertebral osteophytosis of three lumbar vertebrae (photo: M. Najjar).*

scored as 3 (30–34 years) following Lovejoy et al. (1985). Therefore, this individual is estimated to have been 30–35 years of age at her time of death. *Pathologies:* None.

Burial 4: F102 Burial 2, Locus F102.05.56 (observed by MN and MP)

Description of the remains: The remains were found in an undisturbed cist grave below the entrance to the later F102 Church (see p. 153; fig. 5.72). This is an almost complete skeleton, missing only few bones. Most of the bones, however, are not well-preserved. *Age and sex:* Sex of this individual was estimated using morphological features of the pelvis and cranium. The traits of the left and right pelvis bones ranged from ambiguous to probable male. The cranium, on the other hand, displayed primarily male and probable male morphology. Based on this information, the individual was categorized as a probable male. Age estimation relied on degeneration of the right pubic symphysis, which had a Todd (1920) score of 7 (35–39 years of age). Other age indicators such as dental eruption and epiphyseal union confirm the adult age at death of this male. *Pathologies:* Najjar noted some moderate osteoarthritis in some joints, however the joints affected are not identified. His original report also included a photograph of arthritic degeneration of the articular facets and vertebral osteophytosis of three lumbar vertebrae (fig. 10.1).

Burial 5: C101 Church Burial 1, Locus C101.01.46 (observed by MN)

Description of the remains: The remains were found in an undisturbed cist grave inserted below the pavement in the nave of the C101 Church (p. 243–45; figs. 7.23–25). *Age and sex:* Najjar noted that the primary ossification centres of the pelvic bones and vertebrae have not fused together, and the proximal epiphysis of the femur is not fused. Fusion of the femur's proximal epiphysis starts at 12 years of age (Scheuer and Black 2000). The three pelvic ossification centres begin fusing at 5 years of age. Inspection of a photograph of this burial confirms that Najjar actually meant that the bodies of the vertebrae had not fused to the neural arches, a process which occurs from about 3–5 years of age (Sheuer and Black 2000). Based on these indicators, this juvenile was around 5 years of age when he or she died. *Pathologies:* None.

Burial 6: C101 Church Burial 2, Locus C101.01.62 (observed by MN)

Description of the remains: The remains were found in an undisturbed cist grave inserted below the pavement in the nave of the C101 Church. This individual was well-preserved, and most of the bones were recovered (pp. 245–47; figs. 7.27–28). In addition, a mass of black, slightly curled hair (25 g) was associated with the skull.

Fig. 10.2 *Burial 7 (C101 Church Burial 3), poorly healed right femur (photo: M. Najjar).*

Age and sex: Najjar noted that the long bones had unfused epiphyses, and that the root formation of the teeth, especially the third molars, was incomplete. Age estimation based on these vague observations is difficult. The earliest long bone epiphysis to begin fusing is the distal humerus, at 11 years of age (Scheuer and Black 2000). Najjar does not note which teeth have incomplete root formation, nor is it clear whether he is only referring to permanent teeth rather than deciduous teeth, which have root completion by 5 years of age (Moorrees et al. 1963b). If he is referring to permanent teeth, the earliest teeth to complete their root formation are the incisors, by approximately 8 years of age (Moorrees et al. 1963a). The third molar, the last tooth to complete formation, begins forming 9.5–10 years old (Moorrees et al. 1963a). Therefore, the unfused long bones, the present but incomplete third molar, and the incomplete root formation suggest that this individual was anywhere from 8 to 11 years age at the time of death. Sex estimation was not possible with this individual since it is a juvenile, but the artefacts associated with the burial (spindle whorls, jewellery, doll, mirror) are more appropriate to a female (see pp. 385–98).
Pathologies: None.

Burial 7: C101 Church Burial 3, Locus C101.01.56 (observed by MN)

Description of the remains: The remains were found within a wooden coffin in an undisturbed cist grave inserted below the pavement in the nave of the C101 Church (p. 249; fig. 7.31). In general the bones of this individual are extremely robust, and all skeletal bones are present. At the time of discovery, the desiccated remains of the individual's brain were recovered from inside the skull. The slightly spongy tissue had retained the general shape and surface sulci and gyri of a human brain, but it had shrunken to 0.09 × 0.08 m and weighed only 30 g (fig. 7.32). Several patches of black membranous material may be fragments of the meninges. Remains of human brain tissue from desiccated rather than waterlogged corpses apparently are rare (S. O'Connor et al. 2011). The brain was deposited with Prof. A.C. Aufderheide of the University of Minnesota for study. A mass of black hair (125 g), possibly mixed with a woollen shroud, was found associated with the skull. Najjar reconstructed the height of the individual at 1.75 m.
Age and sex: Najjar observed that, based on the morphological features of the skull and the deep and narrow shape of the sciatic notch, the remains are without doubt those of an adult male. Najjar did not attempt age estimation.
Pathologies: Najjar noted a large fracture on the mid-shaft of the right femur that had healed improperly and resulted in *myositis ossificans*, according to the photograph (fig. 10.2).

Burial 8: C101 Church Burial 4, Locus C101.01.73 (observed by MN and MP)

Description of the remains: The remains were found in an undisturbed grave cut into the soil below the pavement in the nave of the C101 Church. Other than the skull, the skeleton was moist and extremely fragile and began to crumble immediately upon exposure. Most of the bones were recovered, including the skull and mandible, but in a fragmented state (p. 250, figs. 7.33, 10.3).
Age and sex: Sex estimation was accomplished through observing cranial and pelvic morphology. Most of the pelvic and cranial indicators scored as probable female or ambiguous, suggesting that

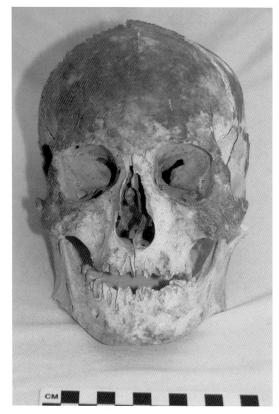

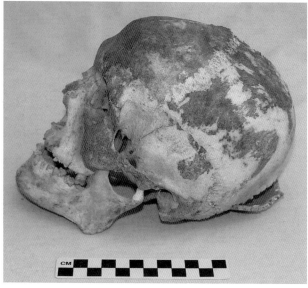

FIG. 10.3 *Burial 8 (C101 Church Burial 4), skull (photo: J.P. Oleson).*

this is a probable female. The pubic symphysis and auricular surfaces of the pelvis were too degraded for age estimation, however, the retroauricular area of the auricular surface scored as phases 4–6 (35–49 years) based on the standards of Lovejoy et al. (1985). Cranial suture closure also was observed for age estimation (Meindl and Lovejoy 1985). The lateral-anterior sutures had an overall score of 5 (mean = 41.1, range = 23–68 years), and the vault score was 6 (mean = 34.7, range = 27–48 years). These combined indicators provide a likely age estimate of 35–45 years old at death.

Pathologies: At the time of death, this individual had an active infection resulting in bone loss on the anterior and superior portion of the body of the fourth lumbar vertebra. This bone loss only very slightly affected the portion of the inferior of the third lumbar vertebra. Slight to moderate vertebral osteophytosis, generally resulting from vertebral disk degeneration, was observed on the lower thoracic (T10–T12) and lumbar vertebrae. The third lumbar vertebra displayed a Schmorl's node on its inferior surface as a result of disk rup-

ture. The left and right twelfth ribs also displayed healed fractures. This adult female had extensive dental wear, particularly in the right mandibular and maxillary molars.

Burial 9: C101 Church Burial 5, Locus C101.01.63 (observed by MN and MP)

Description of the remains: The remains were found within a wooden coffin in an undisturbed grave cut into the soil below the pavement in the nave of the C101 Church. Although fragmented, the skeleton is relatively complete (pp. 251; fig. 7.34). A matt of black hair (65 g) was found in association with the skull.

Age and sex: Sex estimation relied upon pelvic and cranial morphology. The pelvic traits scored on the male end of the spectrum, and the cranial traits ranged between ambiguous to male. This individual was determined to be a male based on these features. Age estimation was based on degeneration of the pubic symphysis and auricular surface. The left pubic symphysis received a Todd (1920) score

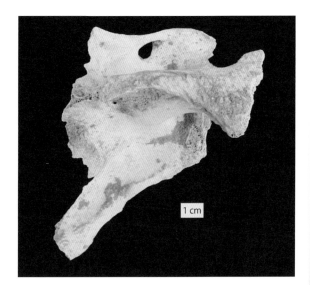

FIG. 10.4   *Burial 10 (B100 Nabataean Burial), bony bridging of the coracoid process and superior border of the right scapula (photo: M. Perry).*

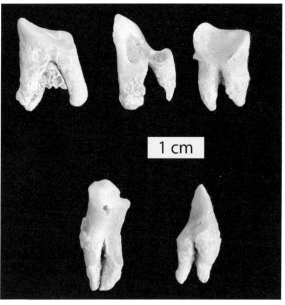

FIG. 10.5   *Burial 10 (B100 Nabataean Burial), examples of extreme dental wear of the upper and lower molars (photo: M. Perry).*

of 5 (27–30 years). In addition, the left and right auricular surfaces were scored following Lovejoy et al. (1985), with the left scoring as a 3 (30–34 years) and the right as a 2 (25–29 years). These pelvic indicators suggest that this individual was anywhere between 25 and 34 years at his time of death.
Pathologies: None, except for impacted upper and lower third molars and significant wear on the right upper first molar.

Burial 10:   Cist tomb underneath B100 Church, Locus B100.E.37 (observed by MN and MP)

Description of the remains: The remains were found in and around a cist tomb beneath the later church apse, several months after they had been disturbed by looters (pp. 176–77; figs. 6.15–16). The bones found in the spoil heap around the grave were very fragmented due to the disturbance, but the bones in general were in good condition. The lower portion of the skeleton survived *in situ* within the cist grave, including both right and left tibiae, fibulae, and the bones of the feet in full articulation. Toenails were still *in situ* on one of the feet. The right scapula has an ossified superior transverse ligament between the coracoid process and the superior border of the scapular body (fig. 10.4).

Age and Sex: Skull and pelvic morphology such as mastoid size and obtuse angle of the mandibular ramus point to this individual being a probable male. Age was estimated based on degeneration of the pubic symphyses and auricular surfaces of this individual. The Todd scores (Todd 1920) were 5 for the left symphysis (27–30) and 4 for the right symphysis (30–35). The Suchey-Brooks scores were 4 for both symphyses (mean = 35.2, range = 23–57) (Brooks and Suchey 1990). In addition, the right auricular surface had the characteristics of someone 40–44 years of age (Lovejoy et al. 1985). Therefore, it appears that this male is 35–45 years of age.
Pathologies: This middle-adult male had developed many pathological lesions by the time of his death. He had very poor dental health, with extreme asymmetrical dental wear down to and often past the cemento-enamel junction (fig. 10.5). Some teeth were completely worn down to the point that only root stubs remained within the socket. This dental wear had resulted in the exposure of numerous pulp chambers, which caused abscesses to form in the maxillary alveolar bone near the apices of the right second premolar, the right canine, and the left first and second premolars. The extreme wear made observation of other dental pathologies dif-

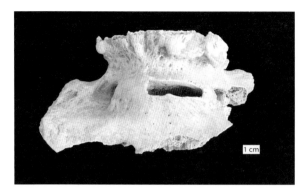

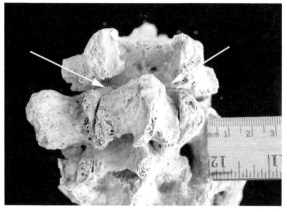

FIG. 10.6 *Burial 10 (B100 Nabataean Burial), anterior view of the fusion of the fifth lumbar vertebra to the sacrum indicative of ankylosing spondylitis (photo: M. Perry).*

FIG. 10.7 *Burial 10 (B100 Nabataean Burial), posterior view of the spondylolytic fracture through the pedicles of the 4th lumbar vertebra. Arrows point to the bilateral fracture sites (photo: M. Perry).*

ficult, but two dental enamel hypoplasias (DEHs) were observed in the upper right second incisor, suggesting he had suffered from, and survived, two periods of stress at approximately 3–4 years of age.

In addition to poor dental health, many joints showed signs of advanced osteoarthritis, sometimes with extensive spicule formation, in the left and right shoulder, elbow, wrist, knee, and ankle joints. In the case of the right elbow, cartilage deterioration had progressed to the point of bone-on-bone contact displayed by eburnation with grooving. The articulations of the left and right clavicles with the scapula and sternum have been extensively remodelled due to inflammation and soft tissue stress at these joints. In addition, the synovial joints between the superior and inferior articular facets of the lumbar vertebrae also show spicule formation and porosity surrounding the joint surface.

The bodies of the vertebrae display the greatest pathology and degeneration. The fifth lumbar vertebra is fused to the sacrum, primarily between the transverse processes and sacral alae and on the left side of the vertebral body (fig. 10.6). The superior edge of the body has extensive spicule formation that appears to originally fuse the fourth and fifth lumbars, but was broken post-mortem. A number of lower thoracic vertebrae, those inferior to the 5th thoracic vertebra, also were fused along the left side of the vertebral body. In all cases, the disk space between the bodies was not compromised. These are classic indicators of ankylosing spondylitis (Ortner 2003). In addition, other observable tho-

racic, lumbar, and cervical vertebrae show evidence of extensive osteophytes along the edges of the vertebral bodies. The fourth lumbar vertebra had a spondylolitic fracture through the left and right pedicles of the neural arch just behind the body (fig. 10.7). The fractured ends show resorption, but the vertebral body does not display evidence of anterior slippage indicative of spondylolysthesis.

Two other anomalies include a healed greenstick fracture of the first metatarsal of the left foot and a healed possible comminuted fracture of the left first rib. The foot fracture seemed to have resulted from bending forces, potentially from stepping on a hard object causing the midshaft of the metatarsal to bend dorsally to the point that it fractured. The fracture of the sternal end of the first rib is rare, and it would likely have involved the left clavicle and potentially the sternal body. It is possible that a blow directly inferior to the medial clavicle could have resulted in the fracture of the rib without involving the clavicle, but the force would have to have been spread over a small area.

Burial 11: E125 Domestic complex, E125.19.26 (observed by MP)

Description of the remains: This burial took place after collapse of the E125 structures, at an undetermined date, but probably prior to the 20th century. The body was laid in a fetal position on its right side with the head oriented NNW then covered with earth and cobbles. The skeleton consists of a few extremely friable, poorly preserved fragments, primarily from the lower body. The skeletal material was cracked significantly due to natural taphonomic processes and had extensive breakage. A few skeletal elements from this burial also displayed signs of burning, concentrated around the left and right knees. The distal right and left femorae, the anterior side of the left tibia, portions of the frontal bone, and the right patella were burned black, although they showed no evidence of warping or of shielded surfaces (burn patterns that indicate the presence of soft tissue at the time of burning). An unsided rib fragment also had been burnt black, but it displayed no warping or heat-related cracking. Bone exposed to heat generally turns black after the organic component becomes carbonized and the natural oils have burned away (Correia 1997). The colour of the burnt bone, the lack of cracking, warping, or any sign of soft tissue at the time of burning suggests that the skeleton was exposed to heat after decomposition was complete. *Age and sex:* Despite the fragmentary nature of the skeletal remains, enough of the left os coxa, particularly the greater sciatic notch, existed for sex estimation. The wide opening of the sciatic notch indicated that this individual was a female. The auricular surface of the left ilium unfortunately was too degraded for age estimation, and no other portions suitable for sex estimation were recovered. All of the observable elements had fused epiphyses indicating that this individual was older than approximately 22 years old at the time of death, i.e., an adult individual.

Pathologies: None, other than significant dental wear.

10.A.2. Analysis

The small sample size of human burials at Hawara/Hauarra limits the contribution they can make to our understanding of disease, health, and death in the site's Nabataean and Byzantine communities. In addition, many of the paleopathology analyses were limited. It is not clear that the exclusion of some pathology indicators from Najjar's report (e.g., dental enamel hypoplasias, porotic hyperostosis) meant that he did not find any within the

sample or that he did not record these anomalies at all. Furthermore, without a complete inventory of the skeletal remains it is difficult to know, for example, what percentage of available preserved knee joints displayed osteoarthritis.

It is notable that seven out of 12 individuals (58%) displayed no pathologies at all. The main pathologies recorded in the sample resulted from age-related degeneration: osteoarthritis of the joints in two individuals, vertebral osteophytosis in three individuals, and extensive dental wear in three individuals, one of whom subsequently developed secondary infections of the exposed pulp cavity leading to multiple abscesses. Only two individuals, the Nabataean period Burial 11 from underneath the B100 church and the early modern Burial 12 from the E125 domestic area, had signs of non-specific infections. A healed but misaligned femoral fracture was suffered by one of the adult males (Burial 7) interred in the C101 church. It is surprising that the fracture was not set properly. Treatment of bone fractures was a common part of Greco-Roman medicine (e.g., Hipppocrates, *On Fractures*), and previous investigations of individuals from contemporary sites in the Near East show signs of the proper setting of fractured bones (e.g., Perry 2002a: 246). The fractures of the left and right rib 12, the lowest rib in the ribcage, such as those experienced by the 35–45 year old woman from Burial 8 (C101 Church Burial 4), commonly results from accidental falls (Galloway 1999).

The poor dental health experienced by some of the subjects, represented by substantial dental wear and subsequent abscess formation, probably resulted from the contamination of food with the wind-blown sand typical of the region. This wear, however, is a counter-indicator for another common dental pathology, dental caries (cavities). The development of carious lesions and tooth wear are influenced primarily by the consistency and characteristics of the diet consumed at the site (see Larsen 1997: 66). Populations consuming foods, and additives—such as grit from stone food-processing tools or from the environment—that result in notable dental wear, tend to have lower rates of caries than groups in low-wear dental environments. Researchers have suggested that dental wear may remove cariogenic bacteria in the grooves of the bite surfaces of teeth, halting the development of carious lesions (Powell 1985). Individuals who lived in the maritime port of Aila, approximately 70 km south of Hauarra along the *Via Nova Traiana*, during the fourth and fifth centuries had similar levels of dental wear and almost no cavities (Perry 2002a), as did fifth- to eighth-century AD individuals from Khirbat as-Samra in northern Jordan (Nabulsi 1998). In addition, the Early Bronze Age groups who buried their dead at Bab edh-Dhra near the southern end of the Dead Sea also had low caries frequencies and notable dental wear (Bentley and Perry 2008; Ortner et al. 2008). Therefore, it seems that this pattern of dental wear with low caries frequencies occurs in numerous environments within Jordan, probably from a combination of environmental or food preparation-related sand and grit inclusions in food.

The excavation of the individuals interred within the C101 Church at Hauarra increases the available sample of individuals buried within ecclesiastical structures in the Near East. Church burials in this region in antiquity generally were limited to donors to the church, priests and their family members, and other church officials (see Tsafrir 1988: 157–58, 171, and above pp. 242–43, below pp. 396–97). The hypothesis that individuals buried in the church had better access to resources, and thus better health, than the general population was tested at Rehovot, ancient Ruheibeh. At that site, no health or disease disparities between these two groups could be documented, suggesting either that the moderate disease load they carried (compared to other populations) was typical of all socioeconomic levels, or that church burial did not denote greater socioeconomic status (Perry 2002a: 270–71). If the former hypothesis is correct, it is possible that the picture created by the church burials at Hauarra reflects that of the general population (excepting the effects of sampling bias).

10.A.3. Summary

The very limited view of Nabataean and Byzantine Hawara/Hauarra allowed by the burials excavated at the site suggests a relatively healthy population, presuming that all pathologies were duly recorded during their initial study. These individuals rarely suffered from infections or other biological stressors that would impact the skeletal system. Most of the pathologies resulted from age-related degeneration, not unexpected for the region, although only two individuals were possibly over the age of 45. The one post-antique individual recovered (from the E125 domestic complex) did not display any major differences from the ancient individuals at the site. The poorly-set femur of the individual in Burial 7 may indicate the lack of proper health care and medical treatment at Hauarra during the Byzantine period.

10.B. FAUNAL REMAINS (M. Finnegan)

10.B.1. Introduction

This section reports on all the animal bones recovered from Humayma, Jordan, during the excavations from 1989 through 2005. It includes inventory, description, identification, analysis, and comparisons of the recovered faunal remains. An abbreviated report on faunal remains recovered between 1989 and 1995 appeared in *HEP* 1: 44–49; this report incorporates and expands upon the data presented there. The fauna are associated with occupation levels that range in date from the Early Nabataean (late first century BC) to Early Islamic period (650–750 AD). Site background and archaeological analyses of the various areas are found elsewhere in this volume and *HEP* 1. Accounts of the architectural history of the Roman Fort (E116) and *vicus* (E125, E128), the Umayyad *Qasr* or Manor House (F103), and some other miscellaneous small excavation areas will be presented in subsequent volumes, but the animal bones from those areas are included in the bones presented here. Additionally, I analyze what these remains offer to the larger archaeological picture and present a number of comparisons between the animals represented at Humayma and other selected sites. Comparisons between or among Roman, Byzantine, and Early Islamic sites provide useful insights into changing subsistence strategies and land use during these little-known time periods in Southern Jordan.

During the field seasons from 1989 to 2005, excavations of areas A104, A107, A115, A117, A118 (Tombs), A127 (Byzantine Farm-house), B100

(Nabataean Tomb, Byzantine Church and Early Islamic house), B126 (Byzantine Church), C101 (Byzantine Church and Early Islamic squatters), C119 (Byzantine Church), C124 (Nabataean Campground), E077 (Late Roman Bath), E116 (Roman Fort), E121 (Roman Structure), E122 (Roman and Early Islamic House), E125 (Nabataean and Late Roman Houses and Shrine), E128 (Nabataean or Roman mudbrick structure), F102 (Byzantine Church and Early Islamic squatters), and F103 (Abbasid Family Manor House) resulted in the recovery of 84,038 animal bones and bone fragments (plus fish and shell). Data for 55 fragments from Fields "6" (N = 1), A111 (N = 2), E122 (N = 14), and E077 "TR 01" (N = 38) was compromised, so Table 10.2 (at the end of this chapter, pp. 359–64) reports on 83,983 bones or bone fragments. The most significant areas with respect to fauna recovery were B100, C101, E116, E125, E128, F102, and F103, which generated 80,401 pieces (Tables 10.3–5; pp. 365–69). In the field, bones were bagged and labelled daily with bucket numbers that could later be cross-referenced back to associated ceramics and other datable artefacts. These bagged bones were transported to the field laboratory at the al-Mureighah regional secondary school, where most of the fish and shell remains were extracted and sent to specialists for their analysis (see Reese, pp. 344–51, for marine molluscs). The remaining materials (more than 83,000 pieces) were sent to the Osteological Laboratories at Kansas State University for further sorting and analysis.

10.B.2. Methods Used in the Analysis

In our laboratories the faunal remains from each bag were dry-brushed, washed when necessary, and separated into generalized categories such as large, medium, or small mammals, reptiles, birds, etc. Bones possessing diagnostic morphologic features were further identified, when possible, to family, genus, and species. All bones were examined for butcher marks, spalls, rodent or carnivore gnawing, and evidence of burning. Worked bone or bone tools, separated from the assemblage, were washed, repaired, and registered. Those few bones that had not been adequately separated in the field laboratory, and bones of special interest

(e.g., possessing pathological conditions) were also separated from the main body of bone for further and special analysis. Bones that were so incomplete or fragmentary that they could only be assigned to general groups (e.g., "small mammal") were recorded as representing one of the broad groups and then re-bagged. Those bones that, when cleaned, showed enough fine morphology for positive or near positive identification but could not be immediately identified without the aid of further research, were sidelined for further study. In addition to identification atlases and other published reports, we were aided by an extensive comparative collection. Primary references are included in the cited literature, particularly Boessneck 1969 and Schmid 1972. Invertebrates were separated and packaged for shipment to researchers specializing in these areas. All data were recorded on laboratory faunal forms and transferred to Microsoft Excel spreadsheets for summary tabulation and statistical analysis. Due to the paucity of complete elements, few remains were measured, and we conducted no metric analysis.

The general format of this report, for both fieldwork and report writing, follows Clason and Buitenhuis 1978, Finnegan 1978, 1981, West et al. 2000, and Finnegan and Van Sickle 2007. Table 10.2 consists of a categorized list by excavation area of the identified, partially identified, and unidentified animals excavated between 1989 and 2005. For the purpose of this study, all excavation units were grouped into cultural phases as defined by the excavator. While data for all fields are represented, only the primary fields were subjected to sub-field analyses. Very few closed, early habitation contexts were found at Humayma, and virtually every late context contained ceramics from all the periods of occupation at the site. It is possible, although not likely, that some of the later contexts contained animal bone refuse from earlier periods, but we had no means to identify such hypothetical contamination. As a result, we have to assume that the bones belong to the later part of the date range for each structure. This assumption makes it difficult to trace the details of diachronic changes in animal use and management, but, nevertheless, some patterns appear. Similarities and differences can be seen among the various structures and occupation periods, and changes in percentages of animal types may reflect both shifts in animal use and adaptations to environmental limitations across time. All dates are AD unless noted as BC. The major fields accounting for most of the data span a number of periods: B100, Nabataean to Early Islamic (ca. 100–750); C101, Byzantine to Early Islamic (ca. 550–750); E116, Roman to Early Byzantine (early 2nd to early 5th century); E125, Nabataean to Early Byzantine (1st century AD to mid-4th century); F102, Nabataean to Early Islamic (1st century to mid-8th century); F103, Early Islamic (ca. 680–750).

The number of identified specimens (NISP) and their percentages have been calculated for each taxon by excavation field. Table 10.2 (pp. 359–64) displays for each animal category and each field category the number of animal pieces, the percent of the field total, and percent of the overall total. Table 10.3 (pp. 365–66) displays the same information for the major fields, those with the largest number of faunal remains: B100, C101, E116, E125, F102, and F103. Table 10.4 (pp. 367–68) displays the same major field data, but sifted further by exclusion of unidentified pieces. Finally, Table 10.5 (p. 369) takes the data in Table 10.3, but reduces the number of major animal categories to exclude cells with habitually low values.

Several basic assumptions were involved in our treatment of the data and subsequent analysis: the sample excavated from each deposit in each field is assumed to be representative; the rate of deposition of sediment in each type of deposit is assumed to be comparable between time periods and fields; each kind of element (e.g., distal tibia) for each animal is assumed to have the same probability of being deposited, recovered, and identified in each successive time period or spatially across the site. While these assumptions were not tested and cannot be upheld with current taphonomic literature, they do provide some elements of validity and were therefore followed in this final report.

10.B.3. Bone Condition and Preservation

Although often displaying significant breakage and extensive cultural modification as a result of human processing (heavy fracturing and green bone breaks) and later taphonomic activity, on the whole,

the surfaces of bones recovered from Humayma are in good to excellent condition relative to natural taphonomic factors (fig. 10.8). Bone surfaces are generally clear, and both spiral and transverse fractures for most areas show no signs of rounding due to hydraulic movement and sub-aerial sand-blasting. Weathering, involving split line cracks and exfoliation, is minimal, ranking Stage 2 or lower on the Behrensmeyer (1978) scale. Much of the assemblage is basically unweathered. Weathering is directly influenced by temperature, precipitation, humidity, sunlight, and length of time on ground surface (White 1992). Although bones recovered from archaeological excavations showed minimal weathering, bones showing the greatest degree of weathering — Stages 3 and 4 — were recovered from a surface survey conducted during earlier field seasons. Several centuries of intense summer solar radiation, trampling by humans and animals, and winter rainfall contributed to the accelerated deterioration of these bone surfaces. The intense weathering of bones found on the surface indicates that deposition in the past of the other bones recovered must have been rapid after meat and marrow were removed. Interestingly, weathering was minimal on sub-adult mammalian individuals and bones of fowl, usually considered more friable than larger, heavier adult mammalian bone. The greatest difficulty encountered in identification and analysis of these remains is found in the significant fracturing of almost all elements due to human behavioural and cultural practices.

The Humayma bones generally display little rootlet damage. The low intensity of root marking left cultural modifications clear. In this hyper-arid environment, even when the site was periodically uninhabited, vegetation did not quickly become established on the surface, and roots did not penetrate the soils to great depths. Evidence of canine biting and chewing is nearly absent or has been masked by further taphonomic degradation. As well, and probably befitting the environment, rodent gnawing is not a predominant feature in these remains.

A few deposits of bones were in such poor condition they could not be identified to genera. Bones associated with levels of mudbrick or decayed mudbrick appear to have suffered the

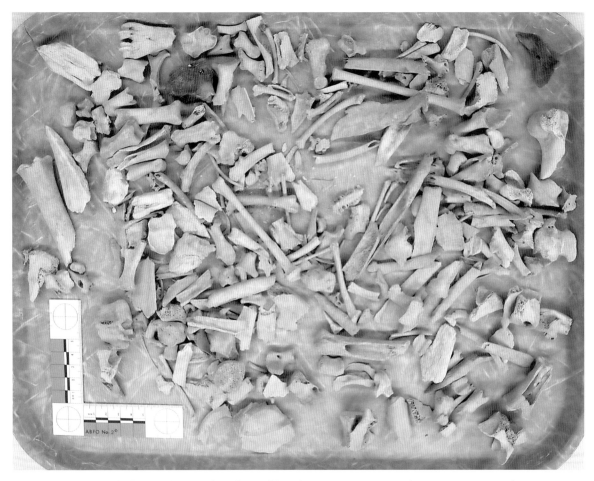

FIG. 10.8 *Bone sample showing the general condition of faunal remains at Humayma (2004.0610: E116.I10.36).*

greatest amount of taphonomic damage over time. Excavating the friable bones from the concrete-like matrix often led to their further destruction. Aside from weathering, fragmentation due to the precipitation of salts (probably led by Na_2Co_3 and $NaCl$) has been observed in some of this collection. Bagging procedures and subsequent transport of bones to Canada or the United States, both unavoidable procedures, led to further minor disintegration of the bone. Of the bones analyzed, 17.18% (NISP = 14,428) were so badly broken as a result of human practices or the archaeological context that they could not be classified beyond basic mammal. They are listed as unidentifiable (usually) mammal bone (Table 10.2). Frequently, bones of certain size and thickness, but lacking specific morphologic features, could only be classified in the general categories of large, medium, and small mammal. Taken together, these three

categories represent 61.91% of all remains (NISP = 51,993), which further limits the overall analysis. Nevertheless, the remaining 17.84% of identifiable bone remains (NISP = 14,984) is slightly or considerably higher than the percentage of identified bone from numerous other archaeological sites. In addition, by invoking and supporting certain assumptions about the medium mammal category, an additional 56.08% of the faunal remains may be realized in this analysis.

Bones belonging to the large mammal category probably represent the cow (*Bos*), horse or donkey (*Equus*), camel (*Camelus*), or possibly large deer (*Cervus*). Bones belonging to the medium mammal category almost certainly represent non-diagnostic fragments of sheep (*Ovis*) and goats (*Capra*). Bones within the non-diagnostic small mammal category include a number of smaller animals and birds, from medium-sized rodents on down.

Within any given category, for example sheep, only one animal was recorded unless the bones identifiable as sheep showed both mature and immature individuals, in which case two animals were recorded. If multiple bones were found (e.g., three left sheep femora), then the number of elements was counted, assuming at least that number of animals to be represented (see Casteel 1977, Nichol and Wild 1984 concerning minimum numbers). As burrowing animals, rodents present a special case. They often represent a later time period, the animal having burrowed into earlier strata prior to death. One locus yielded 60 rodent bones, retrieved from a few adjacent bags. These remains showed no duplication of elements and were judged to represent one individual, probably one that died in its burrow. During excavation of E128 in 2008, a jerboa (sp. *Jaculus*) removed several large ceramic fragments from lower strata during the night and deposited them outside his burrow, on the surface under excavation, a striking example of this process at work (Reeves et al. 2009: 238–39).

Regardless of the method of choice and concomitant assumptions concerning the actual number of animals represented by these remains, it is important to note that various species of animals provide varying amounts of edible meat. Furthermore, while the edible portions may be significant, the remainder of the animal was certainly employed in many other aspects of daily life at Humayma. Typical animal weights have been suggested by Clark and Yi (1983) as follows: sheep, *Ovis aries,* 80 kg; goats, *Capra hircus,* 80 kg; cattle, *Bos taurus,* 625 kg; pigs, *Sus scrofa,* 100 kg. M.C. Hunt (personal communication, 2 May 2007) provides estimates of edible meat yield for both modern and pre-modern eras. By adding the weights suggested by Clark and Yi to the estimated yields for cattle, sheep, pigs, chickens, and ostrich, we generate the values presented in Table 10.6 (p. 370).

10.B.4. Analysis

The categorical nature of the Table 10.5 matrix data (p. 369) suggests application of a chi-square test of independence to analyze the relationship of the variables "bone type" and "field." The chi-square test statistic for the hypothesis that the variables are independent is 259.5875 with p < 0.0001. As a result, it seems that a considerable, significant association is evident between the variables "bone type" and "field." This chi-square test is not based on random areas. These fields were dictated by the observable cultural activities of these earlier human populations — architectural features, surface scatter of ceramic shards and other artefacts — and as such the chi-square test was not generated from a random site sample. The chi-square test does corroborate and reinforces the original decision concerning which areas to expose by the excavation process. In interpreting changes in animal use across time at Humayma, it is important to keep in mind that relatively few closed Nabataean loci have been excavated at the site. In consequence, the Nabataean habits of animal husbandry and food preparation may not be accurately represented in the data sample.

Field recovery and subsequent laboratory analyses of the Humayma animal bones show that approximately 14.37% (N = 12,066) of recovered bone could be identified at the generic or lower taxonomic level. *Capra, Ovis,* and the Sheep/Goat category were the most frequently occurring animal groups (following non-diagnostic medium mammal) identified in the faunal assemblage at Humayma. The largest percentage of bone material within this category is sheep/goat, representing about 43.17% (N = 5,209) if all mature and immature individuals are considered. In addition, at the genus and species level, 4.66% (N = 562) of the identified sample represents sheep (*Ovis aries*) and 6.65% (N = 802) represents goat (*Capra hircus*). This gives an overall percentage of 11.31% of the recovered material representing these animals. The basic criteria for the identification of these animals follow the work of Boessneck 1969 and Boessneck et al. 1964. We are relatively confident that in our sheep/goat category, we have included no animals of the genus *Gazella* or wild forms of sheep and goat, particularly the ibex (*Capra ibex*). Some bone fragments lacked diagnostic features or were too badly damaged to lend themselves to identification at anything other than the general medium mammal category. Nevertheless, it is highly likely that the bones in the medium mammal category (56.07%; N = 47,089) represent either sheep or goats.

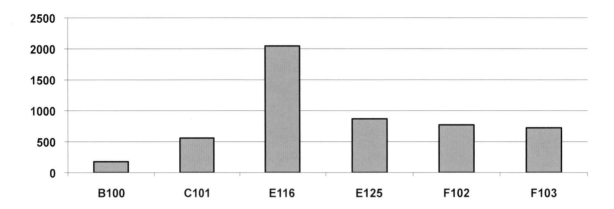

FIG. 10.9   *Distribution of Sheep/Goat across major fields at Humayma. Total = 5144 pieces.*

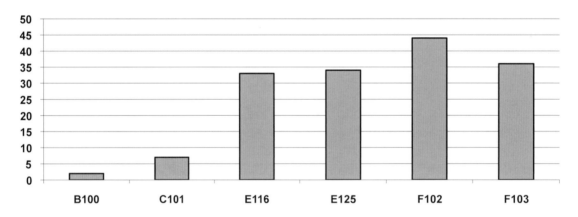

FIG. 10.10 *Distribution of Cattle across major fields at Humayma. Total = 156 pieces.*

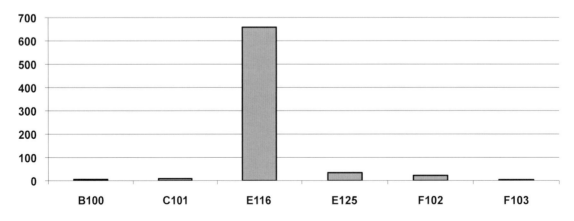

FIG. 10.11 *Distribution of Pigs across major fields at Humayma. Total = 735 pieces.*

Altogether, the four categories encompassing sheep, goats, sheep/goat, and medium mammal (probably representing either sheep or goat) comprises 63.90% (N = 53,662) of the bone assemblage.

The majority of diagnostic sheep/goat bones showed evidence of spalls, or green bone fractures. These types of fractures occur during the butchering process of the animal when heavy blows are delivered against the shafts of long bones and the axial skeleton with sharp tools not unlike cleavers. The majority of sheep/goat bone fragments and spalls recovered from the site included autopodia, metapodials, phalanges, and hoof cores or bones associated with the lower, non-meat bearing portion of the legs. Very likely, one of the first steps in the process of butchering these animals involved removing the lower legs in the region of the autopodia. Disarticulated leg bones were often discarded, most likely after removal of tendons for use in various craft applications, while the meat-bearing portions of the carcass were further processed.

The highest numbers and percentages of diagnostic sheep and goat bones taken together were excavated from Field E116, dating 106–400 (Table 10.5; fig. 10.9). Although the number of diagnostic *Capra* and *Ovis* bones varies greatly among the fields, the ratios between the two animals is approximately equal in fields B100, E125, and C101, which have extensive Nabataean and Byzantine components. The goat to sheep ratio is much higher in the Roman Fort E116 (1.64) and the Early Islamic levels in F103 (1.67) and F102 (1.76). If we assume that the sheep/goat category contains sheep and goats at the same ratio as the identified *Ovis* and *Capra,* Humayma was full of goats in the Roman and Early Islamic periods. This ratio is the opposite of that seen in most modern Bedouin flocks, which focus on the market value of sheep and their by-products rather than their subsistence value (Cribb 1991: 28; Hopkins 1993: 206–7; Campbell and Roe 1998). It appears, then, that a more or less balanced ratio of goats to sheep was replaced by an increase in the proportion of goats during the Roman period, followed by a significant reduction during the Byzantine period, with a subsequent significant rebound during the Early Islamic period.

This significant shift in population patterns of these animals over relatively short periods of time was probably not the result of shifts in climate or environment, but rather a behavioural change in animal husbandry due to dietary preference. It is noteworthy that as Humayma evolved from a small, pastoral-agricultural settlement of the Nabataean period to a busier, larger centre occupied by a Roman garrison, and then to an agricultural settlement owned by the Abbasid family with their wide political connections, goats came to outnumber sheep, despite the fact that sheep generally provide better meat, milk, and fibre. It is possible that the Roman soldiers preferred goat to mutton. Alternatively, the sudden appearance of a large market within the fort for locally produced meat may have exceeded the potential of the regional landscape to provide grazing for increased numbers of sheep, so the ratio of goats, which are more efficient grazers, increased. Relatively stable percentages of slightly higher sheep populations to those of goats usually indicate stable, favourable environmental conditions. When we see a shift of this magnitude from balanced proportions of sheep and goats to a significant increase in goats, we suspect that an equally significant cultural change has had an impact on agrarian life-ways. This is one of the more remarkable changes seen at Humayma through time.

Other than the generalized category of Large Mammal (4.89%; N = 4,103), the remains of *Bos* are relatively low, representing 0.19% (N = 157) of the total faunal material and 1.05% of identified remains (Table 10.2; figs. 10.10, 10.21–22). While we cannot ascribe species to a significant amount of this material, we suggest that it represents *Bos cf. taurus* — domesticated cattle. Cattle figure most prominently during the Roman and Islamic periods and less so during the Byzantine period. As compared to other sites, the low numbers of cattle suggest that either poorer grazing conditions or inadequate cattle husbandry practices existed in the Humayma region during these time periods. This deduction may be further supported by the preference for goat over sheep during the same time periods, noted above. Increased numbers and frequency of cattle seem to be directly associated with increasing proportions of goats to sheep, but inversely proportional to the number and percentage of pigs (figs. 10.15–16,). The clear, significant

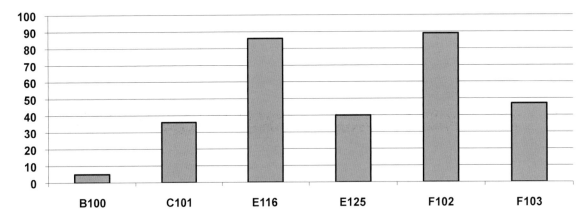

FIG. 10.12 *Distribution of Equids across major fields at Humayma. Total = 303 pieces.*

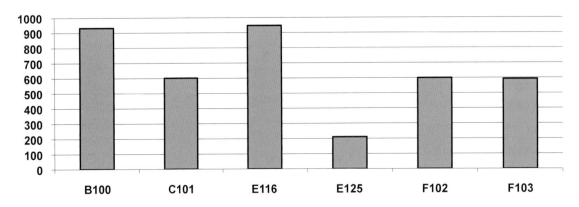

FIG. 10.13 *Distribution of Wild Animal across major fields at Humayma. Total = 3886 pieces.*

numerical increase in *Bos* during the Islamic period is no doubt a replacement for the absent pig, which had been decreasing since Roman times. We also note that the distribution of chicken (*Gallus gallus*) is reduced over time, both numerically and as a percentage of total animals. In this, the reduced distribution of chicken seems to follow the distribution of sheep during the three time periods, but it is near its lowest frequency during the Islamic times. Apparently, increased cattle husbandry provided meat protein in the absence of pig, the significant reduction in the proportion of sheep, and the slight reduction in chicken. This association and its apparent correlation among different food species are based on relatively small numbers and may be purely coincidental. Moreover, at Humayma there does not appear to be a transition from pig to chicken use over time, as was observed at Pella (Köhler 1981), Tell Qarqur

(Finnegan and West 1984), and Tell Nimrin (West et al. 2000).

Although bones and teeth of pig (*Sus*) constitute 0.90% of the total faunal assemblage and 5.01% of the identified bone category, they represent only 0.23% of the identified bones outside the Roman Fort. Pig remains account for 2.19% of all remains in the Fort, and 87.87% of all pig remains are found in the Fort (Tables 10.2–3, fig. 10.11). This chronological pattern is not surprising, since salt pork and bacon were standard foods for Roman soldiers (Davies 1971, 1989: 187–206) and have even been used as an indicator for Romanization (MacKinnon 2001: 649). Pigs were, however, more prevalent in European military sites than in the Near East. The significant presence of oyster shells in the fort is another reflection of Roman military dietary preferences (Davies 1989: 193–94). Bones of pig at the site (N = 750) are most frequently represented by teeth and mandibles, possibly indicating that the meat was not imported from elsewhere already butchered and cured. Remains of the domestic pig were found on the Cavalière Wreck (100 BC; Charlin et al. 1978: 16–17) and the Comacchio Wreck (AD 50; Berti 1990: 120–21, 124–25), apparently preserved by salting or smoking. Although these animals had been quartered before preservation and shipping, a few teeth and mandibles were present on both wrecks. The preponderance of teeth and mandibles at Hauarra, however, makes it unlikely that the meat was imported already butchered and cured.

Since the pig bones reflect immature animals, it is uncertain whether these represent the remains of domesticated or wild animals. Since both wild and domesticated pig varieties lack the capacity to sweat and cool themselves, raising pigs at Humayma would have presented significant problems. The animals would have required shade, significant quantities of water and fodder, and pens far enough from the fort to avoid the problems of smell and water pollution. Pigs, however, clearly were raised in Petra centre in the fourth century (Studer in *EZ* I: 361, 366–67) and at the al-Wuʻayra fort outside Petra in the twelfth century (Brown and Reilly 2010: 132–33). Toplyn (2006: 486–87) asserts that pigs can be raised in areas with less than the supposedly essential 300 mm of precipitation — such as the Roman legionary fortress of Lejjun — as long as there are locally available artificial water sources. The pigs had to be penned, however, rather than grazed. It is possible that the soldiers hunted wild boar in the hills around Humayma to supplement their diet, or that they took advantage of wild animals attracted to the settlement area by garbage, crops, and run-off water from the aqueduct. Although the sample is much smaller, wild boar was not identified at Petra either (Studer in *EZ* I: 361, 366–67). The reasons for drop-off in percentages of pigs over time at Humayma is probably twofold: the introduction of religious taboos against eating pork, and increased demands for clean water sources as the human population grew.

The horse/donkey (*Equus*) is represented by 315 bones (0.38%) of all bone and 2.10% of all identifiable remains (Table 10.2, figs. 10.12, 10.21–22).

Equus remains are more or less evenly distributed over all periods since Roman times. In all probability these bones represent the donkey — the universal beast of burden, especially for the transport of water from the cisterns to the outlying areas. Given their need for high-quality fodder and large quantities of water, it is likely that horses were few in number at Humayma, and that they were kept mainly to confer status (Köhler 1981). Another beast of burden, the camel, was rare at Humayma except during the Roman period, when it flourished (N = 386; 2.58% of identified remains) (Table 10.2). Of camel bones, 99.48% were found in the Roman fort (N = 8) and the nearby civilian settlement (*vicus,* E125) (N = 376). The concentration of camel bones in the *vicus* may indicate that the animals were usually corralled nearby but outside the fort, or simply that the butchering of unneeded or worn-out military mounts took place there. The soldiers may not have consumed camel meat, but even if they did, the butchering of such large animals might well have taken place outside the fort. The overwhelming concentration of camel remains in the Roman period supports Oleson's suggestion (Sherwood et al. 2008b: 175; Oleson 2010: 36–37) that the native cavalry unit (*equites sagittarii indigenae*) mentioned in the *Notitia Dignitatum* as stationed at Hauarra/Humayma was mounted on camels rather than horses. While raising pigs at Humayma would have involved difficulties with heat, maintaining a unit of military horses in good condition would have been virtually impossible because of the absence of appropriate fodder locally. Horses were also much rarer than donkeys and horses at the Roman fort of Lejjun (Toplyn 2006: 489–95).

Chicken (*Gallus gallus*) remains represent 3.28% (N = 2,755) of all faunal remains and 18.38% of the identified remains (Table 10.4). Their distribution shows a considerable presence in Byzantine and Early Islamic levels (B100, F102) and near absence from other periods. Apparently this excellent food resource was supplanted by pork during the Roman period.

While a full report on fish remains is still in preparation, it is worthwhile to point out here that fish seem to have made up a significant part of the diet during a number of periods represented at Humayma. Fish elements or fragments of fish, including fresh-water *Cyprinidae* (carp), were recovered (Tables 10.2–3). The presence of parrot fish probably has more to do with cultural concerns than with diet, and they were most likely specialty items rather than part of the usual diet. Fish remains account for 2,421 pieces (2.89%) of all remains and 16.16% of the identified remains. The use of fish is not well-documented in Nabataean strata (0.85% of their animal diet). This statistic is based on accepting the tomb deposits (A104, A107, A115, A117, A118) and E128 as Nabataean, and half of the deposits in E125 as Nabataean. The representation of fish is also quite low in the Roman to early Byzantine strata in the Roman Fort and *vicus*: 1.50% of the animal remains. The proportion of fish is significantly higher in the Late Byzantine strata in the C101 and C119 churches, at 5.19% of the animal remains, and more or less the same in the Late Byzantine to Early Islamic structures B100, A127, and F102, at 6.45%. The proportion of fish is much lower again in the Early Islamic structures E122 and F103, at 1.70%.

One interpretation of these statistics is that the importation of fish to Humayma did not become important until the later Byzantine period, possibly as a result of the conversion of much of the local population to Christianity, which encouraged the consumption of fish at special commemorative meals and at certain times of the year (Snyder 1985: 24–26, 91–92). Unlike pigs and cattle, fish could not have been raised locally. Most likely the fish were brought in from the Aqaba region, 80 km away, as smoked, salted, or dried fillets. Fish represent the highest level of wild animal utilization at Humayma, although the carp could have been farmed in freshwater pools at Aqaba. Another possible interpretation, however, is that fish bones suffer differential taphonomic survival, and the soils in the earlier deposits did not promote preservation, skewing the remains found through excavation. The time depth between Roman and Late Byzantine periods, however, may not be sufficient to account for a taphonomic loss, and it is likely that fish was simply not a significant dietary factor outside of the Late Byzantine period.

Large birds (*Aves*, other than identified *Gallus*), and small and medium unidentified bird categories account for 2.01% (N = 1,690) of overall faunal remains and appear to be evenly divided among the time periods. Some of these represent very large birds, for example the ostrich. Ostrich represents a source for eggs, egg shells, and hides, as well as for meat. Ostrich egg shell fragments are frequent in occupation levels at the site (N = 371; many more fragments were undoubtedly not recognized). The remains of smaller birds may be the result of natural death or predation by other wild or domesticated animals such as cats and/or dogs.

Wild animals other than fish (amphibians, *Aves*, carnivores, *Cervus*, gazelle, Large Bird, *Lepus*, Medium Rodent, Ostrich, Reptile, Rodent, Small Bird, Small Rodent, and Turtle) are poorly represented at Humayma (1.82% of total remains N = 1,531; fig. 10.13), that is, rare to virtually nonexistent. At Petra the proportion is twice as large (4%; Studer in *EZ* I: 361, 366–67), but remains of wild species were rare at the Lejjun fort (Toplyn 2006: 495–98). It seems odd that some of the larger meat- and hide-bearing cervids and gazelles are not better represented in this collection. Surely they must have been occasionally hunted and consumed. Bones of large deer appear in the region from Iron I to the Byzantine period, but currently there is very little physical evidence that wild deer were hunted during any time periods at Humayma. Rock art in the wadis east of Humayma testifies to the existence of a variety of domesticated and wild animals (Oleson 2010: 36–37): camel, horse, bovine, saluki, ibex, ostrich, and lion. Clearly, there were opportunities for hunting even in this arid environment. One explanation for the paucity of wild animal remains may be behavioural. The meat and hides of the hunted animals may have been differentially treated (butchered and prepared) so as to not mix wild meat and hides with those of domesticated products.

The above data suggest that, unlike subsistence activities at Neolithic sites such as Ain Ghazal and Jericho, the animal husbandry of sheep, goats, and cattle constituted the chief subsistence base at Humayma (sheep, goat and medium mammal categories constitute 63.9%). If hunting occurred, it was a purely ancillary activity and perhaps was associated with a privileged upper class (e.g., see von den Driesch 1993). Faunal evidence suggests that by the earliest settlement, people at Humayma were fully agrarian and largely relied on domesticated sheep and goats for their meat, fat, hides, and milk. Cattle also were used, but to a much lesser extent than the smaller bovids. Although wild pigs were probably locally available in more protected areas, and there may have been some pig-raising at the site, these animals were most heavily raised or hunted and consumed during the Roman period and in the Roman fort. Pigs were used only marginally in the Byzantine period, and not used in the Islamic time period. Medium-sized birds, including chickens, were used during the entire occupation of the site, but with a small dip in the Roman period. Faunal evidence also suggests that the camel was particularly important as a pack animal and possibly a military mount during the Roman period, but that the donkey prevailed in all other periods.

10.B.5. Inter-Site Comparisons

The following sites were selected for faunal comparison with Humayma because the periods of occupation overlap with those of Humayma, and/or they are in geographic proximity to Humayma, or they are located in similar ecological settings. A comparison with the faunal statistics from Petra obviously is important, although the sample is much smaller and is restricted to the fourth and early fifth centuries (Studer in *EZ* I: 359–67) and the twelfth century (Brown and Reilly 2010). There are interesting parallels and contrasts between the faunal remains statistics at Humayma and those of the Byzantine fort at Lejjun, although it is difficult to compare the two sites because of the different manner in which the Lejjun statistics are presented (Toplyn 2006). The percentages of bone remains from Humayma are somewhat comparable to Syrian sites such as Tell Hadidi and Ta'as (Clason and Buitenhuis 1978; Clason 1981). Ta'as was occupied during the Byzantine and early Islamic periods. Tell Hadidi was occupied continuously from roughly 3,250 BC into Roman times (Dornemann 1978, 1985). Other sites for comparison are the Middle Bronze Age settlements at Habuba Kabira (Syria) (Driesch 1993) and in the Refaim Valley (Israel) (Horowitz 1989), Iron Age deposits at Mount Ebal

(Israel) (Horwitz 1986–87), and Hellenistic and Persian occupations at Tel Yoqneam (Israel) (Horowitz and Dahan, 1996). Finally, the more recent, Persian and Hellenistic levels at Tell Nimrin (Jordan) are a suitable comparison (West, et al., 2000).

As at Humayma, sheep and goat husbandry figures heavily in faunal assemblages at all of the comparative sites during all time periods (Table 10.7, fig. 10.14,). The few extreme variations occur during the Hellenistic Period at Tel Yoqneam, and the chronologically mixed sample at Humayma in F102. The low percentage of sheep and goat at Tel Yoqneam was compensated for by significant increases in domestic cattle production. The mixed F102 sample was compensated for largely through increased use of cattle, chicken and fish.

Domesticated cattle dominate the faunal assemblage during the Hellenistic Period at Tel Yoqneam (Table 10.8, fig. 10.15). Domesticated cattle at Humayma generally constitute a higher proportion of identified fauna than in Byzantine Petra, but a much lower proportion than in twelfth-century Petra. The remains are far below the levels recovered at other selected archaeological sites in the region, and it is likely that most of the bones in the Large Mammal category belong to cattle. This assumption greatly increases the percentages of cattle represented at the site, although another possibility is donkey. Even if, however, all the large mammal bone from Humayma represented cattle, the proportion of cattle (5.07%) would still not be comparable to the sites mentioned above. Given the climate of Humayma, this is not surprising, although cattle do appear in the rock art of the Hisma (Jobling 1989a–b; Munro et al. 1997: 100; Oleson 2010: 36).

Following the Roman period at Humayma, percentages of pigs (14.7% of E116 and E125) drop dramatically and remain low (<1% of the identified assemblage) from Byzantine through Islamic times. Pigs were also well represented during Middle Bronze occupations at Refaim Valley (Horwitz 1989), but they are greatly reduced in Middle Bronze levels at Habuba Kabira (Table 10.9, fig. 10.16). Pigs are well represented in Hellenistic occupations at Tel Yoqneam, as at Humayma during the Roman period. The proportion of pigs is surprisingly low in the fort at Lejjun (0.8%; Toplyn

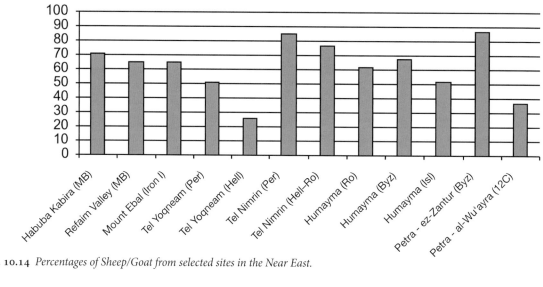

FIG. 10.14 *Percentages of Sheep/Goat from selected sites in the Near East.*

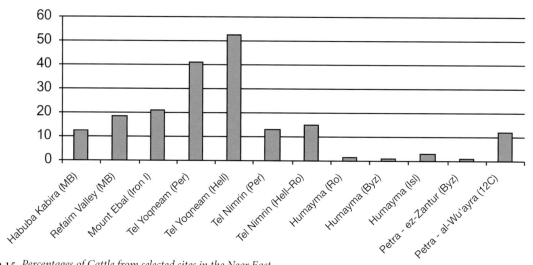

FIG. 10.15 *Percentages of Cattle from selected sites in the Near East.*

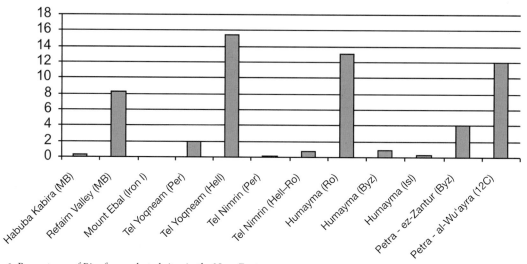

FIG. 10.16 *Percentages of Pigs from selected sites in the Near East.*

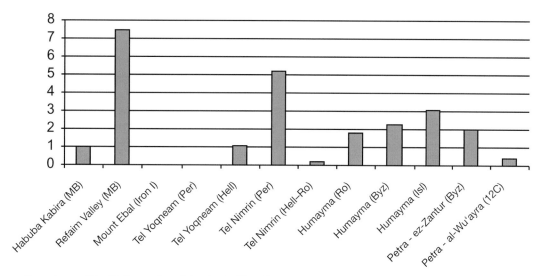

FIG. 10.17 *Percentages of Equids from selected sites in the Near East.*

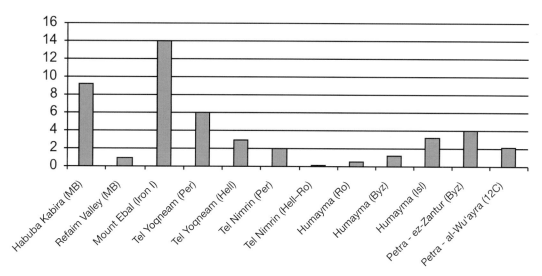

FIG. 10.18 *Percentages of Wild Animal from selected sites in the Near East.*

2006: Table 22.6). Environmental changes over the periods represented at Humayma cannot adequately account for this significant shift away from pig husbandry. Nor does a religious conviction alone support the significant change. As the settlement prospered and grew during the Byzantine and Islamic periods, one expects that the ground cover and associated natural sources of moisture may have been reduced by the consumption of local desert shrubs and trees on the al-Sharah escarpment for fuel. This would have reduced or eliminated the microenvironment needed by pigs.

While there is no obvious broad environmental explanation for this pattern in pig use, change in the microenvironment may have been a significant contributing factor. Other sites in the region of similar time periods have apparently continued higher levels of pig production (up to 30%) even into Byzantine/Umayyad levels (Köhler 1981).

Equid remains reach their highest representation (ca. 4.5%) during the Byzantine Period at Humayma, and they vary between 1.7% and 3.1% during other time periods there. Equid representation is also low at the other selected sites, but

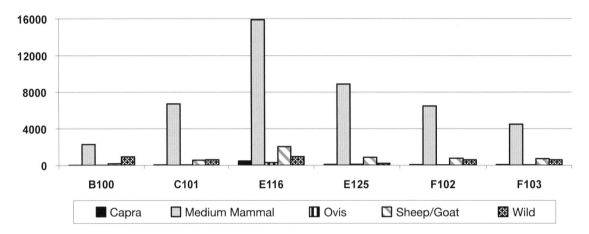

FIG. 10.19 *Regular distribution of medium animals (Capra, Medium Mammal, Ovis, Sheep/Goat, Wild) across major fields at Humayma.*

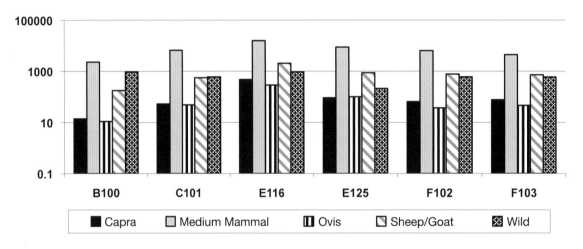

FIG. 10.20 *Logarithmic distribution of medium animals (Capra, Medium Mammal, Ovis, Sheep/Goat, Wild) across major fields at Humayma.*

it reaches 7.5% during the Middle Bronze Age at Refaim Valley (Table 10.10, fig. 10.17). The high percentage of equids at Refaim Valley may represent wild forms, rather than the domesticated forms of later time periods.

Wild fauna (as defined above) are poorly represented at Humayma, and the actual numbers of these animals are quite low (Table 10.2). Together, they constitute less than 1% of the total identified Humayma faunal assemblage, but vary somewhat by time period. The Humayma percentage of wild animals compares most closely with Middle Bronze Age levels at Refaim Valley and with Hellenistic occupations at Tel Yoqneam (Table 10.11, fig. 10.18).

Although the faunal lists for Humayma and Hadidi are similar in that ovicaprid husbandry is prominent, there are also differences. A greater number of types of wild animals have been found at Hadidi and Ta'as than have been found at Humayma. While we have identified *Bos taurus* at Humayma, we have not yet identified there the *Bos* (wild cattle) found at Hadidi. Bones of the hare (*Lepus capensis*) and possibly the gazelle (*Gazella* sp.) were identified in very small numbers at Humayma, and several common species of mice were absent. The lack of wild fauna at Humayma is paralleled at Tell Nimrin. The paucity of bones of wild animals at Humayma indicates a lifestyle

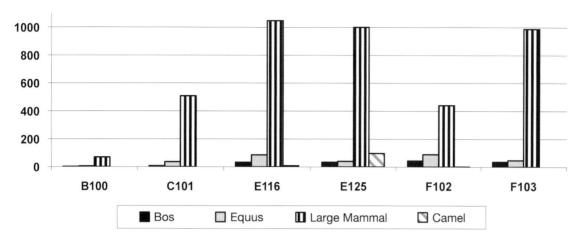

FIG. 10.21 *Regular distribution of large animals (Bos, Equus, Large Mammal, Camel) across major fields at Humayma.*

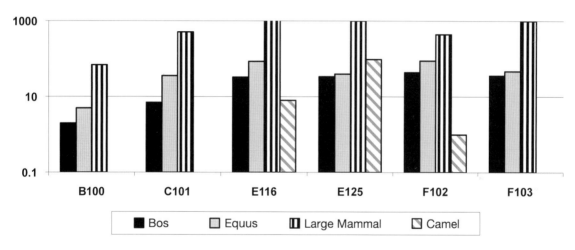

FIG. 10.22 *Logarithmic distribution of large animals (Bos, Equus, Large Mammal, Camel) across major fields at Humayma.*

largely dependent on agriculture and animal husbandry, rather than hunting. Parker reports very similar results from the Roman fort sites on the Kerak plateau (Parker 2005: 416–17). Sheep and goat were the most important sources of meat, and the soldiers raised chickens and pigs as a supplement. There were smaller numbers of cattle, donkeys, mules, horses, and camels.

10.B.6. Conclusions

The types and frequencies of animal remains found at Humayma compare favourably with those at other sites located along the Rift Valley for roughly the same time periods. Neither in Jordan nor Israel, however, have excavations provided the extensive

number of wild species that have been compiled for Syrian sites to the north (Finnegan and West 1984). Humayma lacks significant evidence for the bones of wild animals that could have been used for meat, pelts, ornamentation, or all three. This paucity suggests that the inhabitants of Humayma, from the time of the original Nabataean foundation onward, devoted themselves primarily to the use of domesticated herds, and that they only occasionally used wild animal resources. Although other sites such as Qarqur (Finnegan and West 1984) and Pella (Köhler 1980, 1981) suggest a change from pig to chicken husbandry over time, with a fairly stable as well as dominant reliance on sheep/goat husbandry, the Humayma fauna provide no evidence for this shift in the economy.

10.C. INVERTEBRATE REMAINS FROM HUMAYMA FIELDS C124, F102, B100, AND C101 (D. S. Reese)

This section deals with the invertebrates (marine shells, fresh-water shells, land snails, and fossils) from four fields at Humayma excavated in 1991–93 and 1996: Field C124 (Middle Nabataean to Late Roman Campground), Field F102 (Late Byzantine Church, Islamic House, Ottoman squatters), Field B100 (Byzantine Church, Islamic House, Ottoman squatters), and Field C101 (Late Byzantine Church, Early Islamic squatters). Future volumes will deal with the shells from the other fields at Humayma. The deposits producing remains are dated by the latest datable pottery or coins. In a few cases the deposits are dated by context, even though the pottery preserved comes from earlier periods. Most of the deposits, in fact, produced much residual pottery of earlier periods. Most of the shells discussed here are from Early Islamic (Umayyad and Abbasid, AD 640–969) or Late Islamic (AD 969–1516) deposits.

Shells were bagged separately from the beginning of the excavation. In some cases, shells were mistakenly included with the animal bones and M. Finnegan has passed these on to the present author. Occasionally, shells were noted on the excavation database but were not passed on to me. In some cases these were shells that were given registry numbers and had to remain in Jordan. In other cases, particularly in the early years of excavation, the database label "shells" was inadvertently applied to both invertebrates and bird (particularly ostrich) eggshells.

The material is presented in the Catalogue in order of marine gastropods, marine bivalves, fresh-water bivalves, land snails, and fossils.

10.C.1. Marine Shells

There are 157 marine shells available for study: Field C124, seven, dating Middle Nabataean to Late Roman (four deposits); Field F102, 26, including two Late Byzantine (two deposits), 11 Early Islamic (five deposits), one Late Islamic, and 12 Ottoman (three deposits); Field B100, 57, including one Byzantine, one Late Byzantine, 33 Early Islamic (11 deposits), 12 Late Islamic (four deposits), and 10 Ottoman (three deposits); Field C101, 67, including three Late Byzantine (three deposits), 60 Early Islamic (15 deposits), two Late Islamic (one deposit), and two Ottoman (one deposit).

Humayma is located 46 km as-the-crow-flies from Aqaba on the Red Sea. By the old land route the distance is about 70 km. The site is 190 km from the Mediterranean Sea, but there are no Mediterranean invertebrates in the collection. It should be noted that the three Byzantine churches produced only seven Byzantine-dated marine shells. The cut *Pinctada* fragment from the F102 Room G floor may have been inlay in a piece of furniture or mosaic. The B100 Room G dump *Cypraea,* collected dead on a beach, may have been an ornament. Eighteen (11.5%) of the marine shells were definitely picked up already dead on the beach, suggesting a degree of ancient touristic interest in Aila commensurate with the behaviour of young Bedouin boys from Humayma today: C124, one *Chamelea?* (Middle Nabataean); F102, 11: *Crepidula, Tridacna* fragment, *Glycymeris* fragment (all from one Ottoman deposit), *Anomia* (Early Islamic); B100, seven: bivalve fragment (Late Islamic), *Cerithium* (Late Islamic), *Donax* (Early Islamic), *Glycymeris* (Probe 01), *Cypraea* (Late Byzantine), *Conus* and *Spondylus* (one Ottoman deposit); and C101, seven: *Cypraea, Charonia,* and *Glycymeris* (one Early Islamic deposit), *Glycymeris* (Early Islamic), *Cypraea pantherina/tigris* (Late Islamic), *Nerita* (Early Islamic), *Conus* (Ottoman).

10.C.2. Shell Objects

Twenty-one marine shell artefacts were found. There are six ornaments from Field F102: *Nerita* (nerite) with an apical hole and an *Engina* with a man-made hole on the body from Room A2 (Early Islamic), and a *Conus/Strombus* ring from F102 Room A1 (Ottoman). An Ottoman floor produced a holed *Cypraea,* a *Conus* (cone shell) ground-down and holed at the apex, and a water-worn *Glycymeris* (dog cockle) fragment with a natural hole at the umbo (bivalve "beak").

There are six shell ornaments from Field B100: *Cypraea tigris* lip fragment possibly cut along lip (Late Islamic), water-worn *Cypraea* with an open dorsum from Room G (Late Byzantine), holed *Cerithium* (cerith, horn shell) from Room B (Early Islamic), ground-down and holed *Nerita* from Room B (Early Islamic), and holed and worked *Cypraea* and holed *Cerithium* from Room D (Ottoman).

There are five shell ornaments from Early Islamic deposits in Field C101: holed *Nerita* and water-worn *Cypraea* with open dorsum from the Nave, *Cypraea* lip fragment with the dorsum possibly cut off from the Northeast room, *Nerita* with a natural gastropod-bored hole from the Northwest room , and a *Tectus* or *Pinctada* bead from the far southeast room.

Possible *Pinctada* inlay fragments are known from Field F102: Room G (Late Byzantine) and Trench 01, two pieces (Early Islamic).

Not seen are a possibly sawn and smoothed gastropod piece from F102 Room D (Early Islamic) and a shell ring fragment from the C101 Nave (Early Islamic).

Mediterranean or Red Sea *Glycymeris* holed at the umbo are known from numerous Iron Age and later sites (Reese 1995a: 265–66, 2002: 277–78, 2008: 455, Reese et al. 2002: 461). Holed *Conus* are known from several sites (Reese 2002: 280; Reese et al. 2002: 460) and holed *Nerita* are known from a Roman grave in Amman (Reese 1987: 48) and Busayra (Reese et al. 2002: 461). Shell rings are also known from Busayra and Petra (Reese et al. 2002: 462).

10.C.3. *The Major Marine Shells*

The food shells include *Tectus dentatus* (and the similar related *Trochus niloticus,* both top shells), *Crassostrea* (oyster), and probably several of the rare forms.

There are 26 *Tectus,* distributed as follows: C124, one (Middle Nabataean); F102 Trench 01, one (Early Islamic); B100, four: Room E (Early Islamic), Probe 01 (Early Islamic), Room B (Early Islamic), and Room H (Late Islamic); C101, 21: Nave, six samples with seven MNI (five Early Islamic), Northeast room, 10 MNI (four Early Islamic deposits), Southeast room (Late Islamic), Northwest room, two (Early Islamic), and Southwest room (Ottoman). *Tectus* are the major invertebrate found

at the other Humayma fields, although *Tectus* and *Trochus* are not common at most Jordanian sites located some distance from the Red Sea. One *Tectus* fragment was found in a mid- to late sixteenth-century locus in Jerusalem (Reese 2008: 459). Four samples at Busayra yielded fragments, and the Parr excavations at Petra produced one *Trochus* (Reese et al. 2002: 461).

There are 16 cowrie remains, of both a small type (mainly *C. turdus*) and a large form (*C. tigris,* tiger cowrie, or *C. pantherina,* panther cowrie). Most are modified and were probably used as personal ornaments (smaller forms) or as decorative hangings or in some utilitarian manner (*C. tigris/pantherina*). They come from the following locations: F102 Nave (small *Cypraea,* holed, Ottoman); B100, eight: Room E (*C. tigris/ pantherina* fragment, Byzantine), Room E (small *Cypraea* fragment, Early Islamic), Room E (*C. tigris* lip fragment, possibly cut along lip, Late Islamic), Room D (small *Cypraea* with hole at anterior end and ground-down ventral, Ottoman); Room B (two small *Cypraea,* Early Islamic), Room G (small *Cypraea* with open dorsum, Late Byzantine), Room H (*C. tigris* fragment, Late Islamic); C101, seven: Nave (two small *Cypraea,* open dorsum; fragment, Early Islamic), Northeast room (two small *Cypraea,* one with dorsum possibly cut off, and one *C. tigris* fragment, three Early Islamic deposits), Southeast room (*C. tigris/pantherina* fragment, Late Islamic), and far southwest room (small *Cypraea,* Early Islamic).

Both small and large cowries, often modified, are known from numerous Iron Age and later sites in the Levant (Reese 1995a: 267–68, 2002: 278–79, 2008: 459, Reese et al. 2002: 458; Kovács 2008).

The 14 *Pinctada margaritifera* (black-lipped pearl oyster) might have been a food item secondarily used as a source of inlay. They are known from C124, Late Roman; F102, four: Trench 01 (Early Islamic), Nave (Ottoman), Room G (Late Byzantine and Early Islamic deposits in Trench 05, all possibly from the same individual), outside West Facade (Late Islamic); B100, eight: Room E (one Early Islamic and two Late Islamic deposits), Room, D (Ottoman), Room L (Ottoman), Room B (Early Islamic), Room I (Early Islamic), West Courtyard (Ottoman); and the C101 Nave (Early

Islamic and a second possible fragment similarly dated).

Pinctada have been found at a number of Iron Age and later Near Eastern sites (Reese 1987: 48, pl. XLII.2, 1995a: 271, 1995b: 97, 2008: 458, Reese et al. 2002: 459–60). Humayma Fields E116 and F103 yielded a number of fragments with cut edges, mainly of Late Byzantine or Early Islamic dates. Examples with cut edges are also known from Jerusalem (Reese 1995a: 271, fig. 9; 2008: 458–59).

It is unclear if six of the seven *Tridacna* (giant clams) were brought to the site for food (one was definitely picked up dead) or to be used as small containers. They come from: C124 (Middle Nabataean); F102: Trench 01 (Early Islamic) and Nave (water-worn; Ottoman); B100: Room E (Late Islamic, two), Probe 01 (Early Islamic), Room H (Early Islamic, two), and C101 Nave (Early Islamic).

Tridacna are known from Iron Age and later sites in the Levant (Reese 1995a: 268, 2002: 279–80, 2008: 459, Reese et al. 2002: 454).

10.C.4. Fresh-Water Bivalves

Two related Early Islamic deposits in F102 Room D (Trench 06) produced remains of three *Chambardia rubens arcuata* (formerly called *Aspatharia rubens*). *Chambardia* must come from the Nile River, 400 km away (as-the-crow-flies).

A large fresh-water bivalve fragment comes from B100, Room E (Late Islamic). The C101 Southeast room yielded a fresh-water bivalve fragment (Late Islamic). The Northwest room produced a fresh-water bivalve and an *Unio* fragment (Early Islamic). The Southwest room produced a fresh-water bivalve fragment (Ottoman).

There are 18 *Chambardia* samples from Jerusalem ranging in date from the mid-first to the nineteenth centuries. There are 15 individuals of this large fresh-water bivalve. The only worked example here is a possible sixteenth-century hinge fragment that has a drilled hole below the umbo (Reese 2008: 460).

Chambardia are known from numerous other Near Eastern sites (Reese 2008: 460), including Roman and later Haifa, Sede Boqer and Nessana in Israel, and Pella, Jerash, and Amman in Jordan (Reese et al. 1986; Reese 1995a: 272), a

fragment from the Early Islamic pastoral camp at Nahal 'Oded, south of the Ramon Crater in Israel (Horwitz et al. 1997: 108), and remains from Umayyad Tall Jawa in Jordan (Reese 2002: 286–87).

10.C.5. Land Snails

Only 28 land snails were seen, with ten from F102 (seven Early Islamic in three deposits, and three Ottoman in two deposits), 16 from B100 (one Byzantine, 11 Early Islamic in five deposits, one Late Islamic, three Ottoman in one deposit), and two from Early Islamic C101 (two deposits). While six are the edible *Helix*, most are too small to have been eaten. The bright colour of many shells suggests that they are more recent intrusions.

10.C.6. Fossils

There are seven fossil bivalves in the collection (six *Gryphaea*, one oyster mould), with five Early Islamic and two Late Islamic. None were modified and all are probably to be considered to be natural kick-ups from the limestone bedrock at the top of the escarpment north of the site. Some fossils from archaeological sites in Jordan were modified to serve as ornaments (Reese 2002: 281–82, Reese et al. 2002: 442–46).

10.C.7. Catalogue
    (all dimensions are in millimetres)

10.C.7.a. Field C124 (Middle Nabataean to Late Roman Campground)

Middle Nabataean: Gastropod body fragment (weathered exterior, 37 × 18, max. T 3.75) (1996.0531). *Tridacna* distal body fragment (pres. H 70.25, pres. W 60.25) (1996.0043). *Chamelea* distal fragment (water-worn, pres. H 24, pres. W 23.75) (1996.0043).
Early Roman: *Tectus columella* fragment (very large) (1996.0033).
Roman: *Cerithium* (complete, L 29.75, W 15.75) (1996.0039).
Late Roman: *Fusus* (open lower whorl on labial side, L 32.75, W 11.75) (1996.0045). *Pinctada* body fragment (21.25 × 15.75) (1996.0045).

10.C.7.b. Field F102 (Late Byzantine Church, Islamic House, Ottoman squatters)

Trench 01:
Dump (Early Islamic). *Tectus* (two fragments, one medium MNI) (1992.0309). Three *Pinctada*, flat roughly triangular piece, possible inlay, broken distal, smoothed exterior and interior, L 40.25, max. W 24, T 2.25 (1992.0308.01); distal fragment (smoothed and scored interior, pres. H 16.75, pres. W 24.75) (1992.0309); body fragment (11.25 × 12.75) (1992.0478). *Tridacna* hinge area fragment (very large, pres. H 58, pres. W 62.5 five (1991.0393). Land snail (no colour, slight gloss) (1992.0382). Not seen (database): sea shell; five shell fragments (1992.0414, 1991.0439, 1991.0510, 1992.0157).

Room A:
Rubble and soil (Early Islamic). Fossil *Gryphaea* (weathered, broken distal, pres. L 21.25, W 14) (1992.0045). Not seen (database): sea shell fragment (1992.0044).
Rubble fill (Early Islamic). Not seen (database): two shell fragments (1993.0104).

Room A1:
Fill (Early Islamic). Not seen (database): 21 shell fragments (1991.0106, 0163).
Possible floor (Early Islamic). Not seen (database): five shell fragments (1991.0184).
Lens of sandy soil (Late Islamic). Not seen (database): shell fragment (1991.0321).
Ash layer (Ottoman). Ring made from *Conus/ Strombus* (broken, nicely cut, ring ext. D 28.75, ring int. D 18.5, max. Th 8) (1991.0183.02). Not seen (database): four shell fragments (1991.0190, 0265).

Room A2:
Fill (Early Islamic). *Nerita* (worn or water-worn, hole at apex, L 19) (1991.0178.01; photo only seen by Reese). *Engina bimaculata* (ground-down body and holed, worn apex, L 17.25, W 12.75, ground-down area 6.75 × 5.75, hole 2.75 × 2.75 (1991.0216.01). Not seen (database): two shell fragments (1991.0189, 0270).
Weathering deposit (Early Islamic). Not seen (database): two shell fragments (1991.0223).

Earth floor (Early Islamic). Not seen (database): 2 shell fragments (1991.0273).

Nave:
Sandy fill (Early Islamic by context). Not seen (database): shell fragment (1991.0145).
Packed brown fill (Late Islamic). Not seen (database): five shell fragments (four small) (1991.0148, 0180, 0214).
Collapse (Ottoman). Not seen (database): possible oyster fragment (1991.0112), seven shell fragments (1991.0047, 0112, 0346, 0347, 1995.0258).
Loose soil fill (Ottoman). Large gastropod internal columella fragment (pres. L 27, pres. W 9.25) (1991.0182).
Floor (Ottoman). *Cypraea* (holed on side of dorsum, glossy, L 24) (1991.0377.04; only photo seen by Reese). *Conus* (ground-down and holed at apex, broken lip, L 12.25, W 11.75, ground-down area 4.75 × 4.75, hole 1.25 (1991.0334.01b). *Drupa* (small, L 21.75, W 12.5) (1991.0453). *Crepidula* (water-worn, medium, L 31, W 23.75) (1991.0258). Gastropod inner columella fragment (medium/large, pres. L 38.5, pres. W 20.25) (1991.0361). *Pinctada* hinge fragment (pres. H 42.25, pres. W 25) (1991.0453). *Tridacna* hinge area fragment (water-worn, recent breaks, 50 × 24) (1991.0361). *Glycymeris* hinge fragment (water-worn, natural hole at umbo, medium/large, pres. H 18, pres. W 29.75, hole 5.75 × 2.75 (1991.0334.01a). *Barbatia* distal/side fragment (medium) (1991.0377). *Venus* distal/side fragment (medium/large) (1991.0453). Land snail (no colour or gloss) (1991.0361). Not seen (database): oyster fragment (1991.0302); oyster or mother-of-pearl (1991.0225); seven shell fragments (1991.0334, 0362, 0497).

Room B:
Floor (Early Islamic). Not seen (database): two sea shells (complete) and eight sea shell fragments (1992.0299, 0301, 0425).
Windblown sand (Ottoman). Not seen (database): sea shell (1993.0096).

Room D:
Ash deposit (Early Islamic by context). Not seen (database): sea shell (1992.0267).

Floor (Early Islamic). Land snail (large, has gloss) (1992.0381).

Earth fill (Early Islamic). *Chambardia* hinge fragment (left) (1992.0534). Not seen (database): shell fragments (1992.0557).

Dump layer (Early Islamic). *Tectus* body fragment (medium) (1992.0558). *Crassostrea* (L 56.25, W 47.25) (1992.0558). *Chambardia* fragments (two left MNI based on hinges) (1992.0558, 1993.0038). Not seen (database): "cup or bowl carved from the body of a conch, probably *Strombus tricornis,* broken, incomplete, L 92, W 65, H 2, approximately half the circumference is carefully sawn and smoothed, the rest is broken" (1992.0558.08).

Surface fill (Ottoman). Two land snails (larger no colour, some gloss; smaller, colour and gloss) (1992.0243). Not seen (database): sea shell and sea shell fragment; three shell fragments; six snail fragments (1992.0093, 0103, 0156, 0266).

Room F1:
Below *tabun* (Early Islamic). Not seen (database): sea shell (1992.0291).

By *tabun* (Ottoman). Not seen (database): sea shell (1992.0148).

Room F2:
Fill (Early Islamic). Five land snails (three *Helix*) (1991.0137, 0155). Not seen (database): oyster and oyster fragment (1991.0034, 0045); 10 shell fragments (1991.0150, 0188, 0292, 0314, 0441).

Room G:
Soil and rubble fill (Late Byzantine). *Pinctada* distal fragment (has brown exterior, has one cut side, pres. H 35.75, pres. W 58.25, cut edge 37.5) (1992.0170).

Burial 1, fill (Late Byzantine). Not seen (database): perforated shell (1992.0482).

Loose rubble and soil fill (Late Byzantine). Gastropod internal columella (small piece, L 13.25, W 7.75) (1992.0472).

Fill in bin (Early Islamic). *Pinctada* body fragment (20.75 × 21) (1992.0152).

Cistern area:
Collapse above cistern (Early Islamic). Not seen (database): sea shell (1993.0253).

Clay sealing on roof of cistern (Early Islamic). *Anomia* (water-worn, L 16.75, W 16.25) (1993.0251).

Outside West Facade:
Dump (Late Islamic). *Pinctada* fragment (1993.0297). Not seen (database): sea shell (1993.0296).

10.C.7.c. Field B100 (Byzantine Church, Islamic House, Ottoman squatters)

Room E (Apse):
Fill around tomb marker (Byzantine). *Cypraea tigris/pantherina* body fragment (has colour and gloss, small piece) (1992.0454). Land snail (has slight colour and gloss, broken lip) (1992.0454).

Occupation debris (Early Islamic). *Tectus* body fragment (medium) (1992.0325). *Cypraea* ventral/lip fragment (pres. L 24.24) (1992.0325). *Pinctada* edge fragment (23.75 × 52) (1992.0281). *Barbatia* distal/side fragment (medium) (1992.0281). Land snail (1992.0238). Fossil *Gryphaea* (worn, broken distal, pres. L 13.75, W 10.75) (1992.0238).

Packed earth fill (Early Islamic). *Donax* distal/side fragment (water-worn, medium) (1991.0461). Two land snails (no colour or gloss, small; colour and gloss, medium) (1991.0461). Not seen (database): shell (1991.0460).

Rubble fall (Late Islamic). *Pinctada* hinge fragment (large, pres. H 55, pres. W 37) (1992.0087). *Tridacna* hinge fragment (about one-half valve, small/medium, pres. H 75.5, pres. W 58.25) (1992.0051). Fossil *Gryphaea* (H 26.75, W 18.5) (1992.0083).

Soil on pavement (Late Islamic). Conus (has colour and gloss, small, L 14.25, W 9) (1992.0197). *Ancilla* (has slight colour and gloss, slightly broken lip, L 12.15, W 5.5) (1992.0197). *Pinctada* body fragment (42.75 × 23.75) (1992.0197). Bivalve distal fragment (very water-worn, H 15.75, W 16) (1992.0236).

Rubble and soil fill (Late Islamic). *Cypraea tigris* lip fragment (has colour and gloss, pres. L 61, possibly cut along lip for 42 mm) (1991.0100). *Cerithium* (water-worn, broken mouth area, L 15.75, pres. W 8.5) (1991.0127). *Tridacna* (two body fragments: medium/large, 19 × 23.25; pres. H 21.25, pres. W 31.25, one MNI) (1991.0129, 0136). Large fresh-water bivalve distal/body fragment (pres. H 38.75, pres. W 44.75) (1991.0100). Not seen (database): conch shell (1991.0003).

Room D:
Rubble and soil fill (Ottoman). *Pinctada* (two fragments: hinge, pres. H 33.25, pres. W 50.75; distal, pres. H 42.75, pres. W 33) (1992.0350). *Cypraea* (hole at anterior end, ground-down ventral and lacking most of lip, L 23.25, W 17, hole 1.75 × 2.25) (1992.0350). *Cerithium erythraeonense* (hole opposite mouth, broken lip, L 49.75, W 21.25, hole 6.75 × 6.25) (1992.0350).

Probe 01 in Courtyard:
Fill above pavement (Early Islamic). *Tectus* distal fragment (very large) (1993.0061). *Tridacna* distal fragment (very worn, thick, H 24.25, W 48.25) (1993.0016). *Glycymeris* distal fragment (water-worn, H 11.75, W 13) (1993.0063).
Fill below pavement (Early Islamic). *Cerithium* distal end (very water-worn, medium) (1991.0475). *Tapes* (slightly broken, left, H 32.25, pres. W 45.5) (1991.0406).

Probe 02 in southwest corner of Courtyard:
Packed earth floor above pavement (Early Islamic). Not seen (database): sea shell (1993.0174).
Below upper church pavement (Early Islamic). *Lambis* or *Charonia* columella fragment (pres. L 29, max. W 22) (1993.0203).

West end – Room L:
Tumble (Ottoman). *Pinctada* body fragment (delaminating, 20.5 × 22) (1992.0119). Not seen (database): sea shell (1992.0071).

East end – Room B:
Lens of ash above pavement (Early Islamic). *Tectus* body fragment (medium/large) (1991.0144).
Sandy fill above pavement (Early Islamic). *Crassostrea* fragment (medium) (1991.0173, probably joins 1991.0207).
Fill (Early Islamic). *Cerithium* (hole opposite mouth, small, L 16.25, W 7.5, hole 3.25 × 2.75) (1991.0198). *Pinctada* body fragment (19.75 × 10.25) (1991.0219). *Crassostrea* fragment (medium) (1991.0207, probably joins 1991.0173). Chama (H 27, W 16.75) (1991.0207).
Dumped material below pavement (Early Islamic). *Nerita* (worn, ground-down and holed on body, L 22.5, W 15.75, ground-down area 13.5 × 10.25, hole

4.25 × 4.75) (1991.0385). 2 *Cypraea turdus* (L 25.5, W 17, H 12.25; L 25.75, W 16, H 12.75) (1991.0404). Land snail (no color or gloss, small) (1991.0462). Not seen (database): shell (1991.0342).

Room G:
Occupation debris dump below pavement (Late Byzantine). *Cypraea* (water-worn, open dorsum, has gloss, L 41.75, W 14.25, H 7.75, opening 13 × 8.25) (1992.0092).
Fill around wall foundation (Byzantine). Not seen (database): sea shell (1992.0283).

Room H:
Fill (Late Islamic). *Tectus* columella fragment (large) (1991.0434). *Cypraea tigris* body/lip fragment (has some colour and gloss, medium) (1991.0433). Gastropod internal columella fragment (two pieces, medium/large) (1991.0505). *Helix* apical fragment (has much colour) (1991.0488). Fossil *Gryphaea* (L 23.75, W 13.75) (1991.0434).

Room I:
Fill (Early Islamic). *Nerita* (worn, L 22, W 16.75) (1991.0194). *Charonia* body fragment (thin, pres. L 49.25, pres. W 52.5) (1991.0232). *Lambis* (two large fragments: body/lip, pres. L 58.25, pres. W 53.5; inner body, pres. L 86.75, pres. W 34.25) (1991.0236). *Cerithium* (slightly broken apex, open mouth, L 28.75, W 10.5) (1991.0236). Two gastropod columellas (L 39.25, max. W 20.5; L 49.25, max. W 16.25) (1991.0236). *Pinctada* (two small body fragments) (1991.0194). Two *Tridacna* (left, broken right, small/medium, H 65.75, pres. W 94.75; 1991.0194; body fragment, thick, very large, pres. H 39.25, pres. W 31.25, 1991.0218). *Chamelea* distal/side fragment (thick, large) (1991.0218). *Tapes* distal/side fragment (medium) (1991.0218). *Helix* apical fragment (has colour and gloss) (1991.0218). Two fossil *Gryphaea* (two worn: L 13.5, W 8; L 18.75, W 12.5) (1991.0236).

Exterior of building (southeast corner):
Dump (Early Islamic). *Lambis* body fragment (21.25 × 24) (1991.0128). *Mytilus* body fragment (medium) (1991.0128). Six land snails (1991.0137, 0155). Not seen (database): two cowrie fragments (one discarded) (1991.0406, 0155).

West Courtyard outside door to Room K:
Rubbish beneath packed surface (Ottoman). *Conus* (water-worn, stones in mouth, small, L 25.25, W 11.75) (1992.0193). *Nerita* lip fragment (has colour and gloss, small, W 11) (1992.0193). *Strombus* (broken mouth, small, L 20.25, W 11.25) (1992.0391). *Pinctada* distal fragment (thin, H 31.75, W 27.75, Th 1.75) (1992.0361). *Spondylus* (upper valve, vermetids inside, broken side, medium/large, H 53.25, pres. W 43.5) (1992.0165). *Astarte* distal/side fragment (medium) (1992.0193). Three land snails (1992.0193, 0490). Not seen (database): mussel shell (1992.0122).

10.C.7.d. Field C101 (Late Byzantine Church, Early Islamic squatters)

Nave:
Silt below paving, above Burial one (Late Byzantine). *Tectus* distal fragment (very large) (1992.0463).
Below pavement and above Burial 5 (Late Byzantine). *Thais/Purpura* body fragment (medium, pres. H 26.5, pres. W 27.5) (1992.0609).
Soil below Burial 4 (Late Byzantine by context). *Barbatia* (right, H 34, W 44.75) (1993.0069).
Fill below pavement and above Burial 4 (Late Byzantine). *Tectus* body fragment (medium) (1993.0005). Not seen (database): sea shell; two shell fragments (1992.0592, 0603).
Soils above pavement (Early Islamic). *Tectus* (seven fragments, three burnt gray, one medium MNI) (1991.0254, 0317, 0382, 1992.0107). *Nerita* (dorsum fragment with lip, has roughly circular hole in centre body made from exterior, burnt light grey/light brown, recent breaks, pres. L 19, pres. W 13.25, hole 3 × 3.25) (1992.0135.01). *Nerita* (brown, has gloss, L 16.25, W 11.75) (1992.0344). *Conus* (broken distal, broken lip area, pitted, pres. L 35.75, pres. W 20.5) (1991.0422). Two *Cypraea* (water-worn, one-half, open dorsum, smoothed dorsal area, L 25.5, W 7, 1992.0344; fragment, no colour, has gloss, large, 1992.0107). Two *Charonia* (four body fragments: one water-worn, three fresh, two MNI) (1991.0254, 0317, 0378). *Lambis* body fragment (medium) (1991.0420). Large gastropod columella fragment (1991.0279). Cassid body fragment (thick, pres. L 19, pres. W 12.75) (1992.0344). Gastropod columella (medium/large) (1992.0344). *Pinctada* (two small

fragments) (1991.0422). Two *Crassostrea* valves (H 47, W 31.5, 1992.0344; distal fragment, pres. H 22.75, pres. W 26, 1991.0418). *Glycymeris* (water-worn, H 48.25, W 48.75) (1991.0203). *Barbatia helblingi* distal/side fragment (left, medium) (1992.0107). Not seen: shell finger ring fragment with parallel grooves on exterior, L 40, Th 3 (1992.0376.01). Not seen (database): three shells and two shell fragments (1991.0318, 0446, 1992.0058, 0253).
Lens of ash on pavement (Early Islamic). Not seen (database): 17 shell fragments (1992.0240, 0432).
Compacted silt below paving in apse (Late Byzantine). *Cerithium* (has gloss, L 19, W 6.25) (1992.0512). *Tridacna* body fragment (small piece, pres. H 34.25, pres. W 28.25) (1992.0512). *Crassostrea* (H 50.75, W 41.25) (1992.0500). Not seen (database): four sea shells and two shell fragments (1992.0466, 0514, 0543).
Fill above Burial 1 (Late Byzantine). *Tectus* (three fragments, medium) (1992.0501). Cassid distal body fragment (large) (1992.0501). Not seen (database): two sea shells (1992.0546).
Below pavement and above Burial 3 (Late Byzantine). two *Tectus* (three fragments: one below apex, one body, one distal, two MNI, one medium, one very large) (1992.0542, 0588). Not seen (database): sea shell fragment (1992.0551).
Below pavement and above Burial 2 (Late Byzantine). *Tectus* (two fragments: body, distal, very large) (1992.0563). *Pinctada?* fragment (1992.0563). Not seen (database): two sea shell fragments (1992.0568).

Northeast Room (Room 2, Sacristy):
Tumble (Early Islamic). *Tectus* (three fragments: one apex, two body; one slightly pitted exterior medium) (1991.0352). *Nerita* (worn, L 22.75, W 16.25) (1991.0076). *Helix* apical fragment (has colour and gloss) (1991.0061).
Naturally deposited silt (Early Islamic). *Tectus* (two fragments: body, columella, one MNI) (1991.0133, 0135). *Cypraea* lip fragment (lacks dorsum, possibly cut off, medium/large) (1991.0133).
Soil with ash pockets (Early Islamic by context). *Cypraea turdus* (L 27.25, W 17.75, H 12.75) (1991.0172).
Ashy soil around *tabun* (Early Islamic). *Tectus* (three body fragments: one medium, one large, two MNI) (1991.0205, 1991.0246, 1991.0425). *Conus*

(apical part, burnt black, large, pres. L 28.5, W 23.75) (1991.0339). *Chicoreus* (two burnt gray fragments: distal columella, body) (1991.0229). Large gastropod body fragment (1991.0425). *Mytilus*? nacre edge fragment (12.75 × 18.5) (1991.0294). Not seen (database): shell fragment (1991.0263).

Fill below paving (Late Byzantine). Six *Tectus* (54 fragments: three apex, six columella, four distal, 41 body, one burnt gray, six MNI) (1991.0448, 0466, 0467, 0469, 0471, 0472, 1992.0059, 0106, 0110, 0114, 0129, 0131, 0136, 0137, 0142, 0175). *Cypraea tigris* fragment (1991.0471). *Conus* (worn, small, L 13.75, W 8.75) (1991.0472). *Drupa* (small, L 17.25, W 12.25) (1992.0114). *Bittium* (broken apex, broken lip, small, pres. L 15.75, pres. W 6.25) (1991.0448). *Spondylus* (upper valve, body fragment, burnt gray/brown, pres. H 19.25, pres. W 18.75) (1991.0448). *Venus* hinge fragment (pres. H 15.75, pres. W 20) (1992.0059). *Anomia* (broken distal, pres. H 20.25, pres. W 19.5) (1992.0106).

Southeast room (Room 3):
Tumble (Early Islamic). *Strombus* (broken body/mouth, no colour or gloss, L 37.75, pres. W 20.5) (1991.0023).
Soil on pavement (Early Islamic). *Glycymeris* (water-worn, recently broken side, H 48.25, pres. W 42) (1991.0085).
Fill (Early Islamic). *Tectus* distal fragment (very large) (1992.0202). *Cypraea tigris/pantherina* (water-worn, one-half, lacks dorsum, medium, pres. L 44) (1992.0400). Fresh-water bivalve distal fragment (pres. H 34.75, pres. W 29) (1992.0400).

Northwest entrance room (Room 4):
Tumble (Early Islamic). Not seen (database): mother-of-pearl; three shells (1992.0039, 0203, 0261)
Lenses of occupation debris above floor (Early Islamic). Two *Tectus* (eight fragments, two very large distal, one burnt black, two MNI) (1993.0261, 0266, 0279, 0315). *Trochus* body fragment (medium) (1992.0400). *Nerita* (gastropod-bored near apex, L 22, W ca. 20) (1993.0261.01; only photo seen by Reese). *Charonia* (two upper body fragments: pres. L 74.75, pres. W 59.5; pres. L 28, pres. W 36.25) (1993.0262, 0264). Two gastropod internal columella fragments (pres. L 17.75, pres. W 10.25;

medium, pres. L 34.75, pres. W 14.25) (1993.0264). *Unio* distal fragment (medium) (1993.0355). Fresh-water bivalve (right, broken, medium) (1993.0280, 0281). Fossil oyster internal mould (slightly broken, pres. H 21.5, pres. W 20.25) (1993.0316). Not seen (database): three sea shells, seven sea shell fragment, two shells and two shell fragments (1993.0161, 0278, 0282, 0378).

Southwest room (Room 5):
Occupation deposit (Early Islamic). *Tectus* fragment (medium) (1992.0377). *Conus* (water-worn, broken lip, L 31.75, pres. W 20.25) (1992.0306). Fresh-water bivalve fragments (medium) (1992.0590). Not seen (database): four sea shells (1992.0502, 0503, 0591).

Far southeast room (Room 6):
Fill against east wall of church (Early Islamic). *Tectus* or *Pinctada* nacre bead (roughly rectangular, concave shape, slightly delaminated, L 9.25, W 8.75, hole 1.25 × 1.5) (1992.0428). *Cypraea* fragment (no colour or gloss, small, no dorsum, L 21.25) (1992.0428). *Conus* (worn, slightly broken lip, small, L 15.25, W 10.75) (1993.0112). *Glycymeris* hinge fragment (very large) (1993.0064). Land snail (has some colour and gloss, very small) (1993.0157).

10.D. PLANT REMAINS (J. Ramsay)

10.D.1. Introduction

This section examines and interprets the archaeobotanical assemblage recovered from the site of Humayma during six seasons of excavation of structures and contexts dating from the Early Nabataean period through the Roman, Byzantine, Early Islamic, and Ottoman periods (1995, 1996, 1998, 2000, 2002, and 2005). In addition, the report makes reference to the results of the analysis of plant remains excavated in 1989, 1991, 1992, and 1993 (published in Oleson 1997, 2010: 37–45). The analysis focuses on both the diversity of the plant remains and the reasons this material was deposited. The main issues are the following: which crops were being exploited and why; what was the nature and extent of agricultural irrigation, if any; whether wild plant species provide evidence for agricultural techniques during the various periods of occupation at Humayma; and whether there is evidence of trade in plant products. Unlike the artefacts from Humayma, which for the most part are being published in the report volumes that deal with the structures with which they were associated, the botanical remains for the entire site are published together here. Given the relatively small size of the sample, and the nature of the material, which reflects the natural resources of the site as well as the cultural preferences of the resident population, it seemed more effective to present and analyze it as a unit. In addition, the report was ready early in 2010, and it made no sense to delay its publication until the appearance of the volume that treats the structures that yielded the majority of the samples.

The plant remains analyzed consisted of charred seeds, fruit, nut, and other plant parts, mainly cereal grain and chaff. The samples were recovered from all areas of the excavation and were associated with artefacts dating to all periods of occupation at the site (Table 10.12, pp. 373–76). Since few of the contexts, however, were closed and tightly dated, we have had to assume that the fragile botanical remains most likely were deposited along with the latest of the artefacts in each context. This assumption may not be correct in all instances. All samples were processed in the field during the excavation seasons, retrieved from the soil by means of the flotation technique. This technique was the most efficient and cost effective available, given the size of the site and the type of soil matrix (Wagner 1988). The dry flotation samples from the 1.0 mm sieve were sorted under a Wild Heerbrugg stereoscopic microscope using up to 40× magnification. The carbonized seeds, grains, fruit, and all other material that could be identified as plant fragments, except for charcoal, were removed for further identification. Of the 153 samples that were processed, 100 samples (65%) included carbonized plant remains (cereals, legumes, or fruit/nut). Of these samples, 60 included crop items, either cereals or legumes, and 64 had remains of fruit and/or nut species.

Identification of the recovered botanical material was accomplished using the personal archaeobotanical reference collection of A.C. D'Andrea at the Department of Archaeology at Simon Fraser University, comparing morphological characteristics of the carbonized specimens with modern material from the reference collection. Reference was also made to drawings and pictures from reference seed atlases (Cappers et al. 2006; Anderberg 1994; Berggren 1969, 1981; Beijerinck 1947; Feinbrun-Dothan 1978, 1986; Zohary 1966, 1972; Post 1932), and consultation with colleagues.

10.D.2. List of Samples and Identified Taxa

The 153 samples processed came from seven excavation areas (Table 10.12): a Roman period house (E125); a Roman fort (E116); a Nabataean and Roman building (E128); a Late Roman bath building (E077); and an Abbasid *qasr*, or fortified manor house (F103). Two samples from a tomb near a Nabataean watchtower (A02) and a domestic complex (E122) were processed, but neither contained botanical remains. Analysis of the samples identified 55 plant taxa of either seeds and/or plant parts (chaff and nut material), including 37 wild species, six cereals, five legumes, and six fruit/nut species.

In an earlier study of botanical material from Humayma, John Shay analyzed archaeobotanical samples from 40 loci recovered during the excavation seasons of 1989 and 1991–93. Only 12.5% of the 40 samples examined contained seeds. He identified several crop species and 30 types of wild plant seeds from the Late Roman Bath building (E077), the Byzantine Lower Church (C101), an Umayyad/Early Abbasid house built on top of a Byzantine church (B100), and an Umayyad house built on top of a Byzantine church (F102) (Oleson 1997; *HEP* 1: 37–45). Of the 611.5 charred seeds Shay examined, 39 were cereals, one was a legume, 21.5 were tree and vine crops, 282.5 were wild species, and 267.5 were unidentified seeds. Of these seeds, only 10.2% belonged to domesticated species such as cereals, tree crops, vines, and other fruits. The most abundant cereal item identified in Shay's study was barley, and several unidentified grasses also appeared in the assemblage. The only legume was chick-pea. Fig was the most represented tree crop, and there was only sparse evidence of date, olive, and grape (Oleson 1997). A wide variety of wild species was identified, the most abundant being white broom (*Retama raetam*), mouse-ear chickweed (*Cerastium* sp.), plantain (*Plantago* sp.), medick (*Medicago scutellata*), and several members

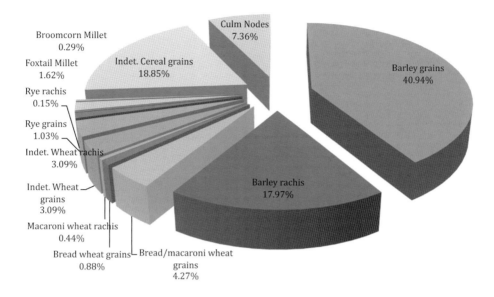

FIG. 10.23 *Percentage of cereal crops represented at Humayma.*

of the goosefoot family (*Chenopodiaceae*) (Oleson 1997; *HEP* 1: 38–39).

The present study examined 153 samples, 91.5% of which contained botanical remains, totalling 2,020 seed and plant parts. The preservation of botanical material was generally quite good for the crop items, except for a few cases in which identification to species level was unfeasible. For example, in several cases it was not possible to identify the wheat grains recovered to species level; as a result they were grouped in a *Triticum* L. sp. category (as seen in samples 58 and 67). Domesticated barley (*Hordeum vulgare* L.), however, characterized by being pointed at both the apex end and the embryo end, and by being rounded on the ventral surface and angular on the dorsal surface, was positively identified and appears definitively in many samples (i.e., samples 49, 58, 76).

Perhaps as a result of the larger, more diverse sample, domesticated plants (cereals, legumes, and tree and vine crops) constituted a significantly larger proportion of the species identified, equalling 53.3%. As in Shay's study, barley grains constitute the highest proportion of the cereals in the archaeobotanical assemblage (40.9%) (fig. 10.23). Also recovered were a significant proportion of barley rachis (18.0%), a large number of unidentified cereal grains (18.85%), several culm

nodes (7.4%), and the remaining approximately 15% is composed of wheats (bread and macaroni), millets (foxtail and broomcorn), and rye.

There has been a far greater recovery of legume species in the current study than in Shay's, which identified only one chick-pea. The present study identified 73 legume samples, of which 42 (57.5%) unfortunately were indeterminate legumes, while 19 (26%) were lentils, and the remaining 12 (16.4%) were faba beans, chick-peas, vetchlings, and bitter vetch (fig. 10.24).

The tree and vine crops present in the samples analyzed here also add to Shay's study. Of the 323 fruit and nut specimens recovered, figs (*Ficus carica* L.), olives (*Olea europaea* L.), grapes (*Vitis vinifera* L.), dates (*Phoenix dactylifera* L.) and walnuts (*Juglans regia* L.) were identified. The most abundant fruit seed recovered in both studies was fig — in this report, 276 seeds, 85.5% of the tree and vine crop assemblage. Naturally, it must be taken into account that each fig fruit can produce anywhere from 10–75 seeds per fruit, which can skew the results to make fig appear to have a greater representation than in reality (Rixford 1918; Condit 1969; Valdeyron, and Lloyd 1979). All other tree and vine species constitute a much smaller percentage of the total assemblage, i.e., grape 6.2%, date 4.0%, olive 2.8% (fig. 10.25).

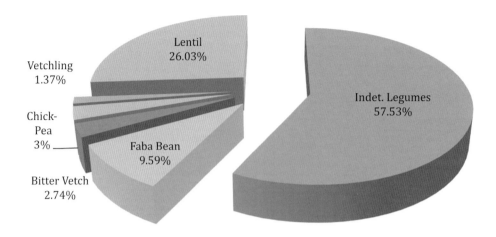

FIG. 10.24 *Percentage of legumes represented at Humayma.*

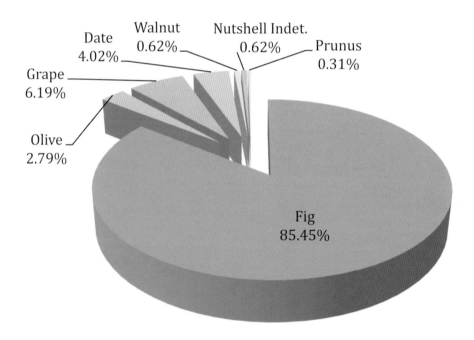

FIG. 10.25 *Percentage of tree and vine crops represented at Humayma.*

The analysis identified 660 seeds of wild species present at Humayma; 331 of these were identified as *Beta* sp. (beet). Since *Beta* sp. represented
just over half of the wild species found, it was
dealt with separately so as not to bias the percent
representation of the rest of the wild species (fig.
10.26). Unidentified grass species dominate the
assemblage of wild species that account for greater
than 2% of the adjusted total (not including *Beta*
sp.), with 33.21% of the total species present, and
ryegrass accounts for 11.4%. Alkana is the next most
common (17.94%), followed by Lucerne/Medicks
(8.40%), Mallows (8.02%), Plantian (4.58%), White
Broom (3.82%), Catchfly (3.82%), and Goosefoot

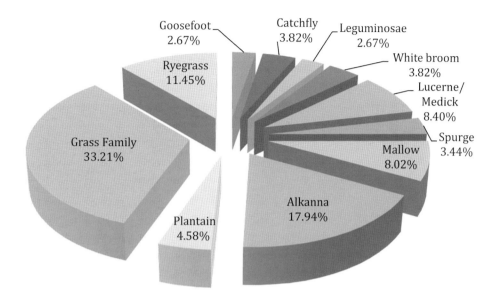

FIG. 10.26 *Percentage of wild plants with greater than 2 percent representation at Humayma (except beet).*

(2.67%). None of the other wild species present constitute greater than 2% of the total, with most representing less than 1%.

Although it is likely that many other plants were grown and used at Humayma, most would not have come in contact with fire and consequently would only have a small chance of being preserved. In contrast, crop species and any associated weeds were susceptible to charring through cooking fires, parching ovens, and kitchen waste disposal regimes.

The following are some of the more common wild species identified and their ecological habitats. *Lolium temulentum* (L.) appears mainly in fields of cereal crops. *Silene* (L.) sp. is associated generally with cultivated fields, sandy soils, and ocean spray; it is also known to grow in vineyards and orchards. *Chenopodium* L. sp. is a common weed in tilled and irrigated fields; it has been cultivated in the past as a bread plant. The seeds of *Chenopodium* are also used medicinally, since they are both highly nutritive and possess large amounts of vitamin C. *Phalarus* (L.) sp. appears in fields and as a weed in crop fields (Blamey and Grey-Wilson 1993). It is apparent from the large number of weeds typically associated with crops that cultivation was being carried out during several occupation periods (e.g.,

Late Roman, Byzantine and Umayyad) in the surrounding hinterlands.

A number of wild species in the sample are associated with fallow fields, roadsides, and waste places. *Alkana* (Tausch.) sp. appears mainly in rocky habitats, waste ground, and roadsides. One alkana species (*Alkana lehmanii* L.) contains a red dye and may have been used in textile production (Blamey and Grey-Wilson 1993). However, as the reference collection did not contain this species, it is difficult to determine if this species is represented at Humayma. *Medicago* (L.) sp. is found in cultivated or fallow fields and roadsides, and *Galium* sp. is associated with grassy habitats, roadsides and olive groves. There is also a good representation in the sample of *Malva* (L.) sp., which is often found in association with waste sites, roadsides, and abandoned fields. This species was also used in the ancient Near East as a mouthwash and an anti-inflammatory.

In addition, there are several weed and wild species that are associated with wet or moist environments. These include *Carex* (L.) sp., which grows in damp or marsh-like environments; *Rumex* (L.) sp., which occurs in swamps and other damp places; *Cladium* P. Br. sp., which is found only in swamps; and *Epilobium* (L.) sp. that generally grows on riverbanks or adjacent to water.

10.D.3. *Interpretation of the Sample*

The representation of archaeobotanical remains is biased by a variety of factors that affect them during all phases of deposition, so it is important to understand all the biases that have affected the sample (Boardman and Jones 1990). The actual plant remains recovered archaeologically and discussed above represent material that was not consumed by the population. If consumed, the material would not have been incorporated in the archaeological record. Furthermore, the carbonization of seeds is not just a process of preservation but also a process of destruction. The final assemblage after charring is determined by the differential preservation rates of each species, and therefore it is difficult to ascertain the original composition of a sample. In consequence, caution must be used when interpreting fossilized assemblages (Wilson 1984; Boardman and Jones 1990). Bias also results from the recovery and sampling techniques utilized. Since population centres in general were not self-sufficient units independent of the area they occupied, it is also essential to examine the role of the surrounding region in order to understand the economy of the site. The concept of how Humayma functioned in the regional economy of the Hisma will be examined only briefly in this report, but it will form the foundations of future research.

The majority of the species identified represent cereals, associated chaff, legumes, fruits, and weeds (Tables 10.12–15; pp. 373–80); most were preserved through carbonization. The botanical remains from Humayma appear to represent various stages of crop processing, including the early stages of crop processing that are rarely detected on archaeological sites. In consequence, it is possible that those samples containing a large quantity of crop by-products such as rachis and culm nodes were deposited in close proximity to either threshing floors or a coarse sieving area. The situation may also indicate that the material is a secondary deposit (fill) that was originally taken from an area where early crop processing took place. Another possible explanation is that the material represents animal dung collected for use as a fuel.

At Humayma, barley (*Hordeum vulgare*) dominates the crop seed assemblage in all periods. As a drought-tolerant species appropriate to the mediocre local soil conditions, it is likely that barley was grown locally at Humayma throughout all occupation periods. In the Early Byzantine period barley appears to be present in greater quantities, possibly representing a more intense local production. Samples from the Ottoman period contained significant quantities of the by-products of crop processing (rachis and culm nodes) (Table 10.14, p. 379), although this may simply be an artefact of preservation or sampling. Barley could be used for groats, biscuits, animal feed, and perhaps beer. The presence of both wheat grain (*Triticum aestivum/ durum*) and wheat chaff indicate that wheat was locally grown and threshed, but the evidence is not as strong as it is for barley. Both rye (*Secale* sp.) and the millet species (*Setaria* sp. and *Panicum* sp.) do not make an appearance until the Byzantine through Islamic periods (Umayyad, Abbasid, and Ottoman). These species are usually found in Africa and may have made in-roads into the Near Eastern economy through the caravan trade.

Lentils (*Lens* sp.) and various legumes constitute the majority of the pulses. Several of the legume species, such as bitter vetch (*Vicia ervilla*), are commonly used as animal fodder, and at Humayma they may have been used to supplement the meagre local pasturage. Lentils are widely cultivated for both human and animal consumption. Like the cereals, legumes either were not intensively cultivated in early occupation periods at Humayma, or they simply were missed in the archaeological contexts sampled.

The most common and identifiable fruits and nuts at the site were figs, olives, grapes, and dates, which were represented through all periods at the site. Fig (*Ficus carica*) has the strongest representation in all occupations period, but, like the rest of the tree and vine crops, it appears to taper off in the Islamic periods (see Table 10.14). It is likely that grapes (*Vitis vinifera*) were being cultivated in small quantities locally in irrigated plots. The pips are present, and one winepress was identified 1.79 km west of the settlement centre (Structure no. 51; *HEP* 1: 149–50). It is also plausible that grapes were imported, as Humayma was a major centre on the local trade route. Olives are identified as *Olea europea,* since they most closely resemble

FIG. 10.27 *Beta sp. seed found in a cache of 302 beet seeds in the Roman Fort (scale: 2 mm).*

this species in the comparison collections and the drawings (Beijerinck 1947). Additional support for the identification of olives as the domesticated variety are the need to provision a relatively large population, and accounts in the early Islamic historians of an olive grove planted by one of the Abbasid overlords of Humayma (*HEP* 1: 61). Figs, being part of the traditional Near Eastern crop complex (wheat, barley, legumes, olives, figs, and dates), could have either been grown locally or brought in by caravan, as figs travel well when dried. Local Bedouin occasionally plant fig trees in the area today. Small quantities of date (*Phoenix dactylifera*) and walnut (*Juglans regia*) were found, but due to the small numbers identified, it is not clear whether these were grown locally or brought in by caravans. Wild date palms can be seen in isolated valleys on the outskirts of the site today.

Plant remains may reveal a change in irrigation practices, as indicated by crop choice, seed size/shape, and characteristic wild species (Miller 1995). There are indications that during the Byzantine through early Islamic periods localized, small-scale irrigation may have been practiced, as some of the weed seeds recovered are hydrophilic (water-loving), such as *Carex* sp., *Rumex* sp., *Cladium* sp., and *Epilobium* sp. (see Table 10.15, p. 380). In the climate of ancient Humayma, it would have been impossible to irrigate large fields of grain crops, and the inhabitants probably planted these crops in fields observed to have been watered by run-off from the winter rains (*HEP* 1: 404–10).

The restriction of these hydrophilic species to the later periods may simply result from the increase in the frequency of crop material recovered from later period samples (Tables 10.14–15).

It is clear that dry farming was employed at Humayma, as there is a large number of weed species that prefer a dry, rocky or sandy habitat, such as *Alkana* sp, *Retama raetam* and *Plantago* sp. (Table 10.15). If some fields were not intensively irrigated, barley (known to be drought-tolerant) would be a reliable crop choice for a dependant population in an arid environment. Irrigated fields are known to produce plumper cereal grains than dry farming fields (Miller 1995). Unfortunately, the size and shape of the identifiably wheat and barley grains are notably consistent throughout the occupation and can therefore not aid in the identification of irrigated farming practices. The expansion of moist habitats or irrigation ditches may be indicated by an increase in weed species that flourish in wet environments.

A cache of 302 beet seeds was recovered from a second-century AD context at the Roman fort (E116.G52.05; 1996.0286) (fig. 10.27). A few other examples were found in fourth-century contexts in the same excavation area (the *Principia*; E116.G81.24, G81.29), and in the Granary (E116.J01.23). There were also a few examples from Umayyad levels in the Abbasid *qasr* (F103.29.05, 37.07, 75.18). Because of similarities in morphology, it is difficult to determine whether they are wild beet seeds (*Beta vulgaris* ssp. *maritima*) or the domesticated variety (*Beta vulgaris* ssp. *vulgaris*). Domesticated beets, however, are mentioned in Babylonia in the eighth century BC, and later on by Theophrastus (371–287 BC), who described the vegetable as having a thick taproot (Zohary and Hopf 2000: 201). Roman and Jewish sources attest to the domesticated beet being present in the Mediterranean (Zohary and Hopf 2000: 201). Beet has been identified at Roman Berenike, where Cappers (2006: 65) noted that its lifecycle fit in well with the extreme desert conditions. Beet (*Beta vulgaris*) can be cultivated for both its leaves and its roots, so it would have been an appropriate choice for cultivation in any kitchen gardens associated with the Roman Fort. Ancient sources frequently mention soldiers at work planting or harvesting crops (Davies 1989:

52–53, 188; Stallibrass and Thomas 2008; Southern 2007: 113), and root vegetables including beets have been found at several Roman military sites (Davies 1971: 133). The recovery of a large quantity of beet seeds from one location may indicate that these seeds were being stored for future planting.

10.D.4. Conclusions

From the information collected during several seasons of recovery of plant remains at Humayma and from the report produced for the 1997 study (Oleson 1997), a definite flora assemblage has been identified for both the cereal/crop items and the wild species. After having examined these remains, it is possible to provide preliminary hypotheses for the identity of the crops that were being exploited, the nature and extent of agricultural irrigation, and the role of wild species in the agricultural regime. The unequal representation of samples from the various occupation periods, however, allows only preliminary conclusions about diachronic trends.

The cereal crops exploited at Humayma were barley, bread wheat, macaroni wheat, rye, broomcorn millet, and foxtail millet. The barley was a reliable, drought-tolerant species that was used by humans and as a fodder crop for animals. The wheat species were used as flour for bread production in the region and appears to have also been locally produced. There were also various legumes, such as lentil, chick pea, bitter vetch, and horse bean. Legumes were used as a reliable source of protein for both human and animal consumption. The fruits and nuts at Humayma were olives, grapes, figs, dates, and walnuts. Most fruits and nuts species were cultivated by this time, however some, such as walnut may have been gathered from wild species and imported to the region.

The subsistence techniques practiced at Humayma were almost certainly mixed farming and animal husbandry at all periods. It is difficult to determine the scale at which agriculture was being practiced, but plant husbandry appears to take the form of intensive agriculture using both small-scale, local irrigation and dry-farming techniques during all periods of site occupation. More samples would be required to clarify the character of irrigation practices. The large proportion of beet seeds recovered may indicate the presence of local kitchen gardens being used for growing pot herbs in the Roman Fort.

The agricultural techniques of irrigation can be determined using the various wild species present in each period, since several wild species will only live in environmentally specific areas. For example, a very high concentration of *Carex* sp. (sedge) is indicative of wet areas. This could be interpreted in two ways: either the environment as a whole was experiencing a wetter period (not likely in this region), or the material was found in an area of intensive irrigation activity. Wild species potentially can aid in site interpretations. Not only do wild species provide general environmental and agricultural data, but they can also provide specific data on local habitats.

The botanical information acquired from Humayma is providing important information about the type of subsistence strategies (diet and economy) practiced by the population and the type of landscape that was present in this part of the Hisma. This kind of evidence may also be vital in identifying other aspects (culture, economic exchange, and natural environment) of the complex societies that once occupied the region. Additional recovery and analysis is necessary to further address important questions and broaden our knowledge of the economy and environment of the site through its various occupations. Likewise, analysis from other sites of this period would undoubtedly aid in our understanding of the economic and ecological changes through time.

Table 10.2 Number of pieces of each animal type found in each field (1989–2005), with the percent within each field, and percent of the total for all fields.

	A104			A107			A115			A117			A118			TOTAL
	# PIECE	% FIELD	% TOTAL	# PIECE	% FIELD	% TOTAL	# PIECE	% FIELD	% TOTAL	# PIECE	% FIELD	% TOTAL	# PIECE	% FIELD	% TOTAL	
Amphibian	-	-	-	-	-	-	-	-	-	-	-	-	-	-	-	54
Aves	-	-	-	-	-	-	-	-	-	-	-	-	-	-	-	395
Bos	-	-	-	-	-	-	-	-	-	-	-	-	-	-	-	157
Camel	-	-	-	-	-	-	-	-	-	-	-	-	-	-	-	386
Canis	-	-	-	-	-	-	-	-	-	-	-	-	-	-	-	6
Capra	-	-	-	-	-	-	-	-	-	-	-	-	-	-	-	802
Carnivore	-	-	-	-	-	-	-	-	-	-	-	-	-	-	-	8
Cervus	-	-	-	-	-	-	-	-	-	-	-	-	-	-	-	11
Coral	-	-	-	-	-	-	-	-	-	-	-	-	-	-	-	1
Equus	-	-	-	-	-	-	-	-	-	-	-	-	-	-	-	315
Felidae	-	-	-	-	-	-	-	-	-	-	-	-	-	-	-	2
G Gallus	1	0.74	0.04	-	-	-	-	-	-	-	-	-	-	-	-	2755
Gazelle	-	-	-	-	-	-	-	-	-	-	-	-	-	-	-	15
Large Bird	-	-	-	-	-	-	-	-	-	-	-	-	-	-	-	59
L Mammal	1	0.74	0.04	10	0.24	0.01	1	1.59	0.02	2	1.00	0.05	-	-	-	4103
L Ungulate	-	-	-	-	-	-	-	-	-	-	-	-	-	-	-	17
Lepus	-	-	-	-	-	-	-	-	-	-	-	-	-	-	-	20
Mammal	-	-	-	-	-	-	-	-	-	-	-	-	-	-	-	91
Marine Shell	-	-	-	-	-	-	-	-	-	-	-	-	-	-	-	246
Medium Bird	1	0.74	0.04	-	-	-	-	-	-	-	-	-	-	-	-	1146
Med Mammal	88	65.18	0.19	-	-	-	40	63.49	0.08	77	38.50	0.16	15	8.20	0.03	47089
Med Rodent	-	-	-	-	-	-	-	-	-	-	-	-	-	-	-	13
Ostrich	-	-	-	-	-	-	-	-	-	-	-	-	-	-	-	4
Ostrich Egg	-	-	-	-	-	-	2	3.17	0.36	-	-	-	-	-	-	371
Ovis	-	-	-	-	-	-	-	-	-	-	-	-	-	-	-	562
Pisces	-	-	-	-	-	-	14	22.22	0.02	-	-	-	1	0.55	0.04	2421
Reptile	-	-	-	-	-	-	-	-	-	-	-	-	-	-	-	4
Rodent	22	16.30	3.32	-	-	-	-	-	-	-	-	-	6	3.28	0.90	663
Sheep/Goat	-	-	-	1	0.41	-	1	1.59	0.02	-	-	-	-	-	-	5209
Small Bird	-	-	-	-	-	-	-	-	-	-	-	-	-	-	-	94
Sm Mammal	1	0.74	0.04	-	-	-	5	7.94	0.62	-	-	-	1	0.55	0.12	801
Sm Rodent	-	-	-	-	-	-	-	-	-	-	-	-	-	-	-	202
Snail Shell	-	-	-	-	-	-	-	-	-	-	-	-	-	-	-	56
Sus	1	0.74	0.04	-	-	-	-	-	-	-	-	-	-	-	-	750

Table 10.2 (cont.)   Number of pieces of each animal type found in each field (1989–2005), with the percent within each field, and percent of the total for all fields.

	A104			A107			A115			A117			A118			TOTAL
	# PIECE	% FIELD	% TOTAL	# PIECE	% FIELD	% TOTAL	# PIECE	% FIELD	% TOTAL	# PIECE	% FIELD	% TOTAL	# PIECE	% FIELD	% TOTAL	
Turtle	-	-	-	-	-	-	-	-	-	-	-	-	-	-	-	1
Ung Tooth	-	-	-	-	-	-	-	-	-	-	-	-	-	-	-	24
Unidentified	1	0.74	0.04	109	44.67	19.12	-	-	-	-	-	-	-	-	-	570
UN-ID Mammal	19	14.07	0.13	124	50.82	0.15	-	-	-	121	60.50	0.84	160	87.43	1.11	14428
UN-ID Shell	-	-	-	-	-	-	-	-	-	-	-	-	-	-	-	132
Total	135	100.00	0.16	244	100.00	0.29	63	100.00	0.08	200	100.00	0.24	183	100.00	0.22	83983
Total ID	24	17.84	0.03	1	0.41	-	17	26.98	0.11	0	-	-	7	3.83	0.05	14984
Total UN-ID	111	82.16	0.16	243	99.59	0.35	46	99.59	0.07	200	73.02	0.29	176	96.17	0.26	68999

	A127			B100			B126			C101			C119			TOTAL
	# PIECE	% FIELD	% TOTAL	# PIECE	% FIELD	% TOTAL	# PIECE	% FIELD	% TOTAL	# PIECE	% FIELD	% TOTAL	# PIECE	% FIELD	% TOTAL	
Amphibian	-	-	-	5	0.10	9.26	-	-	-	-	-	-	-	-	-	54
Aves	-	-	-	73	1.40	18.48	-	-	-	69	0.75	17.47	3	6.67	0.76	395
Bos	-	-	-	2	0.04	1.27	-	-	-	7	0.08	4.46	-	-	-	157
Camel	-	-	-	-	-	-	-	-	-	-	-	-	-	-	-	386
Canis	-	-	-	14	0.27	1.75	-	-	-	1	0.01	16.67	-	-	-	6
Capra	-	-	-	-	-	-	-	-	-	53	0.57	6.61	-	-	-	802
Carnivore	-	-	-	-	-	-	-	-	-	-	-	-	-	-	-	8
Cervus	2	1.98	18.18	-	-	-	-	-	-	2	0.02	18.18	-	-	-	11
Coral	-	-	-	-	-	-	-	-	-	-	-	-	-	-	-	1
Equus	-	-	-	5	0.10	1.59	-	-	-	36	0.39	17.43	-	-	-	315
Felidae	-	-	-	-	-	-	-	-	-	-	-	-	-	-	-	2
G Gallus	1	0.99	0.04	1018	19.54	36.95	-	-	-	41	0.44	1.49	-	-	-	2755
Gazelle	-	-	-	-	-	-	-	-	-	-	-	-	-	-	-	15
Large Bird	-	-	-	6	0.12	10.17	-	-	-	10	0.11	16.95	-	-	-	59
L Mammal	2	1.98	0.05	69	1.32	1.68	-	-	-	508	5.49	12.38	-	-	-	4103
L Ungulate	-	-	-	-	-	-	-	-	-	-	-	-	-	-	-	17
Lepus	-	-	-	-	-	-	-	-	-	-	-	-	-	-	-	20
Mammal	-	-	-	-	-	-	-	-	-	-	-	-	-	-	-	91
Marine Shell	-	-	-	-	-	-	-	-	-	-	-	-	-	-	-	246
Medium Bird	-	-	-	54	1.04	4.71	-	-	-	37	0.40	3.23	-	-	-	1146
Med Mammal	66	65.35	0.14	2296	44.06	4.88	17	94.44	0.04	6714	72.50	14.26	14	31.11	0.03	47089
Med Rodent	-	-	-	10	0.19	76.92	-	-	-	2	0.02	15.39	-	-	-	13

Table 10.2 (cont.) Number of pieces of each animal type found in each field (1989–2005), with the percent within each field, and percent of the total for all fields.

	A127			B100			B126			C101			C119			TOTAL
	# Piece	% Field	% Total	# Piece	% Field	% Total	# Piece	% Field	% Total	# Piece	% Field	% Total	# Piece	% Field	% Total	
Ostrich	-	-	-	-	-	-	-	-	-	-	-	-	-	-	-	4
Ostrich Egg	-	-	-	-	-	-	-	-	-	-	-	-	-	-	-	371
Ovis	6	5.94	0.25	11	0.21	1.96	-	-	-	49	0.53	8.72	-	-	-	562
Pisces	-	-	-	740	14.20	30.57	1	5.56	0.18	476	5.14	19.66	7	15.56	0.29	2421
Reptile	-	-	-	-	-	-	-	-	-	1	0.01	25.00	-	-	-	4
Rodent	1	0.99	0.15	73	1.40	11.00	-	-	-	21	0.23	3.17	-	-	-	663
Sheep/Goat	-	-	-	177	3.40	3.40	-	-	-	559	6.04	0.67	13	28.89	0.25	5209
Small Bird	-	-	-	5	0.10	5.32	-	-	-	1	0.01	1.06	-	-	-	94
Sm Mammal	2	1.98	0.25	31	0.59	3.87	-	-	-	30	0.32	3.75	-	-	-	801
Sm Rodent	-	-	-	20	0.38	9.90	-	-	-	20	0.22	9.90	-	-	-	202
Snail Shell	-	-	-	-	-	-	-	-	-	-	-	-	-	-	-	56
Sus	-	-	-	6	0.12	0.80	-	-	-	9	0.10	1.2	-	-	-	750
Turtle	-	-	-	-	-	-	-	-	-	-	-	-	-	-	-	1
Ung Tooth	-	-	-	-	-	-	-	-	-	-	-	-	-	-	-	24
Unidentified	-	-	-	53	1.02	9.30	-	-	-	24	0.26	4.21	-	-	-	570
UN-ID Mammal	21	20.79	0.15	538	10.32	3.73	-	-	-	584	6.31	4.05	8	17.78	0.06	14428
UN-ID Shell	-	-	-	5	0.10	3.79	-	-	-	7	0.08	5.30	-	-	-	132
Total	101	100.00	0.14	5211	100.00	0.14	18	100.00	0.02	9261	100.00	0.14	45	100.00	0.14	83983
Total ID	10	9.90	0.01	2124	40.76	0.06	1	5.56	0.01	1324	14.30	0.02	23	51.11	0.07	14984
Total UN-ID	91	90.10	0.13	3087	59.24	0.09	17	94.44	0.25	7937	85.70	0.12	22	48.89	0.07	68999

	C124			E077			E116			E121			E122			TOTAL
	# Piece	% Field	% Total	# Piece	% Field	% Total	# Piece	% Field	% Total	# Piece	% Field	% Total	# Piece	% Field	% Total	
Amphibian	-	-	-	-	-	-	7	0.02	12.96	-	-	-	-	-	-	54
Aves	-	-	-	6	0.86	1.52	105	0.35	26.58	-	-	-	-	-	-	395
Bos	-	-	-	1	0.14	-	33	0.11	21.02	-	-	-	-	-	-	157
Camel	-	-	-	-	-	-	8	0.03	2.07	1	0.98	0.26	-	-	-	386
Canis	-	-	-	1	0.14	-	3	0.01	50.00	-	-	-	-	-	-	6
Capra	2	4.65	0.25	12	1.72	1.50	476	1.57	59.35	-	-	-	1	0.56	0.12	802
Carnivore	-	-	-	-	-	-	2	0.01	25.00	-	-	-	-	-	-	8
Cervus	-	-	-	-	-	-	2	0.01	18.18	-	-	-	-	-	-	11

Table 10.2 (cont.) Number of pieces of each animal type found in each field (1989–2005), with the percent within each field, and percent of the total for all fields.

	C124			E077			E116			E121			E122			TOTAL
	# PIECE	% FIELD	% TOTAL	# PIECE	% FIELD	% TOTAL	# PIECE	% FIELD	% TOTAL	# PIECE	% FIELD	% TOTAL	# PIECE	% FIELD	% TOTAL	
Coral	-	-	-	-	-	-	-	-	-	-	-	-	-	-	-	1
Equus	-	-	-	6	0.86	1.90	86	0.28	27.30	-	-	-	6	3.33	1.90	315
Felidae	-	-	-	-	-	-	1	-	50.00	-	-	-	-	-	-	2
G Gallus	1	2.33	0.04	11	1.58	0.40	500	1.65	18.15	-	-	-	-	-	-	2755
Gazelle	-	-	-	-	-	-	13	0.04	86.67	-	-	-	-	-	-	15
Large Bird	-	-	-	-	-	-	24	0.08	40.63	-	-	-	-	-	-	59
L Mammal	2	4.65	0.05	19	2.73	0.02	1047	3.45	25.52	-	-	-	-	-	-	4103
L Ungulate	-	-	-	-	-	-	14	0.05	82.35	-	-	-	-	-	-	17
Lepus	-	-	-	-	-	-	12	0.04	60.00	-	-	-	-	-	-	20
Mammal	-	-	-	-	-	-	88	0.29	96.70	-	-	-	-	-	-	91
Marine Shell	2	4.65	0.81	-	-	-	190	0.63	77.24	5	4.90	2.03	19	10.56	7.72	246
Medium Bird	1	2.33	0.09	14	2.00	1.22	684	2.25	59.69	-	-	-	1	0.56	0.09	1146
Med Mammal	30	69.77	0.06	531	76.18	1.13	15900	52.42	33.77	11	10.78	0.02	-	-	-	47089
Med Rodent	-	-	-	-	-	-	1	-	7.69	-	-	-	-	-	-	13
Ostrich	-	-	-	-	-	-	-	-	-	-	-	-	-	-	-	4
Ostrich Egg	-	-	-	-	-	-	105	0.35	28.30	-	-	-	4	2.22	1.08	362
Ovis	1	2.33	0.18	6	0.86	1.07	289	0.95	51.42	-	-	-	2	1.11	0.36	562
Pisces	-	-	-	-	-	-	551	1.82	22.76	-	-	-	2	1.11	0.08	2421
Reptile	-	-	-	-	-	-	2	0.01	50.00	-	-	-	-	-	-	4
Rodent	-	-	-	-	-	-	127	0.42	19.16	-	-	-	-	-	-	663
Sheep/Goat	4	9.30	0.08	19	2.73	0.36	2045	6.74	39.26	-	-	-	2	1.11	0.04	5209
Small Bird	-	-	-	-	-	-	64	0.21	68.09	-	-	-	-	-	-	94
Sm Mammal	-	-	-	4	0.57	0.50	221	0.73	27.59	-	-	-	-	-	-	801
Sm Rodent	-	-	-	-	-	-	38	0.13	18.81	-	-	-	-	-	-	202
Snail Shell	-	-	-	-	-	-	28	0.09	50.00	-	-	-	-	-	-	56
Sus	-	-	-	5	0.72	0.67	659	2.17	87.87	-	-	-	-	-	-	750
Turtle	-	-	-	-	-	-	-	-	-	-	-	-	-	-	-	1
Ung Tooth	-	-	-	2	0.29	8.33	-	-	-	-	-	-	-	-	-	24
Unidentified	-	-	-	4	0.57	0.70	124	0.41	21.75	-	-	-	-	-	-	570
UN-ID Mammal	-	-	-	56	8.03	0.39	6820	22.48	47.27	81	79.41	0.56	139	77.22	0.96	14428
UN-ID Shell	-	-	-	-	-	-	64	0.21	48.48	4	3.92	-	4	2.22	3.03	132
Total	43	100.00	0.14	697	100.00	0.83	30333	100.00	0.14	102	100.00	0.14	180	100.00	0.14	83974
Total ID	8	18.60	0.03	69	9.90	0.46	5052	16.66	0.02	1	0.98	-	17	9.44	0.01	14984
Total UN-ID	35	81.40	0.12	628	90.10	0.91	25281	83.34	0.12	101	99.02	0.14	163	90.56	0.13	68999

Table 10.2 (cont.) Number of pieces of each animal type found in each field (1989–2005), with the percent within each field, and percent of the total for all fields.

	E125			E128			F102			F103			TOTAL
	# Piece	% Field	% Total	# Piece	% Field	% Total	# Piece	% Field	% Total	# Piece	% Field	% Total	
Amphibian	-	-	-	-	-	-	42	0.37	77.78	-	-	-	54
Aves	4	0.03	1.01	-	-	-	118	1.04	29.87	17	0.16	4.30	395
Bos	34	0.24	21.66	-	-	-	44	0.39	28.03	36	0.35	22.92	157
Camel	376	2.69	97.40	-	-	-	1	0.01	0.26	-	-	-	386
Canis	-	-	-	-	-	-	1	0.01	66.67	-	-	-	6
Capra	92	0.66	11.47	10	0.64	1.25	65	0.58	8.10	77	0.75	9.60	802
Carnivore	-	-	-	-	-	-	6	0.05	75.00	-	-	-	8
Cervus	-	-	-	-	-	-	4	0.04	36.36	1	0.01	9.09	11
Coral	-	-	-	-	-	-	-	-	-	1	0.01	100	1
Equus	40	0.29	12.70	-	-	-	89	0.79	28.25	47	0.46	14.92	315
Felidae	-	-	-	-	-	-	1	0.01	50.00	-	-	-	2
G Gallus	53	0.38	1.92	6	0.38	0.22	1053	9.32	38.22	70	0.68	2.54	2755
Gazelle	2	0.01	13.33	-	-	-	-	-	-	-	-	-	15
Large Bird	1	0.01	1.69	-	-	-	13	0.12	22.03	5	0.05	8.47	59
L Mammal	1000	7.16	24.37	13	0.83	0.32	441	3.90	10.75	988	9.57	24.07	4103
L Ungulate	-	-	-	-	-	-	-	-	-	3	0.03	17.64	17
Lepus	4	0.03	20.00	-	-	-	1	0.01	5.00	3	0.03	15.00	20
Mammal	3	0.02	3.30	-	-	-	-	-	-	-	-	-	91
Marine Shell	18	0.13	7.32	-	-	-	-	-	-	12	0.12	4.88	246
Medium Bird	133	0.95	11.61	7	0.45	0.61	96	0.85	8.38	118	1.14	10.30	1146
Med Mammal	8860	63.42	18.82	1451	92.36	3.08	6482	57.37	13.76	4497	43.55	9.55	47089
Med Rodent	-	-	-	-	-	-	-	-	-	-	-	-	13
Ostrich	-	-	-	-	-	-	-	-	-	4	0.04	100	4
Ostrich Egg	241	1.73	64.96	-	-	-	10	0.09	2.69	11	0.11	2.96	371
Ovis	101	0.72	17.97	17	1.08	3.02	37	0.33	6.58	46	0.45	8.19	562
Pisces	115	0.82	4.75	7	0.45	0.29	325	2.88	13.42	177	1.71	7.31	2421
Reptile	-	-	-	-	-	-	1	0.01	25.00	-	-	-	4
Rodent	76	0.54	11.46	-	-	-	76	0.67	11.46	261	2.53	39.37	663
Sheep/Goat	869	6.22	16.68	25	1.59	0.48	771	6.82	14.80	723	7.00	13.88	5209
Small Bird	9	0.06	9.57	1	0.06	1.06	1	0.01	1.06	13	0.13	13.83	94
Sm Mammal	210	1.50	26.22	-	-	-	183	1.62	22.85	113	1.09	14.11	801
Sm Rodent	-	-	-	-	-	-	13	0.12	6.44	111	1.07	54.95	202
Snail Shell	-	-	-	-	-	-	-	-	-	28	0.27	50.00	56

Table 10.2 (cont.) Number of pieces of each animal type found in each field (1989–2005), with the percent within each field, and percent of the total for all fields.

	E125			E128			F102			F103			TOTAL
	# PIECE	% FIELD	% TOTAL	# PIECE	% FIELD	% TOTAL	# PIECE	% FIELD	% TOTAL	# PIECE	% FIELD	% TOTAL	
Sus	35	0.25	4.67	9	0.57	1.2	22	0.19	2.93	4	0.04	0.53	750
Turtle	-	-	-	-	-	-	-	-	-	1	0.01	100	1
Ung Tooth	-	-	-	-	-	-	22	0.19	91,67	-	-	-	24
Unidentified	65	0.47	11.40	25	1.59	4.39	150	1.33	26.32	15	0.15	2.63	570
UN-ID Mammal	1626	11.64	11.27	-	-	-	1228	10.87	8.51	2903	28.11	20.12	14428
UN-ID Shell	4	0.03	3.03	-	-	-	3	0.03	2.27	41	0.40	31.06	132
Total	13971	100.00	0.14	1571	100.00	1.87	11299	100.00	13.45	10326	100.00	12.29	83983
Total ID	2042	14.62	0.02	74	4.71	0.49	2683	23.75	17.90	1507	14.59	10.06	14984
Total UN-ID	11929	85.38	0.12	1497	95.29	21.70	8616	76.25	12.49	8819	85.41	12.78	68999

Table 10.3 Number of pieces of each animal type found in the six major fields (1989–2005), percent within each field, and percent of total of the six major fields.

	ALL		B100			C101			E116		
	# PIECE	% TOTAL	# PIECE	% FIELD	% TOTAL	# PIECE	% FIELD	% TOTAL	# PIECE	% FIELD	% TOTAL
Amphibian	54	0.07	5	0.10	0.01	-	-	-	7	0.02	0.01
Aves	386	0.48	73	1.40	0.09	69	0.75	0.09	105	0.35	0.15
Bos	156	0.19	2	0.04	-	7	0.08	0.01	33	0.11	0.04
Camel	385	0.48	-	-	-	-	-	-	8	0.03	0.01
Canis	5	0.01	-	-	-	1	0.01	-	3	0.01	-
Capra	777	0.97	14	0.27	0.02	53	0.57	0.07	476	1.57	0.59
Carnivore	8	0.01	-	-	-	-	-	-	2	0.01	-
Cervus	9	0.01	-	-	-	2	0.02	-	2	0.01	-
Coral	1	-	-	-	-	-	-	-	-	-	-
Equus	303	0.38	5	0.10	0.01	36	0.39	0.04	86	0.28	0.11
Felidae	2	-	-	-	-	-	-	-	1	-	-
G Gallus	2735	3.40	1018	19.54	1.27	41	0.44	0.05	500	1.65	0.62
Gazelle	15	0.02	-	-	-	-	-	-	13	0.04	0.02
Large Bird	59	0.07	6	0.12	0.01	10	0.11	0.01	24	0.08	0.03
L Mammal	4053	5.04	69	1.32	0.08	508	5.49	0.63	1047	3.45	1.23
L Ungulate	17	0.02	-	-	-	-	-	-	14	0.05	0.02
Lepus	20	0.02	-	-	-	-	-	-	12	0.04	0.01
Mammal	91	0.11	-	-	-	-	-	-	88	0.29	0.11
Marine Shell	220	0.27	-	-	-	-	-	-	190	0.63	0.24
Medium Bird	1122	1.40	54	1.04	0.07	37	0.40	0.05	684	2.25	0.85
Med Mammal	44749	55.66	2296	44.06	2.86	6714	72.50	8.35	15900	52.42	19.78
Med Rodent	13	0.02	10	0.19	0.01	2	0.02	-	1	-	-
Ostrich	4	-	-	-	-	-	-	-	-	-	-
Ostrich Egg	367	0.46	-	-	-	-	-	-	105	0.35	0.13
Ovis	533	0.66	11	0.21	0.01	49	0.53	0.06	289	0.95	0.36
Pisces	2384	2.97	740	14.20	0.92	476	5.14	0.59	551	1.82	0.69
Reptile	4	-	-	-	-	1	0.01	-	2	0.01	-
Rodent	634	0.79	73	1.40	0.09	21	0.23	0.03	127	0.42	0.16
Sheep/Goat	5144	6.40	177	3.40	0.22	559	6.04	0.69	2045	6.74	2.54
Small Bird	93	0.12	5	0.10	0.01	1	0.01	-	64	0.21	0.08
Sm Mammal	788	0.98	31	0.59	0.04	30	0.32	0.04	221	0.73	0.27
Sm Rodent	202	0.25	20	0.38	0.02	20	0.22	0.02	38	0.13	0.05
Snail Shell	56	0.07	-	-	-	-	-	-	28	0.09	0.03
Sus	735	0.91	6	0.12	0.01	9	0.10	0.01	659	2.17	0.82
Turtle	1	-	-	-	-	-	-	-	-	-	-
Ung Tooth	22	0.28	-	-	-	-	-	-	-	-	-
Unidentified	431	0.54	53	1.02	0.07	24	0.26	0.03	124	0.41	0.15
UN-ID Mammal	13699	17.04	538	10.32	0.67	584	6.31	0.73	6820	22.48	8.48
UN-ID Shell	124	0.15	5	0.10	0.01	7	0.08	0.01	64	0.21	0.08
Total	80401	100	5211	100	6.20	9261	100	11.52	30333	100	37.72
Total ID	14732	18.23	2124	40.76	2.64	1324	14.30	1.65	5052	16.66	6.23
Total UN-ID	65669	81.68	3087	59.24	3.84	7937	85.70	9.87	25281	83.34	31.44

Table 10.3 (cont.)   Number of pieces of each animal type found in the six major fields (1989–2005), percent within each field, and percent of total of the six major fields.

	E125			F102			F103		
	# PIECE	% FIELD	% TOTAL	# PIECE	% FIELD	% TOTAL	# PIECE	% FIELD	% TOTAL
Amphibian	-	-	-	42	0.37	0.05		-	-
Aves	4	0.03	-	118	1.04	0.15	17	0.16	0.02
Bos	34	0.24	0.04	44	0.39	0.05	36	0.35	0.04
Camel	376	2.69	0.47	1	0.01	-	-	-	-
Canis	-	-	-	1	0.01	-	-	-	-
Capra	92	0.66	0.11	65	0.58	0.08	77	0.75	0.10
Carnivore	-	-	-	6	0.05	0.01	-	-	-
Cervus	-	-	-	4	0.04	-	1	0.01	-
Coral	-	-	-	-	-	-	1	0.01	-
Equus	40	0.29	0.05	89	0.79	0.11	47	0.46	0.06
Felidae	-	-	-	1	0.01	-	-	-	-
G Gallus	53	0.38	0.07	1053	9.32	1.31	70	0.68	0.09
Gazelle	2	0.01	-	-	-	-	-	-	-
Large Bird	1	0.01	-	13	0.12	0.02	5	0.05	0.01
L Mammal	1000	7.16	1.24	441	3.90	0.55	988	9.57	1.23
L Ungulate	-	-	-	-	-	-	3	0.03	-
Lepus	4	0.03	-	1	0.01	-	3	0.03	-
Mammal	3	0.02	-	-	-	-	-	-	-
Marine Shell	18	0.13	0.02	-	-	-	12	0.12	0.01
Medium Bird	133	0.95	0.16	96	0.85	0.12	118	1.14	0.15
Med Mammal	8860	63.42	11.02	6482	57.37	8.06	4497	43.55	5.59
Med Rodent	-	-	-	-	-	-	-	-	-
Ostrich	-	-	-	-	-	-	4	0.04	-
Ostrich Egg	241	1.73	0.30	10	0.09	0.01	11	0.11	0.01
Ovis	101	0.72	0.13	37	0.33	0.05	46	0.45	0.06
Pisces	115	0.82	0.14	325	2.88	0.40	177	1.71	0.22
Reptile	-	-	-	1	0.01	-	-	-	-
Rodent	76	0.54	0.09	76	0.67	0.09	261	2.53	0.32
Sheep/Goat	869	6.22	1.08	771	6.82	0.96	723	7.00	0.90
Small Bird	9	0.06	0.01	1	0.01	-	13	0.13	0.02
Sm Mammal	210	1.50	0.26	183	1.62	0.23	113	1.09	0.14
Sm Rodent	-	-	-	13	0.12	0.02	111	1.07	0.14
Snail Shell	-	-	-	-	-	-	28	0.27	0.03
Sus	35	0.25	0.04	22	0.19	0.03	4	0.04	-
Turtle	-	-	-	-	-	-	1	0.01	-
Ung Tooth	-	-	-	22	0.19	0.03	-	-	-
Unidentified	65	0.47	0.08	150	1.33	0.19	15	0.15	0.02
UN-ID Mammal	1626	11.64	2.02	1228	10.87	1.53	2903	28.11	3.61
UN-ID Shell	4	0.03	-	3	0.03	-	41	0.40	0.05
Total	13971	100	17.38	11299	100	14.05	10326	100	12.84
Total ID	2042	14.62	2.54	2683	23.75	3.33	1507	14.59	1.87
Total UN-ID	11929	85.38	14.84	8616	76.25	10.71	8819	85.41	10.97

Table 10.4   Number of identified pieces of each animal type found in the six major fields (1989–2005), percent within each field, and percent of the total of the six major fields.

	ALL		B100			C101			E116		
	# PIECES	% OF TOTAL	# PIECES	% FIELD TOTAL	% ALL TOTAL	# PIECES	% FIELD TOTAL	% ALL TOTAL	# PIECES	% FIELD TOTAL	% ALL TOTAL
Amphibian	54	0.37	5	0.24	0.03		-	-	7	0.14	0.05
Aves	386	2.62	73	3.44	0.50	69	5.21	0.47	105	2.08	0.71
Bos	156	1.06	2	0.09	0.01	7	0.53	0.05	33	0.65	0.22
Camel	385	2.61	-	-	-	-	-	-	8	0.16	0.05
Canis	5	0.03	-	-	-	1	0.08	0.01	3	0.06	0.02
Capra	777	5.27	14	0.66	0.10	53	4.00	0.36	476	9.42	3.23
Cervus	9	0.06	-	-	-	2	0.15	0.01	2	0.04	0.01
Coral	1	0.01	-	-	-	-	-	-	-	-	-
Equus	303	2.06	5	0.24	0.03	36	2.72	0.24	86	1.70	0.58
Felidae	2	0.01	-	-	-	-	-	-	1	0.02	0.01
Gallus Gallus	2735	18.57	1018	47.93	6.91	41	3.10	0.28	500	9.90	3.39
Gazelle	15	0.10	-	-	-	-	-	-	13	0.26	0.09
Lepus	20	0.14	-	-	-	-	-	-	12	0.24	0.08
Ostrich	4	0.03	-	-	-	-	-	-	-	-	-
Ostrich Shell	367	2.49	-	-	-	-	-	-	105	2.08	0.71
Ovis	533	3.62	11	0.52	0.07	49	3.70	0.33	289	5.72	1.96
Pisces	2384	16.18	740	34.84	5.02	476	35.95	3.23	551	10.91	3.74
Reptile	4	0.03	-	-	-	1	0.08	0.01	2	0.04	0.01
Rodent	634	4.30	73	3.44	0.50	21	1.59	0.14	127	2.51	0.86
Sheep/Goat	5144	34.92	177	8.33	1.20	559	42.22	3.79	2045	40.48	13.88
Snail Shell	56	0.38	-	-	-	-	-	-	28	0.55	0.19
Sus	735	4.99	6	0.28	0.04	9	0.68	0.06	659	13.04	4.47
Turtle	1	0.01	-	-	-	-	-	-	-	-	-
Ungulate Tooth	22	0.15	-	-	-	-	-	-	-	-	-
TOTAL:	14732	100	2124	100	14.42	1324	100	8.99	5052	100	34.29

Table 10.4 (cont.)   Number of identified pieces of each animal type found in the six major fields (1989–2005), percent within each field, and percent of the total of the six major fields.

	E125			F102			F103		
	# PIECES	% FIELD TOTAL	% ALL TOTAL	# PIECES	% FIELD TOTAL	% ALL TOTAL	# PIECES	% FIELD TOTAL	% ALL TOTAL
Amphibian	-	-	-	42	1.57	0.29		-	-
Aves	4	0.20	0.03	118	4.40	0.80	17	1.13	0.12
Bos	34	1.67	0.23	44	1.64	0.30	36	2.39	0.24
Camel	376	18.41	2.55	1	0.04	0.01	-	-	-
Canis	-	-	-	1	0.04	0.01	-	-	-
Capra	92	4.51	0.62	65	2.42	0.44	77	5.11	0.52
Cervus	-	-	-	4	0.15	0.03	1	0.07	0.01
Coral	-	-	-	-	-	-	1	0.07	0.01
Equus	40	1.96	0.27	89	3.32	0.60	47	3.12	0.32
Felidae	-	-	-	1	0.04	0.01	-	-	-
Gallus Gallus	53	2.60	0.36	1053	39.25	7.15	70	4.64	0.48
Gazelle	2	0.10	0.01	-	-	-	-	-	-
Lepus	4	0.20	0.03	1	0.04	0.01	3	0.20	0.02
Ostrich	-	-	-	-	-	-	4	0.27	0.03
Ostrich Shell	241	11.80	1.64	10	0.37	0.07	11	0.73	0.07
Ovis	101	4.95	0.69	37	1.38	0.25	46	3.05	0.31
Pisces	115	5.63	0.78	325	12.11	2.21	177	11.75	1.20
Reptile	-	-	-	1	0.04	0.01	-	-	-
Rodent	76	3.72	0.52	76	2.83	0.52	261	17.32	1.77
Sheep/Goat	869	42.56	5.90	771	28.74	5.23	723	47.98	4.91
Snail Shell	-	-	-	-	-	-	28	1.86	0.19
Sus	35	1.71	0.24	22	0.82	0.15	4	0.27	0.03
Turtle	-	-	-	-	-	-	1	0.07	0.01
Ungulate Tooth	-	-	-	22	0.82	0.15	-	-	-
TOTAL:	2042	100	13.86	2683	100	18.21	1507	100	10.23

Table 10.5 Number of pieces of important animals across the six major fields (1989–2005). This table was used to run a Chi Square analysis of the major material at the site.

	B100	C101	E116	E125	F102	F103	TOTAL
Aves	73	69	105	4	118	17	386
Bos	2	7	33	34	44	36	156
Camel			8	376	1		385
Capra	14	53	476	92	65	77	777
Equus	5	36	86	40	89	47	303
Gallus Gallus	1018	41	500	53	1053	70	2735
Large Bird	6	10	24	1	13	5	59
Large Mammal	69	508	1047	1000	441	988	4053
Marine Shell			190	18		12	220
Medium Bird	54	37	684	133	96	118	1122
Medium Mammal	2296	6714	15900	8860	6482	4497	44749
Ostrich Egg			105	241	10	11	367
Ovis	11	49	289	101	37	46	533
Pisces	740	476	551	115	325	177	2384
Rodent	73	21	127	76	76	261	634
Sheep/Goat	177	559	2045	869	771	723	5144
Small Bird	5	1	64	9	1	13	93
Small Mammal	31	30	221	210	183	113	788
Small Rodent	20	20	38		13	111	202
Sus	6	9	659	35	22	4	735
Unidentified	53	24	124	65	150	15	431
Unidentified Mammal	538	584	6820	1626	1228	2903	13699
TOTAL	5191	9250	30096	13958	11218	10244	79955

Table 10.6   Carcass yield estimates for modern and pre-modern era materials.

Species	Modern			Pre-modern Estimates		
	Dressing Percentage	Bones, %	Meat Yield, %	Dressing Percentage	Bones, %	Meat Yield, %
Cattle (625 kg)	62–64	13–15	63–64	56–58	14–16	63–65
Sheep (80 kg)	52–54	16–18	72–73	48–50	17–19	45–47
Swine (100 kg)	72–74	11–13	55–57	66–68	12–14	48–52
Turkeys	78.6					
Broiler Chickens Male, n = 7	73.1					
Broiler Chickens Female, n = 7	72.8					
Ostrich 10–14 mo, n = 14	58.6					

Table 10.7   Percentages of sheep/goats in identified assemblages (with medium mammal) recovered at selected sites in the Near East.

Site	Time Period	% of sheep/goats
Habuba Kabira	Middle Bronze	71.2
Refaim Valley	Middle Bronze	65.3
Mount Ebal	Iron I	65.0
Tel Yoqneam	Persian	51.0
Tel Yoqneam	Hellenistic	26.0
Tell Nimrin	Late Hellenistic-Roman	76.9
Tell Nimrin	Byzantine	75.5
Tell Nimrin	Islamic	71.0
Humayma	Roman (E116)	61.7
Humayma	Roman (E125)	77.2
Humayma	Byzantine to Early Islamic (F102)	65.1
Humayma	Byzantine (B100, C101)	67.9
Humayma	Early Islamic (F103)	51.7
Petra (ez-Zantur)	Byzantine	87.0
Petra (al-Wu'ayra)	Crusader (12c)	36.3

Table 10.8   Percentages of cattle in identified assemblage recovered from selected sites in the Near East.

SITE	TIME PERIOD	% OF CATTLE
Habuba Kabira	Middle Bronze	12.5
Refaim Valley	Middle Bronze	18.5
Mount Ebal	Iron I	21.0
Tel Yoqneam	Hellenistic	52.5
Tel Yoqneam	Persian	41.0
Tell Nimrin	Persian	12.9
Tell Nimrin	Late Hellenistic-Roman	14.8
Tell Nimrin	Byzantine	16.3
Tell Nimrin	Islamic	14.4
Humayma	Roman (E116)	1.7
Humayma	Roman (E125)	1.8
Humayma	Byzantine to Early Islamic (F102)	1.7
Humayma	Byzantine (B100, C101)	0.5
Humayma	Early Islamic (F103)	3.0
Petra (ez-Zantur)	Byzantine	1.0
Petra (al-Wu'ayra)	Crusader (12C)	11.8

Table 10.9   Percentages of pigs recovered in identified assemblage from selected sites in the Near East.

SITE	TIME PERIOD	% OF PIGS
Habuba Kabira	Middle Bronze	0.3
Refaim Valley	Middle Bronze	8.2
Mount Ebal	Iron I	0.0
Tel Yoqneam	Hellenistic	15.5
Tel Yoqneam	Persian	2.0
Tell Nimrin	Persian	0.1
Tell Nimrin	Late Hellenistic-Roman	0.8
Tell Nimrin	Byzantine	0.7
Tell Nimrin	Islamic	2.3
Humayma	Roman (E116)	13.0
Humayma	Roman (E125)	1.7
Humayma	Byzantine to Early Islamic (F102)	0.8
Humayma	Byzantine (B100, C101)	1.0
Humayma	Early Islamic (F103)	0.3
Petra (ez-Zantur)	Byzantine	4.0
Petra (al-Wu'ayra)	Crusader (12C)	12.0

Table 10.10 Percentages of equids in identified assemblage recovered from selected sites in the Near East.

SITE	TIME PERIOD	% OF EQUIDS
Habuba Kabira	Middle Bronze	1.0
Refaim Valley	Middle Bronze	7.5
Mount Ebal	Iron I	0.0
Tel Yoqneam	Hellenistic	1.1
Tel Yoqneam	Persian	0.0
Tell Nimrin	Persian	5.2
Tell Nimrin	Late Hellenistic-Roman	0.18
Tell Nimrin	Byzantine	0.35
Tell Nimrin	Islamic	0.26
Humayma	Roman (E116)	1.7
Humayma	Roman (E125)	2.0
Humayma	Byzantine-Early Islamic (F102)	3.3
Humayma	Byzantine (B100, C101)	1.2
Humayma	Early Islamic (F103)	3.1
Petra (ez-Zantur)	Byzantine	2.0
Petra (al-Wuʻayra)	Crusader (12C)	0.4

Table 10.11 Percentages of wild fauna in identified assemblage recovered from selected sites in the Near East.

SITE	TIME PERIOD	% OF WILD FAUNA
Habuba Kabira	Middle Bronze	9.2
Refaim Valley	Middle Bronze	<1.0
Mount Ebal	Iron 1	14.0
Tel Yoqneam	Hellenistic	3.0
Tel Yoqneam	Persian	6.0
Tell Nimrin	Persian	<2.0
Tell Nimrin	Late Hellenistic-Roman	0.18
Tell Nimrin	Byzantine	<1.0
Tell Nimrin	Islamic	<1.0
Humayma	Roman (E116)	0.6
Humayma	Roman (E125)	0.3
Humayma	Byzantine-Early Islamic (F102)	2.0
Humayma	Byzantine (B100, C101)	0.3
Humayma	Early Islamic (F103)	3.2
Petra (ez-Zantur)	Byzantine	4.0
Petra (al-Wuʻayra)	Crusader (12C)	2.2

Table 10.12 Catalogue of analyzed flotation samples (arranged by bucket number).

SAMPLE	BUCKET	FIELD/AREA	PERIOD	CONTEXT
010	1995.0010	F103.02.04	MN, UM, AB, OT	Abbasid *qasr*
012	1995.0015	F103.02.16	MN, UM, AB, OT	Abbasid *qasr*
023	1995.0044	E116.H42.05	MN, LR, EB	Roman Fort
007	1995.0104	F103.02.17	UM	Abbasid *qasr*
004	1995.0113	F103.02.13	MN, LN, LB, UM, AB	Abbasid *qasr*
018	1995.0132	F102.16.09	MN, LN, LB, UM, AB	Byzantine Church and Umayyad Structure
014	1995.0137	E116.H41.06	MN, RO, EB	Roman Fort
102	1995.0159	F103.02.13	MN, LR, UM, AB	Abbasid *qasr*
009	1995.0236	E116.H43.08	MN, LR, EB	Roman Fort
005	1995.0281	E116.H42.13	MN, LR, EB	Roman Fort
099	1995.0330	E116.D.17	MN, RO, EB	Roman Fort
021	1995.0336	E116.H40.03	MN, RO	Roman Fort
008	1995.0441	F103.96.08	MN, UM	Abbasid *qasr*
006	1995.0443	F103.92.12	UM	Abbasid *qasr*
100	1995.0454	E116.G41.05	MN	Roman Fort
015	1995.0480	E116.G56.22	MN, EB, MB	Roman Fort
017	1995.0493	E122.02.15	MN	House
001	1995.0527	E116.H41.15	RO, MN	Roman Fort
002	1995.0529	E116.H41.16	MN, RO	Roman Fort
020	1995.0543	E125.05.06	MN, LR, EB, MB	Nab/Roman complex
013	1995.0555	F103.81.01	MN, RO, MB, OT	Abbasid *qasr*
019	1995.0562	E116.H42.22	MN	Roman Fort
101	1995.0562	E116.H42.22	MN	Roman Fort
011	1995.0572	E116.D.16	MN, LN, RO, LR, EB	Roman Fort
003	1995.0591	E122.06.11	MN, RO	Nabataean House
022	1995.0603	F103.81.07	UM, OT	Abbasid *qasr*
016	1995.0697	E116.H42.29	MN, RO	Roman Fort
044	1996.0158	F103.14.09	MN, UM, AB	Abbasid *qasr*
046	1996.0158	F103.14.09	MN, UM, AB	Abbasid *qasr*
030	1996.0251	E116.H52.13	MN	Roman Fort
038	1996.0277	E116.G81.24.3	RO	Roman Fort
040	1996.0286	E116.G52.05	MN, RO	Roman Fort
028	1996.0298	E116.G81.29	MN, LR, EB, MB, LB	Roman Fort
026	1996.0317	E116.H41.33	MN, EB, LR	Roman Fort
035	1996.0346	E116.G81.18	MN, LR, EB	Roman Fort
037	1996.0349	E116.G81.18	MN, LR, EB	Roman Fort
041	1996.0354	E116.G81.18	MN, LR, EB	Roman Fort
034	1996.0357	E116.G81.22	MN	Roman Fort
025	1996.0365	E116.G81.24	MN, RO, EB	Roman Fort

Table 10.12 (cont.)　　Catalogue of analyzed flotation samples (arranged by bucket number).

Sample	Bucket	Field/Area	Period	Context
042	1996.0366	E116.G81.25	LN, RO	Roman Fort
039	1996.0384	E116.H32.08	MN, RO	Roman Fort
031	1996.0402	F103.02G/H.25	UM or later	Abbasid *qasr*
027	1996.0477	E116.H31.08	MN, RO	Roman Fort
033	1996.0492	E116.G80.05	MN, RO	Roman Fort
029	1996.0524	E125.02.08	MN, MB, LB	Nab/Roman complex
043	1996.0524	E125.02.08	MN, UM, AB	Nab/Roman complex
032	1996.0591	E125.02.21.1	UM, AB	Nab/Roman complex
024	1996.0679	E116.G81.33	MN, LR, EB	Roman Fort
045	1996.0692	E116.H42.30	MN, RO	Roman Fort
098	1996.0704	E077.04.12	MN, LN, EB, UM	Bath Building
064	1998.0032	F103.78.16.1	MN, MB	Abbasid *qasr*
066	1998.0068	F103.29.05	MN, MB, UM, OT	Abbasid *qasr*
049	1998.0097	F103.37.08	MB	Abbasid *qasr*
144	1998.0173	E125.06.12	MN, LR, EB	Nab/Roman complex
132	1998.0174	E125.06.12	ER, RO, LR	Nab/Roman complex
134	1998.0174	E125.06.12	ER, RO, LR	Nab/Roman complex
063	1998.0195	E125.07.04	MN, EB	Nab/Roman complex
154	1998.0205	F103.75.18	MN, MB, OT	Abbasid *qasr*
059	1998.0221	F103.42.00	MB, UM, OT	Abbasid *qasr*
060	1998.0240	F103.37.10	MB, OT	Abbasid *qasr*
055	1998.0242	F103.37.07	MB	Abbasid *qasr*
058	1998.0250	F103.57.06	UM	Abbasid *qasr*
051	1998.0251	F103.57.06	UM	Abbasid *qasr*
056	1998.0258	F103.01A.12	MN, MB	Abbasid *qasr*
057	1998.0258	F103.75.19	OT	Abbasid *qasr*
052	1998.0350	E125.04B.28	MN, MB	Nab/Roman complex
140	1998.0354	E125.06.17	EB	Nab/Roman complex
152	1998.0381	E125.06.27	MN, EB	Nab/Roman complex
067	1998.0386	E125.02.31	EB	Nab/Roman complex
053	1998.0395	E125.06.31	MN, RO	Nab/Roman complex
050	1998.0398	E125.04B.34	MN, EB	Nab/Roman complex
130	1998.0398	E125.04B.34	ER, RO, LR	Nab/Roman complex
061	1998.0438	E125.06.43	MN, LR, EB	Nab/Roman complex
047	1998.0499	F103.11.01	MN, MB	Abbasid *qasr*
054	1998.0538	E125.08.14	MN, EB	Nab/Roman complex
145	1998.0538	E125.08.14	RO	Nab/Roman complex
062	1998.0543	E125.06.46	MN, MB	Nab/Roman complex
065	1998.0545	E125.07.27	MN, EB	Nab/Roman complex
048	1998.0581	E125.08.13	MN	Nab/Roman complex

Table 10.12 (cont.)   Catalogue of analyzed flotation samples (arranged by bucket number).

SAMPLE	BUCKET	FIELD/AREA	PERIOD	CONTEXT
075	2000.0116	E116.J01.10	RO	Roman Fort
076	2000.0140	E116.J01.23	MN, RO, LR, EB	Roman Fort
071	2000.0185	E116.J02.13	LR	Roman Fort
079	2000.0261	E125.11.04	EB	Nab/Roman complex
081	2000.0265	E125.13.08	EB	Nab/Roman complex
070	2000.0336	E125.07.37	MN	Nab/Roman complex
077	2000.0346	E125.13.12	MN	Nab/Roman complex
069	2000.0427	E116.J02.22	MN	Roman Fort
087	2000.0563	E116.H40.11	LR, EB	Roman Fort
074	2000.0601	E125.14.24	MN, LN	Nab/Roman complex
086	2000.0632	E125.09.44	MN, LR	Nab/Roman complex
088	2000.0665	E125.26.03	MN, LR	Nab/Roman complex
082	2000.0667	E125.26.03	MN	Nab/Roman complex
068	2000.0676	E125.11.11	LN, EB	Nab/Roman complex
078	2000.0697	E125.12.51	MN	Nab/Roman complex
073	2000.0701	E125.22.44	EN, MN	Nab/Roman complex
083	2000.0707	E125.11.32	MN, LN, RO	Nab/Roman complex
080	2000.0776	E125.pipe probe.08	EB?	Nab/Roman complex
085	2000.0814	E116.H39.54	RO, EB	Roman Fort
084	2000.0817	E116.H39.50	RO	Roman Fort
097	2000.0861	E116.L01.09	RO, LR	Roman Fort
072	2000.0869	E116.J02.25	LR, EB	Roman Fort
089	2000.HWS	A02.T01.10	MN, LR, EB	Tombs
090	2000.HWS	A02.T01.06	MN, LR, EB	Tombs
096	2002.0058	F103.87.14	UM	Abbasid *qasr*
091	2002.0061	F103.27.08	N/D	Abbasid *qasr*
093	2002.0075	F103.16.05	UM	Abbasid *qasr*
092	2002.0174	F103.40.10	UM	Abbasid *qasr*
095	2002.0267	F103.39.06	UM	Abbasid *qasr*
094	2002.0290	F103.08.09	UM	Abbasid *qasr*
106	2004.0038	E125.30.06	MN	Nab/Roman complex
127	2004.0052	E125.29.38	MN	Nab/Roman complex
104	2004.0353	E116.62.09	MN, RO	Roman Fort
109	2004.0414	E116.I07.16	MN, RO, EB	Roman Fort
135	2004.0456	E116.N06.16	RO, EB	Roman Fort
110	2004.0489	E116.N01.23	RO	Roman Fort
128	2004.0489	E116.N01.23	RO	Roman Fort
107	2004.0502	E125.14.54	MN, RO, LR, EB	Nab/Roman complex
105	2004.0611	E116.I10.27	MN, RO, EB	Roman Fort
125	2004.0611	E116.I10.27	MN, RO, EB	Roman Fort

Table 10.12 (cont.)   Catalogue of analyzed flotation samples (arranged by bucket number).

Sample	Bucket	Field/Area	Period	Context
103	2004.0624	E116.N01.39	MN	Roman Fort
108	2004.0629	E116.N01.40	MN	Roman Fort
147	2005.0039	E125.20.501	MN, RO	Nab/Roman complex
112	2005.0088	E125.20.511	LR	Nab/Roman complex
121	2005.0094	E125.16.505	ER, RO, LR, EB	Nab/Roman complex
148	2005.0135	E125.24.508	MN, RO	Nab/Roman complex
114	2005.0142	E125.20.522	MN, RO	Nab/Roman complex
116	2005.0150	E125.20.520	ER, RO	Nab/Roman complex
115	2005.0151	E125.20.521	MN, RO	Nab/Roman complex
142	2005.0152	E125.15.505	MN, LN, RO, LR	Nab/Roman complex
120	2005.0154	E125.16/08.514	ER, RO, MB, LB	Nab/Roman complex
111	2005.0170	E125.20.525	ER, RO	Nab/Roman complex
113	2005.0183	E125.28.501	ER, RO	Nab/Roman complex
133	2005.0205	E128.15.10	ER, RO	Nab/Roman building
117	2005.0221	E125.22.512	ER, RO, LR, EB	Nab/Roman complex
119	2005.0252	E128.15.21	ER, RO	Nab/Roman building
118	2005.0264	E128.15.26	LR, EB	Nab/Roman building
129	2005.0328	E116.I18.06	MN, RO	Roman Fort
150	2005.0330	E116.J13.10	MN, RO	Roman Fort
131	2005.0342	E116.I18.09	RO	Roman Fort
122	2005.0345	E116.I18.08	LR, EB	Roman Fort
136	2005.0355	E116.N06.14	MN, RO, LR, EB	Roman Fort
139	2005.0404	E116.J21.05	LR, EB	Roman Fort
138	2005.0468	E116.N12.03	LR, EB	Roman Fort
151	2005.0490	E116.J26.05	MN, RO	Roman Fort
149	2005.0501	E116.J25.12	MN, RO, EB	Roman Fort
143	2005.0523	E116.J24.22	MN, EB	Roman Fort
123	2005.0607	E116.I14.07	RO	Roman Fort
126	2005.0627	E116.N03.23	MN, RO	Roman Fort
124	2005.0630	E116.N02.27	RO	Roman Fort
137	2005.0636	E116.I29.08	LR, EB	Roman Fort
153	2005.0670	E116.N02.30	MN, RO	Roman Fort
146	2005.0721	E116.J17.09	RO	Roman Fort

Table 10.13 List of identified taxa.

CATEGORY	SCIENTIFIC NAME	COMMON NAME
CEREALS	*Hordeum vulgare* L.	Barley
	Triticum aestivum L.	Bread Wheat
	Triticum durum Desf.	Macaroni Wheat
	Secale L. *sp.*	Rye
	Setaria (L.) *Beauv. sp.*	Foxtail Millet
	Panicum L. *sp.*	Broomcorn Millet
LEGUMES	*Vicia ervilia* L.	Bitter Vetch
	Lens culinaris Medik.	Lentil
	Vicia faba L.	Horse Bean
	Cicer arietinum L.	Chick pea
	Lathryus L. *sp.*	Vetchling
FRUIT AND NUT	*Olea europaea* L.	Olive
	Vitis vinifera L.	Grape
	Ficus carica L.	Fig
	Phoenix dactylifera L.	Date
	Juglans regia L.	Walnut
	Prunus L. sp.	Prunus
WILD AND WEED SPECIES	*Rumex* L. sp.	Dock/Sorrel
	Chenopodium L. sp.	Fat Hen (*C. album*)
	Suaeda Forssk. ex J.F. Gmel. sp.	Seablite
	Beta L. sp.	Beet
	Atriplex L. sp.	Orache
	Amaranthus L. sp.	Pigweed
	Cerastium L. sp.	Mouse-ear chickweed
	Silene L. sp.	Cathfly/Campion
	Adonis L. sp.	Pheasant's Eye
	Fumaria L. sp.	Fumitory
	Retama raetam (Corynella) DC. sp.	White broom

Table 10.13 (cont.)   List of identified taxa.

Category	Scientific Name	Common Name
Wild and Weed Species (cont.)	*Astragulus* L. sp.	Milk-vetch, Wild-lentil
	Melilotus P. Mill. sp.	Melilot
	Trigonella L. sp.	Trigonellas/Fenugreek
	Medicago L. sp.	Lucerne/Medick
	Trifloium L. sp.	Clover
	Coronilla L. sp.	Scorpion vetch
	Oxalis L. sp.	Sorrel
	Geranium L. sp.	Geranium
	Erodium L'Her. ex Ait. sp.	Stork's bill
	Euphorbia L. sp.	Spurge
	Malva L. sp.	Mallow
	Viola L. sp.	Violet
	Epilobrium L. sp.	Willowherb
	Galium L. sp.	Woodruff/Bedstraw
	Alkanna Tausch sp.	Alkanna
	Arnebia Forssk. sp.	Arnebia
	Ajuga L. sp.	Bugle
	Scutellaria L. sp.	Skullcaps
	Plantago L. sp.	Plantain
	Lolium temulentum L.	Ryegrass
	Phalaris L. sp.	Canary Grass
	Carex L. sp.	Sedge
	Cladium P. Br. sp.	Sawgrass
	Rubus L. sp.	Berry
	Hypericum L.sp.	St. John's Wort
	Androsace MaximaL.	Greater Rockjasmine

Table 10.14 Summary of botanical data for Humayma by period (crop species only). Numbers of seeds.

PERIOD	MN	MN-RO	ER-LR	MN-EB	MN-MB	UM	AB	OT
NUMBER OF SAMPLES	12	12	18	30	10	7	6	4
Hordeum vulgare L.	12	2	13	135	57	33	2	24
Hordeum vulgare L. –rachis	12	-	8	16	7	3	10	66
Triticum aestivum/durum L.	-	-	1	26	-	1	-	1
Triticum aestivum L. rachis	1	-	2	1	-	-	-	2
Triticum durum L. rachis	-	-	-	2	-	-	-	1
Triticum sp.- Wheat grain	10	2	1	2	1	3	1	1
Triticum sp.- Wheat rachis	9	-	-	8	1	3	-	-
Secale sp.	-	-	-	-	2	1	-	-
cf. *Secale* sp. -	-	-	-	-	-	-	-	4
cf. *Secale* sp. Rachis	-	-	-	-	-	-	-	1
Setaria sp.	-	-	-	4	-	1	2	4
Panicum sp. L.	-	-	-	-	-	-	-	2
Cereal Grain indet.	12	2	8	66	23	4	-	13
Culm node	3	2	7	7	2	7	2	20
Vicia sp.- Legume	-	-	1	4	-	-	-	1
Vicia faba	1	-	-	4	2	-	-	-
Vicia ervilla -	-	-	-	1	1	-	-	-
Cicer arietinum L.	-	-	1	-	1	-	-	-
Lathryus sp.	-	-	1	-	-	-	-	-
Large Legume	1	1	5	10	9	1	3	6
Lens sp.	1	-	1	15	1	1	-	-
Ficus carica L.	117	17	30	71	34	2	4	1
Olea europaea L.	1	-	1	7	-	-	-	-
Vitis vinifera -	1	2	2	8	4	1	1	1
Phoenix dactylifera	3	1	2	4	3	-	-	-
Juglans regia L.	-	-	-	1	1	-	-	-
nutshell indet.	1	-	1	-	-	-	-	-
Prunus sp.	-	-	1	-	-	-	-	-
TOTALS	185	29	86	392	149	61	25	148

Table 10.15 Summary of botanical data by period for Humayma (weed/wild species only; *Beta* sp. may be domesticated). Numbers of seeds.

Period	MN	MN-RO	MN-RO	MN-EB	MN-MB	UM	AB	OT
Number of Samples	12	12	18	30	10	7	6	4
Rumex sp.	1	-	-	-	-	-	-	-
Chenopodium sp.	1	1	-	2	-	-	2	1
Sueda sp.	-	-	-	-	-	1	-	-
Beta sp.	-	302	-	6	13	10	-	-
Atriplex sp.	-	-	-	-	1	-	-	-
Amaranthus sp.	1	-	1	-	-	-	-	-
Caryophyllaceae	2	-	-	-	-	-	-	-
Cerastium sp.	-	-	-	-	-	-	1	-
Silene sp.	5	-	1	1	-	1	2	-
Adonis sp. Type	-	-	-	-	-	-	1	-
Fumaria sp.	1	-	-	1	-	2	-	1
Leguminosae	-	1	-	5	1	-	-	-
Retama raetam	-	-	-	7	-	1	-	2
Astragalus sp.	-	-	-	1	-	-	-	-
Melilotus sp.	2	-	-	-	-	4	-	-
Trigonella sp.	-	-	-	1	-	-	-	1
Medicago sp.	1	-	2	8	3	7	-	1
Trifloium sp.	1	-	-	3	-	-	1	-
Coronilla sp.	2	-	-	-	-	2	-	-
Oxalis sp.	-	-	-	1	-	-	-	-
Geranium sp.	-	-	-	-	-	2	1	-
Erodium sp.	2	-	-	-	-	-	-	-
Euphorbia sp.	-	-	-	9	-	-	-	-
Malva L. sp.	8	-	1	2	7	-	2	1
Viola sp.	1	-	-	2	2	-	-	-
cf. epilobium sp.	-	-	-	1	-	-	-	-
Galium sp.	-	-	-	2	-	-	-	1
Alkanna sp.	15	1	2	25	3	1	-	-
Arnebia sp.	1	-	-	-	-	-	-	-
Ajuga sp.	1	-	-	1	-	-	-	-
Scutellaria sp.	-	-	-	-	1	-	-	-
Plantago sp.	8	-	1	2	1	-	-	-
Gramineae	9	2	-	22	15	32	1	6
Lolium temulentum	5	-	1	8	1	9	-	6
Phalaris sp.	-	-	-	1	1	-	-	-
Cyperaceae	-	-	-	-	2	-	-	1
Carex sp.	-	-	-	1	-	3	1	1
Cladium sp.	-	-	-	1	1	-	-	-
Rubus sp.	1	-	-	-	-	-	-	-
Hypericum sp.	-	-	-	1	-	-	-	-
Androsace maxima	1	-	-	-	-	-	-	-
Unidentified seed pod/nut	-	-	-	1	-	-	-	0
Unidentified seeds	57	20	18	97	44	21	15	13
TOTALS	**126**	**327**	**27**	**212**	**96**	**96**	**27**	**34**

Chapter 11

Tomb Groups

by Leslie Shumka, John P. Oleson, and Jennifer Ramsay

11.A. INTRODUCTION TO THE PRESENTATION OF THE NON- CERAMIC FINDS

The disturbed and scrappy character of most of the occupation deposits associated with the structures presented in this volume meant that the vast majority of the non-ceramic objects found were of little intrinsic interest beyond the information they indirectly provided concerning day-to-day activities at the site. In addition to large quantities of potsherds, usually mixed chronologically, most strata yielded only small fragments of hydrated glass, corroded iron fasteners or fittings, and occasional clippings of bronze or lead sheeting, only a small portion of which repaid registration and presentation here. Less frequent were examples of the material gathered in Chapters 12 and 13: stone beads, reused architectural mouldings, fragments of rotary querns, fragments of inscriptions, bronze or bone cosmetic tools, lamps, candelabra fittings, small sculpture, and miscellaneous fittings. The exceptions were the assemblages of artefacts associated with the two burials found in F102 and with Burials 1 to 5 in C101, and the hoard of coins and jewellery found outside the settlement area. In order to preserve the contextual value of the finds from these seven closed or coherent deposits, they are presented together in Chapters 11 and 12, apart from the other catalogued objects of similar

type. The large cache of marble chancel screen and ambo fragments found scattered around the C101 Church constitutes another important deposit, but it fits easily into the scheme of presenting the stone objects field by field in Chapter 13. The artefacts recovered from the Nabataean burial in B100 and from the necropolis tombs were so few in number and the contexts so disturbed that they are presented with the appropriate object groups in the general catalogue. The glass artefacts are presented separately, in Chapter 14. Within each chapter and subcategory, the artefacts from the various fields are presented in the same order as the presentation of the fields in Chapters 3 to 9, with the exception of the glass objects, which are organized differently.

11.B. TOMB GROUPS

11.B.1. F102, Burials 1 and 2 *(J.P. Oleson)*

The two burials were found in cist graves in front of the central door to the F102 Church, but well below the ground level associated with the Church (see pp. 151–53). Nothing in the graves marks these individuals out as Christians, and they may have been interred several centuries before the Church was built. Both bodies had been laid on their backs, heads at the west end of the cists, arms crossed at the wrists. Scraps of coarse brown cloth remained from their clothing or shrouds, and there was a

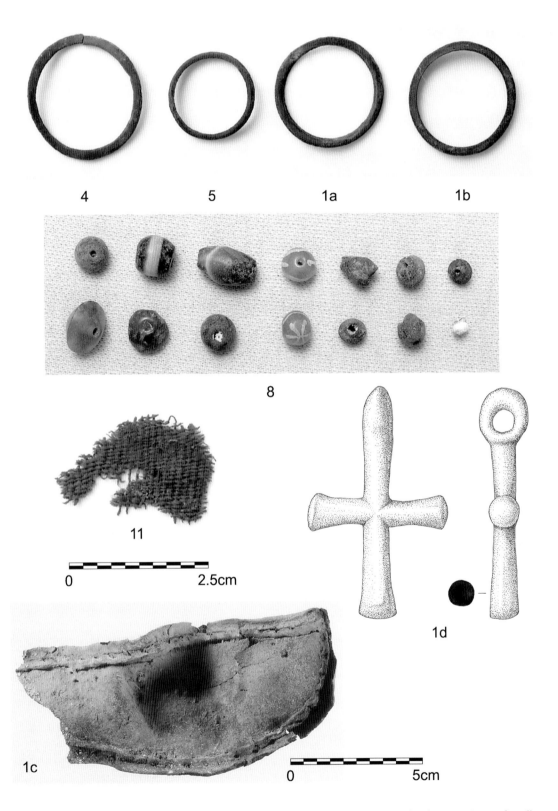

FIG. 11.1 *F102 Burial 1: Nos. 4, 5, 1a, 1b, finger rings. No. 8, six stone beads and eight glass beads. No. 11, Scrap of woollen cloth. F102 Burial 2: No. 1c, sole of a leather shoe or sandal. C101 Burial 1: No. 1d, bronze cross (B. Seymour).*

fragment of a leather sandal by one foot in Burial 2. There were traces of a wooden coffin around Burial 1. The graves were adjacent to each other, and on the same orientation, but there is no obvious reason to believe that the individuals were related.

F102, Burial 1

The grave contained the skeleton of a female 30–35 years of age (see pp. 322–23). Many of the parallels for artefacts found in this grave date to the Late Roman or Byzantine period, but the burial is not necessarily that late.

1. (1992.0482.01; fig. 11.1.1a–1b). Four plain silver rings, all approximately the same size, were found with the bones of left hand: two unbroken (illustrated), one complete but broken, one broken and about 80% complete; no visible markings, badly tarnished. D 0.02 m, Th 0.002 m. The two complete rings weigh 0.3 g and 0.2 g. The rings were made from a thin, slightly flattened rod of metal, bent, overlapped, and hammered.

Gold and silver would seem to be the most desirable materials for finger rings, but in fact they were made from a variety of materials. Finger rings made from thin copper alloy wire were quite common at the Roman period cemetery at the Queen Alia airport, and iron rings, usually with a bezel, were found in 12 graves (Ibrahim and Gordon 1987: 25–26, pl. xv, figs. 1–2). Bronze rings were found in Early Islamic deposits at Yoqne'am (Ben-Tor et al. 1996: 229–30). Simple bronze and iron rings and one silver ring made of plain wire were found in an Early Byzantine chamber tomb at Kabul (Galilee) (Vitto 2011: 122) and in Byzantine tombs at Khirbet al Karak (Delougaz and Haines 1960: pl. 45 nos. 10–18). Iron rings with a bezel and simple silver wire rings were common in the necropolis of Dura-Europos (Toll 1946: 122) and were found in Jerusalem (Geva 2006: 273). Bronze and silver rings were found in Byzantine and Mamluk contexts at en-Gedi (Chernov 2007: 514–17). Rings of iron, bronze, bone, marine shell, amber, and silver were found in various contexts at Hesban; dates are not given, but Roman and Byzantine parallels are cited. Some were just twists of wire, others had a bezel (Ray et al. 2009: 253–66). Bronze, iron, and silver rings were found at Caesarea Palaestinae (Patrich

2008: 421–22). Marine shell rings are also known from Busayra and Petra (Reese et al. 2002: 462).

2. (1992.0482.02). Iron finger ring, found with bones of left hand; corroded. D 0.02 m, 1.4 g. It is not clear whether it had an oval bezel like the iron ring on the right hand. Parallels: see no. 1.

3. (1992.0482.03). Copper alloy finger ring, found with bones of left hand; corroded. The hoop (D 0.019 m, Th 0.001 m, 0.7 g) is made from a flattened wire, which thickens at the top to support a circular copper alloy bezel (D 0.08 m). Parallels: see no. 1.

4. (1992.0482.04; fig. 11.1.4). Plain silver ring, found with bones of right hand: complete, tarnished. D 0.021 m, Th 0.001 m, 0.2 g. The ring is very similar to the one found on the right hand, but is slightly larger. This ring, too, was made from a thin, slightly flattened rod of metal, bent, overlapped, and hammered. Parallels: see no. 1.

5. (1992.0482.05; fig. 11.1.5). Plain silver ring, found with bones of right hand. D 0.016 m, Th 0.001 m, 0.2 g. The ring is very similar to those found on the left hand, but thinner. This ring, too, was made from a thin, slightly flattened rod of metal, bent, overlapped, and hammered. Parallels: see no. 1.

6. (1992.0482.08). Iron finger ring, found with bones of right hand; corroded. The hoop (D 0.019 m, Th ca. 0.002 m, 1.2 g) appears to have been made of a slightly flattened iron strip, to which an oval plate (L 0.011 m, W 0.009 m) was welded as a bezel. No design is visible on the corroded bezel. Parallels: see no. 1.

7. (1992.0482.09). Fragments of one or possibly two amber beads, doughnut-shaped. D 0.011 m, Th 0.005 m, 0.7 g; small central perforation, D 0.003 m. The material is broken and decayed, with an opaque surface, but shiny conchoidal fractures in section reveal a rich yellow brown interior colour. The fragments were found below the skull and may have belonged to an earring or hair ornament. Amber and "resin" beads were found with glass beads in an Early Byzantine chamber tomb at Kabul in Galilee (Vitto 2011: 126–28).

8. (1992.0484.01–02; fig. 11.1.8). Six stone beads and eight glass beads, found near the amber beads, all perforated for suspension. Stone beads: two beads of brown- and white-banded agate, one of

them barrel-shaped (D 0.006, H 0.005), the other a cylinder tapering at either end (L 0.011, Th 0.006); one discoid bead of dark red-orange carnelian (D 0.007, Th 0.002); two spherical beads of light orange carnelian (D 0.006) with curved lines etched around the circumference; one bi-conical amethyst bead (D 0.008, H 0.006). Glass beads: one very small, spherical bead of white or degraded glass (D ca. 0.001); four roughly hemispherical beads of a dark blue or black glass, one of them with some light, white banding (D 0.004–0.005); two squat bi-conical beads of dark glass (D 0.004, H 0.003); one drop-shaped bead of dark glass (D 0.004, H 0.006).

For the materials, shapes, and etching technique, see the beads from Burial 2 in the Lower Church (p. 385–87).

9. (1992.0482.10). Thin, triangular agate bead with brown, white, and clear bands. W 0.017 m, H 0.011 m, Th 0.001 m, 0.5 g. The bead, which is perforated across the base of the triangle with a very small hole (D ca. 0.001 m), was found below the right side of the skull near the jawbone and may have belonged to an earring or hair ornament.

I have not found parallels for this atypical shape. For agate beads in general in the Byzantine period, see Delougaz and Haines 1960: pl. 46 (Byzantine tombs at Khirbet al Karak); 'Abbadi 1973: pl. XLII, 2 (Na'ur, Late Roman–Early Byzantine period); Ibrahim and Gordon 1987: 27, pl. XXXII, figs. 1–2 (Amman, 2–3C); Colt 1962: 64–66 (Nessana); Yadin 1963: fig. 44, nos. 7.19–7.34, 7.71, 7.102 (Cave of Letters, 132–36); Magen 1990: figs. 12–13 (Beit 'Einun, 5C).

10. (1992.0482.11). A marine shell ornament was found near the skull, possibly an ear or hair decoration.

Marine shells were fairly common in tombs at the second- to third-century Queen Alia Airport necropolis, Amman (Ibrahim and Gordon 1987: 34, 48–49), including *Glycymeris, Dentalium, Acanthrocardia tuberculata, Cypraea, Cypraea annulus, Strombus, Pinctada margaritifera,* echnoids, *Columbella,* and *Nerita.*

11. (1992.0482.12; fig. 11.1.11). Scrap of woollen cloth, possibly from the shroud; torn, incomplete; L. 0.028 m, W 0.02 m.

F102, Burial 2

The grave contained the skeleton of a male 35–39 years of age (see p. 323). The leather scraps found in this grave do not allow close dating, and any period from Nabataean through Byzantine is possible.

1. (1992.0530.01; fig. 11.1.1c). Sole of a leather shoe or sandal, for the right foot; incomplete, no evidence for a heel; dry and curled. MPL 0.12 m; approximate original length of leather piece (flattened) 0.16 m, W 0.06 m, Th 0.003 m, 25 g. The outer sole is smooth and polished with use, possibly worn through just to the right of where the pressure would fall from the ball of the foot. The edge of the outer sole is folded over on top to meet the carefully cut edges of the insole, which was glued to it. The periphery of the insole has been crimped into a line of large raised holes (D 0.001 m) for thread spaced very regularly every 7 mm, formed by a lapped seam with whip stitching. The remains of sandals found in C101 Burials 1, 4, and 5 show the same method of construction.

The better-preserved sandals from the Cave of Letters are very similar in construction (Yadin 1963: 167–68); Ibrahim and Gordon 1987: 20–21, pl. XL.2 (Amman Airport, 2–3C), sandal "for a child," L 0.16 m, W 0.055 m. Sandals were quite common in the Amman Airport necropolis: see Tombs nos. 4, 6, 10, 14, 39, 76, 82, 89, 93, 95, 97, 103A, 107, 111, 117, 12, 131, 133, 140.

11.B.2. C101, Burials 1–5 (L. Shumka, *with wood identification by J. Ramsay*)

C101, Burial 1

The grave contained the fully articulated skeleton of a child under the age of 12, of undetermined gender, laid out on the back with the head at the west end (for the skeleton, see pp. 244, 323).

1. (1992.0516.02; fig. 11.1.1d). Bronze cross pendant; intact, corroded. L 0.04 m, W 0.03 m, Th 0.009 m. The vertical bar is longer than the horizontal bar, and all four arms flare slightly toward their outer terminations. There is a plain, transverse suspension loop at the top, which at the time of discovery contained traces of cordage. There is a raised, undecorated button on the front

face where the arms intersect, but no other surface decoration.

The cross was found on the ribs and probably had been worn around the neck on a string or leather thong (fig. 7.24). A slightly smaller but otherwise nearly identical bronze cross was found in Burial 2, also the burial of a child, in association with a necklace of beads. Crosses are an obvious personal talisman in a Christian burial, but it may not be coincidental that the only cross pendants found in the C101 burials were both associated with children.

There are many parallels: Abbadi 1973: pl. XLII, 2 (Naʿur, Late Roman–Early Byzantine period); Avni and Dahari 1990: fig. 10 (Luzit, Byzantine period); Colt 1962: pl. XXIII, no. 9 (Nessana, 7C); Davidson 1952: pl. 110, nos. 2075–76 (Corinth, Byzantine period); Israeli 2000: 143a (Tell Hadid, 6C), 143b (Shoham, 6C); Macalister 1911: no. 40, pl. LXXVIII, no. 25, 242, pl. CVII, no. 21 (Gezer, Byzantine period); Nabulsi et al. 2007: 273, fig. 1 (Khirbet as-Samrā, late Byzantine–early Umayyad period); Patrich 2008: 428, fig. 37 (Caesarea Palaestinae, Byzantine); Sellers and Baramki 1953: fig. 23 nos. 121 and 126 (Silet edh-Dhahr, 1–7C); Smith 1973: pl. 28.244 (Pella, Byzantine).

2. (1992.0516.01; fig. 7.25). Leather sandal soles; incomplete, very brittle, shrunken, and curled, approximately 50% of the sole surviving. Remnants of two leather sandals were found in association with the feet. No evidence of wear. A couple of the larger fragments have stitch holes with slight traces of thread preserved. Similar fragments were found in F102, Burial 2; see the discussion there (p. 384).

C101, Burial 2

The grave contained the skeleton of a child 8–11 years old, laid on her back with her head at the west end (for the skeleton, see pp. 245–47, 323–24). The sex could not be determined from the skeleton, but the grave goods are appropriate for a female.

1. (1992.0607.01; fig. 11.2.1a). Approximately 100 assorted stone, glass, and amber beads, of various sizes, shapes, and colours, all pierced for stringing. Most of the beads were found in a cluster near the base of the skull. They were probably suspended around the neck and fell here as the strings decayed. One amethyst sphere (D 0.006 m). Nineteen beads of orange brown carnelian: nine spherical (D ca. 0.008 m), two decorated with etched abstract motifs; three flattened spheres (D 0.007 m); one four-facetted lozenge (L 0.017 m, W 0.007 m); one chisel shape (L 0.019 m, W 0.009–0.04 m); one barrel shape (L 0.007 m); two 12-facetted spheres (D 0.005 m); one melon shape (D 0.008 m). Thirty beads of white and brown banded agate: 25 small barrel-shaped (L 0.006–0.01 m, W 0.006–0.008 m); three large barrel-shaped (L 0.017 m, W 0.009 m); one cylinder (L 0.012 m, W 0.006 m); one fluted drop (L 0.015; 0.006 m). Two beads of black glass: one cylinder (L 0.012 m, W 0.005 m); one sphere (D 0.007 m). Seven beads of light blue glass (and numerous fragments): four cylinders (L 0.012–0.018 m, W 0.004 m); one cube (D 0.004 m); two ribbed cylinders (L 0.01, W 0.003 m). Twenty-two glass beads of various colours: 13 green, spherical (D 0.001–0.004 m); two irregular red spheres (D 0.004 m), one with dark spots; four squat yellow glass spheres (D 0.002 m); one red, white, and blue striped sphere (D 0.004 m); one blue and yellow striped bi-conical (D 0.002 m); one clear squat sphere (D 0.005 m). Four amber beads: two spherical (D 0.005 m), two elongated spheres (D 0.01 m). Approximately 20 glass beads had cracked and broken into fragments.

The beads are an attractive mix of amber, agate, carnelian, glass, and stone, with large and small examples in all media. Shapes and sizes vary considerably, but on the whole they are similar in form to beads produced throughout most of antiquity (cf. Lemaigre 1983: fig. 54), not least of all in Byzantine Transjordan (Ibrahim and Gordon 1987: 26–27). The small collection of beads from the Cave of Letters is very similar in shape and materials (Yadin 1963: 115, fig. 44), as is the larger collection from the necropolis of Dura-Europos (Toll 1946: 125–30). Some are spherical with facets, others rectangular, and still others bi-conical; the smaller beads were probably used as spacers in a manner similar to those on a necklace from the Byzantine church at Khirbet Abu Rîsh (Magen 1992: 43). The Roman and Byzantine beads from Hesban, also found for the most part in tombs, also show many of the same shapes and materials, with the addition of red jasper, smoky quartz, and green serpentine (Ray et al. 2009: 227–42).

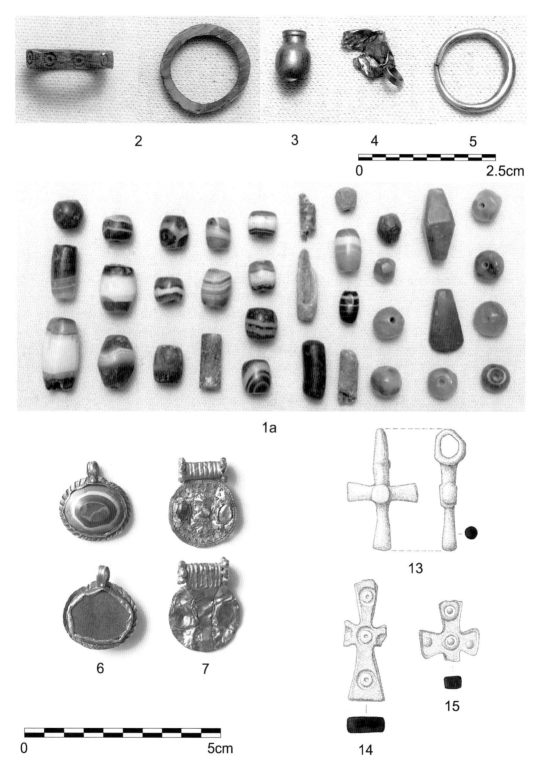

FIG. 11.2   *C101 Burial 2: No. 1a, selection of stone and glass beads. No. 2, bone or ivory finger ring. No. 3, jug-shaped gold bead. No. 4, gold foil pendant or necklace clasp. No. 5, gold ear or nose ring. No. 6, gold and agate pendant. No. 7, gold and carnelian pendant. No. 13, bronze cross pendant (B. Seymour). No. 14, bone cross (B. Seymour). No. 15, bone cross (B. Seymour).*

Craftsmen appear to have found different ways to embellish the beads that they produced: the agate beads were cut and highly polished to bring out the white and brown banding; one of the carnelian beads has an abstract pattern etched into the surface; and a bi-conical glass bead is a vibrant combination of blue with yellow stripes marvered in. The etched beads are part of a long-lived tradition that ran from the Early Bronze Age to the Early Islamic period (De Waele and Haerinck 2006). This bead belongs to Group C, which may have been produced in Sassania and was traded widely around Western Asia and the Middle East. Examples are generally reported from tomb deposits. This, and the two similar beads in F102 Burial 1, are the only examples so far reported from southern Jordan (Eger 2010). It is common for these beads to be represented by only one or two examples in each necklace.

The beads were probably threaded on plaited string, in the same manner as a pendant cross and necklace from the South Cemetery at Khirbet Faynan (Findlater et al. 1998: 78). Whether the beads were all part of one necklace is difficult to say, since most were clustered at the base of the skull. Allowing for shifting of the necklace as the body decomposed, the bronze cross pendant (no. 14) that rested on the sternum may have been strung with them.

There are many parallels for this mix of shapes and materials in the Roman and Byzantine periods: 'Abbadi 1973: pl. xlii, 2 (Na'ur, Late Roman–Early Byzantine period); Davidson 1952: pl. 121, nos. 2415–16 (Corinth, Byzantine period); Ibrahim and Gordon 1987: pl. xxxii, figs. 1–2 (Amman, Roman imperial period); Iliffe 1934: Loculus 1, no. 23 (Tarshiha, late 4C); Magen 1990: figs. 12–13 (Beit 'Einun, 5C); Ray et al. 2009: 227–42 (Hesban, Roman and Byzantine); Vitto 2011: 126–28, fig. 17 (2nd half 4C–ea. 5C); Yadin 1963: fig. 44, nos. 7.19–7.34, 7.71, 7.102 (Cave of Letters, 132–36).

2. (1992.0604.10; fig. 11.2.2). Bone or ivory ring. D 0.016 m, band W 0.003 m, Th 0.002 m. Intact; dark brown discoloration. A ring and dot pattern was drilled into the exterior surface. The ring, found on the middle phalanx of the second finger of the left hand, is modest in design and execution, lacking a bezel or any type of setting,

and embellished only with a pattern of small circles with central dots, at evenly spaced intervals.

There do not seem to be any close parallels for this item in Byzantine Transjordan, but an undecorated bone ring with semi-circular cross section was found at Hesban (Rey et al. 2009: 263–64, fig. 13.17.1). Three examples from Corinth — one of bronze, fifth-century in date, and two of bone dated only as Byzantine — incorporate the same simple bands with ring and dot motif. The small size of these rings suggests that they were intended for children (Davidson 1952: 233, nos. 1835, 1996–97). Findlater et al. (1998: 78) mention a wooden ring found near the left hand of a female interred in the South Cemetery at Khirbet Faynan, but make no mention of any decoration.

3. (1992.0604.01; fig. 11.2.3). Jug-shaped bead with rounded body, narrow neck, and grooved rim. MPL 0.009 m, MPW 0.005 m, 0.5 g. Gilded copper alloy foil around a glass paste or plaster core. Broken, incomplete, part of base and body lost.

This bead is one of three articles of jewellery made from gilded copper alloy (see nos. 4 and 5). There are very few published examples of beads that have been fashioned in this manner, but several gold earrings from a tomb on Jebel Jofeh in Amman show the same technique (Harding 1950: nos. 214, 216, 220, 228, 232). There are glass beads of the same "stylized pomegranate" shape at Hesban (Ray et al. 2009: fig. 13.1.4–5; Roman to Early Islamic). For other parallels see Gath and Rahmani 1977: no. 1, pp. 210–211 (Jerusalem, 3C); Iliffe 1934: Loculus 2, no. 16; Loculus 3, no. 15 (Tarshiha, late 4C); Harding 1950: 92, no. 405 (Jebel Jofeh, Amman, Roman period).

4. (1992.0604.03; fig. 11.2.4). Pendant or necklace clasp, gilded bronze. Bent, torn, incomplete; MPL 0.014 m, MPW 0.008 m, Th 0.004 m, 0.4 g. A thin strap was soldered to one end of the leaf-shaped plate to form a suspension loop.

This object resembles a type of necklace clasp that was used widely in the Mediterranean region (cf. Marshall 1969: nos. 2715, 2736, 2746): a small, leaf-shaped plate was attached to either end of a string of beads, one with an eyelet and the other with a hook to fit in it. A similar clasp composed of two gilded, leaf-shaped pieces was found in a Roman-period tomb in Jerusalem (Rahmani 1960:

145, pl. 21A, ca. 240), another at Palmyra (Mackay 1949: figs. 4 and 4e, post-200). Since both bead no. 3 and this clasp appear to have been damaged before the burial was closed, it is not clear whether these items were part of a necklace worn by the deceased or were interesting scrap collected by her and interred with her for sentimental reasons.

5. (1992.0604.02; fig. 11.2.5). Pair of earrings or nose-rings, gilded bronze. D 0.015 m and 0.013 m, 1.4 g and 1.2 g. The hoops taper strongly in thickness towards each termination (2 mm to 0.5 mm); gilding has worn off the inner surface of one of the hoops.

The two ear or nose-rings are unequal in size and weight. The elongated, tapering hoops were formed of rolled sheet metal, probably over a paste core (cf. Harding 1951). They lack a closure mechanism to prevent them from slipping from position, but the terminations overlap sufficiently to have kept them in position once passed through a piercing. The differential in size and weight might suggest that they are not a matched pair, but a survey of earrings from various historical periods and geographic locations demonstrates that pairs of earrings frequently were not identical (Allason-Jones 1989: nos. 29–30, 56–57, 77–78, 205–6, Roman Britain, Iron Age; Kalavrezou 2003: no. 135). It is also possible that one or both are nose-rings, for which symmetry might not be desired or at least is less important. 'Abbadi (1973: 71) lists three bronze nose-rings among the finds from a Byzantine tomb at Na'ur, although he does not describe them or explain this attribution. The only firmly identified nose-rings from Transjordan were more elaborate in design and much earlier in date, produced by Nabataean jewellers during the first few centuries AD. These are usually composed of a small, sturdy hoop with a fixed, ornate pendant (Rosenthal 1974: pl. 16D; Rosenthal-Heginbottom 1997: 204, pl. 3, no. 19, Oboda, 550).

There is no mention of nose-rings in Byzantine textual sources concerning women's adornments. One of the very few written references comes from the *Mishnah* (*Shabbat* 6.1; redacted in the early third century), in which nose-rings (*nezem*, pl. *n°zamim*) are mentioned as unsuitable for wear by women on the Sabbath. Apparently it was feared the wearer might be tempted to adjust or remove

the ring, thus "carrying a burden" on the Sabbath. Nose rings are mentioned also in *Genesis* 24:47 and *Isaiah* 3:21. It may be that one of the Hauarra hoops was used as a nose-ring, or that it had a removable ornament, as was sometimes the case with earrings (Marshall 1969: pl. LV, nos. 2668–69). There is, however, no pendant in this assemblage that would suit this kind of arrangement. The gold and agate pendant no. 6 is an unlikely candidate, given its weight. Other parallels: Baramki 1931: pl. XIII, no. 1 and no. 7 (Karm al-Shaikh, 4C BC); Tushingham 1972: fig. 26, no. 19, fig. 27, no. 25 (Dhiban, ea. 7C).

6. (1992.0604.18; fig. 11.2.6). Gold and agate pendant. MPW 0.018 m, MPH 0.015 m, Th. 0.004 m. Oval, truncated conical agate stone, with grey, white, and brown banding. The stone, which has been cut and polished to take full advantage of the banding, was held in an open-backed cabochon setting of reddish gold, the edges of which have been folded and rilled to form a twisting, rope-like pattern. The back of the stone has been polished flat and is visible through the setting. A suspension loop was soldered to one long edge of the setting, and the join between loop and cabochon frame is decorated front and back with a single gold ball.

Although shaped and polished agates frequently appear in a variety of settings in the ancient Mediterranean world (Ibrahim and Gordon 1987; Rosenthal-Heginbottom 1997), no close parallels for this pendant from the Near East have been published. Given its reddish colour, the gold has probably been alloyed with copper. An approximate parallel was found in a second- or third-century tomb at Ayn Jawan in Saudi Arabia (al-Ghabban 2010: 402, fig. 239). This pendant carries a hemispherical central garnet, surrounded by a cabochon setting with granulation, surrounded by the backing disk, which carries two pearls and four garnets in cabochon settings. A suspension loop with three raised lines is soldered to the top. Compare also Allason-Jones 1989: pl. 19, no. 36 (Gloucester, 3C), pl. 26, no. 60 (Silchester, 3C); Marshall 1969: pl. LXI, no. 2745 (Roman, 2–3C).

7. (1992.0604.04; fig. 11.2.7). Gold and carnelian pendant. L 0.021 m, W 0.018 m, Th 0.005 m, 1.2 g. Flat gold disk with two cabochon settings for oval stones; the one surviving stone is a carnelian, the other is missing but presumably was also a

carnelian. The gold foil settings were crimped at the edges to hold the stones but were otherwise undecorated. The head, neck, and clothed shoulders of a bearded male worked in relief occupy the centre of the disk, surrounded by two concentric rings of clusters of granulated beads. Damage to the central portion of the face makes it difficult to determine his identity. The edge of the pendant is worked as a plaited wreath. A horizontal gold cylinder (L 0.011) has been soldered to the top edge of the disk as a suspension ring; there are six circumferential grooves, and six beads at either end. The disk was perforated at the lower left and right edges.

This object, a frontlet that was found on the forehead of the deceased at the time of excavation, provides a unique perspective on the integration of the artistic and religious traditions of Transjordan in antiquity. In technique and composition, the frontlet is virtually identical to a pair of earring pendants from Roman Syria, and three others of the early first–mid-second century from the Nabataean necropolis at Mampsis (Kurnub) (Hackens and Winkes 1983: no. 31; Patrich 1984: fig. 3, pl. 6c). All date to the early first or second centuries and are products of the rich Syro-Hellenistic tradition of jewellery making (Hackens and Winkes 1983: no. 31), whose hallmarks are extensive granulation, filigree work, and the use of precious or semi-precious stones on crescent-shaped or circular fields. The arrangement of the stones and other surface details reflect a Nabataean taste for non-figurative images of deities, a preference well-documented by ancient and mediaeval writers (Patrich 1990: 51). The most prominent of the frontlet's surface details are arranged like those on Nabataean betyls, where stylized eyes and noses executed in low relief denote members of the Nabataean pantheon. Among them is al-'Uzza, the tutelary goddess of Petra and counterpart to Aphrodite and Venus (Patrich 1984: 39–42). On the Syrian earrings, a small convex protrusion flanked by two bezels with carnelians gives shape to the face of al-'Uzza. Although the layout of the Hauarra frontlet may reflect this Nabataean tradition, the craftsman has replaced the stylized nose with a small relief portrait. This adaptation is also seen on an earring from the Mampsis necropolis,

where an aedicula-shaped field containing an easily recognizable portrait of Aphrodite Anadyomene stands in place of the godddess' nose (Patrich 1984: 42, fig. 3; cf. Rosenthal-Heginbottom 1997: 202–4, fig. 59.2, Oboda, 550). Patrich (1984: 45) interprets this modification as a reflection of Roman influence on local artistic traditions, which began gathering strength in the late first century BC.

While the frontlet's layout may reflect al-'Uzza imagery, it is clear that the advent of Christianity altered local iconographic traditions sufficiently to allow addition of a humanoid male. The closest parallels appear on a pair of second or third-century gold pendant earrings from Roman Spain, although the two males are clean-shaven (Marshall 1969: no. 2374–75, pl. LII). There is nothing to signify their identity (mythological figure, saint, bishop, or perhaps even an imperial ruler), following as they do the conventions of male portraiture in the Roman and Early Byzantine period: the hair tends to be cropped, the face bearded, the eyes rather wide and expressive, and, in the case of saints or images of Christ, the head has a nimbus. Unfortunately, the damage to the Hauarra frontlet makes it impossible to identify the central figure conclusively. Compare also Allason-Jones 1989: pl. 17, no. 32 (Caerleon, 60/1–ca. 275); Marshall 1969: pl. LXII, nos. 2374–75, pl. LXVIII, nos. 2932–33 (Roman Spain, 3c).

8. (1992.0604.07; fig. 11.3.8). Ivory bottle with stopper; extensive delamination, one side split, many fragments missing; bottle MPL 0.07 m, D 0.025 m; stopper MPL 0.025 m, MPW 0.0175 m. Hollow, cylindrical container; body tapers from top to bottom. Stopper is cylindrical with a projection on its underside that matches the diameter of the bottle opening.

The toiletries, wool-working implements, and (in the case of unmarried females) dolls that frequently occur in ancient burial assemblages for women represent social and familial expectations that they will maintain a respectable appearance, contribute to the economy of the household, and marry well. Whether all such items should be construed as personal possessions of the departed or as items manufactured specifically for funerary purposes is often difficult to ascertain, particularly when the condition is poor. Such is the case with

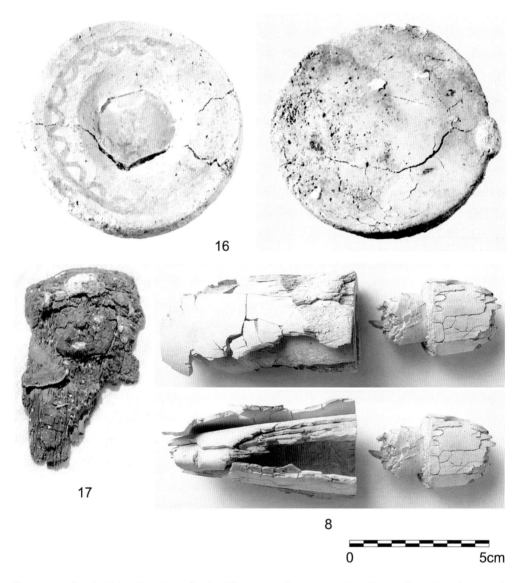

FIG. 11.3   *C101 Burial 2: No. 8, Ivory bottle with stopper, after conservation. No. 16, glass mirror in painted plaster frame. No. 17, carved wooden plaque with human face.*

this poorly-preserved ivory bottle. The original form of the receptacle is clear: an undecorated, tapering cylinder. The container's size and shape are comparable with others from the region that are typically identified as kohl tubes on the basis of small metal sticks and residues found within them. This cylinder was not associated with a kohl stick, but at the time of excavation a tiny lump of a yellow crystalline substance was detected at the very bottom of the container. This matter turned to dust before it could be analyzed, and there is no means

of determining whether it was it was the remains of eye make-up or a salt deposit that resulted from the ivory's deterioration. Galena-derived kohl and malachite were the most widely-used substances for lining the eyes, but written and material sources make clear that women also used blue (Hirschfeld 2006: 182) or a yellowish or saffron-coloured eyeliner (Ovid, *Ars am.* 3.204; Cyprian, *De habitu* 15).

Comparanda for the bottle are to be found among the many bone, wood, and steatite kohl tubes excavated by Petrie at Karanis (Petrie: 1927:

26–28 pl. xxiii, no. 37, Late Roman; cf. no. 38, no provenance, Coptic), which date from the Bronze Age to the Byzantine period. In the South Cemetery at Khirbet Faynan, wooden tubes were discovered in two separate female inhumations in which skeletal orientation and grave offerings were analogous to the Humayma burial and its contents. In one of these burials the wooden tube was found immediately on top of the deceased's right pelvis, while in the other the deceased cradled the tube in her right hand (Findlater et al. 1998: 78, figs. 7 and 9, Late Roman–Early Byzantine). Brashler (1995: 465, and 467, fig. 9) mentions but does not describe in detail a bone "make-up bottle" with decorative banding at one end that was among the contents of a Late Roman–Early Byzantine 14-person tomb at Umm al-Jimal. This bottle is virtually identical to those from Khirbet Faynan, in size and decoration, and was found together with a small plaster mirror that was identified inaccurately as a make-up palette. Compare also: Hirschfeld 2006: fig. 13.29.1 ('En Tamar, 1–3c); Ibrahim and Gordon 1987: no. 13515 (Amman, Roman imperial period); McNicoll et al. 1982: no. 94, pl. 134, no. 5 (Pella, Late Roman period); Colt 1962: pl. xxi, no. 25–26, pl. xxiv, no. 17 (Nessana, 6–8c).

9. (1992.0604.16; fig. 11.4.9). Ivory spindle whorl. Some delamination, flaking, and discoloration; most of the convex upper surface of the whorl is missing; D 0.033 m, original Th ca. 0.015 m, hole D 0.008 m. Small, disk-shaped spindle whorl. Traces of decoration survive: incised dot-in-circle motifs, radiating at evenly spaced intervals from an incised band around the spindle hole to the outer edge. There are traces of a circumferential band of incised dot-in-circle motifs around the flat side of the whorl.

There were three spindle whorls among the contents of Burial 2, two of ivory (nos. 9–10) and one of wood (no. 11); they were found near the basket on the girl's lap (fig. 7.29). The decoration with incised circumferential lines is very common in the Roman and Byzantine periods. The decoration with lines and dot-in-circle motif is very common on all sorts of small objects in the Late Roman and Byzantine period, and it continues on in Early Islamic steatite vessels and up to the present in the region (Ziolkowski and al-Sharqi 2006).

Comparable examples are a bone whorl from a Byzantine tomb at Na'ur ('Abbadi 1973: 71, pl. xlii, 2), more than a dozen whorls from Jerusalem (Geva 2003: 345, B6–7; Nenner-Soriano 2010; Prag 2008: fig. 157.2; Tushingham 1985: fig. 68.3), another from Mampsis dating ca. 363 (Erickson-Gini 2010: 160, 162), a Late Roman or Byzantine example from En-Gedi (Chernov 2007: 526, fig. 68, "button"), and similarly shaped objects from the Corinth excavations (Davidson 1952: 296, nos. 2551–72). These objects are frequently mis-identified as buttons. Although small, they are now generally regarded as whorls, since small whorls are needed for finer threads (Simak 2005–2006).

There are many parallels from other sites in the region: Colt 1962: pl. xxi, no. 7 (Nessana, 6–8c); Chernov 2007: 525–26 ('En Gedi, Late Roman to Byzantine); Geva 2003: 345, B6–7 (Jerusalem, Roman imperial period); Ibrahim and Gordon 1987: no. 13521, pl. xxviii, no. 1 (Amman, Roman imperial period); McNicoll et al. 1982: no. 7, pl. 132 (Pella, Roman period); Prag 2008: fig. 157.3 (Jerusalem, Roman to Byzantine); Ray et al. 2009: 164–75 (Hesban, Late Roman–Byzantine); Rosenthal-Heginbottom 1997: pl. 5, nos. 61–62 (Oboda, middle Nabataean period); Yadin 1963: pl. 36, fig. 51 (Cave of Letters, 132–36).

10. (1992.0604.15; fig. 11.4.10). Ivory spindle whorl. Considerable delamination and flaking of the ivory, and discoloration; D 0.038 m, Th ca. 0.016 m, hole D 0.009 m. Small, plano-convex spindle whorl. Convex upper side decorated with a random pattern of dot-in-circle motifs; bottom surface smooth. For parallels, see no. 9

11. (1992.0604.17; fig. 11.4.11). Wooden spindle whorl. D 0.038 m, Th 0.018 m, hole D 0.01 m. Plano-convex spindle whorl. The upper surface is convex, with a central hole for insertion of the spindle. There are incised concentric grooves around the spindle hole and around the outer edge; the lower surface is flat and carefully smoothed. The simple decoration is typical of the many known wooden spindle whorls. The decoration with incised circumferential lines is very common in the Roman and Byzantine periods on both wooden and ivory spindle whorls.

There are many parallels from the region: Baginski and Shamir 1995: 31 (Nahal 'Omer, Early

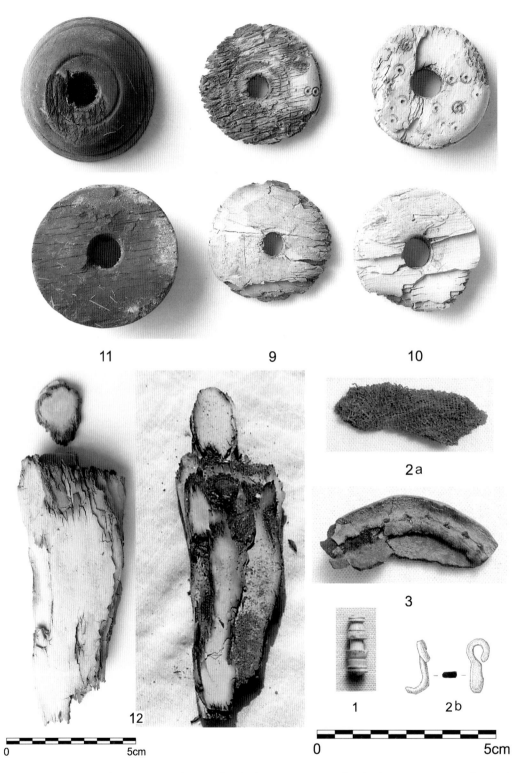

11   9   10

2a

3

1   2b

0   5cm   0   5cm

FIG. 11.4 *C101 Burial 2: No. 11, wooden spindle whorl. No. 9, ivory spindle whorl. No. 10, ivory spindle whorl. No. 12, ivory figurine or doll. Right, condition immediately after excavation. Left: condition after consolidation. C101 Burial 3: No. 2a, fragment of textile. C101 Burial 4: No. 1, head of a bone pin. No. 2b, bronze hooked clasp (B. Seymour). No. 3, fragment of leather sandal sole.*

Islamic); Colt 1962: pl. XXV, nos. 1–2, 5–6, 10–11 (Nessana, ca. 5C); Ibrahim and Gordon 1987: no. 13521, pl. XXVIII, no. 1 (Amman, Roman imperial period); McNicoll et al. 1982: no. 7, pl. 132 (Pella, Roman period); Rosenthal-Heginbottom 1997: pl. 5, nos. 61–62 (Oboda, middle Nabataean period); Shamir 1999: 99 ('En Rahel, 1C), 2005: 109–10 (Mo'a, early Roman); Yadin 1963: pl. 36, fig. 51 (Cave of Letters, 132–36). See also the discussion for no. 9.

12. (1992.0604.13; fig. 11.4.12). Ivory figurine or doll. Poorly-preserved; extensive flaking and delamination; no discernible anatomical features remain other than the outlines of the head, which has become detached from the body; MPL 0.13 m, MPW 0.025 m, Th. 0.018 m. Figurine or doll composed of a flat sheet of ivory with features apparently carved in relief on one surface. The head sat on rounded shoulders, and the armless body tapered to a point where the feet should have been.

A thorough understanding of this artefact is impossible, since it was found in poor condition and delaminated rapidly after excavation. When first uncovered, the outlines of a human head and torso could be discerned. All surface detail on the head and trunk had already disappeared except for a small rosette on the right side of the chest (now lost), so interpretation of the iconography and function must remain speculative. Nevertheless, the figurine's dimensions (taken at the time of excavation) fall within the range for worked bone and ivory dolls produced throughout the Roman world in the second through fifth centuries (cf. Elderkin 1930: 472–75, Rome, Early Christian era; Hübner 1992: 92–98, Palestine; Manson 1987: 24–25, figs. 6–7; Shumka 1999: 615–18, pls. 222–23, Poggio Gramignano; St. Clair 2003: 108–10, fig. 42–43, pl. 51–52, Rome).

Roman dolls are often articulated at the shoulders and hips and normally have modelled faces, coiffures, breasts, and incised Venus folds or pubic triangles. Byzantine-era dolls are seldom jointed (although a few examples have articulated arms) and are easily distinguished by their distinctive facial features: wide, expressive eyes (see the example in Dautermann-Maguire et al. 1989: no. 145, Egypt), elongated triangles for noses, and mouths rendered by means of two or three short horizontal lines. Three examples of this type were found in Early Islamic contexts at Tel Yoqne'am (Agadi 1996). Alternatively, facial features, breasts, and pudenda are sometimes created by judiciously placed rosettes, which are formed from dot-in-circle patterning. The best example of a doll executed in this manner is a stylized bone specimen from Khirbet el-Minyeh (Rahmani 1981: pl. 15B, 6–7C), where incised ring and dot clusters convey the anatomical features of the female body (Rahmani 1981: pl. 15A, el-Burj, Byzantine). The el-Minyeh doll (H 0.165 m) is taller than the Hauarra figurine, yet in general form it is the closest parallel. Also similar is a group of worked bone figurines produced in Seleucia on the Tigris during the first two centuries of the Christian era. These are not dolls, but representations of an oriental mother-goddess or perhaps one of her acolytes (Van Ingen 1939: 340–45). Generally, they are voluptuous, nude adult females with wasp-waists, full hips, Venus folds, pubic triangles, and upswept hair. Some have arms jointed at the shoulder. Complete figurines are 0.11–0.14 m in height. Compare also Colt 1962: pl. XXI, no. 16, pl. XXIX, no. 5 (Nessana, ca. 7–8C); Pitarakis 2009: fig. 29 (Egypt, Fatimid era).

In the final analysis, we cannot state absolutely whether the figurine in our assemblage is a doll or a small statuette of the type seen at Seleucia, but the age and probable gender of the owner suggest the former. It is clear, however, that the figurine is part of the strong bone and ivory carving tradition of this region.

13. (1992.0604.11; fig. 11.2.13). Bronze cross pendant. Intact, L 0.032 m, W 0.02 m, Th. 0.009 m, 10 g. The vertical bar is longer than the horizontal bar, and all four arms flare slightly toward their outer terminations. There is a plain, transverse suspension loop at the top. There is a raised, undecorated circle on the front face where the arms intersect, but no other apparent surface decoration.

Three crosses were found in Burial 2, one of bronze (no. 13) and two of bone (nos. 14–15). The bronze cross was found as part of the compact lump of beads found lying at the base of the skull, so it may have been part of a necklace. A slightly larger but otherwise nearly identical bronze cross constituting the only grave good recovered from C101 Burial 1 (above, no. 1) was found in the same position. Crosses are an obvious personal talisman in a Christian burial, but it may not be coinciden-tal that the only two cross pendants found in the C101 burials were both associated with children. For parallels see above C101 Burial 1 no. 1 (p. 384).

14. (1992.0604.08; fig. 11.2.14). Bone cross. Outer portion of both side arms missing; top end corroded; MPL 0.03 m, MPW 0.012 m, Th 0.004 m. The cross was cut from a flat sheet of bone and decorated on the front surface with five incised circles with central dot, one on each arm and one at the intersection. The arms flare markedly toward their outer ends. No apparent suspension hole.

This simple type of cross is quite common in the Byzantine Near East. For parallels, see Colt 1962: pl. XXIII, no. 8, pl. XX, no. 26 (Nessana, 7c); Davidson 1952: pl. 110, nos. 2073–74, 2080–82, pl. 111, no. 2097 (Corinth, Byzantine period); Hayes 1972: fig. 56, nos. 311e, 312, 321, 325, 329 (North Africa, ca. 480–540); Israeli 2000: 142 (Tarshiha, el-Makr, Beth Shean, Ramle, and Shoham, 6–7c); Magen 1990: figs. 12–13 (Beit 'Einun, 5Hc); Nabulsi 2010 (Khirbat as-Samrā, Byzantine); Rahmani 1964: pl. 15A (Kfar Dikhrin, late 4–ea. 6c).

15. (1992.0604.09; fig. 11.2.15). Bone cross. One end of vertical arm broken off; MPL 0.015 m, W 0.015 m, Th 0.035 m. Same design as no. 14, but smaller, and apparently with stubbier proportions. Parallels: see no. 14.

16. (1992.0604.05; fig. 11.3.16). Mirror. Intact; light abrasion at the lower left edge; several cracks on front and back surfaces; D 0.083 m, Th 0.010 m, 60 g. Mirror consisting of a circular frame of cream coloured plaster with a central depression (D 0.04 m) framing an irregular, slightly convex glass fragment (0.035 m × 0.030 m) that was set into the plaster while it was wet; there is a small rounded projection at one point along the edge. The rim (W 0.02 m) was decorated with a circle holding inward facing semi-circles in matte black paint; the back surface was undecorated.

The convex surface and small size of the glass, along with the absence of tinning on the back of the glass, indicate that the object was of little practical use as a mirror. Was it intended as a burial substi-tute for a piece of grooming equipment that women used regularly, or did it have an entirely different purpose? In fact, the mirror belongs to an extensive group of mirrors with plaster, pottery, or limestone frames, sometimes referred to as mirror plaques, that were produced throughout *Palaestina Tertia* in the Late Roman and Byzantine periods. These items began to appear on the antiquities market in the late nineteenth century, and they have since turned up in excavations, e.g. at Wadi Faynan (Findlater et al. 1998: 77–78, Late Roman–Byzantine period), En-Gedi (Chernov 2007: 520–21, pl. 7, Byzantine), Khirbet as-Samrā (Nabulsi 2000, 2010; Nabulsi et al. 1998: fig. 2d, 2007: 278, Late Byzantine–Early Umayyad period), Umm al-Jimal (Brashler 1995: 467, fig. 8, Late Roman–Early Byzantine), Nessana (Colt 1962: pl. XXVI.9–11), Luzit (Avni and Dahari 1990: fig. 7, Byzantine period); Yavneh Yam (Fischer and Saar 2007: fig. 1, Byzantine period); Gezer (Macalister 1911: no. 242, fig. 201, Byzantine period); Kfar Dikhrin (Rahmani 1964: fig. 4.1–2, 5c); and Bethany (Saller 1957: pl. 130b, no. 4, Byzantine pe-riod). Compare also Bianchi 2002: LA-47b-d (no provenance, 5–6c).

Rahmani (1964: 57) created a typology of these mirrors, assigning them to five groups: zoo-morphic, anthropomorphic, architectural, round and simple, and round with elaborate decorative elements. Most have one or more perforations for hanging, an inset piece of glass (or sometimes several), and incised, painted, or raised decoration. Their function is a matter of some debate. Moulton (1919–20) regarded them as belonging to a group of religious and funerary artefacts that were used in baptisteries and tombs. He supported Cré's claim (1894) that the disks were used as containers for crumbs of Eucharist bread, somewhat like a monstrance, even though written evidence for this practice is largely anecdotal. For instance, during his first consecration of the sacrament Saint Basil of Caesarea (300–379) is alleged to have separated the host into three segments; he placed one in a ritual object, consumed one, and reserved a third for the time of his death in the hope that it would be buried with him (Moulton 1919–20: 78). This theory of the mirror-plaque's purpose has not received widespread acceptance.

Other scholars (e.g. Israeli 1974; Lubin 1993; Rahmani 1964; Watson 2001: 479–80) ascribe an apotropaic function to the mirrors. Throughout classical antiquity individuals used reflective devic-es to avert the evil eye or to turn malevolent forces back upon the source. Fischer and Saar (2007: 83), for instance, assign an apotropaic function to a terracotta mirror that was found in the excavation of a Byzantine bath complex at Yavneh-Yam. Their interpretation owes much to Dunbabin's observations that apotropaic symbols are often found in bathing contexts where physically attractive bodies were a natural target for the jealous eye (Dunbabin 1989: 33–46; Fischer and Saar 2007: 85). In mortuary contexts, according to this theory, the mirrors that were placed among grave goods were intended to obviate any evil forces at work in the afterlife. In Christian contexts especially, protection against malevolent forces appears to have been reinforced in two ways. Concentric circles are sometimes thought to have had the power to avert the evil, and thus were added to mirror rims (Dautermann-Maguire et al. 1989: 5–7). Similarly, small crosses were often included among the burial goods for good measure; Macalister (1911: 387) discovered small metal crosses in Tombs 40 and 242 at Gezer, and Rahmani (1964: 59) claims that there are other cases where mirrors and crosses occur together, as they do in Burial 2. Plainly, such articles would have been intended to provide security for the deceased and a modicum of reassurance for family members who were uneasy about the eternal welfare of the loved one (Rahmani 1964: 60). This interpretation as an apotropaic object seems preferable.

17. (1992.0604.06; fig. 11.3.17). Carved wooden plaque with human face. Broken, incomplete; extensive cracking, flaking, and discoloration; original gold leaf now detached; MPL 0.07 m, W 0.03 m. Traces of gold leaf adhered to the surface at the time of discovery. A face carved in low relief occupies the upper portion of the plaque, the only part preserved. Although poorly preserved, it appears to show an expressionless, clean-shaven individual wearing a headpiece with a central medallion. The lower portion of the plaque has been lost below a diagonal break.

This artefact deteriorated very rapidly after removal from the tomb, with the result that the facial features blurred and most of the gold leaf broke up and became detached. In spite of its relatively poor state, the outlines of the face of a clean-shaven male or a female remain. Following

the conventions of Near Eastern art (Avi-Yonah 1961: 10; Rosenthal 1976: 97), the eyes of the individual are unusually large and peer out from under the brim of a headdress that sits low on the brow. The hat resembles the imperial Roman *stemma,* headgear that has its artistic origins in the diadems and crowns of Persian kings, which Hellenistic and Roman luminaries later adopted and adapted (Rousseau 2004: 6). Physical and literary evidence for Early Byzantine *stemmata* is limited, but the iconography of imperial rulers from the age of Justinian onward demonstrates that they were essentially arch-shaped and heavily jewelled bands, sometimes embellished with an enamel portrait just below the peak, and with jewelled pendants (*pendilia*) that hung from either side of the head near the temples (Rousseau 2004: 6–7, fig. 6, Ravenna, 548). It is impossible to determine how elaborate the *stemma* on the Humayma plaque originally was; the remains of a *pendilium* with traces of gold leaf at the left temple suggest that the artist intended to simulate the precious metal of costly headpieces. An additional embellishment is a slightly raised oval, also with traces of gold leaf, adorning the centre of the hatband. Portraits of emperors wearing such regalia were executed in a variety of media, and highly detailed examples can be seen in a mosaic portrait of Justinian from the Basilica of San Vitale in Ravenna (Stout 1994: fig. 5.10) and on a ceremonial six-*solidus* medallion for Maurice (582–602). These *stemmata* are identical, apart from the cross that is positioned prominently at the peak of Maurice's crown (Grierson 1982: pl. 1, no. 2, Constantinople, 491–510), and they bear a strong similarity to the headdress on the plaque. See also Bates 1971: pl. 1, nos. 116, 123, 128 (Sardis, 527–557/8).

Portraits of *Augustae,* like those of their husbands, also show the women wearing *stemmata* with *pendilia*. The crown of the imperial female was much more ornate, despite being influenced by similar cultural and artistic traditions. In addition to being fashioned from gold or silver, it was embellished with pearls and precious gems and owes much to the sumptuously decorated tiaras worn by Palmyrene women in their funerary portraits (Mackay 1949: 178–79, pl. LX no. 3, 3C; La Follette 1994: 56; Rousseau 2004: 8–9). Two well-known ivory plaques from Constantinople depicting Ariadne (ca. 450–515), consort of Zeno, provide particularly good evidence for variations on the feminine *stemmata* (Angelova 2004: figs. 1–2; Rousseau 2004: 10). A mosaic in the Basilica of San Vitale shows Justinian's wife, Theodora (ca. 500–548), wearing an ornate crown that is comparable in form to her husband's (Stout 1994: fig. 5.11). The similarity of these head-dresses to that on the Humayma plaque is arresting, but the closest parallel is a hat worn by an anonymous Palmyrene woman of the third century in her funerary portrait (Mackay 1949: pl. LX, no. 3). Painted portraits reveal that pearl-encrusted caps embellished with other ornaments remained fashionable throughout much of the Byzantine era and even the Middle Ages (Mackay: 1949: 179). While it remains difficult to ascertain the gender of the figure on the Humayma plaque, or to recover an identity, there is no mistaking the style of the distinctive headdress worn by this individual.

The function of this object is uncertain. The gender of the individual cannot be firmly established, and the face is too severe-looking for a child's plaything, following as it does the conventions of formal portraiture. It should be noted, however, that while this individual's *stemma* resembles those of imperial rulers and their consorts, its general outline is also similar to the headgear worn by married couples in middle Byzantine art. Particularly good representations are found in miniatures from a twelfth-century copy of the John Skylitzes manuscript in Madrid (Kalavrezou 2003: fig. 18; Vikan 1990: fig. 1). Based on written and iconographic evidence from this same period, Pitarakis (2009: 195) speculates that funerary and commemorative portraits of individual females, sometimes wearing wedding wreaths or jewelled *stemma* and accompanied by parents, may signal that they died as virgins. Naturally, one wonders when such portraits first begin to appear, and if the Humayma plaque with its small portrait is an early prototype of this type of iconography.

Discussion of Burial 2

The burial of this young female in such a prominent location in the main aisle of the Lower Church, and the richness of the grave goods, unprecedented at Hauarra, are curious circumstances and raise many questions. What was her identity, her family's position in the community, and why was the C101 Church chosen as her final resting place? Children or infant burials within church precincts and complexes are not well-attested in southern Jordan, although they are common enough elsewhere. There are parallels at Khirbet as-Samrā (Nabulsi and Humbert 1996; Nabulsi et al. 1998), Oboda (Negev 1997: 135–37), and Be'er Sheva (Sodini 1986: 237). Privileged burials within a church were relatively common in the churches in the Negev, particularly after 630, but rare elsewhere (Sodini 1986; Goldfus 1997). When they do occur they are usually those of clerics, abbots, or other high-ranking ecclesiastics (Negev 1974: 407). A few exceptions are found in the central Negev where, around AD 541, burials in the South Church complex at Oboda began to include laypersons; among these was an unnamed child found beneath the floor of the atrium's eastern porch (Negev 1997: 135–37). At Nessana, the deaths of five children are recorded in epitaphs associated with the North Church (Colt 1962: 169, 180, 186; Negev 1974: 407); two may be linked to the Justinianic plague that swept through the area in 541, while the causes of death in the other cases are unknown.

The Hauarra girl appears to belong to a select group of children whose families were granted special permission to bury them within churches or their annexes. The significance of the Church's consent in these cases is controversial, because it appears to contravene the prohibitions on burials within communities and houses of worship set out in the great corpus of Roman law commissioned by Justinian and published between 529 and 534 (*Cod. Theod.* IX.17.6; *Dig.* 47.12.3; *Cod. Just.* III.44.12; *Epitome Legum* XI.39.43). Archaeological evidence from *Palaestina Tertia* demonstrates that intramural burials commenced not long after the Edict of Milan (Ivison 1996: 102). Ivison also cites the tombs in the forum area of Corinth as an example of this development, but it now seems that the forum burials were outside the Late Roman and Byzantine city wall. In his survey of inhumations within eastern churches, including many in Syria, the Negev, and Arabia, Sodini (1986: 233) notes that there was strong opposition to inhumations in churches, even before the passage of the Theodosian Law of 381 which forbade burials in *apostoleia* and *martyria*. Despite this resistance, the practice of interring prominent ecclesiastics within church precincts persisted into the eighth century.

Aside from location, the preparation and disposition of the girl's body is consistent with mortuary practices in other communities in Transjordan and elsewhere in the Late Roman and Byzantine period, for example at the Greek port town of Kenchreai (Rife et al. 2007). Like adults, children were generally clothed, shod, and wrapped in shrouds before being laid to rest. They were placed in tombs or graves with an east–west orientation, with the head at the west end. According to Talbot (2009: 300), the burial assemblages of sub-adults in the Byzantine period tend to be rather spartan, containing single items of jewellery or an apotropaic object. If her claim is true, generally speaking, then the rich and eclectic nature of the grave goods from the Lower Church is all the more striking. To be sure, the disparity between Talbot's claim and the size of our assemblage may simply reflect a regional difference in funerary practices, or the affluence of the girl's family. It is interesting that the burial of a 14–15 year-old girl in a shaft tomb in the Khirbat as-Samrā Site C Cemetery was also far richer than the surrounding tombs (Nabulsi et al. 2009: 170).

In addition to the burial of the young girl, there were five other undisturbed graves in the Nave (see pp. 241–52), one disturbed burial (Burial 6) in the north aisle, and perhaps one or more uninvestigated disturbed burials in the south aisle. The seemingly random locations of the burials were marked by pavers with crosses. The construction of the cists, placement of the bodies (head laid at the west end) and their dispositions (completely extended, with hands crossing or almost crossing the pelvis) attest to a general uniformity of funerary practice. The other burials, however, had few or no grave offerings. In Burial 1, a bronze cross and fragments of leather sandals are the only artefacts associated with the remains of a child under the age of 12, indicating that the mere fact of death during sub-adulthood did not ensure rich grave offerings. Both children, however, in contrast to the

other burials, were furnished with cross pendants. In Burials 3 and 5, wooden coffins held the well-preserved skeletons of adult males. Although wood was undoubtedly an expensive commodity, the associated artefacts are extremely humble. Burial 5 contained a single iron nail and leather fragments in the area of the feet. The body of a female between the ages of 25 and 30 was found in Burial 4. A pair of degraded leather sandals, a small clasp or pendant, and a bone pin that was used to secure the shroud were the only artefacts found with the burial. The identities of the adult individuals are unknown, but they must have been notables in the community or the congregation to have warranted such a prominent place of interment. The meagreness of the funerary goods consequently indicates typical burial customs, or special piety rather than poverty. Indeed, undisturbed church burials at Oboda and Nessana reveal the same sort of modesty. The elaborate assemblage associated with the girl in Burial 2 is strikingly exceptional.

In addition to the distinguished location of the girl's grave and the size of her burial assemblage, the eclectic nature of the objects provides a wonderfully rich impression of a vibrant Trans-Jordanian culture in the Byzantine period, particularly with respect to economy, trade, technology, and religion. The relative economic prosperity of the girl's family in the small desert settlement of Hauarra is reflected clearly in the gold and gilded-copper jewellery, the figured plaque with its gold leaf embellishment, and the ivory spindle whorls and cosmetic container. Traditionally, household implements such as spindle whorls and toiletries were executed in relatively cheap materials such as bone, stone, and wood, and it has been argued that these have a history of being replaced only when a community experiences considerable economic improvement (Simak 2005–2006). Six other spindle whorls have been found at Humayma, all executed in limestone or steatite. The ivory whorls might have been specially commissioned tomb offerings intended to symbolize the girl's potential contribution to her household's economy, and to make a statement about the family's financial good fortune. Items crafted from precious materials also point to a level of affluence in Hauarra's Christian community, as does execution of the church's carved chancel screen in imported marble (Schick 1995b: 340; below, pp. 450–73). It is interesting to note that Nabulsi et al. (2007: 273) posit a period of general prosperity in the Christian community at Khirbet as-Samrā, too, during the sixth and seventh centuries.

From an artistic and technological standpoint, some grave goods provide excellent evidence for a kind of artistic syncretism — Syrian, Greek, Nabataean, and Roman — that undoubtedly arose from the community's location and role in a strong regional trade network; it was well-situated for cultural and artistic exchange with the Negev and Egypt, along with Palmyra and other points to the east. We see in the form and imagery of the transformed al-ʿUzza frontlet, in the presence of Christian imagery and context, and in the use of the plaster mirror as an apotropaic tool, a melding of different religious traditions. Despite the strenuous objections of church fathers to the use of apotropaic devices (Dickie 1995: *passim*), it is apparent that pagan and Christian practices continued to co-exist in this region long after Christianity had taken root.

In the choice of grave goods we see a clear indication of the value of children to their parents, and the hopes they carried for the future. The rite of passage for most girls was marriage, and it was not unusual for families to place the dolls of unmarried girls in their tombs, even those who had moved well beyond the age at which they would be interested in toys. Such was the case of Maria, who married the emperor Honorius in February 398. Maria's mother allegedly prevented immediate consummation of the marriage because the bride was only about ten years old, but when she died in 407, almost aged 20, she was buried with her dolls in the manner of other virgin girls (Elderkin 1932: 475; Manson 1978; Ricotti 1995). There is less material and literary evidence for this practice in the region and period under discussion, but it is evident that the practice was not completely unknown. A few examples demonstrate this point well. Two jointed bone dolls have been discovered in Jerusalem. One dating to the late second century was interred in a lead coffin with a female in her twenties (Rahmani 1960: 147, fig. c); the second is of third-century date and was discovered in a shaft

tomb on the Nablus Road that held the remains of four individuals, one of whom was an infant (Hamilton and Husseini 1935: pl. LXXXII, no. 3). In Tomb 99 at Khirbet as-Samrā, a plaster figurine, approximately 12 cm in length, was found in the hand of a girl aged 12–15 years, while fragments of at least two other figurines were interred with other children (Nabulsi 2000: fig. 1; Nabulsi et al. 1998: 618;). Excavation in the sixth- to eighth-century necropolis near Saqqara uncovered the remains of a young girl with a rag doll in her hand (Quibell 1907: 34, pl. 39.4).

We can only speculate on the impulse behind the rich offerings for the girl's burial, but it most likely was connected with a fervent desire on the part of her grief-stricken parents to ensure that their daughter went tranquilly and comfortably into the afterlife. What better way to achieve this than to seek such an honourable place of interment, to spare no expense in her burial gifts, and to protect her for eternity from malevolent forces. In so doing, this girl's parents also inadvertently provided an invaluable picture of the affluence and diversity of the Christian population of Byzantine Hauarra.

C101 Burial 3

The grave contained the well-preserved skeleton of an adult male, laid out on his back with the head at the west end (for the skeleton, see pp. 249, 324).

1. (1992.0572.01). Fragment of rope; very brittle, broken, incomplete; MPL 0.06 m, D 0.02 m. The fragment of rope was found on top of the coffin, presumably dropped there after it had been used to lower the coffin into the grave. The rope was composed of three strands of twisted twine, each 0.002 m in diameter. Soon after recovery the artefact disintegrated into powder.

2. (1992.0606.02; fig.11.4.2a). Fragments of cloth — probably linen — from the burial shroud. Broken into many small fragments and three larger lumps; very dry, light and brittle. MPL 0.043 m.

3. (1992.0572.02) Fragment of board from coffin. Very fragmented. Identified by J. Ramsay as likely *Cupressus* sp. (*Cupressaceae* Family, Mediterranean Cypress). According to Danin (2004: 20), only one species of *Cupressus* has been

noted in the region covered by *Flora Palaestina* — *C. sempervirens* — which has been noted growing on the north facing slope of soft sandstone in Edom (Danin 2004:20). The wood has also been identified at 14 locations throughout Israel and the Sinai on sites ranging in date from the late Bronze Age to the sixteenth century AD (Fahn et al. 1986: 55).

4. (1992.0572.03). Fragment of board from coffin. Very well-preserved, dense and hard wood. It was difficult to obtain a clear section, but the wood was identified by J. Ramsay as most likely *Acacia* sp. (*Fabaceae* Family, Acacias). Three species of *Acacia* have been identified in the region covered by *Flora Palaestina* (Fahn et al. 1986: 116–18). Danin (2004: 125–26), however, identifies seven species, and it therefore is difficult to determine the species of *Acacia* that is present in the sample. The trees are typically found in *wadis* in hot deserts. Several species have been identified archaeologically from the Negev, Dead Sea area, and Sinai ranging in date from 2000 BC to the seventh century AD (Fahn et al. 1986: 116–19).

C101, Burial 4

The grave contained the badly decomposed skeleton of a 35–45 year old female (for the skeleton, see pp. 250, 324–25). The body had been wrapped in a cloth shroud, which survived only as a dark discoloration on parts of the skeleton, especially the skull.

1. (1993.0062.02; fig. 11.4.1). Bone pin; broken, incomplete, only the head preserved; MPL 0.016 m, D 0.008 m.

The pin, found among the bones of the left hand, may have been used to close up the burial shroud. The head was turned in a series of spool patterns that mirror each other on either side of a deep, flat-bottomed groove. Some decorative material, now lost, may originally have been mounted in the groove. Pins for clothing and hair, both functional and decorative, are ubiquitous in the material culture of this region. Sizes and forms vary according to purpose (e.g., longer pins for hair arrangements), but their general outline is fairly uniform. Shafts are generally straight and taper to a point. Occasionally the shafts show some entasis, and embellishment in the form of

gold leaf (Rahmani 1960: 144, pl. 20E). The finials exhibit the greatest variation, ranging from geometric shapes to intricately worked zoomorphic and anthropomorphic forms. The closest parallels for this pin are found at en-Gedi and Nessana, and all are consistent with the Humayma head in terms of date (Chernov 2007: 526, pl. 67, Late Roman–Early Byzantine; Colt 1962: pl. XXI.10–12, 5–7C). Raised mouldings or necking rings on many other specimens, from the Late Roman through Early Byzantine period, produce in some cases a spool-like effect. More often than not, however, the rings are surmounted by stylized pine-cones (Ibrahim and Gordon 1987: pl. XXIX, 8, Amman, Roman imperial; McNicoll et al. 1982: 92, no. 55, Pella, 2nd half 3–3rd quarter 4C), spheres (Rahmani 1960, pl. 20E), or a zoomorphic head, as is the case with a hairpin from the necropolis at Queen Alia International Airport (Ibrahim and Gordon 1987, pl. XXIX, 7, Roman imperial). Curiously, the spooling on the Humayma pin bears the strongest similarity to elaborately turned couch and chair legs of Greek and Roman date (Richter 1966: passim). This type of ornamentation is also found on a highly-polished furniture joint from Oboda (Rosenthal-Heginbottom 1997: 208, pl. 4, no. 31, Oboda, 1–2C). There was a strong tradition of bone carving in Palestine in this and much later eras (see Goldfus and Bowes 2000), and it is not inconceivable that the individual who crafted the pin simply drew inspiration from carvers working on a much larger scale. Compare also Iliffe 1934: Vestibule, no. 4–5 (Tarshiha, late 4C); Harding 1951: pl. XXXI, no 432 (Amman, Roman period); McDaniel 2006, 108, fig. 6.67 (Lejjun, ca. 363–502); Sellers and Baramki 1953: fig. 19, 252 (Silet edh-Dhahr, Roman–Byzantine periods).

2. (1993.0062.02; fig. 11.4.2b). Bronze hooked clasp; broken, twisted, incomplete; MPL 0.015 m, W 0.007 m, Th 0.003 m. There is a nearly complete, circular loop at one end, partial remains of a second loop or a hook at the other end, oriented perpendicular to the first. The object was found beneath the vertebrae.

It is difficult to assess the function of this item. Patrich (2008: 468, no. 250 and 268, Caesarea, no date) and Rosenthal-Heginbottom (1997: pl. 4, 42, Oboda, 550) both describe hooks that are similar in form to the one from Humayma. The latter suggests (1997: 209) that the Oboda hook, and the fragment of fine chain attached to it, were part of a *polykandelon* or incense burner, while Patrich (2008: 450, no. 259) identifies the Caesarea specimen as a spindle hook, used to catch fibers for twisting (Forbes 1964: 154–55). Since a *polykandelon* chain seems an unlikely burial gift, the spindle seems more likely, made of bone or wood that has since decayed (cf. Davidson 1952: nos. 1223–28, and Patrich et al. 2008: 468, no. 259). The appearance of a spindle in this context would not be unusual, since spinning implements regularly served as indicators of women's industry in burial contexts.

3. (1993.0062.03; fig. 11.4.3). Leather sandals; very brittle, shrunken, and curled; MPL 0.05 m; MPW 0.02 m. Only a small portion of the original footwear remains. The fragments were found in association with the feet. The largest fragment, possibly part of the sole, preserved eight small stitching holes worked into a ridge of leather on the upper surface of the sole. Similar fragments were found in F102, Burial 2; see the discussion there (p. 384).

C101, Burial 5

The grave contained a wooden coffin (Locus 01.63) in less good condition than the coffin in Burial 3. Inside was the skeleton of a 25–34 year old male (for the skeleton, see pp. 251, 325–26). A single iron nail was the only artefact, other than very slight traces of sandals near the feet.

1. (1992.0615.02). Fragment of the long lid board from the coffin. Crumbly. Identified by J. Ramsay as most likely *Crataegus* sp. (*Rosaceae* family, Hawthorn). Three or four species of *Crataegus* are found in Palestine. Unfortunately their wood anatomy is very similar, so they cannot be unambiguously separated (Fahn et al. 1986: 148–50). Hawthorn is the common name given to the genus in Europe. It has an edible fruit that is sold in the markets, especially *C. azarolus,* which is more palatable than *C. aronia.* It seems most likely that this sample is *C. aronia,* as that species is present in Edom according to Danin (2004: 123).

2. (1992.0615.03). Small fragment of coffin board. Identified as most likely *Crataegus* sp. (*Rosaceae* family, Hawthorn). See no. 1.

3. (1992.0615.04). Very fragmentary piece of coffin board. Identified as *Tamarix* sp. (*Tamaricaceae* Family, Tamarisk). Nine species of *Tamarix* have been identified in the region covered by *Flora Palaestina* (Fahn et al. 1986: 165–71). Several of these species are common in hot deserts but in particular *T. aravensis, T. passerinoides,* and *T. nilotica* (Danin 2004: 214–16). *Tamarix* has been identified in archaeological remains from very early periods at 12 locations, mainly in the Negev and the Sinai (Fahn et al. 1986:171).

11.B.3. Conclusions Concerning the C101, F102, and B100 Burials

The construction of the cists, placement of the bodies with the head at the west end, and the arrangement of the corpses completely extended, with hands crossing or almost crossing the pelvis, attest to a general uniformity of funerary practice from the first to the sixth century. Scraps of woollen and linen cloth and of leather attest to interment clothed and shod, or sometimes wrapped in a shroud. Wooden coffins were supplied for at least three of the burials: F102 Burial 1, C101 Burials 3 and 5. The cist containing the Nabataean burial beneath and pre-dating the B100 Church was lined and roofed with slabs of stone, like five of the six burials in the C101 Church. At some point, possibly immediately after placement of the covering slabs, a marker was constructed of upright blocks. The two burial cists outside and pre-dating the F102 church were simply cut into the hard soil and roofed with stone slabs. Low mudbrick walls may have been built around the cists, to mark them off and to contain a heap of earth. C101 Burial 4 was not lined with stone slabs, but it is otherwise no different from the other burials in that church. Each of the C101 burials was marked by a cross carved in the pavement above its approximate location. There were two crosses above Burial 2, which may be significant given the richness of the grave goods.

This method of burial, in both lined and un-lined cists, was common in Jordan during the periods represented at Humayma, for both Christians and non-Christians: e.g., Wadi Faynan (Findlater et al. 1998: 72), Amman airport (Ibrahim and Gordon 1987), Umm al-Jimal (Brashler 1995;

Cheyney et al. 2009), Khirbet as-Samrā (Nabulsi and Humbert 1996; Humbert and Desreumaux 1998: 272–73), Mampsis (Negev 1971), Rehovot in the Negev (Tsafrir 1988: 194–95), and for many Christian burial sites in the Negev (Nagar and Sonntag 2008: 88).

Yet C101 Burial 2 and, to a lesser extent, F102 Burial 1 stand out from the other burials for their extensive range of grave offerings. Since C101 Burial 6 and the B100 burial were too badly disturbed to allow determination of any grave goods, the sample size is seven burials, sufficient to draw some conclusions. In C101 Burial 1, the bronze cross and fragments of leather sandals associated with the remains of a child under the age of 12 indicate that the mere fact of death during sub-adulthood did not ensure rich grave offerings. The wooden coffins in C101 Burials 3 and 5, which held the well-preserved skeletons of adult males, suggest a certain level of affluence, for wood was undoubtedly an expensive commodity, particularly in large planks. But the associated artefacts are extremely humble. Burial 3 contained a small bronze cross, and Burial 5 a single iron nail and leather fragments in the area of the feet. Similarly, the degraded leather sandals, spindle hook, and bone pin used

to secure the shroud of a female, aged 25–30 (Burial 4), are also unassuming. Although the identities of these individuals are unknown, they — like the girl in C101 Burial 2 — must have been notables in the community or the congregation to have warranted a privileged interment. Consequently, the meagre funerary goods indicate typical burial customs, special piety, or religious office rather than poverty. Indeed, undisturbed church burials at Oboda and Nessana reveal the same sort of modest burial goods.

The adult female in F102 Burial 1 was also interred with jewellery, and a marine shell. While these goods are not as rich or varied as those associated with the girl in C101 Burial 2, they still stand out among the sample of intact burials at Humayma. One variation, however, is that this interment was not inside a church and probably predated construction of the adjacent F102 Church. The male in the adjacent tomb was buried without any grave goods, but other tombs in this graveyard (if in fact it is a graveyard) may have contained grave goods. The C101 Burial 2 is clearly anomalous among the C101 burials, but the sample for intact non-church burials is too small for conclusions to be drawn.

Chapter 12

Coins, Metal, Bone, Ivory, Shell, Plaster, and Terracotta Objects

by John P. Oleson, Erik de Bruijn, Dennine Dudley, and Michelle Smith

12.A. HOARD OF COINS AND JEWELLERY
(E. de Bruijn, D. Dudley)

12.A.1. Location and Discovery

During a group hike after hours in the course of the 1991 excavation season, the authors of this report, members of the Humayma Excavation Project staff, discovered by chance a coin and jewellery hoard consisting of five gold *solidi,* eighteen silver drachms, and a pair of large gold hoop earrings, ornamented with gold beads and pearls. The artefacts were presented to Oleson within minutes of their recovery. Preliminary examination indicated that the *solidi* were comparable to those issued by the Eastern Roman Emperor Arcadius (383–408), and that the Sasanian King Yazdegard I (399–420) minted the drachms. The materials were cleaned by Mr. Ibrahim al-Haj Hasan at the Conservation Laboratory of the Department of Antiquities, and in August 1992 the coins and earrings were accessioned by the Jordan Archaeological Museum, Amman. The hoard has been published (de Bruijn and Dudley 1993, 1995; Oleson et al. 1993: 488), but a report is included here for completeness in documenting the excavation and to correct a few minor errors. The coins found in and around the settlement centre are presented in Section 12.B.

The hoard was found 4 km west of the Humayma settlement site on a featureless, sloping, sandy plateau, punctuated with scattered clumps of brush (approximate UTM coordinates, 36R 0722962, 3316647; elev. 1000 m asl). The hoard was found near a dirt track that runs through the hills west of the settlement area, crosses the plateau, and continues on down through the complex of steep wadis and gullies that form the eastern slopes of the Wadi Arabah. No evidence of structural remains was found in the immediate vicinity of the find site, and only possible traces of walls in the neighbourhood, at the northeast edge of the plateau. The presence of small terrace dams in the wadi to the east of the plateau, although undated, suggests some agricultural activity in the area in antiquity, and cave or tent occupation by ancient transient pastoralists is possible. Surface sherding (100% within a 3.0 m radius, and 25% across the entire plateau) yielded scattered ceramic fragments, ranging in date from Middle Nabataean to Ottoman, indicating that the track has been used continuously since antiquity.

At the time of discovery, one oxidized silver drachm, dark-grey in colour, was visible on the surface of the soil and three pearls of one of the earrings also protruded above the surface a few cm to the north; no camera was available to document the context. The remainder of the hoard lay within 0.03 m of the surface, embedded in the wind- and water-deposited sand that forms the ground surface over the entire area of the find site. When the first drachm was lifted, others became visible underneath in a neat stack, some of them still untarnished and bright. Removal of the drachms revealed the gold *solidi* lying beneath. Aside from a small amount of calcium carbonate encrustation, the latter were uncorroded and bright. The earrings lay one on top of the other, adjacent to the coins. One of the gold hoops and some of the pearls were partially coated with a thin encrustation of calcium carbonate. No remains of a container were found, nor was there any evidence that the find site had been marked in any way. The neat and discrete stacking of the two types of coins and the earrings suggests a tight wrapping rather than a loose sack purse.

12.A.2. Catalogue

For each item, the Jordan Archaeological Museum inventory number (beginning with "J") is followed by the Humayma registration number. Drachm die combinations are specified, and Pahlavi legends are given in transliterated form. The locations of any significant features are also given in terms of their relation to the clock face. Cited parallels apply to all the items in each section.

Solidi (fig. 12.1)

1. J16516 (1991.0392.01). 4.34 g. D 2.20 cm. Die orientation 6:00. Obv. *DNABCADI-VSPFAVG.* Draped and cuirassed profile bust of Arcadius facing right and wearing a rosette and jewel diadem with a large jewel in front. Rev. *ONCOBOI-AAVGGGT.* Constantinopolis, mural-crowned and draped facing, head turned to right, right leg bare, seated on a backless lion-headed throne, with ship's prow left, holding a long sceptre and a round shield with legend *VOT/VMVL/X.* In exergue, *AONOB.* All *N*s are reversed.

Parallels: References are to first quinquennial *vota* issues of Arcadius from the Constantinople

mint. *Officina* numbers vary. A variety of Arcadius *solidi* were examined personally by the authors, who would like to thank the curatorial staff of the Department of Coins and Medals, British Museum, for their assistance. Grierson and Mays 1992: nos. 77 and 78, pl. 4; Pearce 1932: 207, nos. 14 and 18; *RIC* 9: 231, nos. 70 c 2 and 70 c 4; Robertson 1982: 472, no. 26 (pl. 92); Sabatier 1955: 102, no. 12; Sear 1988: 356, no. 4219; Tolstoi 1968: 21, no. 21 (pl. 1, no. 21), nos. 22, 23, 24, 25.

2. J16517 (1991.0392.02). 4.35 g. D 2.20 cm. Die Orientation 6:00. Same dies as no. 1.

3. J16518 (1991.0392.05). 4.23 g. D 2.20 cm. Die Orientation 6:00. Same dies as no. 1.

4. J16519 (1991.0392.04). 4.32 g. D 2.10 cm. Die Orientation 6:00. Same dies as no. 1.

5. J16520 (1991.0392.03). 4.24 g. D 2.15 cm. Die Orientation 6:00. Same dies as no. 1.

Drachms (figs. 12.2–4).

The legends, which are often incomplete or only partially legible, are transliterated from Pahlavi. The obverse legend starts at the left side of the globe on the crown and runs counter-clockwise inside the border. Short vowels not written in Pahlavi are supplied in lower case; Pahlavi consonants represented by two letters are underlined. Illegible letters are transliterated in parentheses; missing letters or word elements are placed in square brackets. The different obverse (OS = Obverse Sasanian) and reverse (RS = Reverse Sasanian) dies are given individual numbers. In addition to the published parallels cited, the authors personally examined the collection of Yazdegard I drachms in the Department of Coins and Medals of the British Museum.

6. J16521 (1991.0392.07). 4.00 g. D 2.80 cm. Die Orientation 3:00. Dies: OS2/RS2. Obv. *MaZD(ISN) Ba(G)I RAM<u>SH</u>aT[RI] YaZDaKa[RTI].* Bearded profile bust of Yazdegard I facing right, wearing an ornate crown surmounted by a globe and fronted with a crescent. Rev. Persian fire altar, consisting of a two-course base, column with a garland on

FIG. 12.1 *Finds from hoard: Nos. 1-5, Byzantine counterfeit* solidi *of Arcadius.*

either side, and three-course top, with nine flames flanked by single horizontal crescents above the altar. The altar is flanked by two crowned profile standing figures facing the altar and holding staffs or swords. On the altar column the legend *RAST*. With the coin held so that the altar column is horizontal with the flames on the right, the legend reads from right to left.

Parallels: de Morgan 1933: 701, nos. 164d, 164e, 164f, pl. LXI, nos. 4, 5, 6; Göbl 1971: pl. 9, no. 147; Mitchiner 1978: 164, no. 941; Nikitin 1996: 76, nos. 27, 29, 30; Paruck 1924: 361, no. 305, and 445 (Bartholomaei Collection) pl. XI, no. 10; Sellwood 1985: 116, no. 41; Warden 1972: 275, nos. 14, 28, 34, 37.

7. J16522 (1991.0392.08). 3.26 g. D 2.70 cm. Die Orientation 3:00. Dies: OS3/RS3. Obv. *Ma(Z) DISN (BaGI) RAMSHaT[RI] (Ya)Z[DaKaRTI]*. Obv. as no. 6, except that *BaGI* appears to the lower right of the bust rather than to the left. Rev. as no. 6, except that the letters *AI* appear in the field to the right of the altar.

8. J16523 (1991.0392.09). 4.06 g. D 2.60 cm. Die Orientation 3:15. Dies: OS1/RS1. Obv. *MaZDIS(N) BaG(I) RAMSHaTR[I] [Ya] ZDaKa(R)[TI]*. Obv. as no. 6, except portrait has wider braiding in the beard. Lunate inden-

tation outside border between 7:00 and 8:00 identifies obverses from this die. Rev. as no. 6, except that the letters *RA* appear in the field to the left of the altar.

9. J16524 (1991.0392.10). 4.06 g. D 2.60 cm. Die Orientation 3:00. Dies: OS1/RS1. As no. 8.

10. J16525 (1991.0392.11). 4.00 g. D 2.70 cm. Die Orientation 3:00. Dies: OS4/RS4. Obv. *(MaZ) DISN BaGI RAMSHaTR[I] [Ya]ZDa(KaR)[TI]*. Obv. and rev as no. 8.

11. J16526 (1991.0392.12). 3.61 g. D 2.50 cm. Die Orientation 3:00. Dies: OS3/RS3. As no. 7.

12. J16527 (1991.0392.13). 3.68 g. D 2.70 cm. Die Orientation 3:00. Dies: OS1/RS1. As no. 8.

13. J16528 (1991.0392.14). 3.68 g. D 2.70 cm. Die Orientation 3:00. Dies: OS1/RS1. As no. 8.

14. J16529 (1991.0392.15). 4.04 g. D 2.50 cm. Die Orientation 3:00. Dies: OS1/RS1. As no. 8.

15. J16530 (1991.0392.16). 3.11 g. D 2.60 cm. Die Orientation 3:00. Dies: OS5/RS5. Obv. *MaZD(I) SN BaGI (R)AMSHa(T)[RI] YaZDaKa[RTI]*. Obv. as no. 6. Rev. as no. 6, except the letter A appears in the right field and an indecipherable legend in the left. During photography, a small fragment of the flan that had broken off was inadvertently replaced showing its reverse in

FIG. 12.2 *Finds from hoard: Nos. 6-11, Sasanian drachms of Yazdegard I.*

FIG. 12.3   *Finds from hoard: Nos. 12-17, Sasanian drachms of Yazdegard I.*

FIG. 12.4   *Finds from hoard: Nos. 18-23, Sasanian drachms of Yazdegard I.*

the obverse illustration and its obverse in the reverse illustration.

16. J16531 (1991.0392.17). 4.15 g. D 2.60 cm. Die Orientation 3:00. Dies: OS6/RS6. Obv. *MaZ(D) ISN BaG(I) R(A)MSHaTR[I] YaZDaKa[RTI]*. Obv. as no. 6. Rev. as no. 6, except the letter *A* appears in both right and left fields.

17. J16532 (1991.0392.18). 3.27 g. D 2.70 cm. Die Orientation 3:00. Dies: OS7/RS5. Obv. *MaZD(ISN) BaGI (RA)MSHaT[RI] (YaZDa)[KaRTI]*. Obv. as no. 6. A thin ridge extending from the king's nose to the right may indicate a crack in this die. Rev. as no. 15, with the letters *AI* in the right field and the letter *A* in the left.

18. J16533 (1991.0392.019). 3.51 g. D 2.60 cm. Die Orientation 3:00. Dies: OS5/RS5. As no. 15.

19. J16534 (1991.0392.020). 4.28 g. D 2.60 cm. Die Orientation 3:00. Dies: OS8/RS7. Obv. *(MaZDISN BaGI RAMSHa)T(RI YaZDaKaRTI)*. Obv. as no. 6, except crown has a central turret and lacks the trefoil adornment at the rear. Rev. as no. 6, with traces of a legend that includes the letter *A* in right field. Flame displaced to the right.

20. J16535 (1991.0392.21). 4.16 g. D 2.80 cm. Die Orientation 3:00. Dies: OS1/RS1. As no. 8.

21. J16536 (1991.0392.22). 3.24 g. D 2.70 cm. Die Orientation 3:00. Dies: OS9/RS8. Obv. *MaZDI(SN) BaGI RAMSHaT[RI] YaZ[DaKaRTI]*. Obv. as no. 6, except crown lacks trefoil decoration at rear. Rev. as no. 6, with letters *RA* in left field and *AI* in the right. Right hand attendant wears a scabbard. Altar is slightly elongated.

22. J16537 (1991.0392.23). 4.15 g. D 2.75 cm. Die Orientation 3:00. Dies: OS1/RS6. Obv. as no. 8. Rev. as no. 16, with letters *RA* in left field and *A* in the right.

23. J16538 (1991.0392.06). 3.92 g. D 2.60 cm. Die Orientation 3:00. Dies: OS1/RS1. As no. 8.

Earrings (fig. 12.5.1).

1. J16539 (1991.0392.024, 25). Matched pair of pearl and gold bead hoop earrings. Each earring weighs 17.5 g and consists of an oval hoop ca. 4.5 cm long and 2.6 cm wide formed by a smooth gold rod (D 4.0 mm) terminating at either end in a loop (interior D 2.0 mm, exterior D 4.0 mm). The rod was formed of three twists of gold wire (each D 1.0 mm). Five irregular ("baroque") pearls are strung on the hoop, separated by four gold beads (D 8.0–9.0 mm), each with five hemispherical protrusions bordered by granulated decoration consisting of a row of four or five tiny spheres (D 0.5–2.0 mm). The pearls vary in colour; they are strung in a random arrangement that includes pale shades of cream, yellow, and grey, along with white. The pearls and beads occupy slightly more than half of the circumference of the hoop. The loop at one end of the hoop is finished with a wrapping of six turns of wire, the other by a single turn of wire that then continues behind the pearls and beads and holds them in place with a further wrapping of nine turns. The arrangement of the pearls is roughly symmetrical by size, with the centre pearl apparently selected for its teardrop shape. The fasteners that attached the earrings to the earlobes are missing.

Parallels: Allason-Jones 1989: pl.1; Doxiadis 1995 106, fig.75, Cairo CG33248; al-Ghabban 2010: 403, fig. 242; Hackens 1976: 122–23; Hanfmann 1975: 312–13, pl. XLIX; Kraeling 1938: 208, pl. XXXVII.c; Musche 1988: pls. XIV, XV, CIII; Ramage and Ramage 2009: 265, fig. 8.15.

12.A.3. Discussion of the Coins

Arcadius, born in 377, was the elder son of Theodosius I and his first wife, Aelia Flacilla. Created Augustus in 383, he inherited the eastern half of the Empire after his father's death in 395, his younger brother Honorius taking the western portion. He died in 408 and was succeeded by his young son, Theodosius II. From 383, coins were struck for him in both the western and eastern por-

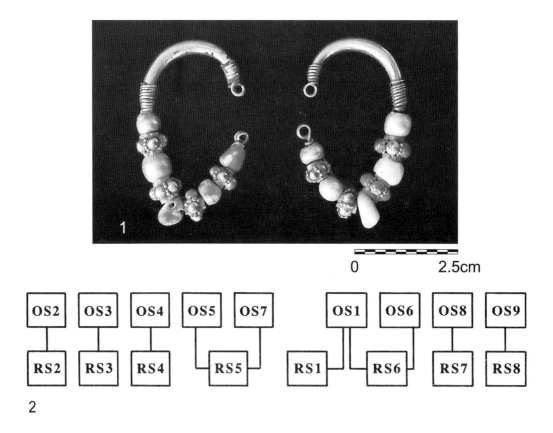

FIG. 12.5 *Finds from Hoard: No. 1, Pair of pearl and gold bead hoop earrings (1991.0392.024, 25; Photo: S. Coliton). No. 2: Chart of dies and die links of the Sasanian drachms.*

tions of the Empire, but in the East, *solidi* were only struck at Constantinople and Thessalonica (Carson 1970: 186). These mints used either a profile or helmeted and cuirassed facing bust of the emperor on the obverse, while a common reverse shows a seated Constantinopolis either holding a globe and Victory or a shield bearing a *vota* inscription (*RIC* 10: 63–67, pls. 1–2).

Yazdegard I, probably a son of Shapur III, inherited the Sasanian throne from Varahran IV in 399. He appears to have been designated heir before the latter's death, as his name appears on the reverse of some of his predecessor's coins (Paruck 1976: 94). He maintained generally peaceful relations with the Romans, signing a treaty of peace and friendship with them in 408/9, and being designated as guardian of Arcadius' son Theodosius II (Greatrex 2002: 32–34; Procopius, *Pers.* 1.2.1–10; Agathias, *Hist.* 1.26.6–7 (157.5–13). Assassinated by dissident nobles in 420, he was succeeded by his

son Varahran V. The silver drachm, struck on a large, thin flan, and leaving a wide border, is by far the most common issue of Sasanian rulers, who are distinguished by the unique form of their crowns. While the obverse portrays the crowned ruler surrounded by a legend, the reverse shows some variation of the Persian fire altar, with or without attendants. Mitchiner lists fifteen definite and two uncertain mintmarks for the coinage of Yazdegard I, including that of Airan Khurra Shahpuhr, or Susa (Mitchiner 1978: 139–46). The year of issue or the regnal year does not appear on Sasanian coins until well after Yazdegard's reign.

The obverse and reverse of the Humayma *solidi* resemble those of Arcadius' first quinquennial *vota* issue from the Constantinople mint. There are, however, significant differences that call into question the authenticity of the coins. The face of the obverse bust bears little resemblance to other portraits of Arcadius or to other members of the family of Theodosius I. The artist has idealized the face, which more closely resembles that seen on *solidi* of Constantius II (Hackens 1976: 124, no. 57). Other minor differences in hair style, in the folds of the drapery, and in the position of the tails and use of rosettes on the diadem all fall within the range of acceptable variation found among similar issues struck from different dies.

The portrait of Constantinopolis on the reverse of the Humayma *solidi* is more crudely executed than the image seen on comparable coins. The face is scarcely detailed, and, while the headdress has been described as a mural crown, it could as well be a careless depiction of the more commonly seen crested helmet. The throne has lion heads at its sides, but these have become stylized into a pattern of bumps, while the ship's prow at the left is only sketchily portrayed and has been confused with the leg of the throne. The shield held by Constantinopolis is round rather than the normal oval shape, and it appears to be floating, as it does not rest on the arm of the throne. The figure's left hand does not hold the top of the shield as on comparable *solidi*. Unlike the clearly executed *vota* legends on other coins, where the letters are quite legible and are carefully arranged in four lines, the legend on the shield of the Humayma *solidi* has been reduced almost to an abstract design. Of the customary legend *VOT/V/MVL /X*, the *V* and *T* of the first line are represented by mere vertical strokes, the numeral *V* has been conflated with the letter *V*, the *M* appears as a squiggle, the *L* resembles a *T* lying on its side, and the whole inscription occupies three lines rather than the normal four.

The obverse and reverse legends also demonstrate that the die carver paid less attention to the cutting of the lettering than to the carving of the obverse portrait. On the obverse, the legend duplicates the formula and spacing used on comparable *solidi*, but the letters are badly cut and not of uniform size. The letter *B*, larger than the other letters, is mistakenly used instead of an *R* in the name of the emperor, and the letters *PF* are barely recognizable. All letters have serifs, all *A*'s have crossbars, and the letter *N* is oriented properly. On the reverse, the initial *C* of the word *CONCORDIA* has been omitted, a large *B* has been used instead

of an *R,* and an *O* instead of a *D*. The letter *T* is used instead of the Greek letter number *G* to indicate the *officina* of the mint. In the exergue, a rudimentary *A* is used instead of an initial *C* in the mintmark *CONOB,* and the final *B* is placed horizontally on its back. All the letters have serifs, but the *A*'s do not have crossbars, and the letter *N* is reversed each time it is used. Although Pearce (1931: 4) notes two coins of this *vota* type with the reading "ARCAPIVS" on the obverse, misspellings on regular issues are rare (Kent 1991: 40).

The disparity in quality between the carving of the portrait and the letter cutting suggests that the legends were considered less important than the portraiture, and that the die carver took less care in producing them. This may not have been unusual, since Latin was not the principal language in the eastern Empire. In addition, it was the iconography that would have served to identify and authenticate the coins. It is possible that the dies were produced by an artist who, while skilled at figural representations, may have been illiterate or unfamiliar with Latin letters. Alternatively, two individuals may have been involved in the carving of the dies for the Humayma *solidi*, a skilled master artist who sculpted the portraits, and a less-skilled letter-cutter, or apprentice, who was delegated to cut the legends. In view of the difference in quality between the obverse and reverse portraits, and the slight differences in the letters used in the obverse and reverse legends, it is even possible that each die was produced separately by two craftsmen or sets of craftsmen.

The diameter of the Humayma *solidi* varies from 2.10 to 2.20 cm. There is no correlation between the diameter of each coin and its weight. Diameters of comparable Arcadius *solidi* vary from 2.05 to 2.20 cm and also show no correlation between coin weight and diameter. The Humayma *solidi* thus do not stand out among other Arcadius *solidi* in terms of size.

The weight of the five Humayma *solidi* ranges from 4.23 to 4.35 g, with a mean weight of 4.30 g. Eleven Arcadius *solidi* of a comparable type (R = Constantinopolis with *vota* shield or globe) in the British Museum collection range in weight from 4.23 g to 4.47 g, with a mean of 4.41 g. The mean weight of these comparable coins exceeds the mean weight of the Humayma *solidi* by 0.11 g. Other non-*vota* issues of Arcadius from Constantinople and other mints range as low as 4.35 g, but most *solidi* weigh between 4.40 and 4.50 g. It is coins heavier than average that tend to disappear into savings hoards, suggesting that the Humayma *solidi* were destined for spending. Alternatively, they were received as payment for goods or services, and the hoard does not constitute deliberate long-term savings.

All the Humayma *solidi* were struck using the same pair of dies. No die links have been found with other Arcadius *solidi* from the Constantinople mint. The accuracy of the orientation of the die axis suggests that care was taken to ensure correct registration. During the Empire the practice was to position the reverse die so that it either faced 6:00, as in the case of the Humayma *solidi*, or 12:00 (Hill: 1922: 40). The reverse die could have been recessed into the punch as a socket that fit over the stock supporting the obverse die, as shown by a pair of steel dies for an *aureus* of Faustina II (Hill 1922: 16). Alternatively, the dies could have been hinged, as seen in a pair of iron dies for an *aureus* of Constans I as Caesar, with an Antioch mint-mark, found in Beaumont-sur-Oise, France. These dies were probably the property of a counterfeiter (Hill 1922: 15).

Comparison of the iconography and letter-forms of the Humayma *solidi* with those of published Arcadius *solidi*, as well as with examples held by the British Museum, suggests two alternatives. The first is that the *solidi* come from some unknown or temporary provincial mint that employed unpractised engravers and letter cutters, and that they were struck for Arcadius' first quinquennial *vota* celebrations in 387. The fact that the hoard contained only five *solidi* could be significant, for both Procopius and Zacharias of Mytilene state that five gold *solidi* were distributed to soldiers as a *vota* donative (Procopius, *Arc.* 24.27–9; Zacharias of Mytilene, *Chron.* 7.8), while Julian gave five *solidi* and a pound of silver to every soldier on his accession (Ammianus Marcellinus 20.4.18). An unknown mint seems highly unlikely, however, as the mintmark of the Constantinople mint is used, the coins show no evidence of wear or circulation, and they were found with Sasanian drachms that can be dated no earlier than 399.

A second alternative is preferable, that the Humayma *solidi* are ancient imitations. As Heideman notes, the "term *imitation* refers to a copy of a well reputed coin type in circulation by an authority or an individual not entitled to use that specific image. It thus differs from the terms counterfeit or forgery. Imitations are not produced in order to deceive the public but only to set money in circulation for various reasons. Imitations are usually of a known quality, counterfeits are not" (Heideman 1998: 108, note 16). The bright and untarnished appearance of the *solidi* indicates high-quality gold and suggests that there was no intent to pass off base metal copies as authentic coins. It should be noted as well that the *solidi* are of good enough quality and appearance to have circulated with little problem, especially among the illiterate and semi-literate. Given the isolation of the find site, the fact that the coins were discovered and excavated under controlled circumstances, and the mineral encrustation on some of the *solidi*, modern forgery is ruled out.

If the metallic content of a forgery is of acceptable purity, and the weight of the coin falls within, or close to, the range known for legitimate issues, the intent of the counterfeiter is not so much to defraud as to put precious metal into circulation by using the form and iconography of a commonly-accepted standard without paying the required taxes and fees to have it officially minted. It is clear that, for gold coinage, the Byzantine *solidus* enjoyed pre-eminence as a readily-accepted medium of exchange both within and outside the Empire, and that it would be the obvious coin to copy for anyone who wished to mint gold unofficially.

As for the silver coins, the attribution of the drachms to Yazdegard I is based on the design of the crown and the use of his name in the obverse legend. A round-topped crown with a central turret, anterior crescent, and globe on top is specific to Yazdegard I (Sellwood 1985: 51, no. 7). The obverse legend, for Sasanian issues typically incomplete or abbreviated, forms part of the formula *MaZDISN BaGI RAMSHaTRI YaZDaKaRTI MaLKAN MaLKA AIRAN,* "Worshipper of [Ahura] Mazda, Joy of the Empire, the Divine Yazdegard, King of Kings of Iran" (Göbl 1971: Table xv; Mitchiner 1978: 149; Paruck 1924: 96). Prominence is given to an epithet typical of Yazdegard I and his son Varahran V, *RAMSHaTRI,* which usually extends from the right shoulder to the right tip of the crescent of the crown, but on some coins extends well beyond this (Göbl 1971: Table xv; Paruck 1924: 96). The name of the king is never given in its entirety, and the epithets *MaLKAN MaLKA* or *MaLKAN MaLKA AIRAN* are not used, with the possible exception of fig. 12.4.19 (OS8). Although the obverse legend here is for the most part illegible, it is much longer than those of the other Humayma drachms and likely represents a more complete version. It is clear that the iconography was more important than the legend, for on all the obverse dies the legend was cut after the portrait, and the words are crammed in between portrait elements or overlap onto them.

Differences in the tilt of the crown, the braiding of the king's beard, the spacing of decorative elements attached to the crown or appearing behind the bust, and in the placement of words serve to distinguish the nine obverse dies. Some features of the Humayma obverse dies seem to be unique. The most noticeable of these is the trefoil decoration that extends towards the left from the lower rear of the cap of the crown. This detail appears on all the drachms except fig. 12.4.19 (OS8), where it is clearly absent. It may not be present on fig. 12.2.7 and 12.2.11 (OS3), although it is more likely that here the detail is concealed by a fault in striking. The trefoil does not appear on any of the other drachms of Yazdegard I that we have studied.

A second significant difference is the absence of the turret on the side of the cap of the crown on most of the Humayma obverses. Again fig. 12.4.19 (OS8) is an exception. The remainder of the drachms show a cap that is adorned with pearls or jewels rather than the stepped turret. Die OS8 thus appears to bear a closer relationship to the obverse dies used for comparable drachms than to the remainder of the Humayma obverse dies, although no exact correspondence has been found.

The reverses are directly comparable to one specific type of Yazdegard I drachm depicting a fire altar guarded by two crowned attendants and with the flames flanked by single crescents without dots. Where the crown of the attendants is clearly shown, it resembles the crown on the obverse. The attendants appear to hold ceremonial staffs rather

than swords, although the right-hand attendant on fig. 12.4.21 (RS8) is clearly wearing a scabbard.

In addition to the epithet *RAST,* "the just," which can be distinguished to a greater or lesser degree on the altar columns, the reverses of many of the Humayma drachms display single or double letters in the right and left fields, between the border and the lower body of the attendants. Reverse legends are all read from right to left holding the coin with the altar flames pointing to 3:00. On the left side, the Pahlavi letters *RA* (figs. 12.2.8, 10; 12.3.12–13; 12.4.21–23) or *A* (figs. 12.2.9; 12.3.14–16, 12.4.18, 20) are visible. On the right side, the Pahlavi letters *AI* (figs. 12.2.7, 12.3.17, 12.4.21) or *A* (figs. 12.3.15–16; 12.4.18–19, 12.4.22–23) can be seen. The poor quality of the striking has obscured these letters on some of the coins. In general, the letters are difficult to distinguish from the apparel of the attendants, which they overlap, but it appears that the letters are reproduced on the coins struck from most of the reverse dies.

The letters on the left may form part of one of the many abbreviated legends that can appear on the reverse of Yazdegard I drachms. Since the word must contain a long Pahlavi *A,* the most likely candidates are *[NU]RA,* "fire," or a repetition of the obverse epithet *RA[MSHaTRI]* (Mitchiner 1978: 164; Paruck 1924: 96–97). The letters in the right field appear to be a mintmark. On the coinage of Yazdegard I, mint names, if shown, usually appear in abbreviated form to the left or right of the altar flames, and later on in the right field parallel to the altar column between the right-hand attendant and the border (Göbl 1971: 23). The most complete and clearest depiction of this mintmark, *AI,* appears on fig. 12.4.21. This mintmark is attested for Yazdegard I, and identifies a mint in the city of Airan Khurra Shahpuhr, or Susa, in the province of Khuzastan, or Susiana (Mitchiner 1978: 140; Paruck 1924: 133–34). As the mintmark *AIRA* is also used by this mint, it is possible that the two groups of letters should be read together, and that the Humayma drachms provide evidence of a transitional method of indicating the mint, as the location of the mintmark moves from either or both sides of the altar flames to its final position in the right field.

It is difficult to distinguish individual carvers and letter cutters responsible for the iconography and legends of the various obverse and reverse dies. First of all, it is apparent that the craftsmen adhered closely to prescribed models, ensuring a high degree of similarity among the various dies. Secondly, the use of very thin flans often results in degraded images and illegible legends, since there is not enough metal to fill the recesses of both dies. As the Humayma drachms show, reverses in particular suffer from this phenomenon, for when the flan is struck, the available material is driven down into the obverse die. Shifting of the flan between hammer blows on the punch results in overstrikes and further blurring.

The shape of the drachms is only roughly circular and sometimes significantly elongated. Diameters vary from 2.50 to 2.80 cm. There is no correlation between diameter and coin weight. Other comparable drachms of Yazdegard I have similar shapes and range in diameter from 2.41 to 2.80 cm. They also show no correlation between coin size and weight. In terms of size, the Humayma drachms fall well within the known limits.

No discernable pattern of groups based on weight is found among the drachms. Coin weight ranges from a low of 3.11 g to a high of 4.28 g; the mean weight is 3.79 g. Four Yazdegard I drachms in the British Museum collection that have reverses of the "flanking single crescents" type range in weight from 3.56 g to 4.19 g, with a mean of 3.98 g. The variation in weight could be explained as the result of mutilation or wear, but there is no obvious evidence for the former, and most of the Humayma drachms show very little evidence of wear or circulation. It appears that variation in the weight of individual flans was not important, and that the coinage was produced *al marco*. As Paruck (1924: 37) observes, the "aim was not that coins should be struck of such and such a weight, but that so many coins should be struck out of such and such a quantity of metal."

Nine obverse dies (OS1 to OS9) and eight reverse dies (RS1 to RS8) were used to strike the 18 Humayma Sasanian drachms. The coins fall into ten groups based on the die combinations used (fig. 12.5.2). The group using OS1 and RS1 contains seven coins, the largest group coming from a single pair of dies. The combinations OS3/RS3 and OS5/RS5

each are found on two coins; all other combinations occur only once. None of the dies match or can be linked to comparable, published Yazdegard I drachms, but a few examples of die linking were found among the Humayma drachms themselves.

Two reverses were used with more than one obverse die. RS5 was used with OS5 (figs. 12.3.15 and 12.4.18) and with OS7 (fig. 12.3.17). RS6 was used with both OS6 (fig. 12.3.16) and OS1 (fig. 12.4.22). Links based on a reverse are not common, as the normal pattern is that several successive reverse dies are used with one obverse die. The obverse die is sunk in the anvil, while the reverse die is set in a punch that receives the hammer blows and consequently wears out much faster (Göbl 1971: 34). Two possible explanations suggest themselves; one, that a new reverse die was brought into use shortly before the failure of an obverse die, and two, that a new reverse die was brought into use shortly before a new version of an obverse die replaced an older version, perhaps at the beginning of a new regnal year.

One obverse die was used with more than one reverse die; OS1 was used with both RS1 (figs. 12.2.8–9; 12.3.12–14; 12.4.20, 23) and RS6 (fig. 12.4.22). As already mentioned, one of these reverses, RS6, was also used with another obverse, OS6 (fig. 12.3.16), and thus there exists a complex relationship among these four dies. Since the year of issue or regnal year does not appear on Sasanian coinage until after the reign of Yazdegard I, the possible chronology of this relationship cannot be determined.

It may be, however, that the die linking was more a matter of work practices within a specific mint than a chronological phenomenon. Unlike many Roman issues, no provision appears to have been made to ensure the correct orientation of the die axis on Sasanian drachms (Paruck 1924: 47). This lack of an indexing mechanism is corroborated by fig. 12.2.8, which shows a reverse die orientation of 3:15, rather than the typical 3:00. It is, therefore, possible that in a busy mint where a number of loose punch reverse dies were in use, no attempt was made to co-ordinate the use of any particular reverse with a specific obverse die, but that chance governed which punch would be picked up by a workman assigned to work at one of the anvils.

Obverse/reverse combinations could thus change from day to day without any relationship to wear.

Unlike the *solidi*, the Humayma drachms appear to be legitimate issues. The thin flans were difficult to counterfeit in plated base metal, and contemporary forgeries are much less common than among Roman coins (Sellwood 1985: 53) The iconography, legends, and physical measurements compare closely to those of other drachms of Yazdegard I, and the coins are struck by one of the major mints, Susa, associated with his coinage. Despite the use of different obverse and reverse dies, the coins show a notable uniformity in the aspects of the iconography and legends that distinguishes them from comparable issues. The Humayma drachms form a cohesive group, indicating that they were minted during the same period. Only fig. 12.4.19 (OS8/RS7), a coin heavier than any of the others (4.28 g), exhibits significant differences. As this coin shows some atypical evidence of wear, it may represent a slightly earlier issue from the same mint. Furthermore, the use of nine different obverse dies and eight different reverse dies to produce the 18 Humayma drachms makes it extremely unlikely that the coins are forgeries. A counterfeiter would simply not go to the time-consuming and expensive effort of creating so many dies. The use of a large number of closely-related dies is indicative of an important and busy official mint. Final confirmation of the authenticity of the coins and their attribution to the Susa mint could be provided by the non-destructive analysis of the silver alloy used in the production of the flans. Gordus, for example, has found that neutron activation analysis of the gold-impurity levels and silver fineness of drachms can assist in identifying issues of particular rulers or from particular mints (Gordus 1974: 143–48).

12.A.4. Discussion of the Earrings

It has not been possible to find exact parallels for the earrings in the Humayma hoard. While it is always possible that the Humayma examples were not worn as earrings, in their shape and mirrored symmetry they have more similarities with this type of jewellery than with other forms. Hoop earrings have a long tradition in the Near East, beginning with crescent-shaped gold hoops recovered in Early Dynastic (third millennium BC) levels at Ur and continuing to the present day (Hyslop 1971: 4–5). The use of pearls in adornment was also widespread in antiquity and thus offers no indication of the origin of the earrings. The techniques of granulation and wire wrapping are common in jewellery of many Near Eastern and Mediterranean cultures and periods, a few of which are considered below. Even the shape of the gold beads offers no clues, as there are numerous ancient examples of gold beads with a "collar" at either side. It seems more likely, however, that the source of the earrings lies with that of (one set of) the coins, than with roughly similar forms from elsewhere, for example South Arabia (e.g., Turner 1973: plate LIV).

Sasanian jewellery offers no close parallels. Musche (1988: 331) notes that a preference for large earrings is a special feature of Sasanian jewellery and there are many varieties of hoop earrings that use pearls, gold beads, and granulation, but none match the Humayma examples. Musche's Type 3.2.2 consists of a round hoop with two terminal loops and two spherical beads with granulation attached to the bottom of the hoop. His Type 4 consists of a crescent-shaped hoop with a closing attachment by which it was suspended from the ear (Musche 1988: pl. CIII). An examination of the Arsacid predecessors of these types also reveals some similarities with the Humayma earrings. For example, granulation and the use of gold beads and pearls are common, especially with thick crescent shapes. Some of these have small loops and heavy wire wrappings at the ends of the crescents, comparable to those of the Humayma earrings. Musche's Type 7.3.2.3 is such an example, and it shows a hinged element attached between the two terminal loops, by which the earring was fastened to the ear. His Type 7.3.2.8 has a similar fastener, and it is heavily ornamented with gold beads, granulation, and recesses for precious stones (Musche 1988: 79–80, pl. XV). Nevertheless, the profiles and sections of the crescent elements of all of these earrings are quite different from the Humayma examples.

Two first- or second-century Roman earrings, said to have been found in Syria, demonstrate the use of gold beads and granulation (Hackens 1976: 113, n. 50). In contrast with the Humayma earrings, here it is the tube of the hoop that is decorated with granulation, while the beads are left plain, but there is a similarity in the techniques used. A mosaic of the fourth century from Sepphoris shows a female wearing hoop earrings with pearls and (apparently) gold beads (Gardiner 1991: 246, fig. 6-90). Whether this depicts a common local jewellery type or results from the shape of the *tesserae* cannot be determined. In any case, while one pearl does appear as threaded on the hoop near the top, the bottom pearl clearly is pendant, unlike the strung pearls on the Humayma earrings. Two gold hoop earrings with gold balls soldered to the exterior were found in a second- or third-century tomb at Ayn Jawan in Saudi Arabia (al-Ghabban 2010: 403, fig. 242). Although the balls are not strung on the body of the hoop, the effect is similar, and as on the Humayma earrings there is a gap between loops at the two ends of the hoop. These earrings seem to be part of the same long tradition as the Humayma examples.

Much closer comparisons can be found in the hoop earrings that appear in numerous panel portraits from Egypt, ranging in date from the early first (e.g., Doxiadis 1995: 53, fig. 36, Cairo 33268) to the early third century (e.g., Doxiadis 1995: 30, fig. 28; British Museum EA65343). Of course, it is not known whether these depictions represent actual ownership of such jewels, or just an idealized mark of status, but they must have depicted an easily recognized and respected fashion object. It is not apparent if any of the surviving examples of earrings come from the identical burial contexts as the painted images (cf. Doxiadis 1995: 235), so the identification of types is somewhat speculative. Images of pearl hoops are most commonly found in second century paintings. Some of the closest parallels to the Humayma earrings may be found in a portrait from Egyptian Hawara of the Hadrianic period (Allason-Jones 1989: pl. 1; Petrie 1913 Doxiadis 1995: 58, fig. 42, British Museum EA74712) and the portrait of an elderly woman from Akhim dating to the Antonine period (Doxiadis 1995: 154, fig. 95, NY Met 09.181.5). Unfortunately, mummy portraits went out of use in the mid-third century (Borg, in Riggs 2002: 106), so they do not contribute contemporary comparisons for the Humayma earrings.

These artistic representations also provide clues as to how the Humayma earrings were worn.

The presence of loops in the wire wrapping suggests that each hoop was closed by another wire that also fastened the earring to the ear. Experimentation has confirmed that, when suspended from a hanger attached between the loops, the Humayma earrings will hang with the curve of pearls displayed and the plain gold towards the back — similar to the Egyptian paintings mentioned above. In this configuration, however, the Humayma earrings are suspended with the long axis approximately horizontal, and all known Egyptian portrait examples show the oval hanging lengthwise. It seems highly unlikely, although not impossible, that one eye and the gold shaft of the hoop actually pierced the ear. While this method would display the pearls in correct orientation, it would eliminate the reason for the wire eyes. Alternatively, the earrings may be related to first- to third-century types in which beaded hoops are attached to the ear with a second loop formed by a long wire fastener that bends to follow the curve of the decorative element (Hackens 1976: 122–23, n. 56; e.g., Marshall 1969: fig. 2679, and Doxiadis 1995: 235). It is not readily apparent that the almost completely closed hoop of the Humayma earrings would fit with this type of attachment, although the wire eye at the pearl end could have provided the closure with counterbalance to assist in the correct angle of display.

Parallels may also be drawn with fifth- to sixth-century pearl and gold bead earrings found with other jewellery during excavation of the Cathedral propylaea at Jerash, in northern Jordan (Kraeling 1938: 208, pl. xxxvii; National Archaeological Museum, Amman J21, formerly PAM 41.578). Each earring consists of a vertical section (L 3.4 cm), half of which divides an oblong circle of gold wire (2.0 × 2.2 cm). Both are strung with white pearls and turquoise separated by small, granulated gold beads and turns of gold wire. At the bottom of each circle is a garnet bead. The upper ends of the circle terminate in small loops that are connected to the centre of the vertical section by a granulated fastener. These elements are suspended from a hoop (1.3 × 1.4 cm) with a small loop at each end. The earrings differ from the Humayma examples in details of their design and in the use of colourful garnet and turquoise beads. Furthermore, the perforated nature of the Jerash jewellery reflects the new styles that, prompted by social and economic upheavals, shifted away from heavy forms to lighter, less expensive pierced-work (Yeroulanou 1999: 192–93). The heavy weight of the Humayma earrings seems indicative of a more financially stable era. Nevertheless, both the Jerash jewellery and the Humayma earrings seem to derive from a common tradition in their use of pearls separated by gold beads decorated with granulation, wire wrapping, double-eyed hoops, and separate attachment elements, as well as in the general impression of opulence.

It is clear that many points of similarity connect the Humayma earrings to jewellery of the East, whether Roman or Persian. But these likenesses are probably more a reflection of a continuous interchange of techniques and cultural influence, as well as of regional trends and personal preference in taste and design, all of which ignore political boundaries. No convincing parallels have yet been found that could provide a definitive answer to the question of where and when the Humayma earrings were created.

12.A.5. Conclusions Regarding the Hoard

The absence of any structures near the find site makes it clear that this sloping plain was used only for transit and temporary occupation. The discovery of ceramic material from many successive periods shows that this transient use was continuous rather than an isolated phenomenon. The plateau probably served as a campsite along a trading route connecting ancient Hauarra, situated on the *Via Nova Traiana,* with settlements further to the west, and ultimately to the Mediterranean coast.

The nature of the contents of the hoard and its arrangement in careful stacks when found indicate that this was not an accidental assemblage of individual elements. The coins and earrings were probably contained in a purse of cloth or leather that decomposed over time, as no evidence of a more substantial container was found. The uncirculated nature of the coins and the uniformity of the issues suggest that this collection was not a normal mercantile purse, which usually contains a variety of circulated denominations. In addition, the firm wrapping that kept the coins in a stack argues that

the contents were not readily accessible, unlike a typical coin purse. Although the inclusion of the earrings may suggest a bullion hoard, the uniformity of the coins and their uncirculated nature is quite different from the variety of worn issues normally seen in such a hoard. It seems most probable that the Humayma hoard represents a purse containing a sum of money recently received as a payment or assembled for some major purchase. The purchasing power of the hoard was substantial, since the annual cost of maintaining a soldier in the fifth century was four *solidi* (Burnett 1977: 4).

The owners of hidden valuables generally conceal them in the hope of safeguarding them and recovering them in the future. It is clear that anyone deliberately concealing valuables on the plateau would have had to mark their location in some conspicuous way if they were to be recovered, either by burying them near some easily-recognized natural feature, such as a tree or large shrub, or by constructing an artificial marker. It is unlikely, however, that the vegetation of the area 1,500 years ago differed much from that of the present day: sparse, indistinguishable clumps of jointed saltbush. Any artificial marker in this area would have drawn attention and thus defeated the purpose of concealment. The purse may have been hastily hidden during a sudden emergency, such as a raid, during which the owner was killed. Accidental loss is another explanation for the deposition of the hoard, as a small purse, once dropped, would be very difficult to recover in this landscape. The featureless topography of the plateau makes the find site difficult to locate today, even in daylight and although now marked with a small stone cairn.

The practice of copying currency was not uncommon in antiquity (Grierson 1956). Barbarian tribes and states imitated imperial coinage, striking gold coins in the name of the current emperor, and in the third and fourth centuries, the volume of such copies reached a new high, with examples coming from northwest Europe, the Danube area, the Caucasus area, and even India (Burnett 1977: 6; Christ 1967: 75; Grierson and Mays 1992: 70). Christ notes that for German examples, circulation was not just restricted to that area of Germany beyond the borders of the Empire, but that such coins were also used in Roman settlements and camps.

It is quite likely that the origin of the Humayma *solidi* is to be found outside the boundaries of the Empire. Cribb has observed that most of the *solidi* found along the Silk Route are ancient counterfeits or copies (personal communication, July 1993, Joe Cribb, Curator of South Asian Coins, Department of Coins and Medals, British Museum). A Sasanian origin for the dies used for the Humayma *solidi* would explain the relative unfamiliarity of the die carvers with Byzantine letter shapes and numismatic iconography. Conclusive evidence could perhaps be obtained through the non-destructive analysis of the gold alloy used in the Humayma *solidi*, and its comparison to analyses of alloys used in other gold coinage of the period.

The effort and cost involved in producing a set of dies might account for the discrepancy in date between the *solidi* and the drachms, since it is likely that a counterfeiter would continue to use a particular die set much longer than an official mint. The fact that the *solidi* were found in association with Sasanian silver drachms raises a further interesting but speculative possibility. The Sasanian kings struck virtually no gold coins, preferring silver, although Byzantine *solidi* may have circulated as well. Burnett (1977: 15–16) notes that a king of Sri Lanka, when visited by Byzantine and Persian merchants, is supposed to have taken the lack of Sasanian gold coins as a sign of the inferiority of the Sasanian king to the Roman emperor. Varahran IV, the predecessor of Yazdegard I, introduced a gold coin corresponding to the *solidus*, although of slightly lower weight (Göbl 1971: 28). Since such Sasanian gold coinage is now very rare, it may have been less readily accepted than the *solidus*, leading an enterprising counterfeiter to re-strike Sasanian gold coins as *solidi*. The one example of a gold dinar of Yazdegard I that was examined by de Bruijn, however, only weighs 4.06 g, and its diameter is 2.05 cm, both slightly less than comparable measurements for the Humayma *solidi* (British Museum, no. 69 12-3-1 1699SR). Alternatively, the counterfeiter simply produced passable imitations of *solidi* of Arcadius at the appropriate weight and dimensions.

Yazdegard's accession date provides a *terminus post quem* of 399 for the deposition of the hoard. The drachms do not provide dates, and no established chronology for Yazdegard I issues exists, so any attempt at precise dating must be tentative. The location of the mintmark, whether *AI* in the right field, or *AIRA* transitionally split between the right and left fields, indicates that the drachms do not belong to Yazdegard's earliest issues, which show the mintmark to the side or on both sides of the altar flame. Since the drachms were found with imitations of *solidi* of Arcadius, the Humayma hoard could date anytime within the first decade of Yazdegard's reign.

Although the Humayma earrings were found together with datable Roman and Sasanian coins, this does not automatically provide a secure date for the manufacture of the earrings. Jewellery can continue in use for several generations, being kept as an heirloom or for its monetary value. Since the elements of the Humayma earrings that closed the hoops and allowed attachment to the ears are missing, the earrings may have been acquired or retained for their intrinsic worth. Since they were still together and in good condition, it is unlikely that they had been out of use for long. Based on the comparative material, a date somewhere between the second and fifth centuries is most likely. In the absence of closer parallels, a definite origin cannot be identified. Further research may determine whether the owner of the hoard obtained the earrings during travel within the Sasanian or Roman empires.

The first two decades of the fifth century appear to have been a generally peaceful interlude in the constant wars that embroiled the Roman Empire and the Sasanians, facilitating international movement and trade (Greatrex 2002: 35–36; Sellwood 1985: 112). A law of 408/9 restricted cross-border trade to the cities of Nisibis, Callinicum, and Artaxata (with some exception for Persian ambassadors), officially confining the predominant area of contact to the region that now includes eastern Turkey, northern Syria, and northwestern Iraq (*Codex Iustinianus*. 4.63.4; Greatrex 2002: 33–36; Maeir 2000: 178). But finds of Sasanian artefacts and coins in the southern Levant, such as the T. Istaba seal from Beth Shean/Scythopolis and the Humayma hoard, while not plentiful, indicate that cross-border contact was much more pervasive and wide-spread, and not just limited to official trading centres (Maeir 2000: 165–69). Since the value of ancient precious metal coins was determined by their bullion content, borders did not hinder their use, as they do for modern token currencies. Sasanian silver coinage was readily accepted in the markets of the Empire, thanks to its substantial silver content (Harl 1996: 307–8).

It is difficult to deduce much about the owner from the contents of the Humayma hoard itself. In addition to merchants and traders, many soldiers, ambassadors, ecclesiastical officials, pilgrims, prisoners of war, and mercenaries made their way across the frontier between the Empire and the Sasanian realm (Maeir 2000: 179–80). As the coins and jewellery represent a substantial amount of wealth, they are not typical of what might be found in an ordinary merchant's purse, so the owner may have been of higher rather than lower status. While the presence of earrings — if in fact they were in use at the time of loss — might suggest that the owner of the hoard was a woman, both men and women in Sasanian Persia commonly wore earrings. The presence of both *solidi* and Sasanian drachms strongly suggests that the owner travelled in both Roman and Sasanian territory, and the large number of issues from Susa may indicate a recent visit to that city. The fact that the hoard includes both imitations of *solidi*, possibly of Sasanian manufacture, and authentic Sasanian drachms may make a Persian owner more likely.

Although the identity of the owner can no longer be recovered, the real significance of the hoard is that it links ancient Hauarra to the trade network and caravan routes that interconnected the Roman and Persian worlds. In doing so, it provides archaeological confirmation for the literary evidence of political, commercial, and ecclesiastical contact between the Byzantine and Sasanian regimes in the early fifth century (Shahid 1989: 25 n. 10; Trimingham 1979: 161).

12.B. COINS FOUND IN THE SETTLEMENT CENTRE (J.P. Oleson)

12.B.1. Introduction and Analysis

The soil in and around Humayma has a deleterious effect on copper, bronze, and silver coins. Coins exposed on the surface are often moderately well-preserved, but those recovered during excavation

normally are encased in a very hard, sandy corrosion deposit that frequently has affected the original surfaces. Unfortunately, the surfaces of the coins found in 1991 and 1992 generally did not survive the traditional form of acid cleaning provided at that time by the Conservation Department of the Department of Antiquities; those coins are listed here as illegible after cleaning. The high proportion of illegible coins noted for B100 is due to the fact that numerous coins were found there in 1991 and 1992. Some of the coins cleaned by the Department could be partially identified by eye prior to the acid treatment, although the detail was not clear enough for photographic recording. Since even these coins were completely illegible after their treatment, no photographs have been included here, even though a partial identification appears in some of the entries. After her arrival in 1993, our conservator Judy Logan developed an effective method of removing this encrustation with a combination of chemical and mechanical cleaning, based on a procedure suggested by Dr. Pierre Bikai (Logan, in Oleson et al. 1999: 445). Her intervention allowed the recovery of information from all but the most corroded coins, and the stabilization of the coins suitable for display. Ongoing monitoring has shown that the condition of the cleaned coins has remained stable for 19 years for those cleaned in 1993.

The coins are presented here by excavation area and locus. The catalogue numbers run in a single series through this section, regardless of excavation area. I have included entries for the illegible coins (without illustration) as well, since their simple presence in the archaeological deposits provides a certain type of information. In the descriptions of the types, "rt." indicates "facing right." Where given, weights are those taken after cleaning, unless cleaning was not necessary.

Forty of the 78 coins recovered could be identified, although a few of these were only tentatively identified on the basis of faint details and general dimensions. The listing in Table 12.1 assumes that the tentative dates are correct. The chronological range and frequencies are not surprising for this region and for the structures represented in this volume: Nabataean, 10 examples; Roman, 1; Early Byzantine, 19; Byzantine, 9. Only one post-Byzantine coin was found; it was illegible but was attributed to the

Table 12.1   Distribution of coins by period and excavation area. A** indicates the various Necropolis tomb sites.

	RANDOM	A**	B100	C101	C119	C124	F102	TOTAL
Aretas II or III			1					1
Aretas IV		1	2			1		4
Rabbel II						2		2
Nabataean						2	1	3
Elagabalus				1				1
Constantine and/or Licinius	1	2						3
Jovian		1						1
Constantius II		1	1					2
Valentinian I or II, Valens, or Gratian		1						1
House of Constantine			9	1			2	12
Anastasius I							2	2
Justinian I			1					1
Byzantine, late 5–6c	1			3		1	1	6
Modern			1					1
Illegible			23	5	1		9	38
Total	2	6	38	10	1	6	15	78

late nineteenth or early twentieth century on the basis of the dimensions and regularity of the flan. Although the non-hoard sample is larger (N=113) and the proportion of unidentified coins smaller (N=23), the statistics for the coins found by the ez-Zantur excavation are quite similar to those for Humayma (*EZ* I: 91–92). The Limes Arabicus Project produced similar proportions of Byzantine to Late Byzantine coins, but only one Nabataean coin (Betlyon, in Parker et al. 2006: 413–44). The absence of Nabataean coins is not surprising, since most of the survey coins were recovered in the Early Byzantine fort at Lejjun. The absence of Early Islamic and modern coins underlines the isolation of the Humayma community in the post-Byzantine period, and the reliance of its inhabitants on self-sufficiency or barter. Even at the commencement of excavation at Humayma in 1989, many of the local Bedouin workers had infrequent access to Jordanian currency. Overall, the relatively small number of coins recovered suggests a low intensity of com-

mercial activity in the areas concerned. Over the whole site between 1989 and 2005, 281 coins were found, 108 of them from the Roman Fort (E116), 16 from the *vicus*. Clearly the occupants of the fort were more committed to a money economy than the occupants elsewhere in ancient Hawara/Hauarra. In contrast to Aqaba and the Limes Arabicus Project sites, the Fort and *vicus* at Humayma also produced a significant number of second- and third-century coins (to be published in *HEP* 3).

Not surprisingly, 6 of the 10 Nabataean coins were found in the Necropolis (A104–A115, A117–A119) and the Nabataean Campground (C124), both of which were originally areas of Nabataean activity. The Byzantine coins from the Necropolis probably were deposited during the later re-use of the tomb shafts. The general absence of second- and third-century issues from the structures reported on in this volume is not surprising, given their construction in the Byzantine period and their later re-use. The four Nabataean coins recovered from B100 and F102 are a heritage of the intensive Nabataean occupation of the same areas, particularly B100. The 20 Byzantine coins from B100, C101, and F102 probably reflect activities associated with the churches in those areas. Although the majority of the coins found in B100 were illegible, the overall total of 38 coins is well beyond the totals for C101 (10 coins) and F102 (15 coins). The central location of B100 may have attracted various activities before and after the construction of the church that resulted in the loss of coins.

The mint could be determined more or less securely for only eight coins. Of these, three were struck in Alexandria (nos. 10, 11, 13; A113.T1–T5), one in Alexandria or Antioch (no. 9; A104.T1), one in Antioch (no. 8; C124), two in Constantinople (nos. 37, 54; B100), and one in Rome (no. 12; A113.T1–T5). It is likely that nos. 21 and 25 (F102) were also struck in Constantinople. The prevalence of eastern mints is not surprising, nor is the presence of a coin from Rome. The same pattern is seen in the Limes Arabicus Project coins (Betlyon, in Parker et al. 2006: Table 19.2). The coins are illustrated at 100%.

12.B.2. Random Surface Finds

1. (1991.0096.01). Surface, 80 m NW of C101. Bronze coin; corroded. Obv. Male head rt. Rev. Male nude standing left with staff or spear in left hand. D. 0.019 m; die orientation 5:00; 2.6 g. Probably *IOVICONSERVATORI* type of Constantine or Licinius; e.g., *RIC* 7: 422–23, 680; Bruck 1961: 44–48.

2. (1991.0290.01). Surface find by worker "in the settlement centre." Copper half *follis;* surface clean but worn; small cutting missing out of rim; D 0.02 m, 2.5 g. Reverse carries a K, indicating a half *follis* of the post-498 reform (Wroth 1908: xiii; Grierson 1982: 4). Late 5–6c.

12.B.3. C124 (Nabataean Campground)

3. (1996.0536.01; fig. 12.6.3). C124.01A.03. Bronze coin, possibly of Aretas IV; corroded. D 0.017 m; 1.95 g. Obv. Male head with tousled hair, rt. Rev. two crossed cornucopias with long,

back-curving terminations. 9 BC–AD 40? Cf. Meshorer 1975: no. 73A (4/3 BC); Huth 2010: 32, no. 78 (9 BC–AD 40).

4. (1996.0033.01; fig. 12.6.4). C124.03.01. Small bronze coin, Nabataean; badly corroded, lumpy flan D 0.014 m; 1.15 g. Obv. Male head rt., margin of heavy dots? Rev. illegible, margin of heavy dots? Cf. Meshorer 1975: 30–30a, Obodas III, 21/20 BC; cf. Huth 2010: 34, no. 85 (Aretas IV, 9 BC–AD 40).

5. (1996.0007.01; fig. 12.6.5). C124.01.05. Bronze coin of Rabbel II. D 0.02 m; die orientation: 1:00; 2.94 g. Obv. Iugate heads of Rabbel II and Gamilat rt. Rev. Two crossed cornucopiae below Nabataean inscription "Rabbel/Gamilat." AD 101/2. Meshorer: 1975: 111, Type 163A; Huth 2010: 40, no. 99.

6. (1996.0018.01; fig. 12.6.6). C124.01.13. Bronze coin of Rabbel II. D 0.015; die orientation 7:00; 2.15 g. Obv. Iugate heads of Rabbel II and Hagru rt., within margin of dots. Rev. Two cornucopiae framing Nabataean inscription "Rabbel/Hagru." AD 103–106. Meshorer 1975: 164; Huth 2010: 40, no. 101.

7. (1996.0016.01; fig. 12.6.7). C124, surface south of Square 01. Small, badly corroded bronze coin, with slightly irregular, lumpy flan, probably Nabataean. D 0.017 m; 2.45 g.

8. (1996.0026.01; fig. 12.6.8). C124, surface south of Square 01. Byzantine copper follis, possibly of Justinian; worn and corroded. D 0.03 m; 13.05 g. Obv. probably a profile head. Rev. M, with cross above, star to the left and right. In exergue:]ΛS. The mint mark may have been ΘΥΠΟΛS, indicating Antioch (Grierson 1982: 22); cf. Bellinger 1966: 139, nos. 212a.2, 212a.3, 212c, pl. 36, 537–539. Probably sixth century.

12.B.4. The Necropolis

9. (1992.0166.01). Tomb A104.T1; surface spoil around shaft. Bronze coin of Valentinian I or II, Valens, or Gratian. D 0.015 m; die orientation 6:00; 0.9 g. Obv. Male head rt. *]PFAVG.* Rev. Victory advancing left, possibly *SECVRITAS*

Fig. 12.6   *Coins from C124. No. 3 (1996.0536.01): Bronze coin, possibly of Aretas IV. No. 4 (1996.0033.01): Small bronze coin, possibly Nabataean. No. 5 (1996.0007.01): Bronze coin of Rabbel II. No. 6 (1996.0018.01): Bronze coin of Rabbel II. No. 7 (1996.0016.01): Small, badly corroded bronze coin, probably Nabataean. No. 8 (1996.0026.01): Byzantine copper* follis.

FIG. 12.7 *Coins from the Necropolis. No. 10 (1992.0599.01): A113.T1-T5; bronze coin of Constantine I. No. 11 (1992.0599.02): Tomb complex A113.T1-T5; bronze coin of Jovian. No. 12 (1992.0599.03): Tomb complex A113.T1-T5; bronze coin of Constantine. No. 13 (1992.0599.04): Tomb complex A113.T1-T5; bronze coin of Constantius II. No. 14 (1992.0599.05): Tomb complex A113.T1-T5; bronze coin, possibly of Aretas IV.*

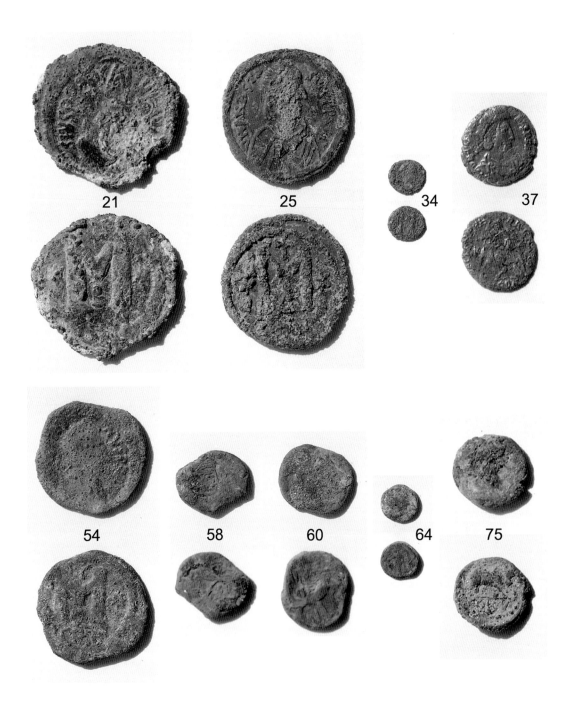

FIG. 12.8 *Coins from various areas. No. 21 (1992.0170.01): F102.05.08; copper* follis *of Anastasius I. No. 25 (1992.0473.01): F102.05.50; copper* follis *of Anastasius I. No. 34 (1991.0345.01): B100.B.29; bronze coin, probably House of Constantine. No. 37 (1991.0345.04): B100.B.29; bronze coin of Constantius II. No. 54 (1992.0351.01): B100.D.01; copper* follis *of Justinian I. No. 58 (1992.0236.02): B100.E.22; bronze coin of Aretas IV. No. 60 (1992.0416.01): B100.E.31; bronze coin, probably Aretas IV and Shuqailat. No. 64 (1992.0226.01): B100.G.05; corroded bronze coin, probably Aretas II or III. No. 75 (1992.0589.01): C101.05.02; bronze coin of Elagabalus.*

REIPUBLICAE. Struck at Alexandria or Antioch, 367–383? Cf. *RIC* 9: 281 no. 36, 288 no. 49 (Antioch, 367–383), 298 no. 3, 5 (Alexandria, 364–367); Bruck 1961: 64–66.

10. (1992.0599.01; fig. 12.7.10). Tomb complex A113. T1–T5. Bronze coin of Constantine I. D 0.02 m; die orientation 12:00; 2 g. Obv. Head of Constantine rt. *CONSTANTI/N[VS MAX AVG*. Rev. 2 soldiers flanking and facing standard. *GLOR/IAEXERC/ITVS*. Exergue: *SMALA*. Letters made up of wedge shapes. Struck in Alexandria, 335–337. *RIC* 7: 712, no. 65.

11. (1992.0599.02; fig. 12.7.11). Tomb complex A113. T1–T5. Bronze coin of Jovian as Augustus. D 0.02 m; die orientation 12:00; 2.6 g. Obv. Male head with diadem rt. Rev. Wreath with ribbon below, cross in jewel above, within: *VOT/V*. Struck in Alexandria 361–363. *RIC* 8: 546 no. 92.

12. (1992.0599.03; fig. 12.7.12). Tomb complex A113. T1–T5. Bronze coin of Constantine. D 0.02 m; die orientation 6:00; 3.4 g. Obv. Constantine, diademed head rt. *]TINVSPFAVG*. Rev. Sol standing left with radiate crown, Victory on globe in left hand. *SOLIINV/I/CTOCOMITI*. In exergue: *T*? Struck in Rome, 316. *RIC* 7: 302 no. 50.

13. (1992.0599.04; fig. 12.7.13). Tomb complex A113.T1–T5. Bronze coin of Constantius II. D 0.02 m; die orientation 12:00; 2.8 g. Obv. Head of Constantius II rt. with pearl diadem. *DNCONSTAN/TIVSPFAVG*. Rev. Helmeted soldier to left spearing fallen horseman. *FELTEMP/REPARATIO*. Exergue: *ALEA*. Struck in Alexandria, 340–351. *RIC* 8: 544 no. 80.

14. (1992.0599.05; fig. 12.7.14). Tomb complex A113.T1–T5. Bronze coin, possibly of Aretas IV. Corroded; D 0.01 m, 3.3 g. Obv. two superimposed heads? Rev. two crossed cornucopiae? AD 39/40? Cf. Meshorer 1975: 105 nos. 112–14.

12.B.5. F102 (Byzantine Church and Early Islamic House)

15. (1995.0049.01). F102.00.00. Bronze coin with irregular, thick, slightly dished flan; worn and corroded. D 0.017 m; 2.7 g. Obv. Two

facing heads? Rev. Two crossed cornucopiae? Nabataean? 1C AD.

16. (1991.0184.01). F102.01.19. Bronze coin; corroded and broken; illegible. D 0.01 m; 1.6 g.

17. (1992.0552.01). F102.01.52. Small bronze coin; illegible after cleaning. D 0.02 m; 2.2 g.

18. (1991.0377.01). F102.03.24. Bronze coin. D 0.02 m; die orientation 1:00; 1.5 g. Obv. Head rt. Rev. Soldiers. Possibly *GLORIAE EXERCITVS* type. House of Constantine, 4C. Cf. Bruck 1961: 26–27.

19. (1991.0507.01). F102.03.27 Bronze coin; corroded; illegible. D 0.01 m; 4 g.

20. (1992.0017.02). F102.05.01. Copper alloy coin; illegible after cleaning. D 0.03 m; 7.7 g. Possibly a sixth-century *follis*.

21. (1992.0170.01; fig. 12.8.21). F102.05.08. Copper follis of Anastasius I; corroded, D 0.04 m; die orientation 7:00; 15.5g. Obv. Head of Anastasius rt. *DNANAST]A/SIVSPPAVG*. Rev. *M*, with * on either side, cross above, and *B* below. Exergue illegible. Probably struck at Constantinople, 498–518. Wroth 1908: I, p. 4, nos. 20–22, pl. I.9; Bellinger 1966: 19, no. 23b.1, pl. 3, Constantinople, 498–518; cf. Grierson 1982: pl. 4.72.

22. (1992.0310.01. F102.05.29. Bronze coin; illegible after cleaning. D 0.01 m.

23. (1992.0310.03). F102.05.29. Bronze coin; corroded. D 0.02 m; die orientation possibly 12:00; 1.0 g. Obv. Head rt. *]CONS[*. Rev. Wreath. House of Constantine, 4C.

24. (1992.0214.01). F102.05.34.01 Bronze coin fragment; illegible. D 0.01 m; 0.8 g.

25. (1992.0473.01; fig. 12.8.25). F102.05.50. Copper *follis* of Anastasius I. D 0.036 m; die orientation 5:00; 18 g. Obv.: Head of Anastasius rt. *DNANASTA/SIVSPPAVG*. Rev.: *M*., with cross above and * on either side; beneath, possible *A*. Exergue illegible. Probably struck in Constantinople, 491–518. Wroth 1908: I, p. 4, nos. 18–19; Bellinger 1966: 18, no. 23a.2, pl. 3, Constantinople, 498–518; cf. Grierson 1982: pl. 4.72.

26. (1992.0478.01). F102.05.52 Small bronze coin; illegible after cleaning. D 0.02; 1.2 g.

27. (1992.0103.01). F102.06.01. Bronze coin; illegible after cleaning. D 0.01 m; 1.7 g.

28. (1992.0268.01). F102.06.06. Bronze coin; illegible after cleaning. D 0.01; 1.1 g.

29. (1993.0253.01). F102.07.10. Bronze coin; illegible after cleaning. D 0.02 m; 1.3 g.

12.B.6. B100 (Byzantine Church and Early Islamic House)

30. (1992.0071.01). B100.22.05. Bronze coin; corroded, illegible. D 0.02 m; 4.3 g.

31. (1991.0408.01). B100.B.00. Bronze coin; corroded. D 0.02 m; 1.3 g. Obv. Head rt., and *]PFAVG[*. Rev. illegible. Probably House of Constantine, 4C.

32. (1991.0207.01). B100.B.15. Bronze coin; corroded, illegible. D 0.01 m; 0.8 g.

33. (1991.0377.02). B100.B.24. Bronze coin; corroded, illegible. D 0.01 m; 1.7 g.

34. (1991.0345.01; fig. 12.8.34). B100.B.29. Bronze coin; corroded. D 0.01 m; die orientation 7:00; 1.7 g. Obv. diademed male head rt. Rev. 2 female figures facing each other. Probably *VICTORIA AVGVSTORVM* issue. House of Constantine, 4C. Cf. Bruck 1961: 80–81.

35. (1991.0345.02). B100.B.29. Bronze coin; corroded. D 0.02 m; 3 g. Obv. male head rt. *...] PFAVG?* Rev. Illegible. House of Constantine? 4C?

36. (1991.0345.03). B100.B.29. Bronze coin; corroded, illegible. D 0.02 m; 1.3 g.

37. (1991.0345.04; fig. 12.8.37). B100.B.29. Bronze coin of Constantius II; corroded. D 0.02 m; die orientation 6:00; 1.9 g. Obv. diademed head rt. *DNCONSTANTI/VSPFAVG.* Rev. soldier to left attacking fallen horseman. *FELTEMPRE/ PARATIO.* In exergue *CON[.* Probably struck at Constantinople, 351–355. *RIC* 8: 458 no. 124; Bruck 1961: 16–20.

38. (1991.0345.05). B100.B.29. Bronze coin; corroded, illegible. D 0.01; 1 g.

39. (1991.0345.07). B100.B.29. Bronze coin; corroded, illegible. D 0.01 m; 1.3 g.

40. (1991.0357.01). B100.B.29. Bronze coin; corroded, illegible. D 0.02 m; 1.6 g.

41. (1991.0357.02). B100.B.29. Corroded bronze coin; D 0.02 m, 1.4 g. Probably House of Constantine, 4C.

42. (1991.0357.03). B100.B.29. Bronze coin; corroded, illegible. D 0.01 m, 1 g.

43. (1991.0357.04). B100.B.29. Bronze coin; corroded, illegible. D 0.01 m, 1.2 g.

44. (1991.0357.05). B100.B.29. Bronze coin; corroded, illegible. D 0.02 m, 0.7 g.

45. (1995.0385.01). B100.B.29. Bronze coin; corroded. D 0.02 m, 1.3 g. Probably House of Constantine.

46. (1991.0385.02). B100.B.29. Bronze coin; corroded, illegible. D 0.02 m, 0.2 g.

47. (1991.0385.03). B100.B.29. Bronze coin; corroded, illegible. D 0.02 m, 2.4 g.

48. (1991.0385.04). B100.B.29. Bronze coin; corroded, illegible. D 0.01 m, 2.1 g.

49. (1991.0385.05). B100.B.29. Bronze coin; corroded, illegible. D 0.01 m, 1.2 g.

50. (1991.0404.02). B100.B.29. Bronze coin; corroded, illegible. D 0.022 m, 1 g.

51. (1991.0436.01). B100.B.31. Bronze coin; corroded. D 0.02 m, Die orientation 12:00, 1.1 g. Obv. Head rt. Rev. *VOT[...* in wreath. House of Constantine, 4C.

52. (1991.0436.02). B100.B.31. Bronze coin; corroded. D 0.02 m, 4.6 g. Probably House of Constantine, 4C.

53. (1991.0437.01). B100.B.32. Bronze coin; corroded. D 0.02 m, 1.8 g. Probably House of Constantine, 4C.

54. (1992.0351.01; fig. 12.8.54). B100.D.01. Copper *follis* of Justinian I. D 0.03 m, die orienta-

tion 6:00, 10 g. Obv. Head of Justinian rt. *DNIVSTINI]/ANVSP[PAVG.* Rev. *M* flanked on either side by stars, or star and cross, gamma (?) below, *CON* in exergue. Struck in Constantinople, 527–538. Wroth 1908: I, p. 29, nos. 30–31, pl. 5.3; Bellinger 1966: 79, no. 28c.5, pl. 14, Constantinople, 527–538.

55. (1991.0356.01). B100.E.05. Possible small coin; broken, very badly corroded. D 0.01 m, 0.8 g.

56. (1992.0187.02). B100.E.12. Bronze coin; corroded, illegible. D 0.01 m, 1.3 g.

57. (1992.0279.01)). B100.E.21. Bronze coin; corroded, illegible. D 0.01 m, 2.0 g.

58. (1992.0236.02; 12.8.58). B100.E.22. Bronze coin; corroded. D 0.02 m, 2.1 g. Obv. Head of Aretas IV rt. Badly struck, with back portion of head off the flan. Rev. Crossed cornucopiae. Close to Meshorer 1975: no. 71, 4/3 BC, which has the same linear style.

59. (1992.0280.01). B100.E.23. Bronze coin; corroded, illegible. D 0.01 m, 0.5 g.

60. (1992.0416.01; fig. 12.8.60). B100.E.31. Bronze coin; corroded. D 0.02 m, 4 g. Obv. illegible. Rev. Crossed cornucopiae with tassels. Probably Aretas IV and Shuqailat. AD 39/40. Cf. Meshorer 1975: nos. 112–114.

61. (1992.0025.01). B100.F.01; found while sweeping top of Wall 02. Bronze coin; corroded, very regular circular shape and thin flan; illegible. D 0.021 m, 3.7 g. Probably late 19C or ea. 20C.

62. (1991.0066.01). B100.F.03. Bronze coin; corroded. D 0.01 m, 1.6 g. Probably House of Constantine, 4C.

63. (1992.0092.01). B100.G.05. Bronze coin; corroded, illegible. D 0.02 m, 5.3 g.

64. (1992.0226.01; fig. 12.8.64). B100.G.05. Corroded bronze coin; D 0.01 m, 2.4 g. Probably Aretas II or III. Obv. Male head? Rev. Standing winged female. Cf. Meshorer 1975: no. Sup. 1, p. 86, pl. I, of Aretas II or III. This parallel is said to be of silver, but the associated bronze issues are similiar.

65. (1992.0327.01). B100.G.08. Bronze coin; corroded, illegible. D 0.02 m, 2.1 g.

66. (1992.0287.01). B100.G.09A. Bronze coin; corroded, illegible. D 0.01 m, 2.2 g.

67. (1992.0594.01). B100.M.07. Bronze coin; corroded, illegible. D 0.01 m, 2.7 g.

12.B.7. C101 (Byzantine Church)

68. (1992.0003.01). C101.01.00. Bronze coin; corroded, illegible. D 0.01 m, 0.9 g.

69. (1992.0466.01). C101.01.37. Bronze coin. D 0.01 m; 1 g. Obv. Diademed male head rt. *]PFAVG.* Rev. Illegible. Probably House of Constantine, 4C.

70. (1991.0170.01). C101.02.15. Bronze coin; corroded, illegible. D 0.01 m, 1.5 g.

71. (1991.0307.01). C101.02.18. Copper *follis.* D 0.032 m; 8.6 g. Obv. illegible. Rev. *M*; to left, *ANNO*; exergue, *]EU* (?). After 538/9, before 668 (Wroth 1908: I, p. cx; Grierson 1982: 25); probably sixth-century.

72. (1992.0209.01). C101.04.05. Bronze coin; corroded, illegible. D 0.01 m, 0.2 g.

73. (1992.0209.02). C101.04.05. Fragments of bronze coin; corroded, illegible.

74. (1993.0162.01). C101.04.24. Bronze coin; corroded, illegible. D 0.01 m, 0.8 g.

75. (1992.0589.01; fig. 12.8.75). C101.05.02. Bronze coin of Elagabalus. D 0.02 m, die orientation 12:00, 6.6 g. Obv. Head of Elagabalus rt. Inscription illegible. Rev. Togate founder (of Petra colony) plowing *pomerium* with steer, to right. P(etra) in front of oxen. In exergue, *COLON[I.* Struck in Petra by Elagabalus in 221/222. Ben-Dor 1948; Spijkerman 1978: 236–37, no. 56, pl. 18.11.

76. (1992.0598.01). C101.05.02. Copper *follis.* D 0.02 m. Obv. Illegible. Rev. *M.* 6C.

77. (1992.0204.01). C101.05.03. Copper *follis.* D 0.03, die orientation 7:00, 14.3 g. Obv. head. Rev. *M*, with * on either side. 6C.

12.B.8. C119 (Byzantine Church)

78. (1993.0443.01). C119.02.08. Small bronze coin; illegible. D 0.02 m, 1.1 g.

12.C. METAL OBJECTS (J.P. Oleson. M. Smith)

12.C.1. Introduction and Analysis

The metal artefacts (other than coins) are presented here by excavation field, and within that category by metal: copper alloy (all are bronze), then iron. Within each metal category the artefacts are arranged by type, more or less from the most elaborate to the least. The metal tomb goods are presented separately in Chapter 11. The catalogue numbers run in a single series through this chapter section, regardless of excavation area.

As a collection, the metal objects are not particularly numerous or remarkable, with the possible exception of the Early Islamic censer handle. There is a mix of more elaborate and more mundane bronze objects, most of which date to the Roman and Byzantine periods, suitable as furnishings in houses and churches, along with cosmetic instruments. It is interesting that two statuettes and a statuette base were found, along with an elaborately decorated Early Islamic censer handle. The iron objects are all functional, serving for the most part as construction fasteners or harness fittings, but with two modern scissors, and one possible medical instrument. Only one sword or knife fragment was recovered, and one iron arrow point. An iron forging bloom was found in F102, but it was probably brought in from E116. The intensive occupation and reoccupation of the structures clearly resulted in the removal of most of the metal artefacts.

A000 (random surface find) Bronze: statuette handle or pendant.

F102 Bronze: figured censer handle, figured vessel handle, hair ring, spike, mirror, *polykandela* hook and chains. Iron: arrow point, knife blade, scissors, nails, door or furniture fittings, forging bloom.

B100 Bronze: buckle, vine leaf attachment, statuette base, spike, *kohl* dipper, scale armour, tent needle. Iron: scissors, medical instrument.

C101 Bronze: statuette, oil lamp, *polykandela* hooks and chains, *kohl* dipper, cosmetic spoon, vessel handle. Iron: nails. Lead: clamp.

No metal objects were registered from the C119 Church, but several tiny fragments of bronze chain were found that probably belonged to *polykandela*, and a fragment of a fibula or vessel handle. No ancient metal artefacts were found in the Necropolis, and the Campground produced only one possibly ancient folded bronze strap. The excavations in the B126 Church did not produce ancient metal artefacts, but very few undisturbed strata were removed from that structure.

Scraps of iron and bronze were frequently found in layers of rubbish in the three main excavation areas; they are mentioned in the report of the stratigraphy within the structures and are not recorded here. Lead is quite rare at the site, which is not surprising, since there is no source for the metal in this area of the Near East. Very small lead clippings and drips were found in two loci in B100 and two in F102, but it is not obvious with what sort of artefacts they were originally associated. Small clippings and drips of lead were found in four loci in the C101 Church, along with a fragment of a lead clamp used in one of the chancel screens. Setting iron architectural clamps was probably the main use of lead at the site, followed by repair clamps for ceramic and steatite vessels. The only lead artefacts registered by the Humayma Excavation Project are a lead clamp found in the Late Roman bath (E077) and a section of the lead pipe that carried water to the bath from Pool 64 (*HEP* 1: 334). There are no obvious discrepancies or patterns in the types of metal finds found in the structures reported on in this volume, other than a general absence of metal finds from the Necropolis and Campsite, which is understandable given their character, and a slightly higher number of *polykandela* fragments from the C101 Church.

12.C.2. Field A (Region surrounding the habitation centre)

1. (1991.0016.01; fig. 12.9.1). Bronze statuette of standing female, with attachment ring on her back; corroded, broken, incomplete; H 0.03 m, W 0.01 m, ring D 0.006 m, Th 0.001 m.

Possibly a handle for the filler hole lid of a lamp, or for the lid of a small vessel. Turned in to Oleson by a local Bedouin man, who reported that it came from "somewhere north of the site." The female is draped, facing front, with right arm across her chest, her left arm at her waist, possibly holding a round object in her hand. She may be wearing a crown, or she may have a Julia Domna type hair-do. The casting is not crisp, and the modelling has been finished with a graver. Roman or Byzantine.

Two slightly smaller bronze statuettes with the same summary finish, and with identical lugs on the back were found near Petra and purchased by a private collector (Vaelske 2005–2006): a naked Venus Capitolina type and a standing Harpokrates. Vaelske, who dates the objects to the third century, interprets them as personal amulets designed to be suspended from a chain or string. The position of the lug on the Harpokrates figurine seems too low to allow suspension in a vertical position, and the lugs on all three figurines seem larger and heavier than necessary for such a function. Alternatively, the figurines could have served as handle attachments on lids for small vessels or lamps. Bronze lamps generally had lids with a perforated, projecting lug that fit between two similar lugs on the rim of the filler hole, forming a simple hinge; for Byzantine examples, see Bouras and Parani 2008: 44–53, 62. The Humayma statuette would have had to be standing on a small disk lid, now lost. Although the subject matter is different, a small bronze dolphin with an attachment ring beneath its tail, found in a sixth- to early seventh-century context at Pella is at a similar scale and may have served a function similar to that of our statuette (Smith and Day et al. 1989: pl. 51.19).

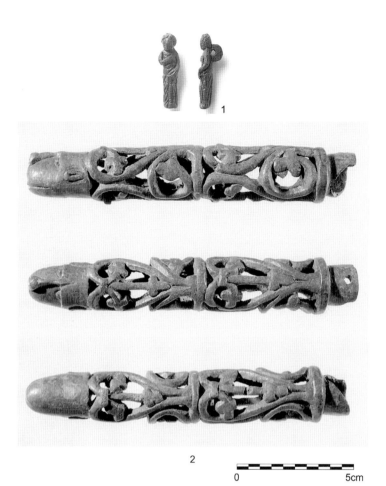

FIG. 12.9   *No. 1: Bronze statuette or pendant of standing female, with attachment ring. Random find near settlement centre. No. 2: Bronze handle from an incense burner, from F102.A2.25; top, side, and bottom views.*

The identity of the Humayma figure remains uncertain. She makes the same gesture of modesty as the naked Venus, but she is definitely clothed. Isis or Tyche are the most likely identifications.

12.C.3.   F102 (Byzantine Church and Early Islamic House)

2.   (1991.0273.01; figs. 12.9.2–12.10). F102.A2.25. (M. Smith, J.P. Oleson). Bronze handle from an incense burner; broken at former join with body of censer L 0.14 m, W of head at termination 0.02 m, H of head at termination, 0.019 m, Head L 0.029, 147.28 g. Mid-8–9C.

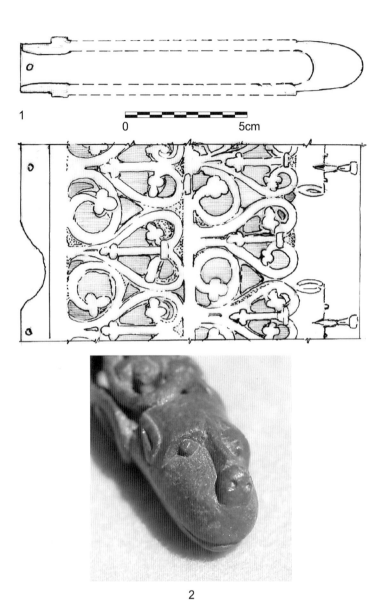

FIG. 12.10 *No. 1: Bronze handle from an incense burner, F102.A2.25; section and expanded drawing (P. Denholm). No. 2: Detail of lionesse's face.*

Archaeological Museum. It has been mentioned in print in Oleson et al. 1993: 480, and Smith 2007.

The handle has the form of a hollow cylinder, the walls composed of an openwork pattern of vines and tendrils. The distal end terminates in the stylized head of a feline, probably a lioness (fig. 12.10.2), the proximal end in a smooth-walled, slightly inset continuation of the cylinder that originally fit into a socket on the censer. A cylindrical hole (D 0.004 m) for a rivet or other fastener penetrates the wall at the top of the inset tube near its termination; the bottom portion of the tube has broken off diagonally at the point where a second hole would have accommodated the fastener. The hollow interior of the handle continues 0.8 m into the lioness' head. The object appears to have been cast by the lost-wax method and then finished by cold working with a chisel and rasp. The interior surface is very rough.

The symmetrical features of the lioness were cast in low relief, then accentuated or finished with the chisel and rasp. The bulging eyes are set beneath low, heavy brows that taper off level with the ears. The ears, formed by oblong loops with a central slit, lie flat against the sides of the head. The long, low bridge of the nose springs from the centre of the brow at the juncture of two deep lines; it widens as it descends the rounded, sloping muzzle, terminating in a wide, stubby snout with two deep nostrils. The mouth is formed by a long, narrow slit running horizontally across the lower third of the face from points well below and just forward of each eye. The large upper lip is not elaborated; the underside of the jaw and head is a smooth surface that follows the curve of the handle proper.

The lioness lacks legs or paws, and its head springs directly from the body of the handle, which

At the time of discovery, the object was in solid, stable condition but the interior and exterior surfaces were covered with a layer of corrosion, obscuring details of the design. A Department of Antiquities conservator removed the corrosion from the exterior during the winter of 1991, revealing a very well-preserved metal surface, with the original finishing marks clearly visible. There was some further cleaning in 1994, and in 2004 Judy Logan treated a few spots of bronze disease. Since 1992 the object has been on display in the Aqaba

is fashioned into two closely similar sections of an openwork design composed of curling vines with trefoil leaves (fig. 12.10.1). A circumferential half-round moulding at the mid-point of the handle separates the two sections; a second half-round moulding appears at the base of the handle, just above the inset. Two tall pairs of vines spring from each base moulding and turn back upon themselves to form symmetrical, heart-shaped frames that contain two short and one long vine sprout, each of which terminates in a trefoil. A narrow band appears to bind each group of vines at the point where they touch. Single vines with a terminal leaf spring from the ring and turn back upon themselves to fill the open spaces between tall, heart-shaped frames. The two tall pairs of tendrils in each of the two panels are approximately on line with each other and with the top and bottom of the lioness' head.

Although the decoration of the handle has an appealing energy, the finishing was not particularly careful. The modelling of the leaves and tendrils is rudimentary, and the openwork areas have been finished only roughly with a rasp or file. Except for the nose, the modelling of the feline head barely rises above the surface of the terminal knob of the handle. Chisel and rasp marks are especially evident around the animal's ears, which have been produced by cutting down into the surface of the knob.

No exact parallels are known for the Humayma handle, but several bronze censers of the Umayyad or Abbasid period from Jordan and the surrounding region show instructive parallels to the handle and suggest the design of the lost censer body. The closest parallel is the handle of a bronze censer now in the Malcove Collection (Campbell 1985: 86, 8–10C; Evans and Ratliff 2012: 180, fig. 122B, 8C), identified as Coptic and dated to the eighth to tenth century on the basis of the style of reliefs on the lid. The handle is a hollow cylinder with three gridded openwork panels. It terminates in an animal head with the same abstract features as the Humayma lioness, but identified as a ram by the horns that curl down the side of the head behind the deep-set eyes. The long, smooth muzzle terminates in a mouth rendered by a wide horizontal slit. The proximal end of the handle was recessed like that of the Humayma handle, to fit into a socket in the

circular censer body. The body was decorated with an openwork pattern of human and animal figures among abstract vines and trees. A similar censer from Egypt now in the Louvre (Bréhier 1936: pl. 44; Atil, Chase, Jett 1985: 59, fig. 20; Evans and Ratliff 2012: 180–81, fig. 122C), dated from the eighth to the tenth century, is covered with an openwork pattern of stylized vines with five-leaf clusters similar to that of the Humayma handle. The handle of this piece is missing, but the socket remains, into which the inset base of the handle would have fit.

Another close parallel is a bronze censer excavated from a mid-seventh-century domestic structure on the Amman Citadel in 1949 (Harding 1951; Allen 1986: 27, fig. 19; Evans and Ratliff 2012: 218, fig. 150A). Allan suggests that the object may have been made in Syria, although he does not justify this attribution. The handle is a smooth, hollow (?) cylinder, undecorated except for the distal termination, which is a ram's head cast in low relief and finished with a chisel. The animal has the same heavy brow, long nasal bridge, prominent nostrils, wide, slit-like mouth, and smooth, rounded muzzle as the Humayma lioness. Identification as a ram rather than a lioness, however, is made possible by the presence of horns executed in low relief that curl down and around the ears on either side of the head. The horn on the left side is better preserved and is marked with diagonal slashes that resemble the striations on a ram's horn. Three rounded flanges project from the proximal end of the handle, allowing it to be attached with rivets to the wall of a cylindrical, three-footed censer. The vertical wall of the censer has been worked in low relief into a stylized pattern that resembles tendrils and trefoil leaves. The same pattern appears on the lid, which has the shape of a dome supported by arched windows. The handle seems slightly too large for the body of the censer, and the alloy appears to be different (Tamari, in Allen 1986: 27), so it may have been intended for some other object. Nevertheless, the style of the animal head on the handle and the design of the tendril and leaf motif on the body are both echoed by the Humayma handle.

The pattern on the domed bronze lid of a censer found at Umm al-Walid (Bujard and Schweizer 1992: 17; Bisheh et al. 2000: 81; Evans and Ratliff 2012: 152, fig. 100) finds some close parallels at

Humayma, although not with the Humayma censer handle. A network of narrow, beaded bands criss-crosses the surface of the dome, framing openwork four-petal rosettes designed to allow the smoke to escape. An almost identical pattern can be seen on the early eighth-century frescoes in the main room of the Abbasid family manor house at Humayma (Field F103; Oleson et al. 1995: 346, figs. 26–27; Foote 1999, 2007: 461).

As with most of the examples cited above, the Humayma handle most likely was mounted on a censer with a cylindrical body, three feet, and a hinged, domed lid. Numerous examples of this type of censer (*mijmar, mabkhara*), dating from the eighth to the fourteenth century, have been found in Islamic contexts (Kühnel 1920; Aga-Oglu 1945; Allen 1986: 25–34). Incense played an important role in the religious ceremonies of both Byzantine and Coptic society (Pfister 1914), and in early Islam it was burned in mosques (Hillenbrand 1991: 666). There are also references to the use of incense at luxurious banquets, for example, by the Abbasid caliph al-Ma'mun (813–833) (Baer 1983: 44). The Islamic tradition of three or four-footed censers with rod handles often terminating in an animal head, along with the habit of using incense in religious rituals, appears to have been borrowed from the Copts (Aga-Oglu 1945: 28–29; Bouras and Kazhdan 1991; Hillenbrand 1991: 666; Taft and Kazhdan 1991). In fact, it can be difficult to distinguish the Coptic from the Early Islamic examples (Aga-Oglu 1945: 29; Baer 1983: 45). A sixth-century Coptic example in the Malcove Collection has a smooth handle terminating in a ram's head (Campbell 1985: 84). Although the horns curl around the ears in the same manner as those on the Amman handle, the head is otherwise much more realistic. The stylized vines with three-lobed leaves, however, that form the openwork of the domed lid on the circular censer body, have a generic resemblance to those of the Humayma handle. An entire crouched antelope or gazelle in realistic style forms the termination of an openwork handle for an elaborate censer with square body now in the Freer Gallery (Baer 1983: 46; Atil, Chase, Jett 1985: 58–61). This piece is attributed to Egypt and dated to the eighth or ninth centuries. Technical analysis revealed that the castings had been reworked with

tools, and that the handle and body of the censer, which clearly belong together, were nevertheless composed of different copper alloys. Allen (1986: 32–33) suggests that a Hellenistic incense burner from Afghanistan is part of the same tradition of animal protomes, but the design is in fact very different, and the chronological gap insurmountable.

Lions appear frequently in the arts of the Umayyad period, the lioness less often. The animal symbolized strength and power, and it could serve both as a symbol for the constellation Leo and as a metaphor for daring and strength, depending on the composition (Kindermann 1960; Smith 2007: 708). In the Umayyad period, the vine scroll evolved from its Late Antique utilisation as a background element into a major architectonic and iconographic feature, loosely representing the Qur'anic and early Hadith idea of Paradise (Flood 2001: 57–113).

The mid-eighth- to ninth-century archaeological context of the Humayma censer handle fits well with the parallels cited above. The handle could, of course, be earlier than the Phase IV or V context, and given the many Coptic parallels, it might even be a survival from the furnishings for the church. The Amman censer was found in a clearly eighth-century structure, but the handle may be reused, taken from an earlier censer, possibly Coptic. In summary, the Humayma handle could have been in use in the F102 church for ecclesiastical purposes, or it could have been used for secular purposes in the F102 Early Islamic house, or, given its relatively luxurious character, in the neighbouring Abbasid family manor house.

3. (1991.0042.01; fig. 12.11.3). F102.01.08. Draped female bust, bronze, projecting from a flat, circular ring; broken, incomplete. Bust H 0.024 m. The disk (W 0.01) has a shallow groove just inside its inner margin, while the outer margin had at least one square perforation. The disk seems to have supported some kind of bronze lattice-work, of which one fragment remains. The bust projects as if it served as a handle, and the face and garment folds have been worn away by abrasion. There is a knob at the top of the head. The style of the head is very generic, but it is likely to be Byzantine in date.

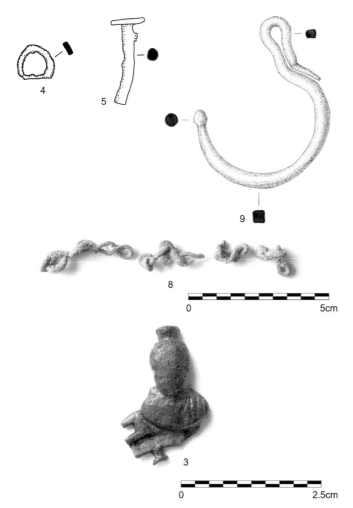

FIG. 12.11 *No. 3: Draped female bust attachment or handle, bronze, F102.01.08. No. 4: Bronze ring, F102.01.51. No. 5: Heavy bronze nail or pin, F102.03.05. No. 8: Bronze chain, F102.01.17. No. 9: Bronze suspension hook, possibly for a* polykandelon, *F102.05.29 (B. Seymour).*

This casting may have served as part of the lower attachment plate for the handle of an elaborate bronze vessel. Comparison can be made with the handle attachment of a biconical bronze jug found in a second- or first-century BC tomb at ʻEn Gedi (Hadas 1994: 6*, fig. 23.22, colour pl. 12). A male bust formed the base of the handle. The back of the bust connects with the wall of the vessel, while the handle terminates in a bevelled knob at top of head.

4. (1992.0477.01; fig. 12.11.4). F102.01.51. Bronze ring; outer D 0.013 m, inner D 0.007 m. A strip of bronze (W 0.004 m, Th 0.002 m), slightly thickened at one end (W 0.006 m) has been

rolled up to form an approximately circular ring with one flat side. Since the inner diameter is too small for use as a finger ring, it may have been used as a hair ring or as reinforcement for a rope or leather strap.

5. (1991.0090.01; fig. 12.11.5). F102.03.05. Heavy bronze nail or pin; broken, tip missing. MPL 0.003 m, W of head 0.014 m, Th of shaft 0.005 m. The nail has a thick, flat, circular head and a shaft circular in section.

6. (1991.0216.02). F102.01.12.2. Three small clippings of a bronze rod; MPL 0.052 m, Th 0.002 m. One section has been given a twist around its long axis.

7. (1991.0115.02). F102.01.12A. Very fine bronze chain; broken, incomplete; MPL ca. 0.015 m, W 0.004 m. The chain was made by bending short lengths of a thin wire (D 0.001) in loops facing opposite directions.

This simple type of chain, appropriate for necklaces or bracelets, light *polykandela,* or for fittings on light bronze vessels, is very common in the Byzantine and Early Islamic period. In a frequent variation the wire is twisted so the loops are at 90 degrees to each other along the long axis of the link. See below no. 8.

There are parallels at Petra (Fiema et al. 2001: 373), En-Gedi (Chernov 2007: 523, Late Roman or Byzantine), Jerash (Zayadine 1986: 152–53, 7–8Cc or earlier), Beth Sheʻarim (Avigad 1976: 214, fig.101.2, Byzantine), and Caesarea Palaestinae (Patrich et al. 2008: 460, fig. 255, Byzantine?).

8. (1991.0163.01; fig. 12.11.8). F102.01.17 Bronze chain; broken, incomplete; MPL 0.10 m, Th 0.006 m. The links, formed by bending each end of a wire (D 0.002 m) into a loop oriented at 90 degrees to the other, are ca. 0.01 m long. There is one larger loop 0.015 m long. See above, no. 7. There are close parallels at Petra (Fiema

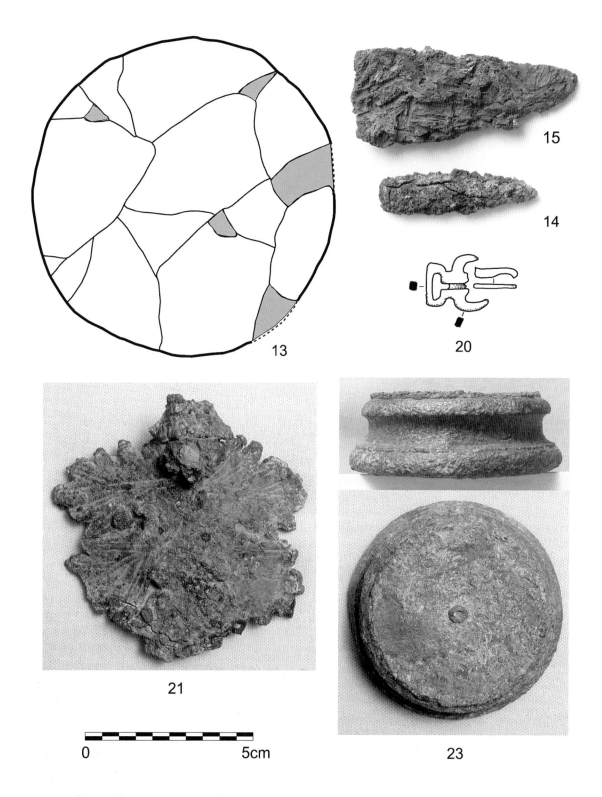

FIG. 12.12 *No. 13: Bronze mirror (?) disk, F102.05.01. No. 14: Iron spear point (1991.0270.01), F102.01.24. No. 15: Tip of an iron knife or sword blade (1991.0377.03), F102.03.24. No. 20: Small bronze buckle with iron tongue (1991.0345.06), B100.B.29. No. 21: Bronze handle attachment for a lamp or a vessel, shaped like a vine leaf (1991.0404.01), B100.B.29. No. 23: Bronze base for a statuette (1991.0342.01), B100.B.29.*

et al. 2001: 373, 4–5c) and at Hippos/Susita (Mlynarczyk 2011: figs. 3–4, 1st half 8c)

9. (1992.0310.02; fig. 12.11.9). F102.05.29. Bronze suspension hook, possibly for a *polykandelon*; L 0.06 m. The hook, hammered out of a rod (D 0.004 m), varying in width from 0.002–0.004 m, forms a wide half-circle (D 0.043 m), tapering toward the outer end, where it terminates in a bulb (D 0.003 m). The other end of the rod has been bent to form a suspension loop, terminating in a slightly flattened plate. *Polykandela* suspension chains often incorporated long, thin rods with a hook at either end that could connect with other rods, or with conventional chains, or with the disk holding the lamps. Remains of *polykandela* were also found in C101 (pp. 441–42, nos. 35–38), and fragments of the lamps they held were found in all the churches except B126 (pp. 519–51).

There are numerous Byzantine parallels in the Eastern Mediterranean: the closest is at Petra, Fiema et al. 2001: 373 (4–5c); see also Bailey 1996: 107–9, pls. 141–50 (6–7c); Bouras and Parani 2008: 90–94; Colt 1962: Pl. XXII.36 (Nessana, Byzantine); Davidson 1952: pl. 63, no 860; (Corinth, Byzantine); McNicoll et al. 1982: 135–36 (Pella, 717–749); Mlynarczyk 2011 (Hippos/Susita, 1st half 8c); Politis et al. 2012: 252–53 (Deir 'Ain 'Abata, 5–7c); Waldbaum 1983: 101–2, nos. 589–601 (Sardis, Early Byzantine); Zayadine 1986: 152–53 (Jerash, 1st half 8c).

10. (1991.0375.01). F102.04.16. Small, rectangular fragment of bronze sheet with rounded corners; MPL 0.02 m, MPW 0.015 m.

11. (1991.0386.01). F102.03.24. Thin bronze pin with one hooked end; broken, incomplete; MPL 0.032 m, W 0.002 m, Th 0.004 m. Possibly part of a fibula.

12. (1991.0453.01). F102.03.29. A small clipping of bronze, shaped like a half circle; broken, incomplete; D 0.008 m, Th 0.003 m.

13. (1992.0017.01; fig. 12.12.13). F102.05.01. Thin bronze disk. Corroded, broken, 95 percent complete; D 0.09 m, Th 0.0015–0.0085 m. No surface decoration could be seen. It is likely

that this is a mirror disk. A slightly smaller bronze mirror disk was found in a tomb in the Amman Airport necropolis (Ibrahim and Gordon 1987: Pl. XVII.2, XLIX.4; 2–3c), a slightly larger one in the Jason tomb in Jerusalem (Rahmani 1967: 91, no.1, pl. 24c, late 1c BC–ea. 1c), and another in the Dura-Europos necropolis (Toll 1946: 122–23, pre-256). The tinned bronze mirror disks in the Cave of the Letters had handles soldered on (Yadin 1963: 125, fig. 48-9, pl. 38; ea. 2c). An iron mirror disk was found at 'En-Gedi (Chernov 2007: 521–21).

14. (1991.0270.01; fig. 12.12.14). F102.01.24. Iron projectile point; broken and incomplete; MPL 0.046 m, W 0.009–0.002 m, Th 0.005 m. The lanceolate point swells gently from the flat butt end, then tapers in a curve to the point. Other than this item and no. 15 below, remains of weaponry are absent from both the churches and the Early Islamic structures built on them.

15. (1991.0377.03; fig. 12.12.15). F102.03.24. Tip of an iron knife or sword blade; broken, incomplete; MPL 0.067 m; MPW 0.028 m, Th 0.005–0.002 m. The blade tapers in a curve from the wide end toward the point. The thick layer of corrosion products carries deep impressions of chaff.

16. (1991.0495.01; fig. 12.13.16). F102.04.16; wedged in between rocks in the north baulk above the Locus 20 stone floor. Iron scissors with midpoint pivot; heavily corroded, broken halfway along the blades but complete; L 0.20 m, W 0.017–0.65 m. The pivoting scissors design is post-antique, and the artefact is most likely Ottoman in date. A similar pair, probably of the same date, was found in B100 (p. 441, no. 30). Similar examples have been found in late contexts at Beth She'arim (Avigad 1976: 215, fig. 102.3), Tel Yoqne'am (Ben-Tor et al. 1996: 232–33: No. 77), Khirbet Shema' (Meyers et al. 1976: pl. 8.2.7), and Sardis (Waldbaum 1983: 63 no. 241, pl. 17).

17. (1992.0558.07; fig. 12.13.17). F102.06.24. Miscellaneous iron hardware for a door, furniture, or tools; all badly corroded; 173 g. 1 straight iron nail, complete; L 0.07 m, head D 0.021 m.

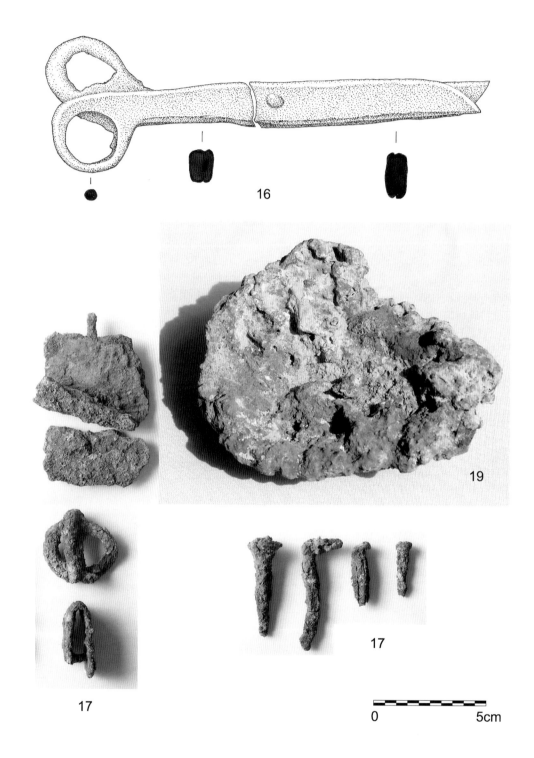

FIG. 12.13 *No. 16: Iron scissors (1991.0495.01), F102.04.16 (B. Seymour). No. 17: Miscellaneous iron hardware (1992.0558.07), F102.06.24. No. 19: Iron forging bloom (1991.0191), F102.03.14.*

1 nail with an offset oval head, complete; L 0.08 m, head L 0.026 m, W 0.015 m, shaft 0.006 m square. 1 similar nail, broken, incomplete; MPL 0.045 m. 1 nail with point hammered over at 90 degrees, broken; L 0.048 m, Th 0.005 m, head D 0.004 m. 1 iron spike with a 90 degree bend, broken, incomplete; MPL 0.105 m, Th 0.012 m. 1 trapezoidal iron plate, broken, possibly incomplete; MPW 0.046–0.035 m, MPL 0.075 m, Th 0.004 m. A short, thin tang (L 0.02, Th 0.003) has been welded to one side of the narrower end of the plate, projecting 0.01 beyond its edge. The wider end of the plate shows two thicknesses of metal. The corrosion layer on the opposite side preserves the pattern of wood grain. 1 iron ring (D 0.033 m, Th 0.005 m) attached to an iron rod (MPL 0.07 m, Th 0.005 m) bent around it to form a loop and splayed at the ends. 1 iron strap, broken, incomplete; MPL 0.055 m, W 0.005 m, Th 0.002 m. The strap had been bent around a wooden object 0.006 m thick and fastened by a rivet. Iron nails with an offset head are common at Humayma, probably because they were easier to produce than nails with a circular head welded to the shaft.

18. (1993.0038.02). F102.06.24A. Iron object of undetermined function, possibly two links of a chain, possibly a door latch; broken, corroded, incomplete; MPL ca. 0.085 m, MPW ca. 0.024 m, Th ca. 0.012 m. Exposed and damaged during looting. It appears to consist of a flattened loop of metal, expanding slightly at either end, one end slightly larger than the other. Another loop or curved element projects upward from the narrow end of the loop.

19. (1991.0191; fig. 12.13.19). F102.03.14. Iron forging bloom; L 0.136 m, W 0.11 m, Th 0.065 m. 840 g. Roughly oval, cup-shaped forging bloom composed of glassy and ferrous slag. Very similar to the numerous forging blooms found in the forge area in the Roman Fort, Area H (Oleson et al. 1999: 419–20). These cup-shaped blooms form in a forge near the *tuyer* carrying in air from the bellows (Unglik 1997; Sim 1998). Since it is an isolated find, this bloom may have been recovered from the fort and transported to F102 as a curiosity.

12.C.4. B100 (Byzantine Church and Early Islamic House)

20. (1991.0345.06; fig. 12.12.20). B100.B.29. Small bronze buckle with iron tongue; corroded, broken, incomplete; MPL 0.027 m; buckle W 0.026 m; strap attachment W 0.01 m; tongue L 0.02 m. The strap attachment is straight, slightly narrower than the buckle frame, which forms an oval. This could be a fitting for an animal harness, or for body armour. Compare Davidson 1952: 266, 270, nos. 2175–76, pl. 113 (Corinth, 4–6c or 8c), D'Amato and Sumner 2009: fig. 167, 173–75 (Vindonissa, 2c).

21. (1991.0404.01; fig. 12.12.21). B100.B.29. Bronze handle attachment for a lamp or a vessel, shaped like a five-lobed vine leaf; corroded, incomplete; MPH 0.076 m, W 0.077 m, Th 0.003 m. The broken attachment lugs at the top suggest that the leaf either stood upright as the handle of a large bronze lamp or was soldered to the belly of a vessel to hold one end of a swing handle. The front side of the leaf is convex, modelled in relief to imitate the curves of a leaf, and a network of veins has been chiselled in. The concave back side is undecorated.

Tall handles shaped like a vine leaf, acanthus leaf, or a palmette appear on larger, more elaborate terracotta lamps from the later Hellenistic period through the third century, e.g., Sussman 2006 (Tel Aviv, 1st half 2CcBC), Hellmann 1985: l3–4, no. 1 (Athens, late 2c–ea.1c BC), Bailey 1988: 336, pl. 76, Q2688 (Benghazi, manufactured at Cnidus, 70–80), 205–6, pl. 29, Q1855 (Tripoli, 150–200). The pretentiousness, detailing, and glazing show that these lamps were imitations of metal lamps, of which only a few survive. The best parallel, although not precisely like the Humayma leaf, was found at Khirbet edh-Dharih (Durand 2011: 59, no. 50, fig. 9; 1c AD?). There are a few other approximate parallels in metal: Bailey 1996: 9, pl. 5, Q3552 (3–2c BC, from Egypt), 28, pl. 29, Q3627 (1c, unknown origin), 43, pl. 54, Q 3685 (50–150, origin unknown).

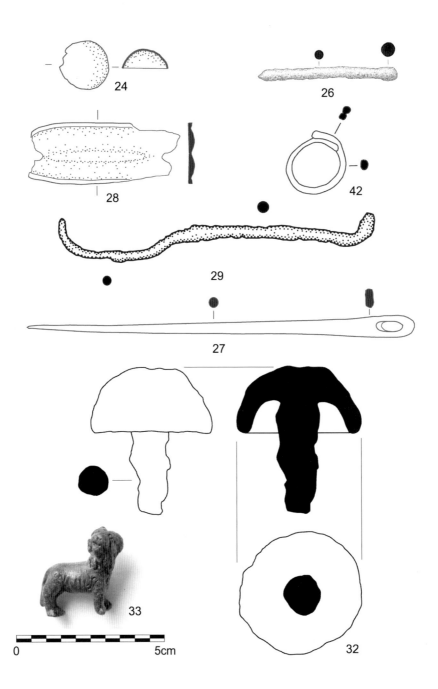

Fig. 12.14 *No. 24: Bronze nail cover (?)(1993.0174.01), B100.19 P02.04. No. 26: Bronze dipper (1993.0203.01), B100.19 P02.09 (B. Seymour). No. 27: Long bronze needle (1995.0277.01), B100.21.00. No. 28: Leaf-shaped bronze plate (1992.0193.01), B100.22.15. No. 29: Bronze medical instrument (?) (1992.0537.01), B100.F.14. No. 32: Head of an iron spike (1992.0086), B100.E.11 (B. Seymour). No. 33: Bronze figurine of a lion (1991.0317.01), C101.01.08. No. 42: Small bronze ring (1993.0048.01), C101.01.69.*

23. (1991.0342.01; fig. 12.12.23). B100.B.29. Bronze base for a statuette; corroded; lower D 0.063 m, upper D 0.050 m, H 0.021 m. The base, typical of small bronzes of the Roman imperial period, has the profile of an Ionic column base (two tori separated by scotia, with a fillet at the top and above the lower torus). The upper surface is flat and smooth, except for a low, projecting knob (D 0.004 m) in the centre with a central depression, presumably to anchor the statuette. The base was hollow cast, but poorly centred in the mould, so one wall is markedly thinner than the other and has corroded through. For similar examples, see Weber 2006: 26 no. 3, pl. 2B–D (Damascus, 1C), Walsh 1990: 228, fig. 29 (Augst, late 2C), and Mitten and Doeringer 1967: 239 no. 232 (origin unknown, AD 20–30).

24. (1993.0174.01; fig. 12.14.24). B100.19 P02.04. Thin, circular bronze sheet, dished to a near hemisphere; incomplete; D 0.016 m, H 0.006 m, Th 0.005 m. The original edge is preserved around approximately half the object. Since there is no mark of an attachment on the inside face, this may be the cover for a nail head or a boss.

25. (1993.0174.02). B100.19 P02.04. Small bronze strap or clipping from a sheet; bent, broken, incomplete. From the broken end (W 0.014 m, Th 0.005 m) the strap widens gradually to a termination at two pointed projections (MPL 0.047, W 0.019). There is a circular nail hole (D 0.002 m) through the strap just inside the V formed by the projections. The object may have served as decoration or as a reinforcing strap on a piece of furniture.

26. (1993.0203.01; fig. 12.14.26). B100.19 P02.09. Bronze cosmetic dipper. The circular shaft is broken at one end, and terminates with a bulbous head at the other; MPL 0.046 m, D of shaft 0.003 m, D of head 0.004 m. Most likely a cosmetic instrument, originally with a dipper knob or small scoop at the other end, for perfumes, *kohl*, or unguent. This type of artefact was common in the Roman and Byzantine Near East, for example at Nessana (Colt 1962: pl. XXIII.3–6), en-Gedi (Chernov 2007: 509–10;

Hadas 1994: 3*), the Amman Airport necropolis (Ibrahim and Gordon 1987: 28–29, pl. XVI, 2–3C), Hesban (Ray et al. 2009: figs. 12.2.1, 12.4.1), Jerash (Zayadine 1966a: 266, pl. XXVI), and Dura-Europos (Toll 1946: 123–24).

27. (1995.0277.01; fig. 12.14.27). B100.21.00. Long bronze needle with large, oblong eye; L 0.13 m, D in middle 0.003 m. The object appears to be machine made, so it is probably an Ottoman period artefact for sewing tent material. A slightly longer Mamluk or Ottoman example was found at Yoqne'am (Ben-Tor et al. 1996: 223–24: pl. 18.5.3). Ancient bronze and iron examples of similar large needles found at other sites were probably used for the same purpose: iron, Cave of the Letters (Yadin 1963: 89, fig. 32.31, pl. 25.31); bronze, Qaryat al-Faw (al-Ghabban 2010: 361, fig. 216), Samaria (Crowfoot et al. 1957: fig. 105.3), Caesarea Palaestinae (Patrich 2008: 458, fig. 221, 467, fig. 221, Byzantine), Corinth (Davidson 1952: 176, pl. 78, no. 1239, Byzantine).

28. (1992.0193.01; fig. 12.14.28). B100.22.15. Small, leaf-shaped bronze plate; broken, incomplete; MPL 0.05 m, W 0.019 m, Th 0.002 m. A central, longitudinal groove is framed by two low, rounded ridges, and a smaller groove along each long edge sets off a raised margin. The object is broken at both ends, at the site of some perforations. The object resembles the end of a cosmetic instrument, but holes make little sense in that context. It is more likely a fragment of armour, a strap fitting, or a pendant (cf. James 2004: 86 fig. 40, 92, fig. 42.230–38). For a cosmetic instrument see the references in no. 39 (p. 442), and Waldbaum 1983: 107–8, nos. 640–41 (Sardis).

29. (1992.0537.01; fig. 12.14.29). B100.F.14. Bronze rod with a hook at one end and an offset (L 0.03 m, depth 0.005 m) at the other; corroded, complete; L 0.095 m, Th 0.02 m. The shape and size resemble those of the medical instrument called a bone elevator or lever (Milne 1907: 133–35, pl. XLI.1), but the finish does not seem fine enough, and medical instruments seem unlikely in this context. Nevertheless, if

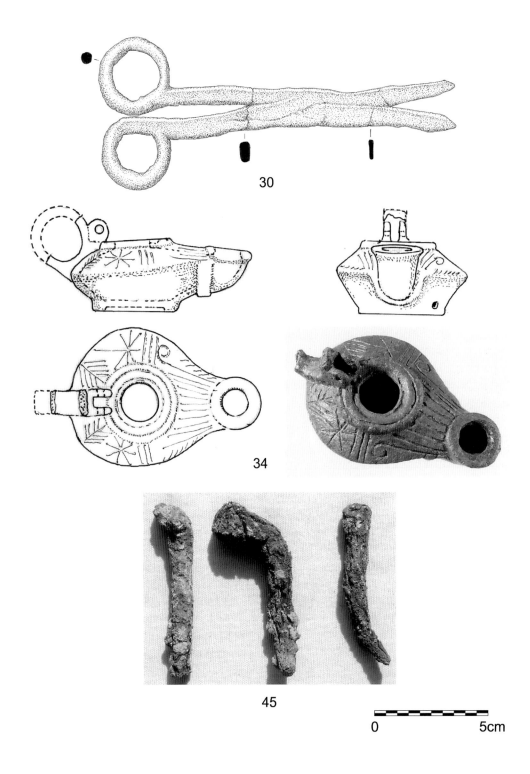

FIG. 12.15 *No. 30: Iron scissors (1993.0231.01), B100.13.00 (B. Seymour). No. 34: Bronze oil lamp (1991.0126.01), C101.02.13 (P. Denholm). No. 45: Iron nails (1991.0254.02, 317.02, 382.01), C101.01.08.*

this is in fact a medical tool, it reinforces the identification of the stone tablet from C101 as a grinding tablet for medicines (p. 508–9, no. 8).

30. (1993.0231.01; fig. 12.15.30). B100.13.00. Pair of iron scissors with central pivot, corroded, broken, complete; L 0.157 m, W at finger holes 0.065 m, Th at pivot 0.01 m. The finger holes have a circular outline; the blades widen slightly at the hinge hole, then taper to sharp points. The pivoting scissors design is post-antique, and the artefact is most likely Ottoman in date. See above, p. 435, no. 16, for an example from F102. Similar examples have also been found in late contexts at Beth She'arim (Avigad 1976: 215, fig. 102.3), Tel Yoqne'am (Ben-Tor et al. 1996: 232–33: No. 77), Khirbet Shema' (Meyers et al. 1976: pl. 8.2.7), and Sardis (Waldbaum 1983: 63 no. 241, pl. 17).

31. (1991.0357.06). B100.B.29. Iron fitting; broken, complete; L 0.061 m, Th of shaft 0.006 m, D of loops 0.013 m. Short rod with a loop at each end, one parallel to its length, the other perpendicular to it. Possibly a harness fitting.

32. (1992.0086; fig. 12.14.32). B100.E.11. Head of an iron spike; corroded, broken, incomplete; MPL 0.05 m, D of head 0.042 m; shaft 0.005 × 0.005 m. The head of the heavy spike is hemispherical and hollow beneath. It may have provided decorative finish to a door or piece of heavy furniture.

12.C.5. C101 (Byzantine Church)

33. (1991.0317.01; fig. 12.14.33). C101.01.08. Small bronze figurine of a lion; corroded; L 0.03 m, H 0.028 m, Th 0.012 m. The animal is standing, head erect and to the right, tail down against the legs. The stance and torso are dog-like, but the curls of a heavy mane are clear. Presumably the small figurine was originally attached by its feet to a bronze vessel or an article of furniture, possibly part of the church furnishings. For small bronze lions see Mitten and Doeringer 1967: 101 no. 99 (Greek, ca. 500 BC?), 184 no. 188 (Etruscan, 550–500 BC), 290 no. 284 (Roman, 1C BC–1C AD).

34. (1991.0126.01; fig. 12.15.34). C101.02.13. Bronze oil lamp; ring handle broken and incomplete, hinged lid missing; L 0.094 m, W 0.06 m, H 0.04 m. The heavy nozzle terminates in a collar below the well-defined shoulder. The shoulder is decorated with incised lines: longitudinal between the nozzle and heavy rings around the filler hole, the two longest with curled terminations, then three vertical lines on either side, then two eight-pointed stars, then two fishbone motifs next to the ring handle. The body is not completely symmetrical. The lamp, which may have formed part of the church furnishings, has a close resemblance to the Early Byzantine terracotta lamps at Petra (Grawehr 2006: 340–49, Type L; cf. in particular nos. 493–94, 502–3, and 511, AD 363), so it should date to the late fourth century. It is not common for bronze lamps to resemble so closely a ceramic design, since the material allowed greater elaboration of handles and nozzles. There are some elaborate Byzantine designs, several with decorative crosses, in Bouras and Parani 2008: 44–55, 60–63. Bronze lamps are not common in Jordan, but another one was found in a mid-second-century (or earlier) context at Khirbet edh-Dharih (Durand 2011: 49–50, no. 49, fig. 8; Villeneuve 1990: 371, pl. I.2).

35. (1991.0025.01; fig. 12.16.35). C101.01.00. Bronze hook and chain, probably part of a polykandelon; MPL 0.055 m, W 0.01 m, rod Th 0.002 m. A bronze rod was bent into a hook at both ends; three chain links are attached to the upper hook, which was bent into an almost completely closed circle. *Polykandela* suspension chains often incorporated long, thin rods with a hook at either end that could connect with other rods, or with conventional chains, or with the disk holding the lamps. *Polykandela* fittings were also found in F102, and fragments of the glass lamps they held were found in all the churches except B126. There are numerous parallels in the Eastern Mediterranean; see F102, no. 9 (pp. 433, 435, 441, 517).

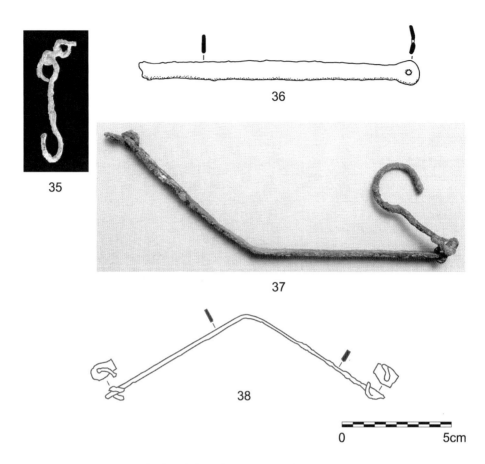

FIG. 12.16 *No. 35: Bronze hook and chain from* polykandelon *(1991.0025. 01), C101.01.00. No. 36:*
Bronze suspension strap for a polykandelon *(1996.0499.01), C101.02.00. No. 37: Bronze*
hook and suspension strap for polykandelon *(1993.0261.02), C101.04.26. No. 38: Bronze*
suspension strap for a polykandelon *(1991.0025.02), C101.01.00.*

36. (1996.0499.01; fig. 12.16.36). C101.02.00. Bronze suspension rod for a *polykandelon;* broken, incomplete; MPL 0.13 m, W 0.01 m, Th 0.002 m. A thin, flat, undecorated strip with a circular suspension lug at each end, perforated for attachment to a chain. See no. 35 above for parallels.

37. (1993.0261.02; fig. 12.16.37). C101.04.26. Bronze hook and suspension strap for *polykandelon;* corroded, incomplete; MPL 0.17 m, W 0.06 m, Th 0.01 m. Bracket L 0.15, slightly bent; eye at one end connected to two links of chain; eye at other end connected to a hook by two links of chain. For this type of suspension bracket, see Fiema et al. 2001: 373 (Petra, 4–5C) and Bailey 1996: 107–9 no. Q3933MLA (Lampsacus, 6–7C).

38. (1991.0025.02; fig. 12.16.38). C101.01.00. Bronze support strap for a *polykandelon*. Small attachment holes at each end still contain small portions of the bronze support chain. L 0.13 m, W 0.01 m, Th 0.005 m. See nos. 35–37 above.

39. (1992.0110.01). C101.02.42. Bronze cosmetic instrument with elongated, leaf-shaped spoon; broken, incomplete; MPL 0.05 m, W 0.01 m. This type of instrument was common in the Roman and Byzantine periods; see Ray et al. 2009: fig. 12.2.1, 12.4.1 (Hesban); Waldbaum 1983: 107–8, nos. 640–41 (Sardis, Late Roman to Early Byzantine).

40. (1993.0389.02; fig. 12.17.40). C101.04.33. Bronze dip-stick for *kohl* or some other cosmetic sub-

stance; broken, incomplete; MPL 0.067 m, D 0.002–0.005 m. The circular shaft swells at one end to a bulbous termination. A similar object was found in B100 (p. 439, no. 26). This type of artefact was common in the Roman and Byzantine Near East, for example at Nessana (Colt 1962: pl. XXIII.3–6), en-Gedi (Chernov 2007: 509–10; Hadas 1994: 3*), the Amman Airport necropolis (Ibrahim and Gordon 1987: 28–29, pl. XVI), Hesban (Ray et al. 2009: figs. 12.2.1, 12.4.1), Jerash (Zayadine 1966a: 266, pl. XXVI), and Dura-Europos (Toll 1946: 123–24).

41. (1991.0294; fig. 12.17.41). C101.02.22. Bronze vessel handle; broken, incomplete; MPL 0.05 m, W 0.02 m. The object is rectangular in section, with a sharp bend in the middle, and a rectangular attachment plate at one end. The other end is broken off. The object could have served as the handle of a small bronze vessel, perhaps a juglet; cf. Davidson 1952: pl. 49, no. 522, 523 (Corinth); Negev 1997: 209, no. 43, pl. 4.43 (Oboda).

42. (1993.0048.01; fig. 12.14.42). C101.01.69. Found in the fill above Burial 4, but probably not part of the grave goods. Small bronze ring formed from a wire with overlapped ends; D 0.02 m, Th 0.003 m.

43. (1992.0110.02). C101.02.42. Flat, thin, crescent-shaped scrap of bronze sheet; MPL 0.03 m, MPW 0.01 m.

44. (1991.0125.01). C101.04.00. Small scrap of bronze; D 0.017 m; 5 g.

45. (1991.0254.02, 317.02, 382.01; fig. 12.15.45). C101.01.08. 7 iron nails, bent at either the head or the point; corroded; L 0.08 m to 0.065 m. Some of the nails appear to have had circular heads, the others heads pounded to one side (see above p. 436, no. 17).

46. (1992.0565.01). C101.05.10. 2 iron nails, one with bent tip, the other with bent shaft; corroded; L 0.08 m, head D 0.022 m; L 0.017 m, head D 0.026 m.

12.D. BONE, IVORY, SHELL, PLASTER, AND TERRACOTTA OBJECTS
(J.P. Oleson)

12.D.1. Introduction and Analysis

This miscellany of material does not show any particular patterns, and the level of craftsmanship is mediocre. Most of the objects could have been produced locally, and items 10 and 16 appear to be the scraps left behind from a craft process. Bone pins are a very common artefact in the Roman, Late Roman, and Byzantine Near East. The moulded plaster (no. 12) may somehow have migrated to C101 from the Abbasid Manor house (F103), after departure of the family. The catalogue numbers run in a single series through this chapter section, regardless of excavation area.

12.D.2. F102 (Byzantine Church and Early Islamic House)

1. (1991.0183.02; fig. 12.17.1). F102.01.18. Finger ring cut from tubular body of a pinkish white seashell; broken, incomplete; ring D 0.029 m, band Th 0.008 m. The exterior surface is the original smooth surface of the *Conus/Strombus* shell. Compare no. 15 below. A shell ring with naturally glossy surface was found at Hesban (Ray et al. 2009: 265, fig. 13.17.3, Roman or Byzantine).

2. (1991.0484.01; fig. 12.18.2). F102.03.27. Late Byzantine potsherd with graffito on outside surface engraved before firing; broken, incomplete; MPL 0.09 m, MPW 0.06 m. Possibly storage ware. Colour: outer surface black, inner surface dark grey, no slip. The text may read μπ[… .

3. (1993.0038.01; fig. 12.17.3). F102.06.24a. Two cylindrical ivory beads; complete, splitting along the grain; H 0.008 m, D 0.013 m, and H 0.007 m, D 0.014 m.

4. (1992.0157.01). F102.01.34. Painted plaster; brownish white; broken, incomplete; MPL 0.06 m, MPW 0.05 m, Th 0.011 m. Two intersecting black lines were painted on the exterior surface.

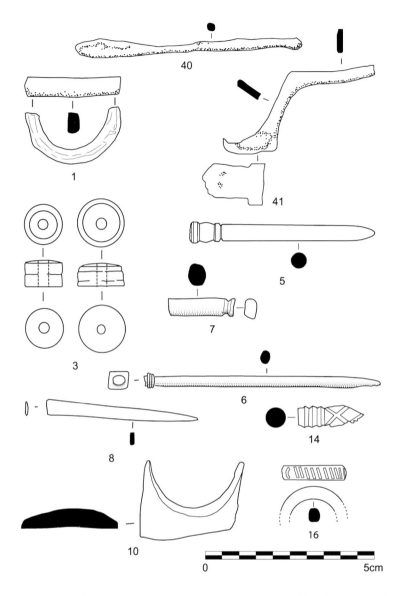

FIG. 12.17 *No. 40: Bronze dip stick (1993.0389.02), C101.04.33. No. 41: Bronze vessel handle (1991.0294), C101.02.22. No. 1: Finger ring cut from sea shell (1991.0183.02), F102.01.18. No. 3: Two cylindrical ivory beads (1993.0038.01), F102.06.24a. No. 5: Bone pin (1993.0183.01), B100.01.P01.11. No. 6: Bone pin (1991.0127.01), B100.B.06. No. 7: Bone pin (1991.0136.01), B100.E.06. No. 8: Bone pin or stylus (1991.0239.01), B100.J.03. No. 10: Curving bone panel (1993.0019.01), B100.E.38. No. 14: Bone pin (1992.0368.03), C101.01.25. No. 16: Finger ring cut from a seashell (1992.0376.01), C101.01.25.*

12.D.3. B100 (Byzantine Church
and Early Islamic House)

5.   (1993.0183.01; fig. 12.17.5). B100.01.P01.11. Bone pin with bead and reel decoration at top end, thick point; broken, complete; L 0.055 m, Th 0.005 m. Bone pins used for pinning up the hair or garments are very common in the Roman and Byzantine Near East; most have a simple knob-like head and were formed by turning on a small lathe. Some Byzantine pins found at en-Gedi (Chernov 2007: 526) and Nessana (Colt 1962: pl. XXI.10–12) have more elaborate profiles similar to this one; cf. also Davidson 1952: pl. 79, no. 1264–65. For more parallels see C101 Burial 4, no. 1 (p. 399).

6. (1991.0127.01; fig. 12.17.6). B100.B.06. Bone pin; roughly circular section, with two ridges near the thick end, dull point; MPL 0.07 m, D 0.002–0.005 m. Carelessly finished bone pins are common throughout the Near East in the Roman and Byzantine period, for example at Samaria (Crowfoot 1957: 459, fig. 114 nos. 16, 24).

7. (1991.0136.01; fig. 12.17.7). B100.E.06. Bone pin, circular in section; broken, only head preserved; MPL 0.02 m, D 0.007 m. There is a carelessly carved groove 0.001 m from the flat, top end of the shaft.

8. (1991.0239.01; fig. 12.17.8). B100.J.03. Bone splinter shaped to the form of a flat toothpick or stylus; wide end possibly broken; MPL 0.046 m, W 0.001–0.005 m, Th. 0.002 m. Cf. Davidson 1952: 187, no. 1369, pl. 83, pl. 120, no. 2385 (Corinth, 1–2C).

9. (1992.0236.01). B100.E.22. Bone bracelet; convex outer surface, rounded edges; broken, incomplete; MPL 0.03 m, Th 0.01 m, D cs. 0.07 m.

10. (1993.0019.01; fig. 12.17.10). B100.E.38. Curving panel cut from a dense long bone, W 0.028, L 0.022, Th 0.004. A circular hole (D 0.024 m) has been cut through it, possibly to produce a blank for a button or circular inlay. Half the circular hole is preserved. There are several good parallels from the Palatine, Rome (St. Clair 2003: 64, fig. 7, pl. pl. 6; late 1–ea. 2C); a bone possibly under preparation to produce buttons was found in a Byzantine context at Corinth (Davidson 1952: pl. 69, no. 957). See below no. 17.

11. (1991.0099.01; fig. 6.42). B100.04.06. Wall sherd of large vessel, with decoration or a graffito engraved before firing; broken, incomplete; MPL 0.08 m, MPW 0.03 m. The graffito may represent a bird or an inscription, but it is too fragmentary for decipherment. Core 2.5YR 5/6; slip 7.5YR 7/2; very hard; rough feel and fracture. Temper: common, clear, ill-sorted, sub-rounded. Inclusions: sparse. Voids: none. Surface ribbed.

12.D.4. C101 (Byzantine Church)

12. (1991.0468.01; fig. 12.18.12). C101.01.08. Moulded plaster; broken, 2 fragments preserved; MPL 0.19 m, 0.08 m. The two fragments appear to be thick wall decoration, one the edge of a panel, the other possibly an abstract plant motif. This type of sculpted or moulded plaster decoration has been found elsewhere at Humayma only in the Abbasid family Manor House (F103.02.13), a three-stepped plaster finial with a central arrow. The same motif appears on some of the ivory furniture panels found in the manor house, indicating that the plaster finial belongs there too. Neither artefact has been published. Alternatively, the object could have been part of a Byzantine plaster frieze of stylized plant motifs, similar to that excavated at Maʾaridh, Ctesiphon (Evans and Ratliff 2012: 29, fig. 18A, 6C).

13. (1991.0254.01; fig. 12.18.13). C101.01.08. Late Byzantine potsherd with graffito on outside surface engraved after firing; broken, incomplete; MPL 0.08 m, MPW 0.05 m. Grey-black ware handmade storage jar. The letters may represent numbers: if Greek, κ ν | ν , possibly "20, 50 | 50." If they are Latin, the K seems out of place, but the V with a horizontal line above could be "5,000." Five thousand of anything seems a lot to be accounting for on the outside of even a very large jar, so the letters might be part of an incomplete word or phrase.

14. (1992.0368.03; fig. 12.17.14). C101.01.25. Bone pin; broken, lower portion lost; MPL 0.02 m, D 0.005 m. There are three parallel grooves at top end, a crosshatch pattern below. There are parallels for this treatment at Samaria (Crowfoot 1957: 459, fig. 114 nos. 28–29, 34–37).

15. (1998.0525). C101.01.78. Bone pin or spindle; broken, top and lower portion lost; MPL 0.08 m, D 0.03 m. There was some kind of finial, a wide band, and two narrow bands above the smooth, cylindrical shaft. The wide diameter and lack of a marked taper in the surviving portion of the shaft suggest that this is a spindle rather than a hairpin.

FIG. 12.18 *No. 2: Late Byzantine potsherd with graffito (1991.0484.01), F102.03.27. No. 17: Bone plaque (1993.0266.09), C101.04.28. No. 12: Moulded plaster (1991.0468.01), C101.01.08. No. 13: Potsherd with graffito (1991.0254.01), C101.01.08.*

16. (1992.0376.01; fig. 12.17.16). C101.01.25. Finger ring cut from tubular body of a pinkish white seashell, possibly *Conus/Strombus;* broken, incomplete; original D 0.02 m, W 0.004 m. The exterior surface has been incised with short parallel lines across the width of the band. Compare no. 1 above (p. 443). A shell ring with naturally glossy surface was found at Hesban (Ray et al. 2009: 265, fig. 13.17.3, Roman or Byzantine).

17. (1993.0266.09; fig. 12.18.17). C101.04.28. Bone plaque; broken, incomplete; MPL 0.11 m, W 0.015–0.02 m, Th 0.005 m. The object has been worked from a panel of a long bone, variable in width, narrower toward the centre. The edges have been smoothed, but the back was left unworked. The front side is decorated with three groups of concentric circles: at one end and at the centre, a central dot (D 0.001 m) is surrounded by two incised concentric circles (outer D 0.016 m); there are traces of a third group of circles at the other end. Given the decoration on only one side, this object may have been used as inlay in a piece of furniture. Given the presence of two concentric circles in the pattern, it is less likely that the bone was being used to produce buttons (see above no. 10).

Chapter 13

Ecclesiastical Marble, Inscriptions, and Miscellaneous Stone Finds

by Robert Schick, John P. Oleson, Khaled Al-Bashaireh,
David Graf, Norman Herz, and Gregory D. Rowe

A variety of stone artefacts was found at Humayma from the whole range of its occupation periods, the largest class being ecclesiastical marble. There were, however, numerous other artefact types, including a few inscriptions on stone, numerous architectural elements surviving from destroyed Nabataean structures, a few altars and betyls, a chess piece, a few possible loom weights, door socket stones, and numerous pounding stones and querns. Many of this last class of artefacts may be early modern in date. Numerous steatite cooking vessels were also found. D. Grubisha has prepared a study of the steatite, but she could not complete it in time for inclusion in this volume. It will appear as an article.

13.A. ECCLESIASTICAL MARBLE
(R. Schick)

13.A.1. Introduction

Approximately 268 pieces of marble were found during the twelve excavation seasons from 1991 to 2009 at Humayma, in addition to numerous small chips and flakes. Most of this material was found in and around the C101 Church, but there were a few pieces from the other excavation areas,

particularly B100 and F102, where abandoned churches were reused for habitation, and in the small C119 church. There was no church in the F103 area, the Abbasid family Manor House, so the material found there was carried in for re-use or out of curiosity either during the occupation of that structure, or in the subsequent centuries. This material most likely came from the nearby F102 Church, which is only 100 m away. The one fragment of marble sculpture so far found at Humayma, the midsection of a draped female, possibly a Victory figure or Artemis of Roman imperial date (1993.0198.01; unpublished), also appeared in F103. When intact, the figurine would have been about 0.60 m tall. Possibly some of this ecclesiastical and non-ecclesiastical marble was brought in from other parts of the site to adorn the Manor House. The F103 marble is included here for completeness, as are the eight fragments of ecclesiastical marble found on the surface around the site.

The salvaging of the marble from the churches at Humayma was systematic, but not particularly thorough. The intentional smashing of the large panels suggest that there was no attempt made to salvage them for re-use, either in another church or in a non-ecclesiastical context. Other than the production of small marble objects, for which we have no evidence at the site, the only obvious use of marble fragments is for the production of lime. The alkaline soils at Humayma (*HEP* 1: 355–59) would not have benefitted from the application of lime, which in any case would have been difficult to apply to the light, dusty soil. Alternatively, the lime could have been used for the production of fine plaster, or in craft procedures such as de-hairing hides prior to preservation. Whatever the intended application, it could not have been a particularly urgent need, since so much marble was left behind. In the C101 Church, 214 fragments of marble were found, with a total weight of 172 kg. This is undoubtedly only a small fraction of the original installations, but it is nevertheless substantial. Another 101.5 kg survive from B100, F102, F103, and surface finds. No lime kilns have yet been identified in the settlement centre or its immediate vicinity. A probable ancient lime kiln was found 2.2 km north of the settlement, cut into a limestone ridge adjacent to the aqueduct and the Wadi al-Amghar (*HEP* 1: 99). This seems a long distance to carry the marble fragments, but perhaps the kiln was originally intended for burning the immediately adjacent limestone, and later on was used opportunistically for the marble.

Each marble piece larger than a chip or flake was registered, and most were photographed. All fragments are registered here, but only those with significant remains of mouldings or cuttings are illustrated. The allocation to the various chancel screens of non-joining fragments was done on the basis of thickness, moulding design, and colour of the stone. The breakdown across the site is as follows: C101, 214 fragments; B100, 12 fragments; C119, 8 fragments; F102, 16 fragments; F103, 10 fragments; Area A, 8 fragments. It is striking that no fragments of ecclesiastical marble have so far been found in the Roman Fort (E116), or the *vicus* structures (E125). There were no churches associated with those structures, so the absence of ecclesiastical marble makes sense, and both had gone out of use long before the construction or abandonment of the churches. The E116 and E125 fields are separated from the closest church structures (B100 and B126) by 400 m and 250 m, respectively, so the casual deposit of stones in the modern period is also less likely than elsewhere on the site. Laboratory analy-

sis of selected samples showed that Prokonnesos (Marmara, Turkey), Thasos, and Naxos (Greece) are the probable sources of the marble.

The entries in this catalogue are arranged according to the reconstructed panels or other types of marble furnishings to which the individual fragments originally belonged. The entry for each reconstructed furnishing gives the registration number of the individual marble fragments, the locus where each fragment was found, and the maximum dimensions of the reconstructed object. The marble pieces from the C101 church derive from numerous chancel screen panels and other liturgical furnishings. The marble from the other areas includes elements from the B100, C119, and F102 churches, in addition to other miscellaneous pieces.

Most of the marble fragments and reconstructed furnishings find parallels in other churches throughout the Byzantine world. Five other excavated churches in Jordan provide extensive published corpora of liturgical marble: Mount Nebo (Acconci 1998), the Church of St. Stephen at Umm al-Rasas (Acconci 1994), the Petra Church (Kanellopoulos and Schick 2001), the Jabal Harûn church (Lehtinen 2008), and Deir ʿAin ʿAbata/Lot's Cave (Loverance 2012). The catalogue here for the most part cites parallels only from those five structures, avoiding needless repetition of the further parallels that can be found cited in those five publications. The parallels with the Petra churches are particularly important.

13.A.2. C101 (Byzantine Church)

The C101 Church yielded 214 pieces of marble for registration. Evidence was found for most of the furnishing elements typical of Byzantine churches, with the exception of chancel screen posts. There were also no fragments that could be identified as belonging to a reliquary.

13.A.2.a. Panels

Fragments of a number of different panels were found in the C101 lower church, originating with the chancel screen, the ambo, and the ambo balustrade. The total number of separate panels origi-

1a-b. Panel 1

FIG. 13.1 *C101, Panel 1, view and reconstruction (Drawing: M. Siklenka).*

nally represented may be around 20, but the precise number is not certain, due to the fragmentary state of preservation of most of the panels. Only about 50 percent of the best-preserved panel was recovered, and some panels seem to be represented by only a single fragment.

Open-Work Panels. Fragments of at least four panels survive with lattice open-work in the centre.

C101 Panel 1. Open-work panel (figs. 13.1.1–13.2.1); the lower part is on display in the Aqaba Archaeology Museum. Thirteen pieces, making about half of a panel, were found scattered in the Nave immediately to the west of the Chancel area. One piece (no. 13) was especially blackened by fire; it joined two other pieces that were not blackened. The original dimensions of the panel were 0.73 × 0.55 m; the thickness varied from 0.025 m towards

the top to 0.031 m towards the bottom. The sides have a sharp bevel, while the top and bottom are flat. The preserved portion of the panel has four fastening holes, each about 0.03 m deep and with a diameter of about 0.007 m: 1) on the lower side 0.155 m from the lower right corner with remains of the plug (fig. 13.2.1); 2) on the lower side 0.40 m from the lower right corner with remains of the plug; 3) on the right side 0.18 m up from the lower right corner; 4) on the left side 0.18 m up from the lower left corner.

The panel consists of a border framing a stylized plant at the bottom, a star with eight rays each ending in a small bulb in the upper corners, and a three-ridged circle in the centre with an ovolo at the top enclosing an open-work cross. The panel is identical to C101 Panel 2, with which it forms a matching set. Other panels typically had a wreath in place of the central circle. Parallels to the star motif

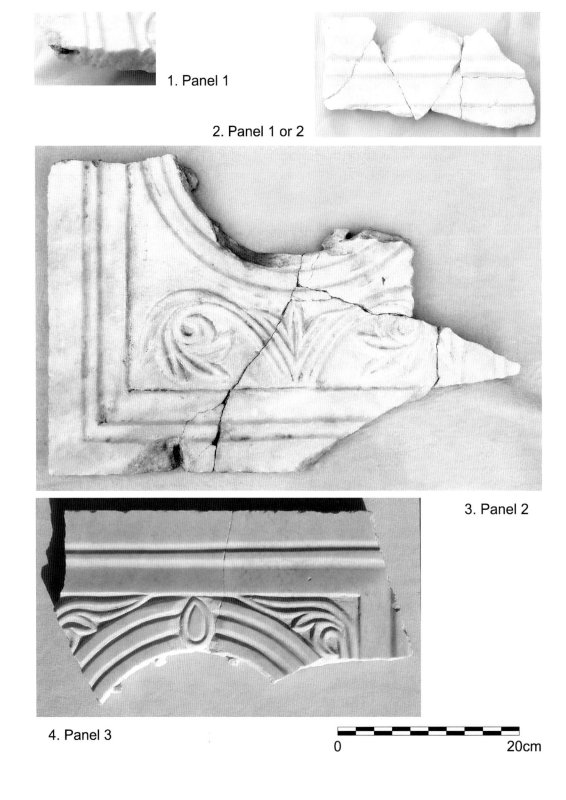

1. Panel 1

2. Panel 1 or 2

3. Panel 2

4. Panel 3

0   20cm

FIG. 13.2 *No. 1: C101, Panel 1, detail of clamp. No. 2: C101, Panel 1 or 2, miscellaneous fragments. No. 3: C101, Panel 2, view. No. 4: C101, Panel 3, view.*

are common (cited in Acconci 1998). This panel is rather small to be one of the chancel screen panels, which typically are ca. 1.15 × 0.90 m, but matches the dimensions of the ambo panels at the Petra Church (Kanellopoulos and Schick 2001: 206), with a width of 0.55 m, the Church of the Lions at Umm al-Rasas (Piccirillo 1992: 208–9), and at Deir ʿAin ʿAbata (Loverance 2012: 338).

1. (1991.0227.01) C101.01.05. Lower right corner. Joins 1991.0227.02 and 03. L 0.19 m, W 0.15 m, Th 0.03 m; 1610 g.

2. (1991.0227.02) C101.01.05. Lower right side. Joins 1991.0227.01, 03, 1991.0419.03. L 0.23 m, W 0.09 m, Th 0.03 m; 1150 g.

3. (1991.0227.03) C101.01.05. Lower right side. Joins 1991.0227.01, 02. L 0.14 m, W 0.12 m, Th 0.03 m; 730 g.

4. (1991.0254.03) C101.01.08. Near upper left corner. Joins 1991.0311.08 and 1991.0446.01. L 0.06 m, W 0.05 m, Th 0.03 m; 100 g.

5. (1991.0295.01) C101.01.08. Centre of left side. Joins 1991.0311.07 and 1991.0447.04. L 0.19 m, W 0.17 m, Th 0.03 m; 1720 g.

6. (1991.0311.07) C101.01.08. Upper left side. Joins 1991.0295.01 and 1991.0311.08. L 0.15 m, W 0.14 m, Th 0.03 m; 975 g.

7. (1991.0311.08) C101.01.08. Upper left corner. Joins 1991.02054.03, 1991.0311.07, 1991.0317.15, 1991.0446.01. L 0.18 m, W 0.16 m, Th 0.03 m; 1320 g.

8. (1991.0317.09) C101.01.08. Lower vertical arm of cross from lattice portion. Joins 1991.0419.03. L 0.08 m, W 0.09 m, Th 0.03 m; 235 g.

9. (1991.0317.15) C101.01.08. Upper left corner. Joins 1991.0311.08. L 0.09 m, W 0.07 m, Th 0.03 m; 230 g.

10. (1991.0317.32) C101.01.08. Lower left corner. Joins 1991.0419.03 and 1991.0447.04. L 0.2 m, W 0.15 m, Th 0.03 m; 1390 g.

11. (1991.0419.03) C101.01.08. Centre of bottom side. Joins 1991.0227.02, 1991.0317.09, 32. L 0.26 m, W 0.17 m, Th 0.03 m; 2270 g.

12. (1991.0446.01) C101.01.08. Centre of top side. Joins 1991.0254.03 and 1991.0311.08. Has hole with metal plug still in place. L 0.2 m, W 0.15 m, Th 0.03 m; 1270 g.

13. (1991.0447.04) C101.01.19. Fragment of marble panel. Lower left corner. Blackened by fire. Joins 1991.0295.01 and 1991.0317.32. L 0.22 m, W 0.14 m, Th 0.03 m; 1300 g.

C101 Panel 2. Open-work panel (fig. 13.2.3); currently on display in the Aqaba Archaeology Museum. Six pieces forming the lower left portion of an openwork panel were found scattered in the central aisle, as well as in Room 4. The maximum preserved dimensions are 0.51 × 0.33 m, although originally the panel would have measured 0.73 × 0.55 m. The panel is between 0.032 and 0.035 m thick. The bottom is flat, while the sides are bevelled. The preserved portion of the panel has two fastening holes: 1) on the left side 0.165 m up from the lower left corner; 2) on the bottom 0.14 m to the right of the lower left corner. The surviving portion of the panel is identical to C101 Panel 1, so the two seem to form a matching set for the ambo.

1. (1991.0468.04) C101.01.08. Lower left corner. Joins 1992.0034.03, 1993.0190.04, 1993.0264.15, and 1993.0266.10. L 0.28 m, W 0.34 m, Th 0.04 m; over 5000 g.

2. (1992.0034.03) C101.01.00. Left centre of bottom. Joins 1991.0468.04, 1993.0190.04. L 0.08 m, W 0.04 m, Th 0.03 m; 190 g.

3. (1993.0190.04) C101.04.25. Centre of bottom. Joins 1991.0468.04, 1992.0034.03, 1993.0264.15, 1993.0266.01, 10. L 0.25 m, W 0.19 m, Th 0.03 m; 2470 g.

4. (1993.0264.15) C101.04.28. Lower centre. Joins 1991.0468.04 m; 1993.0190.04, 1993.0260.10. L 0.13 m, W 0.10 m, Th 0.03 m; 650 g.

5. (1993.0266.01) C101.04.28. Lower right side. Joins 1993.0190.04. L 0.10 m, W 0.07 m, Th 0.03 m; 230 g.

6. (1993.0266.10) C101.04.28. Lower centre. Joins 1991.0468.04, 1993.0190.04, 1993.0264.15. L 0.05 m, W 0.02; Th. 0.04 m; 30 g.

Additional Portions of C101 Panel 1 or Panel 2. Open-work panel; on display in the Aqaba Archaeology Museum. Three other fragments (nos. 1–3) forming a portion of a bevelled border and central open-work cross, with total preserved dimensions of 0.23 × 0.12 × 0.025–0.027 m thick, were found in the Nave. The pieces clearly belonged to either C101 Panel 1 or 2, although they do not join with either one. The fragments are shown placed in the central right portion of the C101 Panel 1 (fig. 13.1b), although they could just as easily have been either the left or right side of C101 Panel 2. There are no fastening holes.

Six other fragments (nos. 4–9; fig. 13.2.2) of a bevelled border of a panel of very light grey marble, with total dimensions of 0.23 × 0.12 × 0.025 m thick were found in Room 4. They could well form the middle right side of C101 Panel 1 or either the left or right side of C101 Panel 2. There are no fastening holes in the extant portion. Front polished, back flat and smooth.

1. (1991.0317.16) C101.01.08. Border of lattice portion. Joins 1991.0317.17, 18. L 0.09 m, W 0.06 m, Th 0.03 m; 215 g.

2. (1991.0317.17) C101.01.08. Horizontal arm of cross from lattice portion. Joins 1991.0317.16. L 0.09 m, W 0.06 m, Th 0.03 m; 185 g.

3. (1991.0317.18) C101.01.08. Centre part of side. Joins 1991.0317.16. L 0.15 m, W 0.14 m, Th 0.03 m; 810 g.

4. (1993.0264.01) C101.04.28. Border. Joins 1993.0264.08. L 0.10 m, W 0.06 m, Th 0.03 m; 190 g.

5. (1993.0264.02) C101.04.28. Border. Joins 1993.0264.04, 14, 1993.0266.02. L 0.06 m, W 0.03 m, Th 0.03 m; 55 g.

6. (1993.0264.04) C101.04.28. Border. Joins 1993.0264.02, 14. L 0.07 m, W 0.06 m, Th 0.03 m; 140 g.

7. (1993.0264.08) C101.04.28. Border. Joins 1993.0264.01, 1993.0266.02. L 0.10 m, W 0.08 m, Th 0.03 m; 220 g.

8. (1993.0264.14) C101.04.28. Border. Joins 1993.0264.02, 04. L 0.08 m, W 0.06 m, Th 0.03 m; 260 g.

9. (1993.0266.02) C101.04.28. Border. Joins 1993.0264.02, 04, 08. L 0.11 m, W 0.09 m, Th 0.03 m; 335 g.

C101 Panel 3. Open-work panel (fig. 13.2.4). Two large pieces of light bluish grey marble forming the border of a third open-work panel, different from C101 Panels 1 and 2, were found immediately west of the Chancel area. The preserved combined dimensions are 0.41 × 0.20 × 0.025 m thick. The panel originally would have been around 0.55 m wide. The top edge has a fastening hole. The front border is polished, while the inset interior portion is not. The back is flat and smooth. The letter A is incised on the back and contains traces of red paint.

The panel consists of a border framing a stylized plant in each corner and a three-ridge circle with an ovolo, enclosing an openwork centre that has broken away completely. This preserved portion would have formed the top of the panel, based on the location of the ovolo at the top of C101 Panel 1. Since the width is too narrow for an average chancel screen panel, like C101 Panels 1 and 2 this would also seem to have been one of the ambo panels.

1. (1991.0253.01) C101.01.08. Upper right corner. Joins 1991.0279.03. L 0.22 m, W 0.19 m, Th 0.025 m; 1980 g.

2. (1991.0279.03) C101.01.08. Centre of top side. Joins 1991.0253.01. L 0.2 m, W 0.21 m, Th 0.025 m; 1870 g.

C101 Panel 4. Open work panel (fig. 13.3.1–2). Six fragments of the border of an open-work panel of light bluish grey marble were found in the Nave west of the Chancel and in Room 4. The pieces do not join, but they all have roughly the same thickness, which is significantly thicker than C101 Panels 1, 2, or 3. The sides are bevelled. The border is different from that of C101 Panel 1 or 2. The border is similar to C101 Panel 3, but these fragments are thicker and so seem to belong to a separate panel. The front border is polished, but not the inset interior. The back is flat and smooth. Two pieces have a fastening hole.

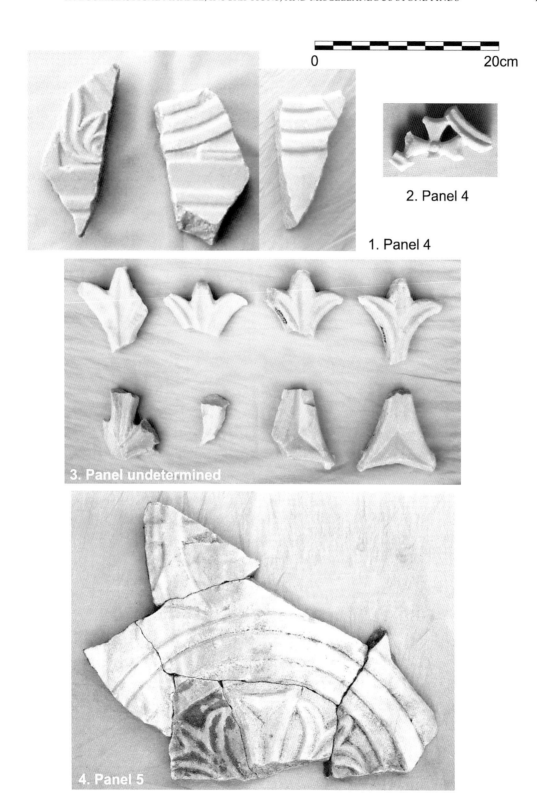

FIG. 13.3   *No. 1: C101, Panel 4, fragments 2 (left), 3 (centre), 8 (right). No. 2: C101, Panel 4, open-work cross.*
No. 3: C101, fragments of crosses and fleur-de-lis from undetermined open-work panels (upper left
to lower right, catalogue nos. 3, 7, 6, 4, and 8, 5, 2, 1). No. 4: C101, Panel 5, fragments.

A seventh fragment probably belongs to this panel as well. It is a fragment of an open-work cross found during surface clearance of Room 7 south of the church. It is clearly different from the open-work portions of C101 panels 1 and 2. It is also too thick to belong to C101 Panel 3, but the thickness corresponds to that of C101 Panel 4.

An eighth fragment found in Room 4 might belong to C101 Panel 4. It has a similar pattern of three concentric circles, but it is somewhat thinner than the other fragments and has a wider flat outer border.

1. (1992.0181.01) C101.01.25. Fragment of panel. L 0.07 m, W 0.07 m, Th 0.04 m; 190 g.

2. (1992.0376.03; fig. 13.3.1) C101.01.25. Probably upper left corner of panel. Front interior with part of stylized leaf and two concentric ridges. L 0.20 m, W 0.07 m, Th 0.034 m; 730 g.

3. (1993.0190.05; fig. 13.3.1) C101.04.25. Centre of panel. Front interior with three curving ridges, fourth ridge parallel to border, forming circular frame for lattice portion in centre. L 0.17 m, W 0.10 m, Th 0.04 m; 1070 g.

4. (1993.0264.10) C101.04.28. Border of panel. One interior side slightly curved, slightly rough, probably secondary cut, small portion of fastening hole 0.007 diameter. L 0.07 m, W 0.07 m, Th 0.03 m; 300 g.

5. (1993.0264.17) C101.04.28. Border of panel. One side slants in 0.03, top third smooth, bottom two thirds rough, fastening hole 0.007 diameter, 0.018 deep, one side secondary cut. L 0.11 m, W 0.10 m, Th 0.03 m; 760 g.

6. (1993.0266.06) C101.04.28. Border of panel. One side slants in 0.03, top half smooth, bottom half rough, portion of fastening hole 0.007 diameter, 0.034 deep. L 0.11 m, W 0.11 m, Th 0.04 m; 665 g.

7. (1993.0051.01; fig. 13.3.2) C101.07.01. Fragment of lattice portion of panel. Three arms of a cross, portion of circle at side of one arm, portion of second circle at side of two other arms. Back mostly broken. Sides smooth to slightly

rough. Front smooth. Light bluish grey. L 0.11 m, W 0.06 m, Th 0.03 m; 145 g.

8. (1993.0264.09; fig. 13.3.1) C101.04.28. Fragment of marble panel. One interior side curved rough, others broken. Back flat, smooth. Front smooth, three curving ridges, fourth ridge at oblique angle, forming circular frame for lattice portion in centre. Light bluish grey. L 0.15 m, W 0.70 m, Th 0.032 m; 465 g.

Additional Fragments of Crosses and Fleur-de-lis from Open-Work Panels. Two fragments of crosses and five fragments of fleur-de-lis from the open-work portions of panels were found scattered immediately west of the Chancel area (fig. 13.3.4). The two arms of open-work crosses (nos. 1 and 2) match that on C101 Panel 1. Whether there could have been fleur-de-lis on C101 Panels 1 or 2 between the crosses, as in C101 panel 5, is uncertain. An eighth fragment, of an open-work cross, found west of the Chancel, is different from the others. It could not have been part of C101 panels 1 or 2.

1. (1991.0279.04) C101.01.08. Arm of cross from lattice portion of marble panel 1, 2, or 3. Sides slightly rough. Back rough with chisel marks. Front smooth. Bluish grey. L 0.09 m, W 0.09 m, Th 0.03 m; 215 g.

2. (1991.0447.03) C101.01.19. Fragment of arm of cross from lattice portion of marble panel 1, 2, or 3. Sides slightly rough. Back flat, smooth; mostly broken. Front smooth. Light grey. L 0.07 m, W 0.07 m, Th 0.03 m; 205 g.

3. (1991.0311.04) C101.01.08. Fragment of fleur-de-lis from lattice portion of marble panel 1, 2, or 3. Sides slightly rough. Back flat, smooth, mostly broken. Front smooth. Very light grey. L 0.09 m, W 0.08 m, Th 0.03 m; 170 g.

4. (1991.0311.09) C101.01.08. Fleur-de-lis from lattice portion of marble panel 1, 2, or 3. Nearly complete. Sides slightly rough. Back rough with chisel marks. Front smooth. Bluish grey. L 0.09 m, W 0.09 m, Th 0.03 m; 180 g.

5. (1991.0311.11) C101.01.08. Fragment of curved stylised leaf from lattice portion of marble panel 1, 2, or 3. Two sides broken, two oth-

ers slightly rough. Back slightly rough. Front preserves trace of central groove. L 0.06 m, W 0.03 m, Th 0.02 m; 35 g.

6. (1991.0468.03) C101.01.08. Fleur-de-lis from lattice portion of marble panel 1, 2, or 3. Nearly complete. Sides slightly rough. Back rough with chisel marks. Front smooth. Light bluish grey. L 0.07 m, W 0.09 m, Th 0.02 m; 175 g.

7. (1992.0330.02) C101.01.28. Fragment of fleur-de-lis of lattice portion of marble panel 1, 2, or 3. Sides slightly rough. Back flat, smooth, mostly broken. Front smooth. Light grey. L 0.09 m, W 0.06 m, Th 0.02 m; 115 g.

8. (1991.0446.02) C101.01.08. Portion of two arms of eight-armed cross/fleur-de-lis from centre of lattice portion of marble panel. Sides slightly rough. Back flat, smooth. Front smooth. Bluish grey. L 0.07 m, W 0.06 m, Th 0.03 m; 140 g.

C101 Panel 5. Panel with central cross (fig. 13.3.4). Six fragments from the centre of a panel were found west of the Chancel area and in Room 4. The dimensions after reassembly are 0.39 × 0.27 × 0.032 m thick. The preserved portion shows three concentric ridges forming a circular frame for a cross with fleurs-de-lis between the arms. The cross and fleurs-de-lis are similar to the cross on the C101 panel 1 and the stray fragments listed earlier. Outside the circular frame is a small part of a cross.

This panel with a cross within concentric ridges is a simple version of a very common type of chancel screen panel; more frequently the circular frame is carved as a wreath, termed a stephanostaurion in Greek. Typically with such a panel, vine tendrils extend from the bottom of the wreath and terminate in crosses (Umm al-Rasas: Acconci 1994: 296–97, 299, no. 22 m; Mount Nebo: Acconci 1998: 514–15, no. 125 m; Petra: Kanellopoulos and Schick 2001: 194–97); Jabal Harûn: Lehtinen 2008: 194–99; Deir 'Ain 'Abata: Loverance 2012: 337, 342, no. 693).

1. (1993.0190.01) C101.04.25. Centre. Joins 1993.0190.02, 03 m; 1993.0261.04. L 0.11 m, W 0.09 m, Th 0.03 m; 565 g.

2. (1993.0190.02) C101.04.25. Centre. Joins 1992.0279.06, 1993.0190.01, 03, 1993.0261.04. L 0.13 m, W 0.10 m, Th 0.03 m; 620 g.

3. (1993.0190.03) C101.04.25. Centre. Joins 1991.0279.06, 1992.0402.01 m; 1993.0190.01, 02, 1993.0261.04 L 0.25 m, W 0.11 m, Th 0.03 m; 1430 g.

4. (1993.0261.04) C101.04.26. Centre. Joins 1993.0190.01, 03. L 0.13 m, W 0.07 m, Th 0.03 m; 485 g.

5. (1992.0402.01) C101.01.25. Middle right. Joins 1993.0190.03. L.0.12 m, W 0.11 m, Th 0.03 m; 590 g.

6. (1991.0279.06) C101.01.08. Middle centre. Joins 1991.0190.02, 03. L 0.17 m, W 0.11 m, Th 0.03 m; 740 g.

C101 Panel 6. Panel with central open-work cross (fig. 13.4.1). Eighteen joining fragments of an unusually thin white panel were mostly found together over the central and north portions of the west steps of the Chancel, near the location of the ambo. The combined dimensions are 0.71 × 0.33 × 0.017–0.026 m thick, around three-quarters the original length but less than half the height. The panel seems to have had a circular open-work centre, from the bottom of which vine tendrils extend and terminate in crosses. This panel is remarkably thin, much thinner than any chancel screen panel, which makes it difficult to consider as either part of the Chancel, or as part of the balustrade of the ambo. Analysis revealed that one of the fragments came from an Anatolian quarry, at Denizli or Prokonnesos (below, p. 491–92).

Two other fragments with a leaf and part of a stem (nos. 19–20) undoubtedly belong to the lower right part of the panel, although they do not join the others (fig. 13.4.1, lower right). One other small fragment (no. 21; not shown) seems to belong to the panel as well, but it does not join the others.

1. (1991.0253.03) C101.01.08. Lower right. Joins 1991.0311.10. L 0.15 m, W 0.12 m, Th 0.02 m; 450 g.

2. (1991.0253.06) C101.01.08. Low centre. Back blackened by fire. Joins 1991.0317.25, 29, 31, 40, 1991.0253.07. L 0.11 m, W 0.07 m, Th 0.02 m; 240 g.

3. (1991.0253.07) C101.01.08. Centre of lower border. Joins 1991.0317.25, 1991.0253.06. L 0.1 m, W 0.07 m, Th 0.03 m; 280 g.

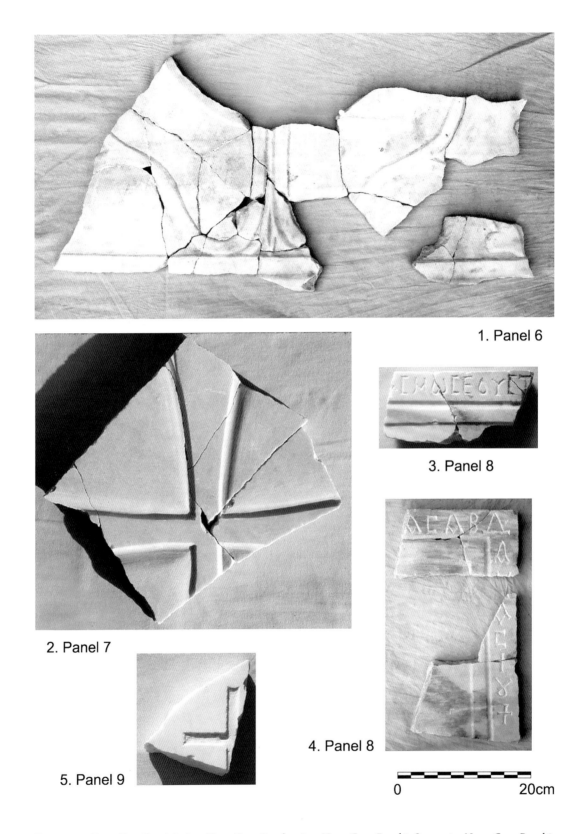

FIG. 13.4 *No. 1: C101, Panel 6, view. No. 2: C101, Panel 7, view. No. 3: C101, Panel 8, Segment 1. No. 4: C101, Panel 8, Segments 2–3. No. 5: C101, Panel 9.*

4. (1991.0254.05) C101.01.08. Lower right centre. Joins 1991.0311.10. L 0.10 m, W 0.06 m, Th 0.02 m; 155 g.

5. (1991.0279.06) C101.01.08. Middle centre. Joins 1991.0190.02, 03. L 0.17 m, W 0.11 m, Th 0.03 m; 740 g.

6. (1991.0311.10) C101.01.08. Lower right. Joins 1991.0253.03, 1991.0254.05, 1991.0317.31. L 0.19 m, W 0.17 m, Th 0.03 m; 1300 g.

7. (1991.0317.25) C101.01.08. Centre of bottom side. Back blackened by fire. Joins 1991.0317.35, 40, 43, and 1991.0253.06, 07. L 0.1 m, W 0.06 m, Th 0.02 m; 255 g.

8. (1991.0317.26) C101.01.08. Lower left centre. Joins 1991.0317.30, 35, 36, 38, 39. L 0.21 m, W 0.1 m, Th 0.02 m; 535 g.

9. (1991.0317.27) C101.01.08. Lower left centre. Joins 1991.0317.30, 31, 39. L 0.10 m, W 0.07 m, Th 0.02 m; 195 g.

10. (1991.0317.29) C101.01.08. Lower centre. Joins 1991.0253.06, 1991.0137.31, 40, 43. L 0.07 m, W 0.03 m, Th 0.02 m; 55 g.

11. (1991.0317.30) C101.01.08. Lower left centre. Joins 1991.0317.26, 27, 36. L 0.16 m, W 0.10 m, Th 0.02 m; 690.

12. (1991.0317.31) C101.01.08. Lower centre. Joins 1991.0253.06, 1991.0311.10, 1991.0317.27, 29. L 0.14 m, W 0.11 m, Th 0.02 m; 615 g.

13. (1991.0317.35) C101.01.08. Centre of bottom side. Joins 1991.0317.25, 26, 38, 39, 43. L 0.06 m, W 0.06 m, Th 0.02 m; 95 g.

14. (1991.0317.36) C101.01.08. Lower left centre. Joins 1991.0317.26, 30, 38. L 0.11 m, W 0.08 m, Th 0.02 m; 260 g.

15. (1991.0317.38) C101.01.08. Left centre of bottom side. Joins 1991.0317.26, 35, 36. L 0.17 m, W 0.16 m, Th 0.02 m; 1000 g.

16. (1991.0317.39) C101.01.08. Lower left centre. Joins 1991.0317.26, 27, 43. L 0.11 m, W 0.07 m, Th 0.02 m; 180 g.

17. (1991.0317.40) C101.01.08. Lower centre. Joins 1991.0317.25, 29, 43, 1991.0253.06. L 0.06 m, W 0.05 m, Th 0.02 m; 90 g.

18. (1991.0317.43) C101.01.08. Lower centre. Joins 1991.0317.25, 29, 35, 39, 40. L 0.05 m, W 0.04 m, Th 0.02 m; 50 g.

19. (1992.0368.01) C101.01.25. Lower right. All sides broken. Back flat, smooth. Front polished border and sunken interior, not polished, with leaf and small portion of stem. White with blue grey streaks. Joins 1992.0368.02. L 0.13 m, W 0.10 m, Th 0.03 m; 530 g.

20. (1992.0368.02) C101.01.25. Lower right. All sides broken. Back flat, smooth. Front polished border with ridge, and interior, not polished. White with blue grey streaks. Joins 1992.0368.01. L 0.10 m, W 0.08 m, Th 0.03 m; 235 g.

21. (1992.0344.02) C101.01.25. Small fragment. All sides broken. Back flat, smooth. Front smooth, slight slant. White with light bluish grey streak. L 0.05 m, W 0.05 m, Th 0.019 m; 75 g.

C101 Panel 7. Panel with central cross (fig. 13.4.2). Five fragments of a thick bluish grey panel with a large cross in the centre were found together in the north part of the area immediately west of the Chancel. The combined dimensions are 0.45 × 0.43 × 0.04 m thick. The thickness is typical for a chancel screen panel, but the design has no exact parallels. This panel is best understood as a chancel screen panel. Two other fragments (nos. 6 and 7, not shown) found in the area west of the Chancel and in Room 4 seem to belong to the same panel, although they do not join.

1. (1991.0317.03) C101.01.08. Part of lower vertical arm of cross. Joins 1991.0317.04, 06. L 0.20 m, W 0.13 m, Th 0.04 m; 1150 g.

2. (1991.0317.04) C101.01.08. Part of lower vertical arm of cross. Joins 1991.0317.03, 05, 06. L 0.22 m, W 0.11 m, Th 0.04 m; 1740 g.

3. (1991.0317.05) C101.01.08. Left horizontal arm of cross. Joins 1991.0317.04, 06 L 0.20 m, W 0.13; Th. 0.04 m; 1990 g.

4. (1991.0317.06) C101.01.08. Right horizontal arm of cross. Joins 1991.0317.03, 04, 05, 41. L 0.39 m, W 0.25 m, Th 0.04 m; 4700 g.

5. (1991.0317.41) C101.01.08. Part of right horizontal arm of cross. Joins 1991.0317.06. L 0.11 m, W 0.07 m, Th 0.04 m; 360 g.

6. (1991.0317.07) C101.01.08. All sides broken. Back flat, smooth. Front flat, smooth. Bluish grey. L 0.15 m, W 0.15 m, Th 0.04 m; 1620 g.

7. (1993.0261.09) C101.04.26. All sides broken. Back flat, smooth. Front flat, smooth. Bluish grey. L 0.17 m, W 0.10 m, Th 0.04 m; 1030 g.

C101 Panel 8. Inscribed border of panel (fig. 13.4.3–4). Seven fragments of the top and right side borders of a panel preserve a portion of a Greek inscription. The three separate segments do not join, but seem to all belong together. All the fragments have the same type of border (W 0.07 m), although the thickness of the top fragments is greater than that of the corner or side fragments. The colour (bluish grey with dark streaks) of these fragments is also distinctive and unlike that of other pieces found at the site. The top pieces were found in the area west of the Chancel, while the corner and side pieces were found in Room 4. Running across the top of Segment 1 are the letters …AC MΩCEOYC T…, and on Segment 2, …ACABΔ, continuing down the right side as AK…. After a gap of unknown length, the inscription continues as …ACIΩ with a cross at the end. The text can be reconstructed as something along the lines of: ΚΑΙ ΜΝΗCΘΗΤΙ ΤΩΝ ΔΟΥΛΩΝ COY …]AC MΩCEOYCT[…]AC ABΔAK[…ANACT]ACIOY. "Lord, Remember Thy Servants […]as, Moses, T[…]as, Abdak[…Anasta]sios. Yiannis Meimaris kindly assisted with the reconstruction and translation. Panels with inscriptions along the top are common enough, as at Jabal Harûn (Fiema and Frösén 2008: 206, 273–78) and Mount Nebo (Acconci 1998: 525–27, no. 150 m; 532–35, no. 168). The letter styles at Jabal Harûn are very similar as well.
Segment 1. Combined dimensions: L 0.182 m, W 0.10 m, Th 0.032–.036 m.

1. (1991.0419.01) C101.01.08. Top border, with seven Greek letters: ΩCEOYCT. Blackened by fire. Joins 1992.0107.02. L 0.15 m, W 0.10 m, Th 0.04 m; 760 g.

2. (1992.0107.02) C101.01.25. Top border. Four Greek letters on top· ACMΩ. Joins 1991.0419.01. L 0.12 m, W 0.10 m, Th 0.03 m; 770 g.

Segment 2. Combined dimensions: L 0.182 m, W 0.10.0 m, Th 0.032–0.036 m. It is not bevelled.

3. (1993.0261.08) C101.04.26. Upper right corner. Three Greek letters, ΔAK; two Greek letters on side, ACIΩ. Joins 1993.0264.11 and 1993.0264.12. L 0.09 m, W 0.09 m, Th 0.03 m; 425 g.

4. (1993.0264.11) C101.04.28. Near top border. Joins 1993.0261.08 and 1993.0264.12. L 0.11 m, W 0.05 m, Th 0.03 m.

5. (1993.0264.12) C101.04.28. Top border. Four Greek letters on top ACAB. Joins 1993.0261.08 and 1993.0264.11. L 0.14 m, W 0.05 m, Th 0.03 m.

Segment 3. Combined dimensions: L 0.225 m, W 0.162 m, Th 0.025 m. The side is broken, so it is not known whether it was bevelled; no fastening holes.

6. (1993.0261.07) C101.04.26. Middle of right border. Two Greek letters and cross on side: IOY. Joins 1993.0266.05. L 0.13 m, W 0.17 m, Th 0.03 m; 995 g.

7. (1993.0266.05) C101.04.28. Middle of right border (currently on display in the Aqaba Museum). Three Greek letters on side: ACI. Joins 1993.0261.07. L 0.11 m, W 0.06 m, Th 0.03 m; 195 g.

Another fragment of a border may belong to this panel, but it does not join and has a slightly different colour. It has preserved a tiny corner of an interior groove, and its top side is slightly bevelled.

8. (1993.0004.01) C101.04.19. Small fragment. Near corner. All sides broken. Back flat, smooth. Front flat, smooth. Grey with dark grey and white streaks. Probably belongs with 1993.0261.07, 08, 1993.0264.11, 12, etc. L 0.11 m, W 0.06 m, Th 0.03 m; 220 g.

C101 Panel 9. Panel with incised cross (fig. 13.4.5). Two pieces found in Room 4 probably belong to the same white marble panel, although they do not join. The larger piece has a large incised cross, with two complete arms 0.072 m long, 0.015 m wide, and 0.02 m deep, and a portion of a third arm. The panel is exceptionally thick, and it looks unlike the other panels at Humayma.

1. (1993.0261.05) C101.04.26. All sides broken. Back flat and smooth, slightly pitted. Front polished, slightly slanted, with portion of cross; two complete arms, L 0.072 m, W 0.015 m, 0.002 m deep, portion of third arm. White. L 0.2 m, W 0.13 m, Th 0.04 m; 1480 g.

2. (1993.0261.06) C101.04.26. One side flat, slightly rough, others broken. Back flat, slightly rough. Front flat, polished. White. L 0.08 m, W 0.06 m, Th 0.04 m; 250 g.

C101 Panel 10. Four fragments that do not join may belong to a single thick panel, or possibly two separate panels (fig. 13.5.1). Portions of the marble show blue-grey banding, and back surfaces of the fragments are coloured light red (close to 10R 6/8). These fragments are similar to the fragments of C101 Panels 11 and 12, although C101 Panel 10 is thicker. The total number of panels represented by the fragments catalogued here as C101 panels 10, 11, and 12 is not certain.

1. (1991.0260.01) C101.02.21. Fragment of panel. One side flat, smooth, others broken. Back flat, smooth, red; front polished border with groove and ridge. Light bluish grey with dark blue streaks. L 0.29 m, W 0.18 m, Th 0.038 m; 3240 g.

2. (1992.0371.02) C101.01.28. Fragment of panel. Corner. One side flat, smooth, second side very slight curve, smooth, others broken. Back flat, smooth, not red. Front polished border with groove and ridge. Light bluish grey with dark blue streaks. L 0.30 m, W 0.18 m, Th 0.035 m; 4060 g.

3. (1991.0253.02) C101.01.08. Fragment of panel. All sides broken. Back flat, smooth, red. Front flat, polished. Light bluish grey with dark grey streaks. L 0.27 m, W 0.12 m, Th 0.037 m; 1760 g.

4. (1991.0317.37) C101.01.08. Fragment of panel. All sides broken. Back flat, smooth, red. Front polished, portion of border and interior. Light bluish grey with dark grey veins. L 0.15 m, W 0.12 m, Th 0.04 m; 1025 g.

C101 Panel 11. Five fragments that do not join all have the same profile as the four fragments of C101 Panel 10, and the marble has the same blue-grey banding, but they are thinner and so seemingly belong to one or two different panels. The back surfaces of two fragments pieces are coloured the same light red (close to 10R 6/8) as those of Panel 10. Two additional pieces (nos. 6–7) that join with each other may belong to this panel, although they might also belong to a separate panel because of their wider flat border. There is the tiny trace of a groove corner in the centre.

1. (1991.0419.02) C101.01.08. Large fragment of panel. All sides broken. Back flat, smooth. Front flat, smooth, has small portion of ridge at one end. Light bluish grey with dark grey veins. Joins 1991.0421.01. L 0.28 m, W 0.14 m, Th 0.03 m; 1520 g.

2. (1991.0421.01) C101.01.08. Border of panel. One side flat, others broken. Back flat, smooth. Front smooth, border with grooves and ridges; interior slightly curved. Light bluish grey with dark grey veins. Joins 1991.0419.02. L 0.19 m, W 0.17 m, Th 0.025–.028 m; 1480 g.

3. (1993.0190.06) C101.04.25. Border of panel. One side flat, others broken. Back flat, smooth. Front polished, border with groove and part of ridge. Very light grey, but without the dark streaks like the others. L 0.10 m, W 0.07 m, Th 0.03 m; 360 g.

4. (1992.0371.01) C101.01.28. Border of panel. One side flat, smooth, others broken. Back flat, smooth, red. Front polished, border with groove and ridge. Light bluish grey with dark blue streaks. May belong with 1992.0371.02, but it is thinner. L 0.13 m, W 0.75 m, Th 0.028 m; 395 g.

5. (1993.0266.07) C101.04.28. Fragment of marble panel. All sides broken. Back flat, smooth, red. Front polished, slightly slanted. Very light grey

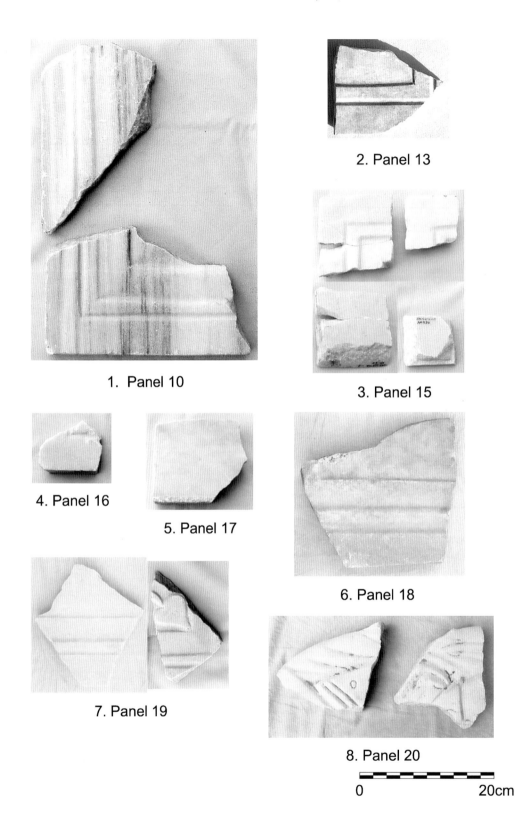

Fig. 13.5 *No. 1: C101, Panel 10. No. 2: C101, Panel 13. No. 3: C101, Panel 15, front surface, no. 1 (right), nos. 2–4 (left) Panel 15, back surface, no. 1 (right), no. 2-4 (left). No. 4: C101, Panel 16. No. 5: C101, Panel 17. No. 6: C101, Panel 18. No. 7: C101, Panel 19, fragments 1, 3. No. 8: C101, Panel 20.*

with dark blue streaks. L 0.24 m, W 0.15 m, Th 0.32 m; 2080 g.

6. (1991.0317.12) C101.01.08. Corner of panel. One side rough, slight bevel in to bottom; others broken. Back flat, smooth, not red; front flat, polished. White with light and dark bluish grey veins. Joins 1991.0317.14. L 0.12 m, W 0.11 m, Th 0.026 m; 725 g.

7. (1991.0317.14) C101.01.08. Corner of panel. All sides broken. Back flat, smooth, not red; front flat, polished, small portion of groove forming corner. White with light and dark bluish grey streaks. Joins 1991.0317.12. L 0.12 m, W 0.11 m, Th 0.026 m; 610 g.

C101 Panel 12. Another large fragment was carved in a marble with blue-grey streaks similar to that of C101 Panels 10 and 11, but the back surface is roughened with chisel marks, and the outer border that is narrower than that seen on the other panels. It seems to belong to yet another panel.

1. (1991.0253.05) C101.01.08. Border of panel. One side flat, slightly rough; others broken. Back flat, rough with chisel marks. Front polished border with grooves and ridges and slanting interior. White with dark blue grey streaks. L 0.20 m, W 0.19 m, Th 0.03 m; 2170 g.

C101 Panel 13. A large fragment of a corner of a panel (0.16 × 0.13 × 0.025 m)(fig. 13.5.2) in white marble. The border, consisting of a narrow border separated with a groove from a wider outer border, is unlike those on any of the other panels, so this should represent yet another panel.

1. (1991.0317.01) C101.01.08. Fragment of panel with portion of a corner. All sides broken. Back flat, smooth, red. Front polished, border with groove and ridge and slightly curving interior. No fastening hole. L 0.16 m, W 0.13 m, Th 0.03 m; 840 g.

C101 Panel 14. Two joining fragments with a bevelled edge do not match any other border fragments.

1. (1991.0317.12) C101.01.08. Fragment of panel near corner. One side rough, slight bevel into bottom; others broken. Back flat, smooth.

Front flat, polished. White with light and dark bluish grey veins. Joins 1991.0317.14. L 0.12 m, W 0.11 m, Th 0.03 m; 725 g.

2. (1991.0317.14) C101.01.08. Fragment of panel near corner. All sides broken. Back flat, smooth, Front flat, polished, small portion of groove forming corner. White with light and dark bluish grey streaks. Joins 1991.0317.12. L 0.12 m, W 0.11 m, Th 0.03 m; 610 g.

C101 Panel 15. Two fragments of corners in light bluish grey marble have similar profiles, which are unlike those of any other fragments (fig. 13.5.3). One side is bevelled with the top part smooth and the bottom part rough. A second side is flat with the top part smooth and the bottom part rough. The second corner fragment consists of three pieces that join, with combined dimensions of 0.12 × 0.11 × 0.033 m thick. It has a fastening hole 0.07 m from the corner, 0.035 m deep, and 0.07 m diameter

1. 98.14.03 (1991.0447.02) C101.01.19. Fragment of panel corner. The front surface is flat and polished and has a border with groove and ridge. The central portion of the back surface is smooth, but three of the edges seem to have been trimmed with a chisel. Might belong to same panel as 1992.0109.01, 02, 04, but it is a bit thinner. L 0.08 m, W 0.077 m, Th 0.032 m.

2. (1992.0109.01) C101.01.26. Fragment of panel corner. The front surface is flat and polished and has a border with groove and ridge. One side edge is slightly bevelled, the surface left rough, and carries a fastening hole with much of lead plug preserved; other sides broken. Back flat, smooth. Joins 1992.0109.02, 04. L 0.11 m, W 0.05 m, Th 0.033 m; 325 g.

3. (1992.0109.02) C101.01.25. Fragment of panel corner. One side sharply bevelled, one-third top smooth, two-thirds bottom rough; second side flat, top half rough, bottom half flat, slightly rough, inset 0.006 m; other sides broken. Back flat, smooth. Front borders with grooves and ridges. Joins 1992.0109.01, 04. L 0.11 m, W 0.07 m, Th 0.033 m; 485 g.

4. (1992.0109.04) C101.01.26. Chip. One side flat, others broken. Back broken, has tiny portion

of fastening hole. Front flat, smooth. Bluish grey. Joins 1992.0109.01, 02. L 0.04 m, W 0.03 m, Th 0.02 m; 20 g.

C101 Panel 16. This fragment of a corner (fig. 13.5.4) has an unusual fastening hole 0.04 m in from the side (D 0.01 m), which penetrates the slab at a slant rather than perpendicular to the side.

1. (1992.0330.01) C101.01.28. Fragment of panel near corner. One side flat, smooth; second side at right angle, bottom 0.016 m slightly rough, top 0.007 m projects 0.007 m. Back smooth, slight curve, thickens at sides. Front polished, border with small part of two grooves at right angle; two fastening holes, one slightly off vertical, 0.012 m diameter, through entire thickness, second slightly off horizontal, ca. 0.009 m diameter. Light bluish grey. L 0.09 m, W 0.07 m, Th 0.025 m; 275 g.

C101 Panel 17. One panel fragment has an unusual plain, projecting rim along one edge (fig. 13.5.5). It does not have a fastening hole. It has a slightly variable thickness of 0.028–0.031 m (not including the rim).

1. (1992.0431.02) C101.01.25. Fragment of panel. Front surface flat, polished, and slanting back slightly, with traces of one side of a groove. Back surface flat, smooth, with a projecting rounded lip (H 0.003 m, W 0.008 m) along one original edge. Two sides flat, one smooth, the other rough, possibly recut; others broken. Grey with dark bluish grey streaks. L 0.14 m, W 0.13 m, Th 0.04 m; 1230 g.

C101 Panel 18. A large unusually thick fragment of panel has a border is unlike any others. It does not have any fastening holes (fig. 13.5.6).

1. (1992.0617.01) C101. Large fragment of thick marble panel. Near corner. One side slightly rough, others broken. Back rough with chisel marks. Front polished border with groove and ridge, interior polished. Weathered. Original catalogue number and context lost; probably from 1992 season in C101. L 0.22 m, W 0.20 m, Th 0.052 m; 3870 g.

C101 Panel 19. These three fragments of a panel border and corner do not join, but they have the same profile and have the same rust orange coloured streaks on the back, suggesting they belong to the same panel (fig. 13.5.7). The corner piece also has a stylized leaf.

1. (1992.0116.01) C101.01.28. Fragment of panel. One side flat, slightly rough with chisel marks; others broken. Back flat, smooth. Front polished border with groove and ridge. Fastening hole 0.026 m deep, D 0.08 m. Light bluish grey. L 0.14 m, W 0.09 m, Th 0.03 m; 690 g.

2. (1993.0264.05) C101.04.28. Fragment of marble panel. One side flat, smooth, others broken. Back flat, smooth, front, border polished with groove and ridge, interior not polished. Light bluish grey. L 0.17 m, W 0.16 m, Th 0.028 m; 1085 g.

3. (1993.0266.08) C101.04.28. Fragment of marble panel. Near corner. All sides broken. Back flat, smooth. Front portion of two sides of polished border with groove and ridge meeting at right angle. Interior corner, not polished, stylized leaf and small part of stem. Light bluish grey. L 0.16 m, W 0.11 m, Th 0.03 m; 605 g.

C101 Panel 20. Two non-joining fragments found in Room 4 have similar complex ridges (fig. 13.5.8).

1. (1993.0264.13) C101.04.28. Fragment of curved panel. One side curved, rough, others broken. Back flat, smooth. Front polished, shows complex ridges and grooves, braid in interior. Very light grey. L 0.17 m, W 0.11 m, Th 0.03 m; 930 g.

2. (1993.0266.04) C101.04.28. Fragment of panel. One side curved, rough, others broken. Back flat, smooth. Front has complex curving ridges and grooves, no clear design. Very light grey. L 0.16 m, W 0.13 m, Th 0.04 m; 1000 g.

C101 Miscellaneous Panel Fragments. Sixty small, non-descript marble fragments were recovered: small fragments and chips of panels, sometimes with portions of grooves or ridges preserved. They do not warrant further discussion but are recorded here for completeness.

1. (1991.0169.01) C101.01.03. Tiny chip of marble panel side. One side flat, smooth, others bro-

ken. Back broken. Front flat, polished. Very light bluish grey. L 0.04 m, W 0.03 m, Th 0.01 m; 10 g.

2. (1991.0227.05) C101.01.05. Fragment of marble panel. All sides broken. Back flat, smooth. Front polished with groove and ridges. White with black veins. Blackened slightly by fire. L 0.12 m, W 0.08 m, Th 0.03 m; 300 g.

3. (1991.0248.01) C101.01.07. Fragment of marble panel. All sides broken. Back flat, smooth. Front flat, smooth, with tiny portion of groove. Light grey. Blackened by fire. Joins 1991.0248.03. L 0.18 m, W 0.15 m, Th 0.03 m; 1245 g.

4. (1991.0248.03) C101.01.07. Small fragment of marble panel. All sides broken. Back flat, smooth. Front flat, smooth. Joins 1991.0248.01. L 0.06 m, W 0.03 m, Th 0.03 m; 100 g.

5. (1991.0254.04) C101.01.08. Small fragment of marble panel. All sides broken. Back flat, smooth. Front smooth with curving ridge. White with dark bluish grey streaks. Burned. L 0.06 m, W 0.05 m, Th 0.03 m; 150 g.

6. (1991.0276.03) C101.01.07. Fragment of marble panel. Probably from border. All sides broken. Back flat, smooth. Front smooth, has small portion of groove. Blackened by fire. L 0.09 m, W 0.09 m, Th 0.03 m; 420 g.

7. (1991.0278.01) C101.01.00. Fragment of marble panel. All sides broken. Back flat and smooth. Front portion of border polished, but rest is left rough. Grey with dark grey patches. L 0.1 m, W 0.09 m, Th 0.02 m; 235 g.

8. (1991.0279.01) C101.01.08. Small fragment of panel. All sides broken. Back, flat, smooth. Front flat, smooth. L 0.7 m, W 0.05 m, Th 0.02 m; 95 g.

9. (1991.0279.05) C101.01.08. Fragment of marble panel. One side polished with curved bottom and smooth flat top, parallel side rough, perhaps secondary cut, others broken. Back flat, polished. Front flat, smooth. Light bluish grey. L 0.09 m, W 0.09 m, Th 0.04 m; 1650 g.

10. (1991.0279.08) C101.01.08. Tiny fragment of panel. All sides broken. Back flat, smooth. Front polished, with grooves and ridge. White. L 0.06 m, W 0.04 m, Th 0.03 m; 55 g.

11. (1991.0311.01) C101.01.08. Fragment of panel. One side flat, slightly rough top half, rough bottom half; others broken. Back flat, smooth. Front polished, border with grooves and ridges. White. L 0.08 m, W 0.05 m, Th 0.03 m; 290 g.

12. (1991.0311.03) C101.01.08. Small fragment of panel. One side rough, perhaps secondary cut, others broken. Back flat, smooth. Front flat, polished. L 0.06 m, W 0.05 m, Th 0.03 m; 105 g.

13. (1991.0311.06) C101.01.08. Fragment of thick marble panel. All sides broken, fastening hole 0.02 deep, 0.01 diameter. Back flat, smooth. Front flat, smooth. L 0.06 m, W 0.06 m, Th 0.04 m; 220 g.

14. (147.1991.0311.12) C101.01.08. Small chip of panel. One side slopes sharply in, others broken. Back broken. Front polished, border with groove and ridge. Bluish grey. L 0.05 m, W 0.04 m, Th 0.02 m; 35 g.

15. (1991.0311.13) C101.01.08. Chip of panel. All sides broken, with tiny piece of lead fastener. Back broken. Front flat, polished. White. L 0.04 m, W 0.04 m, Th 0.01 m; 20 g.

16. (1991.0317.10) C101.01.08. Fragment of panel. All sides broken. Back flat, smooth. Front flat, polished. Bluish grey with dark grey veins. L 0.16 m, W 0.11 m, Th 0.03 m; 715 g.

17. (1991.0317.13) C101.01.08. Small fragment of panel. All sides broken, portion of fastening hole 0.011 diameter. Back flat, smooth. Front flat, polished. Light grey. L 0.06 m, W 0.04 m, Th 0.02 m; 80 g.

18. (1991.0317.19) C101.01.08. Small fragment of panel. One side flat, smooth, others broken, with small portion of fastening hole. Back smooth with slight bevel. Front flat, polished. White to very light grey. L 0.06 m, W 0.04 m, Th 0.02 m; 65 g.

19. (1991.0317.20) C101.01.08. Chip of panel. All sides broken. Back broken. Front polished, part of groove and ridge. Light grey. L 0.08 m, W 0.03 m, Th 0.01 m; 30 g.

20. (1991.0317.21) C101.01.08. Chip of marble panel. All sides broken. Back broken. Front flat, smooth. Light bluish grey. L 0.04 m, W 0.03 m, Th 0.01 m; 25 g.

21. (1991.0317.22) C101.01.08. Small fragment of panel. All sides broken. Back flat, smooth. Front flat, smooth. Bluish grey. Blackened by fire. L 0.06 m, W 0.04 m, Th 0.03 m; 60 g.

22. (1991.0317.23) C101.01.08. Fragment of panel. Near corner. Exterior side flat, smooth, others broken, with fastening hole, diameter 0.009, 0.025 preserved length. Back flat, smooth. Front polished, border with groove and ridge, tiny portion of groove at right angle. Light bluish grey. L 0.11 m, W 0.09 m, Th 0.04 m; 490 g.

23. (1991.0317.24) C101.01.08. Chip of panel. One side curved, polished; others broken. Back broken. Tiny portion of front flat, polished. Light bluish grey. L 0.07 m, W 0.04 m, Th 0.03 m; 60 g.

24. (1991.0317.28) C101.01.08. Tiny fragment of panel. All sides broken. Back flat, smooth. Front polished, with part of groove. Light grey. L 0.03 m, W 0.03 m, Th 0.03 m; 45 g.

25. (1991.0317.33) C101.01.08. Chip of panel. One side polished curved, others broken, small portion of fastening hole, 0.012 diameter. Back broken. Front flat, smooth. Light bluish grey. L 0.08 m, W 0.03 m, Th 0.03 m; 70 g.

26. (1991.0317.34) C101.01.08. Chip of panel. One side polished, curved; others broken. Back broken. Front flat, smooth. Light bluish grey. L 0.05 m, W 0.04 m, Th 0.04 m; 80 g.

27. (1991.0335.03) C101.01.08. Small fragment of panel. All sides broken. Back flat, smooth. Front polished with portions of two grooves and ridges. L 0.08 m, W 0.03 m, Th 0.03 m; 160 g.

28. (1991.0335.04) C101.01.08. Chip of thick panel. All sides broken. Back broken. Front flat, polished. Light bluish grey. L 0.08 m, W 0.04 m, Th 0.04 m; 75 g.

29. (1991.0378.01) C101.01.08. Chip of panel. Two parallel sides flat; others broken. Back broken. Front curved, polished. Oddly shaped but not enough preserved to be sure. Light bluish grey. L 0.04 m, W 0.01 m, Th 0.03 m; 20 g.

30. (1991.0383.01) C101.02.00. Small chip of panel. One side flat, polished, others broken. Back broken. Front flat, polished. Light bluish grey. L 0.08 m, W 0.03 m, Th 0.01 m; 35 g.

31. (1991.0420.01) C101.01.08. Chip of panel. All sides broken. Back broken. Front flat, smooth. Very light grey. L 0.08 m, W 0.04 m, Th 0.01 m; 45 g.

32. (1991.0447.07) C101.01.19. Chip of panel. All sides broken. Back broken. Front flat, smooth. Small portion of fastening hole. Light bluish grey. L 0.05 m, W 0.04 m, Th 0.03 m; 40 g.

33. (1991.0447.08) C101.01.19. Small fragment of panel. One side flat, slightly rough, others broken. Back flat, smooth. Front flat, polished. L 0.04 m, W 0.04 m, Th 0.04 m; 45 g.

34. (1991.0447.09) C101.01.19. Fragment of panel. All sides broken. Back flat, smooth. Front flat, polished. White. L 0.10 m, W 0.08 m, Th 0.02 m; 380 g.

35. (1991.0447.10) C101.01.19. Chip of panel. All sides broken. Back broken. Small part of front surface intact, flat, polished. Light bluish grey. L 0.05 m, W 0.05 m, Th 0.02 m; 45 g.

36. (1991.0470.01) C101.01.19. Small fragment of marble panel. One side flat, rough, perhaps secondary cut; others broken. Back flat, smooth. Front polished with slight curve. White with light bluish grey streaks. L 0.07 m, W 0.06 m, Th 0.02 m; 95 g.

37. (1992.0001.01) C101.04.00. Fragment of panel. All sides broken. Back flat, smooth. Front flat, smooth. Grey. L 0.09 m, W 0.07 m, Th 0.04 m; 430 g.

38. (1992.0034.01) C101.01.00. Small fragment of panel. All sides broken. Back flat, smooth. Front flat, smooth. White. L 0.06 m, W 0.02 m, Th 0.02 m; 30 g.

39. (1992.0034.02) C101.01.00. Chip of panel. One side flat, slightly rough, with portion of fastening hole c. 0.025 L, 0.006 D., others broken. Back broken. Front polished, has small portion of groove. White to light grey. L 0.07 m, W 0.04 m, Th 0.01 m; 40 g.

40. (1992.0107.01) C101.01.25. Fragment of panel. All sides broken. Back flat, smooth. Front smooth, with curving grooves and ridges. Probably part of circular ridges forming frame for centre of panel. Light bluish grey. Slightly blackened by fire. L 0.07 m, W 0.04 m, Th 0.03 m; 175 g.

41. (1992.0107.03) C101.01.25. Small fragment of panel. All sides broken. Back flat, smooth. Front flat, smooth. White with blue-grey streak. L 0.07 m, W 0.04 m, Th 0.03 m; 100 g.

42. (1992.0125.01) C101.01.25. Fragment of marble panel. One bevelled side slants in 0.035 – top half smooth, bottom half rough similar to Panel 1, but border narrower; other sides broken. Back flat, smooth. Front polished border with groove and ridge. Dark bluish grey. L 0.11 m, W 0.06 m, Th 0.028 m; 205 g.

43. (1992.0218.01) C101.01.25. Fragment of panel. All sides broken. Back flat, smooth. Front flat, smooth. Light bluish grey. L 0.07 m, W 0.06 m, Th 0.02 m; 165 g.

44. (1992.0233.01) C101.01.25. Fragment of panel. One side flat, smooth, others broken. Back flat, smooth. Front flat, polished, border with tiny part of groove. Light bluish grey. L 0.09 m, W 0.05 m, Th 0.04 m; 220 g.

45. (1992.0330.03) C101.01.28. Tiny fragment of panel. All sides broken. Back flat, smooth. Front flat, smooth. White. L 0.04 m, W 0.03 m, Th 0.02 m; 30 g.

46. (1992.0344.03) C101.01.25. Fragment of panel. All sides broken. Back flat, rough with chisel marks. Front flat, polished. White with light and dark bluish grey streaks. L 0.11 m, W 0.09 m, Th 0.03 m.

47. (1992.0371.03) C101.01.28. Fragment of marble panel. All sides broken. Back flat, smooth. Front smooth, very slight curve. Very light grey. Blackened slightly by fire. L 0.09 m, W 0.07 m, Th 0.04 m; 305 g.

48. (line drawing 1992.0376.02) C101.01.25. Fragment of panel. One side slightly curved, smooth, others broken. Bottom smooth, slightly curved. Top polished, slants down to interior, small portion of groove. White with dark bluish grey streaks. L 0.06 m, W 0.06 m, Th 0.04 m; 115 g.

49. (1992.0431.01) C101.01.25. Fragment of panel. All sides broken. Back flat, smooth. Front polished, border with groove and ridge. Bluish grey with streaks of white and dark bluish grey. L 0.05 m, W 0.05 m, Th 0.03 m; 130 g.

50. (1992.0431.03) C101.01.25. Small fragment of panel. All sides broken. Back flat, smooth. Front polished, with groove and two ridges. Very light bluish grey. L 0.05 m, W 0.04 m, Th 0.03 m; 90 g.

51. (1992.0435.01) C101.01.00. Small fragment of panel. All sides broken. Back flat, smooth. Front flat, polished. Light bluish grey with dark grey streak. L 0.06 m, W 0.03 m, Th 0.03 m; 40 g.

52. (1992.0544.01) C101.01.50. Small chip. All sides broken. Back unclear broken or flat. Front unclear broken or flat. White. Weathered. L 0.05 m, W 0.02 m, Th 0.03 m; 35 g.

53. (1993.0190.07) C101.04.25. Two fragments of panel. All sides broken. Back flat, smooth. Front flat, smooth. Very light grey. Blackened by fire. L 0.07 m, W 0.06 m, Th 0.04 m; 345 g.

54. (1993.0261.10) C101.04.26. Fragment of panel. All sides broken. Back flat, smooth. Front flat, polished, slants, with tiny portion of groove. White or very light grey. Blackened by fire. L 0.06 m, W 0.05 m, Th 0.02 m; 135 g.

55. (1993.0264.03) C101.04.28. Small chip of panel. One side slants in, top half smooth, bottom half rough, others broken. Back broken. Front flat, polished. Very light grey. L 0.06 m, W 0.04 m, Th 0.02 m; 45 g.

56. (1993.0264.06) C101.04.28. Small fragment of panel. One side slants in 0.035 — top half smooth, bottom rough; others broken. Back flat, smooth. Front flat, polished. Very light grey. L 0.06 m, W 0.06 m, Th 0.03 m; 80 g.

57. (1993.0264.07) C101.04.28. Fragment of thin panel. All sides broken. Back flat, smooth. Front, polished, portion of border with groove and ridge. White with light grey streaks, so different from Panel 6. L 0.07 m, W 0.05 m, Th 0.017 m; 85 g.

58. (1993.0264.16) C101.04.28. Small fragment of panel. All sides broken. Back flat, smooth. Front polished, small portion of ridge and groove. White. L 0.05 m, W 0.04 m, Th 0.03 m; 120 g.

59. (1993.0266.03) C101.04.28. Small chip of panel. All sides broken, portion of fastening hole 0.008 diameter. Back broken. Front flat, smooth. Light bluish grey. L 0.03 m, W 0.02 m, Th 0.03 m; 35 g.

60. (1993.0279.01) C101.04.29. Small fragment of marble panel. All sides broken. Back flat, smooth. Front portions of two curving ridges. White. L 0.05 m, W 0.03 m, Th 0.03 m; 60 g.

13.A.2.b. Hexagonal Ambo Base

Three larger pieces assembled from 17 joining fragments show a distinctive 120 degree angle in plan view (fig. 13.6.1a). The fragments were found mostly west of the Chancel. The 120 degree angle allows the segments to be identified as the base of a hexagonal ambo, which was installed on four circular columns at the northwest corner of the Chancel. A few other small fragments (nos. 19–20) possibly from the ambo base were also found. Michel (2001: 81–87) lists 23 churches in Jordan with traces of ambos, several with hexagonal bases; in addition a seven-sided ambo base was found at Deir 'Ain

'Abata (Loverance 2012). The best preserved was found at the Church of the Lions at Umm al-Rasas (Piccirillo 1992).

1. (1991.0246.01) C101.02.18. Fragment of hexagonal marble ambo base. Two sides polished, bevelled, meet at 120° angle; other sides broken. Back flat, smooth. Front flat, smooth, with incised guidelines parallel to sides and portion of hole 0.023 in diameter that goes through from top to bottom, starting 0.08 m from side, near corner, similar to the hole in 1991.0446.03–04. Joins 1991.0447.01. L 0.17 m, W 0.09 m, Th 0.04 m; 905 g.

2. (1991.0276.01) C101.01.07. Fragment of hexagonal ambo base. One side bevelled, others broken. Back flat, smooth. Front flat, smooth. Lead (?) fastener still in place. Joins 1991.0335.01. L 0.17 m, W 0.17 m, Th 0.04 m; 1700 g.

3. (1991.0279.07) C101.01.08. Fragment of hexagonal ambo base. Joins 1991.0335.02, 1991.0447.06, 1991.0468.02. Dimensions not recorded.

4. (1991.0311.02) C101.01.08. Small chip of corner of hexagonal ambo base. Two sides bevelled; others broken. Back flat, smooth. Front broken. Joins 1991.0335.01, 1992.0344.01. L 0.07 m, W 0.04 m, Th 0.04 m; 80 g.

5. (1991.0317.11) C101.01.08. Fragment of hexagonal ambo base. Joins 1991.0335.02, 1991.0447.05, 1991.0468.02. L 0.09 m, W 0.07 m, Th 0.04 m; 400 g.

6. (1991.0317.42) C101.01.08. Fragment of hexagonal ambo base. Front with incised guideline parallel to side. Joins 1991.0335.01, 1992.0344.01. L 0.15 m, W 0.09 m, Th 0.04 m; 435 g.

7. (1991.0335.01) C101.01.08. Fragment of hexagonal ambo base. One side bevelled, others broken. Back flat, smooth. Front flat, smooth with incised guideline. Joins 1991.0276.01, 1991.0311.02, 1991.0317.42. L 0.13 m, W 0.09 m, Th 0.04 m; 290 g.

8. (1991.0335.02) C101.01.08. Fragment of hexagonal ambo base. Joins 1991.0279.07, 1991.0317.11, 1991.0447.05, 06, 1991.0468.02. L 0.07 m, W 0.06 m, Th 0.04 m; 135 g.

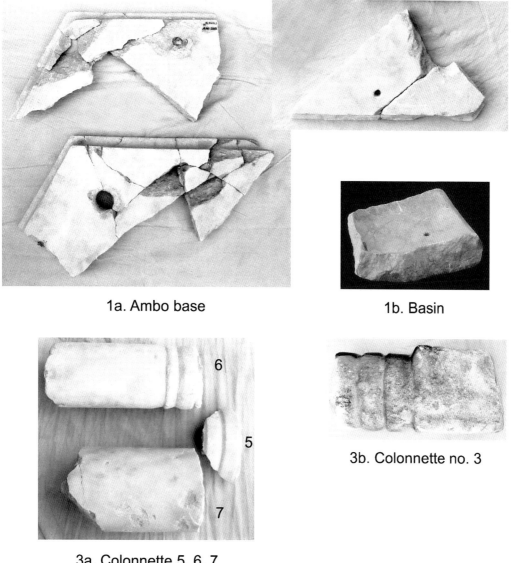

1a. Ambo base

1b. Basin

3a. Colonnette 5, 6, 7

3b. Colonnette no. 3

4. Colonnette

0   20cm

FIG. 13.6   *No. 1a: C101, fragments of Ambo base. No. 1b: C101, Basin. No. 3a: C101, Colonnettes nos. 5, 6, 7. No. 3b: Colonnette no. 3. No. 4: C101, Colonnette no. 4.*

9. (1991.0417.01) C101.01.08. Fragment of hexagonal ambo base. Joins 1991.0446.03, 05, 1991.0468.02. L 0.13 m, W 0.05 m, Th 0.04 m; 380 g.

10. (1991.0446.03) C101.01.08. Fragment of hexagonal ambo base. Front with parallel incised guidelines. Portion of circular hole D 0.026. Joins 1991.0417.01, 1991.0446.04, 05. L 0.11 m, W 0.12 m, Th 0.04 m; 530 g. 0.03–04 have a hole that goes through from top to bottom 0.03 m diameter, starting 0.075 m in from side, near corner; similar to hole in 1991.0246.01.

11. (1991.0446.04) C101.01.08. Fragment of hexagonal ambo base. Two sides meet at 120° angle. Front with parallel incised guidelines, portion of circular hole D 0.026. Portion of fastening hole 0.013 diameter and 0.018 deep and lead (?) fastener starting 0.045 m in from side. Joins 1991.0417.01, 1991.0446.03. L 0.19 m, W 0.14 m, Th.0.04 m; 1280 g.

12. (1991.0446.05) C101.01.08. Fragment of hexagonal ambo base. Front with parallel incised guidelines. Joins 1991.0417.01, 1991.0446.03, 1991.0447.06. L 0.12 m, W 0.07 m, Th 0.04 m; 320 g.

13. (1991.0447.01) C101.01.19. Fragment of hexagonal ambo base. One side polished, bevelled, others broken. Back flat, smooth. Front flat, smooth with incised guideline parallel to side; hole does not go through; D 0.012 m, 0.018 m deep, starting 0.045 m in from side. Joins 1991.0246.01. L 0.26 m, W 0.11 m, Th 0.04 m; 1890 g.

14. (1991.0447.05) C101.01.19. Fragment of hexagonal ambo base. One side polished, bevelled, others broken. Back flat, smooth. Front flat, smooth, has incised guideline. Fragment 05–06 has a hole that does not go through; D 0.012 m, 0.016 m deep, starting 0.035 m from the side. Joins 1991.0317.11, 1991.0335.02. L 0.08 m, W 0.08 m, Th 0.04 m; 250 g.

15. (1991.0447.06) C101.01.19. Fragment of hexagonal ambo base. Joins 1991.0335.02, 1991.0446.05. L 0.07 m, W 0.04 m, Th 0.04 m; 115 g.

16. (1991.0468.02) C101.01.08. Small chip of hexagonal ambo base. Light bluish grey. Joins 1991.0279.07, 1991.0317.11, 1991.0335.02, 1991.0417.01. Dimensions not recorded, 80 g?

17. (1992.0344.01) C101.01.25. Small chip of hexagonal ambo base. Joins 1991.0311.02, 1991.0317.42. L 0.07 m, W 0.03 m, Th 0.03 m; 55 g.

18. (1991.0253.04) C101.01.08. Fragment of marble panel. One side polished, curve 0.025, straight 0.015, others broken. Back flat, smooth. Front flat, smooth. Bluish grey. Perhaps from hexagonal ambo base 11. L 0.22 m, W 0.13 m, Th 0.04 m; 2260 g.

19. (1991.0276.02) C101.01.07. Fragment of panel, possibly base of ambo. One side polished, bevelled, others broken. Back flat, smooth, has E incised. Front flat, smooth. Light bluish grey. Weathered. L 0.17 m, W 0.07 m, Th 0.04 m; 1015 g.

20. (1992.0431.05) C101.01.25. Fragment of marble panel possibly from the ambo base. One side polished and curved, parallel side rough, perhaps secondary cut, others broken with tiny portion of fastening hole. Back flat, smooth. Front flat, polished. Light grey. Blackened by fire. L 0.14 m, W 0.10 m, Th 0.04 m; 1135 g.

21. (1993.0261.03) C101.04.26. Fragment of marble panel possibly from the ambo base. One side polished, bevelled; base 0.015 m flat, top 0.024 m curves in 0.012, others broken. Back flat, smooth. Front, flat, smooth, incised guideline parallel to preserved side. Bluish grey. L 0.21 m, W 0.18 m, Th 0.04 m; 2930 g.

13.A.2.c. Colonnettes

Seven fragments of colonnettes were found in C101. The colonnettes were most likely used to support the Ambo, but could also have been used to support a basin or an altar table, if there was one. The columns generally have a circular cross-section and taper markedly toward the top. Where preserved, the bases consist of a tall, square shaft supporting two narrow, projecting tori below a fascia, all separated by deep grooves, and cut in one piece with the column. Similar bases can be seen in the churches at Petra (Kanellopoulos and Schick 2001: 195–96, 201) and at Jabal Harûn (Lehtinen 2008: 209). No examples of the typical Byzantine flower-like capitals (also carved in one piece with the shaft; cf. Fiema et al. 2001: 196 fig. 7, 201 fig. 23) were found in the churches at Humayma, but a well-preserved example of a shaft and capital was observed in 1993 re-used as a grave marker in the modern Bedouin cemetery 2 km south of the site. It had undoubtedly been salvaged from one of the churches at the site.

1. (1991.0279.02) C101.01.08. Small fragment of the tall, rectangular base and circular shaft of a colonnette. Base: 0.074 high preserved; two faces preserved meeting at right angle; faces flat, slightly rough with chisel marks. Less than quarter of the diameter of the shaft preserved, 0.041 high. Bluish grey marble. L 0.12 m, W 0.03 m, Th 0.02 m; 130 g.

2. (1991.0470.02) C101.01.19. Fragment of colonnette shaft. Quarter of diameter preserved. Top and bottom of shaft broken. Exterior smooth. One spot blackened by fire. Perhaps part of an altar table leg. L 0.04 m, W 0.05 m, Th 0.07 m; 550 g.

3. (1992.0107.04; fig. 13.6.3b) C101.01.25. Base of marble colonnette. Square base, round shaft with grooves above. Base has rough bottom, flat, smooth sides; 0.11 × 0.10 × 0.09 preserved. Shaft diameter 0.095 m; two parallel grooves divide shaft into three segments, each 0.03–0.032 high. White marble, blackened by fire. L 0.26 m, W 0.10 m, Th 0.10 m; 6200 g.

4. (1992.0259.01; fig. 13.6.4) C101.01.25. Fragment of colonnette. Broken at both ends. Circular. Exterior smooth. Bluish grey with lighter and darker bands. L 0.49 m, D 0.08 m; 3880 g.

5. (1993.0189.01; fig. 13.6.5) C101.04.24. Fragment of marble colonnette shaft. Two ridges preserved with groove between. Top and bottom broken. Hole in centre 0.02 diameter. Less than half diameter preserved. Light bluish grey. L 0.12 m, W 0.07 m, Th 0.06 m; 495 g.

6. (1993.0189.02; fig. 13.6.6) C101.04.24. Fragment of marble colonnette shaft with portion of mouldings below capital. Shaft L 0.18 m, tapering slightly to top ridge L 0.02 m, second ridge L 0.03 m, then small curving portion of bottom of capital. Light grey with blue-grey streaks. L 0.25 m; D. 0.10 m; 4300 g.

7. (1993.0189.03; fig. 13.6.7) C101.04.24. Fragment of colonnette shaft; round. Bottom broken. Top broken with hole in centre, hole diameter 0.014, preserved depth 0.022. Very light grey with blue-grey streaks. L 0.21 m; D. 0.12 m; 7500 g.

13.A.2.d. Washbasin and Pedestal

One atypical marble piece is a pedestal with a total height of 0.69 m (fig. 13.7.2). The base is 0.045 m high, with a diameter of 0.25 m at the bottom. The diameter of the shaft narrows from 0.16 m at the bottom to 0.09 m at the top. A ridge 0.04 m high runs around the shaft between 0.145 m and 0.185 m from the bottom. The top has a hole 0.035 m in diameter and 0.015 m deep. A parallel comes from the Petra Church (Fiema et al. 2001: 340–41), although the parallel from Thessaloniki illustrated there is closer to the Humayma example in shape. Other parallels come from Sobeita (Segal 1988: 251) and Mampsis (Negev 1988: 96). The pedestal was probably used to support a washbasin secured to the top by a dowel. A 0.065 m thick basin fragment, which was found close to the pedestal, is an obvious candidate. The fragment is preserved to a height of 0.20 m; the bottom is missing, so any trace of a socket is gone. A small hole was neatly drilled into the interior wall of the basin, but it does not penetrate all the way through the wall. Similar holes surrounding the central pipe hole in the Petra basin were interpreted as holes for rods supporting the vertical water spout. The location of the basin and pedestal immediately west of the Chancel is atypical. At Petra the basin was located in the atrium (Herrmann 2001: 340–41), but the C101 Church, of course, did not have an atrium.

1. (1991.0248.02; fig. 13.6.1b) C101.01.07. Large fragment of basin. Slanted top rim with a slightly projecting exterior lip, smooth; other sides broken. Interior smooth, exterior

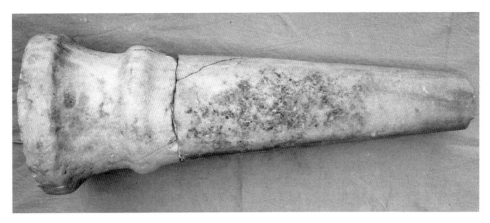

2. Basin support shaft

FIG. 13.7 *No. 2: C101, basin support shaft.*

0   20cm

smooth; small hole 0.008 diameter, 0.010 deep. White to light grey. Exterior slightly blackened by fire. L 0.16 m, W 0.07 m, Th 0.022 m; 3970 g.

2. (1991.0419.04; fig. 13.7.2) C101.01.08. Fragment of basin support shaft. Bottom broken. Top 0.09 diameter with hole c. 0.035 diameter, 0.015 deep. Exterior smooth. Diameter narrows from 0.16 at bottom to 0.09 at top. Light bluish grey. Joins 1991.0419.05 and 0.06. Total height of all three pieces 0.69 m. L 0.465 m; D 0.16 to 0.09 m; more than 5000 g.

3. (1991.0419.05) C101.01.08. Fragment of shaft. Top and bottom broken. Slightly less than half of diameter preserved. Exterior smooth. Joins 1991.0419.04 and 06. White. L 0.16 m, W 0.09 m, Th 0.15 m; 1500 g.

4. (1991.0419.06) C101.01.08. Base of shaft. Bottom flat, rough. 0.045 high base, upper ridge 0.145 to 0.185 high. Exterior smooth. White with light bluish grey streaks. Joins 1991.0419.04 and 05. L 0.0 m, W 0.23 m, Th 0.24 m; 5000 g.

13.A.2.e. Altar Table Top

Two thin fragments of white marble with a curved profile (nos. 1–2) may have belonged to the top of an altar table, although it is also possible that they are fragments of marble basins (cf. B100, p. 477).

Two fragments of thick panels with one curved edge (nos. 3–4) may have been part of an altar table, if not part of the hexagonal ambo base (13.A.2.b).

1. (1991.0022.01) C101.03.00. Small fragment of circular object. One side curved, top slopes in, slightly rough, others broken. Bottom flat, smooth. Top flat, smooth. White. Possibly part of tabletop or altar table top. Similar to and may belong with 1991.0311.05. L 0.09 m, W 0.05 m, Th 0.03 m; 70 g.

2. (1991.0311.05) C101.01.08. Fragment of circular object. One side curved, rough, others broken. Top slopes down from curved side. Back flat, smooth. Front flat, smooth, with tiny portion of lip. Variable thickness. Possibly part of a table top. Similar to and possibly belongs with 1991.0022.01. L 0.09 m, W 0.08 m, Th 0.03 m; 0.0.33 m; 195 g.

3. (1992.0123.01) C101.01.25. Fragment of panel. One side curved 0.025, flat, slanted 0.015 m; opposite side perhaps original, flat, rough or carefully cut; others broken. Back flat, polished. Front flat, polished. Light grey with dark bluish grey streaks. L 0.25 m, W 0.1 m, Th 0.04 m; 2170 g.

4. (1992.0431.04) C101.01.25. Fragment of panel. One side curved, polished; others broken with tiny portion of fastening hole. Back flat,

smooth. Front flat, smooth. Light bluish grey. Like 1991.0276.02, 1991.0279.05, 1992.0431.05. L 0.12 m, W 0.06 m, Th 0.04 m; 610 g.

13.A.2.f. Paving Slabs

No marble pavers were found as part of the C101 church structure, and it seems unlikely that there ever were marble pavers there. Most of the paving in the Nave and Aisles survives, and it is composed of sandstones. Enough of the stepped approach to the Chancel is preserved to show that marble was not used there either. A large fragment of a marble paver recovered from the sub-pavement fill of the Nave represents dump from elsewhere at the site, left with other rubbish prior to the construction of the Church.

1. (1992.0603.01) C101.01.60. Large portion of marble paver. Slightly irregular rectangular shape, somewhat weathered. Three sides probably near original, rough, flat, others broken. Back flat, rough. Front flat, smooth. White. Paver fragment was dumped in sub-church pavement fill. L 0.22 m, W 0.19 m, Th 0.03 m; 2660 g.

13.A.3. B100 (Byzantine Church and Early Islamic House)

Forty-two pieces of marble were found in the B100 excavation area. The fragments are much less numerous than the assemblage from the C101 Church, but they represent a more comprehensive collection of the typical marble furnishings of a Byzantine church. Analysis revealed that two of the fragments came from the Cape Vathy quarry on Thasos (pp. 491–92).

13.A.3.a. Paving Slabs

Fragments of a number of pavers were found associated with the B100 church, suggesting that, unlike the C101 Church, at least part of the B100 Church was furnished with marble paving. They were of white marble and most clustered around 0.035–0.038 m or 0.042 m in thickness. In some cases the fragments could derive from thick panels rather than pavers, but the absence of any surface decoration on either side results in their classification as pavers here. Some could be parts of steps.

1. (1991.0055.01) B100.04.07. Fragment of paver. One edge rough, others broken. Back very rough or broken. Front flat, smooth. White. L 0.12 m, W.0.11 m, Th 0.035 m; 705 g.

2. (1991.0136.03) B100.02.06. Fragment of paver. One side flat, top third smooth, bottom two-thirds rough with chisel marks, second side smooth, others broken. Bottom very rough with chisel marks. Top flat, smooth. White. L 0.13 m, W 0.08 m, Th 0.038 m; 440 g.

3. (1991.0193.01) B100.02.09. Small chip of possible marble step. One side smooth, flat; others broken. Back broken. Front slightly curved, polished. White. L 0.05 m, W 0.03. Th 0.03 m; 50 g.

4. (1991.0442.03) B100.02.11. Large fragment of paver. Corner. One side flat, smooth; second side flat, rough, with parallel chisel marks and rectangular fastening hole, 0.019 × 0.01 × 0.02 m; other sides broken. Back has smooth border, interior raised slightly, rough with chisel marks. Front flat, polished. White. L 0.27 m, W 0.17 m, Th 0.06 m; 6200 g.

5. (1992.0090.01) B100.G.04. Large fragment of marble paver. One side slightly rough, slightly bevelled, one side rough, perhaps original; others broken. Back flat, rough. Front flat, smooth. White. L 0.26 m, W 0.24 m, Th 0.062 m; NA.

6. (1992.0197.01) B100.E.17. Chips from possible paver. White. L NA, W NA, Th NA; 90 g.

7. (1992.0198.01) B100.E.20. Chip of step. One side polished, others broken. Back broken. Front flat, polished. Side at 110° angle to front. White. L 0.06 m, W 0.04 m, Th 0.03 m; 50 g.

8. (1992.0279.03) B100.E.21. Chip of step. One side flat, smooth, others broken. Back broken. Front flat, polished. White. L 0.1 m, W 0.05 m, Th 0.06 m; 195 g.

9. (1992.0367.01) B100.27.12. Fragment of panel or paver. All sides broken. Back flat, smooth. Front flat, polished. White. L 0.1 m, W 0.05 m, Th 0.038 m; 250 g.

10. (1992.0448.01) B100.27.13. Fragment of thick panel or paver. All sides broken. Back flat, smooth. Front flat, polished. White. L 0.06 m, W 0.07 m, Th 0.038 m; 215 g.

11. (1992.0448.02) B100.27.13. Large chip of marble panel or paver. One side slightly bevelled, slightly rough; others broken. Back broken. Front flat, smooth. White. L 0.15 m, W 0.10 m, Th 0.03 m; 655 g.

12. (1992.0448.03) B100.27.13. Fragment of thick panel or paver. One side bevelled; others broken. Back flat, slightly rough. Front flat, polished. White. L 0.12 m, W 0.06 m, Th 0.042 m; 425 g.

13. (1992.0448.05) B100.27.13. Large chip of panel or paver. All sides broken. Back broken. Front flat, smooth. White. L 0.28 m, W 0.17 m, Th 0.04 m; 2320 g.

14. (1992.0451.01) B100.27.15. Fragment of paver. All sides broken. Back flat, slightly rough. Front flat, polished. White. Belongs with 1992.0451.02, 03. L 0.08 m, W 0.07 m, Th 0.042 m; 360 g.

15. (1992.0451.02) B100.27.15. Fragment of paver. All sides broken. Back flat, slightly rough. Front flat, polished. White. Belongs with 1992.0451.01, 03. L 0.06 m, W 0.03 m, Th 0.042 m; 85 g.

16. (1992.0451.03) B100.27.15. Fragment of paver. One side flat, slightly rough, others broken. Back flat, slightly rough. Front flat, polished. White. Belongs with 1992.0451.01, 02. L 0.09 m, W 0.06 m, Th 0.042 m; 290 g.

17. (1992.0611.01) B100.26.87. Fragment of thick panel or paver. One side flat, smooth, others broken. Back flat, smooth. Front flat, polished. White. L 0.09 m, W 0.09 m, Th 0.038 m; 275 g.

18. (1992.0618.01) B100 area. Corner of paver. Two sides, flat top third, rough bottom two thirds, others broken. Back rough with chisel marks.

Front flat, polished. Tag lost; probably from B100 in 1992 season. Light grey with blue-grey streaks. L 0.31 m, W 0.19 m, Th 0.04 m; 3800 g.

13.A.3.b. Panels

Some of these fragments may have served as revetment plaques, others as chancel screen panels. They have been separated out as separate panels on the basis of thickness, decoration, and the colour of the marble.

B100 Panel 1. Three fragments of a thin white panel do not join, but they seem to belong to the same flat, undecorated panel. These undecorated fragments appear to be too thin to have served as pavers, but they may have served as revetment panels on a wall.

1. (1991.0432.03) B100.01.12. Fragment of thin panel. All sides broken. Back flat, smooth. Front flat, smooth. White. L 0.05 m, W 0.04 m, Th 0.01 m; 60 g.

2. (1992.0602.01) B100.26.M.8. Small fragment of thin panel. All sides broken. Back flat, smooth. Front flat, smooth. White. L 0.04 m, W 0.03 m, Th 0.01 m; 25 g.

3. (1993.0172.) B100.01 Pr 1.10. Three joining fragments of a thin panel. One side slightly bevelled; top 0.003 m project out 0.002 m; others broken. Back flat, smooth. Front flat, smooth. White to very light grey. L 0.19 m, W 0.08 m, Th 0.014 m; 355 g.

B100 Panel 2. Two other similar fragments of a white panel are thicker and so seem to belong to a separate flat, undecorated panel. They do not join.

1. (1992.0238.01) B100.E.23. Small fragment of thin panel. All sides broken. Back flat, smooth. Front flat, polished. White. L 0.06 m, W 0.04 m, Th 0.017 m; 75 g.

2. (1993.0230.01) B100.19 Pr 02.06. Fragment of marble panel. All sides broken. Back flat, smooth. Front flat, smooth. White. L 0.08 m, W 0.06 m, Th 0.02 m; 125 g.

B100 Panel 3. Another similar fragment of a white panel is significantly thicker than the previous examples, and so seems to belong to a separate flat, undecorated panel.

1. (1991.0357.07) B100.B.29. Fragment of panel. One side flat, smooth; others broken. Back flat, smooth. Front flat, polished. White. L 0.13 m, W 0.06 m, Th 0.028 m; 330 g.

B100 Panel 4. One fragment of a panel with a border ridge.

1. (1991.0406.01) B100.01.11. Fragment of panel. All sides broken. Back flat, smooth. Front polished, border with ridge and interior. White to light grey. L 0.08 m, W 0.06 m, Th 0.02 m; NA.

B100 Panel 5. One fragment of a panel with a border ridge. The colour of the marble sets it apart from the other, similar panel fragments.

1. (1992.0052.01) B100.E.4. Fragment of panel. One side flat, slightly rough; others broken. Back flat, smooth. Front polished border with groove and ridge. Dark bluish grey front to light bluish grey back. L 0.08 m, W 0.06 m, Th 0.03 m; 275 g.

B100 Panel 6. One fragment of a particularly thick panel.

1. (1992.0448.04) B100.27.13. Fragment of thick panel. One side slightly bevelled, very slightly rough; other sides broken. Back flat, smooth. Front polished, border with tiny portion of groove. White. L 0.06 m, W 0.05 m, Th 0.045 m; 165 g.

B100 Panel 7. Two fragments of thick panels in a different marble. They do not necessarily belong to the same panel.

1. (1992.0086.01) B100.E.11. Fragment of thick panel. All sides broken. Back flat, rough. Front flat, polished, tiny portion of groove. Bluish grey. L 0.20 m, W 0.13 m, Th 0.05 m; 1810 g.

2. (1992.0191.01) B100.27.9. Fragment of panel. All sides broken. Back flat, slightly rough with parallel grooves of chisel marks 0.008 apart. Front flat, smooth with low, flat-topped, slightly curving ridge. Bluish grey. L 0.15 m, W 0.15 m, Th 0.05 m; 1290 g.

B100 Panel 8. One fragment of a thick panel.

1. (1992.0451.04) B100.27.15. Fragment of panel. All sides broken. Back flat, smooth. Front polished, border with groove and ridge. Very light grey. L 0.06 m, W 0.05 m, Th 0.04 m; 190 g.

B100 Panel 9. One fragment of a panel with a polished border.

1. (1992.0451.05) B100.27.15. Fragment of panel. All sides broken. Back flat, smooth. Front polished border with ridge and interior. Light bluish grey. L 0.07 m, W 0.04 m, Th 0.03 m; 120 g.

B100 Pedestal Base (?). This large fragment was part of a square or rectangular base with a narrow vertical fillet below a projecting quarter-round moulding (fig. 13.8.1a). A roughly-finished, low square boss occupies the lower surface (H ca. 0.013 m), separated from the edge of the block by a smoothed surface (W 0.025 m). The boss would have fit into a recess in the supporting slab or step. There is a circular hole in the upper surface, probably for anchoring a pedestal or some other architectural member.

1. (1991.0442.02) B100.2.11. Fragment. One side polished, with fillet below quarter round moulding; other sides broken. Lower surface flat, smooth near side; flat, raised centre. Upper surface flat, polished, with circular hole D 0.033 m, 0.024 m deep. White. L 0.21 m, W 0.1 m, Th 0.06 m; 1840 g.

13.A.3.c. Cube

This cube is too big to have formed part of a mosaic. It is unclear what the function was.

1. (1992.0026.01) B100.G.2. Fragment of small cube. Three sides flat, smooth; one side slightly rough. Bottom rough. Top flat. White. L 0.04 m, W 0.03 m; H 0.03 m; 80 g.

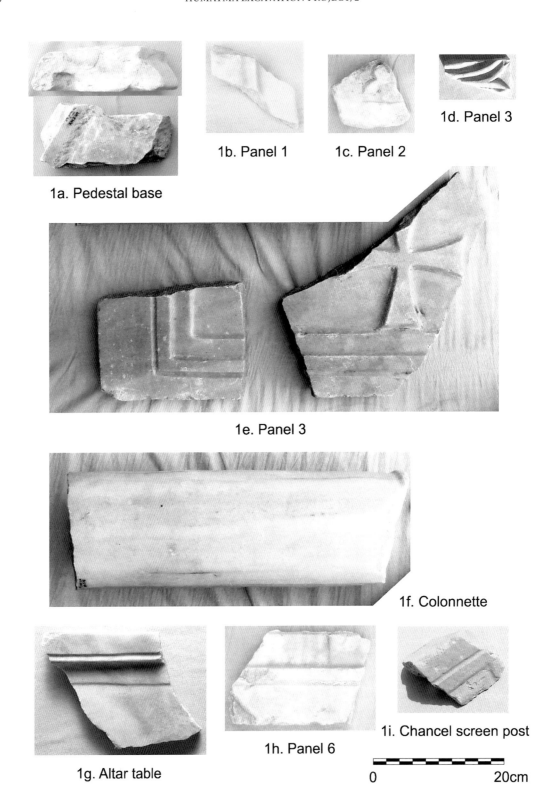

1a. Pedestal base

1b. Panel 1

1c. Panel 2

1d. Panel 3

1e. Panel 3

1f. Colonnette

1g. Altar table

1h. Panel 6

1i. Chancel screen post

0   20cm

FIG. 13.8   *No. 1a: B100, Pedestal base. No. 1b: C119, Panel 1. No. 1c: F102, fragment of Panel 2. No. 1d: F102, fragment of Panel 3. No. 1e: C119, fragments of Panel 3. No. 1f: C119, Colonnette. No. 1g: B100, fragment of altar table. No. 1h: F102, fragment of Panel 6. No. 1i: B100, fragment of chancel screen post.*

13.A.3.d. Basin

The rim of a basin. This is a large, heavy basin, perhaps used for ritual ablutions. A similar fragment was found in C101 (p. 471–72, no. 1).

1. (1991.0370.02) B100.07.05. Rim of bowl or basin; simple rounded rim. Sides broken. Bottom broken. Top side flat, smooth. Exterior, slightly rough with chisel marks. Interior smooth. Bluish grey. Exterior D 0.34 m, Th of wall 0.029. 605 g. Analysis has shown this marble to have come from Thasos-2, Paros-2, Paros-3, or Prokonnesos (pp. 486–90).

13.A.3.e. Altar Table

The mouldings along the edge of this fragment (fig. 13.8.1g) resemble those on the table found in the Petra Church, and the dimensions of the slab are similar (Fiema et al. 2001: 196). The fragments of table slabs found at Jabal Harûn are also similar (Fiema and Frösén et al. 2008: 206–7).

1. (1992.0063.01) B100.G.09. Fragment of possible altar table. Near corner. One side slightly curved, smooth, with some chisel marks, others broken. Back flat, rough with chisel marks. Front polished, thick border with groove and ridge, much thinner slightly curved interior 0.028 thick. Light bluish grey with dark grey patches. L 0.25 m, W 0.22 m, Th 0.05 m; 2720 g.

13.A.3.f. Colonnette

1. (1992.0492.01) B100.01.00. Fragment of colonnette shaft. Top and bottom broken. Exterior smooth, not exactly rounded. Light bluish grey. L 0.09 m, W 0.07 m, Th 0.05 m; 490 g.

13.A.3.g. Chancel Screen Post

This is a fragment of a typical Byzantine chancel screen post, as seen at the Petra Church and Jabal Harûn (Fiema et al. 2001: 198; Fiema and Frösén et al. 2008: 190–93). These posts are square in section, with a plain base, a gumdrop finial, and inset panels on three sides. The fourth side usually was occupied by a deep cutting intended to hold one

end of a chancel screen. A more complete example was found re-used in the Bedouin cemetery south of the site (see p. 484).

1. (98.0161.01; fig. 13.8.1i) B100.00.00). Triangular fragment. Front near corner, smooth, border 3.3 wide, then groove 0.2 deep, then ridge 1.7 wide, then groove 0.3 deep slanting up to interior. One side flat smooth, other broken, top, bottom, back broken. Bluish grey. L 0.12 m, W 0.10 m, Th 0.077 m; 975 g.

13.A.3.h. Miscellaneous Fragments

1. (1991.0432.01) B100.01.12. Small chip of panel. One side flat, polished, others broken. Back broken. Front flat, polished. Light grey. Belongs with 1991.0432.02. L 0.1 m, W 0.04 m, Th 0.02 m; 40 g.

2. (1991.0432.02) B100.01.12. Small chip of panel. One side flat, polished; others broken. Back broken. Front flat, polished. Light bluish grey. Belongs with 1991.0432.01. L 0.04 m, W 0.03 m, Th 0.01 m; 10 g.

3. (1992.0023.01) B100.E.01. Fragment of panel. All sides broken. Back flat, smooth. Front flat, smooth. Bluish grey with dark bluish grey streaks. L 0.15 m, W 0.11 m, Th 0.03 m; 655 g.

5. (1992.0030.01) B100.27.01. Fragment of marble panel. All sides broken. Back flat, smooth. Front flat, polished. Light bluish grey with bluish grey streaks. L 0.08 m, W 0.06 m, Th 0.02 m; 170 g.

6. (1992.0117.01) B100.27.05. Fragment of panel. All sides broken. Back flat, smooth. Front flat, smooth. Very light grey with bluish grey streaks. L 0.14 m, W 0.09 m, Th 0.02 m; 500 g.

13.A.4. C119 (Byzantine Church)

Six fragments of marble were found during the limited excavation in the C119 upper church during the 1993 season. Two pieces were found in general cleanup of the church interior, and four large pieces were found in Room 02, the southeast *pastophorion,* having been dumped there when the marble furnishings of the church were robbed out in antiquity. Two additional marble fragments were found in Square 04 and one in Square 03 during the 2009 season. There are eight panel fragments and one colonnette fragment.

13.A.4.a. Panels

C119 Panel 1. One fragment of a panel or table was found in the surface rubble (fig. 13.8.1b). The fragment is small, but a possible parallel is a panel from Jabal Harûn (Fiema and Frösén 2008: 201–2, no. 289).

1. (1993.0283.01) C119.01.01. Fragment of a panel or table. Front surface has a polished border with groove and ridge framing a recessed interior. Back surface flat but rough, with parallel saw marks. One original side flat, smooth, others broken. Light bluish grey. L 0.12 m, W 0.13 m, Th 0.05 m; 570 g.

C119 Panel 2. One fragment of a second panel was found in the surface rubble.

1. (1993.0345.01) C119.01.01. Fragment of a panel. Front flat, smooth. Back flat, slightly rough. All sides broken. White. L 0.13 m, W 0.01 m, Th 0.04 m; 885 g.

C119 Panel 3. Two fragments of a panel with a cross in relief were found in the southeast *pastophorion* (fig. 13.8.1e). The fragments do not join. At Th 0.05 m these two pieces of a large panel are thicker than typical chancel screen panels. The thick, wide border better suits a table (Acconci 1998: 487–91 m; Patrich 1988: 127–28), although the large cross in the centre is not characteristic of a table.

1. (1993.0381.02) C119.02.05. Large fragment of panel. One side flat, polished, others broken. Back flat, partially slanted, smooth. Front has polished border with groove and ridge, sunken interior, polished, has large cross; two arms complete, L 0.045—0.105, widen at ends; portions of other two arms. Bluish grey. L 0.35 m, W 0.32 m, Th 0.05 m; more than 5000 g.

2. (1993.0381.03) C.119.02.05. Fragment of panel. Probably upper left corner. Two sides flat, one polished, other slightly rough, others broken. Back smooth, partially slanted. Front polished border with groove and ridge, polished sunken interior. Bluish grey. L 0.23 m, W 0.18 m, Th 0.05 m; 4060 g.

C119 Panel 4. One fragment of another panel was found in the southeast *pastophorion.*

1. (1993.0381.05) C119.02.05. Small fragment of panel. Front surface has a polished border with groove; back surface slightly rough. One edge flat, smooth, the others broken. Bluish grey. L 0.10 m, W 0.03 m, Th 0.03 m; 150 g.

C119 Panel 5. One small fragment of a panel was found in the area of the Chancel.

1. (2009.0029.01) C119.04.13. Fragment of a panel. Front surface flat, smooth, polished; curved ridge framing a recessed central panel. Back surface mostly broken, except for a small portion of the smooth original surface with traces of red pigment. All sides broken. Very light grey. L 0.07 m, W 0.085 m, Th 0.037 m; 192 g.

C101 Panel 6. One fragment of a panel was found in the area of the Chancel. The marble colour sets it apart from Panel 5.

1. (2009.030.01) C119.04.13. Fragment of a panel. Front flat, smooth, polished. Back flat smooth. All sides broken. No decorative elements. Light grey with darker streaks. L 0.18 m, W 0.12 m, Th 0.035 m; 1288 g.

C101 Panel 7. One fragment of a panel was found at the west end of the Nave.

1. (2009.0042.01) C119.03.05. Fragment of a panel. Front surface carries traces of a smooth, polished border and portion of a recessed panel. Back surface is rough, with parallel chisel marks. All sides broken. Light grey. L 0.10 m, W 0.10 m, Th 0.033 m; 454 g.

13.A.4.b. Colonnette

C119 Colonnette. One large fragment of a colonnette was found in the southeast Room 2 (fig. 13.8.1f). In 1995, Schick suggested that this was the leg of an ambo (Schick 1995b: 337), but Michel (2001: 145) suggests rather that it was the leg of an altar table, noting that ambos are rare in small churches. Both the top and bottom are broken, so neither the total original height nor the type of base are known. In consequence, as Lehtinen notes (in Fiema and Frösén 2008: 208–10, Reg. nos. 204 and 434, NRS 16 and 17) with regard to four similar colonnette fragments from Jabal Harûn with a shaft diameter around 0.14 m, it is impossible to distinguish between the two types.

This colonnette shaft has a larger diameter than the legs of the altar table in the south apse of the Petra church (Fiema et al. 2001: 195, reg no. 0078 and 0081 m; D 0.10–0.115 m) or a fragment from the bema (Fiema et al. 2001: 201, reg no. 0271 m; D 0.08 m). The diameter of this shaft is only slightly larger than that of two colonnettes from Umm al-Rasas (Acconci 1994: 308–9, no. 61 A–B, L 1.80 m and D 0.133 m; L 1.50 m and D 0.13 m), but it is smaller than the colonnette from a ciborium from Umm al-Rasas (Acconci 1994: 310, no. 63, H 1.76 m, D 0.21 m; Alliata 1994: 314–15, no. 5). It is also smaller than the colonnettes for a ciborium from Mount Nebo (Acconci 1998: 474, no. 6–9, D ca. 0.21–0.25 m), but about the same diameter as other colonnette shafts from Mount Nebo (Acconci 1998: 477, nos. 16–19, D c. 0.15–0.165 m), and larger than other altar table legs from Mount Nebo (Acconci 1998: 480–87, various).

The diameters of four of the colonnettes found in the C101 Church could be determined: no. 3 (1992.0107.04) had a shaft diameter of 0.095 m; no. 4 (1992.0259.01) 0.08 m; no. 6 (1993.0189.02) 0.10 m; no. 7 (1993.0189.03) 0.12 m. See above p. 471.

1. (1993.0381.01) C101.02.05. Large fragment of a colonnette shaft. Top and bottom broken. Slight remnant of rim. Surface smooth and polished. L 0.50 m; D 0.155–0.160 m. White to light grey with grey streaks. More than 5 kg.

13.A.5. F102 (Byzantine Church and Early Islamic House)

Sixteen pieces of marble were found in the F102 excavation area, most of them panels. Because of the re-use of the structure, none of the find spots of the marble appear to have any relation to their original locations.

13.A.5.a. Panels

F102 Panel 1.

1. (1993.13.20; 1991.0042.02) F102.01.08. Fragment of panel. All edges broken, one near original with portion of fastening hole 0.015 deep. Back rough, with parallel grooves of chisel marks. Front flat, smooth. Very light grey with bluish grey streak. L 0.13 m, W 0.09 m, Th 0.025 m; 470 g.

F102 Panel 2.

1. (1991.0359.01; fig. 13.8.1c) F102.04.18. Fragment near corner of panel. All edges broken. Back flat, smooth. Front has portions of border of two sides meeting at right angle, portion of stylized plant. White. L 0.10 m, W 0.09 m, Th 0.034 m; 695 g.

F102 Panel 3. Two fragments of a fleur-de-lis from the centre of an open-work panel like C101 Panel 4.

1. (1991.0439.01; fig. 13.8.1d) F102.01.32. Fragment of panel. All edges broken. Back flat, smooth. Front smooth, with curved ridges and grooves forming fleur-de-lis. Bluish grey. Joins 1991.0439.02. L 0.10 m, W 0.05 m, Th 0.02 m; 165 g.

2. (1991.0439.02) F102.01.32. Small fragment of panel. All edges broken. Back flat, smooth. Front smooth, with portion of stylised plant. Bluish grey. Joins 1991.0439.01. L 0.05 m, W 0.04 m, Th 0.02 m; 55 g.

F102 Panel 4.

1. (1992.0097.01.05) F102.05.05. Small fragment of panel. All edges broken. Back flat, rough. Front flat, polished. Light bluish grey. L 0.04 m, W 0.03 m, Th 0.023 m; 60 g.

F102 Panel 5. Thin panel fragment.

1. (1991.0478.01) F102.01.32. Fragment of thin marble panel. All edges broken. Back flat, smooth. Front flat, smooth. Cream with purple veins. L 0.04 m, W 0.07 m, Th 0.01 m; 25 g.

F102 Panel 6.

1. (1992.0021.01; fig. 13.8.1h). F102.02.04. Fragment of panel. One edge slightly bevelled, smooth, others broken. Back flat, rough, with parallel saw marks. Front smooth border with grooves and ridges. Light bluish grey with dark bluish grey streaks. L 0.21 m, W 0.14 m, Th 0.05 m; 2390 g.

F102 Panel 7.

1. (1992.0291.01) F102.05.23. Fragment of panel. All edges broken. Back flat, smooth. Front polished border with groove and ridge. White. Blackened by fire. The marble has been identified as Prokonnesian. L 0.13 m, W 0.12 m, Th 0.04 m; 960 g.

F102 Panel 8.

1. (1993.0319.01) F102.10.00. Small fragment of marble panel. All edges broken. Back flat, smooth. Front flat, polished. Very light grey. L 0.06 m, W 0.05 m, Th 0.015 m; 50 g.

F102 Panel 9.

1. (1995.0053.02; fig. 13.9.a) F102.15.03. Corner of panel. Two edges flat, others broken. Back rough with chisel marks. Front flat, polished, raised margin and groove, small portion of sunken interior. Light bluish grey, with large crystals (to 0.002). L 0.16 m, W 0.11 m, Th 0.04 m; 1430 g.

F102 Panel 10.

1. (1995.0146.01; fig. 13.9.1a) F102.16.16. Two joining fragments of panel. All edges broken. Back rough with saw marks. Front polished, small portion of border ridge and interior 0.05 m wide, then 3 mm drop to rest of interior. Light bluish grey. L 0.11 m, W 0.09 m, Th 0.03 m; 585 g.

F102 Panel 11.

1. (1995.0060.01; fig. 13.9.1a) F102.00.00. Fragment of marble panel. All edges broken. Back rough. Front border ridge and groove, sunken centre 0.022 thick. Light bluish grey.

Found on surface between F102 and F103, 75 m SW of F102. L 0.11 m, W 0.06 m, Th 0.034 m; 340 g.

F102 Panel 12.

1. (1995.0148.01) F102.17.02. Fragment of marble panel. All edges broken. Back slightly rough, saw marks. Front slightly curved, smooth. Light grey. L 0.16, W 0.12 m, Th 0.025 m; 898 g.

13.A.5.b. Platter or Altar Table

F102 Platter. This fragment could be the rim of either a large white marble platter, or possibly an altar table.

1. (1995.0176.01; fig. 13.9.3) F102.16.21. Fragment of platter or altar table. One edge curved, others broken. Bottom smooth. Top polished. White, fine-grained. L 0.08 m, W 0.05 m, Th 0.01 m; D. 0.45 m; 80 g.

13.A.5.c. F102 Miscellaneous Fragments

Two small chips were also found.

1. (1991.0414.02) F102.01.32. Chip of panel. All edges broken. Back broken. Front polished, portion of border with groove. Light bluish grey. L 0.05 m, W 0.05 m, Th 0.03 m; 65 g.

2. (1993.0253.02. F102.07.10. Chip of panel. All edges broken. Back broken. Front flat and smooth. White to light grey. L 0.04 m, W 0.04 m, Th 0.03 m; 40 g.

13.A.6. F103 (Abbasid Family Manor House)

Seventeen stray pieces of marble were found in the Abbasid family manor house (F103). The overall results of the excavation of this structure will be published in a future volume, but the ecclesiastical marble fragments are included here for the sake of completeness. None of their find spots have any connection with their original locations. The pieces of marble could have come from any one of the churches, although the F102 church is closest.

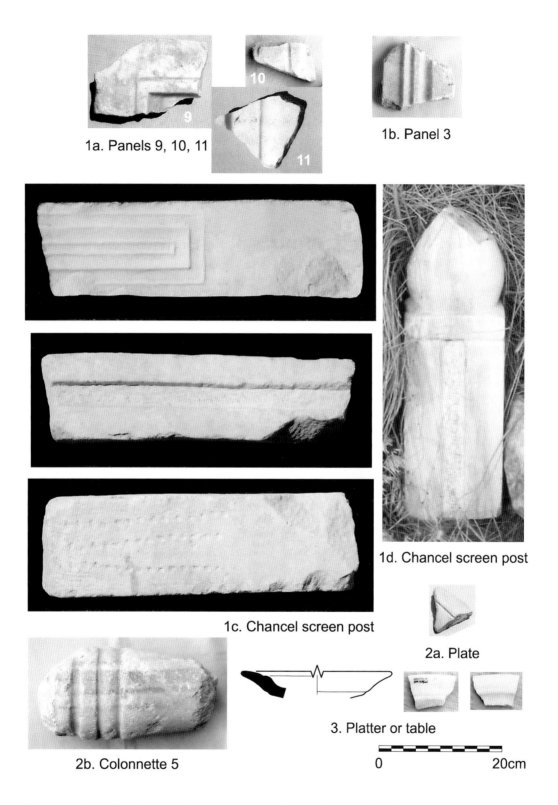

1a. Panels 9, 10, 11

1b. Panel 3

1d. Chancel screen post

1c. Chancel screen post

2a. Plate

3. Platter or table

2b. Colonnette 5

0 20cm

FIG. 13.9 *No. 1a: F102, fragment of Panels 9, 10, 11. No. 1b: F103, fragment of Panel 3. No. 1c: F103, chancel screen post. No. 1d: Colonnette of unknown origin reused in Bedouin cemetery south of Humayma. No. 2a: F103, rim fragment of plate or possible table top. No. 2b: F103, Colonnette 5. No. 3: F102, rim fragment of platter or altar table.*

13.A.6.a. F103 Panel 1

One fragment of a panel was found.

1. (1992.0263.01) F103.Probe 01.04. Fragment of
    a panel. All edges broken. Back flat, smooth.
    Front flat, polished. Very light bluish gray. L
    0.06 m, W 0.05 m, Th 0.03 m; 135 g.

13.A.6.b. F103 Panel 2

This panel fragment has an ovolo and leaf design
similar to C101 Panel 1 and Panel 5.

1. (1993.0128.01) F103.79.00. Small fragment of a
    panel. All edges broken. Back rough. Front has
    portion of ovolo and leaf. Slightly weathered.
    Light bluish grey. L 0.12 m, W 0.10 m, Th 0.04;
    715 g.

13.A.6.c. F103 Panel 3

This panel fragment is exceptionally thin. It has
slight traces of what looks like the start of open-
work decoration. It could have been an open-work
panel like C101 Panels 1 to 4, although it is thinner.
It is unlike any other piece of marble at the site.

1. (1993.0129.01; fig. 13.9.1b) F103.78.00. Fragment
    of thin panel. One edge flat, smooth, second
    interior edge flat, smooth with slight traces of
    start of open-work, other edges broken. Back
    flat, smooth. Front smooth, border with two
    parallel grooves and ridges. Bluish grey with
    dark blue streaks. L 0.12 m, W 0.11 m, Th 0.018
    m; 510 g.

13.A.6.d. F103 Panel 4

One fragment of this panel was found.

1. (1995.0041.01) F103.00. Found 100 m E of
    F103 on surface. Fragment of panel. All edges
    broken. Raised margin on one edge. Back flat,
    smooth. Front polished, with ridge 0.018 m
    wide and 0.005 m high, trace of decorative
    element. Light grey; L 0.10 m, W 0.06 m, Th
    0.003 m; 285 g.

13.A.6.e. F103 Panel 5

One fragment of this panel was found.

1. (2002.0136.01) F103.39.00. Fragment of panel.
    All edges broken, flat. Back smooth, part rough.
    Top smooth. White. L 0.08 m, W 0.07 m, Th
    0.024; 335 g.

13.A.6.f. F103 Panel 6

One fragment of this panel was found.

1. (2002.0157.01) F103.43.09. Fragment of panel.
    One edge flat, polished, others broken. Back
    flat, rough. Front polished, flat border 0.055 m
    wide then groove 0.005 m deep and ridge 0.012
    m wide and then start of interior flat surface
    0.008 m deep. Bluish grey with darker streaks.
    L 0.07, W 0.105, Th 0.048; 1680 g.

13.A.6.g. F103 Panel 7

Two fragments of this panel were found.

1. (2002.0269.01) F103.47.02. Two pieces of a
    large panel fragment. One edge flat smooth,
    other edges broken. Back broken. Front pol-
    ished. White L 0.10 m, W 0.11, Th 0.04; 635 g.

13.A.6.h. F103 Colonnettes

Five fragments of colonnette shafts were found.

1. (1998.0037.01) F103.18.05. Fragment of shaft.
    Top and bottom broken. Smooth, cylindrical.
    Light bluish grey with dark bluish grey streaks.
    L 0.13 m; D 0.085 m; 1834 g.

2. (1998.0269.01; fig. 13.8.1f) 75.25. Fragment
    of shaft. Smooth, nearly cylindrical. Broken,
    surface nicked. Three small holes (D 0.004 m,
    deep 0.005 m have been drilled into the surface
    0.07 m apart, forming a triangle. Bluish grey. L
    0.29 m; D 0.14–13 m bottom, 0.013–12 m top;
    1000 g.

3. (2002.0005.01) F103.22.00. Fragment of shaft.
    Widest at bottom, slants inwards, groove 0.03
    m from bottom. Grey with dark grey streaks.

About quarter of diameter of oval preserved, D 0.07–0.04 m, H 0.055; 235 g.

4. (2002.0074.01) F103.87.17. Fragment of shaft. Not perfectly circular, small portion of circumference flat. Top, bottom broken. Smooth with parallel chisel marks on flat portion of circumference. Grey with a few dark streaks. H 0.13 m, D 0.09 m; 1935 g.

5. (2002.0134.01; fig. 13.9.2b). F103.87.23. Fragment of strongly tapering colonnette shaft. Top, bottom broken. Bottom 0.13 m has four grooves and three ridges. H 0.27, D 0.13 m bottom, 0.105 m top.

13.A.6.i. Chancel Screen Post

A large fragment of a chancel post was found. It is a standard type that has numerous parallels, e.g. Umm al-Rasas (Acconci 1994: 298–99, no. 29); Mount Nebo (Acconci 1998: 504–5, nos. 97, 98).

1. (98.0269.01; fig. 13.9.1c) F103.75.25. Fragment of bottom of chancel screen post. Rectangular section. Top and bottom broken, many knicks and pitting. Front surface, starting 0.25 m from bottom, as a series of grooves and ridges. U-shaped inner ridge 0.02 m wide, middle and outer ridges 0.025 m wide; one side has straight groove (W 0.04 m, deep 0.01 m. There are three rows of small holes on the back surface, each hole 0.01 m in diameter, a few mm deep. Thirteen holes in each row, not completely parallel (L ca. 0.26 m). It is likely that the post was re-worked to serve as a game board (Mulvin and Sidebotham 2004). This re-use can only have happened once the post was removed from its original position and laid horizontally. Light bluish grey with dark bluish grey streaks. L 0.52 m, W 0.16 m, H 0.14 m.

13.A.6.j. Plate

A fragment of a plate or possible table top was found. It has a parallel at Mount Nebo (Acconci 1998: 492–93, no. 65)

1. (1998.0455.01; fig. 13.9.2a) F103.24.02. Fragment of plate. All edges broken. Top, bottom intact.

Wide border (w 0.045 m) near original edge, with groove (deep 0.01 m) and deep curve to interior. Slight trace of groove on lower surface. White, fine-grained. L 0.08 m, W 0.08 m, Th 0.03 m; 140 g.

3.A.6.k. Step

A small chip was found that most likely was part of a step.

1. (1992.0315.01) F103.00. Chip from a step? One edge flat, smooth, others broken. Back broken. Front flat, smooth, Grey to dark grey. L. 0.06m, W 0.03, Th 0.03; 80 g.

13.A.7. Ecclesiastical Marble from Other Areas

A small number of small fragments of ecclesiastical marble have been recovered from the surface here and there around the site (designated as Area A). For the most part, they probably were dropped in the course of salvage from church structures, or moved from their original site and left by visitors in the more recent period. Several surface fragments were subjected to source analysis (see p. 488).

Area A. Miscellaneous Panels.

1. (1992.0540.02) A00.00.00. Fragment of panel. Surface find south of Reservoir 68. All edges broken. Back rough with chisel marks. Front smooth, border with groove and ridges and interior with portion of stylised leaf. White with blue grey veins. Roughened by weathering. L 0.16 m, W 0.11 m, Th 0.05 m; 1630 g.

2. (1993.0448.01) A00.00.00. Surface find northwest of B100. Fragment of panel. All edges broken. Back flat, smooth. Front flat, polished. Very light grey with dark grey streaks. L 0.11 m, W. 0.07 m, Th 0.03 m; 285 g.

3. (1993.0448.02) A00.00.00. Surface find northwest of B100. Fragment of panel. All edges broken. Back flat, smooth. Front flat, smooth. Light bluish grey. L 0.11 m, W 0.06 m, Th 0.03 m; 285 g.

4. (1995.0394.01) A115.00.00. Surface find east of Tomb A115. Fragment of thick marble panel. One edge flat, others broken. Back rough, mostly broken. Front flat, border ridge and groove. White with large crystals. Weathered. L 0.07 m, W 0.06 m, Th 0.055 m; 230 g.

Area A. Chancel Screen Post.

This is a fragment of a typical Byzantine chancel screen post, as seen at the Petra Church and Jabal Harûn (Fiema et al. 2001: 198; Fiema and Frösén et al. 2008: 190–93). These posts are square in section, with a plain base, a gumdrop finial, and inset panels on three sides. The fourth side usually was occupied by a deep cutting intended to hold one end of a chancel screen, as seen here. A well-preserved example was found in F103, and a very fragmentary example in the B100 structure.

1. (Uncatalogued; fig. 13.9.1d) A00.00.00; seen in 1986 re-used in the Bedouin cemetery south of the site. Upper portion of a square chancel screen post with gumdrop finial. Bluish grey marble. Shaft 0.16 × 0.16 m, MPH 0.48 m; deep groove down the centre of one side, W 0.037.

Area A. Miscellaneous.

1. (1991.0026.01) A00.00.00. Fragment of column shaft. Surface find near Reservoir 68. Top, bottom broken; exterior round, smooth; about one third of diameter preserved, not exactly round. White with light bluish grey streaks. L 0.13 m, W 0.08 m, Th 0.07 m, D 15 m; 975 g.

2. (1992.0540.01) A00.00.00. Found on surface south of Reservoir 68. Corner of paver. Two edges flat, rough, form corner; others broken. Back flat, slightly rough. Front flat, smooth. Roughened by weathering. White. L 0.07 m, W 0.06 m, Th 0.04 m; 225 g.

3. (1993.0425.01) D120.01.00. Although found in an excavation area, this is treated as a random surface fragment. Fragment of panel or paver. All edges broken, perhaps one near original flat. Back rough, perhaps broken. Front rough, perhaps broken. Weathered. White. L 0.09 m, W 0.05 m, Th 0.04 m; 195 g.

Area E. Panel.

1. (1995.0588.01) E.00. Surface find between E121 and E116. Small fragment of a panel. All edges broken. Back smooth. Front polished, with portion of a groove. Bluish white with large crystals. L 0.07 m, W 0.04 m, Th 0.025 m ; 102 g.

13.A.8. Conclusions: Scope and Character of the Assemblage

A few general observations are in order. Almost all of the marble was either pure white or else white to light grey with dark grey veins, and it originated in quarries in the eastern Mediterranean (see the reports of al-Bashaireh and Herz, pp. 485–92). There was no marble in the earlier Nabataean–Roman structures that could have been available for reuse in the churches. Importing the marble would have been a significant expense for the church builders, but the ubiquitous presence of marble in most every church site in the region shows that marble furnishings were *de rigeur*. Only in central Jordan were major deposits of oil shale sometimes used as a cheaper local source of material in place of imported marble for panels and columns in churches, as at Lejjun (Schick 1987), where oil shale was used exclusively; at other sites oil shale was used alongside marble, as at Mount Nebo (Acconci 1998), Umm al-Rasas (Acconci 1994), and Deir ʿAin ʿAbata (Loverance 2012).

No sandstone or limestone was used for any of the panels or other liturgical elements, other than the reliquary in the B126 Church (pp. 315–18), although some reused marl conduit blocks were used as steps and as the base for the chancel screen panels in the C101 church, and fossiliferous limestone blocks, characteristic of local quarries near Maʿan, were used throughout the site for mouldings and steps in Nabataean structures now lost (see pp. 497–501).

The majority of marble pieces found at Humayma were recovered from the C101 Church, although most of the marble furnishings there had been removed before the fire destruction of the building, leaving out of consideration additional pieces that presumably were found during the 1962 clearance and subsequently lost. The bulk of the marble from

C101 was used for panels and colonnettes for the chancel screens and the ambo, the standard uses for marble in Byzantine churches in general. There was no remaining trace of the altar, unless a few pieces of marble that might have belonged to a table can be attributed to it. The washbasin and pedestal from C101 was an uncommon type of furnishing.

The few pieces of marble found in B100, C119, and F102 are enough to indicate that those churches also had the standard set of marble furnishings. Many fewer pieces of marble were recovered from the B100 Church than from the C101 church, but they represented a wider range of furnishings, including pavers and chancel screen posts.

The decorative motifs on the various panels — central cross within a circular wreath frame, stylized plants, vine tendrils, fleur-de-lis, crosses, etc. — are commonly found in other churches in the region (parallels are cited above under the individual pieces), showing that the Humayma churches had standard sets of panels, deriving from the same workshops as the other churches in the region. The various marble elements as a whole, and notably the four open-work panels from C101 and other ornately carved pieces, e.g., C101 Panel 20, are of a quality that matches the marble furnishings in other churches of the region. Clearly the church-builders of Hauarra did not skimp when furnishing their structures.

13.A.9. *Provenance Determination of the Marbles by X-Ray Diffraction, Petrography, and Stable Isotopes*
(K. Al-Bashaireh)

Introduction

This work aimed at determining the provenance of white marble samples excavated at the archaeological site of Humayma. The samples were characterized by X-ray diffraction, petrography, and stable isotope analyses. The data collected was compared to the main references of white marbles used in antiquity. The results showed that Prokonnesos (Marmara, Turkey), Thasos, and Naxos (Greece) are the probable sources of the samples.

Provenance studies of archaeological lithic materials have become a major topic of archaeological

research. The archaeometric goal of provenance studies is to locate with confidence the geographic and geologic source of the deposits that provided the raw materials for the manufacture or the carving of an artefact or a building material (Rapp 1985). In this way, lithic materials can provide direct information on the exploitation and use of raw materials from specific sources in antiquity, and the data can elucidate economic, social, and political aspects of ancient societies.

Because of its aesthetic qualities, marble has been one of the most valuable commonly-used lithic materials since early antiquity. Marble is moderately hard to work, but it can hold fine details (Goffer 2007: 60). As early as the Neolithic in Greece, marble was used in jewellery, figurines, and grave goods (Herz and Garrison 1998). Later on, it was used for building construction and architecture elements, sculptures, temples, large sarcophagi, monuments, scrolls, acanthus, and bowls (Herz 1987, 1992; Herz and Garrison 1998; Baietto et al. 1999; De Nuccio et al. 2002; Maniatis et al. 2010). Greeks and Romans preferred pure white marble for statuary and for architectural applications (Rapp and Hill 1998; Lazzarini et al. 1997).

Since the locations and approximate periods of operation of the major marble quarries in Greece, Italy, and Turkey are known from archaeological, inscriptional, and literary evidence, the determination of provenance aids in dating the fabrication of a marble artefact (Manfra et al. 1975; Herz 1985). This information in turn provides information about the contemporary trade routes, exchange patterns, distribution and diffusion in antiquity, and the technology of mining and transportation (Manfra et al. 1975; Bruno et al. 1998; Herz 1985; Rapp 1985; Rapp and Hill 1998). In addition, provenancing marble gives insight into changing aesthetic tastes (Herz 1992) and can reveal modern forgeries or ancient copies of original works (Polikreti 2007).

Since there are no sources of high-quality marble in the region (see al-Bashaireh 2011: 317; Fischer 1988: 162, 1998), both white and coloured marble was imported to most Near Eastern archaeological sites for use for building and sculpture (Capedri et al. 2004: 27). During the Roman and Byzantine periods in the region of modern Jordan, marble was used for architecture and sculpture in the cities of the Decapolis League (al-Bashaireh 2011: 317, 321), in Petra (Reid 2005), at Humayma, and in most of the Byzantine churches at various sites around the region (Michel 2001; Fiema et al. 2001).

Materials

Six marble samples of archaeological interest were selected by Oleson for source analysis by the author (fig. 13.10). The description and context of the samples is given in Table 13.1. Two of the samples have been catalogued elsewhere in this chapter: no. 1 (1991.0370.02) is a fragment of a basin found in B100 (p. 477); no. 2 (1992.0291.01) is a fragment of Panel 7 found in F102 (p. 480).

Analytical Techniques

Since many of the ancient marble quarries in the Mediterranean yielded white marble, it is difficult to differentiate among them based on their macroscopic characteristics, especially when dealing with artefacts that have polished surfaces. Although macroscopic characteristics such as gray streaks or large grains may assist in the sourcing of some marbles, the application of analytical techniques allows the most reliable identification of most marble sources. The stable isotope analysis of carbon and oxygen has been the technique most widely used, although this analysis by itself is not enough to distinguish among all of the Mediterranean white marble sources (Herz 1987: 42). Therefore, many studies combine analysis of stable isotopes with one or more further techniques, including petrography (Lazzarini and Antonelli 2003; al-Bashaireh 2011), trace elements (Matthews 1997), strontium isotopes (Brilli et al. 2005), and electron spin resonance (ESR), which is sometimes referred to as electron paramagnetic resonance (EPR) (Polikerti and Maniatis 2002; Attanasio et al. 2003).

The Humayma samples were characterized by means of x-ray diffraction (XRD), optical petrography, and stable carbon and oxygen isotopes. Analyses were carried out on bulk samples that represent the components of the marbles. The results of these analyses were compared to the main reference databases of Mediterranean marbles exploited

in antiquity, based on carbon and oxygen isotopes and other techniques (see, for instance, Herz 1987; Moens et al. 1988, 1990; Asgari and Matthews 1995; Gorgoni et al. 2002; Capedri et al. 2004; Attanasio et al. 2008).

An XRD analysis was carried out on powdered samples using a Shimadzu Lab X, 6000 X-Ray Diffractometer at the laboratories of the Department of Archaeology and Anthropology at Yarmouk University, Irbid, Jordan. Powder diffraction patterns were obtained under the following conditions: CuKα radiation (λ=1.5418Å) with 30kV, 30mA energy, and Graphite Monochromatic.

Thin-section examinations by a Leica DMLSP polarizing microscope were used to identify a number of petrographic parameters with important diagnostic significance for marble: fabric, maximum grain size (MGS) of calcite or dolomite grains and their boundary shapes (GBS) (Lazzarini et al. 1980; Moens et al. 1988; Gaggadis-Robin 2009). Thin sections were prepared according to the standard procedures (Camuti and McGuire 1999: 3–5) in the workshop of the Department of Archaeology and Anthropology at Yarmouk University.

The isotopic analyses of carbonates were measured using an automated carbonate preparation device (KIEL-III) coupled to a gas-ratio mass spectrometer (Finnigan MAT 252). The results were expressed in terms of $\delta^{13}C$ or $\delta^{18}O$ and measured in parts per mil (‰) relative to the international reference standard PDB (Faure 1986). The precision of the isotopic ratio is ±0.1‰ for $\delta^{18}O$ and ±0.06‰ for $\delta^{13}C$ (1 sigma), and the measurements were calibrated based on repeated measurements of NBS-19 and NBS-18. Isotope analyses were carried out at the Environmental Isotope Laboratory, Department of Geosciences at the University of Arizona (Tucson, AZ).

Results and Discussion

XRD analysis. The XRD results of the samples distinguish Sample 6 from the rest of the samples (fig. 13.11.1). The mineralogical composition of Samples 1, 2, 3, 4, and 5 is calcite, while that of Sample 6 is dolomite. The major source of the dolomitic marbles in antiquity was Thasos-3 (Cape Vathy, Greece), a quarry that provided material widely used in the

FIG. 13.10 *Marble samples for analysis, nos. 1–6.*

The calcitic Samples 1, 2, and 3 have sutured to embayed grain boundaries and a heteroblastic fabric, where the large grains (2.9–3.9 mm) are embedded in a matrix of finer ones (fig. 13.11.2). They form the mortar fabric, a diagnostic feature of the Prokonnesian marble from the island of Marmara, Turkey (Lazzarini 1980: 176–80; Gorgoni et al. 2002: 118). Sample 5 shows a variable size and distribution of coarser grains, which are, however, present in the form of irregular bands or patches in areas that alternate with the finer ones (fig. 13.11.3). This abnormal feature came across in a number of artefacts of Prokonnesian marble (De Nuccio et al. 2002). The above features exclude Paros 2–3 provenance and most probably indicate Prokonnesos as the source for these samples. Sample 4 has a heteroblastic fabric, embayed grain boundaries, and coarse grains (fig. 13.11.4), while Sample 6 has a homeoblastic fabric and isotropic sutured grain boundaries (fig. 13.11.5). The microscopic features of Samples 4 and 6 might be seen in different marble sources such as Aphrodisias, Thasos, and Paros (Moens et al.1988; Gorgoni et al. 2002). Therefore, they alone cannot assign a provenance for the two samples. The XRD analysis also shows that Sample 6 is Thasos-3 marble, while Sample 4 needs an additional analysis.

Isotopic analysis. The values of oxygen and carbon isotopes are given in Table 13.2 and illustrated graphically in the C–O correlation diagram of Gorgoni et al. (2002: 123). Samples 1, 2, 3, 5, and 6 plot in overlapping isotopic regions (fig. 13.12). Sample 1 pinpoints four probable sources of marbles: Thasos-1, Thasos-2, Paros-2, Paros-3, and Prokonnesos-1. Samples 2, 3, and 5 pinpoint Thasos-2, Thasos-3, and Prokonnesos-1. Sample 5 lies on the border of Thasos-3. The macroscopic and petrographic features of Sample 1 noted above, including the distinctive mortar fabric, sutured to embayed carbonate crystal boundaries, MGS of 2–4 mm, and the light grey colour exclude Paros-2 and

Mediterranean region. In contrast, the western Mediterranean sources of dolomitic marbles were used primarily on a local basis (Tykot et al. 1998). The characteristics of Sample 6 are compatible with those of Thasos-3 marble, which is dolomitic, white, and large-grained (see petrographic analysis below; Herrmann and Newman 1998). Therefore, the most probable source of Sample 6 is Thasos-3. The XRD analysis shows the presence of traces of quartz in all of the samples except Sample 6 and traces of dolomite in Samples 4 and 5. Because Paros marble does not contain dolomite (Capedri et al. 2004: 532–34), the Paros source can be excluded as a source for Samples 4 and 5.

Petrographic analysis. Table 13.2 presents the values of the maximum grain size of the samples, and fig. 13.11.2–5 illustrates four textural features.

Table 13.1   List of marble samples subjected to source analysis.

Sample	Context	Description
1 (1991.0370.02)	Locus B100.07.05, Byzantine Church	Basin fragment, white
2 (1992.0291.02)	Locus F102.05.23, Byzantine Church	Chancel screen fragment, burned portions
3 (1998.0037.01)	Locus F103.18.05, Abbasid family manor house, probably carried in from ruins of nearby Byzantine Church at F102.	Colonnette fragment, slightly streaked bluish gray.
4 (1998.0161.01)	Surface find, 15m southeast of reservoir no. 67 in the settlement center, probably carried in from ruins of nearby Byzantine Church at B100.	Chancel screen fragment, dark gray color.
5 (2002.0005.01)	Locus F103.22.00, surface find, Abbasid family manor house, probably carried in from ruins of nearby Byzantine Church at F102.	Colonnette fragment, streaked grayish-white.
6 (2002.0136)	Locus F103.39.00, surface find, Abbasid family manor house, probably carried in from ruins of nearby Byzantine Church at F102.	Panel fragment, beige-white.

Table 13.2   Values of carbon $\delta^{13}C$ and oxygen $\delta^{18}O$ isotopes and maximum grain size (MGS) values.

Sample	$\delta^{13}C \pm 0.06(‰)$	$\delta^{18}O \pm 0.1(‰)$	MGS(mm)
1	2.51	-1.05	2.9
2	3.59	-0.86	3.0
3	3.06	-3.68	3.9
4	3.07	-6.59	4.1
5	3.46	-1.70	2.9
6	3.59	-2.29	2.2

Paros-3 and point alternatively either to Thasos-1, Thasos-2, or Prokonnesos-1 as probable sources. The limited diffusion and use made of Thasos-1 and Thasos-2 marbles (Bruno et al. 2002: 297; Gorgoni et al. 2002), and the dolomitic composition of Thasos-3 strongly suggest Prokonnesos-1 as the most probable source of all four of these marbles.

Sample 4 pinpoints Naxos and the border of Prokonnesos-2 isotopic regions. Contrary to the Prokonnesos-1 marble, the Prokonnesos-2 marble has a highly negative $\delta^{18}O$ value; the two types, however, have similar macroscopic and microscopic features (see above, Asgari and Matthews 1995: 128–29; Gorgoni et al. 2002: 126). The petrographic features of Sample 4 exclude Prokonnesos-2 as a probable source; therefore, Naxos remains the probable source of this sample. Taking into consideration that the exploitation of Naxos marble terminated before the Byzantine period, it is probable that this sample was taken from a disused

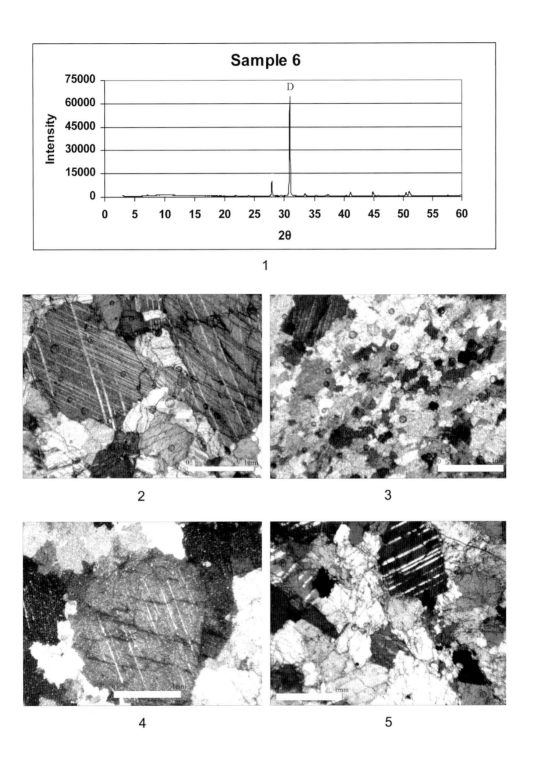

FIG. 13.11 *1: XRD pattern of Sample 6 composed mainly of dolomite (D). Microphotographs showing textural features; bar length = 1mm. 2: Heteroblastic mortar fabric given by some large calcite grains in a matrix of finer grains; typical feature of Prokonnesos marble (Sample 2); 3: Less typical feature of Prokonnesos marble; irregular bands or patches of coarse calcite grains in areas that alternate with the finer ones (Sample 5); 4: Heteroblastic fabric, mosaic, embayed-sutured grain boundaries (Sample 4); 5: Homeoblastic isotropic marble showing sutured grain boundaries of dolomite (Sample 6).*

earlier structure. The provenance of Sample 6 (Thasos-3) was determined on the basis of its dolomitic content. Isotopically, in addition to Thasos-3, Sample 6 plots in Thasos-2 and Prokonnesos-1 isotopic regions. However, because its petrographic features are very different from those of Prokonnesos-1, and because the distribution of Thasos-2 marbles in antiquity was limited, Thasos-3 is the most probable source of Sample 6.

The results of this analysis coincide with the results of previous studies on the provenance of marble uncovered from archaeological sites in Jordan. Al-Bashaireh (2003) found that Prokonnesos-1, Prokonnesos-2, Thasos-3, and Naxos marbles were used in the decoration of the Nymphaeum and Western Baths at Gadara/Umm Qeis. Al-Bashaireh (2011) found that most of the white marble used in the octagonal building at Gadara was Prokonnesian-1 marble. The chancel screens studied by al-Naddaf et al. (2010) were Prokonnesian-1 marble. At Petra, the majority of the marble samples from the small temple studied by Reid (2005) were from Marmara (i.e., Prokonnesian marble). Some marble fragments found in the Jabal Harûn Church were identified as Prokonnesian marble by the project conservator on the basis of visual observation of color and surface, but no scientific analyses were carried out (Fiema and Frösén 2008: 224 n. 17; Fiema, personal communication, January 2012). These fragments were probably taken from the disused monumental structures in Petra. Abu-Jaber et al. (2012) showed that the white marble from the Nabatean Qasr el-Bint and colonnaded street baths at Petra was imported from Thasos, Penteli, Prokonnesos, and Docimeion.

It is noteworthy to mention that because of the ease and low price of quarrying and shipping, the

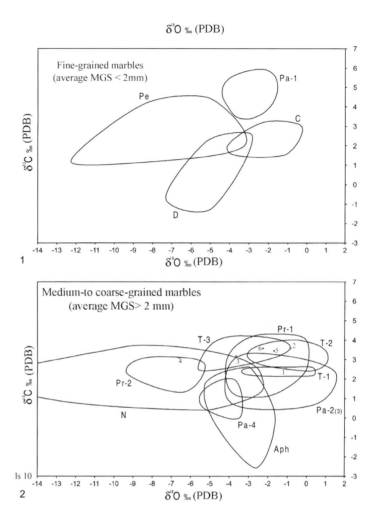

FIG. 13.12 *Position of the samples in the δ18O-δ13C reference diagram for the main Mediterranean marbles of Gorgoni et al. (2002). Legend: T: Thasos (T-1: Fanari district; T-2: Aliki district; T-3: Vathy-Saliara district); D: Docimium (Afyon); N: Naxos; Pa: Paros (Pa-1: Lychnites variety; Pa-2: Chorodaki valley; Pa-3: Aghias Minas valley); Pe: Penteli; C: Carrara; Pr, Marmara (Pr-1, main marble; Pr-2, marble from Camlik area); Aph, Aydin.*

quarries of Prokonnesos were the last to operate in the East, remaining in use into the sixth century AD (there is a good discussion of the Byzantine trade in marbles in Berlinghieri and Paribeni 2011). During the Imperial period, dolomitic marble from Thasos-3 was also commonly used for fine sculpture (Herz 1992). Therefore, this might explain the wide distribution of Prokonnesos and Thasos-3 marbles throughout Jordan. The Byzantine Christian community at Humayma/Hauarra imported the luxurious but common Prokonnesian marble at that

Table 13.3   CAS Marble samples: Description, isotope values, and probable sources.

SAMPLE NO.	CAS NO.	BUCKET NO.	LOCUS	DESCRIPTION	$\delta^{13}C$	$\delta^{18}O$	SOURCE
1	94118	1991.0317	C101.01.08	Chancel screen panel	2.280	-1.895	Denizli, Prokonnesos, or Usak
2	94119	1991.0317	C101.01.08	Chancel screen panel	3.025	-1.526	Prokonnesos
3	94120	1991.0317	C101.01.08	Chancel screen panel	3.373	-1.848	Prokonnesos or Denizli
4	94121	1992.0197	B100.E.17	Paving slab	3.590	-3.278	Thasos, Cape Vathy
5	94122	1992.0197	B100.E.17	Paving slab	3.521	-3.508	Thasos, Cape Vathy
6	94123	1993.0266	C101.04.28	Chancel screen panel	2.497	-2.326	Denizli, Prokonnesos, or Usak
7	94124	no number	Surface find	Chancel screen panel	1.489	-2.230	Aphrodesias, Ephesus, or Mylasa
8	94125	no number	Surface find	Chancel screen panel	2.876	-1.756	Prokonnesos

time for the construction of their churches. The use of imported marbles and the ample number of churches at the site underline the prosperity of Hauarra during the Byzantine period.

13.A.10. A Second Look at the Provenance Determination of the Marble Used at Humayma
(N. Herz, edited by J.P. Oleson)

During August 1994, Norman Herz (University of Georgia), at the request of J.P. Oleson, analyzed eight samples of marble from chancel screens found at Humayma, using stable isotopic ratio analysis (Table 13.3). Although these analyses were carried out 17 years before those of al-Bashaireh, and with a narrower range of methods, the results agree quite closely. Prokonnesos, Thasos, and Naxos are identified as likely sources for the marble, along with an as yet unidentified inland quarry in Anatolia. The analyses were carried out at 50° C, and the results were reported for 25° C, relative to the international PDB standard in parts per mil. CAS indicates Center for Archaeological Services.

The analyses were run through the SPSS (Statistical Package for the Social Sciences) Cluster Program to see which samples should be associated, suggesting a similar provenance. The results of that analysis allow the associations provided in Table 13.4.

The lower the correlation value, the stronger the association. Comparing the results of analysis to the samples in the Classical Quarry Marble Data suggested the following possibilities as sources. Samples no. 4 and 5 (B100) appear to be from Thasos, the quarries at Cape Vathy. They were found to have a high dolomite content, characteristic of marbles from Vathy. To judge from isotopes, Samples no. 2 and 8 (from C101 and surface find) can come from either Prokonnesos or the Carrara classical quarries. Judging from their medium grain size, Prokonnesos may be the better choice. Samples no. 1 and 6 (C101) unfortunately have isotopic values that are not definitive of any one quarry. Most probably they are both from a quarry in Anatolia, with Denizli, Prokonnesos, and Uşak as possibilities. Sample no. 3 (C101) may come from Prokonnesos, although Denizli is also a possibility.

Table 13.4   Correlation coefficients among the CAS marble samples.

CAS NO.	CORRELATION COEFFICIENT
94121 and 94122	0.0577
94119 and 94125	0.0751
94118 and 94123	0.23285
94119/94125 and 94120	0.2401

Sample no. 7 (surface find) is from an Anatolian quarry: Aphrodisias, Ephesus, or Mylasa. Because small fragments were used for the analysis, and the single excavation buckets contained fragments later assigned to a number of panels, attribution to a precise panel is not possible. Samples 1–3 may have belonged to Panels 1, 2, 6, 7, or 10, while Samples 6–8 may have belonged to panels 1, 2, 4, 8, or 10.

In making these assignments of provenance, it must be remembered that no marble quarries from Syria, Israel, or Jordan are included in the database. As far as is known, there were no commercial quarries in that area in classical or post-classical times. The geology makes it unlikely that there were any good local sources available.

13.B. INSCRIPTIONS ON STONE (OTHER THAN ECCLESIASTICAL MARBLE)
(D.F. Graf, G.D. Rowe)

13.B.1. Introduction and Analysis

Only a small number of inscriptions on stone have been found at Humayma, in Nabataean, Latin, and Greek (cf. Oleson, Reeves, Fisher 2002; Oleson et al. 2003: 55; Bevan and Reeves 2010). With one possible exception (*HEP* 1: 336–37), the Nabataean inscriptions on blocks found at or near Humayma have all been funerary in character; there are, however, Nabataean graffiti carved on the bedrock near the betyl niche above Cistern no. 48 south of the site (*HEP* 1: 53) and occasionally on rock faces west and south of the settlement (Reeves 2012). All but one of the Latin inscriptions on stone are public in character, while Greek inscriptions have been found on altars, three tomb steles, and on chancel screens in C101. The chancel screen inscription (C101 Panel 8) is published above, with the ecclesiastical marble (p. 460). It is possible that many more inscriptions once existed, painted directly on blocks of the local sandstone or on their plastered surfaces, but these have now long been lost to weathering. This explanation for the small number of inscriptions has been suggested for Petra as well (Healey 2001: 52). A few painted and incised graffiti in Greek have been found in the Roman Fort and *vicus,* which one would expect to be centres of literacy, while the absence of graffiti from the churches is surprising. Perhaps they were painted and scratched on the interior wall plaster, which has for the most part fallen away and been lost.

13.B.2. Catalogue

1. (1993.0254.01; fig. 13.13.1) A117.T7.00. (D.F. Graf). Inscribed headstone found on surface while cleaning out the tomb shaft. MPL 0.215 m, MPW 0.18 m, Th 0.04 m. It is not clear why the only four inscribed tomb headstones found at Hawara should have all turned up in and around one tomb shaft (A117; nos. 1–4 here). The communal character of the organization of graves around a central shaft or court may have fostered the use of inscribed headstones to identify the individuals interred, while the fact that there were 11 graves in the complex may have increased the odds of survival of inscriptions cut into easily weathered sandstone. The appearance of inscriptions in both Nabataean and Greek, however, may suggest some disparity in origin. The ancient or modern tomb robbers in this part of the necropolis may have tossed "interesting" inscribed slabs in one place, or the simple fact that they had to remove more soil from the central shaft, and the consequent heap of soil around the edges provided the inscribed slabs with the protection from the elements that was lacking elsewhere around the necropolis. The rarity of inscriptions around the whole site of Humayma probably reflects more the use of soft, easily weathered sandstone for inscribing, and of painted inscriptions, than a low level of literacy.

The stone was carved from a natural slab of the local white Disi sandstone; only a portion of the

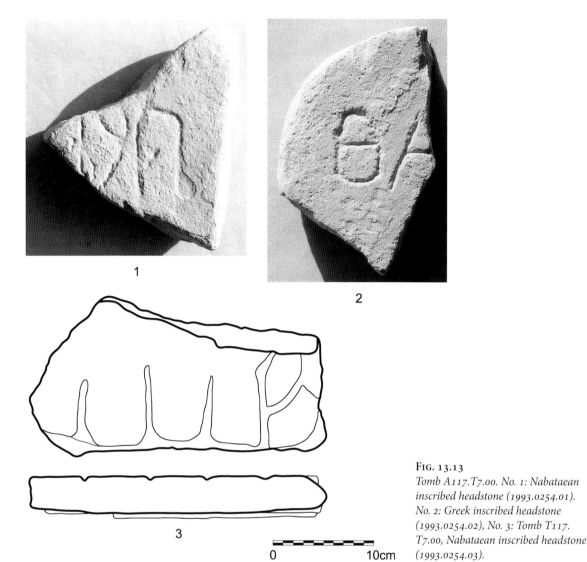

FIG. 13.13
Tomb A117.T7.00. No. 1: Nabataean
inscribed headstone (1993.0254.01).
No. 2: Greek inscribed headstone
(1993.0254.02), No. 3: Tomb T117.
T7.00, Nabataean inscribed headstone
(1993.0254.03).

original right vertical edge survives. Four letters of the epitaph are clear: they read [..]*w' br* [....], "(…) *w*' son of…". The patronym is completely missing. It can be proposed that the initial name should be restored as [*gd*]*w' br* [....]. The name *gdw'* appears only once (Cantineau 1932: 76; Negev 1991: no, 212), but the name *gdw* ("good luck," derived from the name of the divinity *GD,* the Semitic "fortune deity," i.e., "Tyche") is fairly common (al-Khraysheh 1986: 52; Negev 1991: no. 211) and is well-attested in Epigraphic North Arabian (Harding 1971: 154; Safaitic frequently and occasionally in Thamudic). In Palmyrene, it appears as *gdy* (Stark 1971: 81, "divine name used as personal name"). It corresponds to Greek Γάδδος, Γάδος, or Γάδους, frequent in the

Hawran of Syria (Wuthnow 1930: 38). The palaeography of the text suggests a date after 50 AD.

2. (1993.0254.02; fig. 13.13.2). T117.T7. (D.F. Graf). Inscribed headstone found on surface while cleaning out the tomb shaft. MPL 0.23 m, MPW 0.15 m, Th 0.052 m. The stone was carved from a natural slab of the local white Disi sandstone, with dark specks; broken, incomplete; only one original edge survives, approximately one-third of the left side and curving top of the stele. Of the Greek inscription, only two letters survive (H 0.07 m):] ΘΑ…[. Estimating the original width of the stele from the curve of the top, it is possible that 3 or 4 more letters have been lost. The most attractive possibility for filling the lacuna is that ΘΑ- repre-

4

5

FIG. 13.14 *No. 4: Tomb A117.T7.00, Nabataean inscribed headstone (1993.0254.04). No. 5: B126 Church,*
Latin inscribed headstone (2009.0010.01).

sents the first two letters of the name ΘΑ[ΙΜΟΣ], which appears twice at Dura-Europos (Frye et al. 1955: 168, no. 80) and numerous times in the Hawran of Southern Syria (Wuthnow 1930: 52–53; see also ΘΑΙΜΗΣ, but less frequent). It is the Greek version of the Nabataean Aramaic name *tymw*, "servant," which appears throughout the Nabataean kingdom (Cantineau 1932: 155; Negev 1991: no. 1218). It is also a frequent initial component of theophoric (e.g., *tym-dwšr'*, "servant of Dushara") and "basileophoric" names (*tymy-'bdt*, "servant of Obodat;" see Cantineau 1932: 1956, Negev 1991: no. 1224). This makes it possible that ΘΑ[ΙΜΟΣ] is just the initial part of a theophoric name, such as *Taimdusharos*, "servant of [the god] Dushares" (see Wuthnow 1930: 52). There does not seem to be sufficient space above this line for another line of text of the same height, otherwise it could represent the word ἐν[θά]δε — "Here [lies]" — a very common expression in Greek funerary epitaphs in Arabia, including southern Jordan, and often the initial words. For examples, see Sartre 1993: nos. 63 and 67 (Petra), 100 (Khirbet Dharih), 108 (Wadi Arabah). See also Canova 1954: *passim,* esp. nos. 80–81 from Kerak, in which the initial syllable EN- appears in the first line, framing a cross, and the second line begins with -ΘΑΔΕ.... Many of the tomb stelai at Kerak have the same rounded upper shape as this one, and the same general style of lettering. There does not, however, appear to be room for an E and N at the top of the stele.

3. (1993.0254.03; fig. 13.13.3). A117.T7. (D.F. Graf). Inscribed headstone found in the baulk while cleaning out the tomb shaft. MPL 0.24 m, MPW 0.12 m, Th 0.035 m. The stone was carved from a natural slab of the local white Disi sandstone with dark specks; only a portion of the left side of the curving upper termination of the stele may survive, with several letters of a Nabataean inscription. There seems to be a *br* ("son of") to the lower right, followed by several vertical strokes, but nothing else is intelligible.

4. (1993.0254.04; fig. 13.14.4). T117.T7. (D.F. Graf). Fragment of inscribed headstone found in the baulk while cleaning out the tomb shaft. MPL 0.245 m, MPW 0.12 m, Th 0.024 m. The original width was approximately 0.27 m. The stone was carved from a natural slab of the local white sand-

stone with dark specks; only a portion of the curving top of the stele survives, with several letters of a Nabataean inscription preserving the first line with the exception of the first letter to the right, which seems to be completely lost. The visible letters read clearly [...]*hnw š*[..] and I would propose the line should be restored [*k*]*hnw š*[*lm*], "Khnw, Peace!". The personal name is known just once (Cantineau 1932: 106, *CIS* 1358 from the Sinai), but the name *'l-khnw* appears seven times also from the Sinai (Negev 1991: no. 553) and means the "diviner, or priest." The problem with this proposal is that in the space for the missing first letter of the name, there are several lines at 45 degrees, which do not appear to represent a *k*, but the surface of the stone is damaged on the right side and the marks may be secondary.

5. (2009.0010.01; fig. 13.14.5) B126.01.00 (G.D. Rowe). Inscribed sandstone slab, found within the modern barn deposits above the flagstone pavement in the apse of the Church at B126. L 0.33 m, W 0.31 m, Th 0.045 m. Latin is very unusual in the East this late and normally a product of the Roman military or civilian administration. For Humayma it is probably the former. The three partially preserved lines read:

1. *(v)* MONO
2. MENTVṂ
3. DOM·VX

mono/mentum / Dom(itiae) ux(ori)

"tomb for my wife Domitia"

The letter-forms — especially the *M* — reflect the influence of cursive (cf. e.g., *IGLS* 13.1 [Bostra], nos. 9179 and 9190). In line 1 the first letter is offset to the right. In line 2 the final *M* would be illegible without the context. In line 3 an interpunct separates *DOM* from *VX* and the final *X* is damaged but certain.

The stone is broken along all four sides, and the crucial question is whether text is missing, especially to the right. On balance it is preferable to think that the inscription is substantially intact along the top, left, and right, principally because it is easier to take *mono/mentum* as single word than to find separate words appropriate to the context beginning with *mono-* and ending with *-mentum*

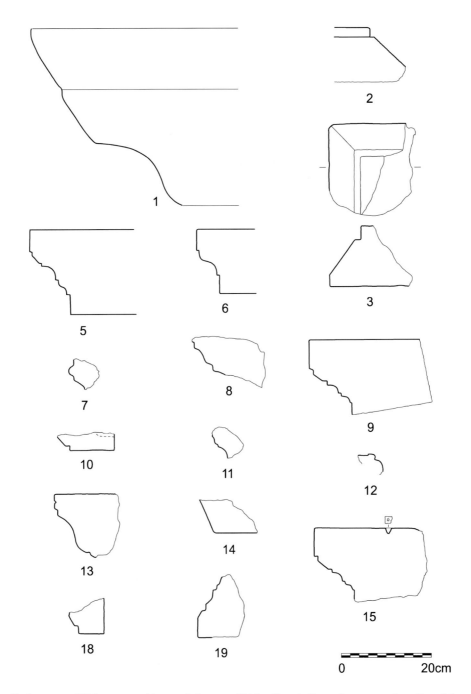

Fig. 13.15 *Profile drawings of Nabataean architectural elements. Thicker lines indicate the preserved portion of the moulding. No. 1: Column capital, sandstone (1992.0620.01); random surface find 150 m west of Reservoir no. 67. No. 2: Pilaster base of sandstone (1992.0621.01); random find in surface rubble 30 m west of Reservoir no. 67. No. 3: Pilaster base or capital of sandstone (1992.0586.01); C101.01.53. No. 5: Moulding of Ma'an limestone (1991.0286.02); F102.01.29. No. 6: Pilaster capital of Ma'an limestone (1991.0185.01); F102.04.01. No. 7: Base moulding of Ma'an limestone (1991.0356.02); B100.01.05. No. 8: Moulding of Ma'an limestone (1993.0183.02); B100.01.11. No. 9: Cornice moulding of Ma'an limestone (1991.0001.01); B100.02.00. No. 10: Moulding of Ma'an limestone (1991.0066.02); B100.E.03. No. 11: Moulding of Ma'an limestone (1991.0070.01); B100.E.03. No. 12: Moulding of Ma'an limestone (1993.0206.01); B100.19 P02.06. No. 13: Moulding of Ma'an limestone (1991.0442.01); B100.E.11. No. 14: Base or capital for a half column, cut in Ma'an limestone (1992.0197.03); B100.E.17. No. 15: Cornice moulding of Ma'an limestone (1992.0279.02); B100.E.21. No. 18: Moulding cut in Ma'an limestone (1992.0227.01); B100.G.05. No. 19: Pilaster base of Umm Ishrin sandstone (1991.0400.01); B100.H.05.*

(*monumentum, testamentum*). For the spelling *monomentum* cf. *AE* 1961, 0015 (≈ HD017707; Cormasa, Boğaziçi, Turkey): *C(aius) Iulius C(ai) f(ilius) Papi/ria natus Cormasa / missicius leci(o) nis(!) / VII eques mono/mentum(!) fecit / sibi et Iulio Iu/cundo liberto / suo.* The abbreviation *ux(or)* is rare but attested (Elliott 1998). On this reading *MONO* in line 1 was centred on the original stone, with approximately two-thirds of an em-space to either side.

The usual developed form of epitaphs with the word *monumentum* is *ille monumentum fecit* (or *posuit*) *sibi et illi,* as in the example from Cormasa above. Here we might imagine *monumentum illi* followed by [*ille fecit*]. Also possible might be *monumentum illius,* on the analogy of the principally Christian form *memoria illius,* though this is unattested.

This is the first private Latin inscription from Humayma (Hauarra). Four small fragments of sandstone tomb markers with pecked inscriptions (3 Nabataean, 1 Greek) are reported on above. Latin is attested at the site only in a barely-legible statue base (?) possibly naming a legate of Legio VI Ferrata, and in an altar dedicated to Jupiter Ammon by a vexillation or *vexillarii* of Legio III Cyrenaica (Oleson et al. 2002 nos. 3 and 4). This inscription is also to be associated with the Roman fort, and is best understood as a gravestone erected by Roman soldier for his peregrine common-law wife, who has taken a name of Roman inspiration, either Domitia or Domitiana (on soldiers' marriages, see Phang 2001).

13.C. ARCHITECTURAL ELEMENTS AND MOULDINGS (J.P. Oleson)

13.C.1. Introduction and Analysis

There are occasional weathered and damaged architectural elements on the surface around the site of Humayma, most of them fragments of columns, bases, and capitals of typical Nabataean design, cut in local Umm Ishrin or Disi sandstone or Ma'an shelly limestone. Several of these are recorded here, along with architectural elements and mouldings encountered in the excavation of the fields published in this volume. Many more Nabataean

architectural elements were encountered in re-use in the Roman Fort (E116), and they will be published with that structure. A significant number of smaller, more carefully cut mouldings executed in the characteristic shelly limestone still quarried around Ma'an, all fragmentary, were found during excavation of the church structures. These were never found re-used as architectural members, but as tumble in the fill within the structures. Out of the 18 fragments recorded here, 12 were found in B100, suggesting once again the presence nearby of a major Nabataean public structure, probably a temple, destroyed or dismantled during the Roman or Byzantine period.

The mouldings all show typical Nabataean motifs, as seen in rock-cut tombs at Petra and mouldings from freestanding architectural monuments here and elsewhere in the Nabataean realm, particularly Oboda and Mampsis. The most comprehensive collection of moulding profiles is found in McKenzie 1990. The mouldings from Hawara use the same collection of profile elements, except for projecting Hellenic entablatures, but frequently in an atypical order. Because of the absence of significant comparative material, it is not yet clear whether variation in the elements of the more elaborate non-Greek mouldings is typical of the work of Nabataean stone-cutters.

13.C.2. Catalogue

Random surface finds

1. (1992.0620.01; fig. 13.15.1). Random surface find 150 m west of Reservoir no. 67. Column capital of local Umm Ishrin red sandstone; broken, incomplete; MPL 0.50 m, MPW 0.45 m, MPH 0.36 m. Approximately two-thirds of a sandstone column capital; the upper and lower surfaces are badly damaged, but the circular outline of the column can be seen, with an outer diameter of approximately 0.40. Beginning from the narrower side, there is a cavetto moulding and two flat fasciae separated by a groove, forming an echinus set at an angle of approximately 55 degrees. This stone was recorded and left *in situ*. The shape is typically Nabataean; cf. Negev 1997: 27.v (Oboda); part of McKenzie 1990: pl. 50.b–c (Petra).

2. (1992.0621.01; fig. 13.15.2). Random find in surface rubble 30 m west of Reservoir no. 67. Pilaster base of the local Umm Ishrin red sandstone; MPL 0.72 m, MPW 0.64 m, Th 0.122 m. The upper and lower surfaces have been finished smoothly. The one surviving original edge carries a low fascia (H 0.02) above an offset and a smooth sloping face at an angle of 43 degrees. There probably was another fascia (H 0.035) directly below. This stone was recorded and left *in situ*. The shape is typically Nabataean; cf. Negev 1997: 27.xb–xc (Oboda).

C101 (Byzantine Church)

3. (1992.0586.01; fig. 13.15.3). C101.01.53. Pilaster base or capital of white Disi sandstone with brown specks; broken, incomplete, one corner preserved MPL 0.19 m, MPH 0.18 m, Th 0.13 m. The wider (bottom?) surface has been smoothed with a chisel and point; the upper surface is slightly smoother. The moulding consists of a fascia (H 0.026 m) below a flat surface at a 55-degree slope, below an inset and another fascia (H 0.03). The shape is typically Nabataean; cf. Negev 1997: 27.xb–xc (Oboda).

B126 (Byzantine Church)

4. (2009.0039.01). B126.01.16. Small fragment of a pilaster base carved from Ma'an limestone; broken incomplete; W 0.057 m, MPH 0.10 m. A small portion survives of the flat surface on either side of a torus; cf. McKenzie 1990: pl. 50.k. The block, found in the soil around the reliquary, is clearly rubble surviving from a Nabataean structure.

F102 (Byzantine Church and Early Islamic House)

5. (1991.0286.02; figs. 13.15.5, 13.16.5). F102.01.29. Fragment of moulding of Ma'an limestone; broken, incomplete; MPL 0.50 m, MPW 0.32 m, H 0.185 m. The base has been roughly finished with a point, somewhat more finely worked for 0.05 m in from the edge. The top surface is smooth. Along the two original sides and back there is a drafted edge for 0.04 m in from the front, worked very smooth, surrounding a recessed area only finished with a point. From top to bottom the mouldings consist

of a vertical fascia (H 0.047 m), a fascia (at an angle of ca. 45 degrees) set off by two grooves, a cavetto, a cyma reversa, and a vertical fascia (H 0.044 m). The individual motifs are all common in Nabataean structures, but the arrangement is odd here, and the cavetto is an atypical addition to the sequence. Cf. McKenzie 1990: 191; Negev 1997: fig. 27.v, vii.

6. (1991.0185.01; figs. 13.15.6, 13.16.6). F102.04.01. Pilaster capital of Ma'an limestone; broken, incomplete; MPL 0.44 m, MPW 0.255 m, H 0.138 m. The wider, top face of the block has been finished to a very smooth surface and polished; the lower surface has been carefully finished with a point. Two finished sides with mouldings have been preserved, meeting at a corner. The mouldings consist of a fascia (H 0.045 m) below a cyma reversa (H 0.052 m), below another fascia (H 0.04 m). The portion of the block opposite the finished, moulded corner has been cut carefully with a point to a flat surface, inset 0.004 m from the adjacent broken portion of the block. The shape is typically Nabataean; cf. Negev 1997: 27.viiia (Oboda); McKenzie 1990: pl. 38.a (lower entablature), 38.b (lower entablature) (Petra).

B100 (Byzantine Church and Early Islamic House)

7. (1991.0356.02; fig. 13.15.7). B100.01.05. Small fragment of base moulding cut in Ma'an limestone; broken, incomplete. Length of curved moulding face is 0.07 m, H 0.06 m. All the other surfaces of the block are broken. Probably from a base similar to McKenzie 1990: pl. 50.e–h, j–k (Petra).

8. (1993.0183.02; fig. 13.15.8). B100.01.11. Small fragment of moulding; Ma'an limestone. Width of moulding 0.11 m; block MPL 0.14 m, MPH 0.06 m. Squared astragal, cyma recta, squared astragal. Common Nabataean moulding; cf. portions of McKenzie 1990: pl. 38.a–h.

9. (1991.0001.01; figs. 13.15.9, 13.16.9). B100.02.00. Cornice moulding; Ma'an limestone. Broken on all but the top and front surfaces, which are smoothly finished; MPL 0.245 m, MPW 0.16m, MPH 0.17 m. Assuming a projecting crowning moulding, from top to bottom the profile consists of a high vertical fascia (H 0.065 m), a back sloping fascia (at an angle of approximately 35 degrees) set off above and below by grooves, two cavettos separated by offsets,

FIG. 13.16 *Nabataean architectural elements. No. 5: Moulding of Ma'an limestone (1991.0286.02); F102.01.29. No. 6: Pilaster capital of Ma'an limestone (1991.0185.01); F102.04.01. No. 9: Cornice moulding of in Ma'an limestone (1991.0001.01); B100.02.00. No. 13: Moulding of Ma'an limestone (1991.0442.01); B100.E.11. No. 17: Pilaster base or capital cut in Umm Ishrin sandstone (1992.0622.01); B100.E.16/27.*

and a vertical fascia (H 0.023 m), First observed on the surface at B100 in 1983; re-examined 1987; accessioned 1991. I have not found precise published parallels; it is odd to have the sloping fascia above two cavettos; cf. no. 15.

10. (1991.0066.02; fig. 13.15.10). B100.E.03. Fragment of moulding; Maʻan limestone; broken, incomplete. The bottom and part of the back surfaces of the block (W 0.08 m, H 0.02 m) are preserved, along with a portion of moulding 0.13 m wide. The surviving profile, an inward sloping fascia above a squared astragal, is close to portions of the 91.0001.01 and 92.0279.01 mouldings, but the fit is not precise. A circular hole (D 0.01 m) has been drilled 0.025 m into the back of the block, perhaps for a clamp. Cf. Negev 1997: fig. 27.7 (Oboda); common as part of the sequences in McKenzie 1990: pls. 28–50 (Petra).

11. (1991.0070.01; fig. 13.15.11). B100.E.03. Small fragment of moulding; Maʻan limestone; broken, incomplete; MPL 0.075 m, MPW 0.045 m, MPH 0.032 m. Squared astragal above a cyma recta, and cavetto.

12. (1993.0206.01; fig. 13.15.12). B100.19 P02.06. Small fragment of moulding; Maʻan limestone; broken, incomplete. Width of moulding face 0.025 m; part of a torus and ridge. The two curved front surfaces have been finished very smoothly, but the upper (?) surface, has a drafted edge around a roughly finished inset recessed 0.002 m. The other faces of the block are broken; MPL 0.09 m, MPH 0.025 m. Probably part of a base, as in McKenzie 1990: pl. 50.e–j.

13. (1991.0442.01; figs. 13.15.13, 13.16.13). B100.E.11. Fragment of moulding; Maʻan limestone; broken, incomplete; MPL 0.29 m, MPW 0.135 m; H 0.135 m. Assuming a projecting moulding, the top surface of the block is very smooth; the mounding includes two narrow, vertical fasciae above a cyma recta, above a narrow torus. There is a narrow band (W 0.02 m) of stone below the moulding that has been finished to a rough but level surface with a point.

14. (1992.0197.03; fig. 13.15.14). B100.E.17. Fragment of a base or capital for a half column; Maʻan limestone; broken, incomplete. One face of the block (MPL 0.13 m, MPH 0.072 m) preserves the original flat, smooth surface. From this surface about 30 degrees is preserved of what must have been a 180-degree half column base or capital. The curving element abuts a level, carefully smoothed face, and tapers from D ca. 0.23 m to D ca. 0.20 m. Cf. Netzer 2003: fig. 222.1 (Petra).

15. (1992.0279.02; fig. 13.15.15). B100.E.21. Fragment of a cornice moulding; Maʻan limestone; broken, incomplete; MPL 0.275 m, MPW 0.27 m, MPH 0.165 m. The block was found in secondary use supporting a marl basin. Assuming a projecting cornice, the upper surface is smooth, except for an approximately square hole (ca. 0.015 m sq.; 0.02 m deep) cut into it 0.175 m in from the front edge. There is a smaller, square recess at the bottom of the hole, suggesting it once accommodated a piece of metal hardware — a clamp or a latch — that has since been pulled out. Below the smooth surface there is a vertical fascia (H 0.065 m), a flat receding fascia, a cavetto offset by grooves, and a cyma reversa. The rest of the block is broken. This moulding is very close in dimensions and profile to 91.0286.01, from Area F102, but there are some small differences in proportions that indicate they did not originate from the same architectural feature. Cf. McKenzie 1990: pl. 34.b, lower mouldings (Palace tomb, Petra); cf. no. 1 above.

16. (1992.0280.03). B100.E.23. A small fragment of a moulding; Maʻan limestone; broken, incomplete; MPL 0.03 m, MPW 0.02 m, MPH 0.02 m.

17. (1992.0622.01; fig. 13.16.17). B100.E.16/27. Pilaster base or capital; Umm Ishrin sandstone; broken, incomplete. The original surfaces are preserved on the top, bottom, and three of the four sloping slides, but there are numerous abrasions. Assuming use as a pilaster base, above the flat base (0.21 m square) the sides slope inward at 45 degrees to an inset below the flat upper surface (0.15 m square); H 0.072 m. There is a shallow, regular circular depression in the upper surface (D 0.06 m, Depth ca. 0.03 m), added when the base was reused as a holy water basin or as a mortar. The block was found reused with the broader side up in the lowest pavement found in the Apse, probably part of the Early Islamic reoccupation of the structure. The base/capital is a typical Nabataean shape; Negev 1997: fig. 27 no. xb (Oboda); Netzer 2003: fig. 222.20 (Petra).

18. (1992.0227.01; fig. 13.15.18). B100.G.05. Fragment of moulding; Maʻan limestone; broken,

incomplete. The original surfaces are preserved on the top and back of the block (Th 0.09 m, H 0.05 m), and for a portion of the moulded face (W 0.19 m). The profile of the moulding, a sloping fascia above a short vertical fascia, is close to portions of the 91.0001.01 and 92.0279.02 mouldings, but the fit is not precise.

19. (1991.0400.01; fig. 13.15.19). B100.H.05. Fragment of a pilaster base; Umm Ishrin sandstone; broken, incomplete; MPL 0.16 m, MPW 0.08 m, MPH 0.08 m. One corner of a small, elaborately moulded column or pilaster base. The bottom surface has been smoothed for 0.02 m in from the front edges, beyond which it is trimmed more roughly with a point. The moulding begins with a fascia (H 0.025 m), above which there are two cavettos or a cavetto below a cyma recta, separated by grooves.

13.D. ALTARS AND POSSIBLE CHESS PIECE
(J.P. Oleson)

13.D.1. Introduction and Analysis

The two altars catalogued below (nos. 1–2) are the only free standing altars in the Nabataean tradition so far found at Humayma. Three altars in the Roman tradition, inscribed with Latin or Greek, were found in the Roman Fort (E116) and *vicus* (E125; Oleson et al. 2002). The possible portable altar (no. 3) is ambiguous, but given the lack of parallels for an altar or betyl of such a small size, it is more likely to have been a chess piece than a religious object. The presence of the two Nabataean altars reused in B100, along with the significant number of Nabataean architectural mouldings in shelly Ma'an limestone found reused in the structure or in the debris around it, reinforce the suggestion that there was a major Nabataean religious structure in the area (see p. 214).

13.D.2. Catalogue

1. (1991.0136.02; fig. 13.17.1). B100.E.06. Small horned altar carved out of the local Disi sandstone, with frequent dark inclusions. The surface has weathered to a pinkish cream colour; the altar base and tips of the horns have been lost (MPH 0.234

m). The body of the altar is a nearly square shaft 0.14 m. by 0.13 m, very smoothly finished, with a protruding square moulding (Th 0.03 m, projecting 0.018 m) surrounding it 0.08 m. from the top. The flat upper surface carries a shallow circular depression (depth 0.015 m) carrying the marks of a small pick or chisel. Above the moulding, each face of the block has been marked with an incised V (MPH 0.06 m; 0.065 m across the top), indicating an altar horn on each corner. The bottom of the V is 0.02–0.03 m above the top of the moulding.

A betyl found at Khirbet edh-Dharih is the same scale, but lacks the upper moulding and horns (Villeneuve and al-Muheisen 2000: 1531, fig. 5). An altar found at Khirbet Tannur is a good parallel (Glueck 1965: 510, pl. 192b). A small (H 0.096 m) ceramic altar with horns at the corners was found in a Nabataean to Early Roman context at Aqaba (Parker 2000: 379, fig. 4). On the function of Nabataean altars, see Healey 2001: 159–59, and *passim;* Patrich 1990: 92–95.

2. (1991.0402.01; figs. 13.17.2). B100.G.04. Horned altar with representation of a deity, carved from the local Disi sandstone; broken, the base and portions of the horns are missing; MPH 0.58 m, W 0.32–0.35 m, Th 0.23 m. The altar has the shape of a thick, rectangular stele, with a pair of projecting crowning mouldings (simple fasciae, projecting 0.007 m) that support a stylized "horn" at each of the four corners. The tips of these horns, now lost, once projected above the top of the altar block, framing a shallow oval basin (0.084 × 0.07 m, Depth 0.02 m) that occupies the top surface of the altar. The outline of the block above the mouldings is oval as well, with diagonal trimming marks around the sides. Thick, soft-looking fillets are represented as suspended from the horns and draped across each of the four faces of the block, thickening markedly at the bottom of the curve, just above the base of the block. No surface modelling or paint has survived to suggest what material these might be intended to represent. The fillets, which are linked to one another at the corners, stand out in relief 0.025 m above the face of the block below the mouldings. On one of the broad sides of the block (probably the front), the fillet frames a weathered oval mass carved in relief (W 0.08 m, H 0.14 m). This may possibly be the head of Tyche, since the

FIG. 13.17 *No. 1: Small Nabataean horned altar from B100.E.06. No. 7: Sandstone slab with incised cross (1993.0390.01);*
C101.04.30. No. 2a–b: Nabataean horned altar with representation of deity, from B100.G.04; front and
left side views.

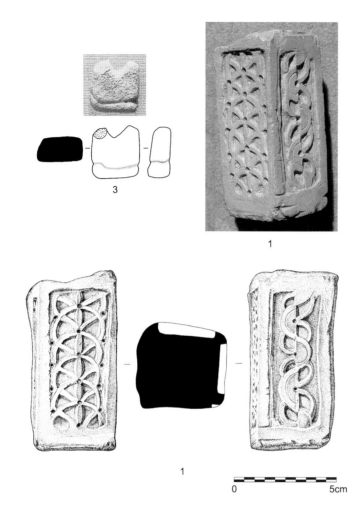

FIG. 13.18 *No. 3. Miniature sandstone altar or betyl, or a chess piece (1991.0407.01). B100.I.06. Drawing and view. No. 1. Carved basin foot (2004.0180.01). E063.00. View and drawing (B. Seymour).*

is much more elaborate (Glueck 1965: 418–20, 506–8). The pendant garlands combined with gods' heads can be seen on the Altar of Dmejr in the Louvre (Ossorio 2009: 48). For a collection of information on representations of Tyche, see Wenning 1987: 357.

3. (1991.0407.01; fig. 13.18.3). B100.I.06. Small carved sandstone object, possibly a miniature altar or betyl, or a chess piece; H 0.025 m, W 0.024 m, Th 0.011 m. Approximately rectangular in section with rounded front edges and a flat base. There is a groove just above base and a deep notch in top, which isolates two horn-like projections. The horns are reminiscent of an altar, and some graffiti at Petra show a similarly abbreviated representation, but there are no known parallels for such a small three-dimensional reproduction (R. Wenning, personal communication, November 2011). Portable but slightly larger eye idols have been found at Petra (Patrich 1990: 83). If the object is in fact a miniature altar, it should date to the Middle Nabataean period.

The object may, however, be the earliest known example of a chess piece of the abstract class, a "rook." The earliest chess pieces so far identified are an ivory set found in ancient Samarkand (Pinder-Wilson 2005: 17; *pace* Cassavoy 2006: 337), in a context of the late seventh or early eighth century. These pieces have life-like human and animal forms, but as a result of religious objections, chess pieces in the Islamic world were transformed into abstract forms early on (Murray 1913: 223–24). There are references in Arabic texts to chess-playing as early as H 23/AD 643, and the game was popular throughout the Islamic world by the end of the Umayyad caliphate (Murray 1913: 186–94). Several early abstract "rooks" from the Middle East are nearly identical to the Humayma object in design, carved in stone, wood, and ivory: Qasr al-Hayr East (wood, 870 AD ± 120; Grabar et al. 1978: vol. 1, p. 189, vol. 2, p. 291, nos. 82–83);

upper portion of the mass carries a series of upright grooves resembling the turrets of a mural crown, as seen on the Tyche relief from et-Tannur (Markoe 2003: 189, fig. 198). The details of the face have been entirely lost. There are no figured representations on the other three sides of the altar, and the back is less carefully finished than the other sides. The block was found re-used in the upper remaining course of the retaining wall at the rear of the apse. The surface is covered with a thick layer of calcium carbonate deposit, possibly in part the remains of a layer of painted and moulded stucco.

There are no particularly close parallels for this altar. The first-century altar of Alexandros Amrou at Khirbet Tannur has a generic resemblance, but

unknown provenance (ivory, 7–9C; Contadini 1995: 123, fig. 26), Nishapur (ivory, 9C; Contadini 1995: 114, fig. 4; Gordon 2009), Egypt (stone, 10C; Contadini 1995 133, fig. 43), Serçe Limani wreck (11C; Cassavoy 2006; Contadini 1995: 130, fig. 42), Egypt (?) (stone, 10–12C; Contadini 1995: 132, fig. 45), Kuwait (?) (stone, 11C; Contadini 1995: 117, fig. 10). Since the Humayma object was found in a seventh-century context, if the identification as a chess piece is correct, it would be the earliest known physical example for the simplified, abstract design, and possibly the earliest known example of a chess piece altogether. Since the game probably was carried westward from India by the movement of merchants and diplomats, it is no surprise that early evidence for it should be found at a site on the busy *Via Nova Traiana*. While resident at Humayma, the Abbasid family had kept itself abreast of events in Syria and Iraq by this same method (*HEP* 1: 61).

13.E. QUERNS (J.P. Oleson)

13.E.1. Introduction and Analysis

Every household in ancient Humayma probably possessed a rotary quern for producing flour. This was a daily task, since bread was the staple of the diet and flour does not keep well. It is consequently surprising that only 19 fragments large enough to deserve registration were recovered in the 5930 buckets recorded between 1991 and 2005; only a few unregistered fragments are noted in the bucket list. Furthermore, only one (unregistered) fragment is recorded from the Fort, although it is well-documented that Roman soldiers ground their own grain (e.g., Davies 1971: 126; Roth 1999: 44–51). Most likely, querns were salvaged or recycled to new owners until they broke, restricting their entrance into the archaeological record. Thirteen of the registered fragments were from runner (upper) stones, while six were from bedding stones; the disproportion is probably in part the result of the relatively small sample, and in part the greater difficulty in differentiating quern bedding stones from small fragments of other types of stone artefact.

The soft or sandy local stones do not seem suitable for the production of efficient querns, but examples were nevertheless recorded made of the local sandstone and marl. Six of the 15 catalogued examples were cut from a black vesicular basalt, which would have served this function much better than the other materials, but which had to be imported at greater expense. There are significant deposits of this stone in Northern Jordan, the Galilee, and the Hejaz, but no source analysis has been carried out. Many of these quern fragments were found near the surface and may derive from the early modern occupation of the site. Until recently, basalt querns were commonly used in the rural areas of Jordan. It is not clear where the sandy limestone used for a number of the querns was obtained.

Of the catalogued quern fragments, 15 came from F102 and four from B100, reflecting the later use of these structures for habitation; only a few small fragments of basalt querns were recorded from the C101, C119, or B126 church structures. It would be difficult to recognize small quern fragments cut in other stones.

13.E.2. Catalogue

F102 (Byzantine Church and Early Islamic House)

1. (1991.0011.01). F102.00.00. Bedding stone for a quern, cut from a black, vesicular basalt; broken, incomplete; MPL 0.09 m, MPW 0.06 m, Th 0.0962 m; original D undetermined. There is no slope to the outer surface, suggesting this is the bedding stone. Cf. 91.0216.01.

2. (1991.0106.01). F102.01.12. Bedding stone for a quern, cut from a black, vesicular basalt; broken, incomplete; MPL 0.08, MPW 0.07, Th 0.06; original D undetermined. There is no slope to the outer surface, suggesting this is the bedding stone. Cf. 91.0216.01.

3. (1991.0216.03). F102.01.12.2. Bedding stone for a quern, cut from black vesicular basalt; broken, incomplete; MPL 0.09 m, MPW 0.08 m, Th 0.06 m, original D ca. 0.35–0.40 m. There is no slope to the outer surface, suggesting this is the bedding stone.

4. (1991.0299.02). F102.01.18. Bedding stone for a quern, cut from a black, vesicular basalt; broken, incomplete; MPL 0.03 m, MPW 0.03 m, Th 0.035 m, D undetermined. There is no slope to the outer surface, suggesting this is the bedding stone. Cf. 1991.0216.01.

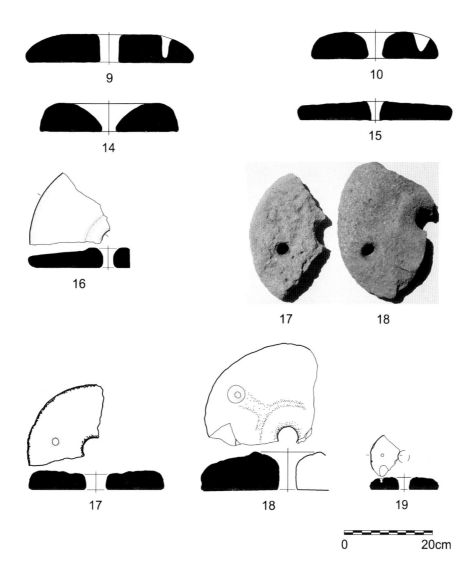

FIG. 13.19 *No. 9: Upper stone of a quern (1991.0302.02); F102.03.20. No. 10: Upper stone of a quern (1991.0029.01); F102.04.01. No. 14: Upper stone of a quern (1995.0072); F102.14.01. No. 15: Upper stone of a quern (1995.0148.02); F102.17.02. No. 16: Upper stone of a quern (1991.0459.01); B100.06.00. No. 17: Upper stone of a quern (1991.0435.01); B100.06.00. No. 18: Upper stone of a quern (1992.0119.01); B100.22.08. No. 19: Upper stone of a quern (1992.0052.02); B100.E.04.*

5. (1991.0299.03). F102.01.18. Runner stone for a quern, carved from a very coarse grained yellow limestone with numerous voids; broken, incomplete; MPL 0.12 m, MPW 0.10 m, Th 0.04 m; original D > 0.24 m.

6. (1991.0365.01). F102.01.30. Runner stone for a quern made of white Disi sandstone; broken, incomplete; MPL 0.12 m, MPW 0.12 m, Th 0.09 m; original D greater than 0.24 m; central hole D ca.

0.018 m. Disi sandstone seems like a poor material for a quern, since it would leave the flour sandy.

7. (1992.0073.01). F102.02.05. Runner stone for a quern, cut from a very rough-grained, light, sandy limestone; broken, incomplete; MPL 0.25, Th 0.10; original D ca. 0.32. Central hole D 0.03; hole for handle, D 0.025. The grinding face is smooth.

8. (1991.0187.01). F102.03.12. Runner stone for a quern, cut from a hard, sandy yellow limestone

with numerous voids; broken, incomplete; original D greater than 0.30, Th 0.06, crank socket D 0.03 m.

9. (1991.0302.02; fig. 13.19.9). F102.03.20. Runner stone for a quern, cut from a hard, very coarse-grained yellow limestone with numerous voids; broken, incomplete; MPL 0.32 m, MPW 0.16 m, Th 0.07 m, D 0.32 m, central pivot hole D 0.035 m, vertical crank socket D 0.02 m. Very similar to the following two stones.

10. (1991.0029.01; fig. 13.19.10). F102.04.01. Runner stone for a quern, cut from a hard, very coarse-grained yellow limestone with numerous voids; broken, incomplete; MPL 0.24 m, MPW 0.15 m, Th 0.06 m; original D 0.30 m; central pivot hole D 0.03 m; vertical crank socket D 0.04 m.

11. (1991.0029.02). F102.04.01. Runner stone for a quern, cut from a hard, very coarse-grained yellow limestone with numerous voids; broken, incomplete; MPL 0.24 m, MPW 0.15 m, Th 0.06 m; original D ca. 0.30 m;

12. (1992.0095.02). F102.05.14. Bedding stone for a quern, cut from black, vesicular basalt; broken, incomplete; MPL 0.24 m, MPW 0.08 m, Th 0.035 m; original D ca. 0.35–0.40 m. There is no slope to the outer surface, suggesting this is the bedding stone. There is a slight lip around the edge. Cf. 91.0216.01.

13. (1993.0211). F102.09.01. Bedding stone (?) for a quern, cut from black, vesicular basalt; broken, incomplete; MPL 0.09 m, MPW 0.08 m, Th 0.028 m; original D ca. 0.35–0.40 m. Both sides are flat, suggesting this is a bedding stone.

14. (1995.0072; fig. 13.19.14). F102.14.01. Runner stone for a quern, cut from a hard, sandy yellow limestone; broken, incomplete; MPL 0.14 m, MPW 0.13 m, Th 0.06 m; original D ca. 0.31 m. No handle hole preserved.

15. (1995.0148.02; fig. 13.19.15). F102.17.02. Runner stone for a quern, cut from a hard, sandy yellow limestone; incomplete, part of one edge lost; D 0.34 m, Th 0.05 m, pivot hole D 0.027–0.04 m. No handle hole preserved. There is a slight ridge around the bottom end of the pivot hole, possibly produced by wear. The stone was cut from a natural slab of limestone and is thicker on one side (Th 0.045 m) than on the other (Th 0.03 m). This stone is thinner than the others found at F102 and more carefully shaped; perhaps it is recent in date.

B100 (Byzantine Church and Early Islamic House)

16. (1991.0459.01; fig. 13.19.16). B100.06.00. Quern runner stone carved from a very hard, fine-grained pink sandstone; broken, incomplete; original D 0.37 m; MPL 0.17 m, MPW 0.016 m, Th 0.032–0.045 m. The lower surface is flat and very smooth; the stone thickens gradually to a marked reinforcement ring surrounding the pivot hole. Soft sandstone seems a poor choice for a quern, but there are parallels at Humayma and other sites in the region.

17. (1991.0435.01; fig. 13.19.17). B100.06.00. Quern runner stone carved from a hard, light yellow limestone with numerous voids; broken, incomplete; original D ca. 0.30 m, MPW 0.18 m, Th 0.45 m, central spindle hole D 0.055 m. Hole in upper surface for upright turning handle, D 0.025 m, 0.02 m deep. There is also a radial inset for a turning bar or frame to support the rynd.

18. (1992.0119.01; fig. 13.19.18). B100.22.08. Quern runner stone cut from black, vesicular basalt; broken, incomplete; D 0.39 m, Th 0.07 m. The central spindle hole (D 0.047 m) is surrounded by a low ridge (W 0.03 m) meant to cup the grain being fed through the spindle hole. There is a hole (D 0.03 m) for a vertical handle toward the periphery.

19. (1992.0052.02; fig. 13.19.19). B100.E.04. Quern runner stone, carved from soft yellow marl; broken, incomplete; MPL 0.10 m, MPW 0.07 m, Th 0.032 m, D 0.16 m. Central spindle hole D 0.025 m. There is a hole (D 0.008 m) for a vertical handle toward the periphery. The impractical dimensions of this quern and the use of the very soft, small grained marl as a material suggests this is a toy. Marl would be an appropriate choice for a toy rather than basalt or limestone because it was easier to carve and the grain allowed fine detail at the small scale. The bottom, grinding surface is polished smooth.

13.F. MISCELLANEOUS STONE OBJECTS
(J.P. Oleson)

13.F.1. Introduction and Analysis

This category contains a very mixed bag of material. The Campground (C124) and Necropolis produced only a few stone or faience beads, the Aqueduct

Pool (E063) an elaborately decorated marl basin foot that probably came from the Abbasid Manor House (F103). The fragment of a large alabaster vessel, the stone slab with an engraved cross, and the small plaque of Africano marble in C101 may all have been furnishings in the Church, while the beads and possible loom weight may stem from the period of later occupation. There are some interesting parallels between F102 and B100 in the miscellaneous stone artefacts, and they all probably belong to the period of later occupation. The F102 structure yielded two door sockets, a scoria polishing stone, six hammer stones, perforated weights (loom weights?), a spindle whorl, mortar, basin, three beads, and a fragment of an alabaster cup. The B100 structure yielded one socket stone, a pestle, a scoria polisher, and three beads. The numerous querns catalogued above round out the picture of two rural residences, probably agricultural in character.

13.F.2. Catalogue

E063 (Nabataean pool at end of aqueduct)

1. (2004.0180.01; fig. 13.18.1). E063.00. Rectangular foot of a low stone table or basin, carved in yellow marl; broken, basin lost; MPH 0.085 m, W 0.042 × 0.039 m. The object was discovered in the wind and rain-deposited silt within the Nabataean pool at the end of the aqueduct (*HEP* 1: 181–87) when that structure was cleared by the Department of Antiquities in 2003. This object should have been included in *HEP* 1: 337, but was omitted in error. The basin was probably square or rectangular in shape, since only two sides of the leg have been carved with decoration. A rectangular panel occupies most of each of two adjacent sides and is occupied by decoration carved in low relief. The decoration was produced by inscribing concentric and intersecting circles, starting from small holes (D 0.002) drilled deep into the stone, then chiselling out some of the outlined shapes. One panel has been finished, but the other appears not to have been fully carved, perhaps because of a mistake in setting out the design. A similar motif and technique appears on a marl stone object found in the Abbasid family manor house (F103; 2002.0237.01; Oleson et al.

2003: 58), which would be a logical point of origin for this object as well. The decoration, too, appears to put the object in the seventh or eighth century. Decorated feet from four circular tripod tables or mortars have been found in the earlier levels of the vicus area at Humayma (E125). carved in sandstone or basalt. The decoration, however, consisted of simple patterns of parallel lines, similar to that on basalt footed mortars of the Byzantine period at En-Gedi (Chernov 2007: 549–52).

I have not found precise parallels for these objects, but a similar use of holes, compass-drawn curves, and cut-backs from a flat surface are seen on an inscribed tombstone in Cairo dated H 220/ AD 857 (O'Kane 2006: 44–45, no. 36), on a ninth-century stone plaque with abstract motifs and stylized vine leaves from Samarra (Ettinghausen and Grabar 1987: 103, fig. 78), and on an eighth-century bone panel from Syria or Egypt that is very similar to the Samarra panel (Hillenbrand 2005: 63, fig. 37).

C124 (Nabataean Campground)

2. (1996.0044). C124.04.01. Polished, teardrop-shaped pebble of a translucent orange/brown stone. Indentations on opposite sides may be the result of an attempt at drilling a perforation. If so, this is unique documentation of stone bead manufacture at Humayma. D 0.014 × 0.010 m. 2 g.

A104.T1 (Necropolis)

3. (1992.0168.01). A104.T1.00; surface spoil around shaft. Glass bead, very dark blue with a horizontal white stripe; D 0.012 m, hole D 0.005 m.

4. (1992.0168.02). A104.T1.00; surface spoil around shaft. Small, irregular bead made from a white quartz pebble; L 0.014 m, W 0.01 m, Th 0.006–0.004 m, perforation D 0.003 m. Two sides of the pebble were abraded to a smooth surface, which was then perforated for suspension.

C101 (Byzantine Church)

5. (1991.0276). C101.01.07. Minute, doughnut-shaped bead of a bright green translucent stone. D 0.004 m, Th 0.002 m. The colour would suggest glass, but the surface remains shiny and unblem-

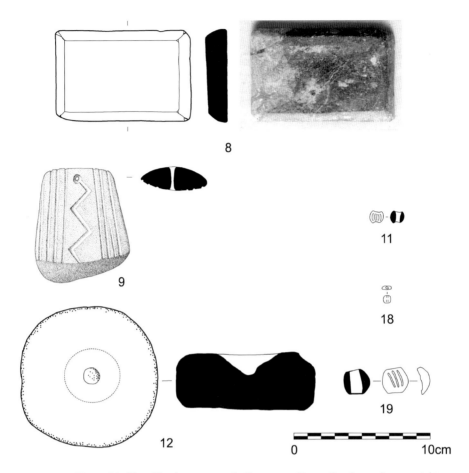

FIG. 13.20 *No. 8. Marble tablet (1992.0184.01). C101.05.03. No. 9. Sandstone loom weight (1992.0333.01). C101.03.19 (B. Seymour). No. 11. Faïence melon bead (1993.0157.02). C101.06.12. No. 12. Stone door socket (1991.0346.01). F102.03.02.01. No. 18. Discoidal faience bead. (1992.0307.01). F102.01.39. No. 19. Spherical faience melon bead (1992.0313.01). F102.01.38.*

ished, and no bubbles are visible on the surface or the interior.

6. (1992.0603.02). C101.01.60. Fragment of a thick-walled vessel of striped brown and white alabaster. MPL 0.085 m, MPW 0.035 m, Th 0.009 m. The exterior surface is highly polished, the interior surface is slightly rough, suggesting a tall closed vessel. The fragment was found in the backfill above the C101 Burial 4, suggesting that it probably was part of the Byzantine levelling fill below the pavement, rather than a fragment of a church furnishing.

7. (1993.0390.01; fig. 13.17.7). C101.04.30. Sandstone slab with incised cross; broken, incomplete; MPL 0.48 m, MPW 0.35 m, Th 0.05 m. Two original edges, one flat, one bevelled, others broken;

back surface roughly finished. The smooth front surface preserves one arm of a neatly incised cross; L 0.155, W 0.02, 0.01 deep. The arm terminates in a small crescent (W 0.07 m). The stone was broken before its re-use as paver. The design and execution of the cross do not resemble the crosses in the Church nave that marked burials.

8. (1992.0184.01; fig. 13.20.8). C101.05.03. Small plaque of mottled black, grey, and red marble, possibly used for grinding medical substances or cosmetics; L 0.10 m, W 0.086 m, Th 0.01; 325 g. All four sides slope inward slightly toward the smooth upper (?) surface (0.09 × 0.073 m). Back surface is smooth as well. Small stone tablets of similar dimensions were often used for grinding or otherwise preparing medical substances or cosmetics

(Milne 1907:169, 171–72). An exotic, colourful type of stone would be appropriate for either purpose. Whetstones also took this shape (Milne 1904: 167), but marble would be ill-suited for such an application. Possibly Africano marble from Teos in Asia Minor, which was quarried during the second and third century (Fant 1989). Another possibility is a similarly colourful marble — *pavonazzetto* — quarried at Dokimeion in Phrygia, which supplied the material for the crater with panther handles in the Petra Church (Fiema et al. 2001: 336–38). If this is in fact a medical tool, it reinforces the identification of the bronze object from B100 as a bone elevator (p. 439, no. 29).

9. (1992.0333.01; fig. 13.20.9). C101.03.19. Sandstone loom weight; ovoid shape, wider at the base than at the top, which is perforated for suspension; L 0.08 m, W 0.08 m, Th 0.017 m; 280 g. There are four parallel grooves on the left side of one surface, three grooves on right, other sides undecorated. The geometric decoration resembles that seen on the Umayyad steatite cooking vessels, so the loom weight may date to the seventh century.

10. (1993.0157.01). C101.06.12. Spherical faience bead; D 0.01 m, hole D 0.004 m. The surface glaze has lost its lustre, but remains as a thin black crust over the granular white interior. Faience beads are common in this region from the Late Bronze Age through the Early Islamic period, and nearly every string of stone beads from the region includes some examples (see next entry).

11. (1993.0157.02; fig. 13.20.11). C101.06.12. Faience melon bead; D 0.01 m, hole D 0.006 m. The surface glaze has lost its lustre, but the moulded decoration of vertical grooves is clear. Faience melon beads, which have a squat spherical shape with grooves running between the two perforation openings are particularly common in this region from the Late Bronze Age through the Early Islamic period.

Parallels: Geva 2003: 447, nos. 3–4, pl. 20.1 (Jerusalem); Ibrahim and Gordon 1987: pl. XXXI.1 (Amman, Byzantine); Patrich 2008: 49, fig. 57 (Caesarea Palaestinae, Byzantine); Toll 1946: 125–30, pl. XXVIII, T7, T40, Dura-Europos, 2–3C).

F102 (Byzantine Church and Early Islamic House)

12. (1991.0346.01; fig. 13.20.12). F102.03.02.01. Socket stone for a door? Thick, discoidal piece of black vesicular basalt with smooth, flat lower surface; D 0.105 m, Th 0.043 m; 650 g. The upper surface is rounded, with a central depression (D 0.01 m; 0.013 m deep) that is smoothed as if used as a pivot. There is another depression on the side of the stone of the same dimensions, but not smoothed. Although more finished looking than most socket stones, this stone nevertheless may have served to seat the lower hinge for a door. A rougher example was found in the Early Islamic house at Jawa (Daviau 2010: 138–40). Compare nos. 13 and 33 below.

13. (1992.0161.01). F102.05.23. Socket stone for a door, fashioned from a naturally smoothed, hard, black sandstone river boulder with two approximately flat sides (0.29 × 0.24 × 0.11 m). There is a hemispherical depression in the centre of one surface (D 0.126 m; 0.04 m deep). There are no signs of abrasion, but the very regular shape suggests the action of a door pivot. A shallow slot 0.10 m wide has been pecked from one side of the depression to the outside of the block, most likely to allow installation of the lower pivot. Compare no. 12 above, no. 33 below.

14. (1992.0558). F102.06.24. Oblong lump of very porous black volcanic scoria, light but very hard; one natural (?) rounded surface and one flat surface for use in grinding or smoothing; L 0.085 m, W 0.066 m, Th 0.035 m; 129.7 g. The stone fits nicely in the hand and probably was formed by chopping a natural scoria nodule in half. A polishing stone of the identical material was found in B100 (below, no. 37).

15. (1992.0242.01). F102.05.26. Spherical flint nodule used as a hammer stone; chips taken out on one side; D 0.10 m; 1270 g.

16. (1992.0535.01; fig. 13.21.16). F102.06.20. Spherical flint nodule used as a hammer stone; chips taken out on one side; D 0.055 m; 330 g.

17. (1992.0558.02; fig. 13.21.17). F102.06.24. Dark grey sandstone river cobble with peck marks at both ends from use as a hammer stone; L 0.11 m, W 0.065 m, H 0.035 m; 555 g.

18. (1992.0307.01; fig. 13.20.18). F102.01.39. Small discoidal faience bead, perforated trans-

Fig. 13.21 *Hammer stones. No. 16: (1992.0535.01), F102.06.20. No. 17: (1992.0558.02), F102.06.24.*
No. 20: (1992.0558.03), F102.06.24; limestone cobbles with solution holes, possibly
used as loom weights. No. 21: (1992.0558.04), F102.06.24. No. 22: (1992.0558.05),
F102.06.24. No. 23: (1992.0558.06), F102.06.24. No. 30: (1992.0101), F102.02.10;
mortar adapted from boulder. No. 35: Sandstone pestle (1992.0350), B100.D.01.

versely; D 0.006 m, Th 0.003 m. The surface still
retains traces of a light green to ivory glaze.

19. (1992.0313.01; fig. 13.20.19). F102.01.38.
Faience melon bead; broken, incomplete; D 0.018,
stringing hole D 0.005 m. The exterior has been
decorated carelessly with diagonal grooves and
coated with a light blue-green glaze. This is a variation on a melon bead. See no. 11 above, and C101
Burial 2, no. 1 (p. 385).

20. (1992.0558.03; fig. 13.21.20). F102.06.24.
Slightly flattened spherical flint nodule with peck-
ing marks on one side from use as a hammer stone;
D 0.12 m; 2060 g.

21. (1992.0558.04; fig. 13.21.21). F102.06.24.
Natural limestone cobble with circular solution
hole; L 0.06 m, W 0.65 m, H 0.05 m, hole D 0.008
m; 320 g. There are a number of other voids that
do not penetrate the block. Possibly used as a loom

weight. Although it is heavy for that purpose, the presence of several other similar artefacts in the same locus supports some sort of collective use.

22. (1992.0558.05; fig. 13.21.22). F102.06.24. Natural limestone cobble with circular solution hole; L 0.06 m, W 0.07 m, H 0.06 m, hole D 0.006 m; 145 g. There are a number of other voids that do not penetrate the block. Possibly used as a loom weight.

23. (1992.0558.06; fig. 13.21.23). F102.06.24. Natural limestone cobble with circular solution hole; L 0.10 m, W 0.07 m, H 0.05 m, hole D 0.05 m; 475 g. There are a number of other voids that do not penetrate the block. Possibly used as a loom weight.

24. (1991.0221.02). F102.01 22. Grinding or hammer stone? A thick, slightly oval disk (D 0.067–0.075 m, Th 0.033 m; 330 g) of a hard black quartzite with a small dimple pecked into the flat upper and lower surfaces. There are peck marks around the entire circumference.

25. (1991.0302.01). F102.03.20. Hard, black sandstone river cobble with signs of use as a hammer stone; L 0.075 m, W 0.07 m, Th 0.04 m; 460 g.

26. (1991.0360.01). F102.04.00. Spherical bead cut from an orange stone, probably carnelian.

27. (1991.0389.01). F102.04.10. Small fragment of a brownish grey alabaster bowl or cup; broken, incomplete; MPL 0.025 m, MPW 0.02 m, Th 0.004 m. Turned on a lathe; two narrow grooves were engraved around the circumference of the vessel, parallel to the rim.

Thin-walled, lathe-turned alabaster vessels with exterior lines are fairly common in first- to third-century contexts in the Roman fort and *vicus* at Humayma. One fragment was also found in the C101 Church, in the fill above Burial 4. The shapes include bowls, cups, plates, and pyxides. This vessel seems to be part of the same tradition, although the usually white stone has been stained. These items were probably imported from Yemen, where there was a long tradition of alabaster vessels of various shapes, although usually with thicker walls. See Hassell 1997; Ibrahim and Gordon 1987: 31, pls. XXIII.2, LII.1; van Beek 1969: 273–76.

28. (1992.0045.01). F102.02.05. Small red-brown sandstone object, shaped like an irregular pyramid; H 0.04 m; base 0.03 m square. Red lines and dots have been painted on the base and may have extended up one or more sides.

29. (1992.0067.01). F102.05.05. Spindle whorl of hard, fine-grained yellow sandstone; chipped; D 0.029 m, Th 0.008 m, hole D 0.005 m; 6.8 g.

30. (1992.0101; fig. 13.21.30). F102.02.10. Mortar adapted from a flat, water-smoothed boulder of very dense, hard, dark red sandstone; 0.29 × 0.25 × 0.11 m. A smooth hemispherical depression (0.125 × 0.11 × 0.057 m deep) has been pounded into the centre of the stone on the naturally concave upper surface.

31. (1993.0371.01; fig. 13.22.31). F102.09.11. Small basin, roughly hollowed out of a block of local Disi sandstone with a punch; broken, incomplete; L 0.245 m, W 0.10 m, H 0.11 m. The capacity of the basin (ca. 1200 cc) is far too small for use by animals, so it may have served for washing, or for the provision of holy water within the church. A slightly larger sandstone basin was found in the Deir 'Ain 'Abata church (Politis 2012: 368, fig. 771).

32. (1991.0221.01, 1991.0313; fig. 13.22.32). F102.01.22, F102.04.11. Steatite cooking pot lid; broken, complete except for small chip; H 0.06 m, D 0.23 m. The handle and attached portion of the lid were found on the floor of Room F2 (Locus 12), while the rest of the lid disk was found 17.2 m away, in Room A2 (Locus 22). Flat, circular lid with diagonal slashes as decoration around the periphery. There is an inset around the circumference of the lower surface to fit with the rim of the pot. The heavy, cubical handle is decorated as a small, masonry structure with crenellations, and arched doors on all four sides. The roof is recessed below the battlements. Now in the Aqaba Archaeological Museum, no. AM107.

I have not found any close parallels for the carefully decorated handle. A steatite lid found at Qasr al-Hayr al-Sharqi in 1971 has a similar heavy, cubical handle, but it slopes inward slightly, and lacks any structural details (K. 'Amr, personal communication, 1992).

B100 (Byzantine Church and Early Islamic House)

33. (1991.0194.02). B100.11.06. Socket stone for door; cut and worn in a yellow marl cobble; broken, incomplete; MPL 0.10 m, MPW 0.09 m, Th 0.055 m. The hole (D 0.037 m; 0.02 m deep), which was started in a natural depression in the stone, is very smooth

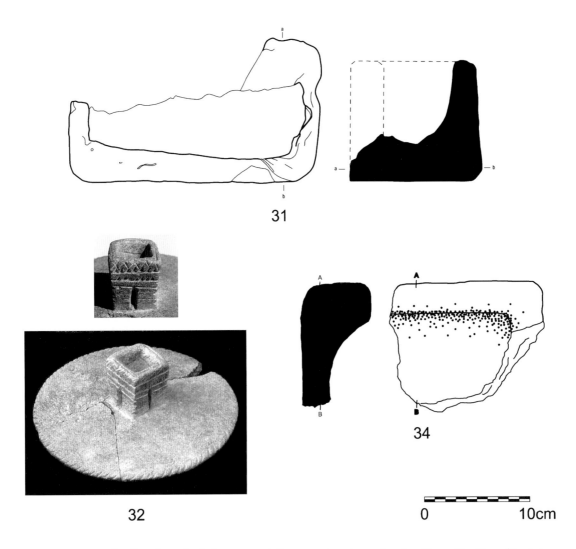

FIG. 13.22 *No. 31: Small sandstone basin (1993.0371.01); F102.09.11; top view and section. No. 32: Steatite cooking pot lid (1991.0221.01, 1991.0313); F102.01.22, F102.04.11. No. 34: Small sandstone basin (1991.0459); B100.06.00.*

and regular in shape, with a few horizontal circumferential striations. Compare nos. 12 and 13 above.

34. (1991.0459; fig. 13.22.34). B100.06.00. Shallow basin carved carefully from a hard, fine-grained light brown sandstone; broken, incomplete; one corner and part of the central recess preserved; MPL 0.14 m, MPW 0.125 m; H 0.07 m. Below the rounded rim the interior wall slopes inward gradually to the basin floor (Th 0.024 m), for a depth of 0.046 m. The basin is too shallow for an animal trough, so it may have been used for ablutions in the Church, or for food preparation.

35. (1992.0350; fig. 13.21.35). B100.D.01. Sandstone pestle shaped from a fragment of Umm

Ishrin sandstone. L 0.122 m, W 0.038 m; H 0.039 m. The naturally square fragment of stone tapers from a larger square end to the smoothly rounded pounding end.

36. (1991.0414). B100.E.01. Pounding or grinding stone shaped from a nodule of Umm Ishrin sandstone; two flat sides and an oval outline; L 0.09 m, W 0.075 m, Th 0.046 m. Peck marks around all the edges.

37. (1991.0385). B100.B.29. Oblong lump of very porous black volcanic scoria, light but very hard; one natural (?) rounded surface and one flat surface for use in grinding or smoothing; broken, incomplete; MPL 0.045 m, MPW 0.035 m, Th 0.035

m; 27.7 g. This is the same material as a polisher found in F102 (above, no. 14).

38. (1992.0197.02). B100.E.17. Small carnelian bead; D 0.006 m, H 0.004 m. Slightly facetted, and flattened at top and bottom; perforated through the short diameter.

39. (1992.0280.02). B100.E.23. Spherical bead carved from green stone; D 0.002 m. Perforated for stringing.

40. (1991.0157.01). B100.11.00. Spherical faience bead; D 0.013 m, hole D 0.004 m. The surface glaze has lost its lustre, but remains as a thin black crust over the granular white interior. Faience beads are common in this region from the Late Bronze Age through the Early Islamic period, and nearly every string of stone beads from the region includes some faience beads. See no. 11 (p. 509, 1993.0157.02) for parallels.

Chapter 14

Glass

by Janet D. Jones

14.A. INTRODUCTION

The fields excavated by the Humayma Project produced nearly 7,000 fragments of glass vessels and window glass. One of the great interests of this glass from the site as a whole is the varied nature of the structures from which it was recovered. This report focuses on the glass from multiple Byzantine churches in Areas B100, B126, C101, C119, and F102, and from Early Islamic domestic structures that succeeded the churches in B100 and F102. There were also a few scraps of wares from the Nabataean campground (C124) and necropolis (Field A), and from the Late Byzantine or Early Islamic farmhouse at A127. The excavation of the A127 structure will be reported in *HEP* 3 (for preliminary information see Oleson et al. 1999: 427–30). These areas provided an interesting mix of luxury wares, utilitarian glass tablewares, and lamps.

The glass in the catalogue has been organized by excavation field, then typologically and chronologically, wherever possible, presenting representative examples of each major type found in that area, with preference for examples from well-stratified contexts. The total number of examples of each type is cited in the discussion for that excavation field. Because of the near absence of full vessel profiles, typological designations are broad to avoid inconsequential distinctions,

except where identification of the full profile is certain. At the beginning of each category there are general comments on the type and discussion of comparative material; rather than being exhaustive in listing parallels, reference is made to the most recent and most complete treatments of the type. The catalogue entries themselves are brief and descriptive. Each fragment had been assigned a publication number, which also serves to identify the illustration, and the original bucket number is provided as well. There is no separate glass registry. Each entry then presents the locus, a short descriptive label, and the dimensions in centimetres. The description provides a fuller account of the object, including colour (if discernible) and surface condition. Any comments about the dating of the fragment are given in the introductory paragraph at the start of the section, along with discussion of the comparanda.

Because of the large numbers of renovations and reoccupations at Humayma and because of the shallow nature of the deposits (many of them fills), most of the strata contained mixed deposits with materials ranging from the Nabataean period to the Abbasid or even Ottoman periods. Thus, dating is most often inferred from the general context of the fragment or from comparative material. Chronological designations given relate to phasing at the nearby site of Aila, as follows: Roman (ca. 63 BC–AD 324), Early Roman/ Nabataean (ca. 63 BC–AD 106), Late Roman (ca. 106–324), Byzantine (ca. 324–630), Early Byzantine (ca. 324–500), Late Byzantine (ca. 500–630), Early Islamic (ca. 630–1170), Umayyad (ca. 630–750). Abbasid (ca. 750–968), Fatimid (ca. 968–1170). These designations differ slightly from those used for the chronological ceramic designations of the Humayma Excavation Project (see above p. 10), but they serve their purpose here.

14.B. OVERVIEW AND ANALYSIS

Overall, the glass from Humayma, like glass finds throughout the region, falls into three broad chronological groups. First are the more sparsely represented earlier types of the Nabataean to Early Roman periods (mid-first century BC into the early second century AD). The glass of this early group at Humayma will be discussed in detail in a later volume that focuses on the areas from which this early glass was recovered: Field E116 (the Roman Fort) and Field E125 (the Nabataean Shrine and Late Roman *vicus*). In brief, this early group includes a higher percentage of luxury wares that probably originated in Egyptian workshops and were transhipped through the port of Aila to other sites in southern Jordan such as Humayma and Petra. Finds from Petra and Aila show that the Nabataean elite, when they used glass at all, appears to have preferred glass from Roman Egypt to that from the Roman Levant (Keller 2006: 42–50; Jones in preparation).

The second broad group of glass at Humayma, and the primary focus of this report, dates from the Byzantine to early Umayyad periods (fourth to seventh centuries). Glass finds at the site are significantly more numerous from the fourth century onward, and there is a marked increase in vessel types originating in the workshops of the Levant. The transition from Late Byzantine to early Umayyad is often difficult to pinpoint because of the continuity in production of both pottery and glass in the region under early Umayyad rule (O'Hea, Aila, in preparation). During this second period, glass-blowing, discovered in the mid-first century BC, had become the norm, and glass production had settled into a mode of relative mass

production. This made glass tablewares more affordable to a wider range of people, who then grew to prefer glass vessels to ceramic, especially for drinking and lighting. Thus, this chronological group is far more numerous and includes a higher percentage of utilitarian tablewares and lamps. The blown glass of this period was thin-walled and fragile and, therefore, far less able to travel any distance. Indeed, there were fewer categories of "export glass" overall, and more evidence of small glass-blowing establishments spread throughout the region in places where enough fuel, the most expensive ingredient in glass-making, was available. This is particularly true of the Levant, where workshops such as that at Jalame were in production for limited periods and then moved on. It is possible, therefore, that residents of Humayma acquired their glass from small glass workshops on the outskirts of Petra. Keller notes that the regional character of the glass at nearby Petra and its indigenous typo-chronological development strongly suggest local production at Petra or, at the very least, itinerant glass-blowers working within the Byzantine province of *Palaestina Tertia* (Keller 2006: 184). There is as yet no evidence for the manufacture of glass at Aila.

The concentration of glass finds at Humayma in this second, later period can also be explained by the proliferation of churches at the site. Unlike the glass finds at Aila or ez-Zantur (Petra) at this time, which come from primarily domestic contexts, the glass finds from the Humayma churches represent a far narrower range of types. There are concentrated finds of lamps and utilitarian tablewares, combined with a few luxury wares such as engraved vessels. These are basic church furnishings. They do not, however, exhibit the high level of luxury found in the church in the port city of Aila, in which was found a cage cup and a concentration of high-quality engraved glass (Jones 2005a: 135–39; Jones 2005b: 180–82). Decoration in this period is more often trailed decoration, frequently in contrasting colours (O'Hea 2003: 136). The central story of glass at Humayma in this period, and overall in terms of numbers of fragments recovered, is the story of developments in lighting and the widespread adoption of the glass lamp by the fourth century in the Levant (O'Hea

2007: 239–46). The first glass lamps were mostly ordinary household vessel types — cups, goblets, and bowls — sometimes with suspension hooks for hanging. These were used intermittently in the second to third centuries, but identification as lamps is difficult because such vessels were primarily drinking vessels. Conical beakers and hemispherical bowls, often with cut grooves and blue blob decoration, became the first widespread lamp type in the fourth century; these also doubled as drinking vessels. By the fifth century, when glass lamps were adopted for lighting at Humayma, they took two forms: 1) the more common cylindrical "tumbler" lamps of the fifth to sixth centuries had three small coil handles applied to the upper body for suspension by means of bronze hangers; 2) bowl-shaped stemmed lamps that could not stand and were meant to be fitted into lamp stands or hangers (*polykandela;* see pp. 295, 433–34), a type that generally dates from the fifth century into the eighth century. Unlike lamps in terracotta, glass lamps were filled with water on which oil and the wick were floated. Glass lamps fuelled with castor oil burned longer and cleaner; the water kept the glass cool and automatically extinguished the lamp when the oil was consumed. The water had the added effect of intensifying the light, so that the entire vessel glowed, casting nearly twice as much light as a terracotta lamp. Ancient authors such as Prudentius (*Cathemerinon* 5) emphasize the otherworldly effect of this illumination. The Humayma churches furnished with multiple glass lamps in *polykandela* would have blazed with light at this period.

The third group of glass at Humayma is a small corpus of late Umayyad (AD 700–750) to Abbasid (AD 750–945) date. This is a thin overlay on the site, primarily confined to areas with Abbasid occupation. In this report, glass of this date comes from houses of Early Islamic date in Area F102. Although the corpus of glass from this period is small, it nevertheless comprises examples of several of the most characteristic vessel types of the period including excellent examples of pincer-decorated and scratch-decorated vessels.

14.C. COMPARANDA

Overall, the most important corpora in terms of comparative material for the Humayma glass include the glass finds from the private houses at Petra ez-Zantur (Keller 2006), from the Petra Great Temple (O'Hea, forthcoming), and from Aila (Aqaba) (Jones, Aila, in preparation; O'Hea, Aila, in preparation) in southern Jordan; from Lejjun (Jones 2006) in central Jordan; from Jerash in northern Jordan (Baur 1938 and Meyer 1987); from Dura Europos in Syria (Clairmont 1963); from Samaria (Crowfoot 1957); from Jalame in western Galilee (Weinberg and Goldstein 1988); from Ramla and Ashqelon in Judaea (Gorin-Rosen 2010; Katsnelson 1999); and from Mezad Tamar in the Negev (Erdmann 1977).

The glass from Petra ez-Zantur ranges in date from the late first century BC to the mid-seventh century AD. Together with glass from other archaeological projects in and around Petra, such as the Petra Great Temple in the city centre, it provides an indispensible typology of glass types and their development in the vicinity of Petra over time. Ez-Zantur is particularly illuminating for its *in situ* deposits of formal glass drinking sets from Late Roman (mid-fourth to early fifth century) domestic contexts. As a site of glass manufacture, Jalame provides valuable comparanda for the Early Byzantine period. The excavator of Jalame originally proposed that glass production at the site was limited to the period from ca. 351 to ca. 383 (Weinberg 1988: 16–19). However, a recent reinterpretation of the evidence from specific phases of the site based on the ceramic finds proposes redating the site to the fifth century (Slane and Magness 2005: 261). The majority of glass finds from Jerash range in date from the Early Byzantine (ca. 324–491) to Late Byzantine (ca. 491–636) periods, with some residual Late Roman material in the mix (Meyer 1987). Dura Europos presents a body of material from a Roman military site with moulded and cut luxury glass strikingly similar to some fragments from Area E and to glass from Aila, just to the south of Humayma; it is important for comparative material from the Roman period up to AD 256. Samaria provides a large number of glass lamps from the monastery and church as well as an important body of intact vessels from tomb groups dated from the third to fifth centuries. Mezad Tamar in the Negev has produced a corpus of utilitarian glass of the third to seventh centuries. Quseir al-Qadim provides an important corpus of export glass of first- to second-century date from a Red Sea port (Meyer 1992). The glass from these sites forms the basis of excavated comparative material for this report.

Major collections at the Corning Museum of Glass, the Toledo Museum of Art, the Metropolitan Museum of Art, the Newark Museum of Art, the Royal Ontario Museum, the Louvre, and the Israel Museum provided additional comparative material.

14.D. PROCESSING

The excavated glass was processed in several stages. Diagnostics were separated from other fragments in a preliminary sort during which all fragments were counted. Diagnostics were then divided according to standard typological categories and counts were taken within each diagnostic category. Characteristic and exceptional fragments were drawn. The total number of fragments from sites reported on in this chapter is approximately 4,540; diagnostics total approximately 1,122 fragments, compared to 3,418 body fragments. The largest concentration of vessel glass at the site comes from a deposit in Room 2 of C119, a Late Byzantine church, from which an area total of 2,491 fragments (1,040 grams: 327 diagnostic and 2,164 undecorated body fragments) were recovered, primarily lamp fragments.

Glass of the Byzantine period at Humayma is fashioned from a thin fabric that is either natural light green or natural light blue-green in colour, occasionally with added decorative threads in a darker green or blue-green. Islamic glass is thicker, either cast or blown, and generally colourless; bright colours, especially deep blues, are frequently encountered, along with thread decoration in contrasting colours.

Much of the Humayma glass, as is usual with glass from this region, is extremely weathered and fragmented. The thin-walled blown vessels of the later Roman and Byzantine period were especially susceptible to the effects of weathering, and this accounts for the poor preservation of the glass and the general lack of complete vessel profiles. There are three dominant types of weathering: a heavy black layer (almost like enamel) over thick, silvery pitted iridescence or a powdery beige layer with scattered brown pits. Where this weathering is lacking (or lost) there is usually either a thin milky or an even thinner filmy layer of iridescence. Many of the fragments are so heavily covered with thick layers of weathering or weathered through so that all traces of colour are obscured. Fragments weathered in this way are generally made of the typical blue green glass of the region and period.

14.E. CATALOGUE

14.E.1. Field A (Necropolis)

Eight small fragments of glass were recovered from surveyed tombs. Three small fragments from Tomb 104 displayed vague traces of moulded or cut decoration but were too small to identify further. No. 1 is a small, thick body fragment from a colourless vessel with the tip of a cut ray or petal preserved. The spherical bubbles and polished surface indicate that this fragment comes from a moulded vessel, possibly with petal decoration. The fragment is too small for definite attribution to a type, but it appears to come from a luxury class of vessels. Decolourized bowls of Flavian to Trajanic date with cut decoration were found nearby in southern Jordan at Aila (Jones, in preparation) and Petra (O'Hea, forthcoming). A simple rim fragment (no. 2) from Tomb 13 in Tomb Group 115 is from a bowl with added amber thread decoration around the rim similar to bowls of Byzantine/early Umayyad date from Petra (Keller 2006: 67, 206 Type VII.11c) and Aila (O'Hea, in preparation).

1. (1992.0166; fig. 14.1.1). A104.00. Body fragment with cut decoration. MPL 2.49 cm, MPW 1.07 cm; Th 0.29 cm. Colourless. Thick body fragment with tip of cut petal or ray preserved.

2. (1992.0597; fig. 14.1.2). A115.13.02. Bowl with thread decoration. D 12.0 cm; MPH 1.68 cm; MPL 3.18 cm; Th 0.17 × 0.09 cm. Pale green. Flaring, irregular simple rim fragment with five revolutions of amber thread below rim.

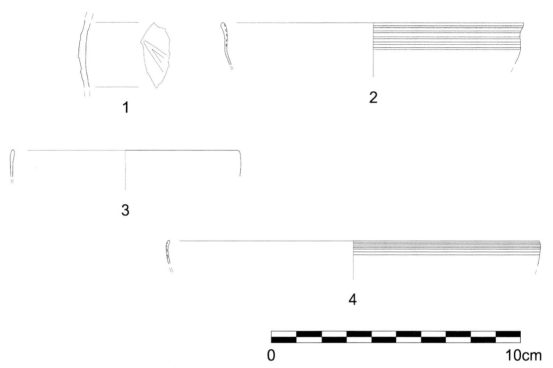

FIG. 14.1 *Glass from the Necropolis and A127.*

14.E.2 Field A127 (Late Byzantine/ Early Islamic House)

One locus in Area A127 produced 17 fragments of utilitarian glasswares, three of which are diagnostic and can be dated to the Late Byzantine/early Umayyad periods. Two, represented by no. 3, are simple incurving rims from small diameter cups or bowls consistent with fifth-century rims from nearby sites (Keller 2006: 67, 206 Types VII.33a and 34a), and one (no. 4) is a larger diameter simple rim of Late Byzantine/early Umayyad date with several revolutions of amber thread below the rim (cf. above, no. 1).

3. (1998.0312; fig. 14.1.3). A127 Probe 01.03. Rim fragment from bowl. D 9.0 cm; MPH 0.95 cm; MPL 2.70 cm; Th 0.06–0.11 cm. Pale bluish-green. Simple rim fragment, incurving.

4. (1998.0312; fig. 14.1.4). A127 Probe 01.03. Rim Fragment from Bowl. D 15.0 cm; MPH 0.85 cm; MPL 1.93 cm; Th 0.03–0.11 cm. Pale bluish-green. Simple rim fragment, incurving, with five revolutions of amber thread below rim.

14.E.3 B100 (Byzantine Church and Early Islamic House)

There were at least five churches at Humayma in the Byzantine period (Fields B100, B126, C101, C119, F102), a large number for a town of its size (see pp. 551–53). The three churches best-preserved and most extensively excavated (B100, C101, C119) produced great concentrations of glass vessel fragments, particularly a dense deposit of 2,491 fragments of broken lamps and other vessels from C119, a deposit accounting for nearly a third of the total finds for the entire site. Altogether, the churches produced over 4,000 fragments of the site total of nearly 7,000 fragments. By far the largest number of fragments represents lamps, particularly the three-handled tumbler lamp common in the fifth to sixth centuries, along with a lesser number of stemmed lamps of similar date.

The B100 structure was most likely functioning as a church from the mid-fifth to the seventh century, from the Byzantine period into the Early Islamic period. Of a total of 326 fragments from the area, 76 were diagnostic. There were 25 fragments of simple rims from utilitarian bowls and cups distributed among flaring (11), straight (8), and incurving (5) profiles. There were only two fragments from rims of closed vessels. As one would expect from a church, there were many tubular (out-folded) rims, mostly likely from lamps. There was one fragment from a cracked-off rim, probably from a lamp.

Simple Rims (nos. 1–2)

1. (1992.0238a; fig. 14.2.1). B100.E.23. Rim Fragment from Bowl. Rim D 12.0 cm; MPH 1.01 cm; MPL 2.70 cm; Rim Th 0.32 cm; Th body 0.05 cm. Colourless. Simple straight rim, thickened; vertical body wall.

2. (1992.0238b; fig. 14.2.2). B100.E.23. Rim Fragment from Bowl. D rim 10.0 cm; MPH 1.14 cm; MPL 1.65 cm; Th rim 0.27 cm; Th body 0.19 cm. Colour uncertain. Simple rim, incurving.

Tubular Rims/Lamps (nos. 3–8)

The largest concentration of rims from open shapes (12) are fragments of out-folded rims (nos. 3–4) common to bowls and to so-called "tumbler" lamps, a type that dates to the fifth to sixth centuries. Tumbler lamps have a deep, cylindrical body with walls tapering downward to a concave base and three small coil handles applied to the upper body and attached to the out-folded rim. The lamps were suspended by these handles using bronze hangers such as those excavated at Pella in association with lamp fragments (Smith and Day 1989: 114–15, fig. 32). Parallels come from Jerash (Baur 1938: fig. 22, no. 380, concave bottom; fig. 23, no. 381f, flared and Meyer 1987: fig. 12, p–r), Mezad Tamar (Erdmann 1977: pl. 1, no. 5b), Shavei Zion (Barag 1967: fig. 16, nos. 21–22), Ashqelon (Katsnelson 1999: 78–79), and Pella (Smith and Day 1989: 114–115, fig. 32 and pl. 60, no. 4).

Other elements from lamps in this deposit include two wick tubes (nos. 5–6), two lamp stems (e.g., no. 7), and nine coil handles of the sort found on hanging tumbler lamps (e.g., no. 8). Internal wick holders such as nos. 5 and 6 represent a common development of the tumbler lamp type

in which an internal wick-holder was applied to the bottom. This type is common in the region with good parallels from Lejjun (Jones 1987: 136, 76; Jones, Aila, in press, no. 104), Mezad Tamar (Erdmann 1977: pl. 1, nos. 3–4), Mt. Nebo (Saller 1941: 315–16), Jerash (Meyer 1987: 205 and fig. 11: Q), Nessana (Harden 1962: 84), Samaria (Crowfoot 1957: 405, 418–19), Pella (Smith and Day 1989: 114–15, fig. 32 and pl. 60: 4), Bet Shean (Hadad 1998: 64, 68, and fig. 1), and Jalame (Weinberg and Goldstein 1988: 85–86, nos. 386–87, wick tubes alone). The Humayma examples have concave bottoms, but variants with stemmed goblet-type feet are known elsewhere (Baur 1938: fig. 20, no. 376).

Lamp stems such as no. 7 come from bowl-shaped stemmed lamps like examples from Jerash (Baur 1938: fig. 17, no. 237; Meyer 1987: 203–5, fig. 11: h–l), Mezad Tamar (Erdmann 1977: pl. 3, no. 151), Khirbet al-Karak (Delougaz and Haines 1960: pl. 60, no. 26), Mt. Nebo (Saller 1956: 30), Lejjun (Jones 1987: 628 and fig. 136: 74–75), Pella (Smith and Day 1989: 114–15; pl. 60: 10), Samaria (Crowfoot 1956: 415, fig. 96: 6), Nessana (Harden 1962, pl. xx, nos. 52 and 54), Bet Shean (Hadad 1998: 69, 72, fig. 4), Umm Qeis, Bosra, and Amman (Dussart 1998: 86–87 type BV1.211, pl.16: 6–8); short-stemmed lamps are known at Jalame (Weinberg and Goldstein 1988: 85–85, nos. 388–90). Stemmed lamps that could not stand were meant to be fitted into *polykandela* such as the one found at Sardis (Saldern 1980: 50–51; pl, 23: 274, 280;Weinberg and Goldstein 1988: 85, no. 184; for *polykandela* finds in the region, see pp. 433–34 above). Lamps of this type generally date from the fifth century into the eighth century.

3. (1995.0430; fig. 14.2.3). B100.21.04. Out-folded rim from lamp/bowl. D rim 12.0 cm; MPH 1.84 cm; MPL 2.96 cm; Th rim 0.65 cm; Th body 0.21 cm. Colour uncertain. Out-folded upright rim forming tubular edge.

4. (1992.0236; fig. 14.2.4). B100.E.22. Out-folded rim from lamp/bowl. D rim 7.0 cm; MPH 0.74 cm; MPL 3.21 cm; Th rim 0.28 cm; Th body 0.05 cm. Colour uncertain. Out-folded upright rim forming compressed tubular edge.

5. (1992.0236; fig. 14.2.5). B100.E.22. Wick tube from lamp. MPH 2.99 cm; D wick tube 1.06

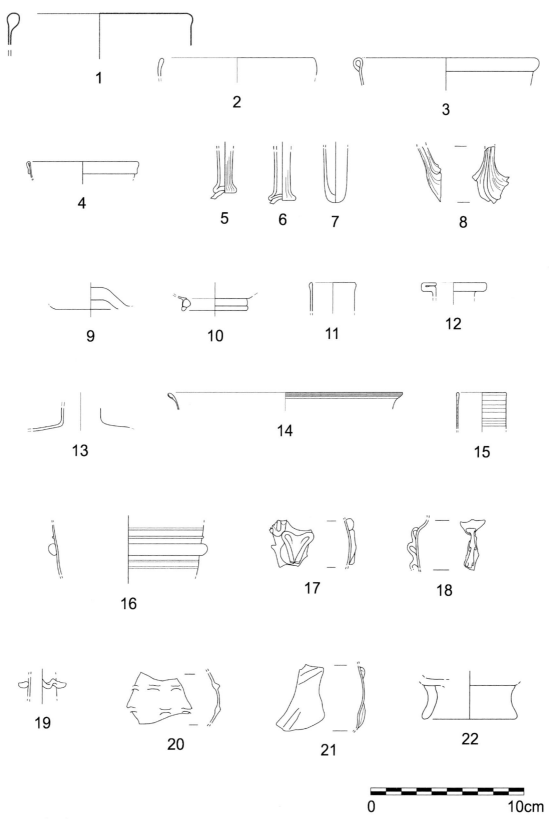

FIG. 14.2 *Glass from B100.*

cm; Th wick tube 0.09 cm; Th body 0.30 cm. Blue green. Wick tube. Cylindrical tube with splaying concave bottom set into lamp with concave base.

6. (1992.0537; fig. 14.2.6). B100.P.14. Wick tube from lamp. MPH 3.28 cm; D wick tube 1.00 cm; Th wick tube 0.11 cm; Th body 0.30 cm. Blue green. Cylindrical wick tube with splaying concave bottom set into lamp with concave base.

7. (1992.0165; fig. 14.2.7). B100.22.15. Stem from lamp. D 1.53 cm; MPH 3.27 cm; Th 0.12 cm. Blue green. Bottom of lamp stem. Cylindrical tube turning inward at bottom; rounded bottom.

8. (1992.0236; fig. 14.2.8). B100.E.22. Coil Handle MPH 3.54; PW 2.18 cm. Blue green. Fragment of coil handle with application end preserved.

Bases (nos. 9–10)

Eight bases were recovered from B100, including one concave base, one rounded base, one solid base, one coil base, and one true base ring from a moulded vessel (see below no. 22). No. 9 is a thick deep concave base similar to bases found on tumbler lamps from Petra of fifth- to seventh-century date (Keller 2006: 74, 225 Type VII.49a–b). No. 10 is a double coil base, splayed out in profile, similar to examples from Khirbat el-Ni'ana, where coil bases of one to five coils in height were found in quantity and produced in local workshops in the fourth to early fifth centuries (Gorin-Rosen and Katsnelson 2007: 75, 88–90, fig. 7, nos. 1–2). These bases are found on a variety of deep bowl and jug types and were very widely distributed in the Mediterranean in the fourth to early fifth centuries.

9. (1992.0414; fig. 14.2.9). B100.G.01. Concave base. D 4.5 cm; MPH 1.74 cm; Th 0.35 × 0.13 cm. Colour uncertain. Fragment of deeply concave base.

10. (1991.0437; fig. 14.2.10). B100.B.32. Coil Base. D 4.0 cm; MPH 0.74 cm; MPL 1.70 cm; Th body 0.11 cm; Th base coil 0.51 cm. Colour uncertain. Fragment of out-splayed coil base with two revolutions of coil.

Closed Shapes (nos. 11–13)

Two rims and three necks from closed shapes were found in area B100. No. 11 is a simple straight rim above straight body wall (see below, no. 13). No. 12 is a flattened infolded rim over a straight cylindrical neck commonly found on unguentaria over a period of centuries. It is similar to rims on pear-shaped unguentaria from a burial cave dated to the first century at Hagosherim (Ovadiah 1999: fig. 3, nos. 9 and 14) and to rims from candlestick unguentaria, such as an unguentarium from 'Ein ez-Zeituna of second- to early third-century date (Winter 2004: 81, fig.3, no. 25). No. 13 is a neck and shoulder fragment from a closed shape with swelling body showing the transition from neck to shoulder. At Petra ez-Zantur globular bottles with rims similar to no. 11 and neck and body profile like no. 13 come from fourth- to seventh-century contexts and represent a bottle type with a period of production extending from the fourth to the eighth centuries (Keller 2006: 74, 227 Type VII.54a).

11. (1992.0414; fig. 14.2.11). B100.G.01. Straight rim from bottle or jar. D 3.0 cm; MPH 1.72 cm; Th 0.19 × 0.13 cm. Colour uncertain. Fragment of straight rim, thickened; straight neck.

12. (1992.0449; fig. 14.2.12). B100.O.00. Infolded bottle rim and neck. D 2.0 cm; MPH 0.85 cm; Th rim 0.97 cm; Th body 0.29 cm. Colour uncertain. Fragment of tubular rim, folded outward, upward, and inward; straight neck.

13. (1992.0187; fig. 14.2.13). B100.E.12. Neck and shoulder fragment. D neck 2.0 cm; MPH 1.15 cm; Th neck 0.17 cm; Th body 0.10 cm. Yellowish-green. Fragment of neck with abrupt transition to horizontal shoulder.

Vessels with Applied Decoration (nos. 14–19)

There are several fragments from Area B100 with applied threads, coils, or bosses.

No. 14 is a flaring simple bowl rim with three revolutions of dark blue thread below the rim, very similar in profile and decoration to a common bowl type dated to the fourth to seventh centuries known from finds at such sites as Petra ez-Zantur

(Keller 2006: 67, 207 Type VII.13c) and Mezad Tamar (Erdman 1977: 132, pl. 6, no. 569).

No. 15 is a simple upright rim from a bottle or jar, with one thick dark blue thread atop rim and nine revolutions of thin dark blue thread below rim probably dated to the fifth or sixth centuries. Close parallels come from the Petra Great Temple (O'Hea, forthcoming: TS 94) and Petra ez-Zantur (Keller 2006: 74, 227 Type VII.54c).

No. 16 is mostly likely from the funnel neck of a large bottle and preserves multiple revolutions of thin thread with one revolution of a thick coil overlying the thin thread. There is similar thread decoration on a wide neck from a globular bottle from Amman dated to the Late Byzantine/Umayyad periods (Dussart 1998: 140–41, pl. 37). Other possible parallels include a tall neck bottle in the Corning Museum of Glass dated to the sixth to seventh centuries (Whitehouse 2001: 174, no. 710)

No. 17 is a body fragment with applied decoration tooled into triangles. This decorative motif appeared on globular bottles and cylindrical flasks of the Early Islamic period (seventh to eighth centuries). An excavated parallel comes from a late eighth-century Abbasid context at Fustat (Foy et al. 2003: 140, fig 2: 25). Examples in collections include flasks of Early Islamic date in the Toledo Museum of Art (Harden 1971: 93, pl. IX E), the Kofler Collection (Carboni 2001: 42 no. 1.8b), and the Constable-Maxwell Collection (Sotheby Park Bernet 1979: 196, no. 347), where elongated widely-spaced triangles alternate pointing upward and downward; a globular bottle in the Kofler Collection with triangles of alternating light (yellow?) and dark (blue) glass (Carboni 2001: 42, no. 1.8a); and an unusual piriform pitcher from the Kofler Collection (Carboni 2001: 28 no. 6), where triangles alternate with disks. These vessels, along with globular bottles decorated with a similarly tooled oxhide-shaped appliqué, were some of the earliest and most numerous glass vessels from the period marking the transition from Byzantine to Early Islamic (Harden 1971: 193; see below F102, no. 43).

No. 18 is a body fragment with a thin decorative looped trail in a darker shade of green. A thin looped trail like this could come from a lamp such as an example of sixth-century date in the Ernesto Wolfe Collection (Stern 2001: 321–22, no. 183). The

trails on this lamp have one larger loop at the top for the attachment of suspension chains.

No. 19 is a neck fragment from a bottle encircled with an applied undulating band or ruffle. These are commonly seen on long-necked globular bottles of the sixth and seventh centuries, such as a complete bottle in the Royal Ontario Museum dated to the sixth century (Hayes 1975: 108, no. 43, pl. 26). Excavated examples come from sixth to seventh-century contexts in Byzantine churches at Khirbat al-Karak (Delougaz and Haines 1960: pl. 59, no. 27) and Jerash (Meyer 1987: 206–7, fig. 11 C–E), and the Byzantine monastery at Samaria (Crowfoot 1957: 418, fig. 99: 1).

14. (1992.0227; fig. 14.2.14). B100.G.05. Rim fragment with thread decoration from bowl. D 15.0 cm; MPH 1.31 cm; Th rim 0.21 cm; Th body 0.04cm. Pale blue green. Fragment of simple flaring rim, with three revolutions of dark blue thread below rim.

15. (1991.0066; fig. 14.2.15). B100.02.03. Rim Fragment with thread decoration from bottle or jar. D 3.0 cm; MPH 2.21 cm; Th rim 0.14 cm; Th body 0.10 cm. Pale blue green. Fragment of simple rim, straight, with one revolution of thick dark blue thread forming rim, and nine revolutions of thin dark blue thread below rim.

16. (1991.0459; fig. 14.2.16). B100.06.00. Rim fragment with thread decoration from jar. MPH 3.29 cm; MPL 3.19 cm; Th rim 0.57 cm; Th body 0.14 cm. Pale blue green. Bottle neck with applied thread decoration: multiple revolutions of thin thread and one revolution of a thick thread or coil of same colour preserved.

17. (1992.0301; fig. 14.2.17). B100.22.15. Body fragment with applied decoration from bottle. MPH 2.90 cm; MPL 2.89 cm; Th body 0.11 cm. Colour uncertain. Body fragment with remains of two applied bosses tooled into triangles.

18. (1992.0188; fig. 14.2.18). B100.E.13. Body fragment with applied decoration. MPH 3.15 cm; MPL 1.65 cm; Th body 0.12 cm. Pale yellowish green. Shoulder and body fragment with thin looping trail in darker yellowish green glass.

19. (1992.0026; fig. 14.2.19). B100.G.02. Neck fragment with wavy trail decoration from bottle. D 3.0 cm; MPH 1.31 cm; Th body 0.09 cm. Blue green. Neck from closed vessel with coil toiled into ruffle around neck.

Vessels with Pinched Decoration (nos. 20–21)

Remains from several vessels with pinched decoration were also found in the Church at B100. No. 20 is an example with two rows of small pinches; no. 21 has larger, longer pinches that are nearly fins; these are not oriented on the same axis.

Smaller pinches as on no. 20 are most commonly seen in single rows decorating the shoulders of small globular bottles ranging in date from the fourth century to the first half of the eighth century (Dussart 1998: 161: BXII.1). Pinches are also a common form of decoration for Early Islamic glass from the seventh to the tenth centuries (Scanlon and Pinder-Wilson 2001: 66). The double row of pinches is less common in the earlier period; one parallel is a bottle also blown into a dip mould in the collection of the Corning Museum of Glass (Whitehouse 2001: 124, no. 628). An example with a double row of pinches comes from an Abbasid context at Pella (O'Hea 2003: 134 and fig. 3). Other vessel shapes with small pinches as decoration include a larger flask from Jerash dated to the early eighth century (Dussart 1998: 158, BX.83, pl. 46) and a hollow-stemmed goblet in the Newark Museum of Art dated to the fifth to early seventh centuries (Auth 1976: 150, no.195).

Larger pinches such as those on no. 21 are variants of those on no. 20, such as those on a globular bottle in the collection of the Corning Museum of Glass dated to the fourth to fifth centuries (Whitehouse 1997: 181, no. 318), on a vessel of late Umayyad date from Aila (O'Hea, in preparation: TS 48), or a cup of Abbasid date from Pella (O'Hea 2003: fig. 3). A complete example with large pinches, almost finned decoration is a bottle of Abbasid date in the Israel Museum (Israeli 2003: 340, no. 443).

20. (1991.0218; fig. 14.2.20). B100.11.08. Body fragment with pinched decoration. MPH 3.12 cm; MPW 3.78 cm; Th body 0.09 cm. Pale blue green. Body fragment from globular vessel

with multiple short pinch marks: six pinches preserved in two rows of three each.

21. (1992.0083; fig. 14.2.21). B100.G.02. Body fragment with pinched decoration. MPL 4.17 cm; MPW 3.03 cm; Th body 0.07 cm. Very pale greenish blue. Body fragment with two long pinches of different orientations preserved.

Moulded Vessels (no. 22)

One fragment from the true base ring of a high-quality cast colourless bowl is similar to late second- to early third-century examples from Dura Europos on which the wall of the bowl curves upward in a continuous profile (Clairmont 1963: 91–92, no. 392).

22. (1992.0528; fig. 14.2.22). B100.G.02. True base ring from moulded vessel. D 5.4 cm; Th 0.47 cm. Colourless with a yellowish tinge. Cast true base ring, slightly out-splayed.

14.E.4. C101 (Byzantine Church)

C101 is a Late Byzantine church dated from the fifth to the mid-seventh centuries. Over 600 fragments of glass vessels were recovered, 242 diagnostic fragments and 365 body fragments. Diagnostic fragments include 55 fragments of simple rounded rims from bowls and cups, 55 fragments from lamps or bowls with out-folded tubular rims, and five fragments from the bases of lamps with wick holders. Other rims include four rims from decorated beakers, five triangular rims, and three cracked-off rims. There were only ten fragments from closed vessels such as bottle and jars.

Simple Rounded Rims (nos. 1–7)

C101 produced 57 fragments from simple rounded bowl and cup rims, of which 32 were from straight rims, seven from flaring rims, and four from distinctive drinking cups in colourless glass with thread decoration around the upper body.

No. 1 is a flaring out-splayed rim from a bowl or plate similar to rims from third- to fourth-century contexts at Petra ez-Zantur (Keller 2006: 53, 208 Type VII.15b). Nos. 2 and 3 are rounded and thickened rims from cups, like no. 4 from B100 above, a tall straight-walled drinking cup known from mid fourth- to late fifth-century contexts at Jerash (Meyer 1987: 189 and fig. 5: S, T, U).

Nos. 4–6 are rim and base fragments from high-quality drinking cup or deep bowl types of long duration. Rims of similar profile can range in date from the first to fourth centuries and beyond. No. 4 is a flaring rim with one very regular revolution of added thread just below the rim. No. 5 is a thicker, more upright rim with similar thread decoration. No. 6 is a slightly incurving rim from a deep bowl with straight walls and one horizontal revolution of thin thread on the upper body. Overall, the rims are very similar to rims from Dura Europos dated to the second to mid third centuries (Clairmont 1963: 54 no. 231, pl. VI), to finds from a Roman well of third- to fourth-century date at Khirbet Ibreiktas (Gorin-Rosin 1998: 55, nos. 5–8), to rims from Petra ez-Zantur, and from a slightly later context at the factory site of Jalame (Weinberg and Goldstein 1988: 44 ff., fig. 4–5).

No. 7 is a tubular base ring from a similar cup decorated with a wide circular trail that is distinctive of this class of drinking cups. This cup type was popular in the western empire from the late second to the fourth centuries. The type is treated comprehensively by Cool and Price (1995: 82–85) in a discussion of parallels from Colchester.

1. (1993.0423; fig. 14.3.1). C101.04.46. Rim fragment from bowl. D 16.0 cm; MPH 1.25 cm; MPL 3.20 cm; Th rim 0.29 cm; Th body 0.03 cm. Pale green. Flaring rim, rounded and thickened; out-splayed walls.

2. (1993.0261; fig. 14.3.2). C101.04.26. Rim fragment from bowl/cup. D 10.0 cm; MPH 1.27 cm; MPL 3.13 cm; Th rim 0.43 cm; Th body 0.16 cm. Pale blue green. Straight rim, rounded and thickened, slightly out turned; straight walls tapering downward.

3. (1993.0005; fig. 14.3.3). C101.01.69. Rim fragment from Bowl/cup. D 14.0 cm; MPH 2.21 cm; MPL 3.69 cm; Th rim 0.44 cm; Th body 0.09 cm. Pale green. Straight rim, rounded and thickened; walls out-splayed.

4. (1991.0212; fig. 14.3.4). C101.02.15. Rim fragment with thread decoration from cup. D 7.0 cm; MPH 1.14 cm; MPL 2.05 cm; Th rim 0.19 cm; Th body 0.09 cm. Colourless. Simple rim, flaring, rounded and thickened; one revolution of thread ca. 1.5 cm below rim.

5. (1992.0464; fig. 14.3.5). C101.01.35. Rim fragment with thread decoration from bowl /cup. D 10.0 cm; MPH 1.73 cm; MPL 2.76 cm; Th rim 0.49 cm; Th body 0.11 cm. Colour uncertain. Straight rim, regular, rounded and thickened, single revolution of thin thread below rim; walls slightly curving.

6. (1993.0046; fig. 14.3.6). C101.06.04. Rim fragment with thread decoration from bowl/cup. D 6.0 cm; MPH 1.84 cm; MPL 2.51 cm; Th rim 0.34 cm; Th body 0.12 cm. Colourless. Slightly out-splayed rim, rounded and thickened; walls straight.

7. (1993.0046; fig. 14.3.7). C101.06.04. Tubular Base Ring. D 5.0 cm; D int. ring 2.80 cm; MPH 0.74 cm; Th base 0.24 cm; Th body 0.09 cm. Colourless. Pushed-in base forming upright tubular base ring; concave bottom decorated with thick circular trail.

Lamps (nos. 8–12)

Fragments from tumbler and stemmed lamps dating to the fifth to seventh centuries make up the majority of glass vessel finds from C101. This is consistent with the identification of the building as a church of the Late Byzantine period. The area produced 55 fragments of out-folded rims common to bowls and to cylindrical tumbler lamps (no. 114a), five fragments of wick holders (no. 114b and 115), three fragmentary stems from hollow stemmed lamps (nos. 116 and 117), and eight small coil handles of the sort seen on tumbler lamps (no. 114a). For a fuller discussion of tumbler lamps see above B100 nos. 3–8.

8a. (1992.0055; fig. 14.3.8a). C101.02.36. Rim, handle, and upper body fragment from tumbler lamp. D 10.0 cm; MPH 3.38 cm; MPL 1.90 cm; Th rim 0.29 cm; Th body 0.07 cm. Blue

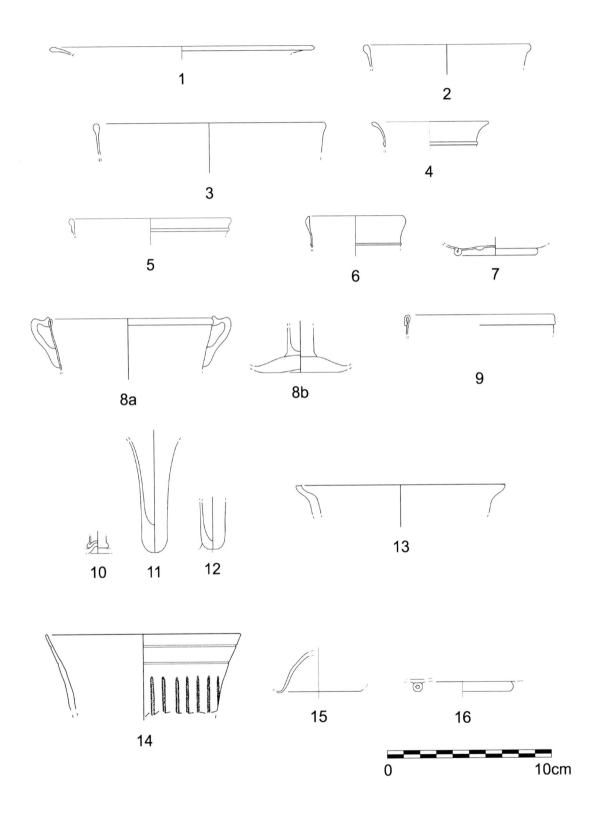

FIG. 14.3   *Glass from C101, nos. 1–16.*

green. Out-folded upright rim forming tubular edge; coil handle applied to upper body, pulled upward and outward, attached to upper part of rim, overlapping top of rim.

8b. (1992.0055; fig. 14.3.8b). C101.02.36. Wick Holder and Concave Base Fragment from Lamp. D base 4.0 cm; Th base 0.78 cm; Th body 0.24 cm; D wick holder 1.50; MPH 1.79; Th wick holder 0.33 cm. Blue green. Concave base, out-splayed walls; cylindrical interior wick holder attached separately at centre of bottom.

9. (1991.0383; fig. 14.3.9). C101.02.00. Out-folded rim fragment from bowl/lamp. D 9.0 cm; MPH 1.15 cm; MPL 1.95 cm; Th rim 0.29 cm; Th body 0.04 cm. Blue green. Out-folded upright rim forming tubular edge; upper part of body wall slightly convex.

10. (1993.0315; fig. 14.3.10). C101.04.31. Wick holder and concave base fragment from lamp. D wick holder 1.0 cm; Th wick holder 0.15 cm; Th base 0.34 cm. Blue green. Concave base with small kick from process of attaching wick holder; interior cylindrical wick holder attached separately at centre of bottom.

11. (1992.0403; fig. 14.3.11). C101.01.28. Hollow stem fragment from lamp. D 1.6 cm; MPH 6.88 cm; Th base 1.60 cm; Th body 0.13 cm. Blue green. Hollow lamp stem, thick bottom, out-splayed walls.

12. (1992.0311; fig. 14.3.12). C101.01.28. Hollow stem fragment from lamp. D 1.49 cm; MPH 2.91 cm; Th base 0.65 cm; Th body 0.21 cm. Blue green. Hollow lamp stem, thick bottom, straight walls; traces of attachment on bottom.

Cracked-Off Rims (nos. 13–14)

Area C101 produced only three fragments from vessels with cracked-off rims. There is evidence for use of vessels with cracked-off rims as both table wares and lamps (Weinberg and Goldstein 1988: 89–91). They are commonly conical or hemispherical and decorated with wheel-cut decoration ranging from a few abraded lines or wheel-cut grooves to facet-

cut designs. Lamps and bowls of this sort were widely distributed throughout the Roman world and usually range in date from the fourth to the early sixth centuries.

No. 13 is a thick rim with no trace of cut decoration close to the trim. It is similar to a rim from a thick walled hemispherical bowl type of fourth century date found at nearby sites such as Petra ez-Zantur (Keller 2006: 204 Type VII.9c) and Lejjun (Jones 2006: 409, fig. 18.8, no. 130).

No. 14 is a fragment from the rim and upper body of a vessel of colourless glass with elongated rice facet cut decoration. It bears a strong resemblance to a facet cut hemispherical bowl from Colchester (Cool and Price 1995: 76–78, no. 412). Such bowls with facets arranged in zones — in both these vessels there are two spaced wheel-cut lines below the rim and then a zone of elongated facets — are widely known in both the western and eastern empire in the second and early third centuries (Cool and Price 1995: 77). Examples in the east include cups of second- to third-century date from Dura Europos (Clairmont 1963: 66, Group d) and Karanis (Harden 1936: 99, 120, no. 317). Harden proposes that the type moved from east to west (Harden 1936: 101).

13. (1991.0448; fig. 14.3.13). C101.02.30. Cracked-off rim fragment from cup or lamp. D 12.0 cm; MPH 2.23 cm; MPL 3.34 cm; Th rim 0.31 cm; Th body 0.40 cm. Blue green. Cracked-off rim, out-splayed; thick straight walls tapering downward.

14. (1993.0064; fig. 14.3.14). C101.06.10. Cracked-off rim fragment from cup with cut decoration. D 13.0 cm; MPH 3.54 cm; MPL 2.08 cm; Th rim 0.15 cm; Th body 0.26 cm. Colourless. Cracked-off rim, slightly out-splayed; straight walls tapering downward; one narrow horizontal lathe-cut groove on rim, a second narrow horizontal lathe-cut groove on upper body, then six wide vertical cut grooves with rounded ends; with associated pushed-in tubular base ring.

Bases (nos. 15–16)

Area C101 produced 39 bases, including 12 tubular base rings, two coil bases, four concave bases, eight

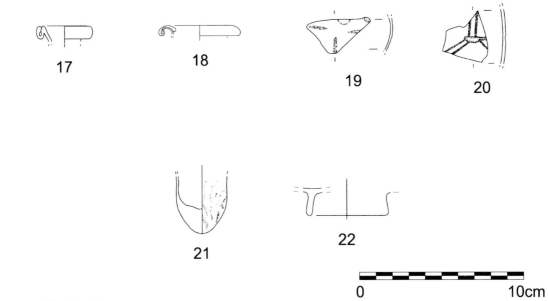

FIG. 14.4 *Glass from C101, nos. 17–22.*

flat bases, two rounded bases, two solid bases, eight true base rings, three stemmed lamp bases (see above), two mould-blown bases, and four high "kicked" bases. No. 15 is representative of the high kicked bases from Area C101. Such bases are fairly rare in the Byzantine period; they are more common in the medieval period. This base is similar to a base from a Byzantine monastery at Deir Ghazali (Avner 2000: 160–61, fig. 26, no. 4). No. 16 is a low tubular base ring of the sort commonly found on deep bowls and cups of the third to fourth centuries, such as nos. 4–6 above (Kletter and Rapuano 1998: 55, no. 8).

15. (1991.0262; fig. 14.3.15). C101.01.00. Kicked base. D 5.0 cm; MPH 2.0 cm; Th 0.07–0.21 cm. Blue green. High, concave kicked base with rounded profile.

16. (1991.0446; fig. 14.3.16). C101.01.08. Coil base. D 6.0 cm; MPH 0.63 cm; MPL 2.61 cm; Th (coil) 0.46 cm; Th body 0.11 cm. Blue green. Coil base formed from one revolution of thick. hollow coil. Thick grey mottled weathering.

Bottles (nos. 17–18)

Area C101 produced 19 fragments from closed vessels, including four rounded rims, six infolded rims,

three neck fragments, and five neck and shoulder fragments. No. 17 is a tubular rim folded outward, downward, and upward to create a collar-like rim similar to a those from Roman period bottles from Caesarea (Israeli 2008: 375, 400, nos. 55–56) and from a small flask in the collection of the Royal Ontario Museum (Hayes 1975: 61–62, no. 163, fig. 7) dated to the second half of the second or early third century. Such rims were reinforced by the extra fold which also served as an anchor for tying on coverings; they were commonly found on bottles used to store or transport liquids. No. 18 is an exaggerated overhanging infolded rim tubular rim similar to an early rim from Jalame (Weinberg and Goldstein 1988: 77, no. 332) and to a type from Petra ez-Zantur dated to the first to fourth centuries (Keller 2006: 229, pl. 21, Type VII.60).

17. (1993.0378; fig. 14.4.17). C101.04.31. Rim fragment from bottle. D 3.0 cm; MPH 0.92 cm; MPL 2.25 cm; Th rim 0.63 cm; Th body 0.16 cm. Yellowish green. Overhanging tubular rim folded outward, downward, outward, and upward.

18. (1993.0113; fig. 14.4.18). C101.04.22. Rim fragment from bottle. D 5.0 cm; MPH 1.24 cm; MPL 3.65 cm; Th rim 0.39 cm; Th body 0.10 cm. Blue green. Broad irregular overhanging

tubular rim, folded outward, downward, outward, upward, and inward.

Incised Decoration (nos. 19–20)

Area C 101 produced two body fragments with lightly incised wheel-cut decoration. The fragments are too small to give a sense of the full decorative scheme, but they most likely belong to the wide range of vessels with cut decoration dating to the third to fourth centuries. No. 21, with its three groups of radiating lines, may come from a common type of two handled cylindrical bottle with linear and facet cut decoration similar to examples in the Corning Museum of Glass (Whitehouse 1997: 266–67, no. 455) and in the Ernesto Wolf Collection (Stern 2001: 162–63, no. 59). Several fragments with similar decoration were found in fourth-century contexts at Petra ez-Zantur (Keller 2006: 235, pl. 22, Type VII.84).

19. (1991.0467; fig. 14.4.19). C101.02.30. Body Fragment with Incised Decoration. MPH 1.66 cm; MPL 3.24 cm; Th 0.20 cm. Colour uncertain. Decorated body fragment with cut elongated grooves and facets; uncertain orientation. Heavy golden weathering layer.

20. (1992.0311; fig. 14.4.20). C101.01.28. Body Fragment with Incised Decoration. MPH 2.45 cm; MPW 2.30 cm; Th 0.26 cm. Colour uncertain. Decorated body fragment with three groups of three cut grooves radiating from central element (now damaged?). Gray weathering layer over silvery iridescence.

Mould Blown Vessels (no. 21)

No. 21 is a lower body fragment from a date-shaped flask. Parallels are commonly dated to the late first to early second centuries but are known from as late as fourth- to fifth-century contexts. The date-shaped vessel is the most common type of mould-blown bottle and was probably used for scented oils or medicines. The largest concentration of finds is from Syro-Palestinian sites, suggesting a locus of production in the region where date production was an important industry (Stern 2001: 53; Stern 1995: 93). The representation of the date on most flasks is naturalistic in shape, perhaps indicating that the moulds into which the glass was blown were cast directly from dates. The vessels are also usually brown or amber in imitation of the normal appearance of dates. Stern notes that such flasks were often found in the graves of women and girls, and often in pairs (Stern 1995: 93, note 188).

21. (1991.0426; fig. 14.4.21). C101.01.08. Lower body fragment from date flask. MPH 2.63 cm; MPW 2.45 × 1.53 cm; Th bottom 1.45 cm; Th body 0.26 cm. Colour uncertain. Lower body fragment with mould-blown decoration preserving the irregular sinuous ridges characteristic of date or almond flasks. Mottled gray and dark brown enamel-like weathering.

Moulded Vessels (no.22)

No. 22 is a true base ring from a moulded colourless vessel very similar in profile to a slightly larger diameter base from Quseir al-Qadim (Meyer 1992: 25, pl. 6, no. 110). Other comparable bases come from early imperial levels at Dura Europos (Clairmont 1963: 18–19, nos. 58–60) and Aila (Jones, in preparation). Colourless luxury table wares are known throughout the Roman world in the early empire and were manufactured in various workshops from the late first into the early second centuries. The Humayma examples were most likely of Egyptian manufacture, although a site of production has not been identified. Such vessels were clearly exported from the southerly Red Sea port of Quseir al-Qadim in this period (Meyer 1992: 11–13; see above B100, no. 22).

22. (1991.0449; fig. 14.4.2). C101.02.30. High base ring. D 8.0 cm; MPH 1.35 cm; MPL 1.35 cm; Th base 0.35 cm; Th body 0.15. Colourless with a yellowish tinge. Low, slightly out-splayed true base ring, applied separately. Beige weathering and iridescence.

14.E.5. C119 (Byzantine Church)

The largest deposit of vessel glass from Humayma comes from a group of related loci in the church in area C119. These loci (C119.02.05–06), located on the floor below a cupboard in the south *pastopho-*

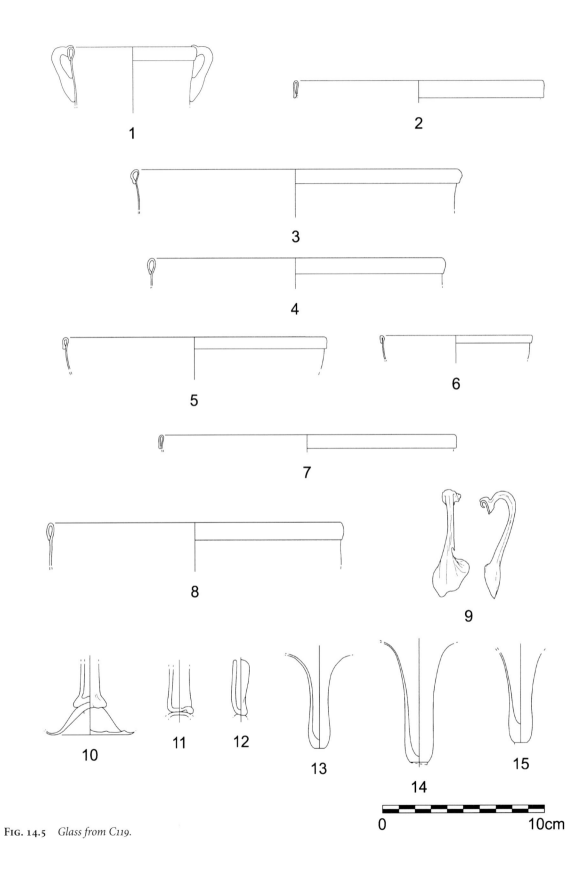

FIG. 14.5   *Glass from C119.*

rion, produced a dense deposit of fragments from broken tumbler lamps and stemmed lamps (189 fragments from out-folded rims, 51 coil handles, three wick holders, and four stem fragments) and other materials (including large marble fragments that overlay the layer of glass) consistent with structural collapse (see p. 307). A selection of rim profiles, wick holders, and hollow stems from the deposit are presented below. It is possible that lamps stored on shelves fell during an earthquake. The 2,382 fragments recovered represent over a third of the total glass produced by the site. Four additional loci in C119 add another 109 fragments to the total.

Dense layers of crushed lamps of the same type have been noted in contemporary Late Byzantine/ Early Islamic period churches at Lejjun (Jones 1987: 627–28; 1996: 412), Jerash (Meyer 1987: 184), Khirbet al-Karak (Delougaz and Haines 1960: 49), Pella (Smith and Day 1989: 70), Petra (O'Hea 2001: 370) and Deir 'Ain 'Abata (O'Hea 2007: 245, 2012). The mostly likely cause of the initial breakage at Lejjun is damage done by an earthquake in 551 (Jones 1987: 627). Such dense accumulations of glass have been variously interpreted, with some musing that such glass was destined for recycling and others wondering if, perhaps, much admired church fittings were deliberately buried to protect them from just that (O'Hea 2007: 246).

Lamps (nos. 1–15)

For a discussion of the tumbler lamp type, see above, B100 nos. 3–8.

1. (1993.0382; fig. 14.5.1). C119.02.06. Tubular rim and coil handle fragment from lamp. D 9.0 cm; MPH 4.0 cm; Th rim 0.52 cm. Pale blue green. Out-folded upright rim forming compressed tubular edge; coil handle applied to body and attached over rim.

2. (1993.0381; fig. 14.5.2). C119.02.06. Out-folded rim fragment from lamp. D 18.0 cm; MPH 0.92 cm; MPL 5.85 cm; Th rim 0.25 cm. Pale blue green. Out-folded upright rim forming tubular edge.

3. (1993.0383; fig. 14.5.3). C119.02.06. Out-folded rim fragment from lamp. D 20.0 cm; MPH 2.43 cm; MPL 2.28 cm; Th rim 0.46 cm; Th body

0.03 cm. Pale blue green. Out-folded upright rim forming tubular edge.

4. (1993.0383; fig. 14.5.4). C119.02.06. Out-folded rim fragment from lamp. D 18.0 cm; MPH 1.58 cm; MPL 3.86 cm; Th rim 0.40 cm; Th body 0.04 cm. Pale blue green. Out-folded upright rim forming tubular edge.

5. (1993.0383; fig. 14.5.5). C119.02.06. Out-folded rim fragment from lamp. D 16.0 cm; MPH 2.18 cm; MPL 6.19 cm; Th rim 0.36 cm; Th body 0.03 cm. Pale blue green. Out-folded upright rim forming tubular edge.

6. (1993.0383; fig. 14.5.6). C119.02.06. Out-folded rim fragment from lamp. D 9.0 cm; MPH 1.39 cm; MPL 4.45 cm; Th rim 0.31 cm; Th body 0.02 cm. Pale blue green. Out-folded upright rim forming tubular edge.

7. (1993.0383; fig. 14.5.7). C119.02.06. Out-folded rim fragment from lamp. D 18.0 cm; MPH 0.82 cm; MPL 5.18 cm; Th rim 0.27 cm; Th body 0.04 cm. Pale blue green. Out-folded upright rim forming tubular edge.

8. (1993.0383; fig. 14.5.8). C119.02.06. Out-folded rim fragment from lamp. D 18.0 cm; MPH 2.49 cm; MPL 2.04 cm; Th rim 0.97 cm; Th body 0.05 cm. Pale blue green. Out-folded upright rim forming tubular edge.

9. (1993.0381; fig. 14.5.9). C119.02.05. Coil handle. MPH 6.27 cm; PW 2.26 cm; D 0.46 cm; Th base 0.61cm. Blue green. Coil handle with small fragment of out-folded rim attached.

10. (1993.0382; fig. 14.5.10). C119.02.06. Wick holder and concave base fragment from lamp. MPH 3.0 cm; D base 4.0 cm; Th body 0.03 cm; cm. D wick holder 2.0 cm; Th wick holder 0.17 cm. Pale blue green. Concave base, out-splayed walls; cylindrical interior wick holder attached separately at centre of bottom.

11. (1993.0382; fig. 14.5.11). C119.02.06. Wick holder and concave base fragment from lamp. MPH 1.39 cm; D wick holder 1.9 cm; Th base 0.38 cm; Th body 0.18 cm. Pale blue green. Concave base; cylindrical interior wick holder attached separately at centre of bottom.

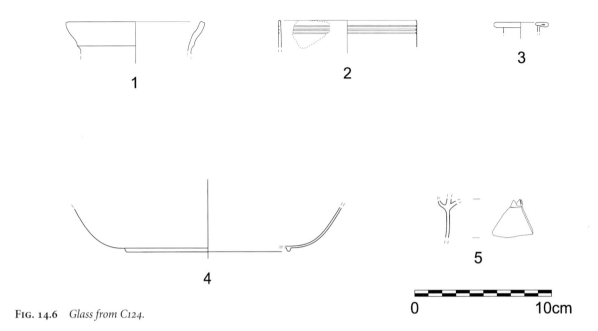

FIG. 14.6 *Glass from C124.*

12. (1993.0383; fig. 14.5.12). C119.02.06. Wick holder and concave base fragment from lamp. MPH 3.26 cm; D wick holder 1.3 cm; Th wick holder 0.27 cm. Pale blue green. Concave base; irregularly shaped, narrow, cylindrical interior wick holder attached separately at centre of bottom.

13. (1993.0382; fig. 14.5.13). C119.02.06. Hollow stem from lamp. MPH 5.44 cm; D stem 1.9 cm; Th body 0.13 cm. Pale blue green. Tubular lamp stem, thick flattened bottom, out-splayed walls.

14. (1993.0383; fig. 14.5.13). C119.02.06. Hollow stem from lamp. MPH 6.85 cm; D stem 2.05 cm; Th body 0.17 cm. Pale blue green. Tubular lamp stem, thick flattened bottom, out-splayed walls.

15. (1993.0382; fig. 14.5.15). C119.02.06. Hollow stem from lamp. MPH 5.38 cm; D stem 1.41 cm; Th body 0.04 cm. Pale blue green. Tubular lamp stem, thick flattened bottom, out-splayed walls.

14.E.6. C124 (Nabataean Campground)

Area C124, a Nabataean campground associated with a cistern, but without habitation structures, was occupied mainly in the first century, but there was probably some dumping of rubbish in later periods (pp. 48–50). Excavation in the area produced a total of 13 glass fragments, of which 10 were diagnostic. The fragments come from an unusually varied group of vessel types including a thick cracked-off rim from a cup or lamp with grooved decoration, a straight rim with multiple horizontal grooves that may come from a conical cup, a tubular bottle rim, and a wall fragment preserving a double fold.

Cracked-off rims (nos. 1–2)

Cracked-off rims are common on drinking cups and lamps with various profiles from hemispherical to conical. No. 1 is a thick rim from a bowl or cup with a wide lathe-cut groove ca. 2.0 cm below the rim. This vessel, probably hemispherical, was most likely meant for use as a lamp, given the rough, thick finish to the rim (Israeli 2008: 381). This rim comes from a common fourth-century type, examples of which are known from Petra ez-Zantur (Keller 2006: 67, 205, Type VII.9b), Caesarea (Israeli 2008: 381–82, 408, nos. 142–44), Ashqelon (Katsnelson 1999: 121, no. 4). No. 2, with its thinner and smoother finish, is most likely from a cup such as a conical example with multiple thin lathe-cut horizontal grooves Caesarea (Israeli 2008: 382–83, 409, no. 149).

1. (1993.0031; fig. 14.6.1). C124.03.00. Cracked-off rim from grooved cup. D 10.0 cm; MPH 2.35 cm; MPL 2.53 cm; Th 0.38 cm. Colourless with greyish green tinge. Very thick, slightly flaring cracked-off rim; wide horizontal lathe-cut groove cut ca. 1.5 cm below rim. Surface well preserved with many horizontal striations from wheel polishing.

2. (1996.0009; fig. 14.6.2). C124.01.06. Cracked-off rim from cup with multiple horizontal grooves. D 10.0 cm; MPH 1.48 cm; MPL 2.0 cm; Th body 0.12 cm. Colourless. Thin straight cracked-off rim with three revolutions of linear cut decoration under the rim. White weathering layer over silver iridescence.

Bottle rim (no. 3)

The single rim from a closed shape from C124 is a flattened infolded rim over a straight cylindrical neck commonly found on unguentaria over a period of centuries. It is similar to rims on piriform unguentaria from a burial cave dated to the first century at Hagosherim (Ovadiah 1999: 223–24, fig. 3, nos. 9 and 14) and to rims from candlestick unguentaria, such as unguentaria from 'Ein ez-Zeituna of second- to mid-third century date (Winter 2006: 81, fig. 3, nos. 25–26).

3. (1996.0537; fig. 14.6.3). C124.01B.04. Infolded rim fragment from unguentarium. D. 4.0 cm; MPH 0.70 cm; MPL 3.91 cm; Th rim 0.32 cm; Th body 0.12 cm. Blue green. Tubular rim folded outward, upward, and inward. Patchy white weathering over areas of iridescence.

Bases (no. 4)

C124 produced three bases, two simple low concave bases, possibly from unguentaria, and one small diameter true base ring that may belong to a colourless plate or bowl. It is similar in profile to a solid base ring on a deep bowl of early imperial date from Alon Shevut (Gorin-Rosen 1999a: 87, fig. 2, no. 7)

4. (1996.0016; fig. 14.6.4). C124.00.00. Low base ring fragment. D 12.0 cm; MPH 3.52 cm; MPL 4.37 cm; Th 0.14 cm. Colourless. Lower body and low true base ring from bowl with tapering

body walls that project far beyond base; base cut or added separately. Surface pitted with silvery iridescence.

Folded Body fragment (no. 5)

This fragment presents several possibilities. It appears to preserve a portion of a double fold in the wall or base of a vessel. It may come from a vessel with a double fold below the rim. This method of articulating the rim is common in the Levant and examples are known from the Early Roman period to the early fifth century with a peak in the fourth century. A site of production of such bowls in the fourth century has been identified at Khirbat el-Ni'ana (Gorin-Rosen and Katsnelson 2007: 81–83). This rim type appears most frequently on deep bowls (cf. Hayes 1975: 120, no, 472; Whitehouse 79, nos. 102–3; Gorin-Rosen 1999b: 66, fig. 8, no. 8). This type was found in quantity at Petra ez-Zantur, where 32 examples were found in mid-fourth- to early fifth-century contexts (Keller 2006: 207–8, Type VII.13d). Earlier examples are known from the Judean Desert (Barag 1962: 208–10), Tripoli (Price 1985: 77, 98, no. 38, fig. 6: 3, no. 38) and Tipasa (Lancel 1967: 20, fig. 29, and 88–90, nos. 174–180). The type is attested at Jalame with more upright profiles than the Aila and Petra examples (Weinberg and Goldstein 1988: 53–54, nos. 108–117). The double fold could be lower on the body of the vessel creating a decorative ridge around the body of the bowl or cup, for example on a bowl of Late Roman to Early Byzantine date from Caesarea (Israeli 2008: 376–77, 403, nos. 84–85). Alternatively, the fragment might come from an unusual base type with a double fold creating a tubular base ring usually on a large shallow bowl, such as those from second-century burials at Horvat 'Eitayim ('Uqsa 2007: 77 fig. 4, nos. 1–2). A smaller diameter base with a pronounced double fold comes from a Late Byzantine period context at Khirbat 'Adasa (Gorin-Rosen 2008: 72, fig. 2, nos. 5 and 6).

5. (1996.0009; fig. 14.6.5). C124.01.06. Folded body fragment. Colour uncertain. Body fragment with portion of double fold preserved. Thick layer of matt gray weathering obscuring colour and fold pattern.

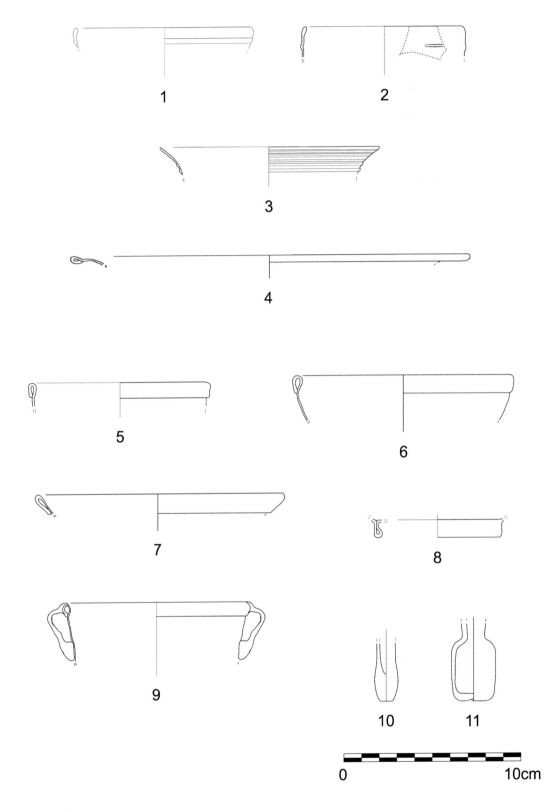

FIG. 14.7 *Glass from F102, nos. 1–11.*

14.E.7 F102 (Byzantine Church and Early Islamic House)

Area F102 included a Byzantine church of mid-seventh-century date that was reoccupied as a habitation in the Umayyad and Fatimid periods, and occupied by squatters in the Ottoman period. Of a total of 1,088 fragments from the area, 461 were diagnostic. The glass from this area is primarily Late Byzantine to early Umayyad in date, with an overlay of finds from the Abbasid periods. There were 39 fragments of simple rims from utilitarian bowls and cups distributed among flaring (4), straight (32), and incurving (3) profiles. There were only two fragments from rims of closed vessels. As one would expect from a church, there were many (131) tubular (out-folded) rims, mostly likely from lamps. There was one fragment from a cracked-off rim, probably from a lamp. One locus, F102.06.24, produced a deposit of glass vessels that included 64 fragments from tubular lamp rims. The Abbasid glass included fragments of pincer- and scratch-decorated vessels, techniques typical of the period.

Bowls with Simple Rounded Rims (nos. 1–3)

Nos. 1 and 2 represent a bowl with a simple rim, usually upright or slightly incurving, with a horizontal rib just below the rim. No. 2 may be an example of an unsuccessful attempt to achieve a single uninterrupted rib below the rim, leaving a long horizontal bubble below the rim. This type of bowl, which seems not to have been widely distributed, is known to have been produced at Jalame and was probably produced there (Weinberg and Goldstein 1988: 45–47, nos. 49–68). Weinberg and Goldstein cite a bowl in the Rockefeller Museum, Jerusalem, preserving the complete profile of a broad shallow bowl with a tubular base ring of medium height (Weinberg and Goldstein 1988: pl. 4-4, no. 70). No. 3 is a simple flaring rim fragment from a bowl with six revolutions of added amber thread decoration around the rim; it is similar to bowls of Byzantine/ early Umayyad date from Petra (Keller 2006: 67, 206, Type VII.11c) and Aila (O'Hea, in preparation).

1. (1992.0423; fig. 14.7.1). F102.05.35. Incurving rim fragment with horizontal rib from bowl. D 10.0 cm; MPH 1.12 cm; MPL 2.75 cm; Th rim 0.29 cm; Th body 0.12 cm. Colour uncertain. Incurving rim, rounded and thickened, low rib below rim. Patchy white weathering and filmy iridescence.

2. (1991.0182; fig. 14.7.2). F102.03.03. Incurving rim fragment with horizontal rib from bowl. D 9.0 cm; MPH 1.67 cm; MPL 2.52 cm; Th rim 0.22 cm; Th body 0.07 cm. Blue green. Incurving rim, rounded and thickened, segment of horizontal low relief rib/broken horizontal bubble below rim. Gray and white mottled weathering layer.

3. (19950148; fig. 14.7.3). F102.17.02. Flaring rim from bowl with contrasting thread decoration. D 12.0 cm; MPH 1.65 cm; MPL 4.61 cm; Th rim 0.12 cm; Th body 0.07 cm. Pale yellowish green. Flaring rim, rounded and thickened; six revolutions of amber thread around rim and upper body; out-splayed walls.

Bowls/Lamps Tubular Rims and Base (nos. 4–8)

These are rims from bowls or lamps with out-folded rims that create tubular collars; the rims can be flaring, upright, or slightly incurving. Body walls are generally convex and curving, tapering downward to create a deep bowl. Such rims are found in quantity at Jalame where associated bases are medium to high tubular base rings like that of no. 8 (Weinberg and Goldstein 1988: 41–44, nos. 12–36). Examples are widely distributed in the region, with good parallels from Hanita (Barag 1978: 11ff, nos. 3–9 and 31–34), Mezad Tamar (Erdmann 1977: 105, 121, and pl. 4, nos. 227–32) and nearby Petra (Keller 2006: 209 Type VII.18). Dates for the type generally range from the third to the fifth centuries.

4. (1992.0481; fig. 14.7.4). F102.06.15. Out-folded rim fragment from bowl. D 22.0 cm; MPH 1.71 cm; MPL 3.28 cm; Th rim 0.43 cm; Th body 0.08 cm. Blue green. Out-folded tubular rim, rounded and thickened, out-splayed until nearly horizontal.

5. (1992.0270; fig. 14.7.5). F102.01.24. Out-folded rim fragment from bowl/lamp. D 10.0 cm; MPH 1.60 cm; MPL 4.27 cm; Th rim 0.37 cm;

Th body 0.07 cm. Pale blue green. Out-folded upright tubular rim cm; convex curving walls.

6. (1992.0169; fig. 14.7.6). F102.05.27. Out-folded rim fragment from bowl/lamp rim. D 12.0 cm; MPH 2.16 cm; MPL 3.76 cm; Th rim 0.52 cm; Th body 0.06 cm. Colour uncertain. Out-folded incurving tubular rim, rounded and thickened; convex curving body walls.

7. (1992.0535; fig. 14.7.7). F102.06.20. Out-folded rim fragment from bowl/lamp rim. D 14.0 cm; MPH 1.12 cm; MPL 3.82 cm; Th rim 0.41 cm. Blue green. Out-folded flaring tubular rim, rounded and thickened; forms wide collar.

8. (1991.0182; fig. 14.7.8). F102.03.13. Tubular base ring. D 7.0 cm; MPH 0.89 cm; MPL 1.60 cm; Th base 0.36 cm; Th body 0.09 cm. Colour uncertain. Pushed-in bottom forming medium high vertical tubular base-ring. Gray weathering layer.

Lamps (nos. 9–11)

Area F102 also produced numerous lamp fragments, over 90 fragments from eight to 10 individual tumbler lamps, and 13 stem fragments from stemmed lamps. For more about lamps, see above, Introduction and B100 nos. 3–8. Nos. 9 and 10 are representative examples of tumbler lamps and stemmed lamps from the area. No. 11, included here as an evolution of the stemmed lamp, is an example of a rectangular stem from a lamp type dated to the late Umayyad period, similar to an example from Bet Shean belonging to Hadad's Type 4 with short, hollow stems (Hadad 1998: 69–72, fig. 4, no. 49).

9. (1991.0115; fig. 14.7.9). F102.01.12a. Out-folded rim fragment with coil handle from tumbler lamp. D 10.0 cm; MPH 2.85 cm; MPL 1.6 cm; Th rim 0.40 cm; Th body 0.07 cm. Blue green. Out-folded tubular rim, rounded and thickened; straight wall tapering downward; short coil handle applied to upper wall and attached to upper part of rim, overlapping top of rim.

10. (1992.0021; fig. 14.7.10). F102.04. Hollow lamp stem. D 2.0 cm; MPH 3.10 cm; Th body 0.20 cm. Blue green. Walls tapering upward; rounded, thickened base; flat break at bottom.

11. (1992.0471; fig. 14.7.11). F102.05.45. Hollow rectangular lamp stem. MPH 4.04 cm; MPW 2.30 × 2.12 cm; Th body 0.26 cm. Colour uncertain. Squared lamp stem with rounded edges; cylindrical neck and sloping shoulder.

Bases (nos. 12–21)

Area F102 produced fragments from 70 bases, including 30 concave bases, eight kicked bases, five rounded bases, seven flat bases, five tubular base rings, three added coil bases, and two true base rings. Disembodied bases are difficult to attribute to particular shapes with certainty, but can be discussed in terms of a range of shapes. These bases belong to vessel types dating from the fourth century into the early Umayyad periods.

No. 12 is representative of small diameter concave bases of Byzantine date from F102. It is similar to an example of third- to fourth-century date from Meron (Feig 2002: 100, fig. 11, no 13). Nos. 13 and 14 are deep concave bases that could come from a variety of vessel shapes. No. 14 is similar to bases on unguentaria from Mt. Gilboa (Gorin-Rosen 1999b: 64, fig. 7, nos. 3–6). No. 15 is a high kicked base most likely from a bottle. The base type is long-lived, seen on cups and bottles ranging in date from the Byzantine into the late medieval period (Erdmann 1977: 103). Possible parallels indicating the range of possibilities include an example from the Byzantine monastery at Deir Ghazali (Avner 2000: 160, fig. 26, no. 4), fourth- to seventh-century examples from Mezad Tamar (Erdmann 1977: 103, fig. 3, nos. 133 and 134), and Abbasid examples from Aila (O'Hea, in preparation: TS 4) as well as a jar base from Ramla (Gorin-Rosen 2010: pl. 10.7: 1b). Nos. 21–23 are thick rounded bases with projecting pontil scars similar to bases from bottles or lamps of fourth- to seventh-century date from Ashqelon (Katsnelson 1999: 78–80, fig. 5, nos. 6–7), Jerash (Meyer 1987: 194, fig. 7 M), and 'Ain ez-Zara/ Kallirrhöe (Dussart 1997: 101, pl. 28: 14). No. 17 is also similar to a base, possibly from a cup, of Late Byzantine to early Umayyad date from Khirbet el-Batiya (Gorin-Rosen 2006: 198, 30, fig. 1, no. 2) and to the base on a two-handled lamp of Umayyad date from Jerash (Meyer 1987: 212, fig. 12 T). No. 19 is a version of a long-lived thickened concave base type commonly found on drinking cups from the region most frequently dated to the fifth to sixth centuries. These cups were manufactured at Jalame (Weinberg and Goldstein 1988: 60–62, fig. 4-23, nos. 162–79). The Humayma examples find good parallels at 'Ain ez-Zara/Kallirrhöe (Dussart 1997: 101, pl. 28: 13b) and at Petra ez-Zantur (Keller 2006: 219, fig. 16 O and R, Type VII.35a). Dussart provides a thorough treatment of the type in the region (1998: 96–98, pl. 21, Type BVIII.121). No. 20 is similar to a rounded base with thinner walls and a slight thickening creating a base ring similar to an Early Byzantine base from Jerash (Meyer 1987: 194, fig. 7 N), and is reminiscent of a cup base from a burial cave at Kabri of late third- to fourth-century date (Stern and Gorin-Rosen 1997: 8, fig. 7: 14). No. 21 is a true base ring of a high quality cast colourless bowl is similar to late second to early third century examples from Dura Europos (see above B100, no. 22).

12. (1991.0359; fig. 14.8.12). F102.04.18. Concave base. D 3.0 cm; MPH 1.40 cm; Th bottom 0.40 cm; Th body 0.28 cm. Dark colour uncertain. Small diameter concave base; ring pontil scar.

13. (1991.0393; fig. 14.8.13). F102.01.31. Concave base. D 8.0 cm; MPH 1.85 cm; Th bottom 0.40 cm; Th body 0.28 cm. Colourless. Large diameter concave base. Heavy gray mottled weathering.

14. (1991.0189; fig. 14.8.14). F102.01.12.2. High concave base. D 4.30 cm; MPH 1.30 cm; Th bottom 0.80 cm; Th body 0.15 cm. Colourless. Concave base with rounded kick; ring pontil scar. Heavy gray mottled weathering.

15. (1992.0151; fig. 14.8.15). F102.05.14. High kicked base. D 4.0 cm; MPH 2.40 cm; Th body 0.10 cm. Blue green. Concave base with steep conical kick; straight body walls. Layer of iridescence.

16. (1992.0292; fig. 14.8.16). F102.05.24. Rounded base. D 2.0 cm; MPH 0.97 cm; Th bottom 0.72 cm; Th body 0.14 cm. Blue green. Rounded base; thick ring pontil scar. Heavy brown weathering layer.

17. (1992.0557; fig. 14.8.17). F102.06.23. Rounded base. D 6.0 cm; MPH 1.70 cm; Th bottom 0.75 cm; Th body 0.14 cm. Blue green. Rounded base; convex curving walls projecting far out from base; deep pontil scar. Heavy brown weathering layer.

18. (1991.0259; fig. 14.8.18). F102.01.23. Flat base. D 7.25 cm; Th bottom 0.95 cm; Th body 0.33 cm. Blue green. Flat base; thick pontil scar. Thick layer of bluish-green iridescence.

19. (1991.0270; fig. 14.8.19). F102.01.24. D 4.0 cm; MPH 1.47 cm; MPL 2.30 cm; Th 0.57 cm. Solid Base. Colourless. Thickened concave base; convex curving body walls. Thick layer of beige weathering.

20. (1992.0173; fig. 14.8.20). F102.05.24. Shallow base ring. D 5.0 cm; MPH 0.70 cm; MPL 2.85 cm; Th 0.07 cm. Yellowish green. Shallow base ring formed from thread well melted into base; convex curving walls projecting far out from base. Thin iridescent layer.

21. (1992.0423; fig. 14.8.21). F102.05.35. Moulded true base ring.. D 5.0 cm; MPH 2.58 cm; MPL 4.04 cm; Th base 0.54 cm; Th bottom 0.32 cm. Colourless. Moulded true base ring, slightly out-splayed. Beige weathering and silvery iridescence.

Bottles (nos. 22–26)

Area F102 produced 28 rim fragments from closed shapes, including simple eight straight or flaring rims and 17 infolded tubular rims. No. 22 is from a jug with a small diameter funnel rim decorated with two revolutions of the thread of the same colour below the rim. It is similar to a jug type with similar and contrasting thread decoration found in small quantities at Jalame (Weinberg and Goldstein 1988: 64–67, fig. 4-27, nos. 208–14). Weinberg and Goldstein cite an example from Samaria for the full profile of globular body, concave base, and strap or coil handle (Weinberg 1988: 65; Crowfoot 1957: 416, fig. 96:9). Examples seem to be more common in the south, with many similar rims known from fourth- to fifth-century contexts at Petra ez-Zantur (Keller 2006: 228, Type VII.57b) and 'Ain ez-Zara/Kallirrhöe (Dussart 1997: 101, pl. 27: 14a–d). No. 23 is an infolded tubular rim from a common type of

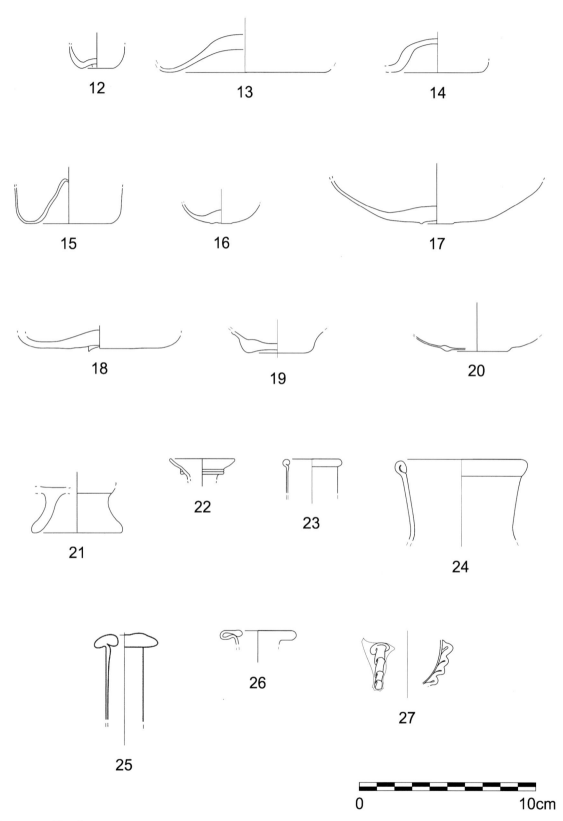

FIG. 14.8 *Glass from F102, nos. 12–27.*

globular bottle like those dating to the sixth century from Caesarea (Israeli 2008: 387, 414, no. 216) or from Ashqelon (Katsnelson 1999: 74, fig. 3: 80). No. 24 is a large diameter version of no. 23 from a jar with a squat conical neck and globular body. It is similar to fourth- to fifth-century jars from Caesarea (Israeli 2008: 380, 406, nos. 120–21). A more squat version of this jar rim dated to the third to seventh centuries can be seen at Petra ez-Zantur (Keller 2006: 231, pl. 21 O, Type VII.66a). Dussart dates the type to the Byzantine/early Umayyad periods (1998: 137–38, pl. 35, Type BX.1132b1). Nos. 25 and 26 are infolded tubular bottle rims. No. 25 is similar to rims on first-century piriform unguentaria such as those from a burial cave at Hagosherim (Ovadiah 1999: 223–24, fig. 7, nos. 5–9, 11, 13–14). No. 26 is a flattened infolded rim over a straight cylindrical neck commonly found on unguentaria over a period of centuries (see above B100 no. 12).

22. (1991.0439; fig. 14.8.22). F102.01.32. Simple rim fragment from funnel mouth bottle. D 3.75 cm; MPH 1.07 cm; Th rim 0.15 cm; Th body 0.20 cm. Blue green. Bottle rim, rounded; small diameter funnel-shaped mouth; two revolutions of thread just above junction of mouth and neck. Thin iridescent layer.

23. (1991.0182; fig. 14.8.23). F102.03.13. Infolded rim fragment from bottle. D 3.0 cm; MPH 1.75 cm; MPL 1.60 cm; Th rim 0.28 cm; Th body 0.08 cm. Blue green. Bottle rim, in-rolled; vertical neck wall. Filmy iridescent layer.

24. (1992.0012; fig. 14.8.24). F102.02.05. Infolded rim, neck, and shoulder fragment from jar. D 7.0 cm; MPH 4.60 cm; MPL 6.02 cm; Th rim 0.53 cm; Th body 0.22 cm. Yellowish green. In-rolled rim and wide neck; vertical body walls; traces of shoulder forming at base of neck. Thin iridescent layer and areas of beige weathering.

25. (1992.0170; fig. 14.8.25). F102.05.08. Infolded rim fragment from bottle. D 2.0–2.2 cm; MPH 1.07 cm; Th rim 0.15 cm; Th body 0.20 cm. Blue green. Bottle rim folded outward, upward, and inward to produce irregular tubular rim; straight cylindrical neck wall. Thick beige weathering layer over filmy iridescence.

26. (1991.0497; fig. 14.8.26). F102.03.16. Infolded overhanging rim fragment from bottle. D 4.0 cm; MPH 1.0 cm; Th rim 0.50 cm; Th body 0.14 cm. Blue green. Bottle rim folded outward, upward, and inward to produce flattened tubular rim. Thick mottled gray and brown weathering layer.

Decorated Body Fragment

No. 27 is a body fragment with a vertical trail of the same colour tooled into projecting loops. This is decorative technique is often found on bowls and cups of the Late Byzantine/early Umayyad period. The Humayma example is similar to a heavier trail on a low bowl from Ramla (Gorin-Rosen 2010: 219, pl. 10.2: 2).

27. (1992.0292; fig. 14.8.27). F102.05.24. Body Fragment with Looping Decorative Handle. MPH 2.53 cm; PW 1.65 cm; Th body 0.09 cm. Blue green. Body fragment with thin decorative coil handle tooled into projecting loops.

Deposit from F102.06.24 (1992.0558) (nos. 28–38)

Room D2 in an Abbasid-period house produced an artefact-rich fill beneath beaten floors that contained a range of glass vessel types of the Late Byzantine to early Umayyad periods. Deposit vessels represent a microcosm of the major types of glass from F102. In all, there were 155 diagnostic and 170 body fragments, including 51 fragments from tubular lamp/bowl rims (five with handles), one cracked-off rim, five concave bases, one rounded base, five closed rims, and one spout from a cupping glass. Some of the metal fittings found in the fill may include lamp hangers.

Bowls with Simple Rims (no. 28)

No. 28 is a simple flaring rim fragment from a bowl with at least four revolutions of added amber thread decoration around the rim; it is similar to bowls of Byzantine/early Umayyad date from Petra (Keller 2006: 67, 206, Type VII.11c) and Aila (O'Hea, in preparation). See above, no. 3.

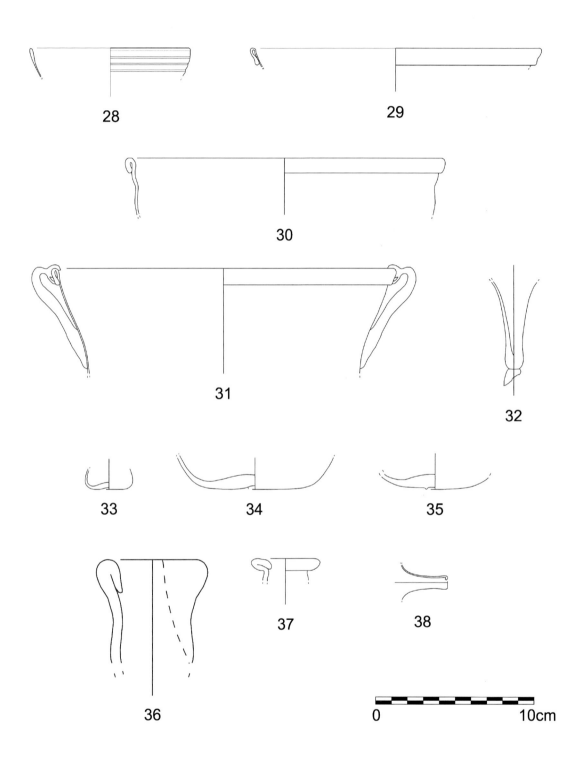

FIG. 14.9 *Glass from F102.06.24, nos. 28-38.*

28. (1992.0558; fig. 14.9).28. F102.06.24. Simple rim fragment with amber thread decoration from bowl. D 10.0 cm; MPH 1.37 cm; MPL 2.10 cm; Th rim 0.21 cm; Th body 0.04 cm. Pale blue green. Straight rim, rounded and thickened; at least four revolutions of thin amber thread around upper body, including one along rim; curving body walls tapering downward. Thick silvery iridescence.

Lamps/Bowls (no. 29–32)

The deposit produced the remains of at least eight tumbler and stemmed lamps (see above, Introduction and B100 nos. 3–8). Very close parallels to the profile of no. 31 are known from excavations of the Painted Tomb at Migdal Ashqelon (Katsnelson 1999: 78, fig. 5, nos. 1–3).

29. (1992.0558; fig. 14.9.29). F102.06.24. Out-folded rim fragment from bowl/lamp. D 18.0 cm; MPH 1.20 cm; MPL 4.39 cm; Th rim 0.4 cm; Th body 0.06 cm. Yellowish green. Out-folded tubular rim, edge rounded and thickened; body wall tapering downward. Thin, patchy layer of milky weathering.

30. (1992.0558; fig. 14.9.30). F102.06.24. Out-folded rim fragment from bowl/lamp. D 20.0 cm; MPH 4.94 cm; MPL 6.47 cm; Th rim 0.65 cm; Th body 0.16 cm. Yellowish green. Out-folded tubular rim creating collar, edge rounded and thickened; straight wall with undulations, tapering downward. Thin layer of silver and brown mottled weathering over filmy iridescence.

31. (1992.0558; fig. 14.9.31). F102.06.24. Out-folded rim and coil handle fragment from tumbler lamp. D 24.0 cm; MPH 4.40 cm; MPL 3.95 cm; Th rim 0.44 cm; Th body 0.04 cm. Yellowish green. Out-folded rim, rounded and thickened, folded outward and downward to create tubular collar; out-splayed wall with slight undulations, tapering downward; coil handle applied to middle body, pulled upward and outward, and attached to upper half of rim, overlapping top of rim. Thin layer of silvery weathering.

32. (1992.0558; fig. 14.9.32). F102.06.24. Hollow Lamp Stem. D base 2.6 cm; MPH 6.43 cm; Th

bottom 1.74 cm; Th body 0.12 cm. Yellowish green. Tubular stem from bowl lamp, tapering downward to thickened bottom; large chunk of pontil remains attached to bottom. Thick layer of silvery weathering.

Bases (no. 33–35)

The deposit produced six low concave to rounded bases. No. 33 is similar to F102, no. 12 (above), and nos. 34–35 are similar to F102, nos. 21–23 (above).

33. (1992.0558; fig. 14.9.33). F102.06.24. Concave base. D 3.0 cm; MPH 1.48 cm; Th bottom 0.22 cm; Th body 0.25 cm. Yellowish green. Concave base; walls tapering upward. Heavy layer of silvery weathering.

34. (1992.0558; fig. 14.9.34). F102.06.24. Concave base. D 6.0 cm; D pontil 1.05 cm; MPH 2.69 cm; Th bottom 0.78 cm; Th body 0.21 cm. Yellowish green. Shallow concave base; out-splayed walls; thick pontil scar. Filmy iridescence.

35. (1992.0558; fig. 14.9.35). F102.06.24. Rounded base. D 6.0 cm; D pontil 1.57 cm; MPH 1.18 cm; Th bottom 0.80 cm; Th body 0.19 cm. Blue green. Rounded base; out-splayed walls; thick pontil scar. Thick layer of silvery iridescence.

Bottles (nos. 36–37)

No. 36 is a heavy tubular rim unlike others from F102; it is similar to an example from Jerash (Dussart 1998: 153–54, pl. 44, Type BX.5321, no. 27) of a type that is most frequently dated to the fourth to sixth centuries. No. 37 is similar to rims on first-century piriform unguentaria such as those from a burial cave at Hagosherim (Ovadiah 1999: 39, fig. 7, nos. 5–9, 11, 13–14; 223–24; see above C124, no. 3, and F102, no. 25).

36. (1992.0558; fig. 14.9.36). F102.06.24. Heavy infolded rim fragment from bottle. D 6.0 cm; MPH 4.0 cm; MPL 4.80 cm; Th rim 0.87 cm; Th body 0.35 cm. Blue green. Straight in-folded bottle rim, thick and irregular; thick straight walls undulating slightly. Silver and brown mottled weathering over filmy iridescence.

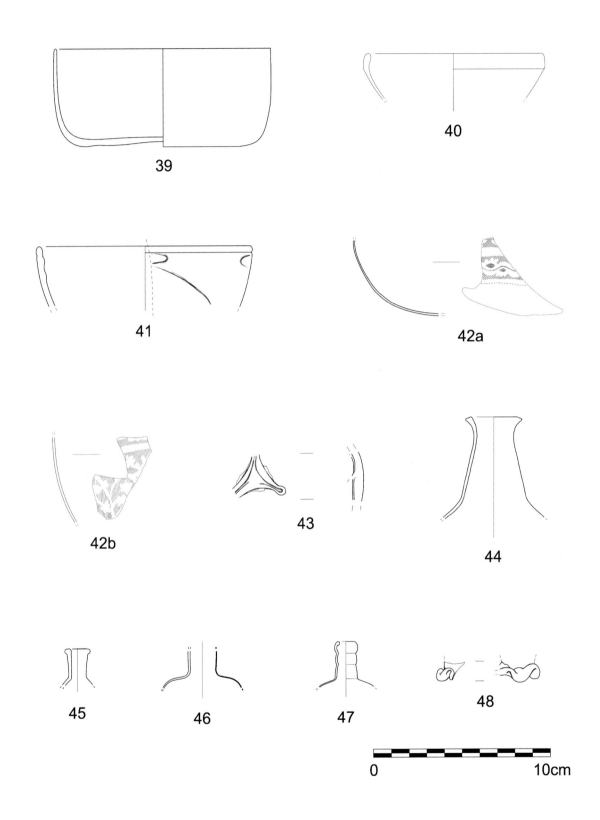

FIG. 14.10 *Glass from F102, nos. 39-48.*

37. (1992.0558; fig. 14.9.37). F102.06.24. Heavy infolded rim fragment from bottle. D 4.0 cm; MPH 1.37 cm; MPL 2.17 cm; Th rim 0.51 cm; Th body 0.24 cm. Yellowish green. Tubular rim folded outward, upward, and inward, then flattened; cylindrical neck. Heavy layer of silvery weathering.

Alembic (no. 38)

No. 38 is a spout from an alembic or alchemical still, a vessel type common to sites of the Islamic period. Similar examples of the Umayyad period are known from Ramla (Gorin-Rosen 2010: 227, pl. 10.2: 21), Caesarea (Pollak 1999: 29; 2003: 165–66, fig. 1, no. 17), and Bet Shean (Hadad 2005: 29, 47–48, pl. 23.453–55). Alembics are known over a wide geographic and chronological range during the Islamic period, for example those found at Fustat in ninth- to eleventh-century contexts (cf. Scanlon and Pinder-Wilson 2001: 56–59, nos. 29a–f) and at Nishapur, dated to the tenth to eleventh centuries (Kröger 1995: 186–88, nos. 241–42). A complete example can be found in the Benaki Museum (Clairmont 1977: 111, pl. XXIII: 87).

38. (1992.0558; fig. 14.9.38). F102.06.24. Spout from alembic. MPL 3.0 cm; D rim 1.20 cm; D break 0.81 cm; Th 0.09 cm. Yellowish green. Tubular feeding tube/spout?; rim rolled inward; walls tapering toward opening. Layer of silvery weathering over filmy iridescence.

Late Umayyad to Abbasid Period Glass from F102

The Early Islamic house in F102 produced a small corpus of primarily Abbasid period glass vessels. As with the late Byzantine–early Umayyad transition, the boundaries between late Umayyad, Abbasid, and early Fatimid glassware are not distinct. There are also regional differences in vessel types and decorative techniques. In general, the tradition of trailed decoration, typical of the Late Byzantine–early Umayyad period, continues in the late Umayyad and Abbasid periods with the trails becoming more prominent and applied in exuberant zigzags, spirals, ruffles, notched-trails, and drawn-out disks (no. 43) (Brosh 2003:

333). New shapes and distinctive new decorative techniques are introduced in the Abbasid period, including mould-blown, pincer, and scratched decoration (O'Hea 2003: 134). Thicker-walled pincer-decorated vessels with geometric designs (no. 41) are common in the Abbasid period and appear to predate rarer scratch-decorated vessels (no. 42a–b). Vessels with cut decoration in high relief are also known from the Abbasid period, but in Jordan these are found rarely and more often in ports such as Aila and Al Mina (O'Hea 2003: 134); none are known from Humayma. Most of the glass of this period is imported.

Undecorated Bowls (nos. 39–48)

No. 39 is a shallow undecorated bowl type in natural coloured glass with simple rim and straight or slightly convex sides; it was in widespread use in the Abbasid period. Examples similar two bowls found in F102 have been found in quantity nearby at Aila (O'Hea, in preparation: TS 192), Caesarea (Pollack 2003: 176, no. 40), Fustat (Scanlon and Pinder Wilson 2001, 21–23, esp. 2b), Raya in the Sinai (Shindo 2003: 181, fig. 2.1), and Nishapur (Kröger 1995: 41–42, nos. 1–3).

No. 40 is an unusual incurving or bevelled rim similar to that on a bevelled bowl with a thickened base of tenth- to eleventh-century date from Sabz Pushan (Kröger 1995: 54, no. 34).

39. (1991.0266; fig. 14.10.39). F102.06.24. Straight rim fragment from low cylindrical bowl. D 12.0 cm; H 6.05 cm; Th rim 0.19 cm; Th base 0.35 cm. Yellowish green. Tubular rim folded outward, upward, and inward, then flattened; cylindrical neck. Heavy layer of silvery weathering.

40. (1992.0156; fig. 14.10.40). F102.06.02. Incurving rim fragment from bowl. D 10.0 cm; MPH 2.03 cm; MPL 1.33 cm; Th rim 0.35 cm; Th body 0.12 cm. Pale green. Thick simple rim, bevelled; body walls tapering downward from bevel. Thin areas of surface iridescence.

Pincer-Decorated Bowl

No. 41 is a rim fragment from a pincer-decorated bowl or cup. The decorative elements seen on the

Humayma fragment, ovals and hatched curving lines, were typical of this type of decoration, which was created by using pincers or tongs to create a decorative scheme on both exterior and interior surface; it is widely known from the early Abbasid period to the late ninth century (O'Hea, Aila, in preparation). Parallels are known nearby at Aila (O'Hea, in preparation) and Petra (Keller 2006: 217, Type VII.28e) and may have been imported from Egypt where they were found in quantity at Fustat (Scanlon and Pinder-Wilson 2001: 80–82, fig. 38). Pincer-decorated vessels from Nishapur have slightly different motifs (Kröger 1995: 95–99, nos. 135–40). This type of decoration is more common on Abbasid glass in the region than cut or scratched decoration, and Lamm posited that it may have originated in Egypt and spread east (Lamm 1939: 2598).

41.   (1992.0422; fig. 14.10.41). F102.06.02. Upright rim and body fragment from pincer-decorated bowl. D 12.0 cm; MPH 3.41 cm; MPL 4.96 cm; Th rim 0.29 cm; Th body 0.31 cm. Yellowish green. Straight rim; body curving convex body walls tapering downward; pincer decoration comprising small oval elements near rim from which two hatched rays extend down diagonally to left and right, and one extends straight down. Heavy layer of brown mottled weathering.

Scratch-Decorated Vessel

Nos. 42a–b are fragments from a scratch-decorated vessel in pale blue green glass, a rare light colour for Abbasid scratch-decorated glass vessels. The appearance of this type of decoration is dated to the mid-ninth century, arising most probably in Syria or Mesopotamia; the Abbasid capital of Samarra is a strong candidate (Carboni 2001: 72–73, 81). Designs were created by etching the surface of the glass with a hard stone that left fine whitish lines that contrasted sharply with the normally dark co-loured glass of this vessel group. The characteristic background hatching of the design is created by scratching closely spaced diagonal lines that set off decorative elements left in reserve. Basic elements include triangles and "rope" motifs that frame floral

components (Carboni 2001: 76–81). The Humayma fragments are carefully cut and show a vine-like element (no. 42a) and branches with lobed leaves (no. 42b) framed by fine diagonal hatching.

42a.   (1992.0169; fig. 14.10.42a). F102.05.27. Lower body fragment from scratch-decorated bowl. MPH 3.44 cm; MPL 5.46 cm; Th 0.14 cm. Pale blue green. Lower body fragment (vessel type uncertain). The lowest part of body is left undecorated; above is a zone of hatching framing a vine-like element with small three-lobed leaves; above this a thin undecorated band with traces of the next band of hatching above. Thin patchy iridescence. From same vessel as 42b.

42b.   (1992.0169; fig. 14.10.42b). F102.05.27. Body fragment from scratch-decorated bowl. MPH 2.24 cm; MPL 4.86 cm; Th 0.14 cm. Pale blue green. Body fragment with wide zone of hatching setting off vegetal motif of branches with lobed leaves; this zone is bordered by a thin undecorated band with traces of next band of hatching above. Thin layer of beige weathering over patchy iridescence. From same vessel as 48a.

Vessel with Applied Decoration

No. 43 is a body fragment from a vessel with applied decoration that included tooled elongated triangles. This decorative motif appeared on globular bottles and cylindrical flasks of the Early Islamic period (seventh to eighth centuries). An excavated parallel comes from a late eighth-century Abbasid context at Fustat (Foy et al. 2001: 140, fig 2: 25). Examples in collections include flasks of Early Islamic date in the Toledo Museum of Art (Harden 1971: 93, pl. IX E), the Kofler Collection (Carboni 2001: 42, no. 1.8b), and the Constable-Maxwell Collection (Sotheby Park Bernet 1979: 196, no. 347), where elongated widely-spaced triangles alternate point-ing upward and downward; a globular bottle in the Kofler Collection with triangles of alternating light (yellow?) and dark (blue) glass (Carboni 2001: 42, no. 1.8a); and an unusual piriform pitcher from the Kofler Collection (Carboni 2001: 28, no. 6) where triangles alternate with disks. These vessels, along with globular bottles decorated with a similarly tooled oxhide-shaped application, were some of the earliest and most numerous glass vessels from the period marking the transition from Byzantine to Early Islamic (Harden 1971: 193; see above, B100, no. 17).

43. (1992.0245; fig. 14.10.43). F102.06.06. Body fragment with applied triangles. MPL 3.08 cm; Th 0.54 cm. Colour uncertain. Thin fragment of body wall with thick applied element tooled into elongated triangle. Thick layer of black weathering.

Bottles (nos. 44–50)

No. 44 comes from a medium-sized bottle with a flaring simple rim and conical neck tapering upward similar in profile to a thick walled example, probably of Abbasid date from Ramla (Gorin-Rosen and Katsnelson 2007: 110, fig. 3: 31). Nos. 45 and 46 are from small bottles with rounded rims and cylindrical necks. The bodies of these bottles are globular or squat and either undecorated or decorated with mould-blown or cut decoration. The type was widely distributed and dates primarily to the Abbasid period, perhaps appearing as early as the late Umayyad period (Gorin-Rosen 2010: 233). Parallels in the region are known from Aila (O'Hea, in preparation: TS119), Ramla (Gorin-Rosen 2010: 233, pl. 10.6: 1–2), Khirbet ʿAdasa (Gorin-Rosen 2008: 72, fig. 2:10), Ras Abu Maʿarif (Gorin-Rosen 1999: 210, fig. 1:21; Gorin-Rosen and Katsnelson 2007: 108–9, fig. 3:25), Caesarea (Pollack 2003: 166–67, fig. 2:23), and Bet Sean (Hadad 2005: 23–24, Pls. 5:103, 6:104–5; 36:725, and 37:747).

No. 47 is from a type of small bottle with a ridged neck common to the Abbasid period. Like the bottles with plain necks above, the type may have originally appeared in the late Umayyad period. This type also had a wide distribution and is well known in the region with good parallels from Aila (O'Hea, in preparation: TS 133, 108, 6), Ramla (Gorin-Rosen 2010: 233–35, fig. 10.6: 7–10), Caesarea (Pollack 2003: 165–67, figs. 1:16, 2:26), Tiberias (Lester 2003: 158, fig. 1:9), Bet Shean (Hadad 2005: 24, Pls. 11:204, 13:269), and Horbat Hermas (Gorin-Rosen 2006: 236, 33, fig. 1:2).

No. 48 is a neck fragment from a bottle encircled with an applied undulating band or ruffle. Two examples of these were found in F102. The Humayma fragments are small and it is impossible to verify the bottle shape, but such trails were normally applied to tall-necked bottles such as a complete bottle in the Royal Ontario Museum dated to the sixth century (Hayes 1975: 108 no. 43, pl. 26). This was a common method for the decoration of bottles from the Roman into the Early Islamic periods. Excavated examples come from sixth- to seventh-century contexts in Byzantine churches at Khirbat al-Karak (Delougaz and Haines 1960: pl. 59, no. 27) and Jerash (Meyer 1987: 206–7, fig. 11 C–E), and the Byzantine monastery at Samaria (Crowfoot 1957: 418, fig. 99:1). Other examples were found at Ramla where they date primarily from the late Umayyad period (Gorin-Rosen 2010: 224). Good parallels for the shape of the trail and diameter of the neck are known from Ramla (Gorin-Rosen 2010: 224, fig. 10.2: 12), Horvat Hermeshit (Winter 1998: 10, 175, fig. 2: 13), Aila (O'Hea, in preparation: TS 196 and 47), and Jerash (Meyer 1987: 206–7, fig. 11 C–E) all of Umayyad date.

44. (1992.0152; fig. 14.10.44). F102.05.20. Rim, neck, and shoulder fragment from bottle. D rim 3.0 cm; MPH 5.58 cm; Th rim 0.38 cm; Th body 0.16 cm. Blue green. Everted irregular cracked-off rim; short wide neck tapering upward; shoulder slanting downward.

45. (1993.0208; fig. 14.10.45). F102.08.01. Rim, neck, and shoulder fragment from bottle. D rim 0.36 cm; MPH 2.10 cm; Th rim 0.36 cm; Th body 0.08 cm. Colourless. Straight simple rim, rounded and thickened; neck tapering downward; rounded shoulder slanting downward.

46. (1992.0151; fig. 14.10.46). F102.05.14. Neck and shoulder fragment from bottle. D 1.50 cm; MPH 1.79 cm; Th neck 0.12 cm; Th body 0.05 cm. Blue. Neck and shoulder fragment. Cylindrical neck; convex curving shoulder with slight depression near the junction between neck and shoulder.

47. (1992.0169; fig. 14.10.47). F102.05.27. Rim, neck, and shoulder fragment from bottle. D 1.0 cm; MPH 2.28 cm; Th rim 0.21 cm; Th body 0.06

cm. Yellowish green. Straight rim, rounded and thickened; cylindrical neck, tapering downward, tooled into three convex segments; convex curving shoulder.

48. (1992.0265; fig. 14.10.48). F102.01.18. Neck fragment with wavy trail decoration from bottle. D 2.0; MPH 0.90; Th thread 0.53; Th body 0.11 cm. Blue green. Fragment of cylindrical neck from bottle; part of one revolution of thick wavy thread decoration; tool marks from application of thread visible. Layer of milky weathering.

Chapter 15

Analysis and Conclusions

by John P. Oleson and Robert Schick

While detailed analysis has been presented above in the chapters concerned with the various structures and artefacts described in this report, it may be helpful to pull the main threads of evidence together here, in one place.

15.A. CHARACTER OF THE CERAMIC CORPUS

The enormous amount of pottery processed for this report yielded no evidence for the local production of wheel-made pottery. The handmade vessels found in the Early Islamic contexts in Fields B100, C101, and F102 may well have been produced locally, and the unbaked clay bowl found in B100 (p. 178, fig. 6.17) is a unique example of a type of ware that may have been fairly common but has now all but disappeared from the archaeological record. For all periods, the fine wares and lamps probably were produced for the most part at Petra or Aila, or imported via those two regional centres. The coarse wares, kitchen wares, and storage wares also find their closest parallels at those two sites.

There are no obvious anomalies in the proportions of the various wares used across the site, or in the shapes or sizes of the vessels recorded. Sherds from the prodigious quantities of first- and second-century Nabataean fine ware imported from Petra continue to appear in all later occupation contexts, as sharp-hoofed sheep and goats

constantly mixed the light, sandy soils. Fine ware dominates the ceramic sample from the Nabataean campground (C124), possibly indicating a special area for hospitality in a tent occupied by a nomadic family. Coarse, kitchen, and storage wares naturally form a larger proportion of the ceramics from the later habitation levels in the B100, C101, and F102 churches.

The chronology of the ceramics recovered during excavation corresponds well with the architectural history of the site (Table 2.2). The large proportion of MN, LN, and LB sherd occurrences (54.5%) highlights both the importance and persistence of the Nabataean occupation of the site, and the construction and heavy use of the churches in the Late Byzantine period. The overwhelming proportion of LN and MN occurrences in Field C124 (81% of the total for that field) underlines the Nabataean character of the occupation of the Campsite area. For the other four excavation fields, UM and AB sherds logged 32.7% of the occurrences, while sherds of the periods FA to OT logged only 4.7%, and 84% of those were found in Field F102. Clearly Fields B100, C101, and F102 were occupied during the Umayyad and Abbasid periods, and the architectural records of these areas reflect the fact. There is, however, much less ceramic evidence for the later periods. There were almost no post-Abbasid sherds in Field C101 (the Lower Church), and the sherds of that period recorded in Field

Table 15.1   The number of "bucket occurrences" by chronological period for excavation fields F102 and F103. Note that most buckets contained sherds from more than one period, so the totals for period or field add up to more than the 1,494 buckets registered.

	MN	LN	ER	RO	LR	EB	MB	LB	UM	AB	FA	AY	MA	OT	No. of BUCKET OCCURRENCES	No. of BUCKETS FOR FIELD
F102	296	184	19	21	10	7	22	385	359	283	52	29	27	70	1,764	509
F103	344	74	7	16	10	16	347	243	411	212	44	41	42	187	1,994	985
Total Occurrences	640	228	26	37	20	23	369	628	770	495	96	70	69	257	3,758	1494

B100 (Byzantine church and Early Islamic House) constitute only 2.9% of the bucket occurrences in that field, indicating abandonment sometime in the ninth century. There was, however, some degree of continued occupation at the Early Islamic farm-house built into the Byzantine church in Field F102, since 10.1% of the bucket occurrences were attributed to the Fatimid through Ottoman periods. The majority of these occur at either end of that long chronological range. There is no obvious practical reason for the concentration of continued occupation in Field F102 rather than Field B100, which was located near a number of cisterns and reservoirs. There was, however, significant occupation in Field F103, the old Abbasid *qasr* during these same periods (Table 15.1), and it may be that there was some collaboration among the inhabitants of this part of the site during the Fatimid through Ottoman periods.

15.B. CHARACTER OF THE NON-CERAMIC ARTEFACTS

Aside from the coin hoard (pp. 403–19) and the array of grave goods recovered from Burial 2 in the C101 Church (pp. 385–98), both anomalous contexts, the non-ceramic artefacts reported on in this volume are typical of other small sites of this period in the region. Coins are not common, which is not surprising, given the rural character of the site, and, as at so many other sites, coins of the House of Constantine predominate. Functional iron objects are

also a dominant category, particularly nails, spikes, door hardware, and harness fittings, but weapons and tools for cutting or piercing are curiously rare. Bronze was reserved for objects of more complex shapes produced by casting. Although a statuette base implies the presence of a work of art, the only figured bronze objects recovered were of mediocre quality and used as a fitting, a pendant, and a censer handle. A bronze lamp, and a bronze vine leaf possibly once part of a lamp or swing handle, also hint at the presence of finer domestic or ecclesiastical furnishings. A few toilet articles were also found, including a mirror disk, along with numerous fragments of *polykandela* chains. Lead objects were absent, aside from small clippings and drips.

Like the ceramics, the glass artefacts presented here find close parallels at both Petra and Aila, and there is no evidence for local production. During the Nabataean period, imports from Egypt were favoured, probably transported through Aila, along with wares produced in the Levant or the Mediterranean world. Glass vessels, particularly for drinking and lighting, were more common in the Byzantine through early Umayyad periods. They were produced at regional workshops, for the most part probably near Petra and Aila. Cylindrical "tumbler" lamps and bowl-shaped stemmed lamps were a typical artefact from Hauarra's churches.

The largest class of stone artefacts is ecclesiastical marble, particularly carved stone chancel screen panels and their fittings. Close parallels are found at Petra, and it would make sense that the ecclesiastical marble was imported through that city via roads across the Negev. The marble itself originated in the Aegean region (Thasos, Naxos, and Prokonnesos), and, given the pattern of the trade in marble objects in the Roman and Byzantine Mediterranean, the panels were probably roughed out close to the quarry. They may then have been imported by sea through Gaza or Rhinocolura to Petra. Stonecutters may have accompanied the expensive, fragile material and finished the panels to order at Petra or Hauarra. The details behind the organization of this difficult, long-distance trade deep into Arabia Petraea are not yet understood, but the fact that few fragments of ecclesiastical marble have been found at Aila (S.T. Parker, oral communication, May 2013) supports the theory of a route through Petra rather than delivery to the port of Aila.

The next largest class of stone artefacts is that of architectural mouldings carved in the local sandstone or in shelly limestone from quarries near Ma'an. All these mouldings, although usually quite fragmentary, appear to have come originally from the impressive public buildings of Nabataean Hawara. There are column and pilaster bases and capitals, crowning or base mouldings, and doorframes. The patterns resemble those of the rock-cut tombs at Petra and the Nabataean architectural members from Oboda and Mampsis, although the occasional re-ordering of the elements suggests production by a local school of stonecutters. The majority of these fragments originated in B100, favouring the possibility that the B100 Church was built over the ruins of a Nabataean temple. The discovery of two Nabataean-type altars re-used as building material in the later habitation structures above the church reinforce this interpretation. One impressive Nabataean moulding was found re-used as a simple paving slab in an Early Islamic pavement in the Apse of the B100 church (p. 173). There is no evidence for the re-use of spolia as architectural members or decoration. They were found lying in the tumble of building collapse, and many were small fragments. A fragment of a sandstone column drum probably originating from the Roman Fort was found in an Umayyad/Abbasid context in F102, but it was being re-used as a mortar rather than as a columnar support (pp. 135–37). A small stone

object that may be one of the earliest known chess pieces also came from an Early Islamic context at B100. Although many more small fragments most likely were not recognized during excavation, the significant number of quern fragments catalogued testifies to the domestic activities taking place in B100 and F102. Some of these querns were cut from local sandstone or marl, but a few were carved from a vesicular basalt that must have been imported from outside the immediate area.

Unfortunately, few ancient inscriptions have survived at Humayma other than concise graffiti pecked into the bedrock in the vicinity of the settlement. Five funerary inscriptions appear in this volume. Given the small size of the sample, it is interesting that all three major languages spoken at the site are represented: Nabataean, Greek, and Latin.

The remaining stone artefacts represent items obviously appropriate to a small, rural settlement centre: door sockets, hammer stones, basins, perforated weights, polishing stones, and beads. One atypical find is a small marble tablet, possibly a pallet for preparing cosmetics or medicines.

15.C. EVIDENCE FOR NABATAEAN HAWARA

The Nabataean origin of Hawara is clear from both literary sources and the evidence of artefacts, and the settlement apparently prospered for more than a century as a small dependency of Petra (*HEP* 1: 50–57). The numerous large and carefully carved Nabataean architectural mouldings found around the site testify to the construction of impressive public buildings. Given the significant number of these mouldings re-used as building material in the Roman Fort, it is likely that the structures for which they were created were destroyed not long before construction of the Fort in the early second century, either by the Romans themselves, or by an earthquake. Although the destruction of houses at Petra and other Nabataean sites has been connected with the Roman invasion of 106 (see *HEP* 1: 57), there is also evidence suggesting such damage may have been caused by an earthquake not long before (Parker 2009c; Alcock et al. 2010: 160). In any case, other than the foundations of a sub-

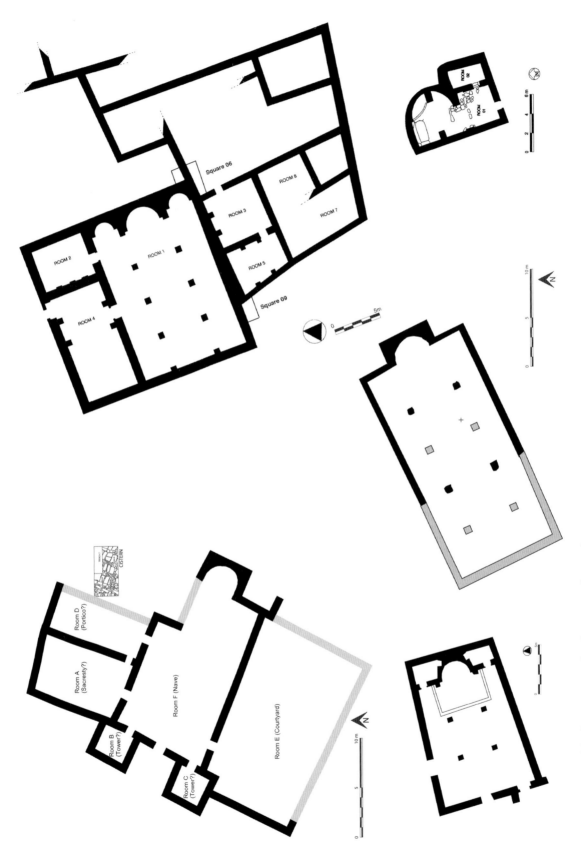

FIG. 15.1   Plan of the five Byzantine churches to a uniform scale.

stantial structure beneath the Late Roman shrine in E125 (Oleson et al. 2008: 312–13), and traces of another structure beneath the Late Roman Bath in E077 (Reeves et al. 2009: 230–35), the major structures of Nabataean Hawara remain undiscovered.

Fortunately, the chance discovery of the Nabataean Campground at C124 provides a glimpse of the non-permanent Nabataean occupation of Hawara and the surrounding region. As at Petra, where evidence has been found for occupation in tents beneath later stone-built houses, Hawara probably started off as a semi-permanent collection of tents whose inhabitants made use of the aqueduct system and reservoirs provided by King Aretas IV (Stucky et al. 1996: 47–50, 88–89; *HEP* 1: 57, 406). The tent dwellers soon constructed cylindrical cisterns for their own use, filled with run-off water like the public reservoirs. Ultimately, houses were constructed around all these cisterns except no. 54, adjacent to the C124 campground (*HEP* 1: 198–202, 307–13, 377–78, 406), leaving us with rare evidence for the early pattern of occupation at the site.

The only visible structures remaining from the Nabataean period at Hawara are the rock-cut tombs in the necropoleis surrounding the site. All but one of these tombs were grave shafts intended for up to eight individuals; the simple design is common at Petra, Hegra, and other Nabataean sites. There seems to have been one chamber tomb at the site (A114.T12–13, pp. 77–78), but the facade has been lost. The elaborate tomb facades seen at Petra and Hegra were not copied at Hawara, probably for a variety of religious, social, or economic reasons: the preference of elite families for habitation and/ or burial at Petra, or the greater sacredness of that site. One subterranean cist grave of Middle or Late Nabataean date was found deep below the B100 complex. The three cist graves found below the F102 complex, of which two were excavated, may be either Late Nabataean or Early Byzantine in date.

Although the arrival of a Roman auxiliary unit of approximately 500 individuals and their official and unofficial wives undoubtedly altered the social and economic patterns of Hauarra, the makeup and trajectory of the community outside the fort need not have changed dramatically. Papyri found at Petra, Sobata, and Nessana, for example, show the survival of Nabataean names well into the sixth

century (*HEP* 1: 468–69). Presumably the locals responded to the construction and staffing of the fort by the provision of services, the sale of grain and livestock, and the small-scale production of leather or metal goods.

15.D. EVIDENCE FOR BYZANTINE HAUARRA

The Roman Fort (E116) has yielded enormous amounts of evidence for Roman and Early Byzantine Hauarra, but this material will be presented in *HEP* 3. Although Byzantine levels were found in two probes dug in houses in the settlement centre that had been built around cylindrical cisterns (*HEP* 1: 307–13), the Humayma Excavation Project did not provide wide exposure of any domestic structure of the Byzantine period. At least some of the many houses that climb up the slope north of the C101 Church should be Byzantine in origin (see fig. 1.2; *HEP* 1: 58–59), but they await excavation. The excavations reported on in this volume, however, did provide rich evidence for ecclesiastical life in Byzantine Hauarra.

Five churches are known at Humayma. The C101 Church is the best preserved. It is marginally the largest of the five church structures at Humayma (fig. 15.1), although it is slightly smaller than the churches in the Negev (Rosenthal-Heginbottom 1982: 231, n. 2). The Church was built around the first half of the sixth century adjacent to a pre-existing building from the Late Nabataean/Roman period, and oriented at 70 degrees. There seems to have been only a single architectural phase; the three apses were an original feature of the Church. The Church continued in use into the seventh century. The tight pottery corpus from Room 5 is particularly valuable for dating the last phase of use of the room, and by extension the Church as a whole, to around 650. The building went out of use while still structurally intact. Later on, the marble and other liturgical furnishings were largely robbed out and part of the building was used for domestic occupation within the Umayyad period, as shown by the oven in Room 2, before the roof and walls of the Church were destroyed in a fire. Unlike the B100 and F102 churches, the C101 church was not re-occupied for housing in the eighth century.

The C119 church is relatively well-preserved, but it has suffered from recent illicit digging. Our limited excavations revealed its architectural features, but little could be recovered about the occupational history. The construction date of the church lies within the sixth or seventh century but cannot be narrowly defined. The nave was oriented at 72 degrees. The southeast *pastophorion* (Room 2) was a storage room for glass lamps and vessels. The pieces of marble that had been dumped there in antiquity point to a deliberate removal of the marble from the church before the major structural collapse of the building occurred. There was no trace of later occupation after the church went out of use at some poorly-defined point within the seventh or eighth century.

The B100 church was not well-preserved, having been extensively built over for housing in the eighth century. It was constructed at some point in the fifth or sixth century, but the precise date cannot be determined; the floor was repaved in a second phase. The nave was oriented to 62 degrees. The church went out of use sometime during the seventh century, possibly due to a fire. A period of abandonment followed, before housing was built into the remains of the structure at the end of the seventh or the beginning of the eighth century.

The F102 church, like the B100 church, was not well-preserved, because it also had been built over for housing in the eighth century. It apparently was constructed in the sixth or seventh century. Unlike all the other churches at Hauarra, the F102 Church was oriented east-southeast (110 degrees) rather than east-northeast. There is no obvious reason for this anomalous orientation, and it possibly had no more significance than the deviation of the other churches to the north of 90 degrees. Whether the church already gone out of use at the time the housing was built in the eighth century, or the new occupants evicted the old, is uncertain.

The B126 church is the least-understood of these ecclesiastical structures. The eastern portion of the church was built over by a barn in the 1960s, and only the small area within this structure could be excavated. Clarification of the overall plan of the church would require the removal of enormous amounts of spoil, and the plan of the possibly anomalous south apse and southeast room

remains obscure because of the modern rebuilding. The nave was oriented more or less at 70 degrees. Nothing was found during the limited excavations that could provide close dates for the construction or abandonment of this church, beyond a general assumption that it must have been constructed in the sixth century and abandoned in the seventh century. The reliquary was the most interesting find, unique at the site, although common enough at other churches in the region.

It is difficult to determine the earliest date for a Christian presence at Hauarra. The construction dates of the churches cannot be more precisely defined than sometime generally around the sixth century, although that possibly could be pushed back into the fifth century. It is unknown which church was constructed first, although the F102 church seems to be later than the others. There is nothing to support an identification of the pre-church Phase II burials in F102 as Christian. A date of around the sixth century for the start of the Christian presence is somewhat later than the evidence for Christians at some other sites in the area, such as Aila, Feinan, and Petra, where a Christian presence can be documented from the fourth century onwards on the basis of the reports of bishops attending church councils or other historical attestations (Michel 2001; Schick 2001). The rural, traditional character of the site may have delayed the arrival of the new religion.

It may well be that all five churches were in use simultaneously in the sixth and early seventh centuries. Five seems a large number of churches for the small population at the site, and it matches or exceeds the number of churches at many other, more populated sites (see Michel 2001, 2011; Schick 2001). Five churches are known at Faynan, but no other site in southern Jordan or the Negev has more churches than Hauarra. Even at the provincial capital and metropolitan See of Petra only four churches have been identified in the core settlement area (the Urn Tomb, the Petra Church, the Ridge Church, and the Blue Chapel). These were supplemented by hermitages in outlying areas re-using some of the Nabataean rock-cut tombs, as well as by the major pilgrimage site of Jabal Harûn to the west. But one can hardly claim that Hauarra was a more important settlement than Petra in the sixth century.

Accounting for the presence of five churches remains a puzzle. By default, one might assume that the five churches were all parish churches with particular congregations. But even taking into account visits by Bedouin living outside the core settlement area, it is difficult to reconstruct a total of more than a couple hundred parishioners (men, women, and children included) supporting the five churches. Whether any of the churches could have been part of a monastery is an open question. The B100, B126, C101, and C119 churches are all surrounded by other buildings that remain largely uninvestigated, although the F102 church and its adjoining rooms form a more isolated structure. Eleven churches existed simultaneously in the large village of Hadeitha – Khirbat as-Samra, north of Amman, which the excavators explain as a mix of specialized pilgrimage centres, parish churches, and commemorative or family chapels (Desreumaux et al. 2011).

There is little evidence that any of the five churches had specific functions that might explain why so many separate structures were needed. No trace of a baptistery was found in any of the churches, but the absence may be the result of incomplete excavation and, in the case of the B100 and F102 churches, their poor preservation. Intramural burials were found only the C101 Church. One might speculate that the people living in the settlement and the Bedouin in the surrounding area belonged to a number of different clans who preferred to have their own separate churches. Along those lines, the C119 church can be seen as a neighbourhood church serving the far west area of the site.

The churches are all reasonably well built, on a par with the other churches in southern Jordan and the Negev. While they are not as elaborate structurally as the Petra Church (Fiema and Frösén 2008), they are certainly built to a higher standard than the hypothetical early mudbrick church at Aila (Parker 2003: 324–25, 332) or the humble church at Lejjun (Schick 1987). The use of expensive imported marble for the liturgical furnishings demonstrates that the Christians had significant financial resources at their disposal, although evidently not enough to justify expensive floor and wall mosaics, or marble columns.

How long the churches continued in use is an important question in determining the situation at the site when the members of the Abbasid family arrived, no later than 705 (Schick 2007). The C101 Church most likely was no longer in use at the time, but it remained structurally intact to a degree that allowed installation of an oven in the Sacristy (Room 2). The B100 Church seems to have gone out of use well before the domestic housing was built there; whether that is also the case for the F102 church is less definite. The dating for the C119 Church is unclear, and nothing can be said about the B126 Church. In any case, there is nothing to point to a continued Christian presence at the site while the three generations of the Abbasid family members lived there, prior to their move to Kufa in 749, at the time of their successful revolution against the Umayyads.

15.E. EVIDENCE FOR EARLY ISLAMIC HUMAYMA

Although the early Islamic architecture reported on in this volume — the houses built over the B100 and F102 churches — is physically less impressive than the Byzantine churches, the structures and their contents provide an important picture of rural life at Humayma during its occupation by the Abbasid family. These structures also provide an important counterpoint to the large Abbasid family manor house (Structure F103), which was very carefully constructed according to a standard plan on a largely unoccupied site toward the end of the seventh or early eighth century (*HEP* 1: 60–62). In contrast, the B100 and F102 houses inserted themselves into roofless and partly collapsed churches in the later seventh or early eighth century, making full use of existing walls and pavements and, where necessary, adding subdivision walls and arches to support new roofs of timber, brushwork, and mud. The same features are seen in the Late Byzantine or Umayyad structures adjacent to the south wall of the C101 Church, Rooms 03 and 05. Bins built up against interior walls were another frequent addition, designed to contain household furnishings, foodstuffs, or animal feed. Some of the bins may have served as feed troughs for domestic animals. *Tabuns* were another common feature.

The B100 nave provided space for several enclosed courtyards that might have been used to accommodate flocks, tools, or crop processing activities, while Room D north of the F102 Church may have been adapted as a partly roofed area for storage of agricultural gear. The re-use of walls, insertion of roofing arches and bins, and a preference for interior mud floors set below the level of soil outside and approached by a high step and threshold are characteristics typical of many Early Islamic houses in Jordan, and they continued to be appear in the structures at Humayma reoccupied by Bedouin families in the twentieth century.

Early Islamic historians suggest that the Abbasid family was interested in agricultural development at the site, possibly including the cultivation of olive trees on an industrial scale. Large-scale cultivation of olives was a typical approach of the Early Islamic villages in Jordan ('Amr and al-Momani 2011; Walmsley 2011). Although there is no direct evidence for agricultural activities in the Early Islamic houses at Humayma, the substantial character of the construction, the utilitarian furnishings and artefacts, and the high proportion of storage wares all suggest permanent occupation and rural activities. The raising of goats, sheep, and camels undoubtedly was an important part of the economy, but the production of grain crops in nearby fields watered by runoff from the winter rains must have been the main basis for subsistence. The economic pattern was probably very similar to that followed by the Nabataeans, once permanent habitation had taken hold at the site (*HEP* 1: 31–50).

The departure of the Abbasid family to Kufa in 749, however, seems to have taken most of the energy out of Humayma, most likely through emigration of the majority of the population (*HEP* 1: 61–62). At F102 in particular there is evidence for continued light occupation through the Mamluk period, but with few architectural initiatives. As noted above, this occupation may have been attracted to F102 by the re-occupation of the nearby Abbasid Manor House (F103) over the same period. By the early Ottoman period the F102 house, too, appears to be in ruins, with squatters using the stubs of walls to shield their *tabuns* from the wind. The complete absence of Ottoman ceramic tobacco pipes may indicate that Ottoman occupation ended by the seventeenth century (Sinibaldi and Tuttle 2011: 448). Only in the twentieth century did the pace of occupation pick up once again, following architectural and economic patterns similar to those seen in Umayyad Humayma.

References

Abbadi, S.
1973   "A Byzantine Tomb from Naʿur." *ADAJ* 18: 69–71.

Abu-Jaber, N.; al-Saad, Z.; Shiyyab, A.; and Degryse, P.
2012   "Provenance of White Marbles from the Nabatean Sites of Qasr Al-Bint and Colonnaded Street Baths at Petra, Jordan." *Mediterranean Archaeology and Archaeometry* 12.1: 21–29.

Acconci, A.
1994   "L'arredo liturgico." Pp. 290–313 in M. Piccirillo, E. Alliata, *Umm al-Rasas Mayfaʿah I. Gli scavi del complesso di santo stefano.* Jerusalem: Studium Biblicum Franciscanum.
1998   "Elements of the Liturgical Furniture." Pp. 468–542 in M. Piccirillo. E. Alliata, *Mount Nebo. New Archaeological Excavations 1967–1997.* Jerusalem: Studium Biblicum Franciscanum.

Adan-Bayewitz, D.
1993   *Common Pottery in Roman Galilee: A Study of Local Trade.* Bar-Ilan Studies in Near Eastern Languages and Culture. Ramat-Gan.

Aga-Oglu, M.
1945   "About a Type of Islamic Incense Burner." *Art Bull* 27: 28–45.

Agadi, S.
1996   "The Bone Objects." Pp. 236–38 in A. Ben-Tor, M. Avissar, Y. Portugali, and G. Berggren, *Yoqneʿam I: The Late Periods.* Qedem Reports, 3. Jerusalem: Hebrew University.

Alcock, S. E. et al.
2010   "The Brown University Petra Archaeological Project: Report on the 2009 Exploration Season in the 'Upper Market'." *ADAJ* 54: 153–66.

Allan, J. W.
1986   *Metalwork of the Islamic World: The Aron Collection.* London: Sotheby's.

Allason-Jones, L.
1989   *Ear-Rings in Roman Britain.* British Archaeological Reports, British Series, 201. Oxford: BAR.

Alliata, E.
1994   "I reliquiari ed altri elementi architettonici." Pp. 312–17 in M. Piccirillo, E. Alliata, *Umm al-Rasas Mayfaʿah I. Gli scavi del complesso di Santo Stefano.* Jerusalem: Studium Biblicum Franciscanum.

Alt, A.
1936   "Der südliche Endabschnitt der römischen Strasse von Bostra nach Aila." *ZDPV* 59: 92–111.

ʿAmr, K.
1992   "Islamic or Nabataean? The Case of a First to Early Second Century AD Cream Ware." *SHAJ* 4: 221–25.
2004   "Beyond the Roman Annexation: The Continuity of the Nabataean Pottery Tradition." *SHAJ* 8: 237–45.

ʿAmr, K., and al-Momani, A.
1999   "The Discovery of Two Additional Pottery Kilns at az-Zurraba/Wadi Musa." *ADAJ* 43: 175–194.

2001   "Preliminary Report on the Archaeological component of the Wadi Musa Water Supply and Wastewater Project (1998–2000)."*ADAJ* 45: 253–85.

2004   "Beyond the Roman Annexation: The Continuity of the Nabataean Pottery Tradition." *SHAJ* 8: 237–45.

2011   "Villages of the Early Islamic Period in the Petra Region." Pp. 305–13 in A. Borrut, M. Debié, A. Papaconstantinou, D. Pieri, and J.-P. Sodini, *Le Proche-orient de Justinien aux Abbassides: Peuplement et dynamiques spatiales. Actes du colloque "Continuités de l'Occupation entre les Périodes Byzantine et Abbasside au Proche-Orient, VIIe–IXe Siècles," Paris, 18–20 octobre 2007.* Bibliothèque de l'antiquité tardive, 19. Turnhout: Brepols.

'Amr, K.; al-Momani, A.; al-Nawafleh, N; and al-Nawafleh, S.
2000   "Summary Results of the Archaeological Project at Khirbat an-Nawafla/Wadi Musa." *ADAJ* 44: 231–56.

'Amr, K., and Schick, R.
2001   "The Pottery from Humeima: The Closed Corpus from the Lower Church." Pp. 107–27 in E. Villeneuve, and P. M. Watson, eds., *La céramique byzantine et proto-islamique en Syrie-Jordanie (IVe–VIIe siècles apr. J.-C.). Actes du colloque tenu à Amman les 3, 4 et 5 décembre 1994.* Beirut: Institut Français d'Archéologie du Proche-Orient.

Anderberg, A.
1994   *Atlas of Seeds,* Part 4, *Resedaceae-Umbelliferae.* Stockholm: Swedish Museum of Natural History.

Angelova, D.
2004   "The Ivories of Ariadne and Ideas About Female Imperial Authority in Rome and Early Byzantium." *Gesta* 43.1: 1–15.

Asgari, N., and Matthews, K. J.
1995   "The Stable Isotope Analysis of Marble from Proconnesos." Pp. 123–29 in Y. Maniatis, N. Herz, Y. Basiakos, eds., *The Study of Marble and other Stones Used in the Antiquity.* London: Archetype.

Atil, E.; Chase, W. T.; and Jett, P.
1985   *Islamic Metalwork in the Freer Gallery of Art.* Washington, DC: Smithsonian Institution.

Attanasio, D.
2003   *Ancient White Marbles, Analysis and Identification by Paramagnetic Resonance Spectroscopy.* Rome: L'Erma di Bretschneider.

Attanasio, D.; Brilli, M.; and Bruno, M.
2008   "The Properties and Identification of Marble from Proconnesos (Marmara Island, Turkey): A New Database Including Isotopic, EPR and Petrographic Data." *Archaeometry* 50: 747–74.

Auth, S.
1976   *Ancient Glass at the Newark Museum.* Newark, NJ: The Newark Museum.

Avigad, N.
1986   *Beth She'arim. Report on the Excavations during 1953–1958,* Vol. III: *Catacombs 12–23.* New Brunswick, NJ: Rutgers University.

Avi–Yonah, M.
1961   *Oriental Art in Roman Palestine.* Studi semitici, 5. Rome: Università di Roma.

Avner R.
2000   "Deir Ghazali: A Byzantine Monastery Northeast of Jerusalem," *'Atiqot* 40: 25–52.

Avni, G., and Dahari, U.
1990   "Christian Burial Caves from the Byzantine Period at Luzit." Pp. 301–14 in G. Bottini et al., eds., *Christian Archaeology in the Holy Lands. New Discoveries. Essays in Honour of Virgilio C. Corbo, OFM.* Jerusalem: Franciscan Printing.

Baer, E.
1983   *Metalwork in Medieval Islamic Art.* Albany, NY: State University of New York.

Bagatti, B.
1985 "Nuova ceramica del Monte Nebo (Siyagha)." *LA* 35: 249–78.

Baginski, A., and Shamir, O.
1995 "Early Islamic Textiles, Basketry, and Cordage from Nahal 'Omer." *Atiqot* 26: 21–42.

Baietto, V.; Villeneuve, G.; Schvoerer, M.;
and Bechtel, F.
1999 "Investigation of Electron Paramagnetic Resonance Peaks in Some Powdered Greek White Marbles." *Archaeometry* 41: 253–65.

Bailey, D. M.
1988 *A Catalogue of the Lamps in the British Museum,* III: *Roman Provincial Lamps.* London: British Museum.
1996 *A Catalogue of the Lamps in the British Museum,* IV: *Lamps of Metal and Stone, and Lampstands.* London: British Museum.

Baly, C.
1935 "S'baita." *PEQ* 67: 171–81.

Barag, D.
1962 "Glass Vessels from the Cave of Horror," *IEJ* 12: 208–214.
1967 "The Glass." Pp. 65–72 in M.W. Prausnitz, *Excavations at Shavei Zion.* Rome: Centro per le Antichità e la Storia dell'arte del Vicino Oriente.
1978 "The Glass Vessels." Pp. 10–34 in D. Barag, "Hanita. Tomb XV, A Tomb of the Third and Early Fourth Century CE," *'Atiqot* 13 (English Series).

Baramki, D. C.
1931 "Note on a Cemetery at Karm al-Shaikh, Jerusalem." *QDAP* 1: 3–9.

Barker, S.
2010 "Roman Builders—Pillagers or Salvagers? The Economics of Deconstruction and Reuse." Pp. 127–42 in S. Camporeale et al., eds., *Arqueología de la construcción, vol. 2.* Merida: Instituto de Arqueología de Mérida.

al-Bashaireh, K.
2003 Determination of Provenance of Marble and Caliche Used in Ancient Gadara (Umm-Qais), N. Jordan. Unpublished Masters Thesis, Department of Earth and Environmental Sciences, Yarmouk University, Irbid, Jordan.
2011 "Provenance of Marbles from the Octagonal Building at Gadara 'Umm-Qais,' Northern Jordan." *Journal of Cultural Heritage* 12(3): 317–322.

Bates, G. E.
1971 *Byzantine Coins.* Archaeological Exploration of Sardis, Vol. I. Cambridge: Harvard University.

Baur, P. V. C.
1938 "Other Glass Vessels." Pp. 513–46 in C.H. Kraeling, *Gerasa: City of the Decapolis.* New Haven, CT: American Schools of Oriental Research.

Behrensmeyer, A. K.
1978 "Taphonomic and Ecologic Information from Bone Weathering." *Paleobiology* 4: 150–62.

Beijerinck, W.
1947 *Zandenatlas der Nederlandsche Flora.* Wageningen.

Bellinger, A. R.
1966 *Catalogue of the Byzantine Coins in the Dumbarton Oaks Collection and the Whittemore Collection,* Vol. 1: *Anastasius I to Maurice, 491–602.* Washington, DC: Dumbarton Oaks Research Library and Collection.

Bellwald, U.
2008 "The Hydraulic Infrastructure of Petra—A Model for Water Strategies in Arid Land." Pp. 47–94 in C. Ohlig, *Cura Aquarum in Jordanien.* Siegburg: DWHG.

Bellwald, U.; al-Huneidi, M.; et al.
2003 *The Petra Siq: Nabataean Hydrology Uncovered.* Amman: Petra National Trust.

Ben-Dor, S.
1948   "Petra Colonia." *Berytus* 9: 41–43.

Bentley, G. R., and Perry, V. J.
2008   "Dental analyses of the Bâb edh-Dhrâ human remains." Pp. 281–96 in D. J. Ortner and B. Frohlich, *The Early Bronze Age I Tombs and Burials of Bâb edh-Dhrâ, Jordan.* Lanham, MD: AltaMira.

Ben-Tor, A.; Avissar, M.; Portugali, Y.; and Berggren, G.
1996   *Yoqneʿam I: The Late Periods.* Qedem Reports, 3. Jerusalem: Hebrew University.

Berggren, G.
1969   *Atlas of Seeds,* Part 2, *Salicaceae-Cruciferae.* Stockholm: Swedish Museum of Natural History.
1981   *Atlas of Seeds,* Part 3, *Cyperaceae.* Stockholm: Swedish Natural Science Research Council.

Berlinghieri, E., and Paribeni, A.
2011   "Byzantine Merchant Ships and Marble Trade: New Data from the Central Mediterranean." *Skyllis: Zeitschrift für Unterwasserarchäologie* 11.1: 64–75.

Bernick, K.
1994   "Basketry, Cordage and Related Artifacts." Pp. 291–317 in J. Aviram et al., eds., *Masada IV. The Yigael Yadin Excavations 1963–1965, Final Reports.* Jerusalem: Israel Exploration Society.

Berti, F.
1990   *Fortuna maris: la nave romana di Comacchio.* Bologna: Nuova alafa.

Bessac, J.-C.
2007   *Le travail de la pierre à Pétra. Technique et économie de la taille rupestre.* Paris: Editions recherche sur les Civilizations.

Bevan, G., and Reeves, M. B.
2010   "A New Nabataean Funerary Inscription from Humayma." *Journal of Semitic Studies* 55: 497–507.

Beyer, H. W.
1925   *Der Syrische Kirchenbau.* Berlin: de Gruyter.

Bianchi, R. S. (ed.)
2002.   *Reflections on Ancient Glass from the Borowski Collection.* Mainz: von Zabern.

Biewers, M.
1992   *L'habitat traditionnel à ʿAima.* Ph.D diss., Lyon.
1993   *L'habitat traditionnel du sud de la Jordanie. Les villages de ʿAima, Dana and Khirbet Nawafleh.* Amman.
1997   *L'habitat traditionnel à ʿAima. Enquête ethnoarchéologique dans un village jordanien.* BAR International Series 662. Oxford: Archaeopress.

Bikai, P. M.
1996   "The Ridge Church at Petra." *ADAJ* 40: 481–89.
2001   "The Excavation Catalogue." Pp. 409–25 in Z. Fiema, C. Kanellopoulos, T. Waliszewski, and R. Schick, *The Petra Church.* Amman: American Center of Oriental Research.
2002   "The Churches of Byzantine Petra." *NEA* 65: 271–76.
2003   "Petra in Jordan: Byzantine Churches and Scrolls." Pp. 115–30 in D. Clark and V. Matthews, eds., *One Hundred Years of American Archaeology in the Middle East. Proceedings of the American Schools of Oriental Research Centennial Celebration, Washington, DC, April 2000.* Boston, MA: American Schools of Oriental Research.

Bikai, P. M., and Perry, M. A.
2001   "Petra North Ridge Tombs 1 and 2: Preliminary Report." *BASOR* 324: 59–78.

Bisheh, G., et al.
2000   *The Umayyads: The Rise of Islamic Art.* Amman: al-Faris.

Blamey, M., and Grey-Wilson, C.
1993 *Mediterranean Wild Flowers*. London: Harper Collins.

Boardman, S., and Jones, G.
1990 "Experiments on the Effects of Charring Cereal Plant Components." *Journal of Archaeological Science* 17: 1–11.

Boessneck, J.
1969 "Osteological Differences Between Sheep (*Ovis aries Linné*) and Goat (*Capra hircus Linné*)." Pp. 331–58 in D. R. Brothwell and E. Higgs, eds., *Science in Archaeology*. New York: Praeger.

Boessneck, J.; Müller, H.-H.; and Teichert, M.
1964 "Osteologische Unterscheidungsmerkmale zwischen Schaf und Ziege." *Kuhn-Archiv* 78, H: 1–2.

Borrut, A.; Debié, M.; Papaconstantinou, A.; Pieri, D.; and Sodini, J.-P. (eds.)
2011 *Le Proche-orient de Justinien aux Abbassides: peuplement et dynamiques spatiales. Actes du colloque "Continuités de l'Occupation entre les Périodes Byzantine et Abbasside au Proche-Orient, VIIe–IXe Siècles," Paris, 18–20 octobre 2007. Bibliothèque de l'antiquité tardive, 19*. Turnhout: Brepols.

Bouras, L., and Kazhdan, A.
1991 "Censer." P. 397 in A. Kazhdan et al., eds., *The Oxford Dictionary of Byzantium*, vol. 1. New York: Oxford University.

Bouras, L., and Parani, M. G.
2008 *Lighting in Early Byzantium*. Washington, DC: Dumbarton Oaks.

Brashler, J.
1995 "The 1994 Umm al-Jimal Cemetery Excavations: Areas AA and Z." *ADAJ* 39: 457–68.

Bréhier, L.
1936 *La sculpture et les arts mineurs byzantins*. Paris: Les Éditions d'Art et d'Histoire.

Brilli, M.; Cavazzini, G.; and Turi, B.
2005 "New Data of 87Sr/86Sr Ratio in Classical Marble: An Initial Database for Marble Provenance Determination." *JAS* 32: 1543–51.

Brooks, S. T., and Suchey, J. M.
1990 "Skeletal Age Determination Based on the *Os Pubis*: A Comparison of the Acsadi-Nemeskeri and Suchey-Brooks Methods." *Human Evolution* 5: 227–38.

Brown, R. M., and Reilly, K.
2010 "A Twelfth Century Faunal Assemblage from al-Wu'ayra in the Southern Highlands of Jordan." *ADAJ* 54: 121–41.

Bruck, G.
1961 *Die spätrömische Kupferprägung*. Graz: Akademische Druck- und Verlagsanstalt.

Brünnow, R. E., and von Domaszewski, A.
1904–9 *Die Provincia Arabia*. 3 vols. Strassburg: Trübner.

Bruno, M.; Cancelliere, S.; Gorgoni, C.; Lazzarini, L.; Pallante, P.; and Pensabene, P.
2002 "Provenance and Distribution of White Marbles in Temples and Public Buildings of Imperial Rome." Pp. 289–300 in J.J. Herrmann, Jr., N. Herz, and R. Newman, eds., *ASMOSIA 5: Interdisciplinary Studies of Ancient Stone, Proceedings of the Fifth International Conference of the Association for the Study of Marble and Other Stones in Antiquity, June 1998*. Boston, MA: Museum of Fine Arts.

Brunwasser, M.
2012 "Burial Customs: Death on the Roman Empire's eastern Frontier." *Archaeology Magazine* 65.5: 24–27.

Bujard, J., and Schweizer, F.
1992 *Entre Byzance et L'Islam: Umm er-Rasas et Umm el-Walid. Fouilles Genevoises en Jordanie*. Geneva: Musée d'art et d'histoire.

Buikstra, J. E., and Ubelaker, D. H.
1994 *Standards for Data Collection from Human Skeletal Remains.* Arkansas Archaeological Series, No. 44. Fayetteville, AR: University of Arkansas.

Burnett, A.
1977 *The Coins of Late Antiquity, AD 400–700.* London: British Museum.

Butler, H. C.
1929 *Early Churches in Syria, Fourth to Seventh Centuries.* Princeton, NJ: Princeton University.

Campbell, S. D. (ed.)
1985 *The Malcove Collection: A Catalogue of the Objects in the Lillian Malcove Collection of the University of Toronto.* Toronto: University of Toronto.

Campbell, S. D., and Roe, A.
1998 "Results of a Preliminary Survey of Livestock Owners." Pp. 189–96 in R. Dutton et al., eds., *Arid Land Resources and their Management: Jordan's Desert Margin.* London: Kegan Paul.

Camuti, K. S., and McGuire, P. T.
1999 "Preparation of Polished Thin Sections from Poorly Consolidated Regolith and Sediment Materials." *Sedimentary Geology* 128: 171–78.

Canivet, P.
2003 "Huarte et les mosaïques d'eglises du IVe siècle au VIe siècle en Syrie Seconde." Pp. 189–97 in N. Duval, ed., *Les églises de Jordanie et leurs mosaïques.* Beirut: Institut Français du Proche-Orient.

Canivet, P., and Canivet, M. T. (eds.)
1987 *Huarte: Sanctuaire chrétien d'Apamène (IVe–VIe S),* vol. 1. Paris: Geuthner.

Canova, R.
1954 *Iscrizioni e monumenti protocristiani del paese di Moab.* Vatican City: Pontificio Isituto di archeologia cristiana.

Cantineau, J.
1932 *Le Nabatéen,* Vol. II: *Choix de texts. Lexiques.* Paris: Leroux.

Capedri, S., and Venturelli, G.
2004 "Accessory Minerals as Tracers in the Provenancing of Archaeological Marbles Used in Combination With Isotopic and Petrographic Data." *Archaeometry* 46: 517–36.

Cappers, R. T. J.
2006 *Roman Foodprints at Berenike: Archaeobotanical Evidence of Subsistence and Trade in the Eastern Desert of Egypt.* Cotsen Institute of Archaeology, Monograph 55. Los Angeles: Cotsen Institute of Archaeology, University of California.

Cappers, R. T. J.; Bekker, R. M.; and Jans, E. A.
2006 *Digitale Zandenatlas Van Nederland.* Groningen Archaeological Studies Vol. 4. Groningen: Barkhuis.

Carboni, S.
2001 *Glass from Islamic Lands: The Al-Sabah Collection, Kuwait National Museum.* New York: Thames and Hudson.

Cassavoy, K.
2004 "The Gaming Pieces." Pp. 329–43 in G. Bass et al., eds., *Serçe Limani, An Eleventh-Century Shipwreck,* Vol. 1: *The Ship and Its Anchorage, Crew, and Passengers.* College Station, TX: Texas A&M University.

Casteel, R. W.
1977 "Characterization of Faunal Assemblages and the Minimum Number of Individuals Determined from Paired Elements: Continuing Problems in Archaeology." *JAS* 4: 125–34.

Charlesworth, D.
1966 "Roman Square Bottles," *JGS* 8: 26–37.

Charlin, G.; Gassend, J.-M.; and Lequément, R.
1978 "L'Épave antique de la Baie de Cavalière (Le Lavandou, Var)." *Archaeonautica* 2: 9–93.

Chernov, E.
2007 "Metal Objects and Small Finds from En-Gedi." Pp. 507–43 in Y. Hirschfeld, ed., *En-Gedi Excavations* II: *Final Report (1996–2002).* Jerusalem: Israel Exploration Society.

Cheyney M., et al.
2009 "Umm al-Jimal Cemeteries Z, AA, BB and CC: 1996 and 1998 Field Reports." *ADAJ* 53: 321–59.

Christ, K.
1967 *Antike Numismatik: Einführung und Bibliographie.* Darmstadt: Wissenschaftliche Buchgesellschaft.

Clairmont, C. W.
1963 *The Excavations at Dura Europos,* Vol. 4, Part 5: *The Glass Vessels.* New Haven, CT: Dura Europos Publications.

Clark, G., and Yi, S.
1983 "Niche-Width Variation in Cantabrian Archaeofauna: A Diachronic Study." Pp. 183–208 in J. Clutton-Brock and C. Grigson, eds., *Animals and Archaeology: 1. Hunters and their Prey.* British Archaeological Reports, Intl. Series, S163. Oxford: BAR.

Clason, A. T.
1981 "The Faunal Remains of Four Prehistoric and Early Historic Sites in Syria as Indicators of Environmental Conditions." Pp. 191–96 in W. Frey and H.-P. Uerpman, eds., *Beiträge zur Umweltgeschichte des Vorderen Orients.* Wiesbaden: Reichert.

Clason, A. T., and Buitenhuis, H.
1978 "A Preliminary Report of the Faunal Remains of Nahr el Homr, Hadidi, and Ta'as in the Tabqa Dam Region in Syria." *JAS* 5: 75–83.

Colt, H. D.
1962 *Excavations at Nessana.* Vol. 1. London: British School of Archaeology in Jerusalem.

Condit, I. J.
1969 *Ficus: The Exotic Species.* Berkeley, CA: University of California Division of Agricultural Sciences.

Contadini, A.
1995 "Islamic Ivory Chess Pieces, Draughtsmen and Dice." Pp. 111–54 in J. Allen, ed., *Islamic Art in the Ashmolean Museum, Part One.* Oxford Studies in Islamic Art, X. Oxford: Oxford University.

Cool, H. E. M., and Price J.
1994 *Roman Vessel Glass from Excavations in Colchester, 1971–85.* Colchester Archaeological Report, 8. Colchester: Colchester Archaeological Trust.

Correia, P. M.
1997 "Fire Modification of Bone: A Review of the Literature." Pp. 275–94 in W. Haglund and M. Sorg, *Forensic Taphonomy: The Postmortem Fate of Human Remains.* Boca Raton, FL: CRC Press.

Cré, L.
1894. "Une découverte eucharistique." *RB* 3: 277–91.

Cribb, R.
1991 *Nomads in Archaeology.* Cambridge: Cambridge University.

Crowfoot, G. M.
1957 "Glass." Pp. 403–22 in J.W. Crowfoot, G.M. Crowfoot, and K. Kenyon, eds., *The Objects from Samaria.* London: Palestine Exploration Fund.

al-Daire, M.
2001 Die fünfschiffige Basilika in Gadara – Umm Qais, Jordanien: Studien zu frühchristlichen Sakralbauten des fünfschiffigen Typus im Orient. PhD dissertation, Johannes Gutenberg-Universität, Mainz.

D'Amato, R., and Sumner, G.
2009   *Arms and Armour of the Imperial Roman Soldier from Marius to Commodus, 112 BC–AD 192.* London: Frontline.

Danin, A.
2004   *Distribution Atlas of Plants in the Flora Palaestina Area.* Jerusalem: Israel Academy of Sciences and Humanities.

Dautermann-Maguire, E.; Maguire, H.; and Duncan-Flowers, M. J.
1989   *Art and Holy Powers in the Early Christian House.* Urbana, IL: University of Illinois.

Daviau, P. M. M.
2010   *Excavations at Tall Jawa, Jordan.* Vol. 4, *The Early Islamic House.* Leiden: Brill.

Davidson, G. W.
1952.   *The Minor Objects. Corinth Vol. XII.* Athens: American School of Classical Studies.

Davies, R. W.
1971   "The Roman Military Diet." *Britannia* 2: 122–42.
1989   *Service in the Roman Army.* Edinburgh: Edinburgh University.

de Bruijn, E., and Dudley, D.
1993   "A Hoard of Byzantine Coins and Jewelry from Humeima: Preliminary Report and Catalogue." *Yarmouk Numismatics* 5: 23–29.
1995   "The Humeima Hoard: Byzantine and Sasanian Coins and Jewelry from Southern Jordan." *AJA* 99: 683–97.

Delhopital, N.
2009   "Monumental Tomb and Simple Pit-Graves at Khirbat Adh-Dharih (Nabataean Period, Jordan): An Archaeo-Anthropological Study." *SHAJ* 10: 805–22.

Delougaz, P., and Haines, R. C.
1960   *A Byzantine Church at Khirbet al-Karak.* Oriental Institute Publications, 85. Chicago: University of Chicago.

de Morgan, J. J. M.
1933   *Numismatique de la Perse antique.* Volume 1 of E. Babelon (ed.), *Traité des monnaies grecques et romaines,* III. *Monnaies orientales.* Paris: Leroux.

De Nuccio, M.; Pensabene, P.; Bruno, M.; Gorgoni, C.; and Pallante, P.
2002   "The Use of Proconnesian Marble in the Architectural Decoration of the Bellona Temple in Rome." Pp. 293–302 in L. Lazzarini, ed., *ASMOSIA 6, Interdisciplinary Studies on Ancient Stones, Proceedings of the Sixth International Conference of the Association for the Study of Marble and other Stones in Antiquity, 15th–18th of June 2000.* Padova: Bottega d'Erasmo.

Desreumaux, A., and Humbert, J.-B.
2003   "Les vestiges chrétiens de Khirbet es-Samra en Jordanie." Pp. 23–34 in N. Duval, ed., *Les églises de Jordanie et leurs mosaïques.* Beirut: Institute Français du Proche-Orient.

Desreumaux, A. et al.
2011   "Des Romains, des Araméens et des Arabes dans le Balqaʿ Jordanien: Le cas de Hadeitha – Khirbet es-Samra." Pp. 285–304 in A. Borrut, M. Debié, A. Papaconstantinou, D. Pieri, and J.-P. Sodini, *Le Proche-orient de Justinien aux Abbassides: Peuplement et dynamiques spatiales. Actes du colloque "Continuités de l'Occupation entre les Périodes Byzantine et Abbasside au Proche-Orient, VIIe–IXe Siècles," Paris, 18–20 octobre 2007.* Bibliothèque de l'antiquité tardive, 19. Turnhout: Brepols.

De Waele, A., and Haerinck, E.
2006   "Etched (Carnelian) Beads from Northeast and Southwest Arabia." *AAE* 17: 31–40.

Dickie, M.
1995.   "Fathers of the Church and the Evil Eye." Pp. 9–34 in H. Maguire, ed., *Byzantine Magic.* Washington, DC: Dumbarton Oaks.

Dolinka, B. J.
2003   *Nabataean Aila (Aqaba, Jordan) from a Ceramic Perspective.* BAR Intl. Series S1116. Oxford: Archaeopress.

Donceel-Voûte, P.
1988   *Les pavements des églises byzantines de Syrie et du Liban. Décor, archéologie et liturgie.* Louvain-la-Neuve: Collège Érasme.

Dorneman, R. H.
1978   "Tell Hadidi: A Bronze Age City on the Euphrates." *Archaeology* 31.6: 20–26.
1985   "Salvage Excavations at Tell Hadidi in the Euphrates River Valley." *Biblical Archaeologist* 48.1: 49–59.

Doxiadis, E.
1995   *The Mysterious Fayum Portraits: Faces from Ancient Egypt.* New York: Abrams.

Dunbabin, K.
1989   "*Baiarum grata voluptas*: Pleasures and Dangers of the Baths." *PBSR* 44: 6–46.

Durand, C.
2011   "Les lampes nabatéennes et romaines de Khirbet edh-Dharih (Jordanie), Ier–IVe s. ap. J.-C." Pp. 43–73 in D. Frangié, and J.-F. Salles, eds., *Lampes antiques du Bilad Es-Sham, Jordanie, Syrie, Liban, Palestine/ Ancient Lamps of Bilad Es-Sham, Actes du colloque international, Pétra-Amman, 6-13 novembre 2005.* Paris: de Boccard.

Dussart, O.
1997   "Les Verres." Pp. 96–102 in C. Clamer et al., *Fouilles Archéologiques de 'Aïn Ez-Zâra/ Callirrhoé villégiature hérodienne.* Beirut: Institut Français d'Archéologie du Proche-Orient.
1998   *Le Verre en Jordanie et en Syrie du sud.* Bibliothéque archéologique et historique, 152. Beirut: Institut Français d'Archéologie du Proche-Orient.

Duval, N.
2003a   "Architecture et liturgie dans la Jordanie byzantine." Pp. 35–114 in N. Duval, ed., *Les églises de Jordanie et leurs mosaïques.* Beirut: Institute Français du Proche-Orient.
2003b   "Les representations architecturales sur les mosaïques chrétiennes de Jordanie." Pp. 211–85 in N. Duval, ed., *Les églises de Jordanie et leurs mosaïques.* Beirut: Institute Français du Proche-Orient.

Eadie, J.
1984   "Humayma 1983: The Regional Survey." *ADAJ* 28: 211–24.

Eadie, J., and Oleson, J. P.
1986   "The Water-Supply Systems of Nabataean and Roman Humayma." *BASOR* 262: 49–76.

Edelstein, G.
2002   "Two Burial Caves from the Roman Period near Tel Qedesh." *'Atiqot* 43: 99–105, 259.

Eger, C.
2010   "Indisch, sassanidisch oder kaukasisch. Zu den Karneolperlen mit Ätzdekor der Gruppe C nach Beck in den östlichen Fernkontakten der Provinz Arabia." *Jahrbuch des römisch-germanischen Zentralmuseums Mainz* 57: 221–78.

Elderkin, K. McK.
1930   "Jointed Dolls in Antiquity." *AJA* 34: 455–49.

Elliott, T.
1998   "Abbreviations in Latin Inscriptions Published in *AE* 1888–1993." Http://www.case. edu/artsci/clsc/asgle/abbrev/latin/. Retrieved 5 January 2012.

Epstein, C., and Tzaferis, V.
1991   "The Baptistry at Sussita-Hippos." *'Atiqot* 20: 89–94.

Erdmann, E.
1977   "Die Glasfunde von Mezad Tamar (Kasr Gehainije) in Israel." *Saalburg Jahrbuch* 34: 98–146.

Erickson-Gini, T.
2010   *Nabataean Settlement and Self-Organized Economy in the Central Negev.* BAR Intl. Series S2054. Oxford: Archaeopress.
2012   "Nabataean Agriculture: Myth and Reality." *Journal of Arid Studies* 86: 50–54.

Ettinghausen, R., and Grabar, O.
1987   *The Art and Architecture of Islam: 650–1250.* New Haven, CT: Yale University.

Evans, H. C., and Ratliff, B. (eds.)
2012   *Byzantium and Islam: Age of Transition, 7th–9th Century.* New York: Metropolitan Museum of Art.

Evans, J., and Millett, M.
1992   "Residuality Revisited." *Oxford Journal of Archaeology* 11.2: 225–40.

Fabian, P., and Goren, Y
2002   "A New Type of Late Roman Storage Jar from the Negev." Pp. 145–53 in J. H. Humphrey, ed., *The Roman and Byzantine Near East, Volume 3.* Journal of Roman Archaeology Supplement 49. Portsmouth, RI: JRA.

Fahn, A.; Werker, E.; and Baas, P.
1986   *Wood Anatomy and Identification of the Trees and Shrubs from Israel and Adjacent Regions.* Jerusalem: Israel Academy of Sciences and Humanities.

Fant, J. C.
1989   "*Poikiloi Lithoi*: The Anomalous Economics of the Roman Imperial Marble Quarry at Teos." Pp. 206–18 in S. Walker and A. Cameron, eds., *The Greek Renaissance in the Roman Empire.* BICS Suppl. 36. London: University of London, Institute of Classical Studies.

Faure, G.
1986   *Principles of Isotope Geology.* 2nd edition. New York: Wiley.

Feig, N.
2002   "Salvage Excavations at Meron." '*Atiqot* 43: 87–107.

Feinbrun-Dothan, N.
1978   *Flora Palaestina: Part III.* Jerusalem: Israel Academy of Science and Humanities.
1986   *Flora Palaestina: Part IV.* Jerusalem: Israel Academy of Science and Humanities.

Fellmann Brogli, R.
1996   "Die Keramik aus den Spätrömischen Bauten." *EZ I*: 219–81.

Fiema, Z.
2012   "Reinventing the Sacred: From Shrine to Monastery at Jabal Hârûn." Pp. 27–38 in L. Nehmé and L. Wadeson, eds., *The Nabataeans in Focus: Current Archaeological Research at Petra.* Supplement to the Proceedings of the Seminar for Arabian Studies, 42. Oxford: Archaeopress.

Fiema, Z., and Comte, M.-C.
2008   "Appendix. The Object from Locus E1.09." Pp. 177–85 in Z. Fiema and J. Frösén, *Petra — The Mountain of Aaron. The Finnish Archaeological Project in Jordan,* Vol. 1: *The Church and the Chapel.* Helsiniki: Societas Scientiarum Fennica.

Fiema, Z., and Frösén, J.
2008   *Petra — The Mountain of Aaron. The Finnish Archaeological Project in Jordan,* Vol. 1: *The Church and the Chapel.* Helsiniki: Societas Scientiarum Fennica.

Fiema, Z.; Kanellopoulos, C.; Waliszewski, T.; and Schick, R.
2001   *The Petra Church.* Amman: American Center of Oriental Research.

Findlater, G.; el-Najjar, M.; Al-Shiyab, A.-H.; O'Hea, M.; and Easthaugh, E.
1998   "The Wadi Faynan Project: The South Cemetery Excavation, Jordan 1996: A Preliminary Report." *Levant* 30: 69–83.

Finkelstein, I.
1995   *Living on the Fringe: The Archaeology and History of the Negev, Sinai and Neighbouring Regions in the Bronze and Iron Ages.* Sheffield: Sheffield Academic.

Finnegan, M.
1978   "Faunal Remains from Bab edh-Dhra, 1975." *AASOR* 43: 51–54.
1981   "Faunal Remains from Bab edh-Dhra and Numeira." *AASOR* 46: 177–80.

Finnegan, M., and Van Sickle, C.
2007   "Analysis of Early Bronze Faunal Remains from the Numeira Town Site and Ras en Numeira, Jordan." Unpublished report to the principal investigators of the Expedition to the Dead Sea Plain, Jordan. 13 August 2007.

Finnegan, M., and West, D. L.
1984   "Faunal Materials Excavated From Tell Qarqur, Syria, 1984." Unpublished report submitted to the directors.

Fischer, M., and Saar, O.-P.
2007.   "A Magical Mirror Plaque from Yavneh-Yam." *IEJ* 57: 83–86.

Fischer, M. L.
1988   "Marble Imports and Local Stone in the Architectural Decoration of Roman Palestine: Marble Trade, Techniques and Artistic Taste." Pp 161–70 in N. Herz and M. Waelkens, eds., *Classical Marble: Geochemistry, Technology, Trade.* Dordrecht: Kluwer Academic.
1998   *Marble Studies: Roman Palestine and the Marble Trade.* Constanz: Universitätsverlag.

Flood, F. B.
2001   *The Great Mosque of Damascus: Studies on the Makings of an Umayyad Visual Culture.* Leiden: Brill.

Foote, R.
1999   "Frescoes and Carved Ivory from the Abbasid Family Homestead at Humeima." *JRA* 12: 423–28.

2007   "From Residence to Revolutionary Headquarters: The Early Islamic Qasr and Mosque Complex at al-Humayma and its 8th–century Context." Pp. 457–66 in T. E. Levy, P. M. M. Daviau, R. W. Younker and M. Shaer, eds., *Crossing Jordan: North American Contributions to the Archaeology of Jordan.* London: Equinox.

Forbes, R. J.
1964   *Studies in Ancient Technology.* Vol. IV. 2nd ed. Leiden: Brill.

Foy, D.; Picon, M.; and Vichy, M.
2003   "Verres omeyyades and abbassides d'origine égyptienne: Les témoignages de l'archéologie et de l'archéometrie." Pp. 138–43 in *Annales du 15ᵉ Congrès de l'Association Internationale pour l'Histoire du Verre, New York--Corning 2001.* Nottingham: Association Internationale pour l'Histoire du Verre.

Frank, F. von
1934   "Explorations in Eastern Palestine, I." *AASOR* 14: 1–113.

Frank, T.
1938   "A New Advertisement at Pompeii." *American Journal of Philology* 59: 224–25.

Freestone, I. C.; Politis, K. D.; and Stapleton, C. P.
2001   "The Byzantine Glazed Pottery from Deir 'Ain 'Abata, Jordan." Pp. 197–206 in E. Villeneuve, and P. M. Watson, eds., *La céramique byzantine et proto-islamique en Syrie-Jordanie (IVe–VIIe siècles apr. J.-C.). Actes du colloque tenu à Amman les 3, 4 et 5 décembre 1994.* Beirut: Institut Français d'Archéologie du Proche-Orient.

Frye R. N.; Gilliam, J. F.; Ingholt, H.; and Welles, C. B.
1955   "Inscriptions from Dura-Europos." *Yale Classical Studies* 14: 127–213.

Fulcherio, E.
2007   "5. Relazione sui resti scheletrici rinvenuti nel reliquario litico ritrovato in loco nella

chiesa della Torre a Umm al-Rasas." Pp. 668–72 in M. Piccirillo, "Ricerca storico-archeologica in Giordania XXVII-2007." *LA* 57: 645–724.

Gaggadis-Robin, V.; Sintes, C.; Kavoussanaki, D.; Dotsika, E.; and Maniatis, Y.
2009   "Provenance Investigation of Some Marble Sarcophagi from Arles with Stable Isotope and Maximum Grain Size Analyses." *Bulletin de Correspondance Hellénique* 51: 133–46.

Galikowski, M.
1992   "Installations Omayyades à Jérash." *SHAJ* 4: 357–61.

Galloway, A.
1999   *Broken Bones: Anthropological Analysis of Blunt Force Trauma.* Springfield, IL: Thomas.

Galvaris, G.
1978   "Some Aspects of the Symbolic Use of Lights in the Eastern Church. Candles, Lamps and Ostrich Eggs." *Byzantine and Modern Greek Studies* 4: 69–78.

Gath, J., and Rahmani, L. Y.
1977   "A Roman tomb at Manahat, Jerusalem." *IEJ* 27: 210–14.

Gatier, P.-L.
2011   "Inscriptions grecques, mosaïques et églises des début de l'époque islamique au proche-orient (VIIe–VIIIe siècles)." Pp. 7–28 in A. Borrut, M. Debié, A. Papaconstantinou, D. Pieri, and J.-P. Sodini, *Le Proche-orient de Justinien aux Abbassides: Peuplement et dynamiques spatiales. Actes du colloque "Continuités de l'Occupation entre les Périodes Byzantine et Abbasside au Proche-Orient, VIIe–IXe Siècles," Paris, 18–20 octobre 2007.* Bibliothèque de l'antiquité tardive, 19. Turnhout: Brepols.

Gerber, Y.
1994   "Nabataean Coarse Ware Pottery." Pp. 286–92 in R. A. Stucky, Y. Gerber, B. Kolb,

and S. G. Schmid, "Swiss-Liechtenstein Excavations at ez-Zantur in Petra 1993: The Fifth Campaign." *ADAJ* 38: 271–92.
1997   "The Nabataean Coarse Ware Pottery: A Sequence from the End of the Second Century BC to the Beginning of the Second Century AD." *SHAJ* 6: 407–11.
1998   "Coarse Ware Pottery from Room 6." Pp. 272–74 in B. Kolb, D. Keller, and Y. Gerber, "Swiss-Liechtenstein Excavations of az-Zantur in Petra, 1997." *ADAJ* 42: 259–77.
2000   "Observations on the 1999 Pottery." Pp. 409–11 in J. Frösén et al., "The 1999 Finnish Jabal Harûn Project: A Preliminary Report." *ADAJ* 44: 395–424.
2001a   "A Glimpse of the Recent Excavations on ez-Zantur/Petra: The Late Roman Pottery and its Prototypes in the 2nd and 3rd Centuries AD." Pp. 7–12 in E. Villeneuve, and P. M. Watson, eds., *La céramique byzantine et proto-islamique en Syrie-Jordanie (IVe–VIIe siècles apr. J.-C.). Actes du colloque tenu à Amman les 3, 4 et 5 décembre 1994.* Beirut: Institut Français d'Archéologie du Proche-Orient.
2001b   "Selected Ceramic Deposits." Pp. 359–66 in Fiema et al., *The Petra Church.* Amman: American Center of Oriental Research.
2001c   "Report on the Pottery." Pp. 427–32 in H. Merklein, R. Wenning, and Y. Gerber, "The Veneration Place of Isis at Wadi as-Siyyagh, Petra: New Research." *SHAJ* 7: 421–32.
2001d   "Observations on the 'Post-Byzantine' Pottery at Jabal Harûn." Pp. 378–79 in J. Frösén et al., "The 1998–2000 Finnish Harûn Project: Specialized Reports." *ADAJ* 45: 377–424.
2002   "Byzantine and Early Islamic Ceramics from Jabal Harûn." Pp. 201–9 in J. Frösén and Z. Fiema, eds., *Petra. A City Forgotten and Rediscovered.* Publications of the Amos Anderson Art Museum, New Series 40. Helsinki: Amos Anderson Art Museum.

Gerostergios, A.
1982   *Justinian the Great. The Emperor and the Saint.* Belmont, MA: Institute for Byzantine and Modern Greek Studies.

2008a "Preliminary Characterization of the Humayma Ceramics." Pp. 331–41 in J. P. Oleson et al., "Preliminary Report on Excavations at al-Humayma, Ancient Hawara, 2004 and 2005." *ADAJ* 52: 309–42.

2008b "The Byzantine and Early Islamic Pottery from Jabal Harûn." Pp. 287–310 in Z. Fiema and J. Frösén, *Petra — The Mountain of Aaron. The Finnish Archaeological Project in Jordan,* Vol. 1: *The Church and the Chapel.* Helsiniki: Societas Scientiarum Fennica.

Gerber, Y., and Holmqvist, V. E.
2008 "The Catalogue of Ceramics from Selected Deposits Associated with The Church and The Chapel." Pp. 311–29 in Z. Fiema and J. Frösén, *Petra — The Mountain of Aaron. The Finnish Archaeological Project in Jordan,* Vol. 1: *The Church and the Chapel.* Helsinki: Societas Scientiarum Fennica.

Genequand, D.
2001 "Wadi al-Qanatir (Jordanie): Un exemple de mise en valeur des terres sous les Omeyyades." *SHAJ* 7: 647–54.

Geva, H.
2003 *Jewish Quarter Excavations in the Old City of Jerusalem,* Vol. 2: *The Finds from Areas A, W and X-2, Final Report.* Jerusalem: Israel Excavation Society.

al-Ghabban, A. I. (ed.)
2010 *Roads of Arabia. Archaeology and History of the Kingdom of Saudi Arabia.* Paris: Somogy Art Publishers.

Ghushah, M. H.
2010 *Kanisat al-Qiyamah.* Ramallah.

Gichon, M.
1974 "Fine Byzantine Wares from the South of Israel." *PEQ* 106: 119–39.

Gilead, I.; Rosen, S.A.; and Fabian, P.
1993 "Horvat Matar (Bir Abu Matar) – 1990/1991." *Excavations and Surveys in Israel* 12: 97–99.

Glueck, N.
1965 *Deities and Dolphins: The Story of the Nabataeans.* New York: Farrar, Straus and Giroux.

Göbl, R.
1971 *Sasanidische Numismatik.* Braunschweig: Klinkhardt & Biermann.

Goffer, Zvi
2007 *Archaeological Chemistry.* 2nd ed. New York: Wiley.

Goldfus, H.
1997 Tombs and Burials in Churches and Monasteries of Byzantine Palestine (324–628 A.D.). Unpublished dissertation, Princeton University.

Goldfus, H., and Bowes, K.
2000. "New Late Roman Bone Carvings from Halusa and the Problem of Regional Bone Carving Workshops in Palestine." *IEJ* 50: 185–203.

Goldfus, H., and Fabian, P.
2000 "Haluza (Elusa)." *Hadashot Arkheologiyot* 111: 93–94.

Gordon, S.
2009 "The Game of Kings." *Saudi Aramco World* 60.4: 18–23.

Gordus, A. A.
1974 "Non-Destructive Analysis of Parthian, Sasanian, and Umayyad Silver Coins." Pp. 143–48 in D.K. Kouymjian, ed., *Near Eastern Numismatics, Iconography, Epigraphy and History: Studies in Honor of George C. Miles.* Beirut: American University.

Gorgerat, L., and Wenning, R.
2013 "The International Aslah Project (2010–2012)." Pp. 223–36 in M. Mouton, S. G. Schmid, eds., *Men on the Rocks: The Formation of Nabataean Petra.* Berlin: DFG ANR.

Gorgoni, C., Lazzarini, L., Pallante, P., and Turi, B.
2002   "An Updated and Detailed Mineropetro-graphic and C-O Stable Isotopic Reference Database for the Main Mediterranean Marbles Used in Antiquity." Pp. 115–31 in J. J. Herrmann, Jr., N. Herz, and R. Newman, eds., *ASMOSIA 5: Interdisciplinary Studies of Ancient Stone, Proceedings of the Fifth International Conference of the Association for the Study of Marble and Other Stones in Antiquity, June 1998*. Boston, MA: Museum of Fine Arts.

Gorin-Rosen, Y.
1997   "Glass Vessels from Burial Caves at Asherat," *'Atiqot* 33: 61–67.
1998   "The Glass Vessels." Pp. 55–56 in R. Kletter and Y. Rapuano, "A Roman Well at Khirbet Ibreiktas." *'Atiqot* 35: 43–59.
1999a   "The Glass Vessels from the Miqveh near Alon Shevut," *'Atiqot* 38: 85–90.
1999b   "The Glass Vessels." Pp. 63–68 in D. Syon, "A Roman Burial Cave on Mt. Gilboa." *'Atiqot* 38: 55–71.
2006   "The Glass Finds from Khirbat el-Batiya (Triangulation Spot 819)." *'Atiqot* 53: 29–36, 198–99.
2008   "The Glass Finds from Khirbat 'Adasa," *'Atiqot* 58: 72–73, 123–24.
2010   "The Islamic Glass Vessels." Pp. 213–64 in O. Gutfeld, *Ramla. Final Report on the Excavations North of the White Mosque*. QEDEM 51. Jerusalem: Hebrew University.

Gorin-Rosen, Y., and Katsnelson, N.
2007   "Glass Production in the Light of the Finds from Khirbat el-Ni'ana." *'Atiqot* 57: 53–154.

Grabar, O., et al.
1978   *City in the Desert: An Account of the Excavations Carried out at Qasr al-Hayr East*. 2 vols. Cambirdge, MA: Harvard University.

Graf, D.
1979   "A Preliminary Report on a Survey of Nabatean-Roman Military Sites in Southern Jordan." *ADAJ* 23: 121–27.

Grawehr, M.
2006   "Die Lampen der Grabungen auf ez-Zantur in Petra." *EZ III*: 261–398.

Greatrex, G., and Lieu, S. N. C. (eds.)
2002   *The Roman Eastern Frontier and the Persian Wars, Part II, AD 363–630. A Narrative Sourcebook*. London: Routledge.

Grierson, P.
1956   "The Roman Law of Counterfeiting." Pp. 240–61 in R. A. G. Carson and C. H. V. Sutherland, eds., *Essays in Roman Coinage presented to Harold Mattingly*. Oxford: Oxford University.
1982   *Byzantine Coins*. Berkeley, CA: University of California.

Grierson, P., and Mays, M.
1992   *Catalogue of Late Roman Coins in the Dumbarton Oaks Collection and in the Whittemore Collection: From Arcadius and Honorius to the Accession of Anastasius*. Washington, DC: Dumbarton Oaks.

Hackens, T.
1976   *Catalogue of the Classical Collection: Classical Jewelry*. Providence, RI: Rhode Island School of Design, Museum of Art.

Hackens, T., and Winkes, R. (eds.)
1983   *Gold Jewelry: Craft, Style, and Meaning from Mycenae to Constantinopolis*. Louvain-la-Neuve: Collège Érasme.

Hadad, S.
1998   "Glass Lamps from the Byzantine through Mamluk Periods at Bet Shean, Israel." *JGS* 40: 63–76.
1999   "Oil Lamps from the Abbasid through the Mamluk Periods at Bet Shean, Israel." *Levant* 31: 203–24.
2005   *Excavations at Bet Shean, 2. Islamic Glass Vessels from the Hebrew University Excavations at Bet Shean*. Qedem Reports, 8. Jerusalem: Hebrew University.

Hadas, G.
1994 "Nine Tombs of the Second Temple Period at 'En Gedi." (Hebrew). 'Atiqot 24 (1994) 1–75.

Haiman, M.
1989 "Western Negev Highlands Emergency Survey." IEJ 39: 173–91.
1995 "Agriculture and Nomad–State Relations in the Negev Desert in the Byzantine and Early Islamic Periods." BASOR 297: 29–53.

Hamilton, R. W., and Husseini, S. A. S
1935 "Shaft Tombs on the Nablus Road, Jerusalem," QDAP 4: 170–74.

Hammond, P. C.
1965 The Excavation of the Main Theater at Petra, 1961–1962: Final Report. London: Colt Archaeological Institute.
1973 The Nabataeans: Their History, Culture and Archaeology. Studies in Mediterranean Archaeology, 37. Gothenburg: Åström.

Hanfmann, G. M. A.
1975 Roman Art. New York: Norton.

Harden, D. B.
1936 Roman Glass from Karanis. Ann Arbor, MI: University of Michigan.
1962 "Glass." Pp. 76–91 in H. Dunscombe Colt, Excavations at Nessana, Vol. 1. London: British School of Archaeology in Jerusalem.
1971 "Ancient Glass, III: Post Roman." Archaeological Journal 128: 78–117.

Harding, G. L.
1950 "A Roman Family Vault on Jebel Jofeh, Amman." QDAP 14: 81–94.
1951 "Excavations on the Citadel, Amman." ADAJ 1: 7–18.
1971 An Index and Concordance of Pre-Islamic Arabian Names and Inscriptions. Near and Middle East Series 8. Toronto: University of Toronto.

Harl, K. W.
1996 Coinage in the Roman Economy, 300 BC to AD 700. Baltimore: John Hopkins University.

Hassell, J.
1997 "Alabaster Beehive-Shaped Vessels from the Arabian Peninsula: Interpretations from a Comparative Study of Characteristics, Contexts and Associated Finds." AAE 8: 245–81.

Hayes, J. W.
1972 Late Roman Pottery. London: British School at Rome.
1975 Roman and Pre-Roman Glass in the Royal Ontario Museum. Toronto: Royal Ontario Museum.
1985 Atlante delle forme ceramiche, I: Ceramica fine romana nel bacino mediterraneo (medio e tardo impero). Encyclopedia dell'arte antica, classica e orientale. Rome: Instituto della Enciclopedia Italiana.

Healey, J. F.
2001 The Religion of the Nabataeans: A Conspectus. Leiden: Brill.

Heidemann, S.
1998 "The Merger of Two Currency Zones in Early Islam. The Byzantine and Sasanian Impact on the Circulation in Former Byzantine Syria and Northern Mesopotamia." Iran 36: 95–112.

Hellmann, M.-C.
1985 Lampes Antiques de la Bibliothèque Nationale, I: Collection Froehner. Paris: Bibliothèque Nationale.

Helms, S.
1990 Early Islamic Architecture of the Desert: A Bedouin Station in Eastern Jordan. Edinburgh: Edinburgh University.

Herz, N.
1985 "Isotopic Analysis of Marble." Pp. 331–51 in G. Rapp Jr., and J. A. Gifford, eds., Ar-

chaeological Geology. New Haven, CT: Yale University.

1987 "Carbon and Oxygen Isotopic Ratios: A Database for Classical Greek and Roman Marble." Archaeometry 29: 35–43.

1992 "Provenance Determination of Neolithic to Classical Mediterranean Marbles by Stable Isotopes." Archaeometry 34: 185–94.

Herz, N., and Garrison, E. G.
1998 Geological Methods for Archaeology. New York: Oxford University.

Hill, G. F.
1922 "Ancient Methods of Coining." Numismatic Chronicle 2: 1–42.

Hillenbrand, R.
1991 "Masdjid (in Central Islamic Lands)." Pp. 644–88 in C.E. Bosthworth et al., eds., Encyclopedia of Islam, new ed., vol. 6. Leiden: Brill.

2005 "The Syrian Connection: Archaic Elements in Spanish Umayyad Ivories." Pp. 49–73 in K. von Folsach and J. Meyer, eds., The Ivories of Muslim Spain. Journal of the David Collection, 2.1. Copenhagen: David Collection.

Hirschfeld, Y.
2006 "The Nabataean Presence South of the Dead Sea: New Evidence." Pp. 167–90 in P. Bienkowski and K. Galor, eds., Crossing the Rift. Resources, Routes, Settlement Patterns and Interaction in the Wadi Arabah. Oxford: Oxbow.

Holmqvist, V. E.
2010 Ceramics in Transition: A Comparative Analytical Study of Late Byzantine–Early Islamic Pottery in Palaestina Tertia. Unpublished PhD thesis, Institute of Archaeology, University College London.

2011 "Ceramic Lamps from Jabal Harûn near Petra. Chronological and Typological Considerations." Pp. 31–41 in D. Frangié, and J.-F. Salles, eds., Lampes antiques du Bilad Es-Sham, Jordanie, Syrie, Liban, Palestine/ Ancient Lamps of Bilad Es-Sham, Actes du colloque international, Pétra-Amman, 6-13 novembre 2005. Paris: de Boccard.

Holmqvist-Saukkonen, V. E.
Forthcoming "Pottery Supply and Exchange: A Techno-Analytical Study of Jabal Harûn Ceramics (ED-XRF, SEM-EDS)." In Z.T. Fiema and J. Frösén, Petra—The Mountain of Aaron II: The Monastery. Helsinki.

Hopkins, D. C.
1993 "Pastoralists in Late Bronze Age Palestine: Which Way Did They Go." BA 56: 200–11.

Horsfield, G., and Horsfield, A.
1938 "Sela-Petra, The Rock of Edom and Nabatene." QDAP 7: 1–42.

Horwitz, L. K.
1986–87 "Faunal Remains from the Early Iron Age Site on Mount Ebal." Tel Aviv 13–14: 173–89.

1989 "Diachronic Changes in Rural Husbandry Practices in Bronze Age Settlements from the Refaim Valley, Israel." PEQ 1989: 44–54.

Horwitz, L. K., and Dahan, E.
1996 "Animal Husbandry Practices during the Historic Periods at Tel Yoqne'am." Pp. 1–15 in A. Ben-Tor, M. Avissar, and Y. Portugali, eds., Yoqne'am, I: The Later Periods. QEDEM, Institute of Archaeology Monographs, 3. Jerusalem: Hebrew University.

Horwitz, L. K.; Tchernov, E.; and Mienis, H.
1997 Faunal Remains from Nahal 'Oded. Appendix One, pp. 107–8 in S.A. Rosen and G. Avni, The 'Oded Sites: Investigations of Two Early Islamic Pastoral Camps South of the Ramon Crater. Beer-sheva: Negev.

Hübner, U.
1992 Spiele und Spielzeug im antiken Palästina. Göttingen: Vandenhoeck & Ruprecht.

Humbert, J.-B., and Desreumaux, A.

1998   *Fouilles de Khirbet es-Samra en Jordanie, I. La voie romaine, Le cimetière, Les documents épigraphiques.* Turnhout: Brepols.

Huth, M.

2010   *Coinage of the Caravan Kingdoms. Ancient Arabian Coins from the Collection of Martin Huth.* New York: American Numismatic Society.

Hyslop, K. R. Maxwell

1971   *Western Asiatic Jewellery c. 3000–612 B.C.* London: Methuen.

Ibrahim, M. M., and Gordon, R. L.

1987   *A Cemetery at Queen Alia International Airport.* Wiesbaden: Harrassowitz.

Iliffe, J. H

1934   "A Rock–Cut Tomb at Tarshiha." *QDAP* 3: 9–16.

Israeli, Y.

1974.   "A Mirror Plaque from the Clark Collection, Jerusalem." *IEJ* 14: 50–60.

2000   "Christian Images and Symbols." Pp. 144–65 in Y. Israeli and D. Mevorah, eds., *Cradle of Christianity.* Jerusalem: The Israel Museum.

2003   *Ancient Glass in the Israel Museum. The Eliahu Dobkin Collection and Other Gifts.* Jerusalem: The Israel Museum.

2008   "The Glass Vessels." Pp. 367–418 in J. Patrich, ed., *Archaeological Excavations at Caesarea Maritima Areas CC, KK, and NN. Final Reports Volume 1: The Objects.* Jerusalem: Israel Exploration Society.

Israeli, Y., and Mevorah, D. (eds.)

2000   *Cradle of Christianity.* Jerusalem: The Israel Museum.

Ivison, E.

1996   "Burials and Urbanism in Late Antique and Byzantine Corinth." Pp. 99–125 in N. Christie and S. T. Loseby, eds., *Towns in Transition: Urban Evolution in Late Antiquity and the Early Middle Ages.* Aldershot: Scolar.

James, S.

2004   *Excavations at Dura-Europos 1928–1937, Final Report VI: The Arms and Armour and Other Military Equipment.* London: British Museum.

Jobling, W. L.

1989a   "'Aqaba–Ma'an Archaeological and Epigraphic Survey." Pp. 16–24 in D. Homès-Fredericq and J. B. Hennessy, eds., *Archaeology of Jordan: III. Field Reports,* Leuven: Peeters.

1989b   "Report of the Eighth Season of the 'Aqaba–Ma'an Archaeological and Epigraphical Survey (January–February 1988)." *Liber Annuus* 39: 253–55.

Johns, J.

1998   "The Rise of Middle-Islamic Hand-Made Geometrically-Painted Ware in Bilad al-Sham (11th–13th c. AD)." Pp. 149–82 in R.-P. Gayraud, ed., *Colloque international d'archéologie islamique.* Cairo: Institut Français d'archéologie orientale.

Johnson, D. J.

1990   "Nabataean Piriform Unguentaria." *ARAM* 2: 235–48.

Jones, J. D.

1987   "The Glass." Pp. 621–53 in S. T. Parker, ed., *The Roman Frontier in Central Jordan. Interim Report of the Limes Arabicus Project, 1980–1985, Vol. II.* BAR International Series, S340 (ii). Oxford: BAR.

2005a   "Glass Vessel Finds from a Possible Early Fourth-Century CE Church at Aila (Aqaba), Jordan." Pp 135–39 in *Annales du 15e Congrès de l'Association pour l'Histoire du Verre, London 2003.* Nottingham: Association pour l'Histoire du Verre.

2005b   "Recently Discovered Cage Cup Fragments from Aqaba." *JGS* 45: 180–82.

2006   "The Glass." Pp. 393–411 in S.T. Parker, ed., *The Roman Frontier in Central Jordan. Final Report on the Limes Arabicus Project, 1980–1989.* Washington, DC: Dumbarton Oaks.

in prep.   "The Roman and Byzantine Glass," in S.T. Parker, ed., *Final Report on the Roman Aqaba Project, vol. 2.*

Kalavrezou, I. (ed.)
2003   *Byzantine Women and their World.* Cambridge, MA: Harvard University.

Kana'an, R., and McQuitty, A.
1994   "The Architecture of al-Qasr on the Kerak Plateau: An Essay in the Chronology of Vernacular Architecture." *PEQ* 126: 127–53.

Kanellopoulos, C., and Schick, R.
2001   "Marble Furnishings of the Apses and the Bema, Phase V." Pp. 193–213 in Z. Fiema et al., *The Petra Church.* Amman: American Center of Oriental Research.

Kareem, J.
1999   "Nabataean to Abbasid Pottery from the First Season of Excavations at Khirbat Nakhil, Jordan." *Levant* 31: 191–202.

Katsnelson, N.
1999   "Glass Vessels from the Painted Tomb at Migdal Ashqelon." *'Atiqot* 37: 67–82.

Keller, D.
2006   "Die Gläser aus Petra." Pp. 1–256 in D. Keller and M. Grawehr, *Petra ez Zantur III.* Terra Archaeologica V. Mainz: von Zabern.

Keller, D. R.; Porter, B. A.; and Tuttle, C. A.
2012   "Archaeology in Jordan, 2010 and 2011 Seasons." *AJA* 116: 693–750.

Kennedy, D., and Bewley, R.
2004   *Ancient Jordan from the Air.* Oxford: Oxbow.

Kent, J. P. C.
1991   "The Coinage of Arcadius (395–408)." *Numismatic Chronicle* 151: 36–57.

Kenyon, K.
1971   "Burial Customs at Jericho." *ADAJ* 16: 5–30.

Khadija, M. M. A.
1974   "Beit Zar'a Tombs (1974)." *ADAJ* 19: 157–63.

Khairy, N.
1982   "Fine Nabataean Ware with Impressed and Rouletted Decorations." *SHAJ* 1: 275–82.
2001   "The Lamps." Pp. 368–70 in Z. Fiema et al., *The Petra Church.* Amman: American Center of Oriental Research.

Khalil, L., and Kareem, J.
2002   "Abbasid Pottery from Area E at Khirbat Yajuz, Jordan." *Levant* 34: 111–50.

al-Khraysheh, F.
1986   Die Personennamen in den nabatäischen Inschriften des Corpus Inscriptionum Semiticarum. Ph.D. Dissertation, Philipps-Universität Marburg/Lahn.

Kindermann, H. K.
1960   "*Al-Asad.*" Pp. 681–83 in C. E. Bosthworth et al,. eds., *Encyclopedia of Islam, new ed.,* vol. 1. Leiden: Brill.

King, G. R. D.
1983   "Two Byzantine Churches in Northern Jordan and their Re-Use in the Islamic Period." *Damazener Mitteilungen* 1: 111–36.

Köhler, I. U.
1981   "Some Preliminary Remarks on the Animal Husbandry of Pella." Unpublished annual report presented to the Directors of the Pella Project.

Köhler-Rollefson, I. U.
1987   "Ethnoarchaeological Research into the Origins of Pastoralism." *ADAJ* 31: 535–42.

Kolb, B., and Keller, D.
2000   "Swiss-Liechtenstein Excavations at az-Zantur/Petra: The Tenth Season." *ADAJ* 44: 355–72.

Kovács, L.
2008   *Vulvae, Eyes, Snake Heads: Archaeological Finds of Cowrie Amulets.* BAR Intl. Ser. S1846. Oxford: Archaeopress.

Kraeling, C. H. (ed.)
1938 *Gerasa: City of the Decapolis.* New Haven, CT: Yale University.

Kröger J.
1995 *Nishapur. Glass of the Early Islamic Period.* New York: Metropolitan Museum of Art.

Krüger, J.
2000 *Die Grabeskirche zu Jerusalem.* Regensburg: Schnell & Steiner.

Kühnel, E.
1920 "Islamisches Räuchergerät." *Berliner Museen* 41.6: 4–8.

Kurdi, H.
1972 "A New Nabataean Tomb at Sadagah." *ADAJ* 17: 85–87.

La Follette, L.
1994 "The Costume of the Roman Bride." Pp. 54–64 in J. L. Sebesta and L. Bonfante, eds., *The World of Roman Costume.* Madison, WI: University of Wisconsin.

Lamm, C. J.
1939 "Glass and Hard Stone Vessels." Pp. 2592–606 in A. U. Pope, ed., *A Survey of Persian Art from Prehistoric Times to the Present,* Vol. 3. London: Oxford University.

Lancel, S.
1967 *Verrerie antique de Tipasa.* Paris: de Boccard.

Larsen, C. S.
1997 *Bioarchaeology.* Cambridge: Cambridge University.

Lazzarini L., and Antonelli, F.
2003 "Petrographic and Isotopic Characterization of the Marble of the Island of Tinos (Greece)." *Archaeometry* 45: 541–52.

Lazzarini, L.; Gorgoni, C.; Pallante, P.; and Turi, B.
1997 "Identification of Ancient White Marble in Rome II: The Portico of Octavia." *Science and Technology for Cultural Heritage* 6: 185–98.

Lehtinen, A.
2008 "Marble Furnishing and Decoration." Pp. 187–234 in Z. Fiema and J. Frösén, *Petra — The Mountain of Aaron. The Finnish Archaeological Project in Jordan,* Vol. 1: *The Church and the Chapel.* Helsiniki: Societas Scientiarum Fennica.

Lemaigre, A. C.
1983. "Chains and Necklaces." Pp. 205–10 in T. Hackens and R. Winkes, eds., *Gold Jewellery. Craft, Style and Meaning from Mycenae to Constantinopolis.* Louvain-la-Neuve: Collège Érasme.

Lenoble, P.; al-Muheisen, Z.; and Villeneuve, F.
2001 "Fouilles de Khirbet edh-Dharih (Jordanie), I: Le cimetière au sud du Wadi Sharheh." *Syria* 78: 89–151.

Lindner, M., et al.
1984 "New Explorations of the Deir-Plateau (Petra) 1982/1983." *ADAJ* 28: 163–81.

Lovejoy, C. O.; Meindl R. A.; Pryzbeck, T. R.; and Mensforth, R. P.
1985 "Chronological Metamorphosis of the Auricular Surface of the *Ilium*: A New Method for the Determination of Adult Skeletal Age at Death." *American Journal of Physical Anthropology* 68: 16–28.

Loverance, R.
2012 "The Marble and Stone Church Furnishings." Pp. 337–47 in K. D. Politis, ed., *Sanctuary of St. Lot at Deir 'Ain 'Abata, Jordan, Excavations 1988-2003.* Amman: Jordan Distribution Agency.

Lubin, M. I.
1993 "Horvat Hermeshit (Neot Qedumim) 1993." *Hadashot Arkheologiyot* 98: 58–60 (Hebrew).

Macalister, R. A. S.
1911 *The Excavation of Gezer 1902–1905 and 1907–1909,* Vol. I. London: Murray.

Mackay, D.
1949 "The Jewellery of Palmyra and its Significance." *Iraq* 11.2: 160–87.

MacKinnon, M.
2001 "High on the Hog: Linking Zooarchaeological, Literary, and Artistic Data for Pig Breeds in Roman Italy." *AJA* 105: 649–73.

Maeir, A. M.
2000 "*Sassania varia Palestiniensia.* A Sassanian Seal from T. Istaba, Israel, and Other Sassanian Objects from the Southern Levant." *Iranica Antiqua* 35: 159–83.

Magen, I.
1990 "A Byzantine Church at Beit 'Einun (Beth 'Anoth) in the Hebron Hills." Pp. 275–86 in G. C. Bottini et al., eds., *Christian Archaeology in the Holy Land. New Discoveries. Essays in Honour of Virgilio C. Corbo, OFM.* Jerusalem: Francisan Printing.
1992 "A Byzantine Church at Beit 'Anun in the Hebron Mountains." *Qadmoniot* 25: 40–44.

Magness, J.
1993 *Jerusalem Ceramic Chronology circa 200–800 C.E.* JSOT/ASOR Monograph Series. Sheffield: University of Sheffield.

Manfra, L.; Masi, U.; and Turi, B.
1975 "Carbon and Oxygen Isotope Ratios of Marbles from some Ancient Quarries of Western Anatolia and their Archaeological Significance." *Archaeometry* 17: 215–21.

Manson, M.
1978 "Histoire d' un mythe: les poupées de Maria, femme d'Honorius." *Mélanges de l'École Française de Rome* 90.2: 863–69.
1987 "Le bambole romane antiche." *Ricerca Folklorica* 16: 15–26.

Mare, W. H.
1991 "The 1998 Season of Excavation at Abila of the Decapolis." *ADAJ* 35: 203–20.

Margalit, S.
1989 "On the Transformation of the Mono-apsidal Churches with Two Lateral Pastophoria into Tri-apsidal Churches." *LA* 39: 143–64.

Markoe, G. (ed.)
2003 *Petra Rediscovered.* New York: Abrams.

Marshall, F. H.
1969 *Catalogue of Jewellery, Greek, Etruscan, and Roman, in the Departments of Antiquities, British Museum.* London: Trustees of the British Museum.

Matthews, K. J.
1997 "The Establishment of a Data Base of Neutron Activation Analyses of White Marble." *Archaeometry* 39: 321–32.

McDaniel, J.
2006 "The Small Finds." Pp. 293–304 in S. T. Parker et al., *The Roman Frontier in Central Jordan. Final Report on the Limes Arabicus Project, 1980–1989.* 2 vols. Washington, DC: Dumbarton Oaks.

McKenzie, J.
1990 *The Architecture of Petra.* Oxford: Oxford University.

McNicoll, A. W., et al.
1982 *Pella in Jordan I. An Interim Report on the Joint University of Sydney and The College of Wooster Excavations at Pella 1979–1981.* Canberra: Australian National Gallery.

McQuitty, A., and Falkner, R.
1993 "The Faris Project: Preliminary Report on the 1989, 1990 and 1991 Seasons." *Levant* 25: 37–61.

Meindl, R. S., and Lovejoy, C. O.
1985 "Ectocranial Suture Closure: A Revised Method for the Determination of Skeletal

Age at Death and Blind Tests of its Accuracy." *American Journal of Physical Anthropology* 68: 87–106.

Melkawi, A.; ʿAmr, K.; and Whitcomb, D. S.
1994 "The Excavation of Two Seventh-Century Pottery Kilns at Aqaba." *ADAJ* 38: 447–68.

Meshorer, Y.
1975 *Nabataean Coins.* Qedem 3. Jerusalem: Hebrew University.

Meyer, C.
1987 "Glass from the North Theater Byzantine Church, and Soundings at Jerash, Jordan, 1982–1983." *BASOR, Supplement 25:* 175–222.
1992 *Glass from Quseir al Qadim and the Indian Ocean Trade.* Studies in Ancient Oriental Civilization No. 53. Chicago, IL: The Oriental Institute of the University of Chicago.

Meyers, E.; Kraabel, A. T.; and Strange, J. F.
1976 *Ancient Synagogue Excavations at Khirbet Shemaʿ, Upper Galilee, Israel 1970–1972.* AASOR 42. Durham: Duke University.

Michel, A.
2001 *Les églises d'époque byzantine et umayyade de la Jordanie, Ve–VIIIe siècle. Typologie architecturale et aménagements liturgiques.* Turnhout: Brepols.
2011 "Le devenir des lieux de culte chrétiens sur le territoire Jordanien entre le VIIe et le IXe siècle: un état de la question." Pp. 233–69 in A. Borrut, M. Debié, A. Papaconstantinou, D. Pieri, and J.-P. Sodini, *Le Proche-orient de Justinien aux Abbassides: Peuplement et dynamiques spatiales. Actes du colloque "Continuités de l'Occupation entre les Périodes Byzantine et Abbasside au Proche-Orient, VIIe–IXe Siècles," Paris, 18–20 octobre 2007.* Bibliothèque de l'antiquité tardive, 19. Turnhout: Brepols.

Miller, N.
1995 "Archaeobotany: Macroremains." Pp. 91–93 in P. E. McGovern, ed., "Science in Archaeology: A review." *AJA* 99: 79–142.

Milne, J. S.
1907 *Surgical Instruments in Greek and Roman Times.* Oxford: Oxford University.

Milson, D.
2003 "The Syrian *technites* Markianos Kyris (†425 CE)." *ZDPV* 119: 15–20.

Milwright, M.
2008 *The Fortress of the Raven: Karak in the Middle Islamic Period (1100–1650).* Leiden: Brill.

Mitchiner, M.
1978 *Oriental Coins and their Values,* Vol. 2: *The Ancient and Classical World 600 BC–AD 650.* London: Seaby.

Mitten, D. G., and Doeringer, S. F.
1967 *Master Bronzes from the Classical World.* Mainz: von Zabern.

Mlynarczyk, J.
2011 "The Fading Lights of a Church…." Pp. 183–210 in D. Frangié, and J.-F. Salles, eds., *Lampes antiques du Bilad Es-Sham, Jordanie, Syrie, Liban, Palestine/Ancient Lamps of Bilad Es-Sham, Actes du colloque international, Pétra-Amman, 6-13 novembre 2005.* Paris: de Boccard.

Moens, L.; Roos, P.; De Rudder, J.; De Paepe, P.; Van Hende, J.; Arechal, R.; and Waelkens, M.
1988 "A Multi-Method Approach to the Identification of White Marbles Used in Antique Artifacts." Pp. 243–50 in N. Herz and M. Waelkens, eds., *Classical Marble: Geochemistry, Technology, Trade.* Dordrecht: Kluwer Academic.

Moens, L.; Roos, P.; De Rudder, J.; De Paepe, P.; Van Hende, J.; and Waelkens, M.
1990 "Scientific Provenance Determination of Ancient White Marble Sculptures, Using Petrographic, Chemical and Isotopic Data." Pp. 111–25 in M. True and J. Podany, eds., *Marble: Art Historical and Scientific Perspectives on Ancient Sculpture.* Los Angeles: The J. Paul Getty Museum.

Moorrees, C. F. A.; Fanning, E. A.; and Hunt, E. E.

1963a "Age Variation of Formation Stages for Ten Permanent Teeth." *Journal of Dental Research* 42: 1490–502.

1963b "Formation and Resorption of Three Deciduous Teeth in Children." *American Journal of Physical Anthropology* 21: 205–13.

Moulton, W. J.

1919–20 "Gleanings in Archaeology and Epigraphy." *AASOR* 1: 66–92.

Mulvin, L., and Sidebotham, S. E.

2004 "Roman Game Boards from Abu Sha'ar (Red Sea Coast, Egypt)." *Antiquity* 301: 602–17.

Munro, N.; Morgan, R.; and Jobling, W.

1997 "Optical Dating and Landscape Chronology at ad-Disa, Southern Jordan, and its Potential." *SHAJ* 6: 97–103.

Murray, H. J. R.

1913 *A History of Chess.* Oxford: Oxford University.

Musche, B.

1988 *Vorderasiatischer Schmuck zur Zeit der Arsakiden und der Sasaniden.* Leiden: Brill.

Musil, A.

1907–8 *Arabia Petraea, II: Edom. Topographischer Reisebericht.* 2 vols. Vienna: Hölder.

1926 *The Northern Hegaz.* 2 vols. New York: American Geographical Society.

Nabulsi, A. J.

1998 "The Byzantine Cemetery in Samra." Pp. 271–79 in J.-B. Humbert, and A. Desreumaux, *Khirbet es-Samra 1, Jordanie: la voie romaine, le cimetière, les documents épigraphiques.* Turnhout: Brepols.

2000 "The Plaster Figurines of Khirbet-es-Samra." Pp. 111–14 in A. Geiger, ed., *Ausstellung: Rettung des Kulturerbes, Projekte rund ums Mittelmeer.* Hamburg: Glöss.

2010 "Khirbat as-Samra Cemetery: Site E, Season 2009." *ADAJ* 54: 217–19.

Nabulsi, A. J., and Humbert, J.-B.

1996 "Excavations in the Byzantine Cemetery at Khirbet as-Samrā: Site B – 1995." *ADAJ* 40: 491–93.

Nabulsi, A. J., et al.

1998 "The 1996 Excavation Season at Khirbet as-Samrā", The Byzantine Cemetery Site B." *ADAJ* 42: 615–19.

2007 "The Ancient Cemetery in Khirbet as-Samrā after the Sixth Season of Excavations (2006)." *ADAJ* 51: 273–81.

2009 "Khirbet as-Samrā Ancient Cemetery: Outline of Site C." *ADAJ* 53: 167–72.

al-Naddaf, M.; al-Bashaireh, K.; and al-Waked, F.

2010 "Characterization and Provenance of Marble Chancel Screens, Northern Jordan." *Mediterranean Archaeology and Archaeometry* 10: 75–83.

Nagar, Y., and Sonntag, F.

2008 "Byzantine Period Burials in the Negev: Anthropological Description and Summary." *IEJ* 58: 79–93.

Najjar, M.

1989 "Abbasid Pottery from el-Muwaqqar." *ADAJ* 33: 305–22.

Negev, A.

1971 "The Necropolis of Mampsis." *IEJ* 21: 110–29.

1972 "Nabataean Sigillata." *RB* 79: 381–98.

1974 "The Churches of the Central Negev. An Archaeological Survey." *RB* 81: 400–22.

1981 *The Greek Inscriptions from the Negev.* Jerusalem: Franciscan Printing.

1986 *The Late Hellenistic and Early Roman Pottery of Nabataean Oboda. Final Report.* Qedem 22. Jerusalem: Israel Exploration Society.

1988 *The Architecture of Mampsis, Final Report,* Vol. II: *The Late Roman and Byzantine Periods.* Qedem 27. Jerusalem: Hebrew University.

1989 "The Cathedral of Elusa and the New Typology and Chronology of the Byzantine Churches in the Negev." *LA* 39: 129–42.

1991 *Personal Names in the Nabataean Realm.* Qedem, 32. Jerusalem: Hebrew University.
1997 *The Architecture of Oboda, Final Report.* Qedem 36. Jerusalem: Hebrew University.

Nehmé, L.
2012 *Pétra. Atlas archéologique et épigraphique: 1, De Bâb as-Sîq au Wâdî al-Farasah.* Paris: Académie des inscriptions et Belles-Lettres.

Nehmé, L.; Arnoux, T.; Bessaac, J.-C.; Braun, J.-P.; Dentzer, J.-M.; Kermorvant, A.; Sachet, I.; and Tholbecq, L.
2006 "Mission archéologique de Mada'in Salih (Arabie Saoudite): Recherches menées de 2001 à 2003 dans l'ancienne Hijra des Nabatéens (1)." *AAE* 17: 41–124.

Nenner-Soriano, R.
2010 "Spindle Whorls." Pp. 276–82 in H. Geva, ed., *Jewish Quarter Excavations in the Old City of Jerusalem,* Vol. 4: *The Burnt House of Area B and Other Studies, Final Report.* Jerusalem: Israel Exploration Society.

Nichol, R. K., and Wild, C. J.
1984 "Numbers of Individuals in Faunal Analysis: The Decay of Fish Bone in Archaeological Sites." *JAS* 11: 35–51.

Nikitin, A. B.
1996 "Sasanian Coins in the Collection of the Museum of Fine Arts, Moscow." *Ancient Civilizations from Scythia to Siberia* 2.1: 71–91.

Nikolsky, V. and P. Figueras
2004 "Descriptive Pottery Catalogue." Pp. 151–215 in P. Figueras, ed., *Horvat Karkur 'Illit. A Byzantine Cemetery Church in the Northern Negev (Final Report of the Excavations 1989-1995).* Beer-Sheva: Ben-Gurion University of the Negev.

O'Connor, S., et al.
2011 "Exceptional Preservation of a Prehistoric Human Brain from Heslington, Yorkshire, UK." *JAS* 38: 1641–54.

Ogden, W.
1888 "Four Days in Petra." *Bulletin of the American Geographical Society* 20.2 (June): 137–52.

O'Hea, M.
2001 "Glass from 1992–4 Excavations." Pp. 370–76 in Z. Fiema et al., *The Petra Church.* Amman: American Center of Oriental Research.
2003 "Some Problems in Early Islamic Glassware." *Annales du 15e Congrès de l'Association Internationale pour l'Histoire du Verre.* Nottingham: Association Internationale pour l'Histoire du Verre.
2007 "Glassware in Late Antiquity in the Near East." Pp. 233–48 in L. Lavan et al., eds., *Technology in Transition, AD.300–650.* Leiden: Brill.
2012 "The Glass." Pp. 293–325 in K. D. Politis, ed., *Sanctuary of St Lot at Deir 'Ain 'Abata, Jordan, Excavations 1988-2003.* Amman: Jordan Distribution Agency.
Forthcoming "The Glass 1998–2006." Chapter 15 in M. J. Joukowsky, ed., *Petra: Great Temple Brown University Excavations 1993-2006,* Vol. III: *Architecture and Material Culture.* JRA Supplement. Providence, RI: Journal of Roman Archaeology.
In prep. "The Islamic Glass," in S. T. Parker, ed. *Final Report on the Roman Aqaba Project, vol. 2.*

Ohlig, C.
2008 *Cura Aquarum in Jordanien.* Siegburg: DWHG.

O'Kane, B.
2006 *Treasures of Islamic Art in the Museums of Cairo.* Cairo: American University in Cairo.

Oleson, J. P.
1990 "Humeima Hydraulic Survey, 1989: Preliminary Field Report." *ADAJ* 34: 285–311.
1994 "The Humeima Excavation Project, Jordan: Preliminary Report of the 1993 Season." *EMC* 13: 141–79.
1997 "Landscape and Cityscape in the Hisma: The Resources of Ancient Al-Humayma." *SHAJ* 6: 175–88.

2010   *Humayma Excavation Project, 1: Resources, History, and the Water-Supply System.* ASOR Archaeological Reports, 15. Boston, MA: American Schools of Oriental Research.

Oleson, J. P.; 'Amr, K.; Foote, R.; Logan, J.; Reeves, M. B.; and Schick, R.
1999   "Preliminary Report of the Al-Humayma Excavation Project, 1995, 1996, 1998." *ADAJ* 43: 411–50.

Oleson, J. P.; 'Amr, K.; Schick, R.; and Foote, R.
1995   "Preliminary Report of the Humeima Excavation Project, 1993." *ADAJ* 39: 317–54.

Oleson, J. P.; 'Amr, K.; Schick, R.; Foote, R.; and Somogyi-Csizmazia, J.
1993   "The Humeima Excavation Project, Jordan: Preliminary Report of the 1991–1992 Seasons." *ADAJ* 37: 461–502.

Oleson, J. P.; Baker, G.; de Bruijn, E.; Foote, R.; Logan, J.; Reeves, M. B.; and Sherwood, A. N.
2003   "Preliminary Report of the al-Humayma Excavation Project, 2000, 2002." *ADAJ* 47: 37–64.

Oleson, J. P.; Reeves, M. B.; Baker, G.; de Bruijn, E.; Gerber, Y.; Nikolic, M.; and Sherwood, A. N.
2008   "Preliminary Report on Excavations at al-Humayma, Ancient Hawara, 2004 and 2005." *ADAJ* 52: 309–42.

Oleson, J. P.; Reeves, M. B.; and Fisher, B. F.
2002   "New Dedicatory Inscriptions from Humayma (Ancient Hawara), Jordan." *Zeitschrift für Papyrologie und Epigraphik* 140: 103–21.

Oleson, M. I., and Oleson, J. P.
1987   "The Utilitarian Wares." Pp. 243–64 in A.M. McCann et al., *The Roman Port and Fishery of Cosa.* Princeton, NJ: Princeton University.

Orssaud, D.
2001   "Les céramiques à glacure monochrome de Qal'at Sem'an (VIIIe–IXe siècles)." Pp. 215–20 in E. Villeneuve, and P. M. Watson, eds., *La céramique byzantine et proto-islamique en Syrie-Jordanie (IVe–VIIe siècles apr. J.-C.). Actes du colloque tenu à Amman les 3, 4 et 5 décembre 1994.* Beirut: Institut Français d'Archéologie du Proche-Orient.

Ortner, D. J.
2003   *Identification of Pathological Conditions in Human Skeletal Remains.* New York: Academic.

Ortner, D. J.; Garofalo, E. M.; and Frohlich B.
2008   "The Paleopathology of the EB IA and EB IB People." Pp. 263–80 in D. J. Ortner and B. Frohlich, *The Early Bronze Age I Tombs and Burials of Bâb edh-Dhrâ, Jordan.* Lanham, MD: AltaMira.

Ossorio, F. A.
2009   *Petra: Splendors of the Nabataean Civilization.* Vercelli: White Star.

Ovadiah, R.
1999   "A Burial Cave of the Hellenistic and Early Roman Periods at Hagosherim." *'Atiqot* 38: 33–47, 223–24.

Papaconstantinou, A., and Talbot, A.-M. (eds.)
2009   *Becoming Byzantine. Children and Childhood in Byzantium.* Cambridge, MA: Harvard University.

Pappalardo, C.
2002   "Il Cortile a Sud della Chiesa di S. Paolo ad Umm al-Rasas – Kastron Mefaa in Giordania." *LA* 52: 385–440.

Parker, S. T.
1976   "Archaeological Survey of the Limes Arabicus: A Preliminary Report." *ADAJ* 21: 19–31.
1986   *Romans and Saracens: A History of the Arabian Frontier.* American Schools of Oriental Research, Dissertation Series, 6. Winona Lake, IN: Eisenbrauns.

2000 "The Roman 'Aqaba Project: The 1997 and 1998 Campaigns." *ADAJ* 44: 373–94.

2002 "The Roman 'Aqaba Project: The 2000 Campaign." *ADAJ* 46: 409

2003 "The Roman 'Aqaba Project: The 2002 Campaign." *ADAJ* 47: 321–33.

2005 "Supplying the Roman Army on the Arabian Frontier." Pp. 415–25 in Z. Visy, *Limes XIX: Proceedings of the XIXth International Congress of Roman Frontier Studies held in Pécs, Hungary, September 2003.* Pécs: University of Pécs.

2006 "Roman Aila and the Wadi Arabah: An Economic Relationship." Pp. 223–30 in P. Bienkowski and K. Galor, eds., *Crossing the Rift: Resources, Routes, Settlement Patterns and Interaction in the Wadi Arabah.* Oxford: Oxbow.

2009a "The Roman Port of Aila: Economic Connections with the Red Sea Littoral." Pp. 79–84 in L. Blue, J. Cooper, R. Thomas, and J. Wainwright, eds., *Connected Hinterlands: Proceedings of the Red Sea Project IV. Held at the University of Southampton September 2008.* Society for Arabian Studies Monographs No. 8. British Archaeological Reports, Intl. Series S2052. Oxford: British Archaeological Reports.

2009b "The Foundation of Aila: A Nabataean Port on the Red Sea." *SHAJ* 10: 685–90.

2009c "*Arabia Adquisita*: The Roman Annexation of Arabia Reconsidered." *Limes XX: Estudios sobre la Frontera Romana. Gladius,* Supplement 13: 1585–92.

Parker, S. T., et al.

1987 *The Roman Frontier in Central Jordan. Interim Report on the Limes Arabicus Project, 1980–1985.* BAR Intl. Ser., S340. Oxford: BAR.

2006 *The Roman Frontier in Central Jordan. Final Report on the Limes Arabicus Project, 1980–1989.* 2 vols. Washington, DC: Dumbarton Oaks.

Parr, P. J.

1970 "A Sequence of Pottery from Petra." Pp. 348–81 in J.A. Sanders, *Near Eastern Archaeology in the Twentieth Century: Essays in Memory of Nelson Glueck.* New York: Doubleday.

Paruck, F. D. J.

1924 *Sasanian Coins.* Bombay: The Times.

Patrich, J.

1984 "Al–Uzza' Earrings." *IEJ* 34: 39–46.

1988 "Architectural Sculpture and Stone Objects." Pp. 97–133 in Y. Tsafrir, *Excavations at Rehovot-in-the-Negev.* Volume I: *The North Church.* Qedem 25. Jerusalem: Hebrew University.

1990 *The Formation of Nabatean Art. Prohibition of a Graven Image among the Nabateans.* Leiden: Brill.

Patrich, J., et al.

2008 *Archaeological Excavations at Caesarea Maritima, Areas CC, KK and NN. Final Reports: The Objects.* Jerusalem: Israel Exploration Society.

Pearce, J. W. E.

1931 "Eugenius and his Eastern Colleagues." *Numismatic Chronicle* 17: 1–27.

1932 The Coinage of the Valentinian and Theodosian Periods." *Spink's Numismatic Circular* 40: 41–46, 121, 201–8, 247–51, 289–96, 340.

Perry, M. A.

2002a Health, Labor, and Political Economy: A Bioarchaeological Analysis of Three Communities in *Provincia Arabia.* Ph.D. Dissertation, Department of Anthropology, University of New Mexico.

2002b "Life and Death in Nabatea: The North Ridge Tombs and Nabataean Burial Practices." *NEA* 65: 265–70.

Perry, M. A., and Jones, G. L.

2008 "Ground-Truthing at Wadi Ramm: A Follow-Up to the 2005 GPR Survey." *ADAJ* 52: 91–104.

Petersen, A.
2001   *A Gazetter of Buildings in Muslim Palestine (Part 1)*. New York: Oxford University.

Petrie, W. M. F.
1927   *Objects of Daily Use*. Publications of the British School of Archaeology in Egypt, 42. London: British School of Archaeology in Egypt.

Pfister, F.
1914   "Rauchopfer." *RE* I.A.1: 267–86.

Phang, S. E.
2001   *The Marriage of Roman Soldiers (13 BC–AD 235). Law and Family in the Imperial Army*. Leiden: Brill.

Piccirillo, M.
1992   "La chiesa dei Leoni a Umm al-Rasas – Kastron Mefaa." *Liber Annuus* 42: 199–225.
1993a   *The Mosaics of Jordan*. Amman: American Center for Oriental Research.
1993b   "La Chiesa del Prete Wa'il a Umm al-Rasas – Kastron Mefaa in Giordania." Pp. 313–34 in F. Manns and E. Alliata, eds., *Early Christianity in Context. Monuments and Documents*. Jerusalem: Franciscan Printing.

Pinder-Wilson, R.
2005   "Ivory Working in the Umayyad and Abbasid Periods." Pp. 13–24 in K. von Folsach and J. Meyer, eds., *The Ivories of Muslim Spain*. Journal of the David Collection, 2.1. Copenhagen: David Collection.

Pitarakis, B.
2009   "The Material Culture of Childhood in Byzantium." Pp. 167–250 in A. Papaconstantinou and A.-M. Talbot, eds., *Becoming Byzantine. Children and Childhood in Byzantium*. Cambridge, MA: Harvard University.

Polikreti, K.
2007   "Detection of Ancient Marble Forgery: Techniques and Limitations." *Archaeometry* 49: 603–19.

Polikreti, K., and Maniatis, Y.
2002   "A New Methodology for the Provenance of Marbles Based on EPR Spectroscopy." *Archaeometry* 44: 1–21.

Politis, K.D. (ed.)
2012   *Sanctuary of Lot at Deir 'Ain 'Abata in Jordan. Excavations 1988–2003*. Amman: Jordan Distribution Agency.

Post, G.
1932   *Flora of Syria, Palastine and Sinai*. Beirut: American.

Prag, K.
2008   *Excavations by K.M. Kenyon in Jerusalem 1961–1967*, Vol. V: *Discoveries in Hellenistic to Ottoman Jerusalem*. Oxford: Oxbow.

Price, J.
1985   "Early Roman Vessel Glass from Burials in Tripolitania: A Study of Finds from Forte Vite and Other Sites Now in the Collections of the National Museum of Antiquities in Tripoli." Pp. 67–106 in D. J. Buck and D. J. Mattingly, eds., *Town and Country in Roman Tripolitania: Papers in Honor of Olwen Hackett*. BAR Intl. Series, S274. Oxford: BAR.
1992   "Hellenistic and Roman Glass. Pp. 415–90 in L.H. Sackett et al., *Knossos: From Greek City to Roman Colony. Excavations at the Unexplored Mansion II*. BAR Supplementary Volume, 21. London: British School of Archaeology at Athens.

Qāqīsh, R. F.
2007   *'Imārat al-Kanā'is wa-Mulaḥaqātihā fī al-Urdun fī al-'Ahdayn al-Bīzanṭī wa-al-Umawī*. (The Architecture of the Churches and their Annexes in Jordan in the Byzantine and Umayyad Periods). Amman: Dār al-Ward.

Quibell, J. E.
1907   *Exavations at Saqqara 1905–1906*. Cairo: Institut Français d'Archéologie Orientale.

Rababeh, S. M.
2005 *How Petra was Built.* BAR Intl. Series, S1460. Oxford: Archaeopress.

Rahmani, L. Y.
1960 "Roman Tombs in Shmuel ha-Navi Street, Jerusalem." *IEJ* 10: 140–48.
1964 "Mirror Plaques from a Fifth Century Tomb." IEJ 14: 50–60.
1967 "Jason's Tomb." *IEJ* 17: 61–100.
1981 "Finds from a Sixth to Seventh Centuries Site near Gaza." *IEJ* 31: 72–80.

Ramage, N. H., and Ramage, A.
2009 *Roman Art: Romulus to Constantine.* 5th ed. Upper Saddle River, NJ: Prentice Hall.

Rapp, G., Jr.
1985 "History, Philosophy, and Perspectives." Pp. 1–23 in G. Rapp, Jr. and J. A. Gifford, eds., *Archaeological Geology.* New Haven, CT: Yale University.

Rapp, G., Jr., and Hill, C. L.
1998 *Geoarchaeology.* New Haven, CT: Yale University.

Ray, P. J. (ed.)
2009 *Hesban 12. Small Finds: Studies of Bone, Iron, Glas, Figurines, and Stone Objects from Tell Hesban and Vicinity.* Berrien Springs, MI: Andrews University.

Reese, D. S.
1987 "The Shells." Pp. 48–49 in M. M. Ibrahim and R. L. Gordon, *A Cemetery at Queen Alia International Airport.* Yarmouk University Publications, Institute of Archaeology and Anthropology Series 1. Wiesbaden: Harrassowitz.
1995a "Marine Invertebrates and Other Shells from Jerusalem (Sites A, C and L)." Pp. 265–78 in I. Eshel and K. Prag, eds., *Excavations by K.M. Kenyon in Jerusalem 1961–1967,* vol. IV. British Academy Monographs in Archaeology 6. Oxford: Oxford University.
1995b "The Shells from Upper Zohar." Pp. 97–98 in R. P. Harper, *Upper Zohar: An Early Byzantine Fort in Palaestina Tertia. Final Report of Excavations in 1985–1986.* British Academy Monographs in Archaeology, 9. Oxford: Oxford University.
2002 "Shells and Fossils from Tall Jawa, Jordan." Pp. 276–91 in P. M. M. Daviau, *Excavations at Tall Jawa, Jordan.* II: *The Iron Age Artefacts.* Culture and History of the Ancient Near East 11/2. Leiden: Brill
2008 "Shells from Jerusalem: Sites B, D, E, J, S and V." Pp. 455–66 in K. Prag, *Excavations by K.M. Kenyon in Jerusalem 1961–1967,* V: *Discoveries in Hellenistic to Ottoman Jerusalem.* Levant Supplementary Series 7. Oxford: Oxbow.

Reese, D. S.; McNamara, K .J.; and Sease, C.
2002 "Fossil and Recent Marine Invertebrates." Pp. 441–69 in P. Bienkowski, *Busayra, Excavations by Crystal-M. Bennett 1971–1980.* British Academy Monographs in Archaeology 13. Oxford: Oxford University.

Reese, D. S.; Mienis, H. K.; and Woodward, F. R.
1986 "On the Trade of Shells and Fish from the Nile River." *BASOR* 264: 79–84.

Reeves, B.; Babbitt, I.; Cummer, K.; Karas, V.; Seymour, B.; and Shelton, A.
2009 "Preliminary Report on Excavations in the Nabataean Town and Roman Vicus at Humayma (Ancient Hawara), 2008." *ADAJ* 53: 229–63.

Reid, S. K.
2005 *The Small Temple: A Roman Imperial Cult Building in Petra, Jordan.* Piscataway, NJ: Gorgias.

Renfrew, J.
1973 *Palaeoethnobotany.* New York: Columbia University.

Richter, G. M. A.
1966 *The Furniture of the Greeks, Etruscans, and Romans.* London: Phaidon.

Ricotti, E. S. P.
1995   *Giochi e giocattoli*. Vita e costumi dei Romani antichi, 18. Rome: Quasar.

Ridgway, H. B.
1876   *The Lord's Land: A Narrative of Travels in Sinai, Arabia Petraea, and Palestine, from the Red Sea to the Entering in of Hamath*. New York: Nelson & Phillips.

Rife, J. L., et al.
2007   "Life and Death at a Port in Roman Greece: The Kenchreai Cemetery Project, 2002–2006." *Hesperia* 76.1: 143–81

Riggs, C.
2002   "Facing the Dead: Recent Research on the Funerary Art of Ptolemaic and Roman Egypt." *AJA* 106: 85–101.

Riwaq
2006   *Riwaq's Registry of Historic Buildings in Palestine*. 3 volumes. Ramallah: Riwaq.

Rixford, G. P.
1918   *Smyrna Fig Culture*. U.S.D.A. Bulletin No. 732. Washington, DC: U.S. Department of Agriculture.

Robertson, A. S.
1982   *Roman Imperial Coins in the Hunter Coin Cabinet, University of Glasgow. V. Diocletian (Reform) to Zeno*. Oxford: Oxford University.

Ronzevalle, S.
1921   "Some Alleged Palestinian Pyxes." *PEF* 53: 172–74.

Rosen, S. A.
1993   "A Roman Period Pastoral Tent Camp in the Negev, Israel." *JFA* 20: 441–51.

Rosenthal, R.
1974   "A Nabatean Nose–Ring from Avdat (Oboda)." *IEJ* 24: 95–96.
1976   "Late Roman and Byzantine Bone Carvings from Palestine." *IEJ* 26: 96–103.

Rosenthal-Heginbottom, R.
1997   "Small Finds from the Excavations (1958–1961)." Pp. 193–214 in A. Negev, ed. *The Architecture of Oboda. Final report*. Jerusalem: Hebrew University.
1982   *Die Kirchen von Sobota und die Dreiapsidenkirchen des Nahen Ostens*. Wiesbaden: Harrassowitz.

Rousseau, V.
2004   "Emblems of an Empire: The Development of the Byzantine Empress's Crown." *Al Masq* 16.1: 5–15.

Rousset, M.-O.
2001   "Les céramique de Hira à décor moulé, incisé ou appliqué monochrome." Pp. 221–30 in E. Villeneuve, and P. M. Watson, eds., *La céramique byzantine et proto-islamique en Syrie-Jordanie (IVe–VIIe siècles apr. J.-C.). Actes du colloque tenu à Amman les 3, 4 et 5 décembre 1994*. Beirut: Institut Français d'Archéologie du Proche-Orient.

Roth, A. M.
1979   "Glass." Pp. 144–82 in D. S. Whitcomb and J. H. Johnson, *Quseir al-Qadim 1978: Preliminary Report*. Cairo: American Research Center in Egypt.

Russell, K. W.
1990   "Household Excavations at Petra." Unpublished ms. held at American Center of Oriental Research, Amman.
1985   "The Earthquake Chronology of Palestine and Northwest Arabia from the 2nd through the Mid-8th Century AD." *BASOR* 260: 37–59.

Roth, J. P.
1999   *The Logistics of the Roman Army at War (264 BC–AD 235)*. Leiden: Brill.

Sabatier, J.
1862   *Description générale des monnaies byzantines frappées sous les empereurs d'Orient depuis Arcadius jusqu'à la prise de Constantinople par Mhomet II*. 2 vols. Paris: Rollin et Feuardent.

al-Salameen, Z., et al.
2011   "New Arabic-Christian Inscriptions from Udhruh, southern Jordan." *AAE* 22: 232–42.

Saldern, A. von
1974   *Glassammlung Hentrich*. Band 3: *Antike und Islam*. Düsseldorf: Kunstmuseum Düsseldorf.
1980   *Ancient and Byzantine Glass from Sardis*. Archaeological Exploration of Sardis, Monograph 6. Cambridge, MA: Harvard University.

Saller, S. J.
1941   *The Memorial of Moses on Mt. Nebo*. Jerusalem: Franciscan.
1957   *Excavations at Bethany (1949–1953)*. Jerusalem: Franciscan.

Sanmori, C.
1998   "The Funerary Practices." Pp 413–24 in M. Piccirillo and E. Alliata, *Mount Nebo. New Archaeological Excavations 1967–1997*. Jerusalem: Studium Biblicum Franciscanum.

Sartre, M.
1993   *Inscriptions de la Jordanie, 4: Petra et la Nabatene meridionale, du Wadi Hasa au Golfe*. Inscriptions greques et latines de la Syrie, 21. Paris: Geuthner.

Sauer, J. A., and Herr, L. G. (eds.)
2012   *Ceramic Finds: Typological and Technological Studies of the Pottery Remains from Tell Hesban and Vicinity*. Hesban 11. Berrien Springs, MI: Andrews University.

Scanlon, G. T., and Pinder-Wilson, R.
2001   *Fustat Glass of the Early Islamic Period. Finds Excavated by the American Research Center in Egypt 1964–1980*. London: Altajir World of Islam Trust.

Scheuer, L., and Black, S.
2000   *Developmental Juvenile Osteology*. New York: Academic.

Schick, R.
1987   "The Church of el-Lejjun." Pp. 353–83 in S. T. Parker, ed, *The Roman Frontier in Central Jordan: Interim Report on the Limes Arabicus Project 1980–1985*. British Archaeological Report, Intl. Series S340. Oxford: BAR.
1995a   *The Christian Communities of Palestine from Byzantine to Islamic Rule: A Historical and Archaeological Study*. Princeton, NJ: Darwin.
1995b   "Christianity at Humeima, Jordan." *Liber Annuus* 45: 319–42.
2001   "Christianity in Southern Jordan in the Byzantine and Early Islamic Periods." *SHAJ* 7: 581–84.
2007   "Al-Humayma and the Abbasid Family." *SHAJ* 9: 345–55.

Schmid, E.
1972   *Atlas of Animal Bones For Prehistorians, Archaeologists, and Quaternary Geologists*. Amsterdam: Elsevier.

Schmid, S. G.
2010   "The International Wadi Farasa Project (IWFP): Preliminary Report on the 2009 Season." *ADAJ* 54: 221–35.

Schmid, S. G., et al.
2008   New Insights into Nabataean funerary practices." Pp. 135–60 in J.M. Córdoba et al., eds., *Proceedings of the 5th International Congress on the Archaeology of the Ancient Near East, Madrid, April 3-8 2006*. Vol. 3. Madrid: UA Ediciones.

Schwartz, J. H.
1995   *Skeleton Keys: An Introduction to Human Skeletal Morphology, Development, and Analysis*. New York: Oxford University.

Sear, D. R.
1988   *Roman Coins and their Values*. 4th rev. ed. London: Seaby.

Sebesta, J. L., and Bonfante, L. (eds.)
1994   *The World of Roman Costume*. Madison, WI: University of Wisconsin.

Sellers, O. R., and Baramki, D. C.

1953	"A Roman–Byzantine Burial Cave in North-
	ern Palestine." *BASOR Supplement* 15–16:
	3–27.

Sellwood, D.; Whitting, P.; and Williams, R.

1985	*An Introduction to Sasanian Coins.* London:
	Spink.

Shahid, I.

1989	*Byzantium and the Arabs in the Fifth Cen-
	tury.* Washington, DC: Dumbarton Oaks.

Shamir, O.

1999	"Textiles, Basketry and Cordage from 'En
	Rahel." *'Atiqot* 38: 91–123.

2005	"Textiles, Basketry, Cordage and Whorls
	from M'oa (Moje Awad)." *'Atiqot* 50: 99–152.

Shereshevski, J.

1991	*Byzantine Urban Settlements in the Negev
	Desert.* Beer-Sheva: Ben-Gurion University
	of the Negev.

Sherwood, A. N.; Oleson, J. P.; de Bruijn, E.;
Bevan, G.; Baker, G.; and Ambrose, H.

2008a	"Preliminary Report of the Humayma
	Excavation Project, 2002, 2004–2005. Part
	I: Geophysical Surveys, *Praetorium* and
	Horreum." *Mouseion* 8: 119–58.

Sherwood, A. N.; Oleson, J. P.; de Bruijn, E.;
and Nikolic, M.

2008b	"Preliminary Report of the Humayma
	Excavation Project, 2002, 2004–2005. Part
	II: Latrine, Plaster Bins/Basins, Hydraulic
	Probes, Weapon-Platform/*Ascensus* and
	Defensive Ditch." *Mouseion* 8: 159–83.

Shumka, L. J.

1999	"A Bone Doll from the Infant Cemetery
	at Poggio Gramignano." Pp. 615–18 in D.
	Soren and N. Soren, eds., *Excavations at
	Lugnano in Teverina.* Rome: L'Erma di
	Bretschneider.

Sidell, J.

2012	"The Eggshells." Pp. 535–36 in K. Politis,
	ed., *Sanctuary of Lot at Deir 'Ain 'Abata in
	Jordan. Excavations 1988–2003.* Amman:
	Jordan Distribution Agency.

Sim, D.

1998	*Beyond the Bloom: Bloom Refining and Iron
	Artifact Production in the Roman World.*
	BAR Intl Series S725. Oxford: BAR.

Simak, E.

2005	"Near Eastern Turned Bone Spindle
	Whorls." *Bead Society of Great Britain
	Newsletter* 81: 7–8.

Simms, S. R.

1988	"The Archaeological Structure osf a Bed-
	ouin Camp." *Journal of Archaeological Sci-
	ence* 15: 197–211.

Sinibaldi, M.

2009	"The Franks in Southern Transjordan and
	the Contribution of Ceramic Studies: A
	Preliminary Report on the Pottery Assem-
	blages of al-Bayda and Wadi Farasa." *ADAJ*
	53: 449–64.

Sinibaldi, M., and Tuttle, C. A.

2011	"The Brown University Petra Archaeo-
	logical Project: 2010 Excavations at Islamic
	Bayda." *ADAJ* 55: 431–50.

Slane, K. W.

1997	"The Fine Wares." Pp. 247–416 in S. Her-
	bert, ed., *Tel Anafa II.i: The Hellenistic and
	Roman Pottery.* Ann Arbor, MI: Kelsey
	Museum, University of Michigan.

Slane, K. W., and Magness, J.

2005	"Jalame Restudied and Reinterpreted,"
	RCRFActa 39: 257–61.

Slane, K. W., and Sanders, G. D. R.

2009	"Corinth: Late Roman Horizons." *Hesperia*
	74: 243–97.

Smith, M. D.
2007 Early Islamic Metalwork in Jordan. Unpublished M.A. Thesis, University of Victoria. Victoria, BC.

Smith, R. H.
1973 *Pella of the Decapolis,* Vol. I, *The 1967 Season of the College of Wooster Expedition to Pella.* Wooster, OH: College of Wooster.

Smith, R. H., and Day, L. P.
1989 *Pella of the Decapolis. Final Report on the College of Wooster Excavations in Area IX, The Civic Complex, 1979–1985.* Wooster, OH: College of Wooster.

Snyder, G. F.
1985 *Ante Pacem: Archaeological Evidence of Church Life Before Constantine.* Atlanta, GA: Mercer University.

Sodini, J.-P.
1986 "Les 'Tombes privilegiées' dans l'orient chretien (à l'exception du diocese d'Egypt)." Pp. 233–43 in Y. Duval and J.-Ch. Picard, eds., *L'inhumation privilegiée du IVe au VIIIe siècle en occident.* Paris: de Boccard.
2003 "La sculpture architecturale des églises de Jordanie." Pp. 123–50 in N. Duval, ed., *Les églises de Jordanie et leurs mosaïques.* Beirut: Institut Français du Proche-Orient

Sotheby Parke Bernet & Co.
1979 *Catalogue of the Constable-Maxwell Collection of Ancient Glass.* New York: Sotheby Parke Bernet Inc.

Southern, P.
2007 *The Roman Army: A Social and Institutional History.* Oxford: Oxford University.

Spijkerman, A.
1978 *The Coins of the Decapolis and Provincia Arabia.* M. Piccirillo ed. Jerusalem: Franciscan Printing.

Stallibross, S., and Thomas, R.
2008 "For Starters: Producing and Supplying Food to the Army in the Roman North-West Provinces." Pp. 1–17 in S. Stallibross and R. Thomas, eds., *Feeding the Roman Army: The Archaeology of Production and Supply in NW Europe.* Oxford: Oxbow.

Stark, J. K.
1971 *Personal Names in Palmyrene Inscriptions.* Oxford: Clarendon.

St. Clair, A.
2003 *Carving as Craft. Palatine East and the Greco-Roman Carving Tradition.* Baltimore, MD: Johns Hopkins University.

Stern, E. J., and Gorin-Rosen Y.
1997 "Burial Caves at Kisra," *'Atiqot* 33: 1–22, 103–35.

Stern, M. E.
1977 *Ancient Glass at the Fondation Custodia (Collection Frits Lugt), Paris.* Academiae Rheno-Traeiectinae Instituto Archaeologico, 12. Groningen: Wolters-Noordhoff.
1995 *The Toledo Museum of Art. Roman Mold-blown Glass: The First through Sixth Centuries.* Rome: "L'Erma" di Bretschneider in Association with the Toledo Museum of Art.
2001 *Roman, Byzantine, and Early Medieval Glass 10 BCE–700 CE.* Ernesto Wolf Collection. Ostfildern-Ruit: Hatje Cantz.

Sternini, M.
2000 "Les verres romains d'après les fouilles italiennes à Carthage (1973–1977)." *Annales du 14ᵉ Congrès de l'Association Internationale pour l'Histoire du Verre.* Lochem: Association Internationale pour l'Histoire du Verre.
2001 "Reperti in vetro da un deposito tardoantico sul Colle Palatino," *JGS* 43: 21–75.

Stout, A.
1994 "Jewelry as a Symbol of Status in the Roman Empire." Pp. 77–100 in J. L. Sebesta and L. Bonfante, eds. *The World of Roman Costume.* Madison, WI: University of Wisconsin.

Stucky, R. A.
1990 "Schweizer Ausgrabungen in ez-Zantur, Petra: Vorbericht der Kampagne 1988." *ADAJ* 34: 249–83.

Sussman, V.
2006 "A Unique Bronze Oil Lamp and Bowl of the Hellenistic Period." *IEJ* 56: 39–50.

Taft, R. F., and Kazhdan, A.
1991 "Incense." P. 991 in A. Kazhdan et al., eds., *The Oxford Dictionary of Byzantium*, vol. 2. New York: Oxford University.

Talbot, A.-M.
2009. "The Death and Commemoration of Byzantine Children." Pp. 283–308 in A. Papaconstantinou and A.-M. Talbot, eds., *Becoming Byzantine. Children and Childhood in Byzantium.* Cambridge, MA: Harvard University.

Todd, T. W.
1920 "Age Changes in the Pubic Bone, I: The Male White *Pubis*." *American Journal of Physical Anthropology* 3: 285–334.
1921 "Age Changes in the Pubic Bone. III: The *Pubis* of the White Female. IV: The *Pubis* of the Female White–Negro Hybrid." *American Journal of Physical Anthropology* 4: 1–70.

Toll, N. P.
1946 *The Excavations at Dura-Europos, Preliminary Report of the Ninth Season of Work, 1935–1936*, Part II. *The Necropolis*. New Haven, CT: Yale University.

Tolstoi, I. I.
1913–14 *Monnaies Byzantines.* St. Petersburg: Galiksi and Vilborĭ.

Tomber, R.
2004 "Amphorae from the Red Sea and Their Contribution to the Interpretation of Late Roman Trade beyond the Empire." Pp. 393–402 in J. Eiring and J. Lund, eds., *Transport Amphorae and Trade in the Eastern Mediterranean: Acts of the International Colloquium at the Danish Institute at Athens, September 26–29, 2002.* Aarhus: Aarhus University.
2008 *Indo-Roman Trade: From Pots to Pepper.* London: Duckworth.

Toplyn, M. R.
2006 "Livestock and *Limitanei*: The Zooarchaeological Evidence." Pp. 463–507 in S. T. Parker et al., *The Roman Frontier in Central Jordan. Final Report on the Limes Arabicus Project, 1980–1989.* 2 vols. Washington, DC: Dumbarton Oaks.

Trimingham, J. S.
1979 *Christianity among the Arabs in Pre-Islamic Times.* London: Longman.

Tsafrir, Y.
1988 "The Northern Church," Pp. 22–77 in Y. Tsafrir et al., *Excavations at Rehovot-in-the-Negev, I: The Northern Church.* Qedem 25. Jerusalem: Hebrew University.

Tsafrir, Y.; Patrich, J.; Rosenthal-Heginbottom, R.; Hershkovitz, I.; and Nevo, Y.
1988 *Excavations at Rehovot-in-the-Negev, I: The Northern Church.* Qedem 25. Jerusalem: Hebrew University.

Tubb, J. N.
1986 "The Pottery from a Byzantine Well near Tell Fara." *PEQ* 118: 51–65.

Turner, G.
1973 "South Arabian Gold Jewellery." *Iraq* 35.2: 127–39.

Tushingham, A. D.
1972 *The Excavations at Dibon (Dhibán) in Moab. The Third Campaign 1952–53.* Annual of the American Schools of Oriental Research Vol. XL. Cambridge, MA: Harvard University.

Tykot, R. H.; Herrmann, J. J., Jr.; van der Merwe, N. J; Newman, R.; and Allegretto, K. O.
2002 "Thasian Marble Sculptures in European and American Collections: Isotopic and

other Analyses." Pp. 188–95 in J.J. Herrmann, Jr., N. Herz, and R. Newman, eds., *ASMOSIA 5: Interdisciplinary Studies of Ancient Stone, Proceedings of the Fifth International Conference of the Association for the Study of Marble and Other Stones in Antiquity, June 1998.* Boston, MA: Museum of Fine Arts.

Unglik, H.
1997 "Metallurgical Study of an Iron Bloom and Associated Finds from Kodlunarn Island." Pp. 181–266 in W. Fitzhugh and J. Olin, *Archaeology of the Frobisher Voyages.* Washington, DC: Smithsonian Institution.

'Uqsa, H. A.
1997 "A Burial Cave from the Roman Period East of Giv'at Yasaf," *'Atiqot* 33: 39–46.
2007 "A Burial Cave at Horvat 'Eitayim," *'Atiqot* 56: 65–79.

Vaelske, V.
2005–6 "Drei Bronzestatuetten aus Petra." *Boreas* 28–29: 133–40, pl. 42.

Valdeyron, G., and Lloyd, D. G.
1979 "Sex Differences and Flowering Phenology in the Common Fig, *Ficus carica* L." *Evolution* 33.2: 673–85.

van der Veen, M., and Fieller, N.
1982 "Sampling Seeds." *JAS* 9: 287–98.

Van de Weghe, N., et al.
2007 "The Triangular Model as an Instrument for Visualising and Analysing Residuality." *JAS* 34: 649–55.

Van Ingen, W.
1939 *Figurines from Seleucia on the Tigris.* Ann Arbor, MI: University of Michigan.

van Lith, S. M. E., and Randsborg, K.
1985 "Roman Glass in the West: A Social Study." *Berichten van de Oudheidkundig Bodemonderzoek Jaargang* 35: 413–532.

Vikan, G.
1990 "Art and Marriage in Early Byzantium," *DOP* 44: 143–63.

Villeneuve, F.
1986 "Khirbet edh-Dharih (1985)." *RBib* 93: 247–52.
1990 "The Pottery from the Oil Factory at Khirbet edh-Dharih (2nd Century AD). A Contribution to the Study of the Material Culture of the Nabataeans." *ARAM* 2: 367–84.
2011 "Dharih (Jordanie méridionale): Village chrétien puis musulman (VIe–IXe siècles) dans les ruines d'un sanctuaire nabatéen." Pp. 315–30 in A. Borrut, M. Debié, A. Papaconstantinou, D. Pieri, and J.-P. Sodini, *Le Proche-orient de Justinien aux Abbassides: Peuplement et dynamiques spatiales. Actes du colloque "Continuités de l'Occupation entre les Périodes Byzantine et Abbasside au Proche-Orient, VIIe–IXe Siècles," Paris, 18–20 octobre 2007.* Bibliothèque de l'antiquité tardive, 19. Turnhout: Brepols.

Villeneuve, F., and al-Muheisen, Z.
2000 "Nouvelles recherches á Khirbet edh-Dharih (Jordanie du Sud, 1996–1999)." *Comptes rendus de l'Académie des Inscriptions et Belles-Lettres* 144.4: 1525–63.

Villeneuve, E., and Watson, P. M. (eds.)
2001 *La céramique byzantine et proto-islamique en Syrie-Jordanie (IVe–VIIe siècles apr. J.-C.). Actes du colloque tenu à Amman les 3, 4 et décembre 1994.* Beirut: Institut Français d'Archéologie du Proche-Orient.

Vitto, F.
2011 "An Early Byzantine-Period Burial Cave at Kabul." *'Atiqot* 66: 107–36.

von den Driesch, A.
1993 "Faunal Remains from Habuba Kabira in Syria." Pp. 52–59 in H. Buitenhuis and A.T. Clason, eds., *Archaeozoology of the Near East: Proceedings of the First International Symposium on the Archaeozoology of South-*

western Asia and Adjacent Areas. Leiden: Universal Book Services.

Wadeson, L.
2011   "The International al-Khubtha Tombs Project (IKTP)." *ADAJ* 55: 213–32.
2012   "The Funerary Landscape at Petra: Results from a New Study." Pp. 99–126 in L. Nehmé and L. Wadeson, eds., *The Nabataeans in Focus: Current Archaeological Research at Petra.* Supplement to the Proceedings of the Seminar for Arabian Studies, 42. Oxford: Archaeopress.

Wagner, G.
1988   "Comparability among Recovery Techniques." Pp. 17–35 in V. Popper and C. Hastorf, eds., *Current Paleoethnobotany: Analytical Methods and Cultural Interpretations of Archaeological Plant Remains.* Chicago, IL: University of Chicago.

Waldbaum, J. C.
1983   *Metalwork from Sardis: The Finds through 1974.* Cambridge, MA: Harvard University.

Waliszewski, T.
2001   "Céramique byzantine et proto-islamique de Khirbet edh-Dharih (Jordanie du Sud)." Pp. 95–106 in E. Villeneuve and P. M. Watson, eds., *La céramique byzantine et proto-islamique en Syrie-Jordanie (IVe–VIIe siècles apr. J.-C.). Actes du colloque tenu à Amman les 3, 4 et 5 décembre 1994.* Beirut: Institut Français d'Archéologie du Proche-Orient.

Walmsley, A.
2001   "Turning East. The Appearance of Islamic Cream Ware in Jordan: The "End of Antiquity." Pp. 305–14 in E. Villeneuve and P. M. Watson, eds., *La céramique byzantine et proto-islamique en Syrie-Jordanie (IVe–VIIe siècles apr. J.-C.). Actes du colloque tenu à Amman les 3, 4 et 5 décembre 1994.* Beirut: Institut Français d'Archéologie du Proche-Orient.

Walmsley, A., and Grey, A. D.
2001   "An Interim Report on the Pottery from Gharandal (Arindela), Jordan." *Levant* 33: 139–64.

Walsh, J.
1990   *Small Bronze Sculpture from the Ancient World.* Malibu, CA: Getty Museum.

Warden, W.B., Jr.
1972   "A Sasanian hoard from Birjand." *Numismatic Circular* 80: 275.

Watson, P.
2001   "The Byzantine Period." Pp. 461–502 in B. MacDonald, R. Adams, and P. Bienkowski, eds. *Archaeology of Jordan.* Sheffield: Sheffield Academic.

Weber, T. M.
2006   *Sculptures from Roman Syria in the Syrian National Museum at Damascus,* Vol. 1: *From Cities and Villages in Central and Southern Syria.* Worms: Werner.

Weinberg, G. D., and Goldstein, S. M.
1988   "The Glass Vessels." Pp. 38–102 in G. D. Weinberg, ed., *Excavations at Jalame: Site of a Glass Factory in Late Roman Palestine.* Columbia, MO: University of Missouri.

Weiss, Z.
1993   "Sepphoris." *NEAEHL* 3: 1324–28.

West, D. L.; Finnegan, M.; Lane, R.; and Kayser, D.
2000   "Analysis of Faunal Remains Recovered from Tell Nimrin, Dead Sea Valley, Jordan." Http://www.case.edu/affil/nimrin/menu/nimrin.htm.

Whitcomb, D.
1987   "Excavations in Aqaba: First Preliminary Report." *ADAJ* 31: 247–66.
1988   "A Fatimid Residence at Aqaba, Jordan." *ADAJ* 32: 207–24.
1989a   "Evidence of the Umayyad Period from the Aqaba Excavations." Pp. 164–84 in M. A. Bakhit and R. Schick, eds., *The History of*

Bilad al-Sham during the Umayyad Period. Proceedings of the Fourth International Conference. Amman: Jordan University.

1989b "Mahesh Ware: Evidence of Early Abbasid Occupation from Southern Jordan." *ADAJ* 33: 269–85.

1990–91 "Glazed Ceramics of the Abbasid Period from the Aqaba Excavations." *Transactions of the Oriental Ceramic Society* 55: 43–65.

2001 "Ceramic Production at Aqaba in the Early Islamic Period." Pp. 297–303 in E. Villeneuve and P. M. Watson, eds., *La céramique byzantine et proto-islamique en Syrie-Jordanie (IVe–VIIe siècles apr. J.-C.). Actes du colloque tenu à Amman les 3, 4 et 5 décembre 1994.* Beirut: Institut Français d'Archéologie du Proche-Orient.

White, T. D.

1991 *Human Osteology.* New York: Academic.

1992 *Prehistoric Cannibalism at Mancos 5MT-UMR-2346.* Princeton, NJ: Princeton University.

Whitehouse, D. B.

1997 *Roman Glass in the Corning Museum of Glass, Volume One.* Corning, NY: Corning Museum of Glass.

1998 *Excavations at ed-Dur (Umm al-Qaiwain, United Arab Emirates), Vol. 1, The Glass Vessels.* Leuven: Peeters.

2001 *Roman Glass in the Corning Museum of Glass, Volume Two.* Corning, NY: Corning Museum of Glass.

Wilson, E. L.

1885 "A Photographer's Visit to Petra." *The Century Illustrated Monthly Magazine* 31.1 (November): 3–27.

1890 *In Scripture Lands: New Views of Sacred Places.* New York: Scribner.

Wilson, D. G.

1984 "The Carbonisation of Weed Seeds and their Representation in Macrofossil Assemblages." Pp. 201–6 in W. van Zeist and W. A. Casparie, eds., *Plants and Ancient Man: Studies in Palaeoethnobotany.* Rotterdam: Balkema.

Winter, T.

2004 "The Glass Vessels from 'Ein ez-Zeituna," *'Atiqot* 51: 77–84.

Wroth, W. W.

1908 *Catalogue of Imperial Byzantine Coins in the British Museum, I.* London: British Museum.

Wuthnow, H.

1930 *Die semitischen Menschennamem in griechischen Inschriften und Papyri des vorderen Orients.* Leipzig: Dietrich.

Yadin, Y.

1963 *The Finds from the Bar-Kokhba Period in the Cave of Letters.* Jerusalem: Israel Exploration Society.

Yavuz, A. B., Bruno, M., and Attanasio, D.

2011 "An Updated, Multi-Method Database of Ephesos Marbles, Including White, Greco Scritto and Bigio Varieties." *Archaeometry* 53(2): 215–24.

Yeroulanou, A.

1991 *Diatrita: Gold Pierced-Work Jewellery from the 3rd to the 7th Century.* Athens: Benaki Museum.

Zayadine, F.

1974 "Excavations at Petra (1973–74)." *ADAJ* 19: 135–50.

1979 "Excavations at Petra (1976–78)." *ADAJ* 23: 185–97.

1986 *Jerash Archaeological Project, I.* Amman: Department of Antiquities.

Zeitler, J. P.

1990 "A Private Building from the First Century BC in Petra." *ARAM* 2: 385–420.

Ziolkowski, M. C., and al-Sharqi, A. S.

2006 "Dot-In-Circle: An Ethnoarchaeological Approach to Soft-Stone Vessel Decoration." *AAE* 17: 152–62.

Zohary, M.
1966   *Flora Palaestina: Part I*. Jerusalem: Israel
        Academy of Science and Humanities,
1972   *Flora Palaestina: Part II*. Jerusalem: Israel
        Academy of Science and Humanities.

Zohary, D., and Hopf, M.
2000   *Domestication of Plants in the Old World*.
        3rd ed. Oxford: Oxford University.

Index

cloth, clothing 52, 152, 247, 250, 381–82, 384, 397–400, 417
coffin 85, 92, 152–53, 242–43, 245, 248–49, 251–52, 324–25, 383, 397–401
coin 43, 45, 48, 50, 52–53, 55, 72, 103, 135, 150, 173, 175, 191, 201, 203, 207–8, 214, 218, 240, 278, 295, 307, 381, 403–15, 417–28, 548
   die link 410, 412, 414
   die-cutter 411–13
Constantine I 420, 421, 423, 425
Constantine, House of 135, 150, 423–27, 548
Constantius II 207, 411, 420, 423–26
cosmetic tool 258, 381, 397, 428, 439, 442
cosmetic pallet 279, 508, 549
cross
   bronze 245, 247, 382, 384–87, 393, 395, 397, 401, 425, 427, 441
   ceramic 236
   ivory, bone 247, 386, 393–94
   stone 91, 111, 222, 232–33, 240–43, 245, 249, 250–51, 271, 307, 310, 397, 400, 451, 453–57, 459–61, 478, 485, 495, 502, 507–8
cubit (*see* module)

D

dirhem (*see* drachma)
doll 247, 324, 389, 392–93, 398
door socket stone 449, 507–9, 511, 549
dot-in-circle motif 391, 393
drachm 403–8, 410, 412–15, 418–19
Dushara 55, 495

E

earring 247, 383–84, 387–89, 403–4, 409–10, 415–19
Elagabalus 278, 420, 424, 427
Elusa (or Halusa) 11, 17, 19, 23, 295
Equites sagittarii indigenae 337
Ethiopia 11

F

faience 102, 141, 506, 508–10, 513
farm-house 159, 218, 329, 425, 548
Faynan (*see* Feinan)
Feinan (ancient Phaino) 552

follis 43, 150, 279, 421–27
forging bloom 132, 428, 436–37
foot (*see* module)
fort, Roman 1–2, 4, 9, 10, 12–13, 16, 24, 30, 51–52, 91, 132, 137, 158, 170, 228, 243, 329–30, 335–39, 343, 352–53, 357–58, 373–76, 420, 437, 450, 492, 497, 501, 504, 511, 516, 549, 551

G

Gaza 549
graffiti 492, 503, 549
granulation 388–89, 415–17
grave (*see* also tomb)
   cist 93, 95, 152–54, 167, 175–77, 233, 240–52, 295, 322–26, 381–401, 492, 551
   shaft 51–92

H

hammer stone 150, 507, 509–11, 549
Hegra 54, 55, 62, 77, 92, 551
Hisma desert 339, 356, 358

I

inscription(s)
   Greek 469, 492, 494–95
   Latin 494–97
   Nabtaean 492–95
Isis 429, 566
ivory 124. 247. 386–87, 389, 390–93, 396–97, 443–45, 503–4, 510

J

Jabal Harûn 13–14, 17–18, 121 152, 170, 192, 214–15, 257, 307, 318, 450, 457, 460, 471, 477–79, 484, 490, 552
Jebel Haroun (*see* Jabal Harûn)
Jericho 54, 338
Jerusalem 13, 295, 345–46, 383, 387, 391, 398, 435, 509, 535
jewellery 52, 135, 247, 324, 381, 387–89, 395–97, 401, 403, 415–19, 485
Jovian 420, 423, 425
Justinian I 395–96, 420–21, 424, 426–27